Readings in Ethical Theory

Readings in Ethical Theory

Selected and Edited by

WILFRID SELLARS and JOHN HOSPERS

Department of Philosophy
University of Minnesota

New York

APPLETON - CENTURY - CROFTS, INC.

Contents

PREFACE ix

INTRODUCTORY

The Elements of Ethics . . . . *Bertrand Russell*   1

I

A SAMPLE ETHICAL THEORY

Utilitarianism . . . . *G. E. Moore*   35

II

MOORE AND THE NATURALISTIC FALLACY

The Indefinability of Good . . . . *G. E. Moore*   63
The Place of Definition in Ethics . . . . . . *G. C. Field*   92
The Naturalistic Fallacy . . . . *W. K. Frankena*   103
Subjectivism and Naturalism in Ethics . . . . . *A. C. Ewing*   115

III

THE DEVELOPMENT OF ETHICAL INTUITIONISM

Ethical Judgments . . . . *Henry Sidgwick*   137
Does Moral Philosophy Rest on a Mistake? . . *H. A. Prichard*   149
The Meaning of "Right" . . . . *Sir David Ross*   163
What Makes Right Acts Right? . . . . . . *Sir David Ross*   174
Different Meanings of "Good" and "Ought" . . . *A. C. Ewing*   210
A Suggested Non-Naturalistic Analysis of Good . *A. C. Ewing*   231
Ethical Intuitionism . . . . *P. F. Strawson*   250

IV

THE NATURALISTIC REJOINDER

Hypostatic Ethics . . . . *George Santayana*   263
The Construction of Good . . . . *John Dewey*   272

Value as Any Object of Any Interest . . . . . *R. B. Perry* 292

The Nature of Goodness . . . . *Sir David Ross* 310

Value and Obligation in Dewey and Lewis . . *Morton G. White* 332

Moral and Non-Moral Values: a Study in the
First Principles of Axiology . . . . . *C. A. Campbell* 340

Some Reflections on Moral-Sense Theories in Ethics . *C. D. Broad* 363

V

THE EMOTIVE THEORY

A Suggestion about Value . . . . . . *W. H. F. Barnes* 391

Critique of Ethics . . . . *A. J. Ayer* 393

Critique of Ayer . . . . *Sir David Ross* 403

Moral Positivism and Moral Aestheticism . . . *E. F. Carritt* 405

The Emotive Meaning of Ethical Terms . . *C. L. Stevenson* 415

The Emotive Theory of Values . . . . . *A. J. Ayer* 430

A Reply to My Critics (Excerpt) . . . . . *G. E. Moore* 432

VI

THE PSYCHOLOGY OF CONDUCT AND THE CONCEPT OF OBLIGATION

Mill and the Hedonistic Principle . . . . . *G. E. Moore* 443

Bishop Butler's Conception of Human Nature . *C. D. Broad* 451

Remarks on Psychological Hedonism . . . . *C. D. Broad* 464

Duty and Interest (Excerpt) . . . . . . *H. A. Prichard* 469

A Criticism of Kant . . . . *G. C. Field* 487

"Ought" and Motivation . . . . *W. D. Falk* 492

Obligation and Motivation . . . . . . *Wilfrid Sellars* 511

Evaluation and Obligation: Two Functions of
Judgments in the Language of Conduct . . . *H. D. Aiken* 518

VII

MORAL FREEDOM, GUILT, AND RESPONSIBILITY

Free Will and Responsibility . . . . . . *A. K. Stout* 537

Ethical Judgments and Avoidability . . . . *C. L. Stevenson* 549

Free-Will and Psychoanalysis . . . . . *John Hospers* 560

Moral Freedom in Recent Ethics . . . . . *H. D. Lewis* 576

Guilt and Freedom . . . . *H. D. Lewis* 597

H. D. Lewis on the Problem of Guilt . . . . *G. A. Paul* 621

VIII

THE PROBLEM OF JUSTIFICATION

Prolegomena to a Theory of the Moral Criterion . *C. A. Campbell* 631
On the Idea of a Philosophy of Ethics . . . . *James Balfour* 645
Ethics as Pure Postulate . . . . *D. C. Williams* 656
Validation and Vindication: An Analysis of the
   Nature and the Limits of Ethical Arguments . *Herbert Feigl* 667
Objectivity in Morals . . . . *William Kneale* 681

SUGGESTED FURTHER READINGS

Books 701
Articles and Essays 703

Preface

The enthusiastic response to *Readings in Philosophical Analysis* has reinforced our conviction that there is a genuine need for collections of important papers and other readings in the various areas of philosophy. The present volume is an attempt to satisfy this need in the field of ethical theory. More specifically, our aim has been to provide a balanced and first-hand account of the theoretical controversies that have developed in ethics since the publication in 1903 of Moore's *Principia Ethica*.

With the exception of a very few cases in which it seemed clear from the beginning that an item belonged in our collection, we have pondered our choices seriously and long. In many cases it was extremely difficult for us to make up our minds. More than one "final" list was scrapped when excluded items made their absence felt, and had it not been for the necessity of meeting a deadline, this process might have gone on indefinitely.

> "In Deliberation, the last Appetite . . . immediately adhaering
> to the action . . . is that wee call the WILL. . . ." *

In this sense only did we "will" the following group of selections rather than any one of a number of lists between which, like Buridan's ass, we hesitated.

Though the volume as a whole is organized by topics rather than by publication date, we have followed, *ceteris paribus*, the chronological order of items within each section, thus reproducing the sequence in which controversy developed. However, we have occasionally seen fit to violate chronological order even here, namely when the logical or pedagogical order of ideas was such that an issue could be more clearly grasped by doing so. For example, in Part VII, the essay "Free-will and Psychoanalysis," though chronologically later, has been placed before the three remaining essays of the section, inasmuch as the empirical material it contains gives body to the more abstract treatment of moral freedom in the remaining essays. And Campbell's "Prolegomena to a Theory of the Moral Criterion," though it appeared much later than the essay by Balfour which follows it, has been placed at the beginning of Part VIII because of its continuity with the closing items of the previous section.

* Thomas Hobbes, *Leviathan*, Part I, Chapter 6, quoted from the Clarendon Press (Oxford) edition, 1909, p. 46.

Teachers who use this book should by no means feel it incumbent upon them to assign the material in the order in which it is presented in this anthology. As a matter of fact, the order in which the selections are printed is the result of highlighting only a few of the complex interrelationships which exist between them. It is useful primarily as a *point d'appui* for the exploration of the controversies within controversies to be found in the literature of ethical theory, but it is not the order in which the selections are necessarily to be read or taught. We can conceive of several equally valid sequences in which the readings might be studied, and have no doubt that colleagues who use the book will think of still others. Since many of the essays deal with a variety of topics, it was by no means obvious in many cases where a given essay belonged, and our grouping has been accompanied by an awareness of the fact that the compartments are not water-tight and many selections bulge their compartments. We hasten to add that we did not begin with the Part headings and look for material appropriate to them; rather the headings varied with the successive lists of essays in a process of mutual accommodation.

Our thanks are due to the many friends and colleagues who have aided and encouraged us in this enterprise, and particularly to Professor William Frankena of the University of Michigan, whose detailed suggestions and comments at all stages have been invaluable, though he must not be held responsible for the contents of the volume. We wish finally to tender our apologies and regrets to those whose essays, sometimes at the last moment, we were obliged to omit; particularly in those cases where permission to reprint had already been secured from both author and publisher. The bibliography at the end of the volume exhibits the richness from which we had to choose, and our publishers have indeed been generous in giving us as much space as they have.

This book should be of particular use in introductory courses in ethics at the senior college level, second courses in ethics, courses in ethical theory, and seminars in moral philosophy and theory of value. It also contains invaluable material for courses and seminars in contemporary philosophy and in philosophical analysis.

We wish to express our deep appreciation to the authors of the articles included in this anthology for their kind permission to reprint, either in full or by way of excerpt, the material here presented. Our gratitude is also extended to the original editors and publishers of these essays for their friendly coöperation. Specific acknowledgment is made on the first page of each section.

W. S.

J. H.

INTRODUCTORY

The Elements of Ethics*

《〜〜》

BERTRAND RUSSELL

I. THE SUBJECT-MATTER OF ETHICS [1]

1. The study of Ethics is perhaps most commonly conceived as being concerned with the questions "What sort of actions ought men to perform?" and "What sort of actions ought men to avoid?" It is conceived, that is to say, as dealing with human conduct, and as deciding what is virtuous and what vicious among the kinds of conduct between which, in practice, people are called upon to choose. Owing to this view of the province of ethics, it is sometimes regarded as *the* practical study, to which all others may be opposed as theoretical; the good and the true are sometimes spoken of as independent kingdoms, the former belonging to ethics, while the latter belongs to the sciences.

This view, however, is doubly defective. In the first place, it overlooks the fact that the object of ethics, by its own account, is to discover true propositions about virtuous and vicious conduct, and that these are just as much a part of truth as true propositions about oxygen or the multiplication table. The aim is, not practice, but propositions about practice; and propositions about practice are not themselves practical, any more than propositions about gases are gaseous. One might as well maintain that botany is vegetable or zoology animal. Thus the study of ethics is not something outside science and co-ordinate with it: it is merely one among sciences.

2. In the second place, the view in question unduly limits the province

* Reprinted by kind permission of the author and the publishers from *Philosophical Essays*, George Allen & Unwin, Ltd., 1910.

The author has requested that the following note be printed in conjunction with this selection: " 'The Elements of Ethics' was written under the influence of Moore's *Principia Ethica*. There are some important points in which, not long after publishing it, I came to disagree with the theory that it advocates. I do not now think that 'good' is undefinable, and I think that whatever objectivity the concept may possess is political rather than logical. I was first led to this view by Santayana's criticisms of my work in his *Winds of Doctrine*, but have since found confirmation in many other directions. I am not, however, quite satisfied with any view of ethics that I have been able to arrive at, and that is why I have abstained from writing again on the subject."

[1] What follows is largely based on Mr. G. E. Moore's *Principia Ethica*, to which the reader is referred for fuller discussions. Sections I. and II. of the following essay are reprinted from the *New Quarterly*, February, 1910; section III. from the *New Quarterly*, May, 1910; section IV. from the *Hibbert Journal*, October, 1908; and sections V. and VI. from the *New Quarterly*, September, 1910.

of ethics. When we are told that actions of certain kinds ought to be performed or avoided, as, for example, that we ought to speak the truth, or that we ought not to steal, we may always legitimately ask for a reason, and this reason will always be concerned, not only with the actions themselves, but also with the goodness or badness of the consequences likely to follow from such actions. We shall be told that truth-speaking generates mutual confidence, cements friendships, facilitates the dispatch of business, and hence increases the wealth of the society which practises it, and so on. If we ask why we should aim at increasing mutual confidence, or cementing friendships, we may be told that obviously these things are good, or that they lead to happiness, and happiness is good. If we still ask why, the plain men will probably feel irritation, and will reply that he does not know. His irritation is due to the conflict of two feelings—the one, that whatever is true must have a reason; the other, that the reason he has already given is so obvious that it is merely contentious to demand a reason for the reason. In the second of these feelings he may be right; in the first, he is certainly wrong. In ordinary life, people only ask *why* when they are unconvinced. If a reason is given which they do not doubt, they are satisfied. Hence, when they do ask *why*, they usually have a logical right to expect an answer, and they come to think that a belief for which no reason can be given is an unreasonable belief. But in this they are mistaken, as they would soon discover if their habit of asking *why* were more persistent.

It is the business of the philosopher to ask for reasons as long as reasons can legitimately be demanded, and to register the propositions which give the most ultimate reasons that are attainable. Since a proposition can only be proved by means of other propositions, it is obvious that not all propositions can be proved, for proofs can only begin by assuming something. And since the consequences have no more certainty than their premisses, the things that are proved are no more certain than the things that are accepted merely because they are obvious, and are then made the basis of our proofs. Thus in the case of ethics, we must ask why such and such actions ought to be performed, and continue our backward inquiry for reasons until we reach the kind of proposition of which proof is impossible, because it is so simple or so obvious that nothing more fundamental can be found from which to deduce it.

3. Now when we ask for the reasons in favour of the actions which moralists recommend, these reasons are, usually, that the consequences of the actions are likely to be *good*, or if not wholly good, at least the best possible under the circumstances. Hence all questions of conduct presuppose the decision as to what things other than conduct are *good* and what *bad*. What is called good conduct is conduct which is a means to other things which are good on their own account; and hence the study of what is good on its own account is necessary before we can decide upon rules of conduct. And the study of what is good or bad on its own account must

be included in ethics, which thus ceases to be concerned only with human conduct.

The first step in ethics, therefore, is to be quite clear as to what we mean by good and bad. Only then can we return to conduct, and ask how right conduct is related to the production of goods and the avoidance of evils. In this, as in all philosophical inquiries, after a preliminary analysis of complex data we proceed again to build up complex things from their simpler constituents, starting from ideas which we understand though we cannot define them, and from premisses which we know though we cannot prove them. The appearance of dogmatism in this procedure is deceptive, for the premisses are such as ordinary reasoning unconsciously assumes, and there is less real dogmatism in believing them after a critical scrutiny than in employing them implicitly without examination.

II. THE MEANING OF GOOD AND BAD

4. Good and Bad, in the sense in which the words are here intended (which is, I believe, their usual sense), are ideas which everybody, or almost everybody, possesses. These ideas are apparently among those which form the simplest constituents of our more complex ideas, and are therefore incapable of being analysed or built up out of other simpler ideas. When people ask "What do you mean by *Good?*" the answer must consist, not in a verbal definition such as could be given if one were asked "What do you mean by *Pentagon?*" but in such a characterisation as shall call up the appropriate idea to the mind of the questioner. This characterisation may, and probably will, itself contain the idea of *good*, which would be a fault in a definition, but is harmless when our purpose is merely to stimulate the imagination to the production of the idea which is intended. It is in this way that children are taught the names of colours: they are shown (say) a red book, and told that that is red; and for fear they should think *red* means *book*, they are shown also a red flower, a red ball, and so on, and told that these are all red. Thus the idea of redness is conveyed to their minds, although it is quite impossible to analyse redness or to find constituents which compose it.

In the case of *good*, the process is more difficult, both because goodness is not perceived by the senses, like redness, and because there is less agreement as to the things that are good than as to the things that are red. This is perhaps one reason that has led people to think that the notion of *good* could be analysed into some other notion, such as *pleasure* or *object of desire*. A second reason, probably more potent, is the common confusion that makes people think they cannot understand an idea unless they can define it— forgetting that ideas are defined by other ideas, which must be already understood if the definition is to convey any meaning. When people begin to philosophise, they seem to make a point of forgetting everything familiar and ordinary; otherwise their acquaintance with redness or any other colour might show them how an idea can be intelligible where definition, in the sense of analysis, is impossible.

5. To explain what we mean by Good and Bad, we may say that a thing is good when on its own account it ought to exist, and bad when on its own account it ought not to exist. If it seems to be in our power to cause a thing to exist or not to exist, we ought to try to make it exist if it is good, and not exist if it is bad. When a thing is good, it is fitting that we should feel pleasure in its existence; when it is bad, it is fitting that we should feel pain in its existence. But all such characterisations really presuppose the notions of good and bad, and are therefore useful only as means of calling up the right ideas, not as logical definitions.

It might be thought that *good* could be defined as the quality of whatever we ought to try to produce. This would merely put *ought* in the place of *good* as our ultimate undefined notion; but as a matter of fact the good is much wider than what we ought to try to produce. There is no reason to doubt that some of the lost tragedies of Aeschylus were good, but we ought not to try to re-write them, because we should certainly fail. What we ought to do, in fact, is limited by our powers and opportunities, whereas the good is subject to no such limitation. And our knowledge of goods is confined to the things we have experienced or can imagine; but presumably there are many goods of which we human beings have absolutely no knowledge, because they do not come within the very restricted range of our thoughts and feelings. Such goods are still goods, although human conduct can have no reference to them. Thus the notion of good is wider and more fundamental that any notion concerned with conduct; we use the notion of good in explaining what right conduct is, but we do not use the notion of right conduct in explaining what good is.

6. A fairly plausible view is that *good* means the same as *desired*, so that when we say a thing is good we mean that it is desired. Thus anything is good which we either hope to acquire or fear to lose. Yet it is commonly admitted that there are bad desires; and when people speak of bad desires, they seem to mean desires for what is bad. For example, when one man desires another man's pain, it is obvious that what is desired is not good but bad. But the supporter of the view that *good* means *desired* will say that nothing is good or bad in itself, but is good for one person and perhaps bad for another. This must happen, he will say, in every case of a conflict of desires; if I desire your suffering, then your suffering is good for me, though it is bad for you. But the sense of *good* and *bad* which is needed in ethics is not in this way personal; and it is quite essential, in the study of ethics, to realise that there is an impersonal sense. In this sense, when a thing is good, it ought to exist on its own account, not on account of its consequences, nor yet of who is going to enjoy it. We cannot maintain that for me a thing ought to exist on its own account, while for you it ought not; that would merely mean that one of us is mistaken, since in fact everything either ought to exist or ought not. Thus the fact that one

man's desire may be another man's aversion proves that *good*, in the sense relevant to ethics, does not mean the same as *desired*, since everything is in itself either good or not good, and cannot be at once good for me and bad for you. This could only mean that its effects on me were good, and on you bad; but here good and bad are again impersonal.

7. There is another line of argument, more subtle but more instructive, by which we can refute those who say that *good* means *desired*, or who propose any other idea, such as pleasure, as the actual *meaning* of good. This line of argument will not prove that the things that are good are not the same as the things that are desired; but it will prove that, if this were the case, it could not be proved by appealing to the *meaning* of the word "good." So far, it might be thought that such an argument could only have a purely logical importance. But in fact this is not so. Many ethical theories have been based upon the contention that "good" means so-and-so, and people have accepted consequences of this contention which, if they had relied upon inspection untrammelled by false theory, they would almost certainly have rejected. Whoever believes that "good" means "desired" will try to explain away the cases where it seems as if what is desired is bad; but if he no longer holds this theory, he will be able to allow free play to his unbiassed ethical perceptions, and will thus escape errors into which he would otherwise have fallen.

The argument in question is this: If any one affirms that the good is the desired, we consider what he says, and either assent or dissent; but in any case our assent or dissent is decided by considering what the good and the desired really are. When, on the contrary, some one gives a definition of the meaning of a word, our state of mind is quite different. If we are told "a pentagon is a figure which has five sides," we do not consider what we know about pentagons, and then agree or disagree; we accept this as the meaning of the word, and we know that we are getting information, not about pentagons, but merely about the *word* "pentagon." What we are told is the sort of thing that we expect dictionaries to tell us. But when we are told that the good is the desired, we feel at once that we are being told something of philosophical importance, something which has ethical consequences, something which it is quite beyond the scope of a dictionary to tell us. The reason of this is, that we already know what we mean by the good, and what we mean by the desired; and if these two meanings always applied to the same objects, that would not be a verbal definition, but an important truth. The analogue of such a proposition is not the above definition of a pentagon, but rather: "A pentagon (defined as above) is a figure which has five angles." Whenever a proposed definition sets us thinking whether it is true in fact, and not whether that is how the word is used, there is reason to suspect that we are not dealing with a definition, but with a significant proposition, in which the word professedly defined has a meaning already known to us, either as simple or as defined in some other way. By applying this test, we shall easily convince ourselves that all hitherto suggested definitions of the good are significant, not merely verbal, propositions; and that therefore, though they *may* be true in fact, they do not give the meaning of the word "good."

The importance of this result is that so many ethical theories depend upon the denial of it. Some have contended that "good" means "desired," others that "good" means "pleasure," others again that it means "conformity to Nature" or "obedience to the will of God." The mere fact that so many different and incompatible definitions have been proposed is evidence against any of them being really definitions; there have never been two incompatible definitions of the word "pentagon." None of the above are really definitions; they are all to be understood as substantial affirmations concerning the things that are good. All of them are, in my opinion, mistaken in fact as well as in form, but I shall not here undertake to refute them severally.

8. It is important to realise that when we say a thing is good in itself, and not merely as a means, we attribute to the thing a property which it either has or does not have, quite independently of our opinion on the subject, or of our wishes or other people's. Most men are inclined to agree with Hamlet: "There is nothing good or bad but thinking makes it so." It is supposed that ethical preferences are a mere matter of taste, and that if X thinks A is a good thing, and Y thinks it is a bad thing, all we can say is that A is good for X and bad for Y. This view is rendered plausible by the divergence of opinion as to what is good and bad, and by the difficulty of finding arguments to persuade people who differ from us in such a question. But difficulty in discovering the truth does not prove that there is no truth to be discovered. If X says A is good, and Y says A is bad, one of them must be mistaken, though it may be impossible to discover which. If this were not the case, there would be no difference of opinion between them. If, in asserting that A is good, X meant merely to assert that A had a certain relation to himself, say of pleasing his taste in some way; and if Y, in saying that A is not good, meant merely to deny that A had a like relation to himself: then there would be no subject of debate between them. It would be absurd, if X said "I am eating a pigeon pie," for Y to answer "that is false: I am eating nothing." But this is no more absurd than a dispute as to what is good, if, when we say A is good, we mean merely to affirm a relation of A to ourselves. When Christians assert that God is good, they do not mean merely that the contemplation of God arouses certain emotions in them: they may admit that this contemplation rouses no such emotion in the devils who believe and tremble, but the absence of such emotions is one of the things that make devils bad. As a matter of fact, we consider some tastes better than others: we do not hold merely that some tastes are ours and other tastes are other people's. We do not even always consider our own tastes the best: we may prefer bridge to poetry, but think it better to prefer poetry to bridge. And when Christians affirm that a world created by a good God must be a good world, they do not mean

that it must be to their taste, for often it is by no means to their taste, but they use its goodness to argue that it *ought* to be to their taste. And they do not mean merely that it is to God's taste: for that would have been equally the case if God had not been good. Thus *good* and *bad* are qualities which belong to objects independently of our opinions, just as much as *round* and *square* do; and when two people differ as to whether a thing is good, only one of them can be right, though it may be very hard to know which is right.

9. One very important consequence of the indefinability of *good* must be emphasised, namely, the fact that knowledge as to what things exist, have existed, or will exist, can throw absolutely no light upon the question as to what things are good. There might, as far as mere logic goes, be some general proposition to the effect "whatever exists, is good," or "whatever exists, is bad," or "what will exist is better (or worse) than what does exist." But no such general proposition can be proved by considering the *meaning* of "good," and no such general proposition can be arrived at empirically from experience, since we do not know the whole of what does exist, nor yet of what has existed or will exist. We cannot therefore arrive at such a general proposition, unless it is itself self-evident, or follows from some self-evident proposition, which must (to warrant the consequence) be of the same general kind. But as a matter of fact, there is, so far as I can discover, no self-evident proposition as to the goodness or badness of all that exists or has existed or will exist. It follows that, from the fact that the existent world is of such and such a nature, nothing can be inferred as to what things are good or bad.

10. The belief that the world is wholly good has, nevertheless, been widely held. It has been held either because, as a part of revealed religion, the world has been supposed created by a good and omnipotent God, or because, on metaphysical grounds, it was thought possible to *prove* that the sum-total of existent things must be good. With the former line of argument we are not here concerned; the latter must be briefly dealt with.

The belief that, without assuming any ethical premiss, we can prove that the world is good, or indeed any other result containing the notion of good, logically involves the belief that the notion of good is complex and capable of definition. If when we say that a thing is good we mean (for example) that it has three other simpler properties, then, by proving that a thing has those three properties we prove that it is good, and thus we get a conclusion involving the notion of *good*, although our premisses did not involve it. But if *good* is a simple notion, no such inference will be possible; unless our premisses contain the notion of good, our conclusion cannot contain it. The case is analogous to the case of elements and compounds in chemistry. By combining elements or compounds we can get a new compound, but no chemical operation will give an element which was not present in the beginning. So, if good is simple, no propositions not containing this notion can have consequences which do contain it.

As a matter of fact, those who have endeavoured to prove that the world as a whole is good have usually adopted the view that all evil consists wholly in the absence of something, and that nothing positive is evil. This they have usually supported by defining *good* as meaning the same as *real*. Spinoza says: [2] "By reality and perfection I mean the same thing"; and hence it follows, with much less trouble than metaphysicians have usually taken in the proof, that the real is perfect. This is the view in "Abt Vogler": "The evil is null, is nought, is silence implying sound."

Whenever it is said that all evil is limitation, the same doctrine is involved; what is meant is that evil never consists in the existence of something which can be called bad, but only in the non-existence of something. Hence everything that does exist must be good, and the sum-total of existence, since it exists most, must be the best of all. And this view is set forth as resulting from the *meaning* of evil.

The notion that non-existence is what is *meant* by evil is refuted exactly as the previous definitions of good were refuted. And the belief that, as a matter of fact, nothing that exists is evil, is one which no one would advocate except a metaphysician defending a theory. Pain and hatred and envy and cruelty are surely things that exist, and are not merely the absence of their opposites; but the theory should hold that they are indistinguishable from the blank unconsciousness of an oyster. Indeed, it would seem that this whole theory has been advanced solely because of the unconscious bias in favour of optimism, and that its opposite is logically just as tenable. We might urge that evil consists in existence, and good in non-existence; that therefore the sum-total of existence is the worst thing there is, and that only non-existence is good. Indeed, Buddhism does seem to maintain some such view. It is plain that this view is false; but logically it is no more absurd than its opposite.

11. We cannot, then, infer any results as to what is good or bad from a study of the things that exist. This conclusion needs chiefly, at the present time, to be applied against evolutionary ethics. The phrase "survival of the fittest" seems to have given rise to the belief that those who survive are the fittest in some ethical sense, and that the course of evolution gives evidence that the later type is better than the earlier. On this basis, a worship of force is easily set up, and the mitigation of struggle by civilisation comes to be deprecated. It is thought that what fights most successfully is most admirable, and that what does not help in fighting is worthless. Such a view is wholly destitute of logical foundation. The course of nature, as we have seen, is irrelevant in deciding as to what is good or bad. *A priori*, it would be as probable that evolution should go from bad to worse, as that it should go from good to better. What makes the view plausible is the fact that the lower animals existed earlier than the higher, and that among men the civilised races are able to defeat and often exterminate the uncivilised. But here the ethical preference of the higher to the lower ani-

[2] *Ethics*, pt. ii. df. vi.

mals, and of the exterminators to the exterminated, is not based upon evolution, but exists independently, and unconsciously intrudes into our judgment of the evolutionary process. If evolutionary ethics were sound, we ought to be entirely indifferent as to what the course of evolution may be, since whatever it is is thereby proved to be the best. Yet if it should turn out that the negro or the Chinaman was able to oust the European, we should cease to have any admiration of evolution; for as a matter of fact our preference of the European to the negro is wholly independent of the European's greater prowess with the Maxim gun.

Broadly, the fact that a thing is unavoidable affords no evidence that it is not an evil; and the fact that a thing is impossible affords no evidence that it is not a good. It is doubtless foolish, in practice, to fret over the inevitable; but it is false, in theory, to let the actual world dictate our standard of good and evil. It is evident that among the things that exist some are good, some bad, and that we know too little of the universe to have any right to an opinion as to whether the good or the bad preponderates, or as to whether either is likely in the future to gain on the other. Optimism and pessimism alike are general theories as to the universe which there is no reason whatever for accepting; what we know of the world tends to suggest that the good and the evil are fairly balanced, but it is of course possible that what we do not know is very much better or very much worse than what we do know. Complete suspense of judgment in this matter is therefore the only rational attitude.

III. RIGHT AND WRONG

12. The ideas of right and wrong conduct are, as we have seen, those with which ethics is generally supposed to be most concerned. This view, which is unduly narrow, is fostered by the use of the one word *good*, both for the sort of conduct which is *right*, and for the sort of things which ought to exist on account of their intrinsic value. This double use of the word *good* is very confusing, and tends greatly to obscure the distinction of ends and means. I shall therefore speak of *right* actions, not of *good* actions, confining the word *good* to the sense explained in section II.

The word "right" is very ambiguous, and it is by no means easy to distinguish the various meanings which it has in common parlance. Owing to the variety of these meanings, adherence to any one necessarily involves us in apparent paradoxes when we use it in a context which suggests one of the other meanings. This is the usual result of precision of language; but so long as the paradoxes are merely verbal, they do not give rise to more than verbal objections.

In judging of conduct we find at the outset two widely divergent methods, of which one is advocated by some moralists, the other by others, while both are practised by those who have no ethical theory. One of these methods, which is that advocated by utilitarians, judges the rightness of an act by relation to the goodness or badness of its consequences. The other method, advocated by intuitionists, judges by the approval or disapproval of the moral sense or conscience. I believe that it is necessary to combine both theories in order to get a complete account of right and wrong. There is, I think, one sense in which a man does right when he does what will probably have the best consequences, and another in which he does right when he follows the dictates of his conscience, whatever the probable consequences may be. (There are many other senses which we may give to the word *right*, but these two seem to be the most important.) Let us begin by considering the second of these senses.

13. The question we have to ask ourselves is: What do we mean by the dictates of the moral sense? If these are to afford a *definition* of right conduct, we cannot say that they consist in judging that such and such acts are *right*, for that would make our definition circular. We shall have to say that the moral sense consists in a certain specific *emotion* of *approval* towards an act, and that an act is to be called right when the agent, at the moment of action, feels this emotion of approval towards the action which he decides to perform. There is certainly a sense in which a man ought to perform any act which he approves, and to abstain from any act which he disapproves; and it seems also undeniable that there are emotions which may be called approval and disapproval. Thus this theory, whether adequate or not, must be allowed to contain a part of the truth.

It is, however, fairly evident that there are other meanings of right conduct, and that, though there is an emotion of approval, there is also a judgment of approval, which may or may not be true. For we certainly hold that a man who has done an action which his conscience approved may have been mistaken, and that in some sense his conscience ought not to have approved his action. But this would be impossible if nothing were involved except an emotion. To be mistaken implies a judgment; and thus we must admit that there is such a thing as a *judgment* of approval. If this were not the case we could not reason with a man as to what is right; what he approves would be necessarily right for him to do, and there could be no argument against his approval. We do in fact hold that when one man approves of a certain act, while another disapproves, one of them is mistaken, which would not be the case with a mere emotion. If one man likes oysters and another dislikes them, we do not say that either of them is mistaken.

Thus there is a judgment of approval,[3] and this must consist of a judg-

---

[3] The judgment of approval does not always coincide with the emotion of approval. For example, when a man has been led by his reason to reject a moral code which he formerly held, it will commonly happen, at least for a time, that his emotion of approval follows the old code, though his judgment has abandoned it. Thus he may have been brought up, like Mohammed's first disciples, to believe it a duty to avenge the murder of relations by murdering the murderer or his relations; and he may continue to *feel* approval of such vengeance after he has ceased to *judge* it approvingly. The *emotion* of approval will not be again in question in what follows.

ment that an act is, in a new sense, right. The judgment of approval is not merely the judgment that we feel the emotion of approval, for then another who disapproved would not necessarily hold our judgment of approval to be mistaken. Thus in order to give a meaning to the judgment of approval, it is necessary to admit a sense of *right* other than approved. In this sense, when we approve an act we judge that it is right, and we may be mistaken in so judging. This new sense is *objective*, in the sense that it does not depend upon the opinions and feelings of the agent. Thus a man who obeys the dictates of his conscience is not always acting rightly in the objective sense. When a man does what his conscience approves, he does what he *believes* to be objectively right, but not necessarily what *is* objectively right. We need, therefore, some other criterion than the moral sense for judging what is objectively right.

14. It is in defining objective rightness that the consequences of an action become relevant. Some moralists, it is true, deny the dependence upon consequences; but that is to be attributed, I think, to confusion with the subjective sense. When people argue as to whether such and such an action is right, they always adduce the consequences which it has or may be expected to have. A statesman who has to decide what is the right policy, or a teacher who has to decide what is the right education, will be expected to consider what policy or what education is likely to have the best results. Whenever a question is at all complicated, and cannot be settled by following some simple rule, such as "thou shalt not steal," or "thou shalt not bear false witness," it is at once evident that the decision cannot be made except by consideration of consequences.

But even when the decision can be made by a simple precept, such as not to lie or not to steal, the justification of the precept is found only by consideration of consequences. A code such as the Decalogue, it must be admitted, can hardly be true *without exception* if the goodness or badness of consequences is what determines the rightness or wrongness of actions; for in so complex a world it is unlikely that obedience to the Decalogue will always produce better consequences than disobedience. Yet it is a suspicious circumstance that breaches of those of the Ten Commandments which people still hold it a duty to obey do, as a matter of fact, have bad consequences in the vast majority of instances, and would not be considered wrong in a case in which it was fairly certain that their consequences would be good. This latter fact is concealed by a question-begging addition of moral overtones to words. Thus, e.g., "Thou shalt do no murder" would be an important precept if it were interpreted, as Tolstoy interprets it, to mean "thou shalt not take human life." But it is not so interpreted; on the contrary, some taking of human life is called "justifiable homicide." Thus murder comes to mean "unjustifiable homicide"; and it is a mere tautology to say, "Thou shalt do no unjustifiable homicide." That this should be announced from Sinai would be as fruitless as Hamlet's report of the ghost's message: "There's ne'er a villain, dwelling in all Denmark, but he's an arrant knave." As a matter of fact, people do make a certain classification of homicides, and decide that certain kinds are justifiable and certain others unjustifiable. But there are many doubtful cases: tyrannicide, capital punishment, killing in war, killing in self-defence, killing in defence of others, are some of these. And if a decision is sought, it is sought usually by considering whether the consequences of actions belonging to these classes are on the whole good or bad. Thus the importance of precepts such as the Ten Commandments lies in the fact that they give simple rules, obedience to which will in almost all cases have better consequences than disobedience; and the justification of the rules is not wholly independent of consequences.

15. In common language the received code of moral rules is usually presupposed, and an action is only called *immoral* when it infringes one of these rules. Whatever does not infringe them is regarded as permissible, so that on most of the occasions of life no one course of action is marked out as alone *right*. If a man adopts a course of action which, though not contrary to the received code, will probably have bad consequences, he is called unwise rather than immoral. Now, according to the distinction we have made between objective and subjective rightness, a man may well act in a way which is objectively wrong without doing what is subjectively wrong, i.e. what his conscience disapproves. An act (roughly speaking, I shall return to this point presently) is *immoral* when a man's conscience disapproves it, but is judged only unwise or injudicious when his conscience approves it, although we judge that it will probably have bad consequences. Now the usual moral code is supposed, in common language, to be admitted by every man's conscience, so that when he infringes it, his action is not merely injudicious, but immoral; on the other hand, where the code is silent, we regard an unfortunate action as objectively but not subjectively wrong, i.e. as injudicious, but not immoral. The acceptance of a moral code has the great advantage that, in so far as its rules are objectively right, it tends to harmonise objective and subjective rightness. Thus it tends to cover all frequent cases, leaving only the rarer ones to the individual judgment of the agent. Hence when new sorts of cases become common, the moral code soon comes to deal with them; thus each profession has its own code concerning cases common in the profession, though not outside it. But the moral code is never itself ultimate; it is based upon an estimate of probable consequences, and is essentially a method of leading men's judgment to approve what is objectively right and disapprove what is objectively wrong. And when once a fairly correct code is accepted, the exceptions to it become very much fewer than they would otherwise be, because one of the consequences of admitting exceptions is to weaken the code, and this consequence is usually bad enough to outweigh the good resulting from admitting such and such an exception. This argument, however, works in the opposite direction with a grossly incorrect code; and it is to be observed that most conventional codes embody some degree of

unwarrantable selfishness, individual, professional, or national, and are thus in certain respects worthy of detestation.

16. What is objectively right, then, is in some way dependent on consequences. The most natural supposition to start from would be that the objectively right act, under any circumstances, is the one which will have the best consequences. We will define this as the *most fortunate* act. The most fortunate act, then, is the one which will produce the greatest excess of good over evil, or the least excess of evil over good (for there may be situations in which every possible act will have consequences that are on the whole bad). But we cannot maintain that the most fortunate act is always the one which is objectively right, in the sense that it is what a wise man will hold that he ought to do. For it may happen that the act which will in fact prove the most fortunate is likely, according to all the evidence at our disposal, to be less fortunate than some other. In such a case, it will be, at least in one sense, objectively wrong to go against the evidence, in spite of the actual good result of our doing so. There have certainly been some men who have done so much harm that it would have been fortunate for the world if their nurses had killed them in infancy. But if their nurses had done so their action would not have been objectively right, because the probability was that it would not have the best effects. Hence it would seem we must take account of probability in judging of objective rightness; let us then consider whether we can say that the objectively right act is the one which will *probably* be most fortunate. I shall define this as the *wisest* act.

The *wisest* act, then, is that one which, when account is taken of all available data, gives us the greatest expectation of good on the balance, or the least expectation of evil on the balance. There is, of course, a difficulty as to what are to be considered available data; but broadly we can distinguish, in any given state of knowledge, things capable of being foreseen from things which are unpredictable. I suppose account to be taken of the general body of current knowledge, in fact the sort of consideration which people expect when they ask legal or medical advice. There is no doubt this brings us nearer to what is objectively right than we were when we were considering the actually most fortunate act. For one thing, it justifies the unavoidable limitation to not very distant consequences, which is almost always necessary if a practical decision is to be reached. For the likelihood of error in calculating distant consequences is so great that their contribution to the *probable* good or evil is very small, though their contribution to the *actual* good or evil is likely to be much greater than that of the nearer consequences. And it seems evident that what it is quite impossible to know cannot be relevant in judging as to what conduct is right. If, as is possible, a cataclysm is going to destroy life on this planet this day week, many acts otherwise useful will prove to have been wasted labour, for example, the preparation of next year's Nautical Almanac; but since we have no reason to expect such a cataclysm, the rightness or wrongness of acts is plainly to be estimated without regard to it.

17. One apparent objection at once suggests itself to the definition. Very few acts are of sufficient importance to justify such elaborate and careful consideration as is required for forming an opinion as to whether they are the wisest. Indeed, the least important decisions are often those which it would be hardest to make on purely reasonable grounds. A man who debates on each day which of two ways of taking exercise is likely to prove most beneficial is considered absurd; the question is at once difficult and unimportant, and is therefore not worth spending time over. But although it is true that unimportant decisions ought not to be made with excessive care, there is danger of confusion if this is regarded as an objection to our definition of objective rightness. For the act which, in the case supposed, is objectively wrong is the act of deliberation, not the act decided upon as the result of deliberation. And the deliberation is condemned by our definition, for it is very unlikely that there is no more beneficial way of spending time than in debating trivial points of conduct. Thus, although the wisest act is the one which, after complete investigation, appears likely to give the most fortunate results, yet the complete investigation required to show that it is the wisest act is only itself wise in the case of very important decisions. This is only an elaborate way of saying that a wise man will not waste time on unimportant details. Hence this apparent objection can be answered.

18. One further addition is required for the definition of the objectively right act, namely, that it must be *possible*. Among the acts whose consequences are to be considered we must not include such as are either physically impossible to perform or impossible for the agent to think of. This last condition introduces difficulties connected with Determinism, which are discussed in Section IV. Ignoring these difficulties, we may say that the objectively right act is that one which, of all that are possible, will probably have the best consequences.

19. We must now return to the consideration of subjective rightness, with a view to distinguishing conduct which is merely mistaken from conduct which is immoral or blameworthy. We here require a new sense of *ought*, which it is by no means easy to define. In the objective sense, a man ought to do what is objectively right. But in the subjective sense, which we have now to examine, he sometimes ought to do what is objectively wrong. For example, we saw that it is often objectively right to give less consideration to an unimportant question of conduct than would be required for forming a truthworthy judgment as to what is objectively right. Now it seems plain that if we have given to such a question the amount and kind of consideration which is objectively right, and we then do what *appears* to us objectively right, our action is, in some sense, subjectively right, although it may be objectively wrong. Our action could certainly not be called a sin, and might even be highly virtuous, in spite of its ob-

jective wrongness. It is these notions of what is sinful and what is virtuous that we have now to consider.

20. The first suggestion that naturally occurs is that an act is subjectively right when it is judged by the agent to be objectively right, and subjectively wrong when it is judged to be objectively wrong. I do not mean that it is subjectively right when the agent judges that it is the act which, of all that are possible, will probably have the best results; for the agent may not accept the above account of objective rightness. I mean merely that it is the one towards which he has the judgment of approval. A man may judge an act to be right without judging that its consequences will be probably the best possible; I only contend that, when he *truly* judges it to be right, then its consequences will probably be the best possible. But his judgment as to what is objectively right may err, not only by a wrong estimate of probable consequences, or by failing to think of an act which he might have thought of, but also by a wrong theory as to what constitutes objective rightness. In other words, the definition I gave of objective rightness is not meant as an analysis of the meaning of the word, but as a mark which in fact attaches to all objectively right actions and to no others.

We are to consider then the suggestion that an act is moral when the agent approves it and immoral when he disapproves it; using *moral* to mean *subjectively* right and *immoral* to mean *subjectively wrong*. This suggestion, it is plain, will not stand without much modification. In the first place, we often hold it immoral to approve some things and disapprove others, unless there are special circumstances to excuse such approval or disapproval. In the second place, unreflecting acts, in which there is no judgment either of approval or disapproval, are often moral or immoral. For both these reasons the suggested definition must be regarded as inadequate.

21. The doctrine that an act is never immoral when the agent thinks it right has the drawback (or the advantage) that it excuses almost all the acts which would be commonly condemned. Very few people deliberately do what, at the moment, they believe to be wrong; usually they first argue themselves into a belief that what they wish to do is right. They decide that it is their duty to teach so-and-so a lesson, that their rights have been so grossly infringed that if they take no revenge there will be an encouragement to injustice, that without a moderate indulgence in pleasure a character cannot develop in the best way, and so on and so on. Yet we do not cease to blame them on that account. Of course it may be said that a belief produced by a course of self-deception is not a genuine belief, and that the people who invent such excuses for themselves know all the while that the truth is the other way. Up to a point this is no doubt true, though I doubt if it is always true. There are, however, other cases of mistaken judgment as to what is right, where the judgment is certainly genuine, and yet we blame the agent. These are cases of thoughtlessness, where a man remembers consequences to himself, but forgets consequences to others. In such a case

he may judge correctly and honestly on all the data that he remembers, yet if he were a better man he would remember more data. Most of the actions commonly condemned as selfish probably come under this head. Hence we must admit that an act may be immoral, even if the agent quite genuinely judges that it is right.

Unreflecting acts, again, in which there is no judgment as to right or wrong, are often praised or blamed. Acts of generosity, for example, are more admired when they are impulsive than when they result from reflection. I cannot think of any act which is more blamed when it is impulsive than when it is deliberate; but certainly many impulsive acts are blamed—for example, such as spring from an impulse of malice or cruelty.

22. In all these cases where reflection is absent, and also in the case of inadequate reflection, it may be said that blame does not belong properly to the act, but rather to the character revealed by the act, or, if to some acts, then to those previous deliberate acts by which the character has been produced which has resulted in the present act. The cases of self-deception would then be dismissed on the ground that the self-deceiver never really believes what he wishes to believe. We could then retain our original definition, that a moral act is one which the agent judges to be right, while an immoral one is one which he judges to be wrong. But I do not think this would accord with what most people really mean. I rather think that a moral act should be defined as one which the agent would have judged to be right if he had considered the question candidly and with due care; if, that is to say, he had examined the data before him with a view to discovering what was right, and not with a view to proving such-and-such a course to be right. If an act is unimportant, and at the same time not obviously less right than some obvious alternative, we shall consider it neither moral nor immoral; for in such a case the act does not deserve careful consideration. The amount of care which a decision deserves depends upon its importance and difficulty; in the case of a statesman advocating a new policy, for example, years of deliberation may sometimes be necessary to excuse him from the charge of levity. But with less important acts, it is usually right to decide even when further reflection might show the present decision to be erroneous. Thus there is a certain amount of reflection appropriate to various acts, while some right acts are best when they spring from impulse (though these are such as reflection would approve). We may therefore say that an act is moral when it is one which the agent would judge to be right after an appropriate amount of candid thought, or, in the case of acts which are best when they are unreflecting, after the amount and kind of thought requisite to form a first opinion. An act is immoral when the agent would judge it to be wrong after an appropriate amount of reflection. It is neither moral nor immoral when it is unimportant and a small amount of reflection would not suffice to show whether it was right or wrong.

23. We may now sum up our discussion of right and wrong. When

a man asks himself: "What ought I to do?" he is asking what conduct is *right* in an objective sense. He cannot mean: "What ought a person to do who holds my views as to what a person ought to do?" for his views as to what a person ought to do are what will constitute his answer to the question "What ought I to do?" But the onlooker, who thinks that the man has answered this question wrongly, may nevertheless hold that, in acting upon his answer, the man was acting rightly in a second, subjective, sense. This second sort of right action we call *moral* action. We held that an action is *moral* when the agent would judge it to be *right* after an appropriate amount of candid thought, or after a small amount in the case of acts which are best when they are unreflecting; the appropriate amount of thought being dependent upon the difficulty and the importance of the decision. And we held that an action is *right* when, of all that are possible, it is the one which will probably have the best results. There are many other meanings of *right*, but these seem to be the meanings required for answering the questions: "What ought I to do?" and "What acts are immoral?"

IV. DETERMINISM AND MORALS

24. The importance to ethics of the free-will question is a subject upon which there has existed almost as much diversity of opinion as on the free-will question itself. It has been urged by advocates of free-will that its denial involves the denial of merit and demerit, and that, with the denial of these, ethics collapses. It has been urged on the other side that, unless we can foresee, at least partially, the consequences of our actions, it is impossible to know what course we ought to take under any given circumstances; and that if other people's actions cannot be in any degree predicted, the foresight required for rational action becomes impossible. I do not propose, in the following discussion, to go into the free-will controversy itself. The grounds in favour of determinism appear to me overwhelming, and I shall content myself with a brief indication of these grounds. The question I am concerned with is not the free-will question itself, but the question how, if at all, morals are affected by assuming determinism.

In considering this question, as in most of the other problems of ethics, the moralist who has not had a philosophical training appears to me to go astray, and become involved in needless complications, through supposing that right and wrong in conduct are the ultimate conceptions of ethics, rather than good and bad, in the *effects* of conduct and in other things. The words *good* and *bad* are used both for the sort of conduct which is *right* or *wrong*, and for the sort of effects to be expected from right and wrong conduct, respectively. We speak of a *good* picture, a *good* dinner, and so on, as well as of a *good* action. But there is a great difference between these two meanings of *good*. Roughly speaking, a *good* action is one of which the probable effects are *good* in the other sense. It is confusing to have two meanings for one word, and we therefore agreed in the previous section to speak of a *right* action rather than a *good* action. In order to decide whether an action is *right*, it is necessary, as we have seen, to consider its probable effects. If the probable effects are, on the whole, better than those of any other action which is possible under the circumstances, then the action is *right*. The things that are good are things which, on their own account, and apart from any consideration of their effects, we ought to wish to see in existence: they are such things as, we may suppose, might make the world appear to the Creator worth creating. I do not wish to deny that right conduct is among the things that are good on their own account; but if it is so, it depends for its intrinsic goodness upon the goodness of those other things which it aims at producing, such as love or happiness. Thus the rightness of conduct is not the fundamental conception upon which ethics is built up. This fundamental conception is intrinsic goodness or badness.

As the outcome of our discussions in the previous section, I shall assume the following definitions. The *objectively right* action, in any circumstances, is that action which, of all that are possible, gives us, when account is taken of all available data, the greatest expectation of probable good effects, or the least expectation of probable bad effects. The *subjectively right* or *moral* action is that one which will be judged by the agent to be objectively right if he devotes to the question an appropriate amount of candid thought, or, in the case of actions that ought to be impulsive, a small amount. The appropriate amount of thought depends upon the importance of the action and the difficulty of the decision. An act is neither moral nor immoral when it is unimportant, and a small amount of reflection would not suffice to show whether it was right or wrong. After these preliminaries, we can pass to the consideration of our main topic.

25. The principle of causality—that every event is determined by previous events, and can (theoretically) be predicted when enough previous events are known—appears to apply just as much to human actions as to other events. It cannot be said that its application to human actions, or to any other phenomena, is wholly beyond doubt; but a doubt extending to the principle of causality must be so fundamental as to involve all science, all everyday knowledge, and everything, or almost everything, that we believe about the actual world. If causality is doubted, morals collapse, since a right action, as we have seen, is one of which the probable effects are the best possible, so that estimates of right and wrong necessarily presuppose that our actions can have effects, and therefore that the law of causality holds. In favour of the view that human actions alone are not the effects of causes, there appears to be no ground whatever except the sense of spontaneity. But the sense of spontaneity only affirms that we can do as we choose, and choose as we please, which no determinist denies; it cannot affirm that our choice is independent of all motives,[4] and indeed introspection tends rather to show the opposite. It is said by the advocates of

---

[4] A *motive* means merely a *cause of volition.*

free-will [5] that determinism destroys morals, since it shows that all our actions are inevitable, and that therefore they deserve neither praise nor blame. Let us consider how far, if at all, this is the case.

26. The part of ethics which is concerned, not with conduct, but with the meaning of good and bad, and the things that are intrinsically good and bad, is plainly quite independent of free-will. Causality belongs to the description of the existing world, and we saw that no inference can be drawn from what exists to what is good. Whether, then, causality holds always, sometimes, or never is a question wholly irrelevant in the consideration of intrinsic goods and evils. But when we come to conduct and the notion of *ought*, we cannot be sure that determinism makes no difference. For we saw that the objectively right action may be defined as that one which, of all that are *possible* under the circumstances, will probably on the whole have the best consequences. The action which is objectively right must therefore be in some sense *possible*. But if determinism is true, there is a sense in which no action is possible except the one actually performed. Hence, if the two senses of possibility are the same, the action actually performed is always objectively right; for it is the only possible action, and therefore there is no other possible action which would have had better results. There is here, I think, a real difficulty. But let us consider the various kinds of possibility which may be meant.

In order that an act may be a *possible* act, it must be physically possible to perform, it must be possible to think of, and it must be possible to choose if we think of it. Physical possibility, to begin with, is obviously necessary. There are circumstances under which I might do a great deal of good by running from Oxford to London in five minutes. But I should not be called unwise, or guilty of an objectively wrong act, for omitting to do so. We may define an act as physically possible when it will occur if I will it. Acts for which this condition fails are not to be taken account of in estimating rightness or wrongness.

27. To judge whether an act is possible to think of is more difficult, but we certainly take account of it in judging what a man ought to do. There is no *physical* impossibility about employing one's spare moments in writing lyric poems better than any yet written, and this would certainly be a more useful employment than most people find for their spare moments. But we do not blame people for not writing lyric poems unless, like FitzGerald, they are people that we feel could have written them. And not only we do not blame them, but we feel that their action may be objectively as well as subjectively right if it is the wisest that *they* could have thought of. But what they *could* have thought of is not the same as what they *did* think of. Suppose a man in a fire or a shipwreck becomes so panic-stricken that he never for a moment thinks of the help that is due to other people,

---

[5] I use *free-will* to mean the doctrine that not all volitions are determined by causes, which is the denial of determinism. Free-will is often used in senses compatible with determinism, but I am not concerned to affirm or deny it in such senses.

we do not on that account hold that he does right in only thinking of himself. Hence in some sense (though it is not quite clear what this sense is), some of the courses of action which a man does not think of are regarded as possible for him to think of, though others are admittedly impossible.

There is thus a sense in which it must be possible to think of an action, if we are to hold that it is objectively wrong not to perform the action. There is also, if determinism is true, a sense in which it is not possible to think of any action except those which we do think of. But it is questionable whether these two senses of possibility are the same. A man who finds that his house is on fire may run out of it in a panic without thinking of warning the other inmates; but we *feel*, rightly or wrongly, that it was possible for him to think of warning them in a sense in which it is not possible for a prosaic person to think of a lyric poem. It may be that we are wrong in feeling this difference, and that what really distinguishes the two cases is dependence upon past decisions. That is to say, we may recognise that no different choice among alternatives thought of at any time would have turned an ordinary man into a good lyric poet; but that most men, by suitably choosing among alternatives actually thought of, can acquire the sort of character which will lead them to remember their neighbours in a fire. And if a man engages in some useful occupation of which a natural effect is to destroy his nerve, we may conceivably hold that this excuses his panic in an emergency. In such a point, it would seem that our judgment may really be dependent on the view we take as to the existence of free-will; for the believer in free-will cannot allow any such excuse.

If we try to state the difference we feel between the case of the lyric poems and the case of the fire, it seems to come to this: that we do not hold an act objectively wrong when it would have required what we recognise as a special aptitude in order to think of a better act, and when we believe that the agent did not possess this aptitude. But this distinction seems to imply that there is not such a thing as a special aptitude for this or that virtue; a view which cannot, I think, be maintained. An aptitude for generosity or for kindness may be as much a natural gift as an aptitude for poetry; and an aptitude for poetry may be as much improved by practice as an aptitude for kindness or generosity. Thus it would seem that there is no sense in which it is possible to think of some actions which in fact we do not think of, but impossible to think of others, except the sense that the ones we regard as possible would have been thought of if a different choice among alternatives actually thought of had been made on some previous occasion. We shall then modify our previous definition of the objectively right action by saying that it is the probably most beneficial among those that occur to the agent at the moment of choice. But we shall hold that, in certain cases, the fact that a more beneficial alternative does not occur to him is evidence of a wrong choice on some previous occasion.

28. But since occasions of choice do often arise, and since there cer-

tainly is a sense in which it is possible to choose any one of a number of different actions which we think of, we can still distinguish some actions as right and some as wrong. Our previous definitions of objectively right actions and of moral actions still hold, with the modification that, among physically possible actions, only those *which we actually think of* are to be regarded as possible. When several alternative actions present themselves, it is certain that we can both do which we choose, and choose which we will. In this sense all the alternatives are possible. What determinism maintains is, that our will to choose this or that alternative is the effect of antecedents; but this does not prevent our will from being itself a cause of other effects. And the sense in which different decisions are possible seems sufficient to distinguish some actions as right and some as wrong, some as moral and some as immoral.

Connected with this is another sense in which, when we deliberate, either decision is possible. The fact that we judge one course objectively right may be the cause of our choosing this course: thus, before we have decided as to which course we think right, either is possible in the sense that either will result from our decision as to which we think right. This sense of possibility is important to the moralist, and illustrates the fact that determinism does not make moral deliberation futile.

29. Determinism does not, therefore, destroy the distinction of right and wrong; and we saw before that it does not destroy the distinction of good and bad: we shall still be able to regard some people as better than others, and some actions as more right than others. But it is said that praise and blame and responsibility are destroyed by determinism. When a madman commits what in a sane man we should call a crime, we do not blame him, partly because he probably cannot judge rightly as to consequences, but partly also because we feel that he could not have done otherwise: if all men are really in the position of the madman, it would seem that all ought to escape blame. But I think the question of choice really decides as to praise and blame. The madman, we believe (excluding the case of wrong judgment as to consequences), did not choose between different courses, but was impelled by a blind impulse. The sane man who (say) commits a murder has, on the contrary, either at the time of the murder or at some earlier time, chosen the worst of two or more alternatives that occurred to him; and it is for this we blame him. It is true that the two cases merge into each other, and the madman may be blamed if he has become mad in consequence of vicious self-indulgence. But it is right that the two cases should not be too sharply distinguished, for we know how hard it often is in practice to decide whether people are what is called "responsible for their actions." It is sufficient that there is a distinction, and that it can be applied easily in most cases, though there are marginal cases which present difficulties. We apply praise or blame, then, and we attribute responsibility, where a man, having to exercise choice, has chosen wrongly; and this sense of praise or blame is not destroyed by determinism.

30. Determinism, then, does not in any way interfere with morals. It is worth noticing that free-will, on the contrary, would interfere most seriously, if anybody really believed in it. People never do, as a matter of fact, believe that any one else's actions are not determined by motives, however much they may think *themselves* free. Bradshaw consists entirely of predictions as to the actions of engine-drivers; but no one doubts Bradshaw on the ground that the volitions of engine-drivers are not governed by motives. If we really believed that other people's actions did not have causes, we could never try to influence other people's actions; for such influence can only result if we know, more or less, what causes will produce the actions we desire. If we could never try to influence other people's actions, no man could try to get elected to Parliament, or ask a woman to marry him: argument, exhortation, and command would become mere idle breath. Thus almost all the actions with which morality is concerned would become irrational, rational action would be wholly precluded from trying to influence people's volitions, and right and wrong would be interfered with in a way in which determinism certainly does not interfere with them. Most morality absolutely depends upon the assumption that volitions have causes, and nothing in morals is destroyed by this assumption.

Most people, it is true, do not hold the free-will doctrine in so extreme a form as that against which we have been arguing. They would hold that most of a man's actions have causes, but that some few, say one per cent, are uncaused spontaneous assertions of will. If this view is taken, unless we can mark off the one per cent of volitions which are uncaused, every inference as to human actions is infected with what we may call one per cent of doubt. This, it must be admitted, would not matter much in practice, because, on other grounds, there will usually be at least one per cent of doubt in predictions as to human actions. But from the standpoint of theory there is a wide difference: the sort of doubt that must be admitted in any case is a sort which is capable of indefinite diminution, while the sort derived from the possible intervention of free-will is absolute and ultimate. In so far, therefore, as the possibility of uncaused volitions comes in, all the consequences above pointed out follow; and in so far as it does not come in, determinism holds. Thus one per cent of free-will has one per cent of the objectionableness of absolute free-will, and has also only one per cent of the ethical consequences.

In fact, however, no one really holds that right acts are uncaused. It would be a monstrous paradox to say that a man's decision ought not to be influenced by his belief as to what is his duty; yet, if he allows himself to decide on an act because he believes it to be his duty, his decision has a motive, i.e. a cause, and is not free in the only sense in which the determinist must deny freedom. It would seem, therefore, that the objections to determinism are mainly attributable to misunderstanding of its purport. Hence, finally, it is not determinism but free-will that has subversive consequences.

There is therefore no reason to regret that the grounds in favour of determinism are overwhelmingly strong.

V. EGOISM

31. We have next to consider an objection to the view that objective rightness consists in probably having the best consequences on the whole. The objection I mean is that of egoism: that a man's first duty is to himself, and that to secure his own good is more imperative than to secure other people's. Extensions of this view are, that a man should prefer the interest of his family to that of strangers, of his countrymen to that of foreigners, or of his friends to that of his enemies. All these views have in common the belief that, quite apart from practicability, the ends which one man ought to pursue are different from those which another ought to pursue.

Egoism has several different meanings. It may mean that every man is psychologically bound to pursue his own good exclusively; it may mean that every man will achieve the best result on the whole by pursuing his own good; it may mean that his own good is the only thing a man ought to think good; and it may mean, lastly, that there is no such thing as the general good at all, but only individual goods, and that each man is only concerned with what is good for himself. These meanings all presuppose that we know what is meant by "*my* good"; but this is not an easy conception to define clearly. I shall therefore begin by considering what it is capable of meaning.

32. "My good" is a phrase capable of many different meanings. It may mean any good that I desire, whether this has any further special relation to me or not. Or, again, it may mean my pleasure, or any state of mind in me which is good. Or it may include honour and respect from others, or anything which is a good and has some relation to me in virtue of which it can be considered *mine*. The two meanings with which we shall be concerned are: (1) any good I desire, (2) any good having to me some relation other than that I desire it, which it does not have to others, of the kind which makes it *mine*, as my pleasure, my reputation, my learning, my virtue, etc.

The theory that every man is psychologically bound to pursue his own good exclusively is, I think, inconsistent with known facts of human nature, unless "my good" is taken in the sense of "something which I desire," and even then I do not necessarily pursue what I desire most strongly. The important point is, that what I desire has not necessarily any such other relation to me as would make it my good in the second of the above senses. This is the point which must now occupy us.

If "my good" means a good which is mine in some other sense than that I desire it, then I think it can be shown that my good is by no means the only object of my actions. There is a common confusion in people's thoughts on this subject, namely the following: If I desire anything, its attainment will give me more or less pleasure, and its non-attainment will give me more or less pain. Hence it is inferred that I desire it on account of the pleasure it would give me, and not on its own account. But this is to put the cart before the horse. The pleasure we get from things usually depends upon our having had a desire which they satisfy; the pleasures of eating and drinking, for example, depend upon hunger and thirst. Or take, again, the pleasure people get from the victory of their own party in a contest. Other people would derive just the same pleasure from the victory of the opposite party; in each case the pleasure depends for its existence upon the desire, and would not exist if the desire had not existed. Thus we cannot say that people only desire pleasure. They desire all kinds of things, and pleasures come from desires much oftener than desires from imagined pleasures. Thus the mere fact that a man will derive some pleasure from achieving his object is no reason for saying that his desire is self-centred.

33. Such arguments are necessary for the refutation of those who hold it to be obvious *a priori* that every man must always pursue his own good exclusively. But, as is often the case with refutations of *a priori* theories, there is an air of logic-chopping about a discussion as to whether desire or the pleasure expected from its satisfaction ought to have priority. Let us leave these questions, and consider whether, as a matter of fact, people's actions can be explained on the egoistic hypothesis. The most obvious instances to the contrary are, of course, cases of self-sacrifice—of men to their country, for example, or of parents to children. But these instances are so obvious that the egoistic theory is ready with an answer. It will maintain that, in such cases, the people who make the sacrifice would not be happy if they did not make it, that they desire the applause of men or of their own consciences, that they find in the moment of sacrifice an exaltation which realises their highest self, etc. etc. etc. Let us examine these arguments. It is said that the people in question would not be happy if they did not make the sacrifice. This is often false in fact, but we may let that pass. Why would they not be happy? Either because others would think less well of them, or because they themselves would feel pangs of conscience, or because they genuinely desired the object to be attained by their sacrifice and could not be happy without it. In the last case they have admittedly a desire not centred in self; the supposed effect upon their happiness is due to the desire, and would not otherwise exist, so that the effect upon happiness cannot be brought in to account for the desire. But if people may have desires for things that lie outside their ego, then such desires, like others, may determine action, and it is possible to pursue an object which is not "my" good in any sense except that I desire and pursue it. Thus, in all cases of self-sacrifice, those who hold the egoistic theory will have to maintain that the outside end secured by the self-sacrifice is not desired. When a soldier sacrifices his life he does not desire the victory of his country, and so on. This is already sufficiently preposterous, and sufficiently

contrary to plain fact. But it is not enough. Assuming that this is the case, let us suppose that self-sacrifice is dictated, not by desire for any outside end, but by fear of the disapproval of others. If this were so there would be no self-sacrifice if no one would know of its non-performance. A man who saw another drowning would not try to save him if he was sure that no one would see him not jumping into the water. This also is plainly contrary to fact. It may be said that the desire for approval, as well as the fear of disapproval, ought to be taken into account; and a man can always make sure of approval by judicious boasting. But men have made sacrifices universally disapproved, for example, in maintaining unpopular opinions; and very many have made sacrifices of which an essential part was that they should not be mentioned. Hence the defender of psychological egoism is driven back on the approval of conscience as the motive to an act of self-sacrifice. But it is really impossible to believe that all who deny themselves are so destitute of rational foresight as this theory implies. The pangs of conscience are to most people a very endurable pain, and practice in wrong-doing rapidly diminishes them. And if the act of self-denial involves the loss of life, the rapture of self-approbation, which the virtuous man is supposed to be seeking, must in any case be very brief. I conclude that the psychology of egoism is only produced by the exigencies of a wrong theory, and is not in accordance with the facts of observable human nature.

Thus when we consider human actions and desires apart from preconceived theories, it is obvious that most of them are objective and have no direct reference to self. If "my good" means an object belonging to me in the sense of being a state of my mind, or a whole of which a state of my mind is a part, or what others think about me, then it is false that I can only desire or pursue my good. The only sense in which it is true is when "my good" is taken to mean "what I desire"; but what I desire need not have any other connection with myself, except that I desire it. Thus there is no truth in the doctrine that men do, as a matter of fact, only desire or pursue objects specially related to themselves in any way except as objects desired or pursued.

34. The next form of egoism to be considered is the doctrine that every man will best serve the general good by pursuing his own. There is a comfortable eighteenth-century flavour about this doctrine—it suggests a good income, a good digestion, and an enviable limitation of sympathy. We may admit at once that in a well-ordered world it would be true, and even that, as society becomes better organised, it becomes progressively truer, since rewards will more and more be attached to useful actions. And in so far as a man's own good is more in his control than other people's, his actions will rightly concern themselves more with it than with other people's. For the same reason he will be more concerned with the good of his family than with that of people with whom he has less to do, and more with the good of his own country than with that of foreign countries. But the scope of such considerations is strictly limited, and every one can easily find

in his own experience cases where the general good has been served by what at any rate appears to be a self-sacrifice. If such cases are to be explained away, it is necessary to alter the conception of "my own good" in a way which destroys the significance of the doctrine we are considering. It may be said, for example, that the greatest of goods is a virtuous life. It will then follow that whoever lives a virtuous life secures for himself the greatest of goods. But if the doctrine means to assert, as it usually does, that self-centred desires, if they are prudent and enlightened, will suffice to produce the most useful conduct, then a refutation may be obtained either from common experience or from any shining example of public merit. The reformer is almost always a man who has strong desires for objects quite unconnected with himself; and indeed this is a characteristic of all who are not petty-minded. I think the doctrine depends for its plausibility, like psychological egoism, upon regarding every object which I desire as *my* good, and supposing that it must be mine in some other sense than that I desire it.

35. The doctrine that my good is the only thing that I ought to think good can only be logically maintained by those who hold that I ought to believe what is false. For if I am right in thinking that my good is the only good, then every one else is mistaken unless he admits that my good, not his, is the only good. But this is an admission which I can scarcely hope that others will be willing to make.

But what is really intended is, as a rule, to deny that there is any such thing as the general good at all. This doctrine cannot be logically refuted, unless by discovering in those who maintain it some opinion which implies the opposite. If a man were to maintain that there is no such thing as colour, for example, we should be unable to disprove his position, provided he was careful to think out its implications. As a matter of fact, however, everybody does hold opinions which imply a general good. Everybody judges that some sorts of communities are better than others; and most people who affirm that when they say a thing is good they mean merely that they desire it, would admit that it is better two people's desires should be satisfied than only one person's. In some such way people fail to carry out the doctrine that there is no such concept as *good;* and if there is such a concept, then what is good is not good *for me* or *for you*, but is simply good. The denial that there is such a thing as good in an impersonal sense is only possible, therefore, to those who are content to have no ethics at all.

36. It is possible to hold that, although there is such a thing as the general good, and although this is not always best served by pursuing my own good, yet it is always right to pursue my own good exclusively. This doctrine is not now often held as regards individuals; but in international politics it is commonly held as regards nations. Many Englishmen and many Germans would admit that it is right for an English statesman to pursue exclusively the good of England, and a German the good of Ger-

many, even if that good is to be attained by greater injury to the other. It is difficult to see what grounds there can be for such a view. If good is to be pursued at all, it can hardly be relevant who is going to enjoy the good. It would be as reasonable for a man on Sundays to think only of his welfare on future Sundays, and on Mondays to think only of Mondays. The doctrine, in fact, seems to have no merit except that it justifies acts otherwise unjustifiable. It is, indeed, so evident that it is better to secure a greater good for A than a lesser good for B, that it is hard to find any still more evident principle by which to prove this. And if A happens to be some one else, and B to be myself, that cannot affect the question, since it is irrelevant to the general maxim who A and B may be.

If no form of egoism is valid, it follows that an act which ought to be performed may involve a self-sacrifice not compensated by any personal good acquired by means of such an act. So unwilling, however, are people to admit self-sacrifice as an ultimate duty that they will often defend theological dogmas on the ground that such dogmas reconcile self-interest with duty. Such reconciliations, it should be observed, are in any case merely external; they do not show that duty *means* the pursuit of one's own interest, but only that the acts which it dictates are those that further one's own interest. Thus when it is pretended that there are *logical* grounds making such reconciliations imperative, we must reply that the *logical* purpose aimed at could only be secured by showing that duty *means* the same as self-interest. It is sometimes said that the two maxims, "You ought to aim at producing the greatest possible good" and "You ought to pursue your own interest," are equally evident; and each is supposed to be true in all possible circumstances and in all possible worlds. But if that were the case, a world where self-interest and the general good might conflict ought not only to be non-existent, but inconceivable; yet so far is it from being inconceivable that many people conceive it to be exemplified in the actual world. Hence the view that honesty is the best policy may be a comfort to the reluctant saint, but cannot be a solution to the perplexed logician. The notion, therefore, that a good God or a future life can be *logically* inferred to remove the apparent conflict of self-interest and the general good is quite unwarrantable. If there were a logical puzzle, it could only be removed by showing that self-interest and the general good *mean* the same thing, not by showing that they coincide in fact. But if the above discussion has been sound, there is no logical puzzle: we ought to pursue the general good, and when this conflicts with self-interest, self-interest ought to give way.

VI. METHODS OF ESTIMATING GOODS AND EVILS

37. In order to complete our account of ethics, it would be natural to give a list of the principal goods and evils of which we have experience. I shall, however, not attempt to give such a list, since I hold that the reader is probably quite as capable as I am of judging what things are good and

what bad. All that I propose to do in this section is to examine the view
that we can never know what is good and what bad, and to suggest methods
to be employed and fallacies to be avoided in considering intrinsic goodness
or badness.

There is a widespread ethical scepticism, which is based upon observation of men's differences in regard to ethical questions. It is said that A
thinks one thing good, and B thinks another, and there is no possible way
in which either can persuade the other that he is wrong. Hence, it is concluded, the whole thing is really only a matter of taste, and it is a waste of
time to ask which is right when two people differ in a judgment of value.

It would be absurd to deny that, as compared with physical science,
ethics does suffer from a measure of the defect which such sceptics allege.
It must be admitted that ultimately the judgment "this thing is good" or
"that thing is bad" must be an immediate judgment, which results merely
from considering the thing appraised, and cannot be proved by any argument that would appeal to a man who had passed an opposite immediate
judgment. I think it must also be admitted that, even after every possible
precaution against error has been taken, people's immediate judgments of
value do still differ more or less. But such immediate differences seem to
me to be the exception: most of the actual differences are of a kind which
argument might lessen, since usually the opinion held is either one of which
the opposite is demonstrable or one which is falsely believed to be itself
demonstrable. This second alternative embraces all false beliefs held because
they flow from a false theory; and such beliefs, though often the direct
contraries of what immediate inspection would lead to, are apt to be a complete bar to inspection. This is a very familiar phenomenon. Sydney Smith,
believed to be always witty, says "pass the mustard," and the whole table
is convulsed with laughter. Much wrong judgment in ethics is of this nature.

38. In regard to the things that are good or bad, in themselves, and
not merely on account of their effects, there are two opposite errors of
this sort to be avoided—the one the error of the philosopher, the other that
of the moralist. The philosopher, bent on the construction of a system, is
inclined to simplify the facts unduly, to give them a symmetry which is
fictitious, and to twist them into a form in which they can all be deduced
from one or two general principles. The moralist, on the other hand, being
primarily concerned with conduct, tends to become absorbed in means, to
value the actions men ought to perform more than the ends which such
actions serve. This latter error—for in theorising it is an error—is so forced
upon us by the exigencies of practice that we may easily come to feel the
ultimate ends of life far less important than the proximate and intermediate
purposes which we consciously endeavour to realise. And hence most of
what they value in this world would have to be omitted by many moralists
from any imagined heaven, because there such things as self-denial and
effort and courage and pity could find no place. The philosopher's error
is less common than the moralist's, because the love of system and of the

intellectual satisfaction of a deductive edifice is rarer than the love of virtue. But among writers on ethics the philosopher's error occurs oftener than the other, because such writers are almost always among the few men who have the love of system. Kant has the bad eminence of combining both errors in the highest possible degree, since he holds that there is nothing good except the virtuous will—a view which simplifies the good as much as any philosopher could wish, and mistakes means for ends as completely as any moralist could enjoin.

39. The moralist's fallacy illustrates another important point. The immediate judgments which are required in ethics concern intrinsic goods and evils, not right and wrong conduct. I do not wish to deny that people have immediate judgments of right and wrong, nor yet that in action it is usually moral to follow such judgments. What I mean is that such judgments are not among those which ethics must accept without proof, provided that (whether by the suggestions of such judgments or otherwise) we have accepted some such general connection of right action with good consequences as was advocated in Section III. For then, if we know what is good and bad, we can discover what is right or wrong; hence in regard to right and wrong it is unnecessary to rely upon immediate inspection—a method which must be allowed some scope, but should be allowed as little as possible.

I think when attention is clearly confined to good and bad, as opposed to right and wrong, the amount of disagreement between different people is seen to be much less than might at first be thought. Right and wrong, since they depend upon consequences, will vary as men's circumstances vary, and will be largely affected, in particular, by men's beliefs about right and wrong, since many acts will in all likelihood have a worse effect if they are generally believed to be wrong than if they are generally believed to be right, while with some acts the opposite is the case. (For example, a man who, in exceptional circumstances, acts contrary to a received and generally true moral rule, is more likely to be right if he will be thought to be wrong, for then his action will have less tendency to weaken the authority of the rule.) Thus differences as regards rules of right action are not a ground for scepticism, provided the different rules are held in different societies. Yet such differences are in practice a very powerful solvent of ethical beliefs.

40. Some differences as to what is good in itself must, however, be acknowledged even when all possible care has been taken to consider the question by itself. For example, retributive punishment, as opposed to deterrent or reformative punishment, was almost universally considered good until a recent time; yet in our own day it is very generally condemned. Hell can only be justified if retributive punishment is good; and the decay of belief in hell appears to be mainly due to a change of feeling on this point.

But even where there seems to be a difference as to ends, this difference is often due to some theory on one side or on both, and not to immediate inspection. Thus in the case of hell, people may reason, consciously or unconsciously, that revelation shows that God created hell, and that therefore retributive punishment must be good; and this argument doubtless influences many who would otherwise hold retributive punishment to be bad. Where there is such an influence we do not have a genuine difference in an immediate judgment as to intrinsic good or bad; and in fact such differences are, I believe, very rare indeed.

41. A source of apparent differences is that some things which in isolation are bad or indifferent are essential ingredients in what is good as a whole, and some things which are good or indifferent are essential ingredients in what is bad as a whole. In such cases we judge differently according as we are considering a thing in isolation or as an ingredient in some larger whole. To judge whether a thing is in itself good, we have to ask ourselves whether we should value it if it existed otherwise than as an ingredient in some whole which we value. But to judge whether a thing ought to exist, we have to consider whether it is a part of some whole which we value so much that we prefer the existence of the whole with its possibly bad part to the existence of neither. Thus compassion is a good of which some one's misfortune is an essential part; envy is an evil of which some one's good is an essential part. Hence the position of some optimists, that all the evil in the world is necessary to constitute the best possible whole, is not logically absurd, though there is, so far as I know, no evidence in its favour. Similarly the view that all the good is an unavoidable ingredient in the worst possible whole is not logically absurd; but this view, not being agreeable, has found no advocates.

Even where none of the parts of a good whole are bad, or of a bad whole good, it often happens that the value of a complex whole cannot be measured by adding together the values of its parts; the whole is often better or worse than the sum of the values of its parts. In all aesthetic pleasures, for example, it is important that the object admired should really be beautiful: in the admiration of what is ugly there is something ridiculous, or even sometimes repulsive, although, apart from the object, there may be no difference in the value of the emotion *per se*. And yet, apart from the admiration it may produce, a beautiful object, if it is inanimate, appears to be neither good nor bad. Thus in themselves an ugly object and the emotion it excites in a person of bad taste may be respectively just as good as a beautiful object and the emotion it excites in a person of good taste; yet we consider the enjoyment of what is beautiful to be better, as a whole, than an exactly similar enjoyment of what is ugly. If we did not we should be foolish not to encourage bad taste, since ugly objects are much easier to produce than beautiful ones. In like manner, we consider it better to love a good person than a bad one. Titania's love for Bottom may be as lyric as Juliet's for Romeo; yet Titania is laughed at. Thus many goods must be estimated as wholes, not piecemeal; and exactly the same applies to evils. In such cases the wholes may be called *organic unities*.

42. Many theorists who have some simple account of the sole good have also, probably without having recognised them as such, immediate judgments of value inconsistent with their theory, from which it appears that their theory is not really derived from immediate judgments of value. Thus those who have held that virtue is the sole good have generally also held that in heaven it will be *rewarded* by happiness. Yet a reward must be a good; thus they plainly *feel* that happiness also is a good. If virtue were the sole good it would be logically compelled to be its own reward.

A similar argument can be brought against those who hold that the sole good is pleasure (or happiness, as some prefer to call it). This doctrine is regarded as self-evident by many, both philosophers and plain men. But although the general principle may at first sight seem obvious, many of its applications are highly paradoxical. To live in a fool's paradise is commonly considered a misfortune; yet in a world which allows no paradise of any other kind a fool's paradise is surely the happiest habitation. All hedonists are at great pains to prove that what are called the higher pleasures are really the more pleasurable. But plainly their anxiety to prove this arises from an uneasy instinct that such pleasures are higher, even if they are not more pleasurable. The bias which appears in hedonist arguments on this point is otherwise quite inexplicable. Although they hold that, "quantity of pleasure being equal, pushpin is as good as poetry," they are careful to argue that quantity of pleasure is *not* equal, but is greater in the case of poetry—a proposition which seems highly disputable, and chiefly commended by its edifying nature. Any one would admit that the pleasure of poetry is a greater good than the pleasure of bathing on a hot day; but few people could say honestly that it is as intense. And even states of mind which, as a whole, are painful, may be highly good. Love of the dead may easily be the best thing in a life; yet it cannot but be full of pain. And conversely, we condemn pleasure derived from the love of what is bad; even if we admit that the pleasure in itself is a good, we consider the whole state of mind bad. If two bitter enemies lived in different countries, and each falsely believed that the other was undergoing tortures, each might feel pleasure; yet we should not consider such a state of things good. We should even think it much worse than a state in which each derived pain from the belief that the other was in torture. It may, of course, be said that this is due to the fact that hatred in general causes more pain than pleasure, and hence is condemned broadly on hedonistic grounds, without sufficient regard to possible exceptions. But the possibility of exceptions to the principle that hatred is bad can hardly be seriously maintained, except by a theorist in difficulties.

Thus while we may admit that all pleasure, in itself, is probably more or less good, we must hold that pleasures are not good in proportion to their intensity, and that many states of mind, although pleasure is an element in them, are bad as a whole, and may even be worse than they would be if the pleasure were absent. And this result has been reached by appealing to ethical judgments with which almost every one would agree. I conclude, therefore, from all that has been adduced in this section, that although some ultimate ethical differences must be admitted between different people, by far the greater part of the commonly observed differences are due either to asking the wrong question (as, e.g., by mistaking means for ends), or to the influence of a hasty theory in falsifying immediate judgments. There is reason to hope, therefore, that a very large measure of agreement on ethical questions may be expected to result from clearer thinking; and this is probably the chief benefit to be ultimately derived from the study of ethics.

43. We may now sum up our whole discussion of ethics. The most fundamental notions in ethics, we agreed, are the notions of intrinsic good and evil. These are wholly independent of other notions, and the goodness or badness of a thing cannot be inferred from any of its other qualities, such as its existence of non-existence. Hence what actually occurs has no bearing on what ought to occur, and what ought to occur has no bearing on what does occur. The next pair of notions with which we were concerned were those of objective right and wrong. The objectively right act is the act which a man will hold that he ought to perform when he is not mistaken. This, we decided, is that one, of all the acts that are possible, which will probably produce the best results. Thus in judging what actions are *right* we need to know what results are *good*. When a man is mistaken as to what is objectively right, he may nevertheless act in a way which is subjectively right; thus we need a new pair of notions, which we called *moral* and *immoral*. A moral act is virtuous and deserves praise; an immoral act is sinful and deserves blame. A moral act, we decided, is one which the agent would have judged right after an appropriate amount of candid reflection,[6] where the appropriate amount of reflection depends upon the difficulty and importance of his decision. We then considered the bearing of determinism on morals, which we found to consist in a limitation of the acts which are *possible* under any circumstances. If determinism is true, there is a sense in which no act is possible except the one which in fact occurs; but there is another sense, which is the one relevant to ethics, in which any act is possible which is contemplated during deliberation (provided it is *physically* possible, i.e. will be performed if we will to perform it). We then discussed various forms of egoism, and decided that all of them are false. Finally, we considered some mistakes which are liable to be made in attempting to form an immediate judgment as to the goodness or badness of a thing, and we decided that, when these mistakes are avoided, people probably differ very little in their judgments of intrinsic value. The making of such judgments we did not undertake; for if the reader agrees, he could make them himself, and if he disagrees without falling into any of the possible confusions, there is no way of altering his opinion.

[6] Or after a small amount in the case of acts which ought to be impulsive.

I

A SAMPLE ETHICAL THEORY

Utilitarianism *

G. E. MOORE

I

ETHICS IS A subject about which there has been and still is an immense amount of difference of opinion, in spite of all the time and labour which have been devoted to the study of it. There are indeed certain matters about which there is not much disagreement. Almost everybody is agreed that certain kinds of actions ought, as a general rule, to be avoided; and that under certain circumstances, which constantly recur, it is, as a general rule, better to act in certain specified ways rather than in others. There is, moreover, a pretty general agreement, with regard to certain things which happen in the world, that it would be better if they never happened, or, at least, did not happen so often as they do; and with regard to others, that it would be better if they happened more often than they do. But on many questions, even of this kind, there is great diversity of opinion. Actions which some philosophers hold to be generally wrong, others hold to be generally right, and occurrences which some hold to be evils, others hold to be goods.

And when we come to more fundamental questions the difference of opinion is even more marked. Ethical philosophers have, in fact, been largely concerned, not with laying down rules to the effect that certain ways of acting are generally or always right, and others generally or always wrong, nor yet with giving lists of things which are good and others which are evil, but with trying to answer more general and fundamental questions such as the following. What, after all, is it that we mean to say of an action when we say that it is right or ought to be done? And what is it that we mean to say of a state of things when we say that it is good or bad? Can we discover any general characteristic, which belongs in common to absolutely *all* right actions, no matter how different they may be in other respects? and which does not belong to any actions except those which are right? And can we similarly discover any characteristic which belongs in common to absolutely all 'good' things, and which does not belong to any thing except what is a good? Or again, can we discover any single

* Reprinted by kind permission of the author and the publisher from *Ethics*, Chaps. 1 and 2. Oxford University Press, 1912.

reason, applicable to all right actions equally, which is, in every case, *the* reason why an action is right, when it is right? And can we, similarly, discover any reason which is *the* reason why a thing is good, when it is good, and which also gives us the reason why any one thing is better than another, when it is better? Or is there, perhaps, no such single reason in either case? On questions of this sort different philosophers still hold the most diverse opinions. I think it is true that absolutely every answer which has ever been given to them by any one philosopher would be denied to be true by many others. There is, at any rate, no such consensus of opinion among experts about these fundamental ethical questions, as there is about many fundamental propositions in Mathematics and the Natural Sciences.

Now, it is precisely questions of this sort, about every one of which there are serious differences of opinion, that I wish to discuss in this book. And from the fact that so much difference of opinion exists about them it is natural to infer that they are questions about which it is extremely difficult to discover the truth. This is, I think, really the case. The probability is, that hardly any positive proposition, which can as yet be offered in answer to them, will be strictly and absolutely true. With regard to *negative* propositions, indeed,—propositions to the effect that certain positive answers which have been offered, are false,—the case seems to be different. We are, I think, justified in being much more certain that some of the positive suggestions which have been made are *not* true, than that any particular one among them *is* true; though even here, perhaps, we are not justified in being *absolutely* certain.

But even if we cannot be justified either in accepting or rejecting, with absolute certainty, any of the alternative hypotheses which can be suggested, it is, I think, well worth while to consider carefully the most important among these rival hypotheses. To realize and distinguish clearly from one another the most important of the different views which may be held about these matters is well worth doing, even if we ought to admit that the best of them has no more than a certain amount of probability in its favour, and that the worst have just a possibility of being true. This, therefore, is what I shall try to do. I shall try to state and distinguish clearly from one another what seem to me to be the most important of the different views which may be held upon a few of the most fundamental ethical questions. Some of these views seem to me to be much nearer the truth than others, and I shall try to indicate which these are. But even where it seems pretty certain that some one view is erroneous, and that another comes, at least, rather nearer to the truth, it is very difficult to be sure that the latter is strictly and absolutely true.

One great difficulty which arises in ethical discussions is the difficulty of getting quite clear as to exactly what question it is that we want to answer. And in order to minimize this difficulty, I propose to begin, in these first two chapters, by stating one particular theory, which seems to me to be peculiarly simple and easy to understand. It is a theory which, so far as

I can see, comes very near to the truth in some respects, but is quite false in others. And why I propose to begin with it is merely because I think it brings out particularly clearly the difference between several quite distinct questions, which are liable to be confused with one another. If, after stating this theory, we then go on to consider the most important objections which might be urged against it, for various reasons, we shall, I think, pretty well cover the main topics of ethical discussion, so far as fundamental principles are concerned.

This theory starts from the familiar fact that we all very often seem to have a choice between several different actions, any one of which we might do, if we chose. Whether, in such cases, we really do have a choice, in the sense that we ever really *could* choose any other action than the one which in the end we do choose, is a question upon which it does not pronounce and which will have to be considered later on. All that the theory assumes is that, in many cases, there certainly are a considerable number of different actions, any one of which we could do, *if* we chose, and between which, therefore, in *this* sense, we have a choice; while there are others which we could not do, even if we did choose to do them. It assumes, that is to say, that in many cases, *if* we had chosen differently, we should have acted differently; and this seems to be an unquestionable fact, which must be admitted, even if we hold that it is never the case that we *could* have chosen differently. Our theory assumes, then, that many of our actions are under the control of our wills, in the sense that *if*, just before we began to do them, we had chosen not to do them, we *should* not have done them; and I propose to call all actions of this kind *voluntary* actions.

It should be noticed that, if we define voluntary actions in this way, it is by no means certain that all or nearly all voluntary actions are actually themselves chosen or willed. It seems highly probable that an immense number of the actions which we do, and which we *could* have avoided, *if* we had chosen to avoid them, were not themselves willed at all. It is only true of them that they are 'voluntary' in the sense that a particular act of will, just before their occurrence, would have been sufficient to *prevent* them; not in the sense that they themselves were brought about by being willed. And perhaps there is some departure from common usage in calling all such acts 'voluntary.' I do not think, however, that it is in accordance with common usage to restrict the name 'voluntary' to actions which are quite certainly actually willed. And the class of actions to which I propose to give the name—all those, namely, which we could have prevented, *if*, immediately beforehand, we had willed to do so—do, I think, certainly require to be distinguished by some special name. It might, perhaps, be thought that almost all our actions, or even, in a sense, *absolutely* all those, which properly deserve to be called 'ours,' are 'voluntary' in this sense: so that the use of this special name is unnecessary: we might, instead, talk simply of 'our actions.' And it is, I think, true that almost all the actions, of which we should generally think, when we talk of 'our actions,' are of this nature; and even that, in some contexts, when we talk of 'human actions,' we do refer exclusively to actions of this sort. But in other contexts such a way of speaking would be misleading. It is quite certain that both our bodies and our minds constantly do things, which we certainly could not have prevented, by merely willing just beforehand that they should not be done; and some, at least, of these things, which our bodies and minds do, would in certain contexts be called actions of ours. There would therefore be some risk of confusion if we were to speak of 'human actions' generally, when we mean only actions which are 'voluntary' in the sense I have defined. It is better, therefore, to give some special name to actions of this class; and I cannot think of any better name than that of 'voluntary' actions. If we require further to distinguish from among them, those which are also voluntary in the sense that we definitely willed to do them, we can do so by calling these 'willed' actions.

Our theory holds, then, that a great many of our actions are voluntary in the sense that we could have avoided them, *if*, just beforehand, we had chosen to do so. It does not pretend to decide whether we *could* have thus chosen to avoid them; it only says that, *if* we had so chosen, we should have succeeded. And its first concern is to lay down some absolutely universal rules as to the conditions under which actions of this kind are *right* or *wrong;* under which they *ought* or *ought not* to be done; and under which it is our *duty* to do them or not to do them. It is quite certain that we do hold that many voluntary actions are right and others wrong; that many ought to have been done, and others ought not to have been done; and that it was the agent's duty to do some of them, and his duty not to do others. Whether any actions, except voluntary ones, can be properly said to be right or wrong, or to be actions which ought or ought not to have been done, and, if so, in what sense and under what conditions, is again a question which our theory does not presume to answer. It only assumes that these things *can* be properly said of some voluntary actions, whether or not they can also be said of other actions as well. It confines itself, therefore, strictly to voluntary actions; and with regard to these it asks the following questions. Can we discover any characteristic, over and above the mere fact that they *are* right, which belongs to absolutely *all* voluntary actions which are right, and which at the same time does not belong to any except those which are right? And similarly: Can we discover any characteristic, over and above the mere fact that they are wrong, which belongs to absolutely *all* voluntary actions which are wrong, and which at the same time does not belong to any except those which are wrong? And so, too, in the case of the words 'ought' and 'duty,' it wants to discover some characteristic which belongs to *all* voluntary actions which *ought* to be done or which it is our duty to do, and which does not belong to any except those which we ought to do; and similarly to discover some characteristic which belongs to *all* voluntary actions which ought *not* to be done and which it is our duty *not* to do, and which does not belong to any except these. To all these questions our theory thinks that it can find a comparatively simple answer. And it is this answer which forms the first part of the theory. It is, as I say, a *comparatively* simple answer; but nevertheless it cannot be stated accurately except at some length. And I think it is worth while to try to state it accurately.

To begin with, then, this theory points out that all actions may, theoretically at least, be arranged in a scale, according to the proportion between the *total* quantities of pleasure or pain which they *cause*. And when it talks of the *total* quantities of pleasure or pain which an action causes, it is extremely important to realize that it means quite strictly what it says. We all of us know that many of our actions do cause pleasure and pain not only to ourselves, but also to other human beings, and sometimes, perhaps, to animals as well; and that the effects of our actions, in this respect, are often not confined to those which are comparatively direct and immediate, but that their indirect and remote effects are sometimes quite equally important or even more so. But in order to arrive at the *total* quantities of pleasure or pain caused by an action, we should, of course, have to take into account absolutely *all* its effects, both near and remote, direct and indirect; and we should have to take into account absolutely *all* the beings, capable of feeling pleasure or pain, who were at any time affected by it; not only ourselves, therefore, and our fellow-men, but also any of the lower animals, to which the action might cause pleasure or pain, however indirectly; and also any other beings in the Universe, if there should be any, who might be affected in the same way. Some people, for instance, hold that there is a God and that there are disembodied spirits, who may be pleased or pained by our actions; and, if this is so, then, in order to arrive at the *total* quantities of pleasure or pain which an action causes, we should have, of course, to take into account, not only the pleasures or pains which it may cause to men and animals upon this earth, but also those which it may cause to God or to disembodied spirits. By the *total* quantities of pleasure or pain which an action causes, this theory means, then, quite strictly what it says. It means the quantities which would be arrived at, if we could take into account absolutely *all* the amounts of pleasure or pain, which result from the action; no matter how indirect or remote these results may be, and no matter what may be the nature of the beings who feel them.

But if we understand the total quantities of pleasure or pain caused by an action in this strict sense, then obviously, theoretically at least, six different cases are possible. It is obviously theoretically possible in the first place (1) that an action should, in its total effects, cause some pleasure but absolutely no pain; and it is obviously also possible (2) that, while it causes both pleasure and pain, the total quantity of pleasure should be *greater* than the total quantity of pain. These are two out of the six theoretically possible cases; and these two may be grouped together by saying that, in both of them, the action in question causes an *excess* of pleasure over pain, or *more* pleasure than pain. This description will, of course, if taken quite strictly, apply only to the second of the two; since an action which causes no pain whatever cannot strictly be said to cause more pleasure than pain. But it is convenient to have some description, which may be understood to cover both cases; and if we describe no pain at all as a *zero* quantity of pain, then obviously we may say that an action which causes some pleasure and no pain, does cause a *greater* quantity of pleasure than of pain, since any positive quantity is greater than zero. I propose, therefore, for the sake of convenience, to speak of both these first two cases as cases in which an action causes an *excess* of pleasure over pain.

But obviously two other cases, which are also theoretically possible, are (1) that in which an action, in its total effects, causes some pain but absolutely no pleasure, and (2) that in which, while it causes both pleasure and pain, the total quantity of *pain* is greater than the total quantity of *pleasure*. And of both these two cases I propose to speak, for the reason just explained, as cases in which an action causes an *excess* of *pain* over *pleasure*.

There remain two other cases, and two only, which are still theoretically possible; namely (1) that an action should cause absolutely no pleasure and also absolutely no pain, and (2) that, while it causes both pleasure and pain, the total quantities of each should be exactly equal. And in both these two cases, we may, of course, say that the action in question causes *no* excess either of pleasure over pain or of pain over pleasure.

Of absolutely every action, therefore, it must be true, in the sense explained, that it either causes an excess of pleasure over pain, or an excess of pain over pleasure, or neither. This threefold division covers all the six possible cases. But, of course, of any two actions, both of which cause an excess of pleasure over pain, or of pain over pleasure, it may be true that the excess caused by the one is *greater* than that caused by the other. And, this being so, all actions may, theoretically at least, be arranged in a scale, starting at the top with those which cause the *greatest* excess of pleasure over pain; passing downwards by degrees through cases where the excess of pleasure over pain is continually smaller and smaller, until we reach those actions which cause no excess either of pleasure over pain or of pain over pleasure: then starting again with those which cause an excess of pain over pleasure, but only the smallest possible one; going on by degrees to cases in which the excess of pain over pleasure is continually larger and larger; until we reach, at the bottom, those cases in which the excess of pain over pleasure is the greatest.

The principle upon which this scale is arranged is, I think, perfectly easy to understand, though it cannot be stated accurately except in rather a complicated way. The principle is: That any action which causes an excess of pleasure over pain will always come higher in the scale *either* than an action which causes a *smaller* excess of pleasure over pain, *or* than an action which causes no excess either of pleasure over pain or of pain over pleasure, *or* than one which causes an excess of pain over pleasure; That any action which causes no excess either of pleasure over pain or of pain over pleasure will always come higher than any which causes an excess of pain over pleasure; and finally That any, which causes an excess of pain over pleasure, will always come higher than one which causes a *greater* excess of pain over pleasure. And obviously this statement is rather complicated. But yet, so far as I can see, there is no simpler way of stating quite accurately the principle upon which the scale is arranged. By saying that one action comes higher in the scale than another, we may mean any one of these five different things; and I can find no simple expression which will really apply quite accurately to all five cases.

But it has, I think, been customary, among ethical writers, to speak loosely of any action, which comes higher in this scale than another, for any one of these five reasons, as causing *more* pleasure than that other, or causing a *greater balance* of pleasure over pain. For instance, if we are comparing five different actions, one of which comes higher in the scale than any of the rest, it has been customary to say that, among the five, this is the one which causes a *maximum* of pleasure, or a *maximum balance* of pleasure over pain. To speak in this way is obviously extremely inaccurate, for many different reasons. It is obvious, for instance, that an action which comes lower in the scale may actually produce much more pleasure than one which comes higher, provided this effect is counteracted by its *also* causing a much greater quantity of pain. And it is obvious also that, of two actions, one of which comes higher in the scale than another, *neither* may cause a balance of pleasure over pain, but both actually more pain than pleasure. For these and other reasons it is quite inaccurate to speak as if the place of an action in the scale were determined either by the total quantity of pleasure that it causes, or by the total balance of pleasure over pain. But this way of speaking, though inaccurate, is also extremely convenient; and of the two alternative expressions, the one which is the most inaccurate is also the most convenient. It is much more convenient to be able to refer to any action which comes higher in the scale as simply causing *more pleasure,* than to have to say, every time, that it causes *a greater balance of pleasure over pain.*

I propose, therefore, in spite of its inaccuracy, to adopt this loose way of speaking. And I do not think the adoption of it need lead to any confusion, provided it is clearly understood, to begin with, that I am going to use the words in this loose way. It must, therefore, be clearly understood that, when, in what follows, I speak of one action as causing more pleasure than another, I shall not mean strictly what I say, but only that the former action is related to the latter in one or other of the five following ways. I shall mean that the two actions are related to one another either (1) by the fact that, while both cause an excess of pleasure over pain, the former causes a greater excess than the latter; or (2) by the fact that, while the former causes an excess of pleasure over pain, the latter causes no excess whatever either of pleasure over pain, or of pain over pleasure; or (3) by the fact that, while the former causes an excess of pleasure over pain, the latter causes an excess of pain over pleasure; or (4) by the fact that, while the former causes no excess whatever either of pleasure over pain or of pain over pleasure, the latter does cause an excess of pain over pleasure; or (5) by the fact that, while both cause an excess of pain over pleasure, the former causes a smaller excess than the latter. It must be remembered, too, that in every case we shall be speaking of the *total* quantities of pleasure and pain caused by the actions, in the strictest possible sense; taking into account, that is to say, absolutely *all* their effects, however remote and indirect.

But now, if we understand the statement that one action causes more pleasure than another in the sense just explained, we may express as follows the first principle, which the theory I wish to state lays down with regard to right and wrong, as applied to voluntary actions. This first principle is a very simple one; for it merely asserts: That a voluntary action is right, whenever and only when the agent could *not*, even if he had chosen, have done any other action instead, which would have caused more pleasure than the one he did do; and that a voluntary action is wrong, whenever and only when the agent *could*, if he had chosen, have done some other action instead, which would have caused more pleasure than the one he did do. It must be remembered that our theory does not assert that any agent ever could have *chosen* any other action than the one he actually performed. It only asserts, that, in the case of all voluntary actions, he *could* have acted differently, *if* he had chosen: not that he could have made the choice. It does not assert, therefore, that right and wrong depend upon what he could *choose*. As to this, it makes no assertion at all: it neither affirms nor denies that they do so depend. It only asserts that they do depend upon what he could have done or could do, *if* he chose. In every case of voluntary action, a man could, *if* he had so chosen just before, have done at least one other action instead. That was the definition of a voluntary action: and it seems quite certain that many actions are voluntary in this sense. And what our theory asserts is that, where among the actions which he could thus have done instead, *if* he had chosen, there is any one which would have caused more pleasure than the one he did do, then his action is always wrong; but that in all other cases it is right. This is what our theory asserts, if we remember that the phrase 'causing more pleasure' is to be understood in the inaccurate sense explained above.

But it will be convenient, in what follows, to introduce yet another inaccuracy in our statement of it. It asserts, we have seen, that the question whether a voluntary action is right or wrong, depends upon the question whether, among all the other actions, which the agent could have done instead, *if* he had chosen, there is or is not any which would have produced more pleasure than the one he did do. But it would be highly inconvenient, every time we have to mention the theory, to use the whole phrase 'all the other actions which the agent could have done instead, *if* he had chosen.' I propose, therefore, instead to call these simply 'all the other actions which he *could* have done,' or 'which were possible to him.' This is, of course, inaccurate, since it is, in a sense, not true that he *could* have done them, if he could not have chosen them: and our theory does not pretend to say whether he *ever* could have chosen them. Moreover, even if it is true that he could *sometimes* have chosen an action which he did not choose, it is pretty certain that it is not always so; it is pretty certain that it is *sometimes* out of his power to choose an action, which he certainly could have done, *if* he had chosen. It is not true, therefore, that *all* the actions which he could have done, *if* he had chosen, are actions which, in every sense, he *could* have done, even if it is true that some of them are. But nevertheless I propose, for the sake of brevity, to speak of them all as actions which he *could* have done; and this again, I think, need lead to no confusion, if it be clearly understood that I am doing so. It must, then, be clearly understood that, when, in what follows, I speak of all the actions which the agent could have done, or all those open to him under the circumstances, I shall mean only all those which he could have done, *if* he had chosen.

Understanding this, then, we may state the first principle which our theory lays down quite briefly by saying: 'A voluntary action is right, whenever and only when no other action possible to the agent under the circumstances would have caused more pleasure; in all other cases, it is wrong.' This is its answer to the questions: What characteristic is there which belongs to *all* voluntary actions which are right, and *only* those among them which are right? and what characteristic is there which belongs to *all* those which are wrong, and *only* to those which are wrong? But it also asked the very same questions with regard to two other classes of voluntary actions—those which *ought* or ought *not* to be done, and those which it is our *duty* to do or not to do. And its answer to the question concerning these conceptions differs from its answer to the question concerning right and wrong in a way, which is, indeed, comparatively unimportant, but which yet deserves to be noticed.

It may have been observed that our theory does *not* assert that a voluntary action is right only where it causes *more* pleasure than any action which the agent could have done instead. It confines itself to asserting that, in order to be right, such an action must cause at least *as much* pleasure as any which the agent could have done instead. And it confines itself in this way for the following reason. It is obviously possible, theoretically at least, that, among the alternatives open to an agent at a given moment, there may be two or more which would produce precisely *equal* amounts of pleasure, while all of them produced more than any of the other possible alternatives; and in such cases, our theory would say, *any one* of these actions would be perfectly right. It recognizes, therefore, that there may be cases in which no single one of the actions open to the agent can be distinguished as *the* right one to do; that in many cases, on the contrary, several different actions may all be equally right; or, in other words, that to say that a man acted rightly does not necessarily imply that, if he had done anything else instead, he would have acted wrongly. And this is certainly in accordance with common usage. We all do constantly imply that sometimes when a man was right in doing what he did, yet he might have been equally right, if he had acted differently: that there may be several different alternatives open to him, none of which can definitely be said to be wrong. This is why our theory refuses to commit itself to the view that an action is right only where it produces *more* pleasure than any of the other possible alternatives. For, if this were so, then it would follow that no two alternatives could ever be *equally* right: some one of them would always have to be *the* right one, and all the rest wrong. But it is precisely in this respect that it holds that the conceptions of 'ought' and of 'duty' differ from the conception of what is 'right.' When we say that a man 'ought' to do one particular action, or that it is his 'duty' to do it, we do imply that it would be wrong for him to do *anything* else. And hence our theory holds that, in the case of 'ought' and 'duty' we may say, what we could not say in the case of 'right,' namely, that an action ought to be done or is our duty, only where it produces *more* pleasure than any which we could have done instead.

From this distinction several consequences follow. It follows firstly that a voluntary action may be 'right' without being an action which we 'ought' to do or which it is our 'duty' to do. It is, of course, always our duty to act rightly, in the sense that, if we don't act rightly, we shall always be doing what we ought not. It is, therefore, true, in a sense, that whenever we act rightly, we are always doing our duty and doing what we ought. But what is not true is that, whenever a particular action is right, it is always our duty to do that particular action and no other. This is not true, because, theoretically at least, cases may occur in which some other action would be quite equally right, and in such cases, we are obviously under no obligation whatever to do the one rather than the other: whichever we do, we shall be doing our duty and doing as we ought. And it would be rash to affirm that such cases never do practically occur. We all commonly hold that they do: that very often indeed we are under no positive obligation to do one action rather than some other; that it does not matter which we do. We must, then, be careful not to affirm that, because it is always our duty to act rightly, therefore any particular action, which is right, is always also one which it is our duty to do. This is not so, because, even where an action is right, it does not follow that it would be wrong to do something else instead; whereas, if an action is a duty or an action which we positively ought to do, it always would be wrong to do anything else instead.

The first consequence, then, which follows, from this distinction between what is right, on the one hand, and what ought to be done or is our duty, on the other, is that a voluntary action may be right, without being an action which we ought to do or which it is our duty to do. And from this it follows further that the relation between 'right' and what ought to be done is not on a par with that between 'wrong' and what ought *not* to be done. Every action which is wrong is also an action which ought not to be done and which it is our duty not to do; and also, conversely, every action which ought not to be done, or which it is our duty not to do, is wrong. These three negative terms are precisely and absolutely coextensive. To say that an action is or was wrong, is to imply that it ought not to be, or to have been, done; and the converse implication also holds. But in the case of 'right' and 'ought,' only one of the two converse propositions holds. Every action which ought to be done or which is our duty, is certainly also right; to say the one thing of any action is to imply the other. But here the converse is not true; since, as we have seen, to say that an action is right is *not* to imply that it ought to be done or that it is our duty: an action may be right, without either of these two other things being true of it. In this respect the relation between the positive conceptions 'right' and 'ought to be done' is not on a par with that between the negative conceptions 'wrong' and 'ought not to be done.' The two positive conceptions are not coextensive, whereas the two negative ones are so.

And thirdly and finally, it also follows that whereas every voluntary action, without exception, must be either right or wrong, it is by no means necessarily true of every voluntary action that it either ought to be done or ought not to be done,—that it either is our duty to do it, or our duty not to do it. On the contrary, cases may occur quite frequently where it is neither our duty to do a particular action, nor yet our duty not to do it. This will occur, whenever, among the alternatives open to us, there are two or more, any one of which would be equally right. And hence we must not suppose that, wherever we have a choice of actions before us, there is always some one among them (*if* we could only find out which), which is *the* one which we ought to do, while all the rest are definitely wrong. It may quite well be the case that there is no one among them, which we are under a positive obligation to do, although there always must be at least one which it would be right to do. There will be one which we definitely *ought* to do, in those cases and those cases only, where there happens to be *only* one which is right under the circumstances—where, that is to say, there are not several which would all be equally right, but some one of the alternatives open to us is *the* only right thing to do. And hence in many cases we cannot definitely say of a voluntary action either that it was the agent's duty to do it nor yet that it was his duty not to do it. There may be cases in which none of the alternatives open to us is definitely prescribed by duty.

To sum up, then: The answers which this theory gives to its first set of questions is as follows. A characteristic which belongs to all right voluntary actions, and only to those which are right, is, it says, this: That they all cause at least *as much* pleasure as any action which the agent could have done instead; or, in other words, they all produce *a* maximum of pleasure. A characteristic which belongs to all voluntary actions, which *ought* to be done or which it is our *duty* to do, and only to these, is, it says, the slightly different one: That they all cause *more* pleasure than any which the agent could have done instead; or, in other words, among all the possible alternatives, it is they which produce *the* maximum of pleasure. And finally, a characteristic which belongs to all voluntary actions which are wrong, or which ought not to be done, or which it is our duty not to do, and which belongs only to these, is, in all three cases the same, namely: That they all cause *less* pleasure than some other action which the agent could have done instead. These three statements together constitute what I will call the first part of the theory; and, whether we agree with them or not, it must, I think, at least be admitted that they are propositions of a very fundamental nature and of a very wide range, so that it would be worth while to know, if possible, whether they are true.

But this first part of the theory is by no means the whole of it. There are two other parts of it, which are at least equally important; and, before we go on to consider the objections which may be urged against it, it will, I think, be best to state these other parts. They may, however, conveniently form the subject of a new chapter.

II

In the last chapter I stated the first part of an ethical theory, which I chose out for consideration, not because I agreed with it, but because it seemed to me to bring out particularly clearly the distinction between some of the most fundamental subjects of ethical discussion. This first part consisted in asserting that there is a certain characteristic which belongs to absolutely *all* voluntary actions which are right, and *only* to those which are right; another closely allied characteristic which belongs to *all* voluntary actions which ought to be done or are duties, and *only* to these; a third characteristic which belongs to *all* voluntary actions which are wrong, ought not to be done, or which it is our duty not to do, and *only* to those voluntary actions of which these things are true. And when the theory makes these assertions it means the words 'all' and 'only' to be understood quite strictly. That is to say, it means its propositions to apply to absolutely every voluntary action, which ever has been done, or ever will be done, no matter who did it, or when it was or will be done; and not only to those which actually have been or will be done, but also to all those which have been or will be *possible*, in a certain definite sense.

The sense in which it means its propositions to apply to *possible*, as well as actual, voluntary actions, is, it must be remembered, only if we agree to give the name 'possible' to all those actions which an agent *could* have done, *if* he had chosen, and to those which, in the future, any agent will be able to do, *if* he were to choose to do them. Possible actions, in this sense, form a perfectly definite group; and we do, as a matter of fact, often make judgements as to whether they would have been or would be right, and as to whether they ought to have been done in the past, or ought to be done in the future. We say, 'So-and-so ought to have done this on that occasion,' or 'It would have been perfectly right for him to have done this,' although as a matter of fact, he did not do it; or we say, 'You ought to do this,' or 'It will be quite right for you to do this,' although it subsequently turns out, that the action in question is one which you do not actually perform. Our theory says, then, with regard to all actions, which were in this sense possible in the past, that they *would have been* right, if and only if they *would* have produced a maximum of pleasure; just as it says that all actual past voluntary actions *were* right, if and only if they *did* produce a maximum of pleasure. And similarly, with regard to all voluntary actions which will be possible in the future, it says that they will be right, if and only if they *would* produce a maximum of pleasure; just as it says with regard to all that will actually be done, that they will be right, if and only if they *do* produce a maximum of pleasure.

Our theory does, then, even in its first part, deal, in a sense, with possible actions, as well as actual ones. It professes to tell us, not only which among actual past voluntary actions *were* right, but also which among those which were possible *would have been* right if they had been done; and not only which among the voluntary actions which actually will be done in the future, *will* be right, but also which among those which will be possible, *would* be right, if they *were* to be done. And in doing this, it does, of course, give us a criterion, or test, or standard, by means of which we could, theoretically at least, discover with regard to absolutely every voluntary action, whichever either has been or will be either actual or possible, whether it was or will be right or not. If we want to discover with regard to a voluntary action which was actually done or was possible in the past, whether it was right or would have been right, we have only to ask: Could the agent, on the occasion in question, have done anything else instead, which would have produced more pleasure? If he could, then the action in question was or would have been wrong; if he could not, then it was or would have been right. And similarly, if we want to discover with regard to an action, which we are contemplating in the future, whether it would be right for us to do it, we have only to ask: Could I do anything else instead which would produce more pleasure? If I could, it will be wrong to do the action; if I could not, it will be right. Our theory does then, even in its first part, profess to give us an absolutely universal *criterion* of right and wrong; and similarly also an absolutely universal *criterion* of what ought or ought not to be done.

But though it does this, there is something else which it does not do. It only asserts, in this first part, that the producing of a maximum of pleasure is a characteristic, which did and will belong, *as a matter of fact*, to all right voluntary actions (actual or possible), and only to right ones; it does not, in its first part, go on to assert that it is *because* they possess this characteristic that such actions are right. This second assertion is the first which it goes on to make in its second part; and everybody can see, I think, that there is an important difference between the two assertions.

Many people might be inclined to admit that, whenever a man acts wrongly, his action always does, on the whole, result in greater unhappiness than would have ensued if he had acted differently; and that when he acts rightly this result *never* ensues: that, on the contrary, right action always does in the end bring about at least as much happiness, on the whole, as the agent could possibly have brought about by any other action which was in his power. The proposition that wrong action always *does*, and (considering how the Universe is constituted) always *would*, in the long run, lead to less pleasure than the agent could have brought about by acting differently, and that right action never *does* and never *would* have this effect, is a proposition which a great many people might be inclined to accept; and this is all which, in its first part, our theory asserts. But many of those who would be inclined to assent to this proposition, would feel great hesitation in going on to assert that this is *why* actions are right or wrong respectively. There seems to be a very important difference between the two positions. We may hold, for instance, that an act of murder, whenever it is wrong, always does produce greater unhappiness than would have followed if the agent had chosen instead some one of the other alternatives, which he could have carried out, *if* he had so chosen; and we may hold that this is true of all other wrong actions, actual or possible, and never of any right ones: but it seems a very different thing to hold that murder and all other wrong actions are wrong, when they are wrong, *because* they have this result—*because* they produce less than the possible maximum of pleasure. We may hold, that is to say, that the fact that it does produce or would produce *less* than a maximum of pleasure is absolutely always a *sign* that a voluntary action is wrong, while the fact that it does produce or would produce a maximum of pleasure is absolutely always a *sign* that it is right; but this does not seem to commit us to the very different proposition that these results, besides being *signs* of right and wrong, are also the *reasons* why actions are right when they are right, and wrong when they are wrong. Everybody can see, I think, that the distinction is important; although I think it is often overlooked in ethical discussions. And it is precisely this distinction which separates what I have called the first part of our theory, from the first of the assertions which it goes on to make in its second part. In its first part it only asserts that the producing or not producing a maximum of pleasure are, absolutely universally, *signs* of right and wrong in voluntary actions; in its second part it goes on to assert that it is *because* they produce these results that voluntary actions are right when they are right, and wrong when they are wrong.

There is, then, plainly some important difference between the assertion, which our theory made in its first part, to the effect that all right
voluntary actions, and only those which are right, do, *in fact*, produce a
maximum of pleasure, and the assertion, which it now goes on to make,
that this is *why* they are right. And if we ask why the difference is important, the answer is, so far as I can see, as follows. Namely, if we say
that actions are right, *because* they produce a maximum of pleasure, we
imply that, provided they produced this result, they *would* be right, *no
matter what other effects they might produce* as well. We imply, in short,
that their rightness does *not* depend at all upon their other effects, but *only*
on the quantity of pleasure that they produce. And this is a very different
thing from merely saying that the producing a maximum of pleasure is
always, as a matter of fact, a *sign* of rightness. It is quite obvious, that, in
the Universe as it is actually constituted, pleasure and pain are by no means
the only results of any of our actions: they all produce immense numbers
of other results as well. And so long as we merely assert that the producing
a maximum of pleasure is a *sign* of rightness, we leave open the possibility
that it is so only because this result does always, as a matter of fact, happen
to coincide with the production of *other* results; but that it is partly upon
these other results that the rightness of the action depends. But so soon
as we assert that actions are right, *because* they produce a maximum of
pleasure, we cut away this possibility; we assert that actions which produced such a maximum *would* be right, even if they did not produce any
of the other effects, which, as a matter of fact, they always do produce.
And this, I think, is the chief reason why many persons who would be inclined to assent to the first proposition, would hesitate to assent to the
second.

It is, for instance, commonly held that some pleasures are higher or
better than others, even though they may not be more pleasant; and that
where we have a choice between procuring for ourselves or others a higher
or a lower pleasure, it is generally right to prefer the former, even though
it may perhaps be less pleasant. And, of course, even those who hold that
actions are only right because of the quantity of pleasure they produce, and
not at all because of the quality of these pleasures, might quite consistently
hold that it is *as a matter of fact* generally right to prefer higher pleasures
to lower ones, even though they may be less pleasant. They might hold
that this is the case, on the ground that higher pleasures, even when less
pleasant in themselves, do, if we take into account all their further effects,
tend to produce more pleasure on the whole than lower ones. There is a
good deal to be said for the view that this does actually happen, as the
Universe is actually constituted; and that hence an action which causes a
higher pleasure to be enjoyed instead of a lower one, will in general
cause *more* pleasure in its *total* effects, though it may cause *less* in its *immediate* effects. And this is why those who hold that higher pleasures are
in general to be preferred to lower ones, may nevertheless admit that mere

quantity of pleasure is always, *in fact*, a correct *sign* or *criterion* of the rightness of an action.

But those who hold that actions are only right, *because* of the quantity of pleasure they produce, must hold also that, *if* higher pleasures did not, in their total effects, produce *more* pleasure than lower ones, then there *would* be no reason whatever for preferring them, provided they were not themselves more pleasant. *If* the *sole* effect of one action were to be the enjoyment of a certain amount of the most bestial or idiotic pleasure, and the *sole* effect of another were to be the enjoyment of a much more refined one, then they must hold that there would be no reason whatever for preferring the latter to the former, provided only that the mere quantity of pleasure enjoyed in each case were the same. And if the bestial pleasure were ever so slightly more pleasant than the other, then they must say it would be our positive duty to do the action which would bring it about rather than the other. This is a conclusion which does follow from the assertion that actions are right *because* they produce a maximum of pleasure, and which does not follow from the mere assertion that the producing a maximum of pleasure is always, *in fact*, a sign of rightness. And it is for this, and similar reasons, that it is important to distinguish the two propositions.

To many persons it may seem clear that it *would* be our duty to prefer some pleasures to others, even if they did not entail a greater *quantity* of pleasure; and hence that though actions which produce a maximum of pleasure are perhaps, *in fact*, always right, they are not right *because* of this, but only because the producing of this result does in fact happen to coincide with the producing of other results. They would say that though perhaps, in fact, actual cases never occur in which it *is* or would be wrong to do an action, which produces a maximum of pleasure, it is easy to *imagine* cases in which it *would* be wrong. *If*, for instance, we had to choose between creating a Universe, in which all the inhabitants were capable only of the lowest sensual pleasures, and another in which they were capable of the highest intellectual and aesthetic ones, it would, they would say, plainly be our duty to create the latter rather than the former, even though the mere quantity of pleasure enjoyed in it were rather less than in the former, and still more so if the quantities were equal. Or, to put it shortly, they would say that a world of men is preferable to a world of pigs, even though the pigs might enjoy as much or more pleasure than a world of men. And this is what our theory goes on to deny, when it says that voluntary actions are right, *because* they produce a maximum of pleasure. It implies, by saying this, that actions which produced a maximum of pleasure *would* always be right, no matter what their effects, in other respects, might be. And hence that it *would* be right to create a world in which there was no intelligence and none of the higher emotions, rather than one in which these were present in the highest degree, provided only that the mere quantity of pleasure enjoyed in the former were ever so little greater than that enjoyed in the latter.

Our theory asserts, then, in its second part, that voluntary actions are right when they are right, *because* they produce a maximum of pleasure; and in asserting this it takes a great step beyond what it asserted in its first part, since it now implies that an action which produced a maximum of pleasure always *would* be right, no matter how its results, in other respects, might compare with those of the other possible alternatives.

But it might be held that, even so, it does not imply that this would be so *absolutely unconditionally*. It might be held that though, in the Universe as actually constituted, actions are right *because* they produce a maximum of pleasure, and hence their rightness does not at all depend upon their *other* effects, yet this is only so for some such reason as that, in this Universe, all conscious beings do actually happen to desire pleasure; but that, if we could imagine a Universe, in which pleasure was not desired, then, in such a Universe, actions would *not* be right because they produced a maximum of pleasure; and hence that we cannot lay it down absolutely unconditionally that in all conceivable Universes any voluntary action would be right whenever and only when it produced a maximum of pleasure. For some such reason as this, it might be held that we must distinguish between the mere assertion that voluntary actions are right, when they are right, *because* they produce a maximum of pleasure, and the further assertion that this *would* be so in all conceivable circumstances and in any conceivable Universe. Those who assert the former are by no means necessarily bound to assert the latter also. To assert the latter is to take a still further step.

But the theory I wish to state does, in fact, take this further step. It asserts not only that, in the Universe as it is, voluntary actions are right *because* they produce a maximum of pleasure, but also that this would be so, *under any conceivable circumstances:* that if any conceivable being, in any conceivable Universe, were faced with a choice between an action which would cause more pleasure and one which would cause less, it would *always* be his duty to choose the former rather than the latter, no matter what the respects might be in which his Universe differed from ours. It may, at first sight, seem unduly bold to assert that any ethical truth can be absolutely unconditional in this sense. But many philosophers have held that some fundamental ethical principles certainly are thus unconditional. And a little reflection will suffice to show that the view that they may be so is at all events not absurd. We have many instances of other truths, which seem quite plainly to be of this nature. It seems quite clear, for instance, that it is not only true that twice two do make four, in the Universe as it actually is, but that they necessarily would make four, in any conceivable Universe, no matter how much it might differ from this one in other respects. And our theory is only asserting that the connexion which it believes to hold between rightness and the production of a maximum of pleasure is, in this respect, similar to the connexion asserted to hold between the number two and the number four, when we say that twice two are four. It asserts that, if any being whatever, in any circumstances whatever, had to choose between two actions, one of which would produce more pleasure than the other, it always would be his duty to choose the former rather than the latter: that this is absolutely unconditionally true. This assertion obviously goes very much further, both than the assertion which it made in its first part, to the effect that the producing a maximum of pleasure is a *sign* of rightness in the case of all voluntary actions, that ever have been or will be actual or possible, and also than the assertion, that in the Universe, as it is actually constituted, actions are right, when they are right, *because* they produce a maximum of pleasure. But bold as the assertion may seem, it is, at all events, not impossible that we should know it to be true.

Our theory asserts, therefore, in its second part: That, if we had to choose between two actions, one of which would have as its sole or total effects, an effect or set of effects, which we may call A, while the other would have as its sole or total effects, an effect or set of effects, which we may call B, then, *if* A contained more pleasure than B, it always would be our duty to choose the action which caused A rather than that which caused B. This, it asserts, would be absolutely *always* true, *no matter what A and B might be like in other respects.* And to assert this is (it now goes on to say) *equivalent* to asserting that any effect or set of effects which contains more pleasure is always *intrinsically better* than one which contains less.

By calling one effect or set of effects *intrinsically better* than another it means that it is better *in itself*, quite apart from any accompaniments or further effects which it may have. That is to say: To assert of any one thing, A, that it is *intrinsically* better than another, B, is to assert that if A existed *quite alone*, without any accompaniments or effects whatever—if, in short, A constituted the whole Universe, it would be better that such a Universe should exist, than that a Universe which consisted solely of B should exist instead. In order to discover whether any one thing is *intrinsically* better than another, we have always thus to consider whether it would be better that the one should exist *quite alone* than that the other should exist *quite alone*. No one thing or set of things, A, ever can be *intrinsically* better than another, B, unless it would be better that A should exist quite alone than that B should exist quite alone. Our theory asserts, therefore, that, wherever it is true that it would be our *duty* to choose A rather than B, if A and B were to be the sole effects of a pair of actions between which we had to choose, there it is always also true that it would be *better* that A should exist quite alone than that B should exist quite alone. And it asserts also, conversely, that wherever it is true that any one thing or set of things, A, is intrinsically better than another, B, there it would always also be our duty to choose an action of which A would be the sole effect rather than one of which B would be the sole effect, if we had to choose between them. But since, as we have seen, it holds that it never could be our duty to choose one action rather than another, unless the total effects of the one contained more pleasure than that of the other, it follows that, according to it, no effect or set of effects, A, can possibly be intrinsically better than another, B, *unless* it contains more pleasure. It holds, therefore, not only that any one effect or set of effects, which contains more pleasure, is always intrinsically better than one which contains less, but also that no effect or set of effects can be intrinsically better than another *unless* it contains more pleasure.

It is plain, then, that this theory assigns a quite unique position to pleasure and pain in two respects; or possibly only in one, since it is just possible that the two propositions which it makes about them are not merely equivalent, but absolutely identical—that is to say, are merely different ways of expressing exactly the same idea. The two propositions are these. (1) That if any one had to choose between two actions, one of which would, in its total effects, cause more pleasure than the other, it always would be his duty to choose the former; and that it never could be any one's duty to choose one action rather than another, unless its total effects contained more pleasure. (2) That any Universe, or part of a Universe, which contains more pleasure, is always intrinsically better than one which contains less; and that nothing can be intrinsically better than anything else, unless it contains more pleasure. It does seem to be just possible that these two propositions are merely two different ways of expressing exactly the same idea. The question whether they are so or not simply depends upon the question whether, when we say, 'It would be better that A should exist quite alone than that B should exist quite alone,' we are or are not saying exactly the same thing, as when we say, 'Supposing we had to choose between an action of which A would be the sole effect, and one of which B would be the sole effect, it would be our duty to choose the former rather than the latter.' And it certainly does seem, at first sight, as if the two propositions were not identical; as if we should not be saying exactly the same thing in asserting the one, as in asserting the other. But, even if they are not identical, our theory asserts that they are certainly *equivalent:* that, whenever the one is true, the other is certainly also true. And, if they are not identical, this assertion of equivalence amounts to the very important proposition that: An action is right, only if no action, which the agent could have done instead, would have had intrinsically better results: while an action is wrong, only if the agent *could* have done other action instead whose total results would have been intrinsically better. It certainly seems as if this proposition were not a mere tautology. And, if so, then we must admit that our theory assigns a unique position to pleasure and pain in two respects, and not in one only. It asserts, first of all, that they have a unique relation to right and wrong; and secondly, that they have a unique relation to *intrinsic value*.

Our theory asserts, then, that any whole which contains a greater amount of pleasure, is always intrinsically better than one which contains a smaller amount, no matter what the two may be like in other respects; and that no whole can be intrinsically better than another unless it contains more pleasure. But it must be remembered that throughout this discussion, we have, for the sake of convenience, been using the phrase 'contains more pleasure' in an inaccurate sense. I explained that I should say of one whole, A, that it contained more pleasure than another, B, whenever A and B were related to one another in either of the five following ways: namely (1) when A and B both contain an excess of pleasure over pain, but A contains a greater excess than B; (2) when A contains an excess of pleasure over pain, while B contains no excess either of pleasure over pain or of pain over pleasure; (3) when A contains an excess of pleasure over pain, while B contains an excess of pain over pleasure, (4) when A contains no excess either of pleasure over pain or of pain over pleasure, while B does contain an excess of pain over pleasure; and (5) when both A and B contain an excess of pain over pleasure, but A contains a smaller excess than B. Whenever in stating this theory, I have spoken of one whole, or effect, or set of effects, A, as containing more pleasure than another, B, I have always meant merely that A was related to B *in one or other of these five ways*. And so here, when our theory says that every whole which contains a greater amount of pleasure is always intrinsically better than one which contains less, and that nothing can be intrinsically better than anything else unless it contains more pleasure, this must be understood to mean that any whole, A, which stands to another, B, in *any one* of these five relations, is always intrinsically better than B, and that no one thing can be intrinsically better than another, unless it stands to it in *one or other* of these five relations. And it becomes important to remember this, when we go on to take account of another fact.

It is plain that when we talk of one thing being 'better' than another we may mean any one of five different things. We may mean either (1) that while both are positively good, the first is better; or (2) that while the first is positively good, the second is neither good nor bad, but indifferent; or (3) that while the first is positively good, the second is positively bad; or (4) that while the first is indifferent, the second is positively bad; or (5) that while both are positively bad, the first is less bad than the second. We should, in common life, say that one thing was 'better' than another, whenever it stood to that other in any one of these five relations. Or, in other words, we hold that among things which stand to one another in the relation of better and worse, some are positively good, others positively bad, and others neither good nor bad, but indifferent. And our theory holds that this is, in fact, the case, with things which have a place in the scale of *intrinsic* value: some of them are intrinsically good, others intrinsically bad, and others indifferent. And it would say that a whole is intrinsically good, whenever and only when it contains an excess of pleasure over pain; intrinsically bad, whenever and only when it contains an excess of pain over pleasure; and intrinsically indifferent, whenever and only when it contains neither.

In addition, therefore, to laying down precise rules as to what things are intrinsically *better* or *worse* than others, our theory also lays down equally precise ones as to what things are intrinsically *good* and *bad* and *indifferent*. By saying that a thing is intrinsically good it means that it would be a good thing that the thing in question should exist, even if it existed *quite alone*, without any further accompaniments or effects whatever. By saying that it is intrinsically bad, it means that it would be a bad thing or an evil that it should exist, even if it existed quite alone, without any further accompaniments or effects whatever. And by saying that it is intrinsically indifferent, it means that, if it existed *quite alone*, its existence would be neither a good nor an evil in any degree whatever. And just as the conceptions 'intrinsically better' and 'intrinsically worse' are connected in a perfectly precise manner with the conceptions 'right' and 'wrong,' so, it maintains, are these other conceptions also. To say of anything, A, that it is 'intrinsically good,' is equivalent to saying that, if we had to choose between an action of which A would be the sole or total effect, and an action, which would have absolutely no effects at all, it would always be our duty to choose the former, and wrong to choose the latter. And similarly to say of anything, A, that it is 'intrinsically bad,' is equivalent to saying that, if we had to choose between an action of which A would be the sole effect, and an action which would have absolutely no effects at all, it would always be our duty to choose the latter and wrong to choose the former. And finally, to say of anything, A, that it is 'intrinsically indifferent,' is equivalent to saying that, if we had to choose between an action, of which A would be the sole effect, and an action which would have absolutely no effects at all, it would not matter which we chose: either choice would be equally right.

To sum up, then, we may say that, in its second part, our theory lays down three principles. It asserts (1) that anything whatever, whether it be a single effect, or a whole set of effects, or a whole Universe, is *intrinsically good*, whenever and only when it either is or contains an excess of pleasure over pain; that anything whatever is *intrinsically bad*, whenever and only when it either is or contains an excess of pain over pleasure; and that all other things, no matter what their nature may be, are intrinsically indifferent. It asserts (2) that any one thing, whether it be a single effect, or a whole set of effects, or a whole Universe, is intrinsically *better* than another, whenever and only when the two are related to one another in one or other of the five following ways: namely, when either (*a*) while both are intrinsically good, the second is not so good as the first; or (*b*) while the first is intrinsically good, the second is intrinsically indifferent; or (*c*) while the first is intrinsically good, the second is intrinsically bad; or (d) while the first is intrinsically indifferent, the second is intrinsically bad; or (e) while both are intrinsically bad, the first is not so bad as the second. And it asserts (3) that, if we had to choose between two actions one of which would have intrinsically better total effects than the other, it always would be our duty to choose the former, and wrong to choose the latter; and that no action ever can be right *if* we could have done anything else instead which would have had intrinsically better total effects, nor wrong, *unless* we could have done something else instead which would have had intrinsically better total effects. From these three principles taken together, the whole theory follows. And whether it be true or false, it is, I think, at least a perfectly clear and intelligible theory. Whether it is or is not of any practical importance is, indeed, another question. But, even if it were of none whatever, it certainly lays down propositions of so fundamental and so far-reaching a character, that it seems worth while to consider whether they are true or false. There remain, I think, only two points which should be noticed with regard to it, before we go on to consider the principal objections which may be urged against it.

It should be noticed, first, that, though this theory asserts that nothing is *intrinsically* good, unless it is or contains an excess of pleasure over pain, it is very far from asserting that nothing is *good*, unless it fulfils this condition. By saying that a thing is *intrinsically good*, it means, as has been explained, that the existence of the thing in question *would* be a good, even if it existed quite alone, without any accompaniments or effects whatever; and it is quite plain that when we call things 'good' we by no means always mean this: we by no means always mean that they *would* be good, even if they existed quite alone. Very often, for instance, when we say that a thing is 'good,' we mean that it is good *because of its effects;* and we should not for a moment maintain that it *would* be good, even if it had no effects at all. We are, for instance, familiar with the idea that it is sometimes a good thing for people to suffer pain; and yet we should be very loth to maintain that in all such cases their suffering *would* be a good thing, even if nothing were gained by it—if it had no further effects. We do, in general, maintain that suffering is good, only *where* and *because* it has further good effects. And similarly with many other things. Many things, therefore, which are *not* 'intrinsically' good, may nevertheless be 'good' in some one or other of the senses in which we use that highly ambiguous word. And hence our theory can and would quite consistently maintain that, while nothing is *intrinsically* good except pleasure or wholes which contain pleasure, many other things really are 'good'; and similarly that, while nothing is *intrinsically* bad except pain or wholes which contain it, yet many other things are really 'bad.' It would, for instance, maintain that it is *always* a good thing to act rightly, and a bad thing to act wrongly; although it would say at the same time that, since actions, strictly speaking, do not *contain* either pleasure or pain, but are only accompanied by or causes of them, a right action is *never intrinsically* good, nor a wrong one *intrinsically* bad. And similarly it would maintain that it is perfectly true that some men are 'good,' and others 'bad,' and some better than others; although no man can strictly be said to *contain* either pleasure or pain, and hence none can be either intrinsically good or intrinsically bad or intrinsically better than any other. It would even maintain (and this also it can do quite consistently), that events which are *intrinsically* good are nevertheless very often bad, and intrinsically bad ones good. It would, for instance, say that it is often a very bad thing for a man to enjoy a particular pleasure on a particular occasion, although the event, which consists in his enjoying it, may be intrinsically good, since it contains an excess of pleasure over pain. It may often be a very bad thing that such an event should happen, because it *causes* the man himself or other beings to have less pleasure or more pain in the future, than they would otherwise have had. And for similar reasons it may often be a very good thing that an intrinsically bad event should happen.

It is important to remember all this, because otherwise the theory may appear much more paradoxical than it really is. It may, for instance, appear, at first sight, as if it denied all value to anything except pleasure and wholes which contain it—a view which would be extremely paradoxical if it were held. But it does *not* do this. It does not deny all value to other things, but only all *intrinsic* value—a very different thing. It only says that none of them *would* have any value if they existed quite alone. But, of course, as a matter of fact, none of them do exist quite alone, and hence it may quite consistently allow that, as it is, many of them do have very great value. Concerning kinds of value, other than intrinsic value, it does not profess to lay down any general rules at all. And its reason for confining itself to intrinsic value is because it holds that this and this alone is related to right and wrong in the perfectly definite manner explained above. Whenever an action is right, it is right only if and because the total effects of no action, which the agent could have done instead, would have had more *intrinsic* value; and whenever an action is wrong, it is wrong only if and because the total effects of some other action, which the agent could have done instead, would have had more *intrinsic* value. This proposition, which is true of *intrinsic* value, is not, it holds, true of value of any other kind.

And a second point which should be noticed about this theory is the following. It is often represented as asserting that pleasure is the only thing which is *ultimately* good or desirable, and pain the only thing which is *ultimately* bad or undesirable; or as asserting that pleasure is the only thing which is good *for its own sake*, and pain the only thing which is bad *for its own sake*. And there is, I think, a sense in which it does assert this. But these expressions are not commonly carefully defined; and it is worth noticing that, if our theory does assert these propositions, the expressions *'ultimately* good' or 'good *for its own sake'* must be understood in a different sense from that which has been assigned above to the expression *'intrinsically* good.' We must not take *'ultimately* good' or 'good *for its own sake'* to be synonyms for *'intrinsically* good.' For our theory most emphatically does *not* assert that pleasure is the only thing *intrinsically* good, and pain the only thing *intrinsically* evil. On the contrary, it asserts that any whole which *contains* an excess of pleasure over pain is *intrinsically* good, no matter how much else it may contain besides; and similarly that any whole which contains an excess of pain over pleasure is *intrinsically* bad. This distinction between the conception expressed by *'ultimately* good' or 'good *for its own sake,'* on the one hand, and that expressed by *'intrinsically* good,' on the other, is not commonly made; and yet obviously we must make it, if we are to say that our theory does assert that pleasure is the only *ultimate* good, and pain the only *ultimate* evil. The two conceptions, if used in this way, have one important point in common, namely, that both of them will only apply to things whose existence *would* be good, even if they existed quite alone. Whether we assert that a thing is 'ultimately good' or 'good for its own sake' or 'intrinsically good,' we are always asserting that it would be good, even if it existed quite alone. But the two conceptions differ in respect of the fact that, whereas a whole which is 'intrinsically good' may contain parts which are *not* intrinsically good, i.e. *would* not be good, if they existed quite alone; anything which is 'ultimately good' or 'good for its own sake' can contain no such parts. This, I think, is the meaning which we must assign to the expressions 'ultimately good' or 'good for its own sake,' if we are to say that our theory asserts pleasure to be the *only* thing 'ultimately good' or 'good for its own sake.' We may, in short, divide intrinsically good things into two classes: namely (1) those which, while as wholes they are intrinsically good, nevertheless contain some parts which are not intrinsically good; and (2) those, which either have no parts at all, or, if they have any, have none but what are themselves intrinsically good. And we may thus, if we please, confine the terms 'ultimately good' or 'good for their own sakes' to things which belong to the second of these two classes. We may, of course, make a precisely similar distinction between two classes of intrinsically bad things. And it is only if we do this that our theory can be truly said to assert that nothing is 'ultimately good' or 'good for its own sake,' except pleasure; and nothing 'ultimately bad' or 'bad for its own sake,' except pain.

Such is the ethical theory which I have chosen to state, because it seems to me particularly simple, and hence to bring out particularly clearly some of the main questions which have formed the subject of ethical discussion.

What is specially important is to distinguish the question, which it professes to answer in its first part, from the much more radical questions, which it professes to answer in its second. In its first part, it only professes to answer the question: What characteristic is there which does actually, *as a matter of fact*, belong to all right voluntary actions, which ever have been or will be done in this world? While, in its second part, it professes to answer the much more fundamental question: What characteristic is there which *would* belong to absolutely any voluntary action, which was right, in any conceivable Universe, and under any conceivable circumstances? These two questions are obviously extremely different, and by the theory I have stated I mean a theory which does profess to give an answer to *both*.

Whether this theory has ever been held in exactly the form in which I have stated it, I should not like to say. But many people have certainly held something very like it; and it seems to be what is *often* meant by the familiar name 'Utilitarianism,' which is the reason why I have chosen this name as the title of these two chapters. It must not, however, be assumed that anybody who talks about 'Utilitarianism' *always* means precisely this theory in all its details. On the contrary, many even of those who call themselves Utilitarians would object to some of its most fundamental propositions. One of the difficulties which occurs in ethical discussions is that no single name, which has ever been proposed as the name of an ethical theory, has any absolutely fixed significance. On the contrary, every name may be, and often is, used as a name for several different theories, which may differ from one another in very important respects. Hence, whenever anybody uses such a name, you can never trust to the name alone, but must always look carefully to see exactly what he means by it.

II

MOORE AND THE NATURALISTIC FALLACY

The Indefinability of Good *

G. E. MOORE

PRINCIPIA ETHICA: PREFACE

IT APPEARS TO ME that in Ethics, as in all other philosophical studies, the difficulties and disagreements, of which its history is full, are mainly due to a very simple cause: namely to the attempt to answer questions, without first discovering precisely *what* question it is which you desire to answer. I do not know how far this source of error would be done away, if philosophers would *try* to discover what question they were asking, before they set about to answer it; for the work of analysis and distinction is often very difficult: we may often fail to make the necessary discovery, even though we make a definite attempt to do so. But I am inclined to think that in many cases a resolute attempt would be sufficient to ensure success; so that, if only this attempt were made, many of the most glaring difficulties and disagreements in philosophy would disappear. At all events, philosophers seem, in general, not to make the attempt; and, whether in consequence of this omission or not, they are constantly endeavouring to prove that 'Yes' or 'No' will answer questions, to which *neither* answer is correct, owing to the fact that what they have before their minds is not one question, but several, to some of which the true answer is 'No,' to others 'Yes.'

I have tried in this book to distinguish clearly two kinds of question, which moral philosophers have always professed to answer, but which, as I have tried to shew, they have almost always confused both with one another and with other questions. These two questions may be expressed, the first in the form: What kind of things ought to exist for their own sakes? the second in the form: What kind of actions ought we to perform? I have tried to shew exactly what it is that we ask about a thing, when we ask whether it ought to exist for its own sake, is good in itself or has intrinsic value; and exactly what it is that we ask about an action, when we ask whether we ought to do it, whether it is a right action or a duty.

But from a clear insight into the nature of these two questions, there appears to me to follow a second most important result: namely, what is

* Reprinted by kind permission of the author and the publisher from *Principia Ethica*, pp. vii–xii, 1–36.

the nature of the evidence, by which alone any ethical proposition can be proved or disproved, confirmed or rendered doubtful. Once we recognise the exact meaning of the two questions, I think it also becomes plain exactly what kind of reasons are relevant as arguments for or against any particular answer to them. It becomes plain that, for answers to the *first* question, no relevant evidence whatever can be adduced: from no other truth, except themselves alone, can it be inferred that they are either true or false. We can guard against error only by taking care, that, when we try to answer a question of this kind, we have before our minds that question only, and not some other or others; but that there is great danger of such errors of confusion I have tried to shew, and also what are the chief precautions by the use of which we may guard against them. As for the *second* question, it becomes equally plain, that any answer to it *is* capable of proof or disproof—that, indeed, so many different considerations are relevant to its truth or falsehood, as to make the attainment of probability very difficult, and the attainment of certainty impossible. Nevertheless the *kind* of evidence, which is both necessary and alone relevant to such proof and disproof, is capable of exact definition. Such evidence must contain propositions of two kinds and of two kinds only: it must consist, in the first place, of truths with regard to the results of the action in question—of *causal* truths—but it must *also* contain ethical truths of our first or self-evident class. Many truths of both kinds are necessary to the proof that any action ought to be done; and any other kind of evidence is wholly irrelevant. It follows that, if any ethical philosopher offers for propositions of the first kind any evidence whatever, or if, for propositions of the second kind, he either fails to adduce both causal and ethical truths, or adduces truths that are neither, his reasoning has not the least tendency to establish his conclusions. But not only are his conclusions totally devoid of weight: we have, moreover, reason to suspect him of the error of confusion; since the offering of irrelevant evidence generally indicates that the philosopher who offers it has had before his mind, not the question which he professes to answer, but some other entirely different one. Ethical discussion, hitherto, has perhaps consisted chiefly in reasoning of this totally irrelevant kind.

One main object of this book may, then, be expressed by slightly changing one of Kant's famous titles. I have endeavoured to write 'Prolegomena to any future Ethics that can possibly pretend to be scientific.' In other words, I have endeavoured to discover what are the fundamental principles of ethical reasoning; and the establishment of these principles, rather than of any conclusions which may be attained by their use, may be regarded as my main object. I have, however, also attempted, in Chapter VI, to present some conclusions, with regard to the proper answer of the question 'What is good in itself?' which are very different from any which have commonly been advocated by philosophers. I have tried to define the classes within which all great goods and evils fall; and I have maintained that very many different things are good and evil in themselves, and that neither class of things possesses any other property which is both common to all its members and peculiar to them.

In order to express the fact that ethical propositions of my *first* class are incapable of proof or disproof, I have sometimes followed Sidgwick's usage in calling them 'Intuitions.' But I beg it may be noticed that I am not an 'Intuitionist,' in the ordinary sense of the term. Sidgwick himself seems never to have been clearly aware of the immense importance of the difference which distinguishes his Intuitionism from the common doctrine, which has generally been called by that name. The Intuitionist proper is distinguished by maintaining that propositions of my *second* class— propositions which assert that a certain action is *right* or a *duty*—are incapable of proof or disproof by any enquiry into the results of such actions. I, on the contrary, am no less anxious to maintain that propositions of *this* kind are *not* 'Intuitions,' than to maintain that propositions of my *first* class *are* Intuitions.

Again, I would wish it observed that, when I call such propositions 'Intuitions,' I mean *merely* to assert that they are incapable of proof; I imply nothing whatever as to the manner or origin of our cognition of them. Still less do I imply (as most intuitionists have done) that any proposition whatever is true, *because* we cognise it in a particular way or by the exercise of any particular faculty: I hold, on the contrary, that in every way in which it is possible to cognise a true proposition, it is also possible to cognise a false one.

When this book had been already completed, I found, in Brentano's 'Origin of the Knowledge of Right and Wrong,' [1] opinions far more closely resembling my own, than those of any other ethical writer with whom I am acquainted. Brentano appears to agree with me completely (1) in regarding all ethical propositions as defined by the fact that they predicate a single unique objective concept; (2) in dividing such propositions sharply into the same two kinds; (3) in holding that the first kind are incapable of proof; and (4) with regard to the kind of evidence which is necessary and relevant to the proof of the second kind. But he regards the fundamental ethical concept as being, not the simple one which I denote by 'good,' but the complex one which I have taken to define 'beautiful'; and he does not recognise, but even denies by implication, the principle which I have called *the principle of organic unities*. In consequence of these two differences, his conclusions as to what things are good in themselves, also differ very materially from mine. He agrees, however, that there are many different goods, and that the love of good and beautiful objects constitutes an important class among them.

[1] 'The Origin of the Knowledge of Right and Wrong.' By Franz Brentano. English Translation by Cecil Hague. Constable, 1902.—I have written a review of this book, which will, I hope, appear in the *International Journal of Ethics* for October, 1903. I may refer to this review for a fuller account of my reasons for disagreeing with Brentano.

I wish to refer to one oversight, of which I became aware only when it was too late to correct it, and which may, I am afraid, cause unnecessary trouble to some readers. I have omitted to discuss directly the mutual relations of the several different notions, which are all expressed by the word 'end.' The consequences of this omission may perhaps be partially avoided by a reference to my article on 'Teleology' in Baldwin's *Dictionary of Philosophy and Psychology*.

If I were to rewrite my work now, I should make a very different, and I believe that I could make a much better book. But it may be doubted whether, in attempting to satisfy myself, I might not merely render more obscure the ideas which I am most anxious to convey, without a corresponding gain in completeness and accuracy. However that may be, my belief that to publish the book as it stands was probably the best thing I could do, does not prevent me from being painfully aware that it is full of defects.

PRINCIPIA ETHICA: CHAPTER I
THE SUBJECT-MATTER OF ETHICS

1. It is very easy to point out some among our every-day judgments, with the truth of which Ethics is undoubtedly concerned. Whenever we say, 'So and so is a good man,' or 'That fellow is a villain'; whenever we ask, 'What ought I to do?' or 'Is it wrong for me to do like this?'; whenever we hazard such remarks as 'Temperance is a virtue and drunkenness a vice'—it is undoubtedly the business of Ethics to discuss such questions and such statements; to argue what is the true answer when we ask what it is right to do, and to give reasons for thinking that our statements about the character of persons or the morality of actions are true or false. In the vast majority of cases, where we make statements involving any of the terms 'virtue,' 'vice,' 'duty,' 'right,' 'ought,' 'good,' 'bad,' we are making ethical judgments; and if we wish to discuss their truth, we shall be discussing a point of Ethics.

So much as this is not disputed; but it falls very far short of defining the province of Ethics. That province may indeed be defined as the whole truth about that which is at the same time common to all such judgments and peculiar to them. But we have still to ask the question: What is it that is thus common and peculiar? And this is a question to which very different answers have been given by ethical philosophers of acknowledged reputation, and none of them, perhaps, completely satisfactory.

2. If we take such examples as those given above, we shall not be far wrong in saying that they are all of them concerned with the question of 'conduct'—with the question, what, in the conduct of us, human beings, is good, and what is bad, what is right, and what is wrong. For when we say that a man is good, we commonly mean that he acts rightly; when we say that drunkenness is a vice, we commonly mean that to get drunk is a

wrong or wicked action. And this discussion of human conduct is, in fact, that with which the name 'Ethics' is most intimately associated. It is so associated by derivation; and conduct is undoubtedly by far the commonest and most generally interesting object of ethical judgments.

Accordingly, we find that many ethical philosophers are disposed to accept as an adequate definition of 'Ethics' the statement that it deals with the question what is good or bad in human conduct. They hold that its enquiries are properly confined to 'conduct' or to 'practice'; they hold that the name 'practical philosophy' covers all the matter with which it has to do. Now, without discussing the proper meaning of the word (for verbal questions are properly left to the writers of dictionaries and other persons interested in literature; philosophy, as we shall see, has no concern with them), I may say that I intend to use 'Ethics' to cover more than this—a usage, for which there is, I think, quite sufficient authority. I am using it to cover an enquiry for which, at all events, there is no other word: the general enquiry into what is good.

Ethics is undoubtedly concerned with the question what good conduct is; but, being concerned with this, it obviously does not start at the beginning, unless it is prepared to tell us what is good as well as what is conduct. For 'good conduct' is a complex notion: all conduct is not good; for some is certainly bad and some may be indifferent. And on the other hand, other things, beside conduct, may be good; and if they are so, then, 'good' denotes some property, that is common to them and conduct; and if we examine good conduct alone of all good things, then we shall be in danger of mistaking for this property, some property which is not shared by those other things: and thus we shall have made a mistake about Ethics even in this limited sense; for we shall not know what good conduct really is. This is a mistake which many writers have actually made, from limiting their enquiry to conduct. And hence I shall try to avoid it by considering first what is good in general; hoping, that if we can arrive at any certainty about this, it will be much easier to settle the question of good conduct: for we all know pretty well what 'conduct' is. This, then, is our first question: What is good? and What is bad? and to the discussion of this question (or these questions) I give the name of Ethics, since that science must, at all events, include it.

3. But this is a question which may have many meanings. If, for example, each of us were to say 'I am doing good now' or 'I had a good dinner yesterday,' these statements would each of them be some sort of answer to our question, although perhaps a false one. So, too, when A asks B what school he ought to send his son to, B's answer will certainly be an ethical judgment. And similarly all distribution of praise or blame to any personage or thing that has existed, now exists, or will exist, does give some answer to the question 'What is good?' In all such cases some particular thing is judged to be good or bad: the question 'What?' is answered by 'This.' But this is not the sense in which a scientific Ethics asks the question. Not one,

of all the many million answers of this kind, which must be true, can form a part of an ethical system; although that science must contain reasons and principles sufficient for deciding on the truth of all of them. There are far too many persons, things and events in the world, past, present, or to come, for a discussion of their individual merits to be embraced in any science. Ethics, therefore, does not deal at all with facts of this nature, facts that are unique, individual, absolutely particular; facts with which such studies as history, geography, astronomy, are compelled, in part at least, to deal. And, for this reason, it is not the business of the ethical philosopher to give personal advice or exhortation.

4. But there is another meaning which may be given to the question 'What is good?' 'Books are good' would be an answer to it, though an answer obviously false; for some books are very bad indeed. And ethical judgments of this kind do indeed belong to Ethics; though I shall not deal with many of them. Such is the judgment 'Pleasure is good'—a judgment, of which Ethics should discuss the truth, although it is not nearly as important as that other judgment, with which we shall be much occupied presently—'Pleasure *alone* is good.' It is judgments of this sort, which are made in such books on Ethics as contain a list of 'virtues'—in Aristotle's 'Ethics' for example. But it is judgments of precisely the same kind, which form the substance of what is commonly supposed to be a study different from Ethics, and one much less respectable—the study of Casuistry. We may be told that Casuistry differs from Ethics, in that it is much more detailed and particular, Ethics much more general. But it is most important to notice that Casuistry does not deal with anything that is absolutely particular—particular in the only sense in which a perfectly precise line can be drawn between it and what is general. It is not particular in the sense just noticed, the sense in which this book is a particular book, and A's friend's advice particular advice. Casuistry may indeed be *more* particular and Ethics *more* general; but that means that they differ only in degree and not in kind. And this is universally true of 'particular' and 'general,' when used in this common, but inaccurate, sense. So far as Ethics allows itself to give lists of virtues or even to name constituents of the Ideal, it is indistinguishable from Casuistry. Both alike deal with what is general, in the sense in which physics and chemistry deal with what is general. Just as chemistry aims at discovering what are the properties of oxygen, *wherever it occurs,* and not only of this or that particular specimen of oxygen; so Casuistry aims at discovering what actions are good, *whenever they occur.* In this respect Ethics and Casuistry alike are to be classed with such sciences as physics, chemistry and physiology, in their absolute distinction from those of which history and geography are instances. And it is to be noted that, owing to their detailed nature, casuistical investigations are actually nearer to physics and to chemistry than are the investigations usually assigned to Ethics. For just as physics cannot rest content with the discovery that light is propagated by waves of ether, but must go on to

discover the particular nature of the ether-waves corresponding to each several colour; so Casuistry, not content with the general law that charity is a virtue, must attempt to discover the relative merits of every different form of charity. Casuistry forms, therefore, part of the ideal of ethical science: Ethics cannot be complete without it. The defects of Casuistry are not defects of principle; no objection can be taken to its aim and object. It has failed only because it is far too difficult a subject to be treated adequately in our present state of knowledge. The casuist has been unable to distinguish, in the cases which he treats, those elements upon which their value depends. Hence he often thinks two cases to be alike in respect of value, when in reality they are alike only in some other respect. It is to mistakes of this kind that the pernicious influence of such investigations has been due. For Casuistry is the goal of ethical investigation. It cannot be safely attempted at the beginning of our studies, but only at the end.

5. But our question 'What is good?' may have still another meaning. We may, in the third place, mean to ask, not what thing or things are good, but how 'good' is to be defined. This is an enquiry which belongs only to Ethics, not to Casuistry; and this is the enquiry which will occupy us first.

It is an enquiry to which most special attention should be directed; since this question, how 'good' is to be defined, is the most fundamental question in all Ethics. That which is meant by 'good' is, in fact, except its converse 'bad,' the *only* simple object of thought which is peculiar to Ethics. Its definition is, therefore, the most essential point in the definition of Ethics; and moreover a mistake with regard to it entails a far larger number of erroneous ethical judgments than any other. Unless this first question be fully understood, and its true answer clearly recognised, the rest of Ethics is as good as useless from the point of view of systematic knowledge. True ethical judgments, of the two kinds last dealt with, may indeed be made by those who do not know the answer to this question as well as by those who do; and it goes without saying that the two classes of people may lead equally good lives. But it is extremely unlikely that the *most general* ethical judgments will be equally valid, in the absence of a true answer to this question: I shall presently try to shew that the gravest errors have been largely due to beliefs in a false answer. And, in any case, it is impossible that, till the answer to this question be known, any one should know *what is the evidence* for any ethical judgment whatsoever. But the main object of Ethics, as a systematic science, is to give correct *reasons* for thinking that this or that is good; and, unless this question be answered, such reasons cannot be given. Even, therefore, apart from the fact that a false answer leads to false conclusions, the present enquiry is a most necessary and important part of the science of Ethics.

6. What, then, is good? How is good to be defined? Now, it may be thought that this is a verbal question. A definition does indeed often mean the expressing of one word's meaning in other words. But this is not the sort of definition I am asking for. Such a definition can never be of ultimate

importance in any study except lexicography. If I wanted that kind of definition I should have to consider in the first place how people generally used the word 'good'; but my business is not with its proper usage, as established by custom. I should, indeed, be foolish, if I tried to use it for something which it did not usually denote: if, for instance, I were to announce that, whenever I used the word 'good,' I must be understood to be thinking of that object which is usually denoted by the word 'table.' I shall, therefore, use the word in the sense in which I think it is ordinarily used; but at the same time I am not anxious to discuss whether I am right in thinking that it is so used. My business is solely with that object or idea, which I hold, rightly or wrongly, that the word is generally used to stand for. What I want to discover is the nature of that object or idea, and about this I am extremely anxious to arrive at an agreement.

But, if we understand the question in this sense, my answer to it may seem a very disappointing one. If I am asked 'What is good?' my answer is that good is good, and that is the end of the matter. Or if I am asked 'How is good to be defined?' my answer is that it cannot be defined, and that is all I have to say about it. But disappointing as these answers may appear, they are of the very last importance. To readers who are familiar with philosophic terminology, I can express their importance by saying that they amount to this: That propositions about the good are all of them synthetic and never analytic; and that is plainly no trivial matter. And the same thing may be expressed more popularly, by saying that, if I am right, then nobody can foist upon us such an axiom as that 'Pleasure is the only good' or that 'The good is the desired' on the pretence that this is 'the very meaning of the word.'

7. Let us, then, consider this position. My point is that 'good' is a simple notion, just as 'yellow' is a simple notion; that, just as you cannot, by any manner of means, explain to any one who does not already know it, what yellow is, so you cannot explain what good is. Definitions of the kind that I was asking for, definitions which describe the real nature of the object or notion denoted by a word, and which do not merely tell us what the word is used to mean, are only possible when the object or notion in question is something complex. You can give a definition of a horse, because a horse has many different properties and qualities, all of which you can enumerate. But when you have enumerated them all, when you have reduced a horse to his simplest terms, then you can no longer define those terms. They are simply something which you think of or perceive, and to any one who cannot think of or perceive them, you can never, by any definition, make their nature known. It may perhaps be objected to this that we are able to describe to others, objects which they have never seen or thought of. We can, for instance, make a man understand what a chimaera is, although he has never heard of one or seen one. You can tell him that it is an animal with a lioness's head and body, with a goat's head growing from the middle of its back, and with a snake

in place of a tail. But here the object which you are describing is a complex object; it is entirely composed of parts, with which we are all perfectly familiar—a snake, a goat, a lioness; and we know, too, the manner in which those parts are to be put together, because we know what is meant by the middle of a lioness's back, and where her tail is wont to grow. And so it is with all objects, not previously known, which we are able to define: they are all complex; all composed of parts, which may themselves, in the first instance, be capable of similar definition, but which must in the end be reducible to simplest parts, which can no longer be defined. But yellow and good, we say, are not complex: they are notions of that simple kind, out of which definitions are composed and with which the power of further defining ceases.

8. When we say, as Webster says, 'The definition of horse is "A hoofed quadruped of the genus Equus," ' we may, in fact, mean three different things. (1) We may mean merely: 'When I say "horse," you are to understand that I am talking about a hoofed quadruped of the genus Equus.' This might be called the arbitrary verbal definition: and I do not mean that good is indefinable in that sense. (2) We may mean, as Webster ought to mean: 'When most English people say "horse," they mean a hoofed quadruped of the genus Equus.' This may be called the verbal definition proper, and I do not say that good is indefinable in this sense either; for it is certainly possible to discover how people use a word: otherwise, we could never have known that 'good' may be translated by 'gut' in German and by 'bon' in French. But (3) we may, when we define horse, mean something much more important. We may mean that a certain object, which we all of us know, is composed in a certain manner: that it has four legs, a head, a heart, a liver, etc., etc., all of them arranged in definite relations to one another. It is in this sense that I deny good to be definable. I say that it is not composed of any parts, which we can substitute for it in our minds when we are thinking of it. We might think just as clearly and correctly about a horse, if we thought of all its parts and their arrangement instead of thinking of the whole: we could, I say, think how a horse differed from a donkey just as well, just as truly, in this way, as now we do, only not so easily; but there is nothing whatsoever which we could so substitute for good; and that is what I mean, when I say that good is indefinable.

9. But I am afraid I have still not removed the chief difficulty which may prevent acceptance of the proposition that good is indefinable. I do not mean to say that *the* good, that which is good, is thus indefinable; if I did think so, I should not be writing on Ethics, for my main object is to help towards discovering that definition. It is just because I think there will be less risk of error in our search for a definition of 'the good,' that I am now insisting that *good* is indefinable. I must try to explain the difference between these two. I suppose it may be granted that 'good' is an adjective. Well 'the good,' 'that which is good,' must therefore be the substantive to

which the adjective 'good' will apply: it must be the whole of that to which the adjective will apply, and the adjective must *always* truly apply to it. But if it is that to which the adjective will apply, it must be something different from that adjective itself; and the whole of that something different, whatever it is, will be our definition of *the* good. Now it may be that this something will have other adjectives, beside 'good,' that will apply to it. It may be full of pleasure, for example; it may be intelligent: and if these two adjectives are really part of its definition, then it will certainly be true, that pleasure and intelligence are good. And many people appear to think that, if we say 'Pleasure and intelligence are good,' or if we say 'Only pleasure and intelligence are good,' we are defining 'good.' Well, I cannot deny that propositions of this nature may sometimes be called definitions; I do not know well enough how the word is generally used to decide upon this point. I only wish it to be understood that that is not what I mean when I say there is no possible definition of good, and that I shall not mean this if I use the word again. I do most fully believe that some true proposition of the form 'Intelligence is good and intelligence alone is good' can be found; if none could be found, our definition of *the* good would be impossible. As it is, I believe *the* good to be definable; and yet I still say that good itself is indefinable.

10. 'Good,' then, if we mean by it that quality which we assert to belong to a thing, when we say that the thing is good, is incapable of any definition, in the most important sense of that word. The most important sense of 'definition' is that in which a definition states what are the parts which invariably compose a certain whole; and in this sense 'good' has no definition because it is simple and has no parts. It is one of those innumerable objects of thought which are themselves incapable of definition, because they are the ultimate terms by reference to which whatever *is* capable of definition must be defined. That there must be an indefinite number of such terms is obvious, on reflection; since we cannot define anything except by an analysis, which, when carried as far as it will go, refers us to something, which is simply different from anything else, and which by that ultimate difference explains the peculiarity of the whole which we are defining: for every whole contains some parts which are common to other wholes also. There is, therefore, no intrinsic difficulty in the contention that 'good' denotes a simple and indefinable quality. There are many other instances of such qualities.

Consider yellow, for example. We may try to define it, by describing its physical equivalent; we may state what kind of light-vibrations must stimulate the normal eye, in order that we may perceive it. But a moment's reflection is sufficient to shew that those light-vibrations are not themselves what we mean by yellow. *They* are not what we perceive. Indeed we should never have been able to discover their existence, unless we had first been struck by the patent difference of quality between the different colours. The most we can be entitled to say of those vibrations is that they are what corresponds in space to the yellow which we actually perceive.

Yet a mistake of this simple kind has commonly been made about 'good.' It may be true that all things which are good are *also* something else, just as it is true that all things which are yellow produce a certain kind of vibration in the light. And it is a fact, that Ethics aims at discovering what are those other properties belonging to all things which are good. But far too many philosophers have thought that when they named those other properties they were actually defining good; that these properties, in fact, were simply not 'other,' but absolutely and entirely the same with goodness. This view I propose to call the 'naturalistic fallacy' and of it I shall now endeavour to dispose.

11. Let us consider what it is such philosophers say. And first it is to be noticed that they do not agree among themselves. They not only say that they are right as to what good is, but they endeavour to prove that other people who say that it is something else, are wrong. One, for instance, will affirm that good is pleasure, another, perhaps, that good is that which is desired; and each of these will argue eagerly to prove that the other is wrong. But how is that possible? One of them says that good is nothing but the object of desire, and at the same time tries to prove that it is not pleasure. But from his first assertion, that good just means the object of desire, one of two things must follow as regards his proof:

(1) He may be trying to prove that the object of desire is not pleasure. But, if this be all, where is his Ethics? The position he is maintaining is merely a psychological one. Desire is something which occurs in our minds, and pleasure is something else which so occurs; and our would-be ethical philosopher is merely holding that the latter is not the object of the former. But what has that to do with the question in dispute? His opponent held the ethical proposition that pleasure was the good, and although he should prove a million times over the psychological proposition that pleasure is not the object of desire, he is no nearer proving his opponent to be wrong. The position is like this. One man says a triangle is a circle: another replies 'A triangle is a straight line, and I will prove to you that I am right: *for*' (this is the only argument) 'a straight line is not a circle.' 'That is quite true,' the other may reply; 'but nevertheless a triangle is a circle, and you have said nothing whatever to prove the contrary. What is proved is that one of us is wrong, for we agree that a triangle cannot be both a straight line and a circle: but which is wrong, there can be no earthly means of proving, since you define triangle as straight line and I define it as circle.'—Well, that is one alternative which any naturalistic Ethics has to face; if good is *defined* as something else, it is then impossible either to prove that any other definition is wrong or even to deny such definition.

(2) The other alternative will scarcely be more welcome. It is that the discussion is after all a verbal one. When A says 'Good means pleasant' and B says 'Good means desired,' they may merely wish to assert that most people have used the word for what is pleasant and for what is desired

respectively. And this is quite an interesting subject for discussion: only it is not a whit more an ethical discussion than the last was. Nor do I think that any exponent of naturalistic Ethics would be willing to allow that this was all he meant. They are all so anxious to persuade us that what they call the good is what we really ought to do. 'Do, pray, act so, because the word "good" is generally used to denote actions of this nature': such, on this view, would be the substance of their teaching. And in so far as they tell us how we ought to act, their teaching is truly ethical, as they mean it to be. But how perfectly absurd is the reason they would give for it! 'You are to do this, because most people use a certain word to denote conduct such as this.' 'You are to say the thing which is not, because most people call it lying.' That is an argument just as good!—My dear sirs, what we want to know from you as ethical teachers, is not how people use a word; it is not even, what kind of actions they approve, which the use of this word 'good' may certainly imply: what we want to know is simply what *is* good. We may indeed agree that what most people do think good, is actually so; we shall at all events be glad to know their opinions: but when we say their opinions about what *is* good, we do mean what we say; we do not care whether they call that thing which they mean 'horse' or 'table' or 'chair,' 'gut' or 'bon' or 'ἀγαθός'; we want to know what it is that they so call. When they say 'Pleasure is good,' we cannot believe that they merely mean 'Pleasure is pleasure' and nothing more than that.

12. Suppose a man says 'I am pleased'; and suppose that is not a lie or a mistake but the truth. Well, if it is true, what does that mean? It means that his mind, a certain definite mind, distinguished by certain definite marks from all others, has at this moment a certain definite feeling called pleasure. 'Pleased' *means* nothing but having pleasure, and though we may be more pleased or less pleased, and even, we may admit for the present, have one or another kind of pleasure; yet in so far as it is pleasure we have, whether there be more or less of it, and whether it be of one kind or another, what we have is one definite thing, absolutely indefinable, some one thing that is the same in all the various degrees and in all the various kinds of it that there may be. We may be able to say how it is related to other things: that, for example, it is in the mind, that it causes desire, that we are conscious of it, etc., etc. We can, I say, describe its relations to other things, but define it we can *not*. And if anybody tried to define pleasure for us as being any other natural object; if anybody were to say, for instance, that pleasure *means* the sensation of red, and were to proceed to deduce from that that pleasure is a colour, we should be entitled to laugh at him and to distrust his future statements about pleasure. Well, that would be the same fallacy which I have called the naturalistic fallacy. That 'pleased' does not mean 'having the sensation of red,' or anything else whatever, does not prevent us from understanding what it does mean. It is enough for us to know that 'pleased' does mean 'having the sensation of pleasure,' and though pleasure is absolutely indefinable, though pleasure is

pleasure and nothing else whatever, yet we feel no difficulty in saying that we are pleased. The reason is, of course, that when I say 'I am pleased,' I do *not* mean that 'I' am the same thing as 'having pleasure.' And similarly no difficulty need be found in my saying that 'pleasure is good' and yet not meaning that 'pleasure' is the same thing as 'good,' that pleasure *means* good, and that good *means* pleasure. If I were to imagine that when I said 'I am pleased,' I meant that I was exactly the same thing as 'pleased,' I should not indeed call that a naturalistic fallacy, although it would be the same fallacy as I have called naturalistic with reference to Ethics. The reason of this is obvious enough. When a man confuses two natural objects with one another, defining the one by the other, if for instance, he confuses himself, who is one natural object, with 'pleased' or with 'pleasure' which are others, then there is no reason to call the fallacy naturalistic. But if he confuses 'good,' which is not in the same sense a natural object, with any natural object whatever, then there is a reason for calling that a naturalistic fallacy; its being made with regard to 'good' marks it as something quite specific, and this specific mistake deserves a name because it is so common. As for the reasons why good is not to be considered a natural object, they may be reserved for discussion in another place. But, for the present, it is sufficient to notice this: Even if it were a natural object, that would not alter the nature of the fallacy nor diminish its importance one whit. All that I have said about it would remain quite equally true: only the name which I have called it would not be so appropriate as I think it is. And I do not care about the name: what I do care about is the fallacy. It does not matter what we call it, provided we recognise it when we meet with it. It is to be met with in almost every book on Ethics; and yet it is not recognised: and that is why it is necessary to multiply illustrations of it, and convenient to give it a name. It is a very simple fallacy indeed. When we say that an orange is yellow, we do not think our statement binds us to hold that 'orange' means nothing else than 'yellow,' or that nothing can be yellow but an orange. Supposing the orange is also sweet! Does that bind us to say that 'sweet' is exactly the same thing as 'yellow,' that 'sweet' must be defined as 'yellow'? And supposing it be recognised that 'yellow' just means 'yellow' and nothing else whatever, does that make it any more difficult to hold that oranges are yellow? Most certainly it does not: on the contrary, it would be absolutely meaningless to say that oranges were yellow, unless yellow did in the end mean just 'yellow' and nothing else whatever—unless it was absolutely indefinable. We should not get any very clear notion about things, which are yellow—we should not get very far with our science, if we were bound to hold that everything which was yellow, *meant* exactly the same thing as yellow. We should find we had to hold that an orange was exactly the same thing as a stool, a piece of paper, a lemon, anything you like. We could prove any number of absurdities; but should we be the nearer to the truth? Why then, should it be different with 'good'? Why, if good is good and indefinable, should

I be held to deny that pleasure is good? Is there any difficulty in holding both to be true at once? On the contrary, there is no meaning in saying that pleasure is good, unless good is something different from pleasure. It is absolutely useless, so far as Ethics is concerned, to prove, as Mr. Spencer tries to do, that increase of pleasure coincides with increase of life, unless good *means* something different from either life or pleasure. He might just as well try to prove that an orange is yellow by shewing that it always is wrapped up in paper.

13. In fact, if it is not the case that 'good' denotes something simple and indefinable, only two alternatives are possible: either it is a complex, a given whole, about the correct analysis of which there may be disagreement; or else it means nothing at all, and there is no such subject as Ethics. In general, however, ethical philosophers have attempted to define good, without recognising what such an attempt must mean. They actually use arguments which involve one or both of the absurdities considered in § 11. We are, therefore, justified in concluding that the attempt to define good is chiefly due to want of clearness as to the possible nature of definition. There are, in fact, only two serious alternatives to be considered, in order to establish the conclusion that 'good' does denote a simple and indefinable notion. It might possibly denote a complex, as 'horse' does; or it might have no meaning at all. Neither of these possibilities has, however, been clearly conceived and seriously maintained, as such, by those who presume to define good; and both may be dismissed by a simple appeal to facts.

(1) The hypothesis that disagreement about the meaning of good is disagreement with regard to the correct analysis of a given whole, may be most plainly seen to be incorrect by consideration of the fact that, whatever definition be offered, it may be always asked, with significance, of the complex so defined, whether it is itself good. To take, for instance, one of the more plausible, because one of the more complicated, of such proposed definitions, it may easily be thought, at first sight, that to be good may mean to be that which we desire to desire. Thus if we apply this definition to a particular instance and say 'When we think that A is good, we are thinking that A is one of the things which we desire to desire,' our proposition may seem quite plausible. But, if we carry the investigation further, and ask ourselves 'Is it good to desire to desire A?' it is apparent, on a little reflection, that this question is itself as intelligible, as the original question 'Is A good?'—that we are, in fact, now asking for exactly the same information about the desire to desire A, for which we formerly asked with regard to A itself. But it is also apparent that the meaning of this second question cannot be correctly analysed into 'Is the desire to desire A one of the things which we desire to desire?': we have not before our minds anything so complicated as the question 'Do we desire to desire to desire to desire A?' Moreover any one can easily convince himself by inspection that the predicate of this proposition—'good'—is positively dif-

ferent from the notion of 'desiring to desire' which enters into its subject: 'That we should desire to desire A is good' is *not* merely equivalent to 'That A should be good is good.' It may indeed be true that what we desire to desire is always also good; perhaps, even the converse may be true: but it is very doubtful whether this is the case, and the mere fact that we understand very well what is meant by doubting it, shews clearly that we have two different notions before our minds.

(2) And the same consideration is sufficient to dismiss the hypothesis that 'good' has no meaning whatsoever. It is very natural to make the mistake of supposing that what is universally true is of such a nature that its negation would be self-contradictory: the importance which has been assigned to analytic propositions in the history of philosophy shews how easy such a mistake is. And thus it is very easy to conclude that what seems to be a universal ethical principle is in fact an identical proposition; that, if, for example, whatever is called 'good' seems to be pleasant, the proposition 'Pleasure is the good' does not assert a connection between two different notions, but involves only one, that of pleasure, which is easily recognised as a distinct entity. But whoever will attentively consider with himself what is actually before his mind when he asks the question 'Is pleasure (or whatever it may be) after all good?' can easily satisfy himself that he is not merely wondering whether pleasure is pleasant. And if he will try this experiment with each suggested definition in succession, he may become expert enough to recognise that in every case he has before his mind a unique object, with regard to the connection of which with any other object, a distinct question may be asked. Every one does in fact understand the question 'Is this good?' When he thinks of it, his state of mind is different from what it would be, were he asked 'Is this pleasant, or desired, or approved?' It has a distinct meaning for him, even though he may not recognise in what respect it is distinct. Whenever he thinks of 'intrinsic value,' or 'intrinsic worth,' or says that a thing 'ought to exist,' he has before his mind the unique object—the unique property of things—which I mean by 'good.' Everybody is constantly aware of this notion, although he may never become aware at all that it is different from other notions of which he is also aware. But, for correct ethical reasoning, it is extremely important that he should become aware of this fact; and, as soon as the nature of the problem is clearly understood, there should be little difficulty in advancing so far in analysis.

14. 'Good,' then, is indefinable; and yet, so far as I know, there is only one ethical writer, Prof. Henry Sidgwick, who has clearly recognised and stated this fact. We shall see, indeed, how far many of the most reputed ethical systems fall short of drawing the conclusions which follow from such a recognition. At present I will only quote one instance, which will serve to illustrate the meaning and importance of this principle that 'good' is indefinable, or, as Prof. Sidgwick says, an 'unanalysable notion.' It is an

instance to which Prof. Sidgwick himself refers in a note on the passage, in which he argues that 'ought' is unanalysable.[2]

'Bentham,' says Sidgwick, 'explains that his fundamental principle "states the greatest happiness of all those whose interest is in question as being the right and proper end of human action" '; and yet 'his language in other passages of the same chapter would seem to imply' that he *means* by the word "right" "conducive to the general happiness." Prof. Sidgwick sees that, if you take these two statements together, you get the absurd result that 'greatest happiness is the end of human action, which is conducive to the general happiness'; and so absurd does it seems to him to call this result, as Bentham calls it, 'the fundamental principle of a moral system,' that he suggests that Bentham cannot have meant it. Yet Prof. Sidgwick himself states elsewhere [3] that Psychological Hedonism is 'not seldom confounded with Egoistic Hedonism'; and that confusion, as we shall see, rests chiefly on that same fallacy, the naturalistic fallacy, which is implied in Bentham's statements. Prof. Sidgwick admits therefore that this fallacy is sometimes committed, absurd as it is; and I am inclined to think that Bentham may really have been one of those who committed it. Mill, as we shall see,[3a] certainly did commit it. In any case, whether Bentham committed it or not, his doctrine, as above quoted, will serve as a very good illustration of this fallacy, and of the importance of the contrary proposition that good is indefinable.

Let us consider this doctrine. Bentham seems to imply, so Prof. Sidgwick says, that the word 'right' *means* 'conducive to general happiness.' Now this, by itself, need not necessarily involve the naturalistic fallacy. For the word 'right' is very commonly appropriated to actions which lead to the attainment of what is good; which are regarded as *means* to the ideal and not as ends-in-themselves. This use of 'right,' as denoting what is good as a means, whether or not it be also good as an end, is indeed the use to which I shall confine the word. Had Bentham been using 'right' in this sense, it might be perfectly consistent for him to *define* right as 'conducive to the general happiness,' *provided only* (and notice this proviso) he had already proved, or laid down as an axiom, that general happiness was *the* good, or (what is equivalent to this) that general happiness alone was good. For in that case he would have already defined *the* good as general happiness (a position perfectly consistent, as we have seen, with the contention that 'good' is indefinable), and, since right was to be defined as 'conducive to *the* good,' it would actually *mean* 'conducive to general happiness.' But this method of escape from the charge of having committed the naturalistic fallacy has been closed by Bentham himself. For

[2] *Methods of Ethics*, Bk. 1, Chap. iii, §§ 2–3. [Chap. iii of Sidgwick's book is reprinted in this volume, pp. 137 ff. The footnote quoted by Moore will be found on p. 139.]

[3] *Methods of Ethics*, Bk. 1, Chap. iv, § 1.

[3a] [See the selection from *Principia Ethica* printed below under the title "Mill and the Hedonistic Principle"].

his fundamental principle is, we see, that the greatest happiness of all concerned is the *right* and proper *end* of human action. He applies the word 'right,' therefore, to the end, as such, not only to the means which are conducive to it; and, that being so, right can no longer be defined as 'conducive to the general happiness,' without involving the fallacy in question. For now it is obvious that the definition of right as conducive to general happiness can be used by him in support of the fundamental principle that general happiness is the right end; instead of being itself derived from that principle. If right, by definition, means conducive to general happiness, then it is obvious that general happiness is the right end. It is not necessary now first to prove or assert that general happiness is the right end, before right is defined as conducive to general happiness— a perfectly valid procedure; but on the contrary the definition of right as conducive to general happiness proves general happiness to be the right end—a perfectly invalid procedure, since in this case the statement that 'general happiness is the right end of human action' is not an ethical principle at all, but either, as we have seen, a proposition about the meaning of words, or else a proposition about the *nature* of general happiness, not about its rightness or goodness.

Now, I do not wish the importance I assign to this fallacy to be mis-understood. The discovery of it does not at all refute Bentham's conten-tion that greatest happiness is the proper end of human action, if that be understood as an ethical proposition, as he undoubtedly intended it. That principle may be true all the same; we shall consider whether it is so in succeeding chapters. Bentham might have maintained it, as Professor Sidg-wick does, even if the fallacy had been pointed out to him. What I am maintaining is that the *reasons* which he actually gives for his ethical propo-sition are fallacious ones, so far as they consist in a definition of right. What I suggest is that he did not perceive them to be fallacious; that, if he had done so, he would have been led to seek for other reasons in support of his Utilitarianism; and that, had he sought for other reasons, he *might* have found none which he thought to be sufficient. In that case he would have changed his whole system—a most important consequence. It is un-doubtedly also possible that he would have thought other reasons to be sufficient, and in that case his ethical system, in its main results, would still have stood. But even in this latter case, his use of the fallacy would be a serious objection to him as an ethical philosopher. For it is the business of Ethics, I must insist, not only to obtain true results, but also to find valid reasons for them. The direct object of Ethics is knowledge and not practice; and any one who uses the naturalistic fallacy has certainly not fulfilled this first object, however correct his practical principles may be.

My objections to Naturalism are then, in the first place, that it offers no reason at all, far less any valid reason, for any ethical principle whatever; and in this it already fails to satisfy the requirements of Ethics, as a scien-tific study. But in the second place I contend that, though it gives a reason

for no ethical principle, it is a *cause* of the acceptance of false principles—
it deludes the mind into accepting ethical principles, which are false; and
in this it is contrary to every aim of Ethics. It is easy to see that if we start
with a definition of right conduct as conduct conducive to general happiness; then, knowing that right conduct is universally conduct conducive
to the good, we very easily arrive at the result that the good is general
happiness. If, on the other hand, we once recognise that we must start our
Ethics without a definition, we shall be much more apt to look about us,
before we adopt any ethical principle whatever; and the more we look
about us, the less likely are we to adopt a false one. It may be replied to
this: Yes, but we shall look about us just as much, before we settle on our
definition, and are therefore just as likely to be right. But I will try to shew
that this is not the case. If we start with the conviction that a definition
of good can be found, we start with the conviction that good *can mean*
nothing else than some one property of things; and our only business will
then be to discover what that property is. But if we recognise that, so far
as the meaning of good goes, anything whatever may be good, we start
with a much more open mind. Moreover, apart from the fact that, when
we think we have a definition, we cannot logically defend our ethical principles in any way whatever, we shall also be much less apt to defend them
well, even if illogically. For we shall start with the conviction that good
must mean so and so, and shall therefore be inclined either to misunderstand
our opponent's arguments or to cut them short with the reply, 'This is
not an open question: the very meaning of the word decides it; no one can
think otherwise except through confusion.'

15. Our first conclusion as to the subject-matter of Ethics is, then,
that there is a simple, indefinable, unanalysable object of thought by reference to which it must be defined. By what name we call this unique object
is a matter of indifference, so long as we clearly recognise what it is and that
it does differ from other objects. The words which are commonly taken
as the signs of ethical judgments all do refer to it; and they are expressions
of ethical judgments solely because they do so refer. But they may refer
to it in two different ways, which it is very important to distinguish, if we
are to have a complete definition of the range of ethical judgments. Before
I proceeded to argue that there was such an indefinable notion involved
in ethical notions, I stated (§ 4) that it was necessary for Ethics to enumerate all true universal judgments, asserting that such and such a thing was
good, whenever it occurred. But, although all such judgments do refer
to that unique notion which I have called 'good,' they do not all refer to
it in the same way. They may either assert that this unique property does
always attach to the thing in question, or else they may assert only that the
thing in question is *a cause or necessary condition* for the existence of other
things to which this unique property does attach. The nature of these two
species of universal ethical judgments is extremely different; and a great
part of the difficulties, which are met with in ordinary ethical speculation,

are due to the failure to distinguish them clearly. Their difference has, indeed, received expression in ordinary language by the contrast between the terms 'good as means' and 'good in itself,' 'value as a means' and 'intrinsic value.' But these terms are apt to be applied correctly only in the more obvious instances; and this seems to be due to the fact that the distinction between the conceptions which they denote has not been made a separate object of investigation. This distinction may be briefly pointed out as follows.

16. Whenever we judge that a thing is 'good as a means,' we are making a judgment with regard to its causal relations: we judge *both* that it will have a particular kind of effect, *and* that that effect will be good in itself. But to find causal judgments that are universally true is notoriously a matter of extreme difficulty. The late date at which most of the physical sciences became exact, and the comparative fewness of the laws which they have succeeded in establishing even now, are sufficient proofs of this difficulty. With regard, then, to what are the most frequent objects of ethical judgments, namely actions, it is obvious that we cannot be satisfied that any of our universal causal judgments are true, even in the sense in which scientific laws are so. We cannot even discover hypothetical laws of the form 'Exactly this action will always, under these conditions, produce exactly that effect.' But for a correct ethical judgment with regard to the effects of certain actions we require more than this in two respects. (1) We require to know that a given action will produce a certain effect, *under whatever circumstances it occurs*. But this is certainly impossible. It is certain that in different circumstances the same action may produce effects which are utterly different in all respects upon which the value of the effect depends. Hence we can never be entitled to more than a *generalisation*—to a proposition of the form 'This result *generally* follows this kind of action'; and even this generalisation will only be true, if the circumstances under which the action occurs are generally the same. This is in fact the case, to a great extent, within any one particular age and state of society. But, when we take other ages into account, in many most important cases the normal circumstances of a given kind of action will be so different, that the generalisation which is true for one will not be true for another. With regard then to ethical judgments which assert that a certain kind of action is good as a means to a certain kind of effect, none will be *universally* true; and many, though *generally* true at one period, will be generally false at others. But (2) we require to know not only that *one* good effect will be produced, but that, among all subsequent events affected by the action in question, the balance of good will be greater than if any other possible action had been performed. In other words, to judge that an action is generally a means to good is to judge not only that it generally does *some* good, but that it generally does the greatest good of which the circumstances admit. In this respect ethical judgments about the effects of action involve a difficulty and a complication far greater than

that involved in the establishment of scientific laws. For the latter we need only consider a single effect; for the former it is essential to consider not only this, but the effects of that effect, and so on as far as our view into the future can reach. It is, indeed, obvious that our view can never reach far enough for us to be certain that any action will produce the best possible effects. We must be content, if the greatest possible balance of good seems to be produced within a limited period. But it is important to notice that the whole series of effects within a period of considerable length is actually taken account of in our common judgments that an action is good as a means; and that hence this additional complication, which makes ethical generalisations so far more difficult to establish than scientific laws, is one which is involved in actual ethical discussions, and is of practical importance. The commonest rules of conduct involve such considerations as the balancing of future bad health against immediate gains; and even if we can never settle with any certainty how we shall secure the greatest possible total of good, we try at least to assure ourselves that probable future evils will not be greater than the immediate good.

17. There are, then, judgments which state that certain kinds of things have good effects; and such judgments, for the reasons just given, have the important characteristics (1) that they are unlikely to be true, if they state that the kind of thing in question *always* has good effects, and (2) that, even if they only state that it *generally* has good effects, many of them will only be true of certain periods in the world's history. On the other hand there are judgments which state that certain kinds of things are themselves good; and these differ from the last in that, if true at all, they are all of them universally true. It is, therefore, extremely important to distinguish these two kinds of possible judgments. Both may be expressed in the same language: in both cases we commonly say 'Such and such a thing is good.' But in the one case 'good' will mean 'good as means,' i.e. merely that the thing is a means to good—will have good effects: in the other case it will mean 'good as end'—we shall be judging that the thing itself has the property which, in the first case, we asserted only to belong to its effects. It is plain that these are very different assertions to make about a thing; it is plain that either or both of them may be made, both truly and falsely, about all manner of things; and it is certain that unless we are clear as to which of the two we mean to assert, we shall have a very poor chance of deciding rightly whether our assertion is true or false. It is precisely this clearness as to the meaning of the question asked which has hitherto been almost entirely lacking in ethical speculation. Ethics has always been predominantly concerned with the investigation of a limited class of actions. With regard to these we may ask *both* how far they are good in themselves *and* how far they have a general tendency to produce good results. And the arguments brought forward in ethical discussion have always been of both classes—both such as would prove the conduct in question to be good in itself and such as would prove it to be good as a means. But that these

are the only questions which any ethical discussion can have to settle, and that to settle the one is *not* the same thing as to settle the other—these two fundamental facts have in general escaped the notice of ethical philosophers. Ethical questions are commonly asked in an ambiguous form. It is asked 'What is a man's duty under these circumstances?' or 'Is it right to act in this way?' or 'What ought we to aim at securing?' But all these questions are capable of further analysis; a correct answer to any of them involves both judgments of what is good in itself and causal judgments. This is implied even by those who maintain that we have a direct and immediate judgment of absolute rights and duties. Such a judgment can only mean that the course of action in question is *the* best thing to do; that, by acting so, every good that *can* be secured will have been secured. Now we are not concerned with the question whether such a judgment will ever be true. The question is: What does it imply, if it is true? And the only possible answer is that, whether true or false, it implies both a proposition as to the degree of goodness of the action in question, as compared with other things, and a number of causal propositions. For it cannot be denied that the action will have consequences: and to deny that the consequences matter is to make a judgment of their intrinsic value, as compared with the action itself. In asserting that the action is *the* best thing to do, we assert that it together with its consequences presents a greater sum of intrinsic value than any possible alternative. And this condition may be realised by any of the three cases:—(*a*) If the action itself has greater intrinsic value than any alternative, whereas both its consequences and those of the alternatives are absolutely devoid either of intrinsic merit or intrinsic demerit; or (*b*) if, though its consequences are intrinsically bad, the balance of intrinsic value is greater than would be produced by any alternative; or (*c*) if, its consequences being intrinsically good, the degree of value belonging to them and it conjointly is greater than that of any alternative series. In short, to assert that a certain line of conduct is, at a given time, absolutely right or obligatory, is obviously to assert that more good or less evil will exist in the world, if it be adopted, than if anything else be done instead. But this implies a judgment as to the value both of its own consequences and of those of any possible alternative. And that an action will have such and such consequences involves a number of causal judgments.

Similarly, in answering the question 'What ought we to aim at securing?' causal judgments are again involved, but in a somewhat different way. We are liable to forget, because it is so obvious, that this question can never be answered correctly except by naming something which *can* be secured. Not everything can be secured; and, even if we judge that nothing which cannot be obtained would be of equal value with that which can, the possibility of the latter, as well as its value, is essential to its being a proper end of action. Accordingly neither our judgments as to what actions we ought to perform, nor even our judgments as to the ends which they ought to produce, are pure judgments of intrinsic value. With regard to the former, an action which is absolutely obligatory *may* have no intrinsic value whatsoever; that it is perfectly virtuous may mean merely that it causes the best possible effects. And with regard to the latter, these best possible results which justify our action can, in any case, have only so much of intrinsic value as the laws of nature allow us to secure; and they in their turn *may* have no intrinsic value whatsoever, but may merely be a means to the attainment (in a still further future) of something that has such value. Whenever, therefore, we ask 'What ought we to do?' or 'What ought we to try to get?' we are asking questions which involve a correct answer to two others, completely different in kind from one another. We must know *both* what degree of intrinsic value different things have, *and* how these different things may be obtained. But the vast majority of questions which have actually been discussed in Ethics—*all* practical questions, indeed—involve this double knowledge; and they have been discussed without any clear separation of the two distinct questions involved. A great part of the vast disagreements prevalent in Ethics is to be attributed to this failure in analysis. By the use of conceptions which involve both that of intrinsic value and that of causal relation, as if they involved intrinsic value only, two different errors have been rendered almost universal. Either it is assumed that nothing has intrinsic value which is not possible, or else it is assumed that what is necessary must have intrinsic value. Hence the primary and peculiar business of Ethics, the determination what things have intrinsic value and in what degrees, has received no adequate treatment at all. And on the other hand a *thorough* discussion of means has been also largely neglected, owing to an obscure perception of the truth that it is perfectly irrelevant to the question of intrinsic values. But however this may be, and however strongly any particular reader may be convinced that some one of the mutually contradictory systems which hold the field has given a correct answer either to the question what has intrinsic value, or to the question what we ought to do, or to both, it must at least be admitted that the questions what is best in itself and what will bring about the best possible, are utterly distinct; that both belong to the actual subject-matter of Ethics; and that the more clearly distinct questions are distinguished, the better is our chance of answering both correctly.

18. There remains one point which must not be omitted in a complete description of the kind of questions which Ethics has to answer. The main division of those questions is, as I have said, into two; the question what things are good in themselves, and the question to what other things these are related as effects. The first of these, which is the primary ethical question and is presupposed by the other, includes a correct comparison of the various things which have intrinsic value (if there are many such) in respect of the degree of value which they have; and such comparison involves a difficulty of principle which has greatly aided the confusion of intrinsic value with mere 'goodness as a means.' It has been pointed out that

one difference between a judgment, which asserts that a thing is good in itself, and a judgment which asserts that it is a means to good, consists in the fact that the first, if true of one instance of the thing in question, is necessarily true of all; whereas a thing which has good effects under some circumstances may have bad ones under others. Now it is certainly true that all judgments of intrinsic value are in this sense universal; but the principle which I have now to enunciate may easily make it appear as if they were not so but resembled the judgment of means in being merely general. There is, as will presently be maintained, a vast number of different things, each of which has intrinsic value; there are also very many which are positively bad; and there is a still larger class of things, which appear to be indifferent. But a thing belonging to any of these three classes may occur as part of a whole, which includes among its other parts other things belonging both to the same and to the other two classes; and these wholes, as such, may also have intrinsic value. The paradox, to which it is necessary to call attention, is that *the value of such a whole bears no regular proportion to the sum of the values of its parts*. It is certain that a good thing may exist in such a relation to another good thing that the value of the whole thus formed is immensely greater than the sum of the values of the two good things. It is certain that a whole formed of a good thing and an indifferent thing may have immensely greater value than that good thing itself possesses. It is certain that two bad things or a bad thing and an indifferent thing may form a whole much worse than the sum of badness of its parts. And it seems as if indifferent things may also be the sole constituents of a whole which has great value either positive or negative. Whether the addition of a bad thing to a good whole may increase the positive value of the whole, or the addition of a bad thing to a bad may produce a whole having positive value, may seem more doubtful; but it is, at least, possible, and this possibility must be taken into account in our ethical investigations. However we may decide particular questions, the principle is clear. *The value of a whole must not be assumed to be the same as the sum of the values of its parts.*

A single instance will suffice to illustrate the kind of relation in question. It seems to be true that to be conscious of a beautiful object is a thing of great intrinsic value; whereas the same object, if no one be conscious of it, has certainly comparatively little value, and is commonly held to have none at all. But the consciousness of a beautiful object is certainly a whole of some sort in which we can distinguish as parts the object on the one hand and the being conscious on the other. Now this latter factor occurs as part of a different whole, whenever we are conscious of anything; and it would seem that some of these wholes have at all events very little value, and may even be indifferent or positively bad. Yet we cannot always attribute the slightness of their value to any positive demerit in the object which differentiates them from the consciousness of beauty; the object itself may approach as near as possible to absolute neutrality. Since, therefore, mere consciousness does not always confer great value upon the whole of which it forms a part, even though its object may have no great demerit, we cannot attribute the great superiority of the consciousness of a beautiful thing over the beautiful thing itself to the mere addition of the value of consciousness to that of the beautiful thing. Whatever the intrinsic value of consciousness may be, it does not give to the whole of which it forms a part a value proportioned to the sum of its value and that of its object. If this be so, we have here an instance of a whole possessing a different intrinsic value from the sum of that of its parts; and whether it be so or not, what is meant by such a difference is illustrated by this case.

19. There are, then, wholes which possess the property that their value is different from the sum of the values of their parts; and the relations which subsist between such parts and the whole of which they form a part have not hitherto been distinctly recognised or received a separate name. Two points are especially worthy of notice. (1) It is plain that the existence of any such part is a necessary condition for the existence of that good which is constituted by the whole. And exactly the same language will also express the relation between a means and the good thing which is its effect. But yet there is a most important difference between the two cases, constituted by the fact that the part is, whereas the means is not, a part of the good thing for the existence of which its existence is a necessary condition. The necessity by which, if the good in question is to exist, the means to it must exist is merely a natural or causal necessity. If the laws of nature were different, exactly the same good might exist, although what is now a necessary condition of its existence did not exist. The existence of the means has no intrinsic value; and its utter annihilation would leave the value of that which it is now necessary to secure entirely unchanged. But in the case of a part of such a whole as we are now considering, it is otherwise. In this case the good in question cannot conceivably exist, unless the part exist also. The necessity which connects the two is quite independent of natural law. What is asserted to have intrinsic value is the existence of the whole; and the existence of the whole includes the existence of its part. Suppose the part removed, and what remains is *not* what was asserted to have intrinsic value; but if we suppose a means removed, what remains is just what *was* asserted to have intrinsic value. And yet (2) the existence of the part may *itself* have no more intrinsic value than that of the means. It is this fact which constitutes the paradox of the relation which we are discussing. It has just been said that what has intrinsic value is the existence of the whole, and that this includes the existence of the part; and from this it would seem a natural inference that the existence of the part has intrinsic value. But the inference would be as false as if we were to conclude that, because the number of two stones was two, each of the stones was also two. The part of a valuable whole retains exactly the same value when it is, as when it is not, a part of that whole. If it had value under other circumstances, its value is not any greater, when it is part of a far more

valuable whole; and if it had no value by itself, it has none still, however great be that of the whole of which it now forms a part. We are not then justified in asserting that one and the same thing is under some circumstances intrinsically good, and under others not so; as we are justified in asserting of a means that it sometimes does and sometimes does not produce good results. And yet we are justified in asserting that it is far more desirable that a certain thing should exist under some circumstances than under others; namely when other things will exist in such relations to it as to form a more valuable whole. *It* will not have more intrinsic value under these circumstances than under others; *it* will not necessarily even be a means to the existence of things having more intrinsic value: but it will, like a means, be a necessary condition for the existence of that which *has* greater intrinsic value, although, unlike a means, it will itself form a part of this more valuable existent.

20. I have said that the peculiar relation between part and whole which I have just been trying to define is one which has received no separate name. It would, however, be useful that it should have one; and there is a name, which might well be appropriated to it, if only it could be divorced from its present unfortunate usage. Philosophers, especially those who profess to have derived great benefit from the writings of Hegel, have latterly made much use of the terms 'organic whole,' 'organic unity,' 'organic relation.' The reason why these terms might well be appropriated to the use suggested is that the peculiar relation of parts to whole, just defined, is one of the properties which distinguishes the wholes to which they are actually applied with the greatest frequency. And the reason why it is desirable that they should be divorced from their present usage is that, as at present used, they have no distinct sense and, on the contrary, both imply and propagate errors of confusion.

To say that a thing is an 'organic whole' is generally understood to imply that its parts are related to one another and to itself as means to end; it is also understood to imply that they have a property described in some such phrase as that they have 'no meaning or significance apart from the whole'; and finally such a whole is also treated as if it had the property to which I am proposing that the name should be confined. But those who use the term give us, in general, no hint as to how they suppose these three properties to be related to one another. It seems generally to be assumed that they are identical; and always, at least, that they are necessarily connected with one another. That they are not identical I have already tried to shew; to suppose them so is to neglect the very distinctions pointed out in the last paragraph; and the usage might well be discontinued merely because it encourages such neglect. But a still more cogent reason for its discontinuance is that, so far from being necessarily connected, the second is a property which can attach to nothing, being a self-contradictory conception; whereas the first, if we insist on its most important sense, applies to many cases, to which we have no reason to think that the third applies also, and the third certainly applies to many to which the first does not apply.

21. These relations between the three properties just distinguished may be illustrated by reference to a whole of the kind from which the name 'organic' was derived—a whole which is an organism in the scientific sense—namely the human body.

(1) There exists between many parts of our body (though not between all) a relation which has been familiarised by the fable, attributed to Menenius Agrippa, concerning the belly and its members. We can find in it parts such that the continued existence of the one is a necessary condition for the continued existence of the other; while the continued existence of this latter is also a necessary condition for the continued existence of the former. This amounts to no more than saying that in the body we have instances of two things, both enduring for some time, which have a relation of mutual causal dependence on one another—a relation of 'reciprocity.' Frequently no more than this is meant by saying that the parts of the body form an 'organic unity,' or that they are mutually means and ends to one another. And we certainly have here a striking characteristic of living things. But it would be extremely rash to assert that this relation of mutual causal dependence was only exhibited by living things and hence was sufficient to define their peculiarity. And it is obvious that of two things which have this relation of mutual dependence, neither may have intrinsic value, or one may have it and the other lack it. They are not necessarily 'ends' to one another in any sense except that in which 'end' means 'effect.' And moreover it is plain that in this sense the whole cannot be an end to any of its parts. We are apt to talk of 'the whole' in contrast to one of its parts, when in fact we mean only *the rest* of the parts. But strictly the whole must include all its parts and no part can be a cause of the whole, because it cannot be a cause of itself. It is plain, therefore, that this relation of mutual causal dependence implies nothing with regard to the value of either of the objects which have it; and that, even if both of them happen also to have value, this relation between them is one which cannot hold between part and whole.

But (2) it may also be the case that our body as a whole has a value greater than the sum of values of its parts; and this may be what is meant when it is said that the parts are means to the whole. It is obvious that if we ask the question 'Why *should* the parts be such as they are?' a proper answer may be 'Because the whole they form has so much value.' But it is equally obvious that the relation which we thus assert to exist between part and whole is quite different from that which we assert to exist between part and part when we say 'This part exists, because that one could not exist without it.' In the latter case we assert the two parts to be causally connected; but, in the former, part and whole cannot be causally connected, and the relation which we assert to exist between them may exist even though the parts are not causally connected either. All the parts of a picture do not have that relation of mutual causal dependence, which certain parts of the body have, and yet the existence of those which do not have it may be absolutely essential to the value of the whole. The two relations are quite distinct in kind, and we cannot infer the existence of the one from that of the other. It can, therefore, serve no useful purpose to include them both under the same name; and if we are to say that a whole is organic because its parts are (in this sense) 'means' to the whole, we must *not* say that it is organic because its parts are causally dependent on one another.

22. But finally (3) the sense which has been most prominent in recent uses of the term 'organic whole' is one whereby it asserts the parts of such a whole to have a property which the parts of no whole can possibly have. It is supposed that just as the whole would not be what it is but for the existence of the parts, so the parts would not be what they are but for the existence of the whole; and this is understood to mean not merely that any particular part could not exist unless the others existed too (which is the case where relation (1) exists between the parts), but actually that the part is no distinct object of thought—that the whole, of which it is a part, is in its turn a part of it. That this supposition is self-contradictory a very little reflection should be sufficient to shew. We may admit, indeed, that when a particular thing is a part of a whole, it does possess a predicate which it would not otherwise possess—namely that it is a part of that whole. But what cannot be admitted is that this predicate alters the nature or enters into the definition of the thing which has it. When we think of the part *itself*, we mean just *that which* we assert, in this case, to *have* the predicate that it is part of the whole; and the mere assertion that *it* is a part of the whole involves that it should itself be distinct from that which we assert of it. Otherwise we contradict ourselves since we assert that, not *it*, but something else—namely it together with that which we assert of it—has the predicate which we assert of it. In short, it is obvious that no part contains analytically the whole to which it belongs, or any other parts of that whole. The relation of part to whole is *not* the same as that of whole to part; and the very definition of the latter is that it does contain analytically that which is said to be its part. And yet this very self-contradictory doctrine is the chief mark which shews the influence of Hegel upon modern philosophy—an influence which pervades almost the whole of orthodox philosophy. This is what is generally implied by the cry against falsification by abstraction: that a whole is always a part of its part! 'If you want to know the truth about a part,' we are told, 'you must consider *not* that part, but something else—namely the whole: *nothing* is true of the part, but only of the whole.' Yet plainly it must be true of the part at least that it is a part of the whole; and it is obvious that when we say it is, we do *not* mean merely that the whole is a part of itself. This doctrine, therefore, that a part can have 'no meaning or significance apart from its whole' must be utterly rejected. It implies itself that the statement 'This is a part of that

[handwritten marginal note: BUT THE 'PART' IS NOT IN QUESTION — KNOWLEDGE IS.]

whole' has a meaning; and in order that this may have one, both subject and predicate must have a distinct meaning. And it is easy to see how this false doctrine has arisen by confusion with the two relations (1) and (2) which may really be properties of wholes.

(*a*) The *existence* of a part may be connected by a natural or causal necessity with the existence of the other parts of its whole; and further what is a part of a whole and what has ceased to be such a part, although differing intrinsically from one another, may be called by one and the same name. Thus, to take a typical example, if an arm be cut off from the human body, we still call it an arm. Yet an arm, when it is a part of the body, undoubtedly differs from a dead arm: and hence we may easily be led to say 'The arm which is a part of the body would not be what it is, if it were not such a part,' and to think that the contradiction thus expressed is in reality a characteristic of things. But, in fact, the dead arm never was a part of the body; it is only *partially* identical with the living arm. Those parts of it which are identical with parts of the living arm are exactly the same, whether they belong to the body or not; and in them we have an undeniable instance of one and the same thing at one time forming a part, and at another not forming a part of the presumed 'organic whole.' On the other hand those properties which *are* possessed by the living, and *not* by the dead, arm, do not exist in a changed form in the latter: they simply do not exist there *at all*. By a causal necessity their existence depends on their having that relation to the other parts of the body which we express by saying that they form part of it. Yet, most certainly, if they ever did not form part of the body, they *would* be exactly what they are when they do. That they differ intrinsically from the properties of the dead arm and that they form part of the body are propositions not analytically related to one another. There is no contradiction in supposing them to retain such intrinsic differences and yet not to form part of the body.

But (*b*) when we are told that a living arm has no *meaning* or *significance* apart from the body to which it belongs, a different fallacy is also suggested. 'To have meaning or significance' is commonly used in the sense of 'to have importance'; and this again means 'to have value either as a means or as an end.' Now it is quite possible that even a living arm, apart from its body, would have no intrinsic value whatever; although the whole of which it is a part has great intrinsic value owing to its presence. Thus we may easily come to say that, *as* a part of the body, it has great value, whereas *by itself* it would have none; and thus that its whole 'meaning' lies in its relation to the body. But in fact the value in question obviously does not belong to *it* at all. To have value merely as a part is equivalent to having no value at all, but merely being a part of that which has it. Owing, however, to neglect of this distinction, the assertion that a part has value, *as a part*, which it would not otherwise have, easily leads to the assumption that it is also different, as a part, from what it would otherwise be; for it is, in fact, true that two things which have a different value must also differ in other respects. Hence the assumption that one and the same thing, because it is a part of a more valuable whole at one time than at another, therefore has more intrinsic value at one time than at another, has encouraged the self-contradictory belief that one and the same thing may be two different things, and that only in one of its forms is it truly what it is.

For these reasons, I shall, where it seems convenient, take the liberty to use the term 'organic' with a special sense. I shall use it to denote the fact that a whole has an intrinsic value different in amount from the sum of the values of its parts. I shall use it to denote this and only this. The term will not imply any causal relation whatever between the parts of the whole in question. And it will not imply either, that the parts are inconceivable except as parts of that whole, or that, when they form parts of such a whole, they have a value different from that which they would have if they did not. Understood in this special and perfectly definite sense the relation of an organic whole to its parts is one of the most important which Ethics has to recognise. A chief part of that science should be occupied in comparing the relative values of various goods; and the grossest errors will be committed in such comparison if it be assumed that wherever two things form a whole, the value of that whole is merely the sum of the values of those two things. With this question of 'organic wholes,' then, we complete the enumeration of the kind of problems, with which it is the business of Ethics to deal.

23. In this chapter I have endeavoured to enforce the following conclusions. (1) The peculiarity of Ethics is not that it investigates assertions about human conduct, but that it investigates assertions about that property of things which is denoted by the term 'good,' and the converse property denoted by the term 'bad.' It must, in order to establish its conclusions, investigate the truth of *all* such assertions, *except* those which assert the relation of this property only to a single existent (1-4). (2) This property, by reference to which the subject-matter of Ethics must be defined, is itself simple and indefinable (5-14). And (3) all assertions about its relation to other things are of two, and only two, kinds: they either assert in what degree things themselves possess this property, or else they assert causal relations between other things and those which possess it (15-17). Finally, (4) in considering the different degrees in which things themselves possess this property, we have to take account of the fact that a whole may possess it in a degree different from that which is obtained by summing the degrees in which its parts possess it (18–22).

The Place of Definition in Ethics *

G. C. FIELD

THIS IS NOT, perhaps, one of the major questions which the moral philosopher has to face. But it is of some interest, and of enough difficulty to lead to certain clear differences of opinion. Everybody is familiar with the classic argument of Prof. Moore that the chief notion in Ethics, that of good, is and must be indefinable. A somewhat similar argument has recently been put forward by Dr. Ross and extended by him to the notion of right. Some members of this Society will remember, also, the lively interchange of opinion which took place at the last Joint Session, one member demanding a definition of the term under discussion, while another denounced this demand as a mere trick of dialectic.

I propose, therefore, to ask the general question suggested by my title. And, in trying to answer it, I do not propose to begin by giving a definition of "definition," and then seeing whether there is any room for the process thus defined in ethical thinking. I prefer to begin at the other end, and ask what processes go on in ethical thinking which might possibly be called definition or which resemble other processes which everyone is agreed in calling definition. If we are clear about what processes can properly go on in ethical thinking, it becomes to a large extent a matter of choice whether we call any of them definition or not. And it will be of help in this investigation if we look for a moment at the use of definition in one or two other branches of knowledge.

(1) Perhaps the most obvious and typical instances of definition are to be found in the definitions of Euclidean geometry. At any rate, it seems probable that this was the type that Aristotle had in mind when he drew up his rules for correct definition.

The place of definition in the Euclidean geometry seems fairly obvious. It is the necessary starting-point of the investigation. We begin with a definition of a figure, and from it, with the aid of certain axioms and postulates of general application, we deduce other properties of that figure and its relations to other figures. We thus have to have a definition to start with. And to arrive at such a definition is not a very difficult process. The

* Reprinted by kind permission of the author, the editor of *Mind* and J. W. Arrowsmith, Ltd., publishers of G. C. Field's *Studies in Philosophy* (University of Bristol Studies No. 3), 1935.

definition of a triangle, for instance, simply states the most obvious feature of a kind of figure with which we are all familiar and of which we have a perfectly distinct idea. In other cases, though the definition is not very difficult to arrive at, it is not quite so obvious as this. The Euclidean definition of a circle, for instance, is not immediately obvious to the beginner in geometry, though the thing defined is perfectly clear and distinct to his mind. He has to stop and think for a moment before he sees that it is true of that sort of figure.

The difficulty is not very great. But it introduces us to a point that will assume more importance later—that is, the point that we may "have an idea of" a circle, and know what we mean by the term before we know the definition, before, that is, we are aware of the particular feature of the circle that a geometrician takes as the definition of it. This would be more obvious if we considered some of the other definitions that Greek mathematicians attempted of the circle, for instance, that it was the largest area that could be contained by a line of given length. I have heard unmathematical people, like myself, express doubts whether that was true of a circle or not. But, in spite of this, they would not have admitted that they did not know, in some sense, what a circle was.

(2) We may consider next the place of definition in zoölogy and botany. I am referring here to the earlier work of classification of species and genera, which was carried out by the older natural historians. The modern biologist, in general, I suppose, is not very much interested in this. But it forms a necessary basis for his subsequent investigations.

The process of definition here is similar to definition in geometry, in that it involves the statement of the general features which distinguish one species or genus from the others. But the place it occupies in the investigation is entirely different. It is certainly not the necessary starting-point of the investigation. It is rather the conclusion of it. And the natural historian does not use his definition as a basis from which to deduce the other properties of the species. Nothing follows from the definition, in the sense in which the conclusions of a geometrical proposition follow.

If it were always necessary to have a clear definition of what we were talking about before starting our investigations on it, it would be difficult to see how the natural historian could ever start his investigations at all. Of course, he has some idea of the things he is talking about, he means something by plant, animal, dog, horse, fish, etc., before he begins to investigate and classify them. Human beings at the pre-scientific stage made some distinctions based on some observable differences between one kind of living being and another. And the first scientists start from that. But there is nothing that we could call a definition. There is only what, for convenience, we may speak of as the vague popular idea of dog, horse, etc.

What is contained in this vague popular idea it would be very difficult to say. Clearly it is based on certain obvious visible characteristics. But which characteristics the unscientific man takes in determining whether he is going to call any particular animal a dog or not it would be almost impossible to determine with any certainty. We might arrive at a conclusion by a long and careful psychological investigation. But the important point to note is that such an investigation would be of no interest at all to the scientist. It would tell him nothing of what he wanted to discover. He simply accepts the fact that we do have vague popular ideas of the different kinds of living creature, and all this does for him is to point to the direction in which he can begin his investigations. But, once begun, he carries on his investigations by observation and experiment in entire disregard of the original idea. He looks for and finds facts which are not dreamed of at the pre-scientific stage, for instance, the facts of internal structure, which are generally taken as the most important features in the definition. These features are not in any sense contained in the original idea, nor could they be said to be implied by or deduced from it. When we arrive at a zoölogical definition we could not in any sense say that this is what we really meant by the term all along. Sometimes, indeed, our definition may contradict the original idea. Most people who know no zoölogy would probably call a whale a fish, like Herman Melville's whalers, or a spider an insect.

There is one more point that we may raise in passing before going on to our main subject. That is the question what light is thrown by these instances on the statement sometimes put forward that there is one kind of definition which consists in an arbitrary statement of what we are going to mean by a certain term. There is clearly no place for this kind of definition in either natural history or geometry. On the other hand, we need not accept the assumption apparently made by Aristotle that there is one and only one right definition for every general term, and that any other definition is wrong. We find, for instance, that the definition of a circle changes in passing from Euclidean geometry to conic sections. But that does not mean that the more elementary definition is wrong. What it does mean is that there is a certain freedom of selection from among the general properties of the thing defined according to the context in which we are going to use the definition.

This freedom of selection, however, is severely restricted. Most obviously it is restricted by the facts. We can only select among the properties that really belong there. It is restricted, again, by the context. If we want to investigate in one particular direction, we may choose the definition that will be most helpful for that investigation. But which definition will actually be most helpful is a matter of fact which we have to discover. And we are restricted by the ordinary use of language. Even if we modify the ordinary idea of what a word means in our final definition (e.g., when we define "fish" so as to exclude whales), we must still keep as near to it as possible. We must not define "fish," for instance, so as to exclude all or most of the creatures usually called fishes. To say, "By 'fish' I am going to mean a two-legged animal with feathers," would be entirely pointless. An arbitrary statement of what I am going to mean by a word, if it is really entirely arbitrary, is not a definition, or even a form of definition. It is merely a way of being silly.

It is possible that definition has sometimes been supposed to be arbitrary because it has been confused with a different process, arbitrary naming. We get a certain amount of that in scientific investigations when we invent a new technical vocabulary. Here, however, the usual process is reversed. Instead of beginning with a word and then arriving at a definition, we get our definition of the general kind of thing that we have discovered in our investigations, and then look about for a name for it. Even here, however, there is generally some reason for the choice of names. But the possibility of this process illustrates one important point, namely, that definition is never merely of names, but always of something that the name means to us. Otherwise we could not, as we clearly sometimes do, arrive at the definition of a class of objects before we find a name for it. Of course, more often we begin with a familiar name which already conveys some meaning to us, and so we are apt to speak loosely at times of defining a name or word. And there is no harm in that as long as we realize that it is only a loose and popular mode of speech.

(3) We now turn to our main subject, definition in ethics. No one doubts, of course, that some of the general terms used in ethics are capable of being defined, even if some of them are believed to be indefinable.

When we consider the work of the moral philosopher in the light of these analogies two or three points seem to come out clearly at the outset. One of these is that it is impossible in ethics to start, as geometry does, with any definitions which will be generally and immediately accepted and recognizably applicable to the objects of our study. If we could find such clear definitions to start with there would be no call for specifically philosophical thinking about the subject at all. It would be quite a different kind of thinking that would be required. What gives rise to the need for philosophical thinking is that we are faced with ideas or notions which, though in common use, are not at all clearly conceived, and therefore not immediately definable. And it is the first, if not the only work of philosophical thinking to make these ideas clear and definite. In this respect the position of definition in ethics is analogous to its position in natural history. It is not the starting-point, but the goal of our inquiries. It comes at the end, not at the beginning of our investigations.

On the other hand, there is one respect in which the situation in ethics is quite different from that in natural history. To the naturalist, as we have seen, the vague popular idea of any kind of animal, with which we start before we know any zoölogy, is of no interest at all except as merely pointing the way at the beginning. He then goes on to study the observable facts, and is not concerned at all to analyse or clarify the original idea. "That's not my idea of an elephant" an unscientific person is reported to have said on hearing the scientific account of this species. To which the zoölogist, quite naturally, replied, "Perhaps not, but it is God's idea." What is contained in "my idea" of an elephant in this sense is completely irrelevant to the studies of the zoölogist.

To the moral philosopher, on the other hand, what is contained in "my idea" of good or right or justice or selfishness is of vital importance. It forms the main part, if not the whole, of the subject of his investigations. At any rate, it is an essential part, and a part which calls for hard and prolonged effort. It seems to me that one of the most frequent causes of error in ethics is that the investigation into the content of the ideas of good, right, etc., which actually are or have been held has not been sufficiently widespread and exhaustive. We have no observable facts, different in kind from these ideas and discoverable by quite different methods, to which we can turn, as the naturalist does, for the real subject of our investigation. The starting-point for ethics is always the moral judgements of mankind and what is implied in them, and we can never entirely get away from these as our main source of knowledge.

The technique of this process of clarifying the vague ideas with which we start would be an interesting subject of study. Though many people have attained a considerable degree of success in the process, there is little explicit discussion of the material that we have for it and the methods by which it should be treated. There is room for a new logic, or perhaps a psychologic of ethics. There are also, no doubt, certain psychological and metaphysical difficulties in the suggestion that it is possible to discover more in an idea than those who entertained the idea were aware of (or had any idea of). The position is not like that of the naturalist, who claims to discover a lot more, and sometimes something quite different, in the fact from what there was in the original idea of it. For here we do not yet know whether there are any facts that we have access to, except by an examination of ideas. But we cannot enter into these problems here. It is an undeniable fact that something of the kind goes on. But there is room for considerable difference of opinion about the correct description of it. I suppose in practice we generally say that we have discovered something more in a person's idea than he knew himself if we find him using it or applying it in a way that would only be justified if this something more was included in it.

There is, however, one point in this connexion on which I should like to say a word, because it is concerned with the interesting question of what the qualities are which make a good moral philosopher. It sometimes seems to be supposed that the only virtues which a philosopher needs are what I might call the logical virtues, a sense of form and system, a passion for coherence and self-consistency, a love of precise definition, a keen eye for fine distinctions of meaning, and kindred qualities. No one, I hope, would undervalue these qualities. But, for the moral philosopher in particular, I would suggest that it is a profound mistake to treat those qualities as the sole, or even the chief qualifications necessary for his task. At the risk of being misunderstood, I would go so far as to say that it is possible to be too exact and consistent, or rather, perhaps, to insist on exactness and consistency inopportunely at the wrong time or the wrong place.

At any rate, we must remember that the development of these virtues is, if I may be allowed the metaphor, a question of sharpening the instrument with which we think. And an instrument, however sharp, is of no value unless there is something to cut with it. Moral philosophy, as I understand it, consists primarily in reflection on moral experience and criticism of moral assumptions. And we cannot reflect on these things until we have got some sort of acquaintance with them. It seems to me that there is a quality required in ethics analogous to what we might call a good nose for facts in the natural scientist. And this is a different quality from the capacity for constructing a consistent and systematic theory to explain the facts, and just as essential.

This does not mean, as I think it is sometimes taken to mean, that the moral philosopher should necessarily have an extensive and intense moral experience of his own, that he should be living a life of continual struggle against temptations, that he should be labouring under a sense of sin, or anything of that kind. Doubtless he must have moral experience of his own, and must take this seriously, not just as an object of idle curiosity. But to be living a life of strong emotional stress and strain, to be going through fierce moral conflicts, would probably be, at the time at any rate, a positive disqualification for reflecting on it. Partly, of course, any strong emotion is unfavourable to reflection while it is being experienced. But what is much more serious, such strong emotional experience would tend to concentrate our attention too exclusively on our own experience, which in the nature of things must be very limited, and pay too little attention to the experience of other people, which is just as essential a part of our data.

The important qualification for a moral philosopher is, therefore, not so much moral experience of his own as a certain sensitiveness and receptivity to the moral experience of other people, and to the moral assumptions or ideas that are taken for granted by the people around him. He must be able, in some way, to let these enter his own mind in the form of assumptions or vague ideas, so that he may be able, then, to make them explicit and interpret and criticize them. We may add that he should be able to do this not only for the ideas current around him, but also for the ideas current in other ages. It is very doubtful whether the highest levels of ethical speculation are attainable without an historical sense.

This is the point at which the possible dangers of premature clear thinking arise. Current moral ideas and assumptions are necessarily vague and inexact, and probably often self-contradictory. But even the contradictions and confusions are part of the data for reflection. We must be able to receive them into our minds in that form before we begin to clear them up and make them definite and self-consistent. If we begin our work of cutting them down on the ground of self-contradiction too soon, if we begin limiting their meaning in order to get at a clear definition too hastily, we may easily find that we have rejected without proper examination some of the most essential parts of our data.

I seem to have wandered from the place of definition in ethics to the place of definiteness in ethics. But it is not all irrelevant, for we may presume that definition is one form of definiteness. At any rate, we have got so far that the first task of the moral philosopher is to make clear and explicit the vague general ideas that are held about the objects with which he deals. He has to discover as much as he can of what is implied by the ways in which the chief moral notions are or have been used. This is a sort of definition. But it is not a sort of definition with which he can rest content. For, as has been suggested, he will find when he has made these implications explicit that they by no means always coincide. Sometimes, indeed, they seem flatly to contradict each other. They, therefore, have to be subjected to progressive examination and criticism, until we finally reach an answer, that satisfies us, to the main question of ethics. This main question may be formulated thus: What sort of facts must we suppose there to be in order to account satisfactorily for human beings having these ideas about them?

Thus the whole of this stage of our investigations consists, in a very real sense, in arriving at definitions. This is not, perhaps, the whole of ethics. For when we have got these results we ought to be able to draw certain conclusions from them by a process of deduction. But it is certainly the most important and the most difficult part. So the place of definition in ethics appears to be co-extensive with the greater part of its field. Further, it is a continuous and progressive process. We have no grounds, except as a matter of temporary convenience in a particular part of the investigation, for picking out one feature as being, in a special sense, the definition. Even in geometry we saw how the sharp Aristotelian distinction between the essence, given in definition, and the properties broke down. And in ethics it is even more obviously untenable.

These considerations will indicate the attitude that should be taken up to the suggestion that we must give definitions before our investigations start. As applied literally to ethics the suggestion is obviously absurd. Definitions are the conclusion of the process, and cannot be demanded at the beginning. To the person who says, "You must state precisely what you mean by your terms before you can discuss them," we must reply, "It is only by discussing them that we can find out what we mean by them."

On the other hand, I think it is possible, on occasions, to carry this refusal to give preliminary definitions too far. At least it ought to be possible to give, if not a definition, a preliminary indication, a kind of sign-post pointing in the direction of the thing we are going to investigate. It might be done by citing one or two typical instances. In fact, this is often the most satisfactory method, though not the only one. But we must always remember that it is only a preliminary indication. The reason why some people are frightened of going even as far as this is that they feel that once they have committed themselves to any such statement, they are bound to hold by it for the rest of the discussion, and that if they restrict or enlarge or modify it in any other way they are thereby convicted of inconsistency and self-contradiction. But in reality it would be a very unfruitful discussion if it did not produce considerable modifications and developments of the notions with which it started.

We may suspect forgetfulness of this truth when we find text-books and courses of lectures giving, as they too often do, an inordinate amount of space at the beginning of their treatment to an attempted definition of their subject. I remember a great teacher, who influenced my early think-ing more than any other single person, who was fond of exercising his acute powers of criticism on these definitions. He would take the definition of a subject given, either verbally or in writing, by one of its exponents and proceed to examine his subsequent treatment of his subject in detail, and show how far he departed in practice from his original definition. As young men we were enormously impressed by these devastating criticisms, and I think we sometimes wondered how any psychologist or economist could bear to go on with the study of a subject which apparently did not really exist. Such criticism was doubtless a valuable warning against taking any preliminary definition too seriously. But beyond that, it seems to me now a singularly unprofitable exercise. I much prefer the method of the Scot-tish professor, who, after discussing for some time various suggestions for distinguishing between logic and epistemology, concluded, "The only really satisfactory definition of these two subjects that I can give you is that logic is the subject on which I shall lecture to you on Mondays, Wednesdays and Fridays, and epistemology the subject on which I shall lecture on Tuesdays, Thursdays and Saturdays." We must hope, however, that by the end of his course the relations between the two had become fairly clear, though probably not expressible by any simple formula.

There remains for examination one question, which to some will seem the most interesting, if not the only interesting part of the discussion. Under what conditions and on what kind of grounds can we pronounce any ethical notion to be indefinable? It seems, if our previous discussion has any truth in it, that such a statement itself admits of a variety of mean-ings. We may mean that our idea of it is indefinable, or that we think of it as something indefinable. What we think it to be is, I suppose, the strict sense of the phrase "what we mean" by any term. But we might also mean that, however we have been accustomed to think of it, it is in fact a simple unanalysable quality which can only be named and not described further. This would mean, according to our account of ethical thinking, that the only way to account for our thinking and speaking thus and thus of it is to suppose it to be such a simple quality. Let us consider these possibilities in order.

We start, it is suggested, with a vague general idea, a consciousness of a sort of a something we do not know exactly what, to which we apply the term in question. Now, in one sense, this is necessarily indefinable. Just because it is a vague general idea, it is different from the clear explicit idea expressed in the definition. The two are not exactly equivalent, as the meaning of two synonyms would be. If arriving at a definition means an advance in knowledge, the words of the definition must express something more than was present in the original idea. That is why a definition is a significant statement at all.

This is, of course, quite different from having a clear and explicit idea of a simple unanalysable quality. We have such ideas, as for instance of any particular colour. But it is obvious that we do not have such ideas of moral facts, at any rate to begin with. If we had there would be no possibility of beginning any discussion about them, indeed no room for philosophical thinking in such questions at all.

There is, however, another possibility that comes somewhere between these two. We may find that in our ordinary use of some moral notion, such as good or right, we use it in a way that implies that it is a simple unanalysable fact about which nothing further can be said. I find it rather difficult to imagine what sort of usage could be said to imply this. But, at any rate, it seems to me clear that we do not in fact use it in this way. It seems certain that our actual use and applications of these notions imply a good many things about them which can be put into words. Consequently they cannot be said to imply that they are indefinable.

So we are left with the possibility about any such notion—let us take "good" as a typical example—that, though we often seem to assume it to be something more, in reality it is only a simple, indefinable quality.

Here, again, I find it difficult to see what sort of proof there could be of this. There is the well-known argument in *Principia Ethica* which argues that good must be indefinable, because, whenever a definition is attempted, we can always ask with significance of the complex so defined whether it is in fact good. I have never been able to find any plausibility in this argument. It is not clear what sort of significance such a question is supposed to have. It may mean that we can never be quite sure of the correctness of any definition that we offer, that the possibility of its being wrong is always in our minds, and that therefore we can still raise questions about it. This is no doubt sometimes true. Indeed, if the process of definition is as we have described, it seems the right and proper attitude to take. But it obviously does not exclude the possibility that the definition may be correct. It is also true, however, that even if we are certain that the definition is correct we can still ask the question significantly, in the sense that we can have something before our minds in asking it. For, whenever the definition is not immediately self-evident, we can still retain a memory in our minds of what we originally meant by the term, namely, our first vague general idea. And, as we have seen, the vague general idea is necessarily different from the more precise idea expressed in the subsequent definition. So we can always put a question about their relation to each other. This, however, applies in many cases in which a definition is admittedly possible. Though I know, for instance, that part of the zoölogical definition of a fish is that it is cold-blooded, I can still attach a meaning to the question, Is a fish a cold-blooded animal?

There is one further point of importance in this connexion. If it were proved in any way that calling a thing good meant that it possessed a simple indefinable quality, it still would not necessarily follow that this was an important or interesting fact. It would only become important if it could be shown that it meant nothing more than that, that there was no further fact that could be asserted about all the things we called good. If there was any further fact or group of facts that could be truly asserted about anything we called good and about nothing else, it is obvious that in any argument or statement we could always substitute this for "good" without saying anything untrue. And if it led us on to further knowledge, it would be a much more interesting and important fact than the mere presence of a simple, indefinable quality.

I think we could find a convincing illustration of this argument by considering once more one of our elementary geometrical ideas. It seems to me clear that what we understand by a circle really has a simple indefinable quality, which we apprehend directly. That is what we think of when we first learn the use of the word, and it remains in our minds even after we have learned the various geometrical definitions. We could always distinguish in our minds between this simple quality, which we should probably speak of in crude language as "what a circle looks like," and any of the facts about that sort of figure given in the definitions. So, when we are faced with Euclid's definition, still more when we are faced with the complicated formula by which a circle is defined in higher branches of mathematics, we could truly say, in a sense, "That is not what we *mean* by circle: that is a further fact *about* it." But no one would think such a statement very valuable, nor would it be regarded as invalidating the mathematician's right to his definitions. If we are interested in extending our mathematical knowledge, the simple, indefinable quality of a circle becomes uninteresting and unimportant.

The distinction, therefore, which Dr. Ross so frequently insists on,[1] between the attribute which we mean by the term and the further attribute or attributes necessarily connected with it, seems to me an unreal one. Partly, it smacks too much of the sharp distinction between essence and properties which we are agreed in abandoning. But also it seems to me to misrepresent the nature of ethical investigation. What we *mean* by "good" (or "right" or any other moral term), in the first place, is the vague indefinite idea with which we start. But this only sets the problem. What we are trying to find is the nature of the facts that we must sup-

---

[1] *The Right and the Good,* Chap. I, *passim* [pp. 163 ff. this volume]; *Aristotelian Society, Supplementary Volume,* X, p. 61.

pose to exist in order to account for the way in which we think about these matters. And anything that we can say about them may equally be taken as part of their definition, in the only sense in which definition is possible in ethics at all. It may be that these considerations point in the direction of the doubts lately raised by Mr. Joseph (in *Some Problems in Ethics*) whether goodness should really be thought of as a quality at all. But that, I believe, is to be the subject of future discussions.

1932.

The Naturalistic Fallacy[*]

〰〰

W. K. FRANKENA

THE FUTURE HISTORIAN of "thought and expression" in the twentieth century will no doubt record with some amusement the ingenious trick, which some of the philosophical controversialists of the first quarter of our century had, of labelling their opponents' views "fallacies." He may even list some of these alleged fallacies for a certain sonority which their inventors embodied in their titles: the fallacy of initial predication, the fallacy of simple location, the fallacy of misplaced concreteness, the naturalistic fallacy.

Of these fallacies, real or supposed, perhaps the most famous is the naturalistic fallacy. For the practitioners of a certain kind of ethical theory, which is dominant in England and capably represented in America, and which is variously called objectivism, non-naturalism, or intuitionism, have frequently charged their opponents with committing the naturalistic fallacy. Some of these opponents have strongly repudiated the charge of fallacy, others have at least commented on it in passing, and altogether the notion of a naturalistic fallacy has had a considerable currency in ethical literature. Yet, in spite of its repute, the naturalistic fallacy has never been discussed at any length, and, for this reason, I have elected to make a study of it in this paper. I hope incidentally to clarify certain confusions which have been made in connexion with the naturalistic fallacy, but my main interest is to free the controversy between the intuitionists and their opponents of the notion of a logical or quasi-logical fallacy, and to indicate where the issue really lies.

The prominence of the concept of a naturalistic fallacy in recent moral philosophy is another testimony to the great influence of the Cambridge philosopher, Mr. G. E. Moore, and his book, *Principia Ethica.* Thus Mr. Taylor speaks of the "vulgar mistake" which Mr. Moore has taught us to call "the naturalistic fallacy," [1] and Mr. G. S. Jury, as if to illustrate how well we have learned this lesson, says, with reference to naturalistic definitions of value, "All such definitions stand charged with Dr. Moore's 'naturalistic fallacy.' " [2] Now, Mr. Moore coined the notion of the nat-

[*] Reprinted by kind permission of the author and the editor from *Mind*, 48, 1939.
[1] A. E. Taylor, *The Faith of a Moralist*, vol. I, p. 104 n.
[2] *Value and Ethical Objectivity*, p. 58.

uralistic fallacy in his polemic against naturalistic and metaphysical systems of ethics. "The naturalistic fallacy is a fallacy," he writes, and it "must
not be committed." All naturalistic and metaphysical theories of ethics,
however, "are *based* on the naturalistic fallacy, in the sense that the commission of this fallacy has been the main cause of their wide acceptance." [3]
The best way to dispose of them, then, is to expose this fallacy. Yet it is not
entirely clear just what is the status of the naturalistic fallacy in the po-
lemics of the intuitionists against other theories. Sometimes it is used as a
weapon, as when Miss Clarke says that if we call a thing good simply because it is liked we are guilty of the naturalistic fallacy.[4] Indeed, it presents this aspect to the reader in many parts of *Principia Ethica* itself. Now,
in taking it as a weapon, the intuitionists use the naturalistic fallacy as if it
were a logical fallacy on all fours with the fallacy of composition, the
revelation of which disposes of naturalistic and metaphysical ethics and
leaves intuitionism standing triumphant. That is, it is taken as a fallacy
in advance, for use in controversy. But there are signs in *Principia Ethica*
which indicate that the naturalistic fallacy has a rather different place in the
intuitionist scheme, and should not be used as a weapon at all. In this aspect, the naturalistic fallacy must be proved to be a fallacy. It cannot be
used to settle the controversy, but can only be asserted to be a fallacy
when the smoke of battle has cleared. Consider the following passages:
(*a*) "the naturalistic fallacy consists in the contention that good *means*
nothing but some simple or complex notion, that can be defined in terms
of natural qualities"; (*b*) "the point that good is indefinable and that to
deny this involves a fallacy, is a point capable of strict proof." [5] These
passages seem to imply that the fallaciousness of the naturalistic fallacy
is just what is at issue in the controversy between the intuitionists and
their opponents, and cannot be wielded as a weapon in that controversy.
One of the points I wish to make in this paper is that the charge of committing the naturalistic fallacy can be made, if at all, only as a conclusion
from the discussion and not as an instrument of deciding it.

The notion of a naturalistic fallacy has been connected with the notion
of a bifurcation between the 'ought' and the 'is,' between value and fact,
between the normative and the descriptive. Thus Mr. D. C. Williams says
that some moralists have thought it appropriate to chastise as the naturalistic fallacy the attempt to derive the Ought from the Is.[6] We may begin,
then, by considering this bifurcation, emphasis on which, by Sidgwick,
Sorley, and others, came largely as a reaction to the procedures of Mill
and Spencer. Hume affirms the bifurcation in his *Treatise:* "I cannot for-

[3] *Principia Ethica*, pp. 38, 64.

[4] M. E. Clarke, "Cognition and Affection in the Experience of Value," *Journal of
Philosophy*, 1938.

[5] *Principia Ethica*, pp. 73, 77. See also p. xix.

[6] "Ethics as Pure Postulate," *Philosophical Review*, 1933 [pp. 656 ff. this volume].
See also T. Whittaker, *The Theory of Abstract Ethics*, pp. 19 f.

bear adding to these reasonings an observation, which may, perhaps, be found of some importance. In every system of morality which I have hitherto met with, I have always remarked, that the author proceeds for some time in the ordinary way of reasoning, and establishes the being of a God, or makes observations concerning human affairs; when of a sudden I am surprised to find, that instead of the usual copulations of propositions, *is*, and *is not*, I meet with no proposition that is not connected with an *ought*, or an *ought not*. This change is imperceptible; but is, however, of the last consequence. For as this *ought*, or *ought not*, expresses some new relation or affirmation, it is necessary that it should be observed and explained; and at the same time that a reason should be given, for what seems altogether inconceivable, how this new relation can be a deduction from others, which are entirely different from it. But as authors do not commonly use this precaution, I shall presume to recommend it to the readers; and am persuaded, that this small attention would subvert all the vulgar systems of morality, and let us see that the distinction of vice and virtue is not founded merely on the relations of objects, nor is perceived by reason." [7]

Needless to say, the intuitionists *have* found this observation of some importance.[8] They agree with Hume that it subverts all the vulgar systems of morality, though, of course, they deny that it lets us see that the distinction of virtue and vice is not founded on the relations of objects, nor is perceived by reason. In fact, they hold that a small attention to it subverts Hume's own system also, since this gives naturalistic definitions of virtue and vice and of good and evil.[9]

Hume's point is that ethical conclusions cannot be drawn validly from premises which are non-ethical. But when the intuitionists affirm the bifurcation of the 'ought' and the 'is,' they mean more than that ethical propositions cannot be deduced from non-ethical ones. For this difficulty in the vulgar systems of morality could be remedied, as we shall see, by the introduction of definitions of ethical notions in non-ethical terms. They mean, further, that such definitions of ethical notions in non-ethical terms are impossible. "The essential point," says Mr. Laird, "is the irreducibility of values to non-values." [10] But they mean still more. Yellow and pleasantness are, according to Mr. Moore, indefinable in non-ethical terms, but they are natural qualities and belong on the 'is' side of the fence. Ethical properties, however, are not, for him, mere indefinable natural qualities, descriptive or expository. They are properties of a different *kind*—non-descriptive or non-natural.[11] The intuitionist bifurcation consists of three statements:—

[7] Book III, part ii, section i.
[8] See J. Laird, *A Study in Moral Theory*, pp. 16 f.; Whittaker, *op. cit.*, p. 19.
[9] See C. D. Broad, *Five Types of Ethical Theory*, ch. iv.
[10] *A Study in Moral Theory*, p. 94 n.
[11] See his *Philosophical Studies*, pp. 259, 273 f.

(1) Ethical propositions are not deducible from non-ethical ones.[12]
(2) Ethical characteristics are not definable in terms of non-ethical ones.
(3) Ethical characteristics are different in kind from non-ethical ones.

Really it consists of but one statement, namely, (3) since (3) entails (2) and (2) entails (1). It does not involve saying that any ethical characteristics are absolutely indefinable. That is another question, although this is not always noticed.

What, now, has the naturalistic fallacy to do with the bifurcation of the 'ought' and the 'is'? To begin with, the connexion is this: many naturalistic and metaphysical moralists proceed as if ethical conclusions can be deduced from premises all of which are non-ethical, the classical examples being Mill and Spencer. That is, they violate (1). This procedure has lately been referred to as the "factualist fallacy" by Mr. Wheelwright and as the "valuational fallacy" by Mr. Wood.[13] Mr. Moore sometimes seems to identify it with the naturalistic fallacy, but in the main he holds only that it involves, implies, or rests upon this fallacy.[14] We may now consider the charge that the procedure in question is or involves a fallacy.

It may be noted at once that, even if the deduction of ethical conclusions from non-ethical premises is in no way a fallacy, Mill certainly did commit a fallacy in drawing an analogy between visibility and desirability in his argument for hedonism; and perhaps his committing *this* fallacy, which, as Mr. Broad has said, we all learn about at our mothers' knees, is chiefly responsible for the notion of a naturalistic *fallacy*. But is it a fallacy to deduce ethical conclusions from non-ethical premises? Consider the Epicurean argument for hedonism which Mill so unwisely sought to embellish: pleasure is good, since it is sought by all men. Here an ethical conclusion is being derived from a non-ethical premise. And, indeed, the argument, taken strictly as it stands, *is* fallacious. But it is not fallacious because an *ethical* term occurs in the conclusion which does not occur in the premise. It is fallacious because any argument of the form "A is B, therefore A is C" is invalid, if taken strictly as it stands. For example, it is invalid to argue that Crœsus is rich because he is wealthy. Such arguments are, however, not intended to be taken strictly as they stand. They are enthymemes and contain a suppressed premise. And, when this suppressed premise is made explicit, they are valid and involve no logical fallacy.[15] Thus the Epicurean inference from psychological to ethical hedonism is valid when the suppressed premise is added to the effect that what is sought by all men is good. Then the only question left is whether the premises are true.

It is clear, then, that the naturalistic fallacy is not a logical fallacy,

[12] See J. Laird, *op. cit.*, p. 318. Also pp. 12 ff.

[13] P. E. Wheelwright, *A Critical Introduction to Ethics*, pp. 40–51, 91 f.; L. Wood, "Cognition and Moral Value," *Journal of Philosophy*, 1937, p. 237.

[14] See *Principia Ethica*, pp. 114, 57, 43, 49. Whittaker identifies it with the naturalistic fallacy and regards it as a "logical" fallacy, *op. cit.*, pp. 19 f.

[15] See *ibid.*, pp. 50, 139; Wheelwright, *loc. cit.*

since it may be involved even when the argument is valid. How does the naturalistic fallacy enter such "mixed ethical arguments" [16] as that of the Epicureans? Whether it does or not depends on the nature of the suppressed premise. This may be either an induction, an intuition, a deduction from a "pure ethical argument," a definition, or a proposition which is true by definition. If it is one of the first three, then the naturalistic fallacy does not enter at all. In fact, the argument does not then involve violating (1), since one of its premises will be ethical. But if the premise to be supplied is a definition or a proposition which is true by definition, as it probably was for the Epicureans, then the argument, while still valid, involves the naturalistic fallacy, and will run as follows:—

> (a) Pleasure is sought by all men.
> (b) What is sought by all men is good (definition).
> (c) Therefore, pleasure is good.

Now I am not greatly interested in deciding whether the argument as here set up violates (1). If it does not, then no 'mixed ethical argument' actually commits any factualist or valuational fallacy, except when it is unfairly taken as complete in its enthymematic form. If it does, then a valid argument may involve the deduction of an ethical conclusion from non-ethical premises and the factualist or valuational fallacy is not really a fallacy. The question depends on whether or not (b) and (c) are to be regarded as ethical propositions. Mr. Moore refuses so to regard them, contending that, by hypothesis, (b) is analytic or tautologous, and that (c) is psychological, since it really says only that pleasure is sought by all men. [17] But to say that (b) is analytic and not ethical and that (c) is not ethical but psychological is to prejudge the question whether 'good' can be defined; for the Epicureans would contend precisely that if their definition is correct then (b) is ethical but analytic and (c) ethical though psychological. Thus, unless the question of the definability of goodness is to be begged, (b) and (c) must be regarded as ethical, in which case our argument does not violate (1). However, suppose, if it be not nonsense, that (b) is non-ethical and (c) ethical, then the argument will violate (1), but it will still obey all of the canons of logic, and it is only confusing to talk of a 'valuational logic' whose basic rule is that an evaluative conclusion cannot be deduced from non-evaluative premises. [18]

For the only way in which either the intuitionists or postulationists like Mr. Wood can cast doubt upon the conclusion of the argument of the Epicureans (or upon the conclusion of any parallel argument) is to attack the premises, in particular (b). Now, according to Mr. Moore, it is due to the presence of (b) that the argument involves the naturalistic fallacy. (b) involves the identification of goodness with 'being sought by all

[16] See C. D. Broad, *The Mind and Its Place in Nature*, pp. 488 f.; Laird, *loc. cit.*
[17] See *op. cit.*, pp. 11 f. [pp. 73 f. this volume]; 19, 38, 73, 139.
[18] See L. Wood, *loc. cit.*

men,' and to make this or any other such identification is to commit the naturalistic fallacy. The naturalistic fallacy is not the procedure of violating (1). It is the procedure, implied in many mixed ethical arguments and explicitly carried out apart from such arguments by many moralists, of defining such characteristics as goodness or of substituting some other characteristic for them. To quote some passages from *Principia Ethica:*—

(*a*) ". . . far too many philosophers have thought that when they named those other properties [belonging to all things which are good] they were actually defining good; that these properties, in fact, were simply not 'other,' but absolutely and entirely the same with goodness. This view I propose to call the 'naturalistic fallacy.' . . ." [19]

(*b*) "I have thus appropriated the name Naturalism to a particular method of approaching Ethics. . . . This method consists in substituting for 'good' some one property of a natural object or of a collection of natural objects. . . ." [20]

(*c*) ". . . the naturalistic fallacy [is] the fallacy which consists in identifying the simple notion which we mean by 'good' with some other notion." [21]

Thus, to identify 'better' and 'more evolved,' 'good' and 'desired,' etc., is to commit the naturalistic fallacy.[22] But just why is such a procedure fallacious or erroneous? And is it a fallacy only when applied to good? We must now study Section 12 of *Principia Ethica*. Here Mr. Moore makes some interesting statements:—

". . . if anybody tried to define pleasure for us as being any other natural object; if anybody were to say, for instance, that pleasure *means* the sensation of red. . . . Well, that would be the same fallacy which I have called the naturalistic fallacy. . . . I should not indeed call that a naturalistic fallacy, although it is the same fallacy as I have called naturalistic with reference to Ethics. . . . When a man confuses two natural objects with one another, defining the one by the other . . . then there is no reason to call the fallacy naturalistic. But if he confuses 'good,' which is not . . . a natural object, with any natural object whatever, then there is a reason for calling that a naturalistic fallacy. . . ." [23]

Here Mr. Moore should have added that, when one confuses 'good,' which is not a metaphysical object or quality, with any metaphysical object or quality, as metaphysical moralists do, according to him, then the fallacy should be called the metaphysical fallacy. Instead he calls it a naturalistic fallacy in this case too, though he recognises that the case is different since metaphysical properties are non-natural [24]—a procedure which

[19] p. 10 [p. 73 this volume].
[20] p. 40.
[21] p. 58, *cf*. pp. xiii, 73.
[22] *Cf*. pp. 49, 53, 108, 139.
[23] p. 13 [p. 75 this volume].
[24] See pp. 38–40, 110–112.

has misled many readers of *Principia Ethica*. For example, it has led Mr. Broad to speak of "theological naturalism." [25]

To resume: "Even if [goodness] were a natural object, that would not alter the nature of the fallacy nor diminish its importance one whit." [26]

From these passages it is clear that the fallaciousness of the procedure which Mr. Moore calls the naturalistic fallacy is not due to the fact that it is applied to good or to an ethical or non-natural characteristic. When Mr. R. B. Perry defines 'good' as 'being an object of interest' the trouble is not merely that he is defining *good*. Nor is the trouble that he is defining an *ethical* characteristic in terms of *non-ethical* ones. Nor is the trouble that he is regarding a *non-natural* characteristic as a *natural* one. The trouble is more generic than that. For clarity's sake I shall speak of the definist fallacy as the generic fallacy which underlies the naturalistic fallacy. The naturalistic fallacy will then, by the above passages, be a species or form of the definist fallacy, as would the metaphysical fallacy if Mr. Moore had given that a separate name.[27] That is, the naturalistic fallacy, as illustrated by Mr. Perry's procedure, is a fallacy, not because it is naturalistic or confuses a non-natural quality with a natural one, but solely because it involves the definist fallacy. We may, then, confine our attention entirely to an understanding and evaluation of the definist fallacy.

To judge by the passages I have just quoted, the definist fallacy is the process of confusing or identifying two properties, of defining one property by another, or of substituting one property for another. Furthermore, the fallacy is always simply that two properties are being treated as one, and it is irrelevant, if it be the case, that one of them is natural or non-ethical and the other non-natural or ethical. One may commit the definist fallacy without infringing on the bifurcation of the ethical and the non-ethical, as when one identifies pleasantness and redness or rightness and goodness. But even when one infringes on that bifurcation in committing the definist fallacy, as when one identifies goodness and pleasantness or goodness and satisfaction, then the *mistake* is still not that the bifurcation is being infringed on, but only that two properties are being treated as one. Hence, on the present interpretation, the definist *fallacy* does not, in any of its forms, consist in violating (3), and has no essential connexion with the bifurcation of the 'ought' and the 'is.'

This formulation of the definist fallacy explains or reflects the motto of *Principia Ethica*, borrowed from Bishop Butler: "Everything is what it is, and not another thing." It follows from this motto that goodness is what it is and not another thing. It follows that views which try to identify it with something else are making a mistake of an elementary sort. For it *is* a mistake to confuse or identify two properties. If the properties really are two, then they simply are not identical. But do those who define ethical

[25] *Five Types of Ethical Theory*, p. 259.
[26] p. 14 [p. 75 this volume].
[27] As Whittaker has, *loc cit.*

notions in non-ethical terms make this mistake? They will reply to Mr. Moore that they are not identifying two properties; what they are saying is that two words or sets of words stand for or mean one and the same property. Mr. Moore was being, in part, misled by the material mode of speech, as Mr. Carnap calls it, in such sentences as "Goodness is pleasantness," "Knowledge is true belief," etc. When one says instead, "The word 'good' and the word 'pleasant' mean the same thing," etc., it is clear that one is not identifying two things. But Mr. Moore kept himself from seeing this by his disclaimer that he was interested in any statement about the use of words.[28]

The definist fallacy, then, as we have stated it, does not rule out any naturalistic or metaphysical definitions of ethical terms. Goodness is not identifiable with any 'other' characteristic (if it is a characteristic at all). But the question is: *which* characteristics are other than goodness, which names stand for characteristics other than goodness? And it is begging the question of the definability of goodness to say out of hand that Mr. Perry, for instance, is identifying goodness with something else. The point is that goodness is what it is, even if it is definable. That is why Mr. Perry can take as the motto of his naturalistic *Moral Economy* another sentence from Bishop Butler: "Things and actions are what they are, and the consequences of them will be what they will be; why then should we desire to be deceived?" The motto of *Principia Ethica* is a tautology, and should be expanded as follows: Everything is what it is, and not another thing, unless it is another thing, and even then it is what it is.

On the other hand, if Mr. Moore's motto (or the definist fallacy) rules out any definitions, for example of 'good,' then it rules out all definitions of any term whatever. To be effective at all, it must be understood to mean, "Every term means what it means, and not what is meant by any other term." Mr. Moore seems implicitly to understand his motto in this way in Section 13, for he proceeds as if 'good' has no meaning, if it has no unique meaning. If the motto be taken in this way, it will follow that 'good' is an indefinable term, since no synonyms can be found. But it will also follow that no term is definable. And then the method of analysis is as useless as an English butcher in a world without sheep.

Perhaps we have misinterpreted the definist fallacy. And, indeed, some of the passages which I quoted earlier in this paper seem to imply that the definist fallacy is just the error of defining an indefinable characteristic. On this interpretation, again, the definist fallacy has, in all of its forms, no essential connexion with the bifurcation of the ethical and the non-ethical. Again, one may commit the definist fallacy without violating that bifurcation, as when one defines pleasantness in terms of redness or goodness in terms of rightness (granted Mr. Moore's belief that pleasantness and goodness are indefinable). But even when one infringes on that bifurcation and defines goodness in terms of desire, the *mistake* is not that one is infringing

[28] See *op. cit.*, pp. 6, 8, 12 [pp. 69, 71, 73 this volume].

on the bifurcation by violating (3), but only that one is defining an indefinable characteristic. This is possible because the proposition that goodness is indefinable is logically independent of the proposition that goodness is non-natural: as is shown by the fact that a characteristic may be indefinable and yet natural, as yellowness is; or non-natural and yet definable, as rightness is (granted Mr. Moore's views about yellowness and rightness).

Consider the definist fallacy as we have just stated it. It is, of course, an error to define an indefinable quality. But the question, again, is: which qualities are indefinable? It is begging the question in favour of intuitionism to say in advance that the quality goodness is indefinable and that, therefore, all naturalists commit the definist fallacy. One must know that goodness is indefinable before one can argue that the definist fallacy *is* a fallacy. Then, however, the definist fallacy can enter only at the end of the controversy between intuitionism and definism, and cannot be used as a weapon in the controversy.

The definist fallacy may be stated in such a way as to involve the bifurcation between the 'ought' and the 'is.' [29] It would then be committed by anyone who offered a definition of any ethical characteristic in terms of non-ethical ones. The trouble with such a definition, on this interpretation, would be that an *ethical* characteristic is being reduced to a *non-ethical* one, a *non-natural* one to a *natural* one. That is, the definition would be ruled out by the fact that the characteristic being defined is ethical or non-natural and therefore cannot be defined in non-ethical or natural terms. But on this interpretation, too, there is danger of a *petitio* in the intuitionist argumentation. To assume that the ethical characteristic is exclusively ethical it to beg precisely the question which is at issue when the definition is offered. Thus, again, one must know that the characteristic is non-natural and indefinable in natural terms before one can say that the definists are making a mistake.

Mr. Moore, McTaggart, and others formulate the naturalistic fallacy sometimes in a way somewhat different from any of those yet discussed. They say that the definists are confusing a universal synthetic proposition about *the good* with a definition of *goodness*.[30] Mr. Abraham calls this the "fallacy of misconstrued proposition." [31] Here again the difficulty is that, while it is true that it is an error to construe a universal synthetic proposition as a definition, it is a *petitio* for the intuitionists to say that what the definist is taking for a definition is really a universal synthetic proposition.[32]

At last, however, the issue between the intuitionists and the definists (naturalistic or metaphysical) is becoming clearer. The definists are all holding that certain propositions involving ethical terms are analytic, tautologous, or true by definition, e.g., Mr. Perry so regards the statement,

[29] See J. Wisdom, *Mind*, 1931, p. 213, note 1.
[30] See *Principia Ethica*, pp. 10 [p. 73 this volume], 16 [p. 75 this volume], 38; *The Nature of Existence*, vol. ii, p. 398.
[31] Leo Abraham, "The Logic of Intuitionism," *International Journal of Ethics*, 1933.
[32] As Mr. Abraham points out, *loc. cit.*

"All objects of desire are good." The intuitionists hold that such statements are synthetic. What underlies this difference of opinion is that the intuitionists claim to have at least a dim awareness of a simple unique quality or relation of goodness or rightness which appears in the region which our ethical terms roughly indicate, whereas the definists claim to have no awareness of any such quality or relation in that region, which is different from all other qualities and relations which belong to the same context but are designated by words other than 'good' and 'right' and their obvious synonyms.[33] The definists are in all honesty claiming to find but one characteristic where the intuitionists claim to find two, as Mr. Perry claims to find only the property of being desired where Mr. Moore claims to find both it and the property of being good. The issue, then, is one of inspection or intuition, and concerns the awareness or discernment of qualities and relations.[34] That is why it cannot be decided by the use of the notion of a fallacy.

If the definists may be taken at their word, then they are not actually confusing two characteristics with each other, nor defining an indefinable characteristic, nor confusing definitions and universal synthetic propositions—in short they are not committing the naturalistic or definist fallacy in any of the interpretations given above. Then the only fallacy which they commit—the real naturalistic or definist fallacy—is the failure to descry the qualities and relations which are central to morality. But this is neither a logical fallacy nor a logical confusion. It is not even, properly speaking, an error. It is rather a kind of blindness, analogous to colour-blindness. Even this moral blindness can be ascribed to the definists only if they are correct in their claim to have no awareness of any unique ethical characteristics and if the intuitionists are correct in affirming the existence of such characteristics, but certainly to call it a 'fallacy,' even in a loose sense, is both unamiable and profitless.

On the other hand, of course, if there are no such characteristics in the objects to which we attach ethical predicates, then the intuitionists, if we may take them at their word, are suffering from a corresponding moral hallucination. Definists might then call this the intuitionistic or moralistic fallacy, except that it is no more a 'fallacy' than is the blindness just described. Anyway, they do not believe the claim of the intuitionists to be aware of unique ethical characteristics, and consequently do not attribute to them this hallucination. Instead, they simply deny that the intuitionists really do find such unique qualities or relations, and then they try to find some plausible way of accounting for the fact that very respectable and trustworthy people think they find them.[35] Thus they charge the intuitionists with verbalism, hypostatisation, and the like. But this half of the story does not concern us now.

[33] See R. B. Perry, *General Theory of Value*, p. 30; cf. *Journal of Philosophy*, 1931, p. 520.
[34] See H. Osborne, *Foundations of the Philosophy of Value*, pp. 15, 19, 70.
[35] *Cf.* R. B. Perry, *Journal of Philosophy*, 1931, pp. 520 ff.

What concerns us more is the fact that the intuitionists do not credit the claim of the definists either. They would be much disturbed, if they really thought that their opponents were morally blind, for they do not hold that we must be regenerated by grace before we can have moral insight, and they share the common feeling that morality is something democratic even though not all men are good. Thus they hold that "we are all aware" of certain unique characteristics when we use the terms 'good,' 'right,' etc., only due to a lack of analytic clearness of mind, abetted perhaps by a philosophical prejudice, we may not be aware at all that they are different from other characteristics of which we are also aware.[36] Now, I have been arguing that the intuitionists cannot charge the definists with committing any fallacy unless and until they have shown that we are all, the definists included, aware of the disputed unique characteristics. If, however, they were to show this, then, at least at the end of the controversy, they could accuse the definists of the error of confusing two characteristics, or of the error of defining an indefinable one, and these errors might, since the term is somewhat loose in its habits, be called 'fallacies,' though they are not logical fallacies in the sense in which an invalid argument is. The fallacy of misconstrued proposition depends on the error of confusing two characteristics, and hence could also on our present supposition, be ascribed to the definists, but it is not really a *logical* confusion,[37] since it does not actually involve being confused about the difference between a proposition and a definition.

Only it is difficult to see how the intuitionists can prove that the definists are at least vaguely aware of the requisite unique characteristics.[38] The question must surely be left to the inspection or intuition of the definists themselves, aided by whatever suggestions the intuitionists may have to make. If so, we must credit the verdict of their inspection, especially of those among them who have read the writings of the intuitionists reflectively, and, then, as we have seen, the most they can be charged with is moral blindness.

Besides trying to discover just what is meant by the naturalistic fallacy, I have tried to show that the notion that a logical or quasi-logical fallacy is committed by the definists only confuses the issue between the intuitionists and the definists (and the issue between the latter and the emotists or postulationists), and misrepresents the way in which the issue is to be settled. No logical fallacy need appear anywhere in the procedure of the definists. Even fallacies in any less accurate sense cannot be implemented to decide the case against the definists; at best they can be ascribed to the definists only after the issue has been decided against them on independent grounds. But the only defect which can be attributed to the definists, *if* the intuitionists are right in affirming the existence of unique

---

[36] *Principia Ethica*, pp. 17 [p. 77 this volume], 38, 59, 61.

[37] But see H. Osborne, *op. cit.*, pp. 18 f.

[38] For a brief discussion of their arguments, see *ibid.*, p. 67; L. Abraham, *op. cit.* I think they are all inconclusive, but cannot show this here.

indefinable ethical characteristics, is a peculiar moral blindness, which is not a fallacy even in the looser sense. The issue in question must be decided by whatever method we may find satisfactory for determining whether or not a word stands for a characteristic at all, and, if it does, whether or not it stands for a unique characteristic. What method is to be employed is, perhaps, in one form or another, the basic problem of contemporary philosophy, but no generally satisfactory solution of the problem has yet been reached. I shall venture to say only this: it does seem to me that the issue is not to be decided against the intuitionists by the application *ab extra* to ethical judgments of any empirical or ontological meaning dictum.[39]

[39] See *Principia Ethica*, pp. 124 f., 140.

Subjectivism and Naturalism in Ethics[*]

A. C. EWING

FOR THE FREQUENCY today of ethical theories of a frankly subjectivist or naturalist type there are several obvious causes. Firstly, the success of the natural sciences as compared with philosophy and the failure of obscurantist opposition in the name of religion have made people very reluctant to admit anything which cannot be subjected to the methods of empirical science. Secondly, the decline of the influence of organized Christianity and the widespread doubts as to the justification of its central theological beliefs have contributed to the rise of scepticism about ethics. This must specially be the case with those who thought that ethics was essentially bound up with religion but have lost their faith in religion. Thirdly, the radical divergence in ethical views between different people and different types of civilization has been realized as never before (and, I think, exaggerated). Fourthly, since the war of 1914–18 there has been a world-wide reaction against rationalism in all spheres so that there is a consequent tendency to regard any *a priori* element in ethics with great suspicion and to connect value-judgements closely with feeling, even sometimes to the expressions of feeling. We must not, however, exaggerate the prevalence of such opinions. When I reviewed the ethical literature published in the world in 1937 and 1938 in order to write a manual on it for the Institut International de Collaboration Philosophique,[1] I found that in the continent of Europe naturalist or subjectivist ethics was decidedly the exception among philosophers, and I noted an assertion in an article by Professor Urban [2] that the objectivity of value can now be regarded as one of the things "we know" in axiology, in the sense that among critical opinion there is a large measure of assent on this point even in America and more markedly in Europe. But the question is still a highly topical one, and both its practical and its philosophical importance are such as to make it specially suitable for discussion. The arguments I shall bring for the objectivity of ethics cannot claim to be original—it is unlikely that I could produce really original arguments on such a well-worn topic—but it is none the less very desirable that readers of *Mind* should have their attention called from time to time

---

[*] Reprinted by kind permission of the author and the editor from *Mind*, 53, 1944.
[1] This was unfortunately never published owing to the German occupation of Paris.
[2] *Journal of Philosophy*, 1937, pp. 588 ff.

to their existence. Unfortunately there are many philosophers whom they will not satisfy, but I can only say what seems to me true and I still cannot help feeling convinced that they ought to satisfy.

But before we can discuss the matter we must arrive at some definition of what is meant by the "objectivity" of ethical judgements. Obviously a person may maintain them to be objective in the usual sense in which the word is used in ethical discussions without maintaining that they ascribe ethical or any sort of intrinsic value to physical objects. What is then meant by "objective"? The simplest way to answer this question is by pointing out what views are excluded by the assertion that "ethical judgments" are "objective." It is clear that, as usually understood, this assertion excludes the following views: (a) that they are not really judgements at all but, e.g. exclamations, commands, or wishes; (b) that, though judgements, they are all false or at least that we are never justified in thinking them true; (c) that, though they are judgements and true judgements, they merely refer to the psychological state or the psychological dispositions of the person who makes them, so that "This is wrong" is the same sort of judgement as "I feel pity for the people in concentration camps," or "I hate Hitler." Any of these three alternative views may be called "subjective" as opposed to "objective." The "objective" view is also often understood as excluding any view which holds ethical judgements to be analyzable exclusively in terms of human psychology, but here a distinction is required between "subjectivism" and "naturalism," understanding by the latter the view which analyzes ethical concepts in purely psychological terms, from which it would follow that ethics was a mere branch of psychology, a natural science. (If ethics were made a branch of some other natural science the ethics of course would still be naturalistic, but I say "psychology" merely because it is the only natural science of which ethics could be made a branch with any show of plausibility.) Now a naturalist theory of ethics need not be subjective. A typical example of a naturalist ethics would be the theory that to say some action is right or some experience good merely means that most men, or most men in a certain group, tend to have a particular kind of feeling about it. On such a view "good" and "right" still stand for objective facts quite independent of the attitude towards them of the person who makes the ethical judgement in question, i.e. they stand for facts about a class of people or people in general. They would still be as objective as the judgement that many Germans admired Hitler or that people are generally distressed by the death of their parents. The forms of naturalist ethics in question do not differ from "non-naturalist" ethics in denying the objectivity of ethics, for judgements of psychology are objective, but in making ethics a branch of a factual science.

I am in full agreement with the usual criticisms of subjectivist views. The simplest form of subjectivism is that according to which "ethical judgements," though genuine judgements, assert only that the person who makes the judgement has or tends to have certain feelings. "This is good" on such a view becomes "I have an emotion of approval in considering this," or "I have a disposition or tendency to feel an emotion of approval when I consider things like this." From such a view a number of consequences would follow which seem to my mind so clearly false as to constitute a sufficient argument to refute any theory of this kind. For it would follow from such a theory (1) that an ethical judgement cannot be false unless the person judging has made a mistake about his own psychology; (2) that two different people never mean the same thing when they make an ethical judgement, for either means "This is approved by *me*"; (3) if I judge something good and you judge precisely the same thing bad our judgements are never logically incompatible with each other; (4) no argument can be in any degree relevant to justifying or casting doubt on an ethical judgement, nor can any citation of empirical facts unless they are facts about the psychology of the person who made the judgement. These arguments apply whether the subjectivist takes ethical judgements to be about one's feelings, about one's thoughts, or about a kind of consciousness which includes both feelings and thoughts. Indeed, if "this is good or right" means, or includes in its meaning, "I think it good or right," the additional objection, besides those already mentioned, arises that "good" or "right" is then defined in terms of itself. "I think this good or right" would become "I think that I think it good or right," thus still presupposing an undefined meaning of "good" or "right."

Thwarted in their attempts to make "ethical judgements" merely judgements about one's own psychology, subjectivists are now mostly inclined to assert that they are imperatives, wishes, or exclamations.* In that case they are neither true nor false and so are not judgements at all, so that, strictly speaking, it is a misnomer to speak of them as "ethical judgements," but I shall for the sake of convenience use this phrase in inverted commas so as to cover such a view, meaning by "judgements" here "real or apparent judgements." To say that "moral judgements" are exclamations is to say that they are expressions of emotion, but this is distinguished from saying that they are judgements about the speaker's emotions. To say "Alas!" is not to assert, though it is to suggest, that I am in distress. Whether this distinction can be maintained is, however, very doubtful. It has been rightly challenged on the ground that it must be admitted at any rate that ethical statements are sentences deliberately constructed by the speaker to express his feelings, and that voluntarily and deliberately to employ a form of language intended to express the fact that I have a particular kind of feeling can hardly be distinguished from asserting that I have the feeling in question.[3] There is a grammatical distinction between "Hurrah!" and "I am glad," but to say "Hurrah!" is really to assert that I am glad. If

---

* [A detailed statement and discussion of this view will be found in Section V of the present volume.—Ed.]

[3] E. F. Carritt, *Philosophy*, Vol. XIII, No. 50, p. 133. [The major portion of this paper, "Moral Positivism and Moral Aestheticism," is reprinted below pp. 405 ff.].

so the exclamational view is indistinguishable from the view which I have discussed and so falls before the objections to which that view is exposed.

But even if the two views can be distinguished we can urge against the exclamational view as against the other that it would lead to the impossible conclusion that if I say something is good and you say it is bad we are never contradicting each other and that no argument nor any citation of empirical facts could be relevant to the refutation of any ethical judgement. It would also make it impossible for an ethical "judgement" to be true or false, which is a further objection. Not only would such "judgements" not be strictly provable (which may be admitted in any case), but nothing whatever could be said in their support. For to say something in their support would be to say something which makes their truth more likely, but they can no more be true according to this view than a blow is true. That in making "ethical judgements" we are at least claiming to assert what is true is surely obvious from a consideration of our psychological attitude when we make them. When I try to decide what I ought to do in a given case I am conscious of trying *to find out something*, not merely of resolving or wanting to do something, and "to try to find something out" is to try to discover what is true about it.

The same objections seem to me quite sufficient as against the view that "moral judgements" really are wishes, commands,[4] or exhortations. Further, I may wish or command something which I know or believe to be wrong, and I may quite well think you ought to do something which I do not wish you and would not dream of commanding you to do, e.g. punish me. Nor is the account of moral judgements as commands compatible with the fact that we can make moral judgements about the past or about the rightness or wrongness of acts which have not yet been done but which we think might be done. This objection cannot be avoided by making them hypothetical commands. Is there the least plausibility in saying that my judgement that the Athenians of classical times did wrong in attacking Melos is to be analyzed as simply saying that, if I had been there, I should have exhorted them not to attack Melos? Besides, I might judge that a historical action was wrong and yet believe (from knowledge of my weaknesses) that I should have advocated it if I had lived at that time or be very doubtful whether I should have had the courage to oppose it. I judge it wrong of Hitler to persecute the Jews, but I am certainly not thereby saying that I should have been brave enough, if I had had the opportunity, to go to Hitler and exhort him not to persecute the Jews. My judgement is certainly not dependent on my believing that I should have been brave enough, and makes a claim which holds independently of any such questions about my character or hypothetical action. If the moral judgement is analyzed as meaning "I would have done so apart from ir-

---

[4] To say that moral "judgments" are commands by the person who makes the "judgment" is different from saying they are judgments that an action is commanded, e.g. by society. The latter view would be naturalist, not subjectivist, and open to the objections to which other naturalist views are exposed, which I shall bring shortly.

relevant motives" the analysis involves a vicious circle, for "irrelevant" can only be understood as "irrelevant to the rightness or wrongness of the act."

The naturalist view which seeks to analyze ethical concepts purely in terms of psychology may, as I have said, take forms in which it could not be described as subjective. This occurs if ethical propositions are regarded as propositions asserting what most people, or people of a certain class, feel, or what will satisfy the desires of these people. Two, as I think, fatal objections to a view of this kind are stated respectively by Professor Broad and Professor Moore. Professor Broad points out that the logical consequences of such a view is "not (as with subjectivism) that in disputes on moral questions there comes a point beyond which we can only say 'de gustibus non est disputandum.' " On the contrary, "the logical consequence is that all such disputes *could* be settled, and that the way to settle them is to collect statistics of how people in fact do feel. And to me this kind of answer seems utterly irrelevant to this kind of question." [5] This objection, brought against the particular view of Hume, would apply to all forms of naturalism which are not subjective, for all such views would equate ethical propositions with propositions about the psychology of men in general or of some class of men and therefore with propositions the truth of which was capable of being determined in this way. We might put it even more strongly and say that it would make ethical propositions identical with propositions about statistics (except that they were vaguely expressed). For the difference between vagueness and definiteness is only the difference between saying "most" and saying "882 out of 1024." Yet ethical propositions, whatever they are, are surely not just vague propositions about statistics.

Professor Moore objects to all naturalistic definitions of "good" that, no matter what the alleged definition is, we can always see that it is quite sensible to ask whether things which have the property put forward in the definition are or are not good, and that therefore the definition is wrong, since, if it were right, to say that a thing which had the defining property was good would be to utter a tautology, and to question whether it was good would be to ask whether what is good is good.[6] This, I think, expresses a valid objection, but one that must be used with care. Obviously, till we have made up our minds whether a definition is correct or not, it may still be on any view a question the answer to which can seriously be doubted whether a thing which possesses the defining property is good or not, and naturalists have thought that they could meet Professor Moore's objection by raising this point. But surely the trouble with the naturalistic definitions is that when we consider them and ask whether what possesses the defining property is always good we are clearly conscious that we are asking not a question about what the term means but the question whether

[5] C. D. Broad, *Five Types of Ethical Theory*, p. 115.
[6] *Principia Ethica*, § 13.

everything which has the defining property has also a different property, signified by "good." The naturalist says that "good" means "desired" or "such that men feel approval of it" or "such as ultimately to satisfy men," but it presents itself to us as a contingent question of empirical fact whether what is approved or desired or will ultimately satisfy us is also good. Perhaps men are so constituted that in fact they only desire or only feel approval of what is in some way good (provided they know what it is like), and perhaps they are so constituted that the good and only the good will ultimately satisfy them, but at least whether they are so constituted is a doubtful empirical question and not one an affirmative answer to which follows from the very meaning of "good." We never, with any of the proposed definitions, reach the stage at which it seems at all plausible (at least except for extraneous, and I think wrong, reasons) to hold that to say a thing is good is just *the same* as to say that the thing has the defining property in question, and before we are entitled to accept a definition (in Professor Moore's sense of the word) that stage must be reached.

We must remember that it is never possible to *prove* that an analysis of a concept is correct though it may be possible to prove that one is incorrect, and therefore in the last resort we are dealing in attempts at analysis forced to fall back upon our consciousness of whether a proposed analysis does or does not express what we mean. For, even if a philosophical analysis also expresses something more than what we mean, it at least must include all that we mean. An analysis may indeed sometimes express what I mean when I think it does not, but I can never be justified in accepting an analysis as an expression of my meaning unless I am in a position to say: "Well, this is what I meant all along, though I did not put it so clearly." Now in the case of naturalistic definitions of "good," so far from my seeing this I see quite definitely the contrary. I see that propositions about good in some senses of "good" are propositions which cannot be analyzed adequately in psychological terms almost as clearly as I see that they cannot be analyzed adequately in terms of physics or mathematics. It is not merely that I have been unable to think of any naturalistic definition which satisfied me but am prepared to leave it an open question whether somebody may not in the future think of one which will satisfy me. On the contrary, I see that "good," "right," "duty," "ought," "morality" are just not the sort of concepts which can ever be analyzed completely in terms of psychology, as I can see that sights cannot be analyzed in terms of sounds (however many correlations we may establish between sights and sounds). There may be senses in which it is sometimes true to say that a man does not know what he means, but I could not use words intelligently at all if I were not, sometimes at least, immediately aware of what I mean. The immediate awareness to which I have appealed so far is of a sort which even the sceptic cannot rule out, the immediate awareness of introspection. For "what I mean" is "what I intend to assert," and I surely can be immediately aware of my own intentions. It is possible for the sceptic to say that I am under a delusion in thinking something good when it is not really good on the ground that we cannot have such non-empirical knowledge, but he cannot deny that I can have empirical knowledge of my own intentions. The difficulty is not to account for this knowledge but to account for the fact that there is any disagreement about the subject, since disagreement implies that either I or the naturalists must be wrong about what we mean. Perhaps it may be explained by the following circumstances.

(1) The naturalists, either because they have a general philosophical outlook which makes them unwilling to admit the existence of any characteristics which cannot be reduced to empirical terms, or for some other reason, think that we could never be justified in asserting that anything was good or bad if we meant anything more by these statements than what could be analyzed in psychological terms. They are therefore forced to hold either that our ethical judgements are analyzable in such a fashion or that these judgements are all mistaken, and they prefer the former of these alternatives. I doubt whether anybody would be inclined to analyze "ethical judgements" naturalistically if he considered merely his state of mind as it seemed to him in making such judgements and was not influenced by other epistemological considerations.

(2) There are certainly some cases of "good" in which "good" might be defined naturalistically. For instance, "strawberries are good" seems to mean only "I (or most people) like strawberries." "This is a good knife" seems only to mean that it is useful for certain purposes, which may be bad or indifferent; I should still call it a good knife if it had not been used for anything but committing murders. Philosophers in the past have usually not paid sufficient attention to the multiplicity of senses in which the same word is used, so people who defined "good" naturalistically may easily have confused different senses of "good," though this is more likely to be the case with earlier than in the contemporary naturalists.

(3) Just as there are some senses of "good" which require a naturalistic definition, so perhaps there are some senses of "definition" in which we might have a naturalistic definition of every sense of "good." Colours could be said to be "definable" in terms of wave-lengths because they are correlated with them, but this would not commit one to saying that the colour as seen was just the wave-length which occurred in its definition. Similarly, it might be possible in a sense to define "good" in terms of a characteristic which always accompanied goodness without holding that goodness just was the characteristic in question. I do not wish to commit myself to the view that such a universally accompanying characteristic could be found, but at least the view that there is such a characteristic is in some of its forms less unplausible than the view that this characteristic is identical with goodness. We must remember that the fact, if it is a fact, that a and bc go together is no proof that bc is identical with a. Suppose a future physiologist were (as is logically possible) to discover a specific modification of the brain which accompanied every good experience or action. The brain-

modification would then be an infallible sign of goodness, but it still certainly would not follow that "good" just *meant* "accompanied by this new brain-modification" or that goodness *was identical with* the property of being thus accompanied. If it were, no people who lived before this physiological discovery could have meant anything by "good." Till recently the different senses of "definition" have not been clearly distinguished, at least with reference to ethics, and even now the most prominent school of naturalistic philosophers, the verificationists, regard as unanswerable, or at any rate take no interest in answering, the question what we mean by a word in any sense in which this can be distinguished from the empirical criteria on account of which the word is applied. It is therefore fair to say that there has been a great deal of confusion in the matter and that it is highly probable that most people who put forward naturalistic definitions of "good" did not mean by "definition" what Professor Moore meant in *Principia Ethica*.

(4) It seems very unsatisfactory to conclude a long discussion with the tame remark that the central concept we have been discussing cannot be defined. But it is important to realize that to say this is not necessarily to exclude the possibility of being able to say more about it but only to exclude the possibility of reducing the central concept of ethics to non-ethical terms.[7] It may be that when we have said that it cannot be thus reduced we shall find ourselves able to say other things of a more positive kind about it, such as that what is good is what is willed by God or is what would be desired by all men if they really knew what it was like. All I wish to deny is that such statements could exhaust the meaning of the term "good." They may be correct descriptions but they are not definitions, at least in the sense under discussion. In that sense some terms must be indefinable, for analysis implies the unanalyzable, but to say a term is indefinable is not to say that we do not know what it means, but only that the concept for which it stands, with which we may still be perfectly familiar, is too ultimate and unique to be analyzed in terms of anything else.

(5) Even philosophers who have insisted on "analysis" have rarely clearly committed themselves to the view that, when they put forward an analysis, they were just giving an account of what people meant in the ordinary sense of "meaning." What they seem often to be doing rather is giving that element in the meaning of a general statement which they take to be true, while rejecting the rest as false, ungrounded or confused, or, alternatively, stating a proposition which they think has the same implications as the original one. We need not, therefore, be very surprised at the disagreement between naturalists and non-naturalists, for the people who disagreed with each other were generally trying to do different things.

---

[7] I do not think that Professor Moore has shown that "good" cannot be analyzed in terms of other ethical concepts together with psychological concepts. I suggested such an analysis in *Mind*, Vol. XLVIII, No. 189, pp. 1 ff. [Reprinted in this volume, pages 231–249, *infra*.—Ed.]

(6) I do not, indeed, altogether rule out the possibility of mistakes of introspection in this connection. Introspective analysis of one's own state of mind is not always easy. All I can say is that when I try to see what I mean when I use ethical terms I find that I have present to my consciousness an idea generically different from any empirical psychological concepts, and that I am as clearly aware of this as I am of what I mean in almost any other case of meaning. I have not yet discussed the possibility that I may be wrong in thinking that this concept applies to anything, a question which could not be answered by introspection alone, but at least I have the concept and believe that it applies. It is for everybody to ask himself whether he too has this concept. That one large class of philosophers are psychologically peculiar in this respect, i.e. that they in concrete ethical experiences have a fundamentally different idea of what good is from other people seems incredible. A circumstance which makes it easier for people to overlook this concept is that the times when we actually have first-hand ethical experience and the times when we discuss philosophically the analysis of good do not usually coincide, and it is perhaps impossible to engage in the two activities exactly simultaneously, so that we are dependent for our ethical experience on memory when we are philosophizing. For we do not have first-hand ethical experience all the time we do what is right or even every time we make judgements about the good, especially when we take the judgements only as examples for a philosophical argument. Some of our judgements as to good and evil are almost parrot-like; some are mere applications of a general principle the truth of which is not intuited, at least at the time, but taken for granted; some involve an insight into the particular case as regards means but presuppose prior judgements as to ends. It is therefore very easy when we investigate these matters philosophically to go wrong because we have not before us at the time a genuine ethical experience, and at the very moment when we have such an experience we are too much concerned with it as a practical issue to philosophize about it. This perhaps explains why good and intelligent men could sometimes put forward quite preposterous ethical theories, e.g. egoistic hedonism.

Some would-be naturalists admit that we can see any naturalistic analysis to be incomplete but attempt to meet the objection by calling in subjectivism as an ally and contending that naturalistic definitions leave out something but only the emotional or hortatory element. On that view an "ethical judgement" is really a psychological judgement plus an exclamation, wish, or command. But this renders them liable to the objections brought against subjectivism. At least this is so if we admit the possibility of distinguishing exclamations, etc., from judgements, a possibility on which I earlier cast doubt.[8] So this dilemma arises: If we have to admit that exclamations, wishes, or commands, since they are the intentional use of words to express our state of mind, must be regarded as assertions about

[8] *Vide* above, p. 123.

the latter, ethical propositions are still on that view nothing but psychological propositions, and the attempt to avoid the objections given above has failed. If, on the other hand, we allow the distinction between exclamations, etc., expressing our state of mind and assertions that our state of mind is so and so, and maintain that the only non-naturalistic part of an ethical judgement is such an exclamation or command, we are, as I have said, liable to all the objections brought earlier against subjectivism. For we have then admitted that, if not the whole "judgement," at any rate the only genuinely ethical part of it is something which can neither be true nor false and which does not contradict the "judgement" by somebody else (who might agree as to all the factual part) that the same thing is bad. Nor does the view in any case really escape the objection it is intended to avoid, namely, that we can see any naturalistic analysis to be incomplete, for it is just as obvious that the element in "ethical judgements" which is capable of being true or false includes more than can be given in any naturalistic analysis as it is that the "judgement" as a whole does so.

Again some naturalists try to escape objections by shifting the meaning of "good." When objections to a particular view of "good" are pointed out they say that, while this view is true of some uses of "good," in the cases where objection is taken "good" is being used in a different sense, though one that is still naturalist or subjectivist. If objections are brought against this second sense, they can then reply in any case where the objections are insuperable that "good" is being used not in this second sense but in the first or a third sense. They may then hope that, whatever particular objection is brought, they can always find some sense of "good" which will avoid this particular objection and that the other objections to which the new definition may be subject will only apply in cases where they could claim that "good" was being used in another sense without exposing themselves to worse objections. For example, if "good" or "right" is defined as that of which most men feel approval and it is then pointed out that a moral reformer or conscientious objector may, without contradicting himself, assert that something is bad or wrong while admitting that most people feel approval of it, the naturalist may try to avoid the difficulty by saying that "good" as used by him in this context means not "what most men approve" but "what I, the speaker, approve." If then it is objected, e.g., that in that case two men never contradict each other when one asserts that A is bad and another that A is good, he may retort that when they do really contradict each other they are using "good" in the first, not the second, sense or in some third sense, e.g. as meaning what will satisfy most men's desires in the long run. But it seems plain to me that the main objections I feel about any naturalist or subjectivist analysis apply to them all and cannot therefore be avoided by putting forward one analysis in one case and another in another case. When I use a sentence such as commonly expresses an "ethical judgement" not parrot-like, but sincerely, and with clear consciousness of what I am doing, it seems quite clear to me that I am asserting something which must be either true or false and which is not merely about my state of mind or dispositions, thus excluding subjectivism, and also that I am asserting something which goes beyond any statement about people's psychology, thus excluding naturalism. The type of theory I am criticizing cannot be saved by shifting one's position, for if an "ethical judgement" excludes one position of the subjectivist kind it excludes them all, and if it excludes one position of the naturalist kind it excludes them all. The same insight shows either the falsity of none or the falsity of all. And it seems perfectly clear to me that, if other people mean at all the same sort of thing when they use ethical words as I do (which assumption, though not strictly provable, is most unlikely to be wrong), no subjectivist or naturalist can possibly give an adequate analysis of what they mean.

What is it that is missing from any naturalist or subjectivist account? Well, I should not like to say the only missing element but at any rate the most important one is the concept of obligation. "Good" in its non-natural sense or senses carries with it the notion that the good thing *ought* not to be wantonly sacrificed but, other things being equal, pursued. Now to-say that I wish for something or that I have a certain kind of emotional feeling about it, or to exclaim in a way which expresses these psychological states, if that can be distinguished from saying that I have them, does not entail that I am under any obligation whatever to produce the objects of this wish or emotion. Nor does the notion of being commanded (or of commanding myself) involve in any way that of being under an obligation unless we presuppose such propositions as that the person who commands has a special claim on me such that I ought to obey him, or that the act commanded is on its own account my duty apart from the fact of its being commanded, which is already to assume the fact of obligation. Similarly, that everybody or most people or some group of people will feel an emotion of approval about me if I do *x* may make me more inclined to do *x* because I like the result, but it is quite incapable of putting me under an obligation to do *x*. The notion of obligation is neither contained in nor deducible from the notion of general approval. On the contrary it is an essential part of the moral consciousness that, if I ought to do something, I ought to do it whether others approve it or not. Obligations need not conflict with the approval of others, and their approval may even be *one* of the factors in helping to determine what I am under an obligation to do, since *other things being equal* I am more likely to do good by doing what is generally approved than by doing what is not so approved. But for obligation to be definable in terms of general approval the latter would have to be *the only* factor which ultimately counted in deciding what we ought to do and this it certainly is not; and we can still even say that indifference to approval is an essential part of the notion of obligation, because *once we grant that something is our duty* it follows that we ought to do it irrespective of whether others approve or not. Their approval is a contingent accident. This point may be made clearer still by considerations such as this. It is obvious that we ought to seek what is good as the only end-in-itself. But it certainly cannot be right to seek the approval of others as the only end-in-itself. And I cannot see what point there could possibly be in doing what other people would approve *if* they knew what I have done when in fact they do not know it, unless there is some other reason besides the approval; yet if something is my duty I clearly ought to do it whether people know of it or not. The same kind of criticism may be brought against all naturalistic definitions of ethical terms. For instance, unless we assume that the desires of men are good not bad desires there is no ground for saying that we ought to do what will satisfy their desires, so we cannot define "good" as "what satisfies desire."

When I say that I or somebody else ought to do certain things and not do others I am stating what I take to be an objective fact. Obligation is what subjectivist and naturalist theories leave out, and to have an ethics without obligation is like playing Hamlet without the Prince of Denmark. The stand against naturalism has usually been made in relation to the notion of "good," but to make it in relation to "ought" would have been to take up an even securer line of defence. Only, if once it is granted that we cannot give a naturalist or subjectivist account of "ought," it is then unreasonable to try to give one of all senses of "good," for it is plain that some meanings of "good" involve a reference to "ought," e.g. at any rate a "good man" in the moral sense seems to mean, chiefly or only, a man who does what he ought. Maybe there are two irreducible ethical concepts, good and ought, both of them incapable of analysis. Whether this is so or not I am leaving an open question, but I insist that at least there is one, ought, and that this notion of ought is either included in or entailed by the notion of good in any sense of "good" in which the good is a rational end of action. That what is good ought to be promoted (where possible without interfering with any other obligation such as the obligation to promote another, greater good) seems to me an *a priori* proposition, though I am doubtful whether it is analytic or synthetic.

The naturalist or subjectivist may, however, now retire to a different position, though one which is rarely stated unambiguously in so many words. He may admit that the naturalist and subjectivist accounts do not give any adequate analysis of the meaning of value judgements, but he may still maintain that value judgements, in so far as they assert anything more than is given in such an analysis, are false or that at least there is no justification for believing them to be true. This is to assume the position of the moral sceptic, and like that of the theoretical sceptic it is irrefutable if held consistently. That anybody can really hold it throughout consistently in his ordinary attitude to matters commonly regarded as of ethical import I find it very hard to believe. If he did he would, I think, be in a position analogous to that of the theoretical sceptic. The theoretical sceptic cannot be refuted and of course he may talk if he likes, but he cannot without inconsistency claim any of his statements to be rationally justified. Similarly, the complete sceptic as to values cannot be refuted and he can still act in accordance with his desires, but he cannot consistently claim that there is any justification for any of his acts, that any one is more rational than any other. (If he replies that "justifiable" only means, say, "conducive to the satisfaction of desires" he has gone back to the naturalist position which we have already discussed.) Some people forget that not only specifically moral acts but even mere acts of ordinary prudence in furtherance of one's own interests presuppose the abandonment of the position of the sceptic. The sceptic as to values is not entitled to believe even the proposition that it is more reasonable to wash his hands in water than in sulphuric acid, for this presupposes that pain is evil, so he has no real ground for not washing his hands in sulphuric acid. To say that he does not like to do so is to give a psychological cause and not a reason, unless we assume that it is good to do what one likes or that our desires ought to be satisfied. If we admit even the judgement that our own pain is evil to be self-evident, there are other judgements as to values, such as that we are under an obligation to further the good of others, which are as evident, so that it is inconsistent to accept the first and reject the second, not indeed in the sense that there is a self-contradiction in doing so but in the sense that if we trust our intuitive awareness of values in the one case we are equally justified in trusting it in the others; if we were to reject it in the one case we should have no less call to reject it in the others.

If a philosopher is not satisfied with this, there is not much more one can say beyond removing positive arguments for naturalism, subjectivism, or scepticism. It is, however, worth while to point out that, if the sceptical view of ethics were adopted, we should have to admit that the human mind can do what is often called "creating a new simple idea." The notion of obligation is on that view the notion of a relation which does not apply to anything and yet is thought by human beings so to apply. We have seen that it cannot be analyzed in empirical, or any non-ethical terms, therefore it is not a compound idea formed by putting together other ideas, nor can it, on the sceptical view, be the fruit of an intuitive insight into the real. But to have to admit that the mind can thus create a new idea off its own bat is repugnant to most philosophers and in a special degree to the type of empiricist philosopher who is inclined to deny the objectivity of ethics. It may be retorted that the "idea of obligation" is no real idea but just a muddle. But this is to say either that sentences about obligation are all meaningless, which is obviously false, or that they really have a purely naturalistic meaning but are wrongly thought by the people who use the words to mean something else, in which case we have abandoned the sceptical view and are back at the position criticized throughout the major portion of this article, namely, the view that a naturalistic analysis of ethical propositions is the correct one. This view, I hope, has been adequately refuted and, if so, we must admit at least that we have an idea of ethical obligation not analyzable without residuum in psychological terms. But, if we have an idea of the relation and it is irreducible, surely the most plausible explanation is that the relation is really present in some cases (though this does not of course prevent us, when we have really found it present on some occasions, thinking wrongly from a false analogy or some other source of error that it is present in others when it is not).

No doubt psychological theories may be put forward as to the origin of ethical from non-ethical ideas, such as the fear of punishment, but even if they originated historically from non-ethical ideas this would not prove that they now contained nothing beyond these ideas. With all new kinds of ideas there must have been a time at which they originated in the race as a whole or in any individual of it from psychological antecedents which did not contain the ideas. Besides, the moral facts of which we are aware when we see that certain actions are right or wrong and certain qualities good or bad are much more certain than could be any psychological theory which claimed to explain them away. Such a theory would rest on the psychology of children and savages, in whom the ideas originated, and the impossibility of obtaining reliable introspective evidence from such subjects makes it of itself highly speculative. The same remarks apply to any theory of ethics based on a study of the way in which children learn the use of ethical terms. In any case if the psychological theory merely tells us what experience preceded the formation of the ethical ideas it is innocuous, while if it claims to analyze them in terms of these non-ethical experiences it is open to the objections already brought against naturalistic theories of ethics.

It remains to deal with the chief positive arguments for naturalism or subjectivism, which I think can be done very quickly. One is based on the striking differences in ethical views between different people. But the differences between the views of savages and those of modern scientists about eclipses, or between the views of different politicians as to the causes and likely effects of recent events, are as great as the differences between the views of savages and of Christians, or the views of democrats and of Nazis, as to ethics. Are we to conclude from this that the scientists are no more right than the savages or that the political events about which the disputes lie have not objectively any causes or effects? If we do not draw this conclusion here, why draw it about ethics? There are also various ways of explaining the differences of view that exist without casting doubt on the objectivity of ethics. In the first place, acts which bear the same name may be very different acts in different states of society, because the circumstances and the psychology of the people concerned are very different, so that it might well be the case that e.g. slavery or polygamy was right (as the course which involved the least evil) in certain more primitive societies and wrong in ours. So the savage and the modern European may often both be right about ethical points over which they dispute, each for the society to which he belongs. Secondly, differences as to ethical judgements are often due to differences of opinion as to matters of fact. If A and B differ as to the likely consequences of an action they may well differ as to whether the action is right or wrong, and this is perhaps the most fertile source of disputes as to what is right. But it is not an ethical difference at all: it is a difference such as arises between rival scientific predictions based on inductive evidence. Differences or apparent differences of opinion caused in either of these two ways obviously constitute no possible argument against the objectivity of ethics.

But there are also genuinely ethical differences, i.e. differences as to our judgements not of fact but of value. These may be explained sometimes by differences in people's experience of life. If I never experience A I cannot realize the intrinsic goodness of A and may therefore wrongly subordinate it to something less good. And we must remember that what is intrinsically good is not a physical thing or a physical act but the experience or state of mind associated with it. Even a long study of philosophical books would not qualify a person to pass a judgement on the intrinsic value of philosophy if he was hopelessly bad at the subject, because then, however many books he read, he would not have a genuinely philosophical experience. Two people who differ as to the esthetic value of a picture may really be judging about different things, their several experiences of it (or, at least, their judgements will be based on different data). Other differences of view may be due to the misapplication of principles accepted on authority or to genuine intellectual confusions such as the philosopher or even the man of common sense could remove. For instance a man may confuse "intrinsically good" and "instrumentally good," or he may confuse "bad" and "wrong" and conclude or assume, e.g., that because lying is always bad (an evil) it is therefore always wrong, while it may be a case of choosing the lesser evil rather than the greater. Or the judgement that something is good or evil on the whole may have been due to concentrating attention on one side of it while ignoring or underestimating the others, as, for instance, militarists concentrate their attention on the heroism which war brings out in men and forget or underestimate war's evils. Lesser degrees of such one-sidedness it is impossible to avoid and yet they may detrimentally influence ethical judgements. To decide what is right in a particular case is often a very difficult matter of balancing the good or evil likely to be produced by one proposed act against that likely to be produced by others.[9] Perhaps if we saw at the same time all the consequences clearly as they would be in their factual character we should always be in agreement as to the degree in which they were good or evil as compared to

[9] I am not here committing myself to the philosophical view called "Ideal Utilitarianism," but on any tenable view such balancing of the consequences must play the predominant part in at least many ethical decisions. Even on Ideal Utilitarianism it will not, in practice, play a part in all, for there will always be many cases where it is right to act on general rules justified by their effects in the past, and also cases where it is obvious that we can do some particular good by an action and impossible to foresee any bad effects to set against the good done.

the consequences of other possible acts, but apart from the difficulty of estimating what the consequences of an act will be, it is practically impossible in cases which are at all complex to keep our attention sufficiently fixed at the same time on all the foreseeable consequences likely to be seriously relevant for good or evil, and consequently we are likely through lack of attention to under-estimate the value or disvalue of some as compared to that of others.

The lack of attention I have mentioned is in some degree inevitable, but it is greatly enhanced by prejudice and desire. It is a commonplace that ethical mistakes are often due to non-intellectual factors. Whether these act only through affecting the attention or whether they can lead to mistaken valuations even in the presence of full attention to the object valued we need not discuss. There is in any case a large class of errors for which some form of "psycho-analysis" (I do not say necessarily the Freudian) is required rather than argument, and another (probably larger) of which it can only be said that the person in question fell into error because he did not steadfastly will to seek the truth and therefore did not fix his attention on points which displeased him. The convictions of some people as to the objectivity of ethics appear to have been shaken by the fact that enthusiastic Nazis seem to have believed that it was their duty to do things which we are convinced are completely wrong, such as ill-treating the Jews, but is there any reason to think that these Nazis really wanted to arrive at the truth as regards the question whether it was right or wrong to send Jews to concentration camps? If not, we need not be surprised that they did not attain the truth which they did not want to seek. So it may well be the case that all differences in people's judgements as to whether certain acts are right or wrong or certain things good or bad are due to factors other than an irreducible difference in ethical intuition. But, even if they should not be, we must remember that ethical intuition, like our other capacities, is presumably a developing faculty and therefore may well be capable of error. But in any case we have said enough to show that ethical differences are quite compatible with the objectivity of ethical judgements.

Differences between philosophers about the general theory of ethics are remarkable and perplexing, but experience shows that very wide philosophical differences are quite compatible with striking agreement as regards the kinds of act judged right, just as radical differences between philosophers in their theories of perception and of physical objects are compatible with complete agreement in ordinary life as to what particular physical objects are in a particular place at a particular time. The differences between philosophers are not mainly differences as to their ethical judgements in concrete ethical situations but as to the general theory explaining these. We may add that the differences between different people and different civilizations as to concrete ethical judgements are commonly exaggerated. David Livingstone says that nowhere had he need to teach the African savages the Decalogue (at least the second table); but there is of course a great inconsistency (not only among savages) in confining to a limited group rules which demand universal extension.

Westermarck contends that objectivity is disproved by the fact that ethical judgements are based on emotion,[10] but he does not even try, as far as I can see, to disprove the view that emotions only provide a psychological condition in the absence of which we should not have been in a fit state ever to intuit the non-natural characteristic of goodness or the non-natural relation of obligation. That we could never have intuited them if we had no emotions may well be true and would perhaps be admitted by most non-naturalists.[11] It may even be that a necessary *a priori* condition is the occurrence of certain emotions. But though the experience of making an ethical judgement will in any case require various psychological conditions in order to be possible, it does not follow that the judgement must be about these conditions. Nobody would argue that ethical judgements must all be really about breathing because breathing is a necessary condition without which we could not make the judgements at all. However, I think it more plausible to hold that the feeling and ethical intuition are correlative than that one is a prior condition of the other, and this view is still easier to square with non-naturalism.

Some people are convinced that there can be no non-natural properties or relations and therefore conclude that good or obligation cannot be such, but I cannot see any way of establishing such a view. On the contrary, if any arguments are ever valid at all there must be at least one non-natural relation, the relation of entailment, and the two corresponding non-natural relational properties of entailing and being entailed by. However could you possibly reduce these to sensible relations or properties? So there is no *a priori* reason for denying that there are other non-natural relations or properties.

But probably the principal reason which makes people inclined to deny the objectivity of ethics is the fact that in ethical argument we are very soon brought to a point where we have to fall back on intuition and that disputants are easily placed in a situation in which there are two conflicting intuitions between which there seems to be no means of deciding by argument. But it is not only ethics but all reasoning which presupposes intuition. I cannot argue A, $\therefore$ B, $\therefore$ C without seeing that A entails B, and this must either be seen immediately or require a further argument. If it is seen immediately it is a case of intuition; if it has to be established by a further argument, this means that another term, D, must be interpolated between A and B such that A entails D and D entails B; and then the same question arises about A entailing D, so that sooner or later we must come to something we see immediately (intuitively) to be true, as the process of interpolation obviously cannot go on *ad infinitum*. We cannot therefore,

[10] *Ethical Relativity*, p. 60.
[11] Once we have ideas of them, however formed, we can on any view apply them without feeling in all our ethical judgments an actual emotion.

whatever we do, get rid of intuition if we are to have any inference at all.

It may, however, be said that at any rate in subjects other than ethics people agree in their intuitions. But outside mathematics or formal logic this is by no means universally true. There is frequent disagreement about matters of fact as to what has happened or will happen or concerning the causes of something, and when we have exhausted the arguments on a given point in these matters there still remains a difference between the ways in which these arguments are regarded by the disputants. In any science where you cannot prove your conclusions but only make them more or less probable there will be different estimates as to the balance of probabilities. As in ethics you have to balance different values against each other in order to decide what you ought to do, so here you have to balance different probable arguments, and in order to do this you must rely at some point or other on an estimate of their strength which cannot itself be further justified by mediate reasoning. Yet, when everything has been said in the way of argument, people may not all agree. Some will attribute more weight to one consideration, others to another, as they do in ethical questions about what is the right act in a given case. Our decision as to which of two probable arguments is the stronger may be influenced by other arguments in turn, but in order to deal with the situation rationally we must also estimate the weight of these other arguments, so that in the last resort it is a matter of insight into their nature which cannot be settled by other arguments *ad infinitum.* Just as in a demonstrative argument you must see intuitively how each step follows from the preceding one, so in the case of a probable argument you must rely on estimates of the degree of probability given by the argument as compared to that given by arguments on the other side, and these estimates, unless the degree of probability can be mathematically calculated, must be intuitive or deduced from estimates which are intuitive. I do not wish to maintain that reasoning in these matters is altogether analogous to that which occurs in dealing with ethical questions, but at any rate it is the case here that as in ethics we are confronted with a situation in which we either see or do not see and cannot logically prove that what we seem to see is true. Yet we cannot surely therefore conclude that the scientific or historical propositions under discussion are really only propositions about the state of mind of the people who assert them or are neither true nor false.

We must therefore have intuition, and in a subject where infallibility is not attainable intuitions will sometimes disagree. It may be that this disagreement is always due to some intellectual mistake which could be removed by reasoning, some lack of experience which could be removed by supplying the experience, some emotional cause which could be removed by psychotherapy, or some moral defect which could be removed by a more sincere and energetic determination to attain the truth as to what one ought to do, though there are cases in ethics as in other subjects where it is, humanly speaking, impossible to remove it. On the other hand, we must not think of intuition as something quite by itself uninfluenced by inference, it is helped by inference but sees beyond what could be proved by inference. And when intuitive ethical views differ use may be made of inference to support one or another of the clashing views, especially by showing that it fits well into a coherent ethical system. It will not settle the question absolutely conclusively, but it can help towards settlement. Perhaps as the result of the inference one of the parties to the dispute may alter his "intuitions." It would be a great mistake to say that, when two people disagree on an ethical question, there is nothing to be done about it or that there is no scope in ethics for inference. But, however this may be, it is clear that no argument is available which could establish the subjectivity of ethics without establishing the similar subjectivity of all other branches of study except mathematics and formal logic, and in the absence of counter-arguments the *prima facie* case for its objectivity is exceedingly strong. Nor have the naturalist arguments proved any more successful.

III

THE DEVELOPMENT OF ETHICAL
INTUITIONISM

Ethical Judgments *

ᵱᵱᢇ᛫ᢇᔛ

HENRY SIDGWICK

§ 1. In the first chapter I spoke of actions that we judge to be right and what ought to be done as being "reasonable," or "rational," and similarly of ultimate ends as "prescribed by Reason": and I contrasted the motive to action supplied by the recognition of such reasonableness with "non-rational" desires and inclinations. This manner of speaking is employed by writers of different schools, and seems in accordance with the common view and language on the subject. For we commonly think that wrong conduct is essentially irrational, and can be shown to be so by argument; and though we do not conceive that it is by reason alone that men are influenced to act rightly, we still hold that appeals to the reason are an essential part of all moral persuasion, and that part which concerns the moralist or moral philosopher as distinct from the preacher or moral rhetorician. On the other hand it is widely maintained that, as Hume says, "Reason, meaning the judgment of truth and falsehood, can never of itself be any motive to the Will"; and that the motive to action is in all cases some Non-rational Desire, including under this term the impulses of action given by present pleasure and pain. It seems desirable to examine with some care the grounds of this contention before we proceed any further.

Let us begin by defining the issue raised as clearly as possible. Every one, I suppose, has had experience of what is meant by the conflict of non-rational or irrational desires with reason: most of us e.g. occasionally feel bodily appetite prompting us to indulgences which we judge to be imprudent, and anger prompting us to acts which we disapprove as unjust or unkind. It is when this conflict occurs that the desires are said to be irrational, as impelling us to volitions opposed to our deliberate judgments; sometimes we yield to such seductive impulses, and sometimes not; and it is perhaps when we do *not* yield that the impulsive force of such irrational desires is most definitely felt, as we have to exert in resisting them a voluntary effort somewhat analogous to that involved in any muscular exertion. Often, again,—since we are not always thinking either of our duty or of our interest,—desires of this kind take effect in voluntary actions without our having judged such actions to be either right or wrong,

* Reprinted from *The Methods of Ethics* (Seventh Edition), pp. 23-38. The Macmillan Co., 1907.

either prudent or imprudent; as e.g. when an ordinary healthy man eats his dinner. In such cases it seems most appropriate to call the desires "non-rational" rather than "irrational." Neither term is intended to imply that the desires spoken of—or at least the more important of them—are not normally accompanied by intellectual processes. It is true that some impulses to action seem to take effect, as we say "blindly" or "instinctively," without any definite consciousness either of the end at which the action is aimed, or of the means by which the end is to be attained: but this, I conceive, is only the case with impulses that do not occupy consciousness for an appreciable time, and ordinarily do not require any but very familiar and habitual actions for the attainment of their proximate ends. In all other cases—that is, in the case of the actions with which we are chiefly concerned in ethical discussion—the result aimed at, and some part at least of the means by which it is to be realised, are more or less distinctly represented in consciousness, previous to the volition that initiates the movements tending to its realisation. Hence the resultant forces of what I call "non-rational" desires, and the volitions to which they prompt, are continually modified by intellectual processes in two distinct ways; first by new perceptions or representations of means conducive to the desired ends, and secondly by new presentations or representations of facts actually existing or in prospect—especially more or less probable consequences of contemplated actions—which rouse new impulses of desire and aversion.

The question, then, is whether the account just given of the influence of the intellect on desire and volition is not exhaustive; and whether the experience which is commonly described as a "conflict of desire with reason" is not more properly conceived as merely a conflict among desires and aversions; the sole function of reason being to bring before the mind ideas of actual or possible facts, which modify in the manner above described the resultant force of our various impulses.

I hold that this is not the case; that the ordinary moral or prudential judgments which, in the case of all or most minds, have some—though often an inadequate—influence on volition, cannot legitimately be interpreted as judgments respecting the present or future existence of human feelings or any facts of the sensible world; the fundamental notion represented by the word "ought" or "right," [1] which such judgments contain expressly or by implication, being essentially different from all notions representing facts of physical or psychical experience. The question is one on which appeal must ultimately be made to the reflection of individuals on their practical judgments and reasonings: and in making this appeal it seems most convenient to begin by showing the inadequacy of all attempts to explain the practical judgments or propositions in which this fundamental notion is introduced, without recognising its unique character as above negatively defined. There is an element of truth in such explanations, in so far as they bring into view feelings which undoubtedly accom-

[1] The difference between the significations of the two words is discussed later.

pany moral or prudential judgments, and which ordinarily have more or less effect in determining the will to actions judged to be right; but so far as they profess to be interpretations of what such judgments mean, they appear to me to fail altogether.

In considering this question it is important to take separately the two species of judgments which I have distinguished as "moral" and "prudential." Both kinds might, indeed, be termed "moral" in a wider sense; and, as we saw, it is a strongly supported opinion that all valid moral rules have ultimately a prudential basis. But in ordinary thought we clearly distinguish cognitions or judgments of duty from cognitions or judgments as to what "is right" or "ought to be done" in view of the agent's private interest or happiness: and the depth of the distinction will not, I think, be diminished by the closer examination of these judgments on which we are now to enter.

This very distinction, however, suggests an interpretation of the notion of rightness which denies its peculiar significance in moral judgments. It is urged that "rightness" is properly an attribute of means, not of ends: so that the attribution of it merely implies that the act judged right is the fittest or only fit means to the realisation of some end understood if not expressly stated: and similarly that the affirmation that anything 'ought to be done' is always made with at least tacit reference to some ulterior end. And I grant that this is a legitimate interpretation, in respect of a part of the use of either term in ordinary discourse. But it seems clear (1) that certain kinds of actions—under the names of Justice, Veracity, Good Faith, etc.—are commonly held to be right unconditionally, without regard to ulterior results: and (2) that we similarly regard as "right" the adoption of certain ends—such as the common good of society, or general happiness. In either of these cases the interpretation above suggested seems clearly inadmissible.[2]

We have therefore to find a meaning for "right" or "what ought to be" other than the notion of fitness to some ulterior end. Here we are met by the suggestion that the judgments or propositions which we commonly call moral—in the narrower sense—really affirm no more than the existence of a specific emotion in the mind of the person who utters them; that when I say 'Truth ought to be spoken' or 'Truthspeaking is right,' I mean no more than that the idea of truthspeaking excites in my mind a feeling of approbation or satisfaction. And probably some degree of such emotion, commonly distinguished as 'moral sentiment,' ordinarily accompanies moral judgments on real cases. But it is absurd to say that a mere state-

---

[2] As, for instance, when Bentham explains (*Principles of Morals and Legislation*, chap. i. § i. note) that his fundamental principle "states the greatest happiness of all those whose interest is in question as being the right and proper end of human action," we cannot understand him really to *mean* by the word "right" "conducive to the general happiness," though his language in other passages of the same chapter (§§ ix. and x.) would seem to imply this; for the proposition that it is conducive to general happiness to take general happiness as an end of action, though not exactly a tautology, can hardly serve as the fundamental principle of a moral system.

ment of my approbation of truth-speaking is properly given in the proposition 'Truth ought to be spoken'; otherwise the fact of another man's disapprobation might equally be expressed by saying 'Truth ought not to be spoken'; and thus we should have two coexistent facts stated in two mutually contradictory propositions. This is so obvious, that we must suppose that those who hold the view which I am combating do not really intend to deny it: but rather to maintain that this subjective fact of my approbation is all that there is any *ground* for stating, or perhaps that it is all that any reasonable person is prepared on reflection to affirm. And no doubt there is a large class of statements, in form objective, which yet we are not commonly prepared to maintain as more than subjective if their validity is questioned. If I say that 'the air is sweet,' or 'the food disagreeable,' it would not be exactly true to say that I mean no more than that I like the one or dislike the other: but if my statement is challenged, I shall probably content myself with affirming the existence of such feelings in my own mind. But there appears to me to be a fundamental difference between this case and that of moral feelings. The peculiar emotion of moral approbation is, in my experience, inseparably bound up with the conviction, implicit or explicit, that the conduct approved is 'really' right—i.e. that it cannot, without error, be disapproved by any other mind. If I give up this conviction because others do not share it, or for any other reason, I may no doubt still retain a sentiment prompting to the conduct in question, or—what is perhaps more common—a sentiment of repugnance to the opposite conduct: but this sentiment will no longer have the special quality of 'moral sentiment' strictly so called. This difference between the two is often overlooked in ethical discussion: but any experience of a change in moral opinion produced by argument may afford an illustration of it. Suppose e.g. that any one habitually influenced by the sentiment of Veracity is convinced that under certain peculiar circumstances in which he finds himself, speaking truth is not right but wrong. He will probably still feel a repugnance against violating the rule of truthspeaking: but it will be a feeling quite different in kind and degree from that which prompted him to veracity as a department of virtuous action. We might perhaps call the one a 'moral' and the other a 'quasi-moral' sentiment.

The argument just given holds equally against the view that approbation or disapprobation is not the mere liking or aversion of an individual for certain kinds of conduct, but this complicated by a sympathetic representation of similar likings or aversions felt by other human beings. No doubt such sympathy is a normal concomitant of moral emotion, and when the former is absent there is much greater difficulty in maintaining the latter: this, however, is partly because our moral beliefs commonly agree with those of other members of our society, and on this agreement depends to an important extent our confidence in the truth of these beliefs.[3] But if, as in the case just supposed, we are really led by argument to a new moral

[3] See Book iii. chap. xi. § 1.

belief, opposed not only to our own habitual sentiment but also to that of the society in which we live, we have a crucial experiment proving the existence in us of moral sentiments as I have defined them, colliding with the represented sympathies of our fellow-men no less than with our own mere likings and aversions. And even if we imagine the sympathies opposed to our convictions extended until they include those of the whole human race, against whom we imagine ourselves to stand as *Athanasius contra mundum*; still, so long as our conviction of duty is firm, the emotion which we call moral stands out in imagination quite distinct from the complex sympathy opposed to it, however much we extend, complicate and intensify the latter.

§ 2. So far, then, from being prepared to admit that the proposition 'X ought to be done' *merely* expresses the existence of a certain sentiment in myself or others, I find it strictly impossible so to regard my own moral judgments without eliminating from the concomitant sentiment the peculiar quality signified by the term 'moral.' There is, however, another interpretation of 'ought,' in which the likings and aversions that men in general feel for certain kinds of conduct are considered not as sympathetically represented in the emotion of the person judging, and thus constituting the moral element in it, but as causes of pain to the person of whom 'ought' or 'duty' is predicated. On this view, when we say that a man 'ought' to do anything, or that it is his 'duty' to do it, we mean that he is bound under penalties to do it; the particular penalty considered being the pain that will accrue to him directly or indirectly from the dislike of his fellow-creatures.

I think that this interpretation expresses a part of the meaning with which the words 'ought' and 'duty' are used in ordinary thought and discourse. For we commonly use the term 'moral obligation' as equivalent to 'duty' and expressing what is implied in the verb 'ought,' thus suggesting an analogy between this notion and that of legal obligation; and in the case of positive law we cannot refuse to recognise the connexion of 'obligation' and 'punishment': a law cannot be properly said to be actually established in a society if it is habitually violated with impunity. But as a more careful reflection on the relation of Law to Morality, as ordinarily conceived, seems to show that this interpretation of 'ought'—though it cannot be excluded—must be distinguished from the special ethical use of the term. For the ideal distinction taken in common thought between legal and merely moral rules seems to lie in just this connexion of the former but not the latter with punishment: we think that there are some things which a man ought to be compelled to do, or forbear, and others which he ought to do or forbear without compulsion, and that the former alone fall properly within the sphere of law. No doubt we also think that in many cases where the compulsion of law is undesirable, the fear of moral censure and its consequences supplies a normally useful constraint on the will of any individual. But it is evident that what we mean when we say that a man is "morally though not legally bound" to do a thing is not merely that he "will be punished by public opinion if he does not"; for we often join these two statements, clearly distinguishing their import: and further (since public opinion is known to be eminently fallible) there are many things which we judge men 'ought' to do, while perfectly aware that they will incur no serious social penalties for omitting them. In such cases, indeed, it would be commonly said that social disapprobation 'ought' to follow on immoral conduct; and in this very assertion it is clear that the term 'ought' cannot mean that social penalties are to be feared by those who do not disapprove. Again, all or most men in whom the moral consciousness is strongly developed find themselves from time to time in conflict with the commonly received morality of the society to which they belong: and thus—as was before said—have a crucial experience proving that duty does not mean *to them* what other men will disapprove of them for not doing.

At the same time I admit, as indeed I have already suggested in § 3 of chap. i., that we not unfrequently pass judgments resembling moral judgments in form, and not distinguished from them in ordinary thought, in cases where the obligation affirmed is found, on reflection, to depend on the existence of current opinions and sentiments as such. The members of modern civilised societies are under the sway of a code of Public Opinion, enforced by social penalties, which no reflective person obeying it identifies with the moral code, or regards as unconditionally binding: indeed the code is manifestly fluctuating and variable, different at the same time in different classes, professions, social circles, of the same political community. Such a code always supports to a considerable extent the commonly received code of morality: and most reflective persons think it generally reasonable to conform to the dictates of public opinion—to the code of Honour, we may say, in graver matters, or the rules of Politeness or Good Breeding in lighter matters—wherever these dictates do not positively conflict with morality; such conformity being maintained either on grounds of private interest, or because it is thought conducive to general happiness or wellbeing to keep as much as possible in harmony with one's fellow-men. Hence in the ordinary thought of unreflective persons the duties imposed by social opinion are often undistinguished from moral duties: and indeed this indistinctness is almost inherent in the common meaning of many terms. For instance, if we say that a man has been 'dishonoured' by a cowardly act, it is not quite clear whether we mean that he has incurred contempt, or that he has deserved it, or both: as becomes evident when we take a case in which the Code of Honour comes into conflict with Morality. If e.g. a man were to incur social ostracism anywhere for refusing a duel on religious grounds, some would say that he was 'dishonoured,' though he had acted rightly, others that there could be no real dishonour in a virtuous act. A similar ambiguity seems to lurk in the common notion of 'improper' or 'incorrect' behaviour. Still in all such cases the ambiguity becomes evident on reflection: and when discovered, merely serves to illustrate further the distinction between the notion of 'right conduct,' 'duty,' what we 'ought' or are under 'moral obligation' to do—when these terms are used in a strictly ethical sense—and conduct that is merely conformed to the standard of current opinion.

There is, however, another way of interpreting 'ought' as connoting penalties, which is somewhat less easy to meet by a crucial psychological experiment. The moral imperative may be taken to be a law of God, to the breach of which Divine penalties are annexed; and these, no doubt, in a Christian society, are commonly conceived to be adequate and universally applicable. Still, it can hardly be said that this belief is shared by all the persons whose conduct is influenced by independent moral convictions, occasionally unsupported either by the law or the public opinion of their community. And even in the case of many of those who believe fully in the moral government of the world, the judgment "I ought to do this" cannot be identified with the judgment "God will punish me if I do not"; since the conviction that the former proposition is true is distinctly recognised as an important part of the grounds for believing the latter. Again, when Christians speak—as they commonly do—of the 'justice' (or other moral attributes) of God, as exhibited in punishing sinners and rewarding the righteous, they obviously imply not merely that God *will* thus punish and reward, but that it is 'right' [4] for Him to do so: which, of course, cannot be taken to mean that He is 'bound under penalties.'

§ 3. It seems then that the notion of 'ought' or 'moral obligation' as used in our common moral judgments, does not merely import (1) that there exists in the mind of the person judging a specific emotion (whether complicated or not by sympathetic representation of similar emotions in other minds); nor (2) that certain rules of conduct are supported by penalties which will follow on their violation (whether such penalties result from the general liking or aversion felt for the conduct prescribed or forbidden, or from some other source). What then, it may be asked, does it import? What definition can we give of 'ought,' 'right,' and other terms expressing the same fundamental notion? To this I should answer that the notion which these terms have in common is too elementary to admit of any formal definition. In so saying, I do not mean to imply that it belongs to the "original constitution of the mind"; i.e. that its presence in consciousness is not the result of a process of development. I do not doubt that the whole fabric of human thought—including the conceptions that present themselves as most simple and elementary—has beeen developed, through a gradual process of psychical change, out of some lower life in which thought, properly speaking, had no place. But it is not therefore to be inferred, as regards this or any other notion, that it has not really the simplicity which it appears to have when we now reflect upon it. It is sometimes assumed that if we can show how thoughts have grown up—if we can point to the psychical antecedents of which they are the natural con-

---

[4] 'Ought' is here inapplicable, for a reason presently explained.

sequents—we may conclude that the thoughts in question are really compounds containing their antecedents as latent elements. But I know no justification for this transference of the conceptions of chemistry to psychology; [5] I know no reason for considering psychical antecedents as really constitutive of their psychical consequents, in spite of the apparent dissimilarity between the two. In default of such reasons, a psychologist must accept as elementary what introspection carefully performed declares to be so; and, using this criterion, I find that the notion we have been examining, as it now exists in our thought, cannot be resolved into any more simple notions: it can only be made clearer by determining as precisely as possible its relation to other notions with which it is connected in ordinary thought, especially to those with which it is liable to be confounded.

In performing this process it is important to note and distinguish two different implications with which the word "ought" is used; in the narrowest ethical sense what we judge 'ought to be' done, is always thought capable of being brought about by the volition of any individual to whom the judgment applies. I cannot conceive that I 'ought' to do anything which at the same time I judge that I cannot do. In a wider sense, however,—which cannot conveniently be discarded—I sometimes judge that I 'ought' to know what a wiser man would know, or feel as a better man would feel, in my place, though I may know that I could not directly produce in myself such knowledge or feeling by any effort of will. In this case the word merely implies an ideal or pattern which I 'ought'—in the stricter sense—to seek to imitate as far as possible. And this wider sense seems to be that in which the word is normally used in the precepts of Art generally, and in political judgments: when I judge that the laws and constitution of my country 'ought to be' other than they are, I do not of course imply that my own or any other individual's single volition can directly bring about the change.[6] In either case, however, I imply that what ought to be is a possible object of knowledge: i.e. that what I judge ought to be must, unless I am in error, be similarly judged by all rational beings who judge truly of the matter.

In referring such judgments to the 'Reason,' I do not mean here to prejudge the question whether valid moral judgments are normally attained by a process of reasoning from universal principles or axioms, or by

[5] In Chemistry we regard the antecedents (elements) as still existing in and constituting the consequent (compound) because the latter is exactly similar to the former in weight, and because we can generally cause this compound to disappear and obtain the elements in its place. But we find nothing at all like this in the growth of mental phenomena: the psychical consequent is in no respect exactly similar to its antecedents, nor can it be resolved into them. I should explain that I am not here arguing the question whether the *validity* of moral judgments is affected by a discovery of their psychical antecedents. This question I reserve for subsequent discussion. See Book iii. chap. i. § 4.

[6] I do not even imply that any combination of individuals could completely realise the state of political relations which I conceive 'ought to' exist. My conception would be futile if it had no relation to practice: but it may merely delineate a pattern to which no more than an approximation is practically possible.

direct intuition of the particular duties of individuals. It is not uncommonly held that the moral faculty deals primarily with individual cases as they arise, applying directly to each case the general notion of duty, and deciding intuitively what ought to be done by this person in these particular circumstances. And I admit that on this view the apprehension of moral truth is more analogous to Sense-perception than to Rational Intuition (as commonly understood): [7] and hence the term Moral Sense might seem more appropriate. But the term Sense suggests a capacity for feelings which may vary from *A* to *B* without either being in error, rather than a faculty of cognition: [8] and it appears to me fundamentally important to avoid this suggestion. I have therefore thought it better to use the term Reason with the explanation above given, to denote the faculty of moral cognition: [9] adding, as a further justification of this use, that even when a moral judgment relates primarily to some particular action we commonly regard it as applicable to any other action belonging to a certain definable class: so that the moral truth apprehended is implicitly conceived to be intrinsically universal, though particular in our first apprehension of it.

Further, when I speak of the cognition or judgment that 'X ought to be done'—in the stricter ethical sense of the term ought [10]—as a 'dictate' or 'precept' of reason to the persons to whom it relates, I imply that in rational beings as such this cognition gives an impulse or motive to action: though in human beings, of course, this is only one motive among others which are liable to conflict with it, and is not always—perhaps not usually—a predominant motive. In fact, this possible conflict of motives seems to be connoted by the term 'dictate' or 'imperative,' which describes the relation of Reason to mere inclinations or non-rational impulses by comparing it to the relation between the will of a superior and the wills of his subordinates. This conflict seems also to be implied in the terms 'ought,' 'duty,' 'moral obligation,' as used in ordinary moral discourse: and hence these terms cannot be applied to the actions of rational beings to whom we cannot attribute impulses conflicting with reason. We may, however, say of such beings that their actions are 'reasonable,' or (in an absolute sense) 'right.'

§ 4. I am aware that some persons will be disposed to answer all the preceding argument by a simple denial that they can find in their consciousness any such unconditional or categorical imperative as I have been

[7] We do not commonly say that particular physical facts are apprehended by the Reason: we consider this faculty to be conversant in its discursive operation with the relation of judgments or propositions: and the intuitive reason (which is here rather in question) we restrict to the apprehension of universal truths, such as the axioms of Logic and Mathematics.

[8] By cognition I always mean what some would rather call "apparent cognition"—that is, I do not mean to affirm the *validity* of the cognition, but only its existence as a psychical fact, and its claim to be valid.

[9] A further justification for this extended use of the term Reason will be suggested in a subsequent chapter of this Book (chap. viii. § 3).

[10] This is the sense in which the term will always be used in the present treatise, except where the context makes it quite clear that only the wider meaning—that of the political 'ought'—is applicable.

trying to exhibit. If this is really the final result of self-examination in any case, there is no more to be said. I, at least, do not know how to impart the notion of moral obligation to any one who is entirely devoid of it. I think, however, that many of those who give this denial only mean to deny that they have any consciousness of moral obligation to actions without reference to their consequences; and would not really deny that they recognise some universal end or ends—whether it be the general happiness, or well-being otherwise understood—as that at which it is ultimately reasonable to aim, subordinating to its attainment the gratification of any personal desires that may conflict with this aim. But in this view, as I have before said, the unconditional imperative plainly comes in as regards the end, which is—explicitly or implicitly—recognised as an end at which all men 'ought' to aim; and it can hardly be denied that the recognition of an end as ultimately reasonable involves the recognition of an obligation to do such acts as most conduce to the end. The obligation is not indeed "unconditional," but it does not depend on the existence of any non-rational desires or aversions. And nothing that has been said in the preceding section is intended as an argument in favour of Intuitionism, as against Utilitarianism or any other method that treats moral rules as relative to General Good or Well-being. For instance, nothing that I have said is inconsistent with the view that Truthspeaking is only valuable as a means to the preservation of society: only if it be admitted that it *is* valuable on this ground I should say that it is implied that the preservation of society—or some further end to which this preservation, again, is a means—must be valuable *per se*, and therefore something at which a rational being, as such, ought to aim. If it be granted that we need not look beyond the preservation of society, the primary 'dictate of reason' in this case would be 'that society *ought* to be preserved': but reason would also dictate that truth ought to be spoken, so far as truthspeaking is recognised as the indispensable or fittest means to this end: and the notion "ought" as used in either dictate is that which I have been trying to make clear.

So again, even those who hold that moral rules are only obligatory because it is the individual's interest to conform to them—thus regarding them as a particular species of prudential rules—do not thereby get rid of the 'dictate of reason,' so far as they recognise private interest or happiness as an end at which it is ultimately reasonable to aim. The conflict of Practical Reason with irrational desire remains an indubitable fact of our conscious experience, even if practical reason is interpreted to mean merely self-regarding Prudence. It is, indeed, maintained by Kant and others that it cannot properly be said to be a man's duty to promote his own happiness; since "what every one inevitably wills cannot be brought under the notion of duty." But even granting [11] it to be in some sense true that a man's volition is always directed to the attainment of his own happiness, it does not follow that a man always does what he believes will be conducive to his

[11] As will be seen from the next chapter, I do not grant this.

own *greatest* happiness. As Butler urges, it is a matter of common experience that men indulge appetite or passion even when, in their own view, the indulgence is as clearly opposed to what they conceive to be their interest as it is to what they conceive to be their duty. Thus the notion 'ought' —as expressing the relation of rational judgment to non-rational impulses— will find a place in the practical rules of any egoistic system, no less than in the rules of ordinary morality, understood as prescribing duty without reference to the agent's interest.

Here, however, it may be held that Egoism does not properly regard the agent's own greatest happiness as what he "ought" to aim at: but only as the ultimate end for the realisation of which he has, on the whole, a predominant desire; which may be temporarily overcome by particular passions and appetites, but ordinarily regains its predominance when these transient impulses have spent their force. I quite recognise that this is a view widely taken of egoistic action, and I propose to consider it in a subsequent chapter.[12] But even if we discard the belief, that any end of action is unconditionally or "categorically" prescribed by reason, the notion 'ought' as above explained is not thereby eliminated from our practical reasonings: it still remains in the "hypothetical imperative" which prescribes the fittest means to any end that we may have determined to aim at. When e.g. a physician says, "If you wish to be healthy you ought to rise early," this is not the same thing as saying "early rising is an indispensable condition of the attainment of health." This latter proposition expresses the relation of physiological facts on which the former is founded; but it is not merely this relation of facts that the word 'ought' imports: it also implies the unreasonableness of adopting an end and refusing to adopt the means indispensable to its attainment. It may perhaps be argued that this is not only unreasonable but impossible: since adoption of an end means the preponderance of a desire for it, and if aversion to the indispensable means causes them not to be adopted although recognised as indispensable, the desire for the end is *not* preponderant and it ceases to be adopted. But this view is due, in my opinion, to a defective psychological analysis. According to my observation of consciousness, the adoption of an end as paramount— either absolutely or within certain limits—is quite a distinct psychical phenomenon from desire: it is a kind of volition, though it is, of course, specifically different from a volition initiating a particular immediate action. As a species intermediate between the two, we may place resolutions to act in a certain way at some future time: we continually make such resolutions, and sometimes when the time comes for carrying them out, we do in fact act otherwise under the influence of passion or mere habit, without consciously cancelling our previous resolve. This inconsistency of will our practical reason condemns as irrational, even apart from any judgment of approbation or disapprobation on either volition considered by itself. There is a similar inconsistency between the adoption of an end and a

[12] Chap. ix. of *The Methods of Ethics.*

general refusal to take whatever means we may see to be indispensable to its attainment: and if, when the time comes, we do not take such means while yet we do not consciously retract our adoption of the end, it can hardly be denied that we 'ought' in consistency to act otherwise than we do. And such a contradiction as I have described, between a general resolution and a particular volition, is surely a matter of common experience.

Does Moral Philosophy Rest on a Mistake? *

H. A. PRICHARD

PROBABLY TO MOST students of Moral Philosophy there comes a time when they feel a vague sense of dissatisfaction with the whole subject. And the sense of dissatisfaction tends to grow rather than to diminish. It is not so much that the positions, and still more the arguments, of particular thinkers seem unconvincing, though this is true. It is rather that the aim of the subject becomes increasingly obscure. 'What,' it is asked, 'are we really going to learn by Moral Philosophy?' 'What are books on Moral Philosophy really trying to show, and when their aim is clear, why are they so unconvincing and artificial?' And again: 'Why is it so difficult to substitute anything better?' Personally, I have been led by growing dissatisfaction of this kind to wonder whether the reason may not be that the subject, at any rate as usually understood, consists in the attempt to answer an improper question. And in this article I shall venture to contend that the existence of the whole subject, as usually understood, rests on a mistake, and on a mistake parallel to that on which rests, as I think, the subject usually called the Theory of Knowledge.

If we reflect on our own mental history or on the history of the subject, we feel no doubt about the nature of the demand which originates the subject. Any one who, stimulated by education, has come to feel the force of the various obligations in life, at some time or other comes to feel the irksomeness of carrying them out, and to recognize the sacrifice of interest involved; and, if thoughtful, he inevitably puts to himself the question: 'Is there really a reason why I should act in the ways in which hitherto I have thought I ought to act? May I not have been all the time under an illusion in so thinking? Should not I really be justified in simply trying to have a good time?' Yet, like Gaucon, feeling that somehow he ought after all to act in these ways, he asks for a *proof* that this feeling is justified. In other words, he asks '*Why* should I do these things?', and his and other people's moral philosophizing is an attempt to supply the answer, i.e. to supply by a process of reflection a proof of the truth of what he and they have prior to reflection believed immediately or without proof. This frame of mind seems to present a close parallel to the frame of mind which originates the Theory of Knowledge. Just as the recognition that the doing of our duty

* Reprinted by kind permission of the editor from *Mind*, 21, 1912.

often vitally interferes with the satisfaction of our inclinations leads us to wonder whether we really ought to do what we usually call our duty, so the recognition that we and others are liable to mistakes in knowledge generally leads us, as it did Descartes, to wonder whether hitherto we may not have been always mistaken. And just as we try to find a proof, based on the general consideration of action and of human life, that we ought to act in the ways usually called moral, so we, like Descartes, propose by a process of reflection on our thinking to find a test of knowledge, i.e. a principle by applying which we can show that a certain condition of mind was really knowledge, a condition which *ex hypothesi* existed independently of the process of reflection.

Now, how has the moral question been answered? So far as I can see, the answers all fall, and fall from the necessities of the case, into one of two species. *Either* they state that we ought to do so and so, because, as we see when we fully apprehend the facts, doing so will be for our good, i.e. really, as I would rather say, for our advantage, or better still, for our happiness; *or* they state that we ought to do so and so, because something realized either in or by the action is good. In other words, the reason 'why' is stated in terms either of the agent's happiness or of the goodness of something involved in the action.

To see the prevalence of the former species of answer, we have only to consider the history of Moral Philosophy. To take obvious instances, Plato, Butler, Hutcheson, Paley, Mill, each in his own way seeks at bottom to convince the individual that he ought to act in so-called moral ways by showing that to do so will really be for his happiness. Plato is perhaps the most significant instance, because of all philosophers he is the one to whom we are least willing to ascribe a mistake on such matters, and a mistake on his part would be evidence of the deep-rootedness of the tendency to make it. To show that Plato really justifies morality by its profitableness, it is only necessary to point out (1) that the very formulation of the thesis to be met, viz. that justice is ἀλλότριον ἀγαθόν,* implies that any refutation must consist in showing that justice is οἰκεῖον ἀγαθόν, i.e. really, as the context shows, one's own advantage, and (2) that the term λυσιτελεῖν ** supplies the key not only to the problem but also to its solution.

The tendency to justify acting on moral rules in this way is natural. For if, as often happens, we put to ourselves the question 'Why should we do so and so?', we are satisfied by being convinced either that the doing so will lead to something which we want (e.g. that taking certain medicine will heal our disease), or that the doing so itself, as we see when we appreciate its nature, is something that we want or should like, e.g. playing golf. The formulation of the question implies a state of unwillingness or indifference towards the action, and we are brought into a condition of willingness by the answer. And this process seems to be precisely what we desire

* [Someone else's good, i.e., advantage.—Ed.]
** [To profit (someone), i.e., to be to someone's advantage.—Ed.]

when we ask, e.g., 'Why should we keep our engagements to our own loss?'; for it is just the fact that the keeping of our engagements runs counter to the satisfaction of our desires which produced the question.

The answer is, of course, not an answer, for it fails to convince us that we ought to keep our engagements; even if successful on its own lines, it only makes us *want* to keep them. And Kant was really only pointing out this fact when he distinguished hypothetical and categorical imperatives, even though he obscured the nature of the fact by wrongly describing his so-called 'hypothetical imperatives' as imperatives. But if this answer be no answer, what other can be offered? Only, it seems, an answer which bases the obligation to do something on the *goodness* either of something to which the act leads or of the act itself. Suppose, when wondering whether we really ought to act in the ways usually called moral, we are told as a means of resolving our doubt that those acts are right which produce happiness. We at once ask: 'Whose happiness?' If we are told 'Our own happiness,' then, though we shall lose our hesitation to act in these ways, we shall not recover our sense that we ought to do so. But how can this result be avoided? Apparently, only by being told one of two things; *either* that anyone's happiness is a thing good in itself, and that *therefore* we ought to do whatever will produce it, *or* that working for happiness is it-self good, and that the intrinsic goodness of such an action is the reason why we ought to do it. The advantage of this appeal to the goodness of something consists in the fact that it avoids reference to desire, and, instead, re-fers to something impersonal and objective. In this way it seems possible to avoid the resolution of obligation into inclination. But just for this rea-son it is of the essence of the answer, that to be effective it must neither include nor involve the view that the apprehension of the goodness of any-thing necessarily arouses the desire for it. Otherwise the answer resolves itself into a form of the former answer by substituting desire or inclination for the sense of obligation, and in this way it loses what seems its special advantage.

Now it seems to me that both forms of this answer break down, though each for a different reason.

Consider the first form. It is what may be called Utilitarianism in the generic sense, in which what is good is not limited to pleasure. It takes its stand upon the distinction between something which is not itself an action, but which can be produced by an action, and the action which will produce it, and contends that if something which is not an action is good, then we *ought* to undertake the action which will, directly or indirectly, orig-inate it.[1]

But this argument, if it is to restore the sense of obligation to act, must presuppose an intermediate link, *viz.* the further thesis that what is good ought to be.[2] The necessity of this link is obvious. An 'ought,' if it is to be

[1] Cf. Dr. Rashdall's *Theory of Good and Evil*, vol. i, p. 138.
[2] Dr. Rashdall, if I understand him rightly, supplies this link (cf. ibid., pp. 135–6).

derived at all, can only be derived from another 'ought.' Moreover, this link tacitly presupposes another, viz. that the apprehension that something good which is not an action ought to be involves just the feeling of imperativeness or obligation which is to be aroused by the thought of the action which will originate it. Otherwise the argument will not lead us to feel the obligation to produce it by the action. And, surely, both this link and its implication are false.[3] The word 'ought' refers to actions and to actions alone. The proper language is never 'So and so ought to be,' but 'I ought to do so and so.' Even if we are sometimes moved to say that the world or something in it is not what it ought to be, what we really mean is that God or some human being has not made something what he ought to have made it. And it is merely stating another side of this fact to urge that we can only feel the imperativeness upon us of something which is in our power; for it is actions and actions alone which, directly at least, are in our power.

Perhaps, however, the best way to see the failure of this view is to see its failure to correspond to our actual moral convictions. Suppose we ask ourselves whether our sense that we ought to pay our debts or to tell the truth arises from our recognition that in doing so we should be originating something good, e.g. material comfort in A or true belief in B, i.e. suppose we ask ourselves whether it is this aspect of the action which leads to our recognition that we ought to do it. We at once and without hesitation answer 'No.' Again, if we take as our illustration our sense that we ought to act justly as between two parties, we have, if possible, even less hesitation in giving a similar answer; for the balance of resulting good may be, and often is, not on the side of justice.

At best it can only be maintained that there is this element of truth in the Utilitarian view, that unless we recognized that something which an act will originate is good, we should not recognize that we ought to do the action. Unless we thought knowledge a good thing, it may be urged, we should not think that we ought to tell the truth; unless we thought pain a bad thing, we should not think the infliction of it, without special reason, wrong. But this is not to imply that the badness of error is the reason why it is wrong to lie, or the badness of pain the reason why we ought not to inflict it without special cause.[4]

It is, I think, just because this form of the view is so plainly at variance with our moral consciousness that we are driven to adopt the other form of the view, viz. that the act is good in itself and that its intrinsic goodness is the reason why it ought to be done. It is this form which has always made

[3] When we speak of anything, e.g. of some emotion or of some quality of a human being, as good, we never dream in our ordinary consciousness of going on to say that therefore it ought to be.

[4] It may be noted that if the badness of pain were the reason why we ought not to inflict pain on another, it would equally be a reason why we ought not to inflict pain on ourselves; yet, though we should allow the wanton infliction of pain on ourselves to be foolish, we should not think of describing it as wrong.

the most serious appeal; for the goodness of the act itself seems more closely related to the obligation to do it than that of its mere consequences or results, and therefore, if obligation is to be based on the goodness of something, it would seem that this goodness should be that of the act itself. Moreover, the view gains plausibility from the fact that moral actions are most conspicuously those to which the term 'intrinsically good' is applicable.

Nevertheless this view, though perhaps less superficial, is equally untenable. For it leads to precisely the dilemma which faces everyone who tries to solve the problem raised by Kant's theory of the good will. To see this, we need only consider the nature of the acts to which we apply the term 'intrinsically good.'

There is, of course, no doubt that we approve and even admire certain actions, and also that we should describe them as good, and as good in themselves. But it is, I think, equally unquestionable that our approval and our use of the term 'good' is always in respect of the motive and refers to actions which have been actually done and of which we think we know the motive. Further, the actions of which we approve and which we should describe as intrinsically good are of two and only two kinds. They are either actions in which the agent did what he did because he thought he ought to do it, or actions of which the motive was a desire prompted by some good emotion, such as gratitude, affection, family feeling, or public spirit, the most prominent of such desires in books on Moral Philosophy being that ascribed to what is vaguely called benevolence. For the sake of simplicity I omit the case of actions done partly from some such desire and partly from a sense of duty; for even if all good actions are done from a combination of these motives, the argument will not be affected. The dilemma is this. If the motive in respect of which we think an action good is the sense of obligation, then so far from the sense that we ought to do it being derived from our apprehension of its goodness, our apprehension of its goodness will presuppose the sense that we ought to do it. In other words, in this case the recognition that the act is good will plainly *presuppose* the recognition that the act is right, whereas the view under consideration is that the recognition of the goodness of the act *gives rise* to the recognition of its rightness. On the other hand, if the motive in respect of which we think an action good is some intrinsically good desire, such as the desire to help a friend, the recognition of the goodness of the act will equally fail to give rise to the sense of obligation to do it. For we cannot feel that we ought to do that the doing of which is *ex hypothesi* prompted solely by the desire to do it.[5]

The fallacy underlying the view is that while to base the rightness of an act upon its intrinsic goodness implies that the goodness in question is that of the motive, in reality the rightness or wrongness of an act has

[5] It is, I think, on this latter horn of the dilemma that Martineau's view falls; cf. *Types of Ethical Theory*, part ii, book i.

nothing to do with any question of motives at all. For, as any instance will show, the rightness of an action concerns an action not in the fuller sense of the term in which we include the motive in the action, but in the narrower and commoner sense in which we distinguish an action from its motive and mean by an action merely the conscious origination of something, an origination which on different occasions or in different people may be prompted by different motives. The question 'Ought I to pay my bills?' really means simply 'Ought I to bring about my tradesmen's possession of what by my previous acts I explicitly or implicitly promised them?' There is, and can be, no question of whether I ought to pay my debts from a particular motive. No doubt we know that if we pay our bills we shall pay them with a motive, but in considering whether we ought to pay them we inevitably think of the act in abstraction from the motive. Even if we knew what our motive would be if we did the act, we should not be any nearer an answer to the question.

Moreover, if we eventually pay our bills from fear of the county court, we shall still have done *what* we ought, even though we shall not have done it *as* we ought. The attempt to bring in the motive involves a mistake similar to that involved in supposing that we can will to will. To feel that I ought to pay my bills is to be *moved towards* paying them. But what I can be moved towards must always be an action and not an action in which I am moved in a particular way, i.e. an action from a particular motive; otherwise I should be moved towards being moved, which is impossible. Yet the view under consideration involves this impossibility, for it really resolves the sense that I ought to do so and so, into the sense that I ought to be moved to do it in a particular way.[6]

So far my contentions have been mainly negative, but they form, I think, a useful, if not a necessary, introduction to what I take to be the truth. This I will now endeavour to state, first formulating what, as I think, is the real nature of our apprehension or appreciation of moral obligations, and then applying the result to elucidate the question of the existence of Moral Philosophy.

The sense of obligation to do, or of the rightness of, an action of a particular kind is absolutely underivative or immediate. The rightness of an action consists in its being the origination of something of a certain kind A in a situation of a certain kind, a situation consisting in a certain relation B of the agent to others or to his own nature. To appreciate its rightness two preliminaries may be necessary. We may have to follow out the consequences of the proposed action more fully than we have hitherto done, in order to realize that in the action we should originate A. Thus we may not appreciate the wrongness of telling a certain story until we realize that we should thereby be hurting the feelings of one of our audi-

---

[6] It is of course not denied here that an action done from a particular motive may be *good;* it is only denied that the *rightness* of an action depends on its being done with a particular motive.

ence. Again, we may have to take into account the relation B involved in the situation, which we had hitherto failed to notice. For instance, we may not appreciate the obligation to give X a present, until we remember that he has done us an act of kindness. But, given that by a process which is, of course, merely a process of general and not of moral thinking we come to recognize that the proposed act is one by which we shall originate A in a relation B, then we appreciate the obligation immediately or directly, the appreciation being an activity of *moral* thinking. We recognize, for instance, that this performance of a service to X, who has done us a service, just in virtue of its being the performance of a service to one who has rendered a service to the would-be agent, ought to be done by us. This apprehension is immediate, in precisely the sense in which a mathematical apprehension is immediate, e.g. the apprehension that this three-sided figure, in virtue of its being three-sided, must have three angles. Both apprehensions are immediate in the sense that in both insight into the nature of the subject directly leads us to recognize its possession of the predicate; and it is only stating this fact from the other side to say that in both cases the fact apprehended is self-evident.

The plausibility of the view that obligations are not self-evident but need proof lie in the fact that an act which is referred to as an obligation may be incompletely stated, what I have called the preliminaries to appreciating the obligation being incomplete. If, e.g., we refer to the act of repaying X by a present merely as giving X a present, it appears, and indeed is, necessary to give a reason. In other words, wherever a moral act is regarded in this incomplete way the question '*Why* should I do it?' is perfectly legitimate. This fact suggests, but suggests wrongly, that even if the nature of the act is completely stated, it is still necessary to give a reason, or, in other words, to supply a proof.

The relations involved in obligations of various kinds are, of course, very different. The relation in certain cases is a relation to others due to a past act of theirs or ours. The obligation to repay a benefit involves a relation due to a past act of the benefactor. The obligation to pay a bill involves a relation due to a past act of ours in which we have either said or implied that we would make a certain return for something which we have asked for and received. On the other hand, the obligation to speak the truth implies no such definite act; it involves a relation consisting in the fact that others are trusting us to speak the truth, a relation the apprehension of which gives rise to the sense that communication of the truth is something owing by us to them. Again, the obligation not to hurt the feelings of another involves no special relation of us to that other, i.e. no relation other than that involved in our both being men, and men in one and the same world. Moreover, it seems that the relation involved in an obligation need not be a relation to another at all. Thus we should admit that there is an obligation to overcome our natural timidity or greediness, and that this involves no relations to others. Still there is a relation involved, *viz.* a relation to our own disposition. It is simply because we can and because others cannot directly modify our disposition that it is our business to improve it, and that it is not theirs, or, at least, not theirs to the same extent.

The negative side of all this is, of course, that we do not come to appreciate an obligation by an *argument*, i.e. by a process of nonmoral thinking, and that, in particular, we do not do so by an argument of which a premiss is the ethical but not moral activity of appreciating the goodness either of the act or of a consequence of the act; i.e. that our sense of the rightness of an act is not a conclusion from our appreciation of the goodness either of it or of anything else.

It will probably be urged that on this view our various obligations form, like Aristotle's categories, an unrelated chaos in which it is impossible to acquiesce. For, according to it, the obligation to repay a benefit, or to pay a debt, or to keep a promise, presupposes a previous act of another; whereas the obligation to speak the truth or not to harm another does not; and, again, the obligation to remove our timidity involves no relations to others at all. Yet, at any rate, an effective *argumentum ad hominem* is at hand in the fact that the various qualities which we recognize as good are equally unrelated; e.g. courage, humility, and interest in knowledge. If, as is plainly the case, ἀγαθά [goods] differ ᾗ ἀγαθά [*qua* goods], why should not obligations equally differ *qua* their obligatoriness? Moreover, if this were not so there could in the end be only one obligation, which is palpably contrary to fact.[7]

Certain observations will help to make the view clearer.

In the first place, it may seem that the view, being—as it is—avowedly put forward in opposition to the view that what is right is derived from what is good, must itself involve the opposite of this, *viz.* the Kantian position that what is good is based upon what is right, i.e. that an act, if it be good, is good because it is right. But this is not so. For, on the view put forward, the rightness of a right action lies solely in the origination

---

[7] Two other objections may be anticipated: (1) that obligations cannot be self-evident, since many actions regarded as obligations by some are not so regarded by others, and (2) that if obligations are self-evident, the problem of how we ought to act in the presence of conflicting obligations is insoluble.

To the first I should reply:

(*a*) That the appreciation of an obligation is, of course, only possible for a developed moral being, and that different degrees of development are possible.

(*b*) That the failure to recognize some particular obligations is usually due to the fact that, owing to a lack of thoughtfulness, what I have called the preliminaries to this recognition are incomplete.

(*c*) That the view put forward is consistent with the admission that, owing to a lack of thoughtfulness, even the best men are blind to many of their obligations, and that in the end our obligations are seen to be co-extensive with almost the whole of our life.

To the second objection I should reply that obligation admits of degrees, and that where obligations conflict, the decision of what we ought to do turns not on the question 'Which of the alternative courses of action will originate the greater good?' but on the question 'Which is the greater obligation?'

in which the act consists, whereas the intrinsic goodness of an action lies solely in its motive; and this implies that a morally good action is morally good not simply because it is a right action but because it is a right action done because it is right, i.e. from a sense of obligation. And this implication, it may be remarked incidentally, seems plainly true.

[handwritten margin note: SUBJ + OBLIGATION OBLIGATION BOTH NECESSARY]

In the second place, the view involves that when, or rather so far as, we act from a sense of obligation, we have no purpose or end. By a 'purpose' or 'end' we really mean something the existence of which we desire, and desire of the existence of which leads us to act. Usually our purpose is something which the act will originate, as when we turn round in order to look at a picture. But it may be the action itself, i.e. the origination of something, as when we hit a golf-ball into a hole or kill someone out of revenge.[8] Now if by a purpose we mean something the existence of which we desire and desire for which leads us to act, then plainly, so far as we act from a sense of obligation, we have no purpose, consisting either in the action or in anything which it will produce. This is so obvious that it scarcely seems worth pointing out. But I do so for two reasons. (1) If we fail to scrutinize the meaning of the terms 'end' and 'purpose,' we are apt to assume uncritically that all deliberate action, i.e. action proper, must have a purpose; we then become puzzled both when we look for the purpose of an action done from a sense of obligation, and also when we try to apply to such an action the distinction of means and end, the truth all the time being that since there is no end, there is no means either. (2) The attempt to base the sense of obligation on the recognition of the goodness of something is really an attempt to find a purpose in a moral action in the shape of something good which, as good, we want. And the expectation that the goodness of something underlies an obligation disappears as soon as we cease to look for a purpose.

The thesis, however, that, so far as we act from a sense of obligation, we have no purpose must not be misunderstood. It must not be taken either to mean or to imply that so far as we so act we have no *motive*. No doubt in ordinary speech the words 'motive' and 'purpose' are usually treated as correlatives, 'motive' standing for the desire which induces us to act, and 'purpose' standing for the object of this desire. But this is only because, when we are looking for the motive of the action, say, of some crime, we are usually presupposing that the act in question is prompted by a desire and not by the sense of obligation. At bottom, however, we mean by a motive what moves us to act; a sense of obligation does sometimes move us to act; and in our ordinary consciousness we should not hesitate to allow that the action we were considering might have had as its motive a sense of obligation. Desire and the sense of obligation are co-ordinate forms or species of motive.

[8] It is no objection to urge that an action cannot be its own purpose, since the purpose of something cannot be the thing itself. For, speaking strictly, the purpose is not the *action's* purpose but *our* purpose, and there is no contradiction in holding that our purpose in acting may be the action.

In the third place, if the view put forward be right, we must sharply distinguish morality and virtue as independent, though related, species of goodness, neither being an aspect of something of which the other is an aspect, nor again a form or species of the other, nor again something deducible from the other; and we must at the same time allow that it is possible to do the same act either virtuously or morally or in both ways at once. And surely this is true. An act, to be virtuous, must, as Aristotle saw, be done willingly or with pleasure; as such it is just not done from a sense of obligation but from some desire which is intrinsically good, as arising from some intrinsically good emotion. Thus, in an act of generosity the motive is the desire to help another arising from sympathy with that other; in an act which is courageous and no more, i.e. in an act which is not at the same time an act of public spirit or family affection or the like, we prevent ourselves from being dominated by a feeling of terror, desiring to do so from a sense of shame at being terrified. The goodness of such an act is different from the goodness of an act to which we apply the term moral in the strict and narrow sense, *viz*. an act done from a sense of obligation. Its goodness lies in the intrinsic goodness of the emotion and of the consequent desire under which we act, the goodness of this motive being different from the goodness of the moral motive proper, *viz*. the sense of duty or obligation. Nevertheless, at any rate in certain cases, an act can be done either virtuously or morally or in both ways at once. It is possible to repay a benefit either from desire to repay it, or from the feeling that we ought to do so, or from both motives combined. A doctor may tend his patients either from a desire arising out of interest in his patients or in the exercise of skill, or from a sense of duty, or from a desire and a sense of duty combined. Further, although we recognize that in each case the act possesses an intrinsic goodness, we regard that action as the best in which both motives are combined; in other words, we regard as the really best man the man in whom virtue and morality are united.

It may be objected that the distinction between the two kinds of motive is untenable, on the ground that the *desire* to repay a benefit, for example, is only the manifestation of that which manifests itself as the *sense of obligation* to repay whenever we think of something in the action which is other than the repayment and which we should not like, such as the loss or pain involved. Yet the distinction can, I think, easily be shown to be tenable. For, in the analogous case of revenge, the desire to return the injury and the sense that we ought not to do so, leading, as they do, in opposite directions, are plainly distinct; and the obviousness of the distinction here seems to remove any difficulty in admitting the existence of a parallel distinction between the desire to return a benefit and the sense that we ought to return it.[9]

[9] This sharp distinction of virtue and morality as co-ordinate and independent forms of goodness will explain a fact which otherwise it is difficult to account for. If we turn from books on Moral Philosophy to any vivid account of human life and action

Further, the view implies that an obligation can no more be based on or derived from a virtue than a virtue can be derived from an obligation, in which latter case a virtue would consist in carrying out an obligation. And the implication is surely true and important. Take the case of courage. It is untrue to urge that, since courage is a virtue, we ought to act courageously. It is and must be untrue, because, as we see in the end, to feel an obligation to act courageously would involve a contradiction. For, as I have urged before, we can only feel an obligation to *act;* we cannot feel an obligation to *act from a certain desire*, in this case the desire to conquer one's feelings of terror arising from the sense of shame which they arouse. Moreover, if the sense of obligation to act in a particular way leads to an action, the action will be an action done from a sense of obligation, and therefore not, if the above analysis of virtue be right, an act of courage.

The mistake of supposing that there can be an obligation to act courageously seems to arise from two causes. In the first place, there is often an obligation to do that which involves the conquering or controlling of our fear in the doing of it, e.g. the obligation to walk along the side of a precipice to fetch a doctor for a member of our family. Here the acting on the obligation is externally, though only externally, the same as an act of courage proper. In the second place there is an obligation to acquire courage, i.e. to do such things as will enable us afterwards to act courageously, and this may be mistaken for an obligation to act courageously. The same considerations can, of course, be applied, *mutatis mutandis,* to the other virtues.

The fact, if it be a fact, that virtue is no basis for morality will explain what otherwise it is difficult to account for, *viz.* the extreme sense of dissatisfaction produced by a close reading of Aristotle's *Ethics.* Why is the *Ethics* so disappointing? Not, I think, because it really answers two radically different questions as if they were one: (1) 'What is the happy life?,' (2) 'What is the virtuous life?' It is, rather, because Aristotle does not do what we as moral philosophers want him to do, *viz.* to convince us that we really ought to do what in our non-reflective consciousness we have hitherto believed we ought to do, or if not, to tell us what, if any, are the other things which we really ought to do, and to prove to us that he is right. Now, if what I have just been contending is true, a systematic account of the virtuous character cannot possibly satisfy this demand. At best it can only make clear to us the details of one of our obligations, *viz.* the obligation to make ourselves better men; but the achievement of this does not help us to discover what we ought to do in life as a whole, and

such as we find in Shakespeare, nothing strikes us more than the comparative remoteness of the discussions of Moral Philosophy from the facts of actual life. Is not this largely because, while Moral Philosophy has, quite rightly, concentrated its attention on the fact of obligation, in the case of many of those whom we admire most and whose lives are of the greatest interest, the sense of obligation, though it may be an important, is not a dominating factor in their lives?

why; to think that it did would be to think that our only business in life
was self-improvement. Hence it is not surprising that Aristotle's account
of the good man strikes us as almost wholly of academic value, with little
relation to our real demand, which is formulated in Plato's words: οὐ γὰρ
περὶ τοῦ ἐπιτυχόντος ὁ λόγος, ἀλλὰ περὶ τοῦ ὅντινα τρόπον χρὴ ζῆν.⁹ᵃ

I am not, of course, *criticizing* Aristotle for failing to satisfy this demand, except so far as here and there he leads us to think that he intends
to satisfy it. For my main contention is that the demand cannot be satisfied, and cannot be satisfied because it is illegitimate. Thus we are brought
to the question: 'Is there really such a thing as Moral Philosophy, and, if
there is, in what sense?'

We should first consider the parallel case—as it appears to be—of the
Theory of Knowledge. As I urged before, at some time or other in the
history of all of us, if we are thoughtful, the frequency of our own and of
others' mistakes is bound to lead to the reflection that possibly we and
others have *always* been mistaken in consequence of some radical defect
of our faculties. In consequence, certain things which previously we
should have said without hesitation that we *knew*, as e.g. that $4 \times 7 = 28$,
become subject to doubt; we become able only to say that we thought we
knew these things. We inevitably go on to look for some general procedure by which we can ascertain that a given condition of mind is really
one of knowledge. And this involves the search for a criterion of knowledge, i.e. for a principle by applying which we can settle that a given
state of mind is really knowledge. The search for this criterion and the
application of it, when found, is what is called the Theory of Knowledge.
The search implies that instead of its being the fact that the knowledge
that A is B is obtained directly by consideration of the nature of A and B,
the knowledge that A is B, in the full or complete sense, can only be
obtained by first knowing that A is B, and then knowing that we knew it
by applying a criterion, such as Descartes's principle that what we clearly
and distinctly conceive is true.

Now it is easy to show that the doubt whether A is B, based on this
speculative or general ground, could, if genuine, never be set at rest. For if,
in order really to know that A is B, we must first know that we knew it,
then really, to know that we knew it, we must first know that we knew
that we knew it. But—what is more important—it is also easy to show that
this doubt is not a genuine doubt but rests on a confusion the exposure of
which removes the doubt. For when we *say* we doubt whether our previous condition was one of knowledge, what we *mean*, if we mean anything at all, is that we doubt whether our previous *belief* was *true*, a belief
which we should express as the *thinking* that A is B. For in order to doubt
whether our previous condition was one of knowledge, we have to think
of it not as knowledge but as only belief, and our only question can be

⁹ᵃ [For no light matter is at stake; the question concerns the very manner in which
human life is to be lived (*Republic*, Bk. I, 352D)—Ed.].

'Was this belief true?' But as soon as we see that we are thinking of our previous condition as only one of belief, we see that what we are now doubting is not what we first *said* we were doubting, *viz.* whether a previous condition of knowledge was really knowledge. Hence, to remove the doubt, it is only necessary to appreciate the real nature of our consciousness in apprehending, e.g. that $7 \times 4 = 28$, and thereby see that it was no mere condition of believing but a condition of knowing, and then to notice that in our subsequent doubt what we are really doubting is not whether this consciousness was really knowledge, but whether a consciousness of another kind, *viz.* a belief that $7 \times 4 = 28$, was true. We thereby see that though a doubt based on speculative grounds is possible, it is not a doubt concerning what we believed the doubt concerned, and that a doubt concerning this latter is impossible.

Two results follow. In the first place, if, as is usually the case, we mean by the 'Theory of Knowledge' the knowledge which supplies the answer to the question 'Is what we have hitherto thought knowledge really knowledge?,' there is and can be no such thing, and the supposition that there can is simply due to a confusion. There can be no answer to an illegitimate question, except that the question is illegitimate. Nevertheless the question is one which we continue to put until we realize the inevitable immediacy of knowledge. And it is positive knowledge that knowledge is immediate and neither can be, nor needs to be, improved or vindicated by the further knowledge that it was knowledge. This positive knowledge sets at rest the inevitable doubt, and, so far as by the 'Theory of Knowledge' is meant this knowledge, then even though this knowledge be the knowledge that there is no Theory of Knowledge in the former sense, to that extent the Theory of Knowledge exists.

In the second place, suppose we come genuinely to doubt whether, e.g., $7 \times 4 = 28$ owing to a genuine doubt whether we were right in believing yesterday that $7 \times 4 = 28$, a doubt which can in fact only arise if we have lost our hold of, i.e. no longer remember, the real nature of our consciousness of yesterday, and so think of it as consisting in believing. Plainly, the only remedy is to do the sum again. Or, to put the matter generally, if we do come to doubt whether it is true that A is B, as we once thought, the remedy lies not in any process of reflection but in such a reconsideration of the nature of A and B as leads to the knowledge that A is B.

With these considerations in mind, consider the parallel which, as it seems to me, is presented—though with certain differences—by Moral Philosophy. The sense that we ought to do certain things arises in our unreflective consciousness, being an activity of moral thinking occasioned by the various situations in which we find ourselves. At this stage our attitude to these obligations is one of unquestioning confidence. But inevitably the appreciation of the degree to which the execution of these obligations is contrary to our interest raises the doubt whether after all these obligations are really obligatory, i.e. whether our sense that we ought not to do certain things is not illusion. We then want to have it *proved* to us that we ought to do so, i.e. to be convinced of this by a process which, as an argument, is different in kind from our original and unreflective appreciation of it. This demand is, as I have argued, illegitimate.

Hence, in the first place, if, as is almost universally the case, by Moral Philosophy is meant the knowledge which would satisfy this demand, there is no such knowledge, and all attempts to attain it are doomed to failure because they rest on a mistake, the mistake of supposing the possibility of proving what can only be apprehended directly by an act of moral thinking. Nevertheless the demand, though illegitimate, is inevitable until we have carried the process of reflection far enough to realize the self-evidence of our obligations, i.e. the immediacy of our apprehension of them. This realization of their self-evidence is positive knowledge, and so far, and so far only, as the term Moral Philosophy is confined to this knowledge and to the knowledge of the parallel immediacy of the apprehension of the goodness of the various virtues and of good dispositions generally, is there such a thing as Moral Philosophy. But since this knowledge may allay doubts which often affect the whole conduct of life, it is, though not extensive, important and even vitally important.

In the second place, suppose we come genuinely to doubt whether we ought, for example, to pay our debts, owing to a genuine doubt whether our previous conviction that we ought to do so is true, a doubt which can, in fact, only arise if we fail to remember the real nature of what we now call our past conviction. The only remedy lies in actually getting into a situation which occasions the obligation, or—if our imagination be strong enough—in imagining ourselves in that situation, and then letting our moral capacities of thinking do their work. Or, to put the matter generally, if we do doubt whether there is really an obligation to originate A in a situation B, the remedy lies not in any process of general thinking, but in getting face to face with a particular instance of the situation B, and then directly appreciating the obligation to originate A in that situation.

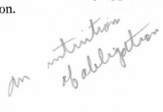

The Meaning of "Right" *

〽〽

SIR DAVID ROSS

THE PURPOSE of this inquiry is to examine the nature, relations, and implications of three conceptions which appear to be fundamental in ethics—those of 'right,' 'good' in general, and 'morally good.' The inquiry will have much in common with the inquiries, of which there have been many in recent years, into the nature of value, and I shall have occasion to discuss some of the more important theories of value; but my object is a more limited one. I offer no discussion, except at most a purely incidental and illustrative one, of certain forms of value, such as economic value and beauty. My interest will throughout be ethical, and value will be discussed only so far as it seems to be relevant to this interest.

I propose to begin with the term 'right.' A considerable ambiguity attaches to any attempt to discuss the meaning of any term. Professor G. E. Moore has well indicated three main objects that such an attempt at definition may have. 'When we say, as Webster says, "The definition of horse is, 'A hoofed quadruped of the genus Equus,' " we may, in fact, mean three different things. (1) We may mean merely: "When I say 'horse,' you are to understand that I am talking about a hoofed quadruped of the genus Equus." This might be called the arbitrary verbal definition. . . . (2) We may mean, as Webster ought to mean: "When most English people say 'horse,' they mean a hoofed quadruped of the genus Equus." This may be called the verbal definition proper. . . . But (3) we may, when we define horse, mean something much more important. We may mean that a certain object, which we all of us know, is composed in a certain manner: that it has four legs, a head, a heart, a liver, etc., etc., all of them arranged in definite relations to one another.' [1]

We must ask ourselves whether, in discussing the meaning of 'right,' we are attempting any one of these kinds of definition, or something different from them all. I certainly do not wish *merely* to indicate a sense in which I propose to use the term 'right.' I wish to keep in touch with the general usage of the word. While other things may be called 'right' (as in the phrases 'the right road,' 'the right solution'), the word is specially

---

* Chapter I of *The Right and the Good*, reprinted by kind permission of the author and the publisher, The Clarendon Press, 1930.
[1] *Principia Ethica*, 8 [p. 71 this volume].

applied to acts, and it is the sense (by general consent a very important one) in which it is so applied that I wish to discuss. But we must be prepared to find that the general usage of the word is not entirely consistent with itself. Most of the words in any language have a certain amount of ambiguity; and there is special danger of ambiguity in the case of a word like 'right,' which does not stand for anything we can point out to one another or apprehend by one of the senses. Even with words that do stand for such things there is this danger. Even if two people find that the things the one calls red are just the things the other calls red, it is by no means certain that they mean the same quality. There is only a general presumption that since the structure of their eyes (if neither is colour-blind) is pretty much the same, the same object acting on the eyes of the two men produces pretty much the same kind of sensation. And in the case of a term like 'right,' there is nothing parallel to the highly similar organization of different people's eyes, to create a presumption that when they call the same act right, they mean to refer to the same quality of it. In point of fact, there is a serious difference of view as to the *application* of the term 'right.' Suppose, for instance, that a man pays a particular debt simply from fear of the legal consequences of not doing so, some people would say he had done what was right, and others would deny this: they would say that no moral value attaches to such an act, and that since 'right' is meant to imply moral value, the act cannot be right. They might generalize and say that no act is right unless it is done from a sense of duty, or if they shrank from so rigorous a doctrine, they might at least say that no act is right unless done from *some* good motive, such as either sense of duty or benevolence.

This difference of view may be due to either of two causes. Both parties may be using 'right' in the same sense, the sense of 'morally obligatory,' and differing as to the further character an act must have in order to have this quality. *Or* the first party may be using 'right' in this sense, and the second in the sense of 'morally good.' It is not clear to me which of these two things is usually happening when this difference of view arises. But it seems probable that both things really happen—that some people fail to notice the distinction between 'right' and 'morally good,' and that others, while distinguishing the meaning of these terms, think that only what is morally good is right. A discussion of the first of these positions only is strictly in point here, where we are discussing the *meaning* of 'right.' It seems to me clear that 'right' does not mean the same as 'morally good'; and we can test this by trying to substitute one for the other. If they meant the same thing we should be able to substitute, for instance, 'he is a right man' for 'he is a morally good man'; nor is our inability to do this merely a matter of English idiom, for if we turn to the sort of moral judgement in which we do use the word 'right,' such as 'this is the right act,' it is clear that by this we mean 'this act is the act *that ought to be done,' 'this act is morally obligatory';* and to substitute either of these

phrases for 'morally good' in 'he is a morally good man' would obviously
be not merely unidiomatic, but absurd. It should be obvious, then, that
'right' and 'morally good' mean different things. But some one might say
that while 'morally good' has a wider application than 'right,' in that it can
be applied to agents as well as to acts, yet when applied to acts they mean
the same thing. I should like therefore to convince him that 'right act'
cannot mean the same as 'act that ought to be done' and *also* the same as
'morally good act.' If I can convince him of this, I think he will see the
propriety of not using 'right act' in the sense of 'morally good act.'

But we ought first to note a minor difference between the meaning
of 'right' and the meaning of 'something that ought to be done' or 'that is
my duty' or 'that is incumbent on me.' It may sometimes happen that
there is a set of two or more acts one or other of which ought to be done
by me rather than any act not belonging to this set. In such a case any act
of this set is right, but none is my duty; my duty is to do 'one or other'
of them. Thus 'right' has a somewhat wider possible application than
'something that ought to be done' or any of its equivalents. But we want
an adjective to express the same meaning as 'something that ought to be
done,' and though we have 'obligatory' at our disposal, that also has its
ambiguity, since it sometimes means 'compulsory.' We should have to say
'morally obligatory' to make our meaning quite clear; and to obviate the
necessity of using this rather cumbrous expression, I will use 'right' in this
sense. I hope that this paragraph will prevent any confusion arising from
this slightly inaccurate usage.

Some might deny the correctness of the distinction just drawn. They
might say that when there are two or more acts one or other of which,
as we say, we ought to do (it not being our duty to do one rather than
another), the truth is that these are simply alternative ways of producing a
single result, and that our duty is, strictly, not to do 'one or other' of the
acts, but to produce the result; this alone is our duty, and this alone is
right. This answer does, I think, fairly apply to many cases in which it *is*
the production of a certain result that we think obligatory, the means
being optional: e.g. to a case in which it is our duty to convey information
to some one, but morally immaterial whether we do so orally or in writing.
But in principle, at any rate, there may be other cases in which it is our
duty to produce one or other of two or more *different* states of affairs,
without its being our duty to produce one of them rather than another;
in such a case each of these acts will be right, and none will be our duty.

If it can be shown that nothing that ought to be done is ever morally
good, it will be clear *a fortiori* that 'morally good' does not *mean* the same
as 'that ought to be done.' Now it is, I think, quite clear that the only acts
that are morally good are those that proceed from a good motive; this
is maintained by those whom I am now trying to convince, and I entirely

agree. If, then, we can show that action from a good motive is never morally obligatory, we shall have established that what is morally good is never right, and *a fortiori* that 'right' does not *mean* the same as 'morally good.' That action from a good motive is never morally obligatory follows (1) from the Kantian principle, which is generally admitted, that 'I ought' implies 'I can.' It is not the case that I can by choice produce a certain motive (whether this be an ordinary desire or the sense of obligation) in myself at a moment's notice, still less that I can at a moment's notice make it effective in stimulating me to act. I can act from a certain motive only if I have the motive; if not, the most I can do is to cultivate it by suitably directing my attention or by acting in certain appropriate ways so that on some future occasion it *will* be present in me, and I shall be able to act from it. My *present* duty, therefore, cannot be to act here and now from it.

(2) A similar conclusion may be reached by a *reductio ad absurdum*. Those who hold that our duty is to act from a certain motive usually (Kant is the great exemplar) hold that the motive from which we ought to act is the sense of duty. Now if the sense of duty is to be my motive for doing a certain act, it must be the sense that it is my duty to do that act. If, therefore, we say 'it is my duty to do act *A* from the sense of duty,' this means 'it is my duty to do act *A* from the sense that it is my duty to do act *A*.' And here the whole expression is in contradiction with a part of itself. The whole sentence says 'it is my duty to-do-act-*A*-from-the-sense-that-it-is-my-duty-to-do-act-*A*.' But the latter part of the sentence implies that what I think is that it is my duty to-do-act-*A* simply. And if, as the theory in question requires, we try to amend the latter part of the expression to bring it into accord with the whole expression, we get the result 'it is my duty to do act *A* from the sense that it is my duty to do act *A* from the sense that it is my duty to do act *A*,' where again the last part of the expression is in conflict with the theory, and with the sentence as a whole. It is clear that a further similar amendment, and a further, and in the end an infinite series of amendments would be necessary in the attempt to bring the last part of the expression into accordance with the theory, and that even then we should not have succeeded in doing so.

Again, suppose that I say to you 'it is your duty to do act *A* from the sense of duty'; that means 'it is your duty to do act *A* from the sense that it is your duty to do act *A*.' Then *I* think that it is your duty to act from a certain motive, but I suggest that *you* should act under the supposition that it is your duty to do a certain thing, irrespective of motive, i.e. under a supposition which I must think false since it contradicts my own.

The only conclusion that can be drawn is that our duty is to do certain things, not to do them from the sense of duty.[2]

---

[2] It should be added, however, that one, and an important one, of our duties is to cultivate in ourselves the sense of duty. But then this is the duty of cultivating in ourselves the sense of duty, and not of cultivating in ourselves, from the sense of duty, the sense of duty.

The latter of these two arguments ([1] and [2]) cannot be used against those who hold that it is our duty to act from some other motive than the sense of duty; the sense of duty is the only motive that leads to the infinite series in question. But the first of the two arguments seems in itself sufficient against *any* theory which holds that motive of any kind is included in the content of duty. And though the second argument does not refute the view that we ought to act from some other motive, it would be paradoxical to hold that we ought to act from some other motive but never ought to act from a sense of duty, which is the highest motive.[3]

Let us now return to the three senses in which Professor Moore points out that we may understand an attempt to define a certain term.[4] So far, the position we have taken up with regard to 'right' includes something of each of the first two attitudes he distinguishes. In using 'right' as synonymous (but for the minor distinction already pointed out)[5] with 'what is my duty,' and as distinct from 'morally good,' I believe I am conforming to what most men (if not all men) usually mean when they use the word. But I could not maintain that they always use the word in this way. I am, therefore, to some extent adopting the first of the attitudes he distinguishes, and expressing my own intention to use 'right' in this sense only. And this is justified by the great confusion that has been introduced into ethics by the phrase 'a right action' being used sometimes of the initiation of a certain change in the state of affairs irrespective of motive, and at other times of such initiation from some particular motive, such as sense of duty or benevolence. I would further suggest that additional clearness would be gained if we used 'act' of the thing done, the initiation of change, and 'action' of the doing of it, the initiating of change, from a certain motive. We should then talk of a right act but not of a right action, of a morally good action but not of a morally good act. And it may be added that the doing of a right act may be a morally bad action, and that the doing of a wrong act may be a morally good action; for 'right' and 'wrong' refer entirely to the thing done, 'morally good' and 'morally bad' entirely to the motive from which it is done. A firm grasp of this distinction will do much to remove some of the perplexities of our moral thought.

The question remains, what attitude we are to take up towards Professor Moore's third sense of 'definition.' Are we to hold that 'right' can be defined in the sense of being reduced to elements simpler than itself? At first sight it might appear that egoism and utilitarianism are attempts to define 'right'—to define it as 'productive of the greatest possible pleasure to the agent' or as 'productive of the greatest possible pleasure to mankind'; and I think these theories have often been so understood by some of those who accept them. But the leaders of the school are not unanimous in so

[3] If any one doubts that it is, I beg him to refer to pp. 164–5, where I give reasons in support of the contention.

[4] Cf. p. 1 [p. 163 this volume].

[5] pp. 3–4.

understanding their theory. Bentham seems to understand it so. He says [6] that 'when thus interpreted' (i.e. as meaning 'comformable to the principle of utility'), 'the words *ought* and *right* . . . and others of that stamp, have a meaning; when otherwise, they have none.' And elsewhere [7] he says 'admitting (what is not true) that the word *right* can have a meaning without reference to utility.' Yet, as Sidgwick points out,[8] 'when Bentham explains (*Principles of Morals and Legislation*, Chap. I, § 1, note) that his fundamental principle "states the greatest happiness of all those whose interest is in question as being the right and proper end of human action," we cannot understand him really to *mean* by the word "right" "conducive to the general happiness"; for the proposition that it is conducive to general happiness to take general happiness as an end of action, though not exactly a tautology, can hardly serve as the fundamental principle of a moral system.' Bentham has evidently not made up his mind clearly whether he thinks that 'right' *means* 'productive of the general happiness,' *or* that being productive of the general happiness is what makes right acts right; and would very likely have thought the difference unimportant. Mill does not so far as I know discuss the question whether right is definable. He states his creed in the form 'actions are right in proportion as they tend to promote happiness,' [9] where the claim that is made is not that this is what 'right' means, but that this is the other characteristic in virtue of which actions that are right are right. And Sidgwick says [10] that the meaning of 'right' or 'ought' 'is too elementary to admit of any formal definition,' and expressly repudiates [11] the view that 'right' means 'productive of any particular sort of result.'

The most deliberate claim that 'right' is definable as 'productive of so and so' is made by Prof. G. E. Moore, who claims in *Principia Ethica* that 'right' means 'productive of the greatest possible good.' Now it has often been pointed out against hedonism, and by no one more clearly than by Professor Moore, that the claim that 'good' just means 'pleasant' cannot seriously be maintained; that while it may or may not be true that the only things that are good are pleasant, the statement that the good is just the pleasant is a synthetic, not an analytic proposition; that the words 'good' and 'pleasant' stand for distinct qualities, even if the things that possess the one are precisely the things that possess the other. If this were not so, it would not be intelligible that the proposition 'the good is just the pleasant' should have been maintained on the one hand, and denied on the other, with so much fervour; for we do not fight for or against analytic propositions; we take them for granted. Must not the same claim be made about the statement 'being right means being an act productive of the

---

[6] *Principles of Morals and Legislation*, Ch. I, § 10.
[7] ib. § 14. 10.
[8] *Methods of Ethics*, ed. 7, 26 n.
[9] *Utilitarianism*, copyright eds., 9.
[10] *Methods of Ethics*, ed. 7, 32 [p. 143 this volume].
[11] ib. 25–6 [p. 139 this volume].

greatest good producible in the circumstances'? Is it not plain on reflection that this is not what we *mean* by right, even if it be a true statement about what *is* right? It seems clear for instance that when an ordinary man says it is right to fulfil promises he is not in the least thinking of the total consequences of such an act, about which he knows and cares little or nothing. 'Ideal utilitarianism' [12] is, it would appear, plausible only when it is understood not as an analysis or definition of the notion of 'right' but as a statement that all acts that are right, and only these, possess the further characteristic of being productive of the best possible consequences, and are right because they possess this other characteristic.

If I am not mistaken, Professor Moore has moved to this position, from the position that 'right' is *analysable* into 'productive of the greatest possible good.' In *Principia Ethica* the latter position is adopted: e.g. 'This use of "right," as denoting what is good as a means, whether or not it is also good as an end, is indeed the use to which I shall confine the word.' [13] 'To assert that a certain line of conduct is, at a given time, absolutely right or obligatory, is obviously to assert that more good or less evil will exist in the world, if it be adopted, than if anything else be done instead.' [14] 'To ask what kind of actions one ought to perform, or what kind of conduct is right, is to ask what kind of effects such action and conduct will produce . . . What I wish first to point out is that "right" does and can mean nothing but "cause of a good result," and is thus always identical with "useful" . . . That the assertion "I am morally bound to perform this action" is identical with the assertion "this action will produce the greatest possible amount of good in the Universe" has already been briefly shewn . . . ; but it is important to insist that this fundamental point is demonstrably certain. . . . Our "duty," therefore, can only be defined as that action, which will cause more good to exist in the Universe than any possible alternative. And what is "right" or "morally permissible" only differs from this, as what will *not* cause *less* good than any possible alternative.' [15]

In his later book, *Ethics*, Professor Moore seems to have to adopt the other position, though perhaps not quite unequivocally. On page 8 [15a] he names as one of the 'more fundamental questions' of ethics the question 'what, after all, is it that we mean to say of an action when we say that it is right or ought to be done?' Here it is still suggested that 'right' is perhaps analysable or definable. But to this question *Ethics* nowhere distinctly offers an answer, and on page 9 [15b] we find, 'Can we discover any single reason,

---

[12] I use this as a well-known way of referring to Professor Moore's view. 'Agathistic utilitarianism' would indicate more distinctly the difference between it and hedonistic utilitarianism.

[13] p. 18 [p. 78 this volume].

[14] p. 25 [p. 83 this volume].

[15] pp. 146–8. *Cf.* also pp. 167, 169, 180–1.

[15a] [p. 35 this volume; p. 7 reset edition of *Ethics*].

[15b] [pp. 8–9 this volume; p. 8 reset edition of *Ethics*].

applicable to all right actions equally, which is, in every case, *the* reason why an action is right, when it is right?' This is the question which Professor Moore in fact sets himself to answer. But the *reason* for an action's being right is evidently not the same thing as its *rightness*, and Professor Moore seems already to have passed to the view that productivity of maximum good is not the definition of 'right' but another characteristic which underlies and accounts for the rightness of right acts. Again, he describes hedonistic utilitarianism as asking, 'can we discover any characteristic, over and above the mere fact that they *are* right, which belongs to absolutely *all* voluntary actions which are right, and which at the same time does not belong to any except those which are right?' [16] This is the question which he describes hedonism as essentially answering, and since his own view differs from hedonism not in logical form but just by the substitution of 'good' for 'pleasure,' his theory also seems to be essentially an answer to this question, i.e. not to the question what is rightness but to the question what is the universal accompaniment and, as he is careful to add,[17] the necessitating ground of rightness. Again, he describes hedonistic utilitarianism as giving us 'a criterion, or test, or standard by which we could discern with regard to any action whether it is right or wrong.' [18] And similarly, I suppose, he regards his own theory as offering a different criterion of rightness. But obviously a criterion of rightness is not rightness itself. And, most plainly of all, he says, 'It is indeed quite plain, I think, that the meaning of the two words' ('duty' and 'expediency,' the latter being equivalent to 'tendency to produce the maximum good') 'is *not* the same; for, if it were, then it would be a mere tautology to say that it is always our duty to do what will have the best possible consequences.' [19] If we contrast this with *Principia Ethica*, page 169, 'if I ask whether an action is *really* my duty or *really* expedient, the predicate of which I question the applicability to the action in question is precisely the same,' we see how much Professor Moore has changed his position, and changed it in the direction in which, as I have been urging, it must be changed if it is to be made plausible. And if it is clear that 'right' does not mean 'productive of the greatest possible good,' it is *a fortiori* clear that it does not *mean* 'productive of the greatest possible pleasure, for the agent or for mankind,' but that productivity of the greatest possible pleasure for the agent or for mankind is at most the ground of the rightness of acts, rightness itself being admitted to be a distinct characteristic, and one which utilitarianism does not claim to define.

But there are theories other than utilitarianism which claim to define 'right.' It would be tedious to try to refute all such theories. With regard to many of them [20] it seems to be enough to ask one's readers whether it is

[16] p. 17 [p. 38 this volume; p. 13 reset edition of *Ethics*].
[17] pp. 44, 54 [pp. 47–48 this volume; p. 29, 35 reset edition of *Ethics*].
[18] p. 43 [p. 47 this volume; p. 28 reset edition of *Ethics*].
[19] p. 173 [p. 107 reset edition of *Ethics*].
[20] e.g. the evolutionary theory which identifies 'right' with 'conducive to life.'

not clear to them on reflection that the proposed definition of 'right' bears in fact no resemblance to what they mean by 'right.' But there is one group of theories to which some reference should be made, *viz.* those that give what may be called a subjective theory of 'right,' that identify the rightness of an act with its tendency to produce either some feeling or some opinion in the mind of some one who contemplates it. This type of theory has been dealt with very thoroughly by Professor Moore,[21] and I should have little or nothing to add to his convincing refutation. But such theories are perhaps even more prevalent with regard to 'good' than to 'right,' and in my fourth chapter I discuss them at some length. I would ask my readers to read the argument there offered, and to reflect whether the refutation I offer [22] of subjective accounts of 'good' does not apply with equal force to subjective accounts of 'right.'

Any one who is satisfied that neither the subjective theories of the meaning of 'right,' nor what is far the most attractive of the attempts to reduce it to simpler objective elements, is correct, will probably be prepared to agree that 'right' is an irreducible notion.

Nor is this result impugned by inquiries into the historical development of our present moral notions from an earlier state of things in which 'what is right' was hardly disentangled from 'what the tribe ordains.' The point is that we can now see clearly that 'right' does not mean 'ordained by any given society.' And it may be doubted whether even primitive men thought that it did. Their thoughts about what in particular was right were to a large extent limited by the customs and sanctions of their race and age. But this is not the same as to say that they thought that 'right' just meant 'what my race and age ordains.' Moral progress has been possible just because there have been men in all ages who have seen the difference and have practised, or at least preached, a morality in some respects higher than that of their race and age. And even the supporters of the lower morality held, we may suspect, that their laws and customs were in accordance with a 'right' other than themselves. 'It is the custom' has been accompanied by 'the custom is right,' or 'the custom is ordained by some one who has the right to command.' And if human consciousness is continuous, by descent, with a lower consciousness which had no notion of right at all, that need not make us doubt that the notion is an ultimate and irreducible one, or that the rightness (*prima facie*) [23] of certain types of act is self-evident; for the nature of the self-evident is not to be evident to every mind however undeveloped, but to be apprehended directly by minds which have reached a certain degree of maturity, and for minds to reach the necessary degree of maturity the development that takes place from generation to generation is as much needed as that which takes place from infancy to adult life.

[21] *Ethics*, Chs. 3, 4.
[22] pp. 80–104.
[23] For this qualification cf. pp. 19–20 [pp. 176–7 this volume].

In this connexion it may be well to refer briefly to a theory which has enjoyed much popularity, particularly in France—the theory of the sociological school of Durkheim and Lévy-Bruhl, which seeks to replace moral philosophy by the 'science des mœurs,' the historical and comparative study of the moral beliefs and practices of mankind. It would be foolish to deny the value of such a study, or the interest of many of the facts it has brought to light with regard to the historical origin of many such beliefs and practices. It has shown with success that many of the most strongly felt repulsions towards certain types of conduct are relics of a bygone system of totems and fetishes, their connexion with which is little suspected by those who feel them. What must be denied is the capacity of any such inquiry to take the place of moral philosophy. The attitude of the sociological school towards the systems of moral belief that they find current in various ages and races is a curiously inconsistent one. On the one hand we are urged to accept an existing code as something analogous to an existing law of nature, something not to be questioned or criticized but to be accepted and conformed to as part of the given scheme of things; and on this side the school is able sincerely to proclaim itself conservative of moral values, and is indeed conservative to the point of advocating the acceptance in full of conventional morality. On the other hand, by showing that any given code is the product partly of bygone superstitions and partly of out-of-date utilities, it is bound to create in the mind of any one who accepts its teaching (as it presupposes in the mind of the teacher) a sceptical attitude towards any and every given code. In fact the analogy which it draws between a moral code and a natural system like the human body (a favourite comparison) is an entirely fallacious one. By analysing the constituents of the human body you do nothing to diminish the reality of the human body as a given fact, and you learn much which will enable you to deal effectively with its diseases. But beliefs have the characteristics which bodies have not, of being true or false, of resting on knowledge or of being the product of wishes, hopes, and fears; and in so far as you can exhibit them as being the product of purely psychological and nonlogical causes of this sort, while you leave intact the fact that many people hold such opinions you remove their authority and their claim to be carried out in practice.

It is often said, in criticism of views such as those of the sociological school, that the question of the validity of a moral code is quite independent of the question of its origin. This does not seem to me to be true. An inquiry into the origin of a judgement may have the effect of establishing its validity. Take, for instance, the judgement that the angles of a triangle are equal to two right angles. We find that the historical origin of this judgement lies in certain pre-existing judgements which are its premisses, plus the exercise of a certain activity of inferring. Now if we find that these pre-existing judgements were really instances of knowing, and that the inferring was also really knowing—was the apprehension of a necessary connexion—our inquiry into the origin of the judgement in question will have established its validity. On the other hand, if any one can show that *A* holds actions of type *B* to be wrong simply because (for instance) he knows such actions to be forbidden by the society he lives in, he shows that *A* has no real reason for believing that such actions have the specific quality of wrongness, since between being forbidden by the community and being wrong there is no necessary connexion. He does not, indeed, show the belief to be untrue, but he shows that *A* has no sufficient reason for holding it true; and in this sense he undermines its validity.

This is, in principle, what the sociological school attempts to do. According to this school, or rather according to its principles if consistently carried out, no one moral code is any truer, any nearer to the apprehension of an objective moral truth, than any other; each is simply the code that is necessitated by the conditions of its time and place, and is that which most completely conduces to the preservation of the society that accepts it. But the human mind will not rest content with such a view. It is not in the least bound to say that there has been constant progress in morality, or in moral belief. But it is competent to see that the moral code of one race or age is in certain respects inferior to that of another. It has in fact an *a priori* insight into certain broad principles of morality, and it can distinguish between a more and a less adequate recognition of these principles. There are not merely so many moral codes which can be described and whose vagaries can be traced to historical causes; there is a system of moral truth, as objective as all truth must be, which, and whose implications, we are interested in discovering; and from the point of view of this, the genuinely ethical problem, the sociological inquiry is simply beside the mark. It does not touch the questions to which we most desire answers.[24]

[24] For a lucid and up to a point appreciative account of the sociological school, and a penetrating criticism of its deficiencies, see ch. 2 of M. D. Parodi's *Le Problème Moral et la Pensée Contemporaine*.

What Makes Right Acts Right? *

SIR DAVID ROSS

THE REAL POINT at issue between hedonism and utilitarianism on the one hand and their opponents on the other is not whether 'right' means 'productive of so and so'; for it cannot with any plausibility be maintained that it does. The point at issue is that to which we now pass, *viz.* whether there is any general character which makes right acts right, and if so, what it is. Among the main historical attempts to state a single characteristic of all right actions which is the foundation of their rightness are those made by egoism and utilitarianism. But I do not propose to discuss these, not because the subject is unimportant, but because it has been dealt with so often and so well already, and because there has come to be so much agreement among moral philosophers that neither of these theories is satisfactory. A much more attractive theory has been put forward by Professor Moore: that what makes actions right is that they are productive of more *good* than could have been produced by any other action open to the agent.[1]

This theory is in fact the culmination of all the attempts to base rightness on productivity of some sort of result. The first form this attempt takes is the attempt to base rightness on conduciveness to the advantage or pleasure of the agent. This theory comes to grief over the fact, which stares us in the face, that a great part of duty consists in an observance of the rights and a furtherance of the interests of others, whatever the cost to ourselves may be. Plato and others may be right in holding that a regard for the rights of others never in the long run involves a loss of happiness for the agent, that 'the just life profits a man.' But this, even if true, is irrelevant to the rightness of the act. As soon as a man does an action *because* he thinks he will promote his own interests thereby, he is acting not from a sense of its rightness but from self-interest.

To the egoistic theory hedonistic utilitarianism supplies a much-needed amendment. It points out correctly that the fact that a certain pleasure will be enjoyed by the agent is no reason why he *ought* to bring it into being rather than an equal or greater pleasure to be enjoyed by another, though,

* Chapter II of *The Right and the Good*, reprinted by kind permission of the author and the publisher, The Clarendon Press, 1930.

[1] I take the theory which, as I have tried to show, seems to be put forward in *Ethics* rather than the earlier and less plausible theory put forward in *Principia Ethica*. For the difference, cf. my pp. 8–11 [pp. 168–170 this volume].

human nature being what it is, it makes it not unlikely that he *will* try to bring it into being. But hedonistic utilitarianism in its turn needs a correction. On reflection it seems clear that pleasure is not the only thing in life that we think good in itself, that for instance we think the possession of a good character, or an intelligent understanding of the world, as good or better. A great advance is made by the substitution of 'productive of the greatest good' for 'productive of the greatest pleasure.'

Not only is this theory more attractive than hedonistic utilitarianism, but its logical relation to that theory is such that the latter could not be true unless *it* were true, while it might be true though hedonistic utilitarianism were not. It is in fact one of the logical bases of hedonistic utilitarianism. For the view that what produces the maximum pleasure is right has for its bases the views (1) that what produces the maximum good is right, and (2) that pleasure is the only thing good in itself. If they were not assuming that what produces the maximum *good* is right, the utilitarians' attempt to show that pleasure is the only thing good in itself, which is in fact the point they take most pains to establish, would have been quite irrelevant to their attempt to prove that only what produces the maximum *pleasure* is right. If, therefore, it can be shown that productivity of the maximum good is not what makes all right actions right, we shall *a fortiori* have refuted hedonistic utilitarianism.

When a plain man fulfils a promise because he thinks he ought to do so, it seems clear that he does so with no thought of its total consequences, still less with any opinion that these are likely to be the best possible. He thinks in fact much more of the past than of the future. What makes him think it right to act in a certain way is the fact that he has promised to do so—that and, usually, nothing more. That his act will produce the best possible consequences is not his reason for calling it right. What lends colour to the theory we are examining, then, is not the actions (which form probably a great majority of our actions) in which some such reflection as 'I have promised' is the only reason we give ourselves for thinking a certain action right, but the exceptional cases in which the consequences of fulfilling a promise (for instance) would be so disastrous to others that we judge it right not to do so. It must of course be admitted that such cases exist. If I have promised to meet a friend at a particular time for some trivial purpose, I should certainly think myself justified in breaking my engagement if by doing so I could prevent a serious accident or bring relief to the victims of one. And the supporters of the view we are examining hold that my thinking so is due to my thinking that I shall bring more good into existence by the one action than by the other. A different account may, however, be given of the matter, an account which will, I believe, show itself to be the true one. It may be said that besides the duty of fulfilling promises I have and recognize a duty of relieving distress,[2] and that

---

[2] These are not strictly speaking duties, but things that tend to be our duty, or *prima facie* duties. Cf. pp. 19–20 [pp. 176–7 this volume].

when I think it right to do the latter at the cost of not doing the former, it is not because I think I shall produce more good thereby but because I think it the duty which is in the circumstances more of a duty. This account surely corresponds much more closely with what we really think in such a situation. If, so far as I can see, I could bring equal amounts of good into being by fulfilling my promise and by helping some one to whom I had made no promise, I should not hesitate to regard the former as my duty. Yet on the view that what is right is right because it is productive of the most good I should not so regard it.

There are two theories, each in its way simple, that offer a solution of such cases of conscience. One is the view of Kant, that there are certain duties of perfect obligation, such as those of fulfilling promises, of paying debts, of telling the truth, which admit of no exception whatever in favour of duties of imperfect obligation, such as that of relieving distress. The other is the view of, for instance, Professor Moore and Dr. Rashdall, that there is only the duty of producing good, and that all 'conflicts of duties' should be resolved by asking 'by which action will most good be produced?' But it is more important that our theory fit the facts than that it be simple, and the account we have given above corresponds (it seems to me) better than either of the simpler theories with what we really think, *viz.* that normally promise-keeping, for example, should come before benevolence, but that when and only when the good to be produced by the benevolent act is very great and the promise comparatively trivial, the act of benevolence becomes our duty.

In fact the theory of 'ideal utilitarianism,' if I may for brevity refer so to the theory of Professor Moore, seems to simplify unduly our relations to our fellows. It says, in effect, that the only morally significant relation in which my neighbours stand to me is that of being possible beneficiaries by my action.[3] They do stand in this relation to me, and this relation is morally significant. But they may also stand to me in the relation of promisee to promiser, of creditor to debtor, of wife to husband, of child to parent, of friend to friend, of fellow countryman to fellow countryman, and the like; and each of these relations is the foundation of a *prima facie* duty, which is more or less incumbent on me according to the circumstances of the case. When I am in a situation, as perhaps I always am, in which more than one of these *prima facie* duties is incumbent on me, what I have to do is to study the situation as fully as I can until I form the considered opinion (it is never more) that in the circumstances one of them is more incumbent than any other; then I am bound to think that to do this *prima facie* duty is my duty *sans phrase* in the situation.

I suggest '*prima facie* duty' or 'conditional duty' as a brief way of referring to the characteristic (quite distinct from that of being a duty

---

[3] Some will think it, apart from other considerations, a sufficient refutation of this view to point out that I also stand in that relation to myself, so that for this view the distinction of oneself from others is morally insignificant.

proper) which an act has, in virtue of being of a certain kind (e.g. the keep-ing of a promise), of being an act which would be a duty proper if it were not at the same time of another kind which is morally significant. Whether an act is a duty proper or actual duty depends on *all* the morally significant kinds it is an instance of. The phrase *'prima facie* duty' must be apologized for, since (1) it suggests that what we are speaking of is a certain kind of duty, whereas it is in fact not a duty, but something related in a special way to duty. Strictly speaking, we want not a phrase in which duty is qualified by an adjective, but a separate noun. (2) *'Prima' facie* suggests that one is speaking only of an appearance which a moral situation presents at first sight, and which may turn out to be illusory; whereas what I am speaking of is an objective fact involved in the nature of the situation, or more strictly in an element of its nature, though not, as duty proper does, arising from its *whole* nature. I can, however, think of no term which fully meets the case. 'Claim' has been suggested by Professor Prichard. The word 'claim' has the advantage of being quite a familiar one in this connexion, and it seems to cover much of the ground. It would be quite natural to say, 'a person to whom I have made a promise has a claim on me,' and also, 'a person whose distress I could relieve (at the cost of breaking the promise) has a claim on me.' But (1) while 'claim' is appropriate from *their* point of view, we want a word to express the corresponding fact from the agent's point of view—the fact of his being subject to claims that can be made against him; and ordinary language provides us with no such correlative to 'claim.' And (2) (what is more important) 'claim' seems inevitably to suggest two persons, one of whom might make a claim on the other; and while this covers the ground of social duty, it is inappropriate in the case of that important part of duty which is the duty of cultivating a certain kind of character in oneself. It would be artificial, I think, and at any rate metaphorical, to say that one's character has a claim on oneself.

There is nothing arbitrary about these *prima facie* duties. Each rests on a definite circumstance which cannot seriously be held to be without moral significance. Of *prima facie* duties I suggest, without claiming com-pleteness or finality for it, the following division.[4]

(1) Some duties rest on previous acts of my own. These duties seem to include two kinds, (*a*) those resting on a promise or what may fairly be

---

[4] I should make it plain at this stage that I am *assuming* the correctness of some of our main convictions as to *prima facie* duties, or, more strictly, am claiming that we *know* them to be true. To me it seems as self-evident as anything could be, that to make a promise, for instance, is to create a moral claim on us in someone else. Many readers will perhaps say that they do *not* know this to be true. If so, I certainly cannot prove it to them; I can only ask them to reflect again, in the hope that they will ulti-mately agree that they also know it to be true. The main moral convictions of the plain man seem to me to be, not opinions which it is for philosophy to prove or dis-prove, but knowledge from the start; and in my own case I seem to find little difficulty in distinguishing these essential convictions from other moral convictions which I also have, which are merely fallible opinions based on an imperfect study of the work-ing for good or evil of certain institutions or types of action.

called an implicit promise, such as the implicit undertaking not to tell lies which seems to be implied in the act of entering into conversation (at any rate by civilized men), or of writing books that purport to be history and not fiction. These may be called the duties of fidelity. (*b*) Those resting on a previous wrongful act. These may be called the duties of reparation. (2) Some rest on previous acts of other men, i.e. services done by them to me. These may be loosely described as the duties of gratitude.[5] (3) Some rest on the fact or possibility of a distribution of pleasure or happiness (or of the means thereto) which is not in accordance with the merit of the persons concerned; in such cases there arises a duty to upset or prevent such a distribution. These are the duties of justice. (4) Some rest on the mere fact that there are other beings in the world whose condition we can make better in respect of virtue, or of intelligence, or of pleasure. These are the duties of beneficence. (5) Some rest on the fact that we can improve our own condition in respect of virtue or of intelligence. These are the duties of self-improvement. (6) I think that we should distinguish from (4) the duties that may be summed up under the title of 'not injuring others.' No doubt to injure others is incidentally to fail to do them good; but it seems to me clear that non-maleficence is apprehended as a duty distinct from that of beneficence, and as a duty of a more stringent character. It will be noticed that this alone among the types of duty has been stated in a negative way. An attempt might no doubt be made to state this duty, like the others, in a positive way. It might be said that it is really the duty to prevent ourselves from acting either from an inclination to harm others or from an inclination to seek our own pleasure, in doing which we should incidentally harm them. But on reflection it seems clear that the primary duty here is the duty not to harm others, this being a duty whether or not we have an inclination that if followed would lead to our harming them; and that when we have such an inclination the primary duty not to harm others gives rise to a consequential duty to resist the inclination. The recognition of this duty of non-maleficence is the first step on the way to the recognition of the duty of beneficence; and that accounts for the prominence of the commands 'thou shalt not kill,' 'thou shalt not commit adultery,' 'thou shalt not steal,' 'thou shalt not bear false witness,' in so early a code as the Decalogue. But even when we have come to recognize the duty of beneficence, it appears to me that the duty of non-maleficence is recognized as a distinct one, and as *prima facie* more binding. We should not in general consider it justifiable to kill one person in order to keep another alive, or to steal from one in order to give alms to another.

The essential defect of the 'ideal utilitarian' theory is that it ignores, or at least does not do full justice to, to the highly personal character of duty. If the only duty is to produce the maximum of good, the question who is to have the good—whether it is myself, or my benefactor, or a person to whom I have made a promise to confer that good on him, or a

[5] For a needed correction of this statement, cf. pp. 22–23 [p. 179 this volume].

mere fellow man to whom I stand in no such special relation—should make no difference to my having a duty to produce that good. But we are all in fact sure that it makes a vast difference.

One or two other comments must be made on this provisional list of the divisions of duty. (1) The nomenclature is not strictly correct. For by 'fidelity' or 'gratitude' we mean, strictly, certain states of motivation; and, as I have urged, it is not our duty to have certain motives, but to do certain acts. By 'fidelity,' for instance, is meant, strictly, the disposition to fulfil promises and implicit promises *because we have made them*. We have no general word to cover the actual fulfilment of promises and implicit promises *irrespective of motive;* and I use 'fidelity,' loosely but perhaps conveniently, to fill this gap. So too I use 'gratitude' for the returning of services, irrespective of motive. The term 'justice' is not so much confined, in ordinary usage, to a certain state of motivation, for we should often talk of a man as acting justly even when we did not think his motive was the wish to do what was just simply for the sake of doing so. Less apology is therefore needed for our use of 'justice' in this sense. And I have used the word 'beneficence' rather than 'benevolence,' in order to emphasize the fact that it is our duty to do certain things, and not to do them from certain motives.

(2) If the objection be made, that this catalogue of the main types of duty is an unsystematic one resting on no logical principle, it may be replied, first, that it makes no claim to being ultimate. It is a *prima facie* classification of the duties which reflection on our moral convictions seems actually to reveal. And if these convictions are, as I would claim that they are, of the nature of knowledge, and if I have not misstated them, the list will be a list of authentic conditional duties, correct as far as it goes though not necessarily complete. The list of *goods* put forward by the rival theory is reached by exactly the same method—the only sound one in the circumstances—*viz.* that of direct reflection on what we really think. Loyalty to the facts is worth more than a symmetrical architectonic or a hastily reached simplicity. If further reflection discovers a perfect logical basis for this or for a better classification, so much the better.

(3) It may, again, be objected that our theory that there are these various and often conflicting types of *prima facie* duty leaves us with no principle upon which to discern what is our actual duty in particular circumstances. But this objection is not one which the rival theory is in a position to bring forward. For when we have to choose between the production of two heterogeneous goods, say knowledge and pleasure, the 'ideal utilitarian' theory can only fall back on an opinion, for which no logical basis can be offered, that one of the goods is the greater; and this is no better than a similar opinion that one of two duties is the more urgent. And again, when we consider the infinite variety of the effects of our actions in the way of pleasure, it must surely be admitted that the claim which *hedonism* sometimes makes, that it offers a readily applicable criterion of right conduct, is quite illusory.

I am unwilling, however, to content myself with an *argumentum ad hominem*, and I would contend that in principle there is no reason to anticipate that every act that is our duty is so for one and the same reason. Why should two sets of circumstances, or one set of circumstances, *not* possess different characteristics, any one of which makes a certain act our *prima facie* duty? When I ask what it is that makes me in certain cases sure that I have a *prima facie* duty to do so and so, I find that it lies in the fact that I have made a promise; when I ask the same question in another case, I find the answer lies in the fact that I have done a wrong. And if on reflection I find (as I think I do) that neither of these reasons is reducible to the other, I must not on any *a priori* ground assume that such a reduction is possible.

An attempt may be made to arrange in a more systematic way the main types of duty which we have indicated. In the first place it seems self-evident that if there are things that are intrinsically good, it is *prima facie* a duty to bring them into existence rather than not to do so, and to bring as much of them into existence as possible. It will be argued in our fifth chapter that there are three main things that are intrinsically good—virtue, knowledge, and, with certain limitations, pleasure. And since a given virtuous disposition, for instance, is equally good whether it is realized in myself or in another, it seems to be my duty to bring it into existence whether in myself or in another. So too with a given piece of knowledge.

The case of pleasure is difficult; for while we clearly recognize a duty to produce pleasure for others, it is by no means so clear that we recognize a duty to produce pleasure for ourselves. This appears to arise from the following facts. The thought of an act as our duty is one that presupposes a certain amount of reflection about the act; and for that reason does not normally arise in connexion with acts towards which we are already impelled by another strong impulse. So far, the cause of our not thinking of the promotion of our own pleasure as a duty is analogous to the cause which usually prevents a highly sympathetic person from thinking of the promotion of the pleasure of others as a duty. He is impelled so strongly by direct interest in the well-being of others towards promoting their pleasure that he does not stop to ask whether it is his duty to promote it; and we are all impelled so strongly towards the promotion of our own pleasure that we do not stop to ask whether it is a duty or not. But there is a further reason why even when we stop to think about the matter it does not usually present itself as a duty: *viz.* that, since the performance of most of our duties involves the giving up of some pleasure that we desire, the doing of duty and the getting of pleasure for ourselves come by a natural association of ideas to be thought of as incompatible things. This association of ideas is in the main salutary in its operation, since it puts a check on what but for it would be much too strong, the tendency to pursue one's own pleasure without thought of other considerations. Yet if pleasure is good, it seems in the long run clear that it is right to get it for ourselves as well as to produce it for others, when this does not involve the failure to discharge some more stringent *prima facie* duty. The question is a very difficult one, but it seems that this conclusion can be denied only on one or other of three grounds: (1) that pleasure is not *prima facie* good (i.e. good when it is neither the actualization of a bad disposition nor undeserved), (2) that there is no *prima facie* duty to produce as much that is good as we can, or (3) that though there is a *prima facie* duty to produce other things that are good, there is no *prima facie* duty to produce pleasure which will be enjoyed by ourselves. I give reasons later [6] for not accepting the first contention. The second hardly admits of argument but seems to me plainly false. The third seems plausible only if we hold that an act that is pleasant or brings pleasure to ourselves must for that reason not be a duty; and this would lead to paradoxical consequences, such as that if a man enjoys giving pleasure to others or working for their moral improvement, it cannot be his duty to do so. Yet it seems to be a very stubborn fact, that in our ordinary consciousness we are not aware of a duty to get pleasure for ourselves; and by way of partial explanation of this I may add that though, as I think, one's own pleasure is a good and there is a duty to produce it, it is only if we *think* of our own pleasure not as simply our own pleasure, but as an objective good, something that an impartial spectator would approve, that we can think of the getting it as a duty; and we do not habitually think of it in this way.

If these contentions are right, what we have called the duty of beneficence and the duty of self-improvement rest on the same ground. No different principles of duty are involved in the two cases. If we feel a special responsibility for improving our own character rather than that of others, it is not because a special principle is involved, but because we are aware that the one is more under our control than the other. It was on this ground that Kant expressed the practical law of duty in the form 'seek to make yourself good and other people happy.' He was so persuaded of the internality of virtue that he regarded any attempt by one person to produce virtue in another as bound to produce, at most, only a counterfeit of virtue, the doing of externally right acts not from the true principle of virtuous action but out of regard to another person. It must be admitted that one man cannot compel another to be virtuous; compulsory virtue would just not be virtue. But experience clearly shows that Kant overshoots the mark when he contends that one man cannot do anything to *promote* virtue in another, to bring such influences to bear upon him that his own response to them is more likely to be virtuous than his response to other influences would have been. And our duty to do this is not different in kind from our duty to improve our own characters.

It is equally clear, and clear at an earlier stage of moral development, that if there are things that are bad in themselves we ought, *prima facie*,

[6] pp. 135-8.

not to bring them upon others; and on this fact rests the duty of non-maleficence.

The duty of justice is particularly complicated, and the word is used to cover things which are really very different—things such as the payment of debts, the reparation of injuries done by oneself to another, and the bringing about of a distribution of happiness between other people in proportion to merit. I use the word to denote only the last of these three. In the fifth chapter I shall try to show that besides the three (comparatively) simple goods, virtue, knowledge, and pleasure, there is a more complex good, not reducible to these, consisting in the proportionment of happiness to virtue. The bringing of this about is a duty which we owe to all men alike, though it may be reinforced by special responsibilities that we have undertaken to particular men. This, therefore, with beneficence and self-improvement, comes under the general principle that we should produce as much good as possible, though the good here involved is different in kind from any other.

But besides this general obligation, there are special obligations. These may arise, in the first place, incidentally, from acts which were not essentially meant to create such an obligation, but which nevertheless create it. From the nature of the case such acts may be of two kinds—the infliction of injuries on others, and the acceptance of benefits from them. It seems clear that these put us under a special obligation to other men, and that only these acts can do so incidentally. From these arise the twin duties of reparation and gratitude.

And finally there are special obligations arising from acts the very intention of which, when they were done, was to put us under such an obligation. The name for such acts is 'promises'; the name is wide enough if we are willing to include under it implicit promises, i.e. modes of behaviour in which without explicit verbal promise we intentionally create an expectation that we can be counted on to behave in a certain way in the interest of another person.

These seem to be, in principle, all the ways in which *prima facie* duties arise. In actual experience they are compounded together in highly complex ways. Thus, for example, the duty of obeying the laws of one's country arises partly (as Socrates contends in the *Crito*) from the duty of gratitude for the benefits one has received from it; partly from the implicit promise to obey which seems to be involved in permanent residence in a country whose laws we know we are *expected* to obey, and still more clearly involved when we ourselves invoke the protection of its laws (this is the truth underlying the doctrine of the social contract); and partly (if we are fortunate in our country) from the fact that its laws are potent instruments for the general good.

Or again, the sense of a general obligation to bring about (so far as we can) a just apportionment of happiness to merit is often greatly reinforced by the fact that many of the existing injustices are due to a social and economic system which we have, not indeed created, but taken part in and assented to; the duty of justice is then reinforced by the duty of reparation.

It is necessary to say something by way of clearing up the relation between *prima facie* duties and the actual or absolute duty to do one particular act in particular circumstances. If, as almost all moralists except Kant are agreed, and as most plain men think, it is sometimes right to tell a lie or to break a promise, it must be maintained that there is a difference between *prima facie* duty and actual or absolute duty. When we think ourselves justified in breaking, and indeed morally obliged to break, a promise in order to relieve some one's distress, we do not for a moment cease to recognize a *prima facie* duty to keep our promise, and this leads us to feel, not indeed shame or repentance, but certainly compunction, for behaving as we do; we recognize, further, that it is our duty to make up somehow to the promisee for the breaking of the promise. We have to distinguish from the characteristic of being our duty that of tending to be our duty. Any act that we do contains various elements in virtue of which it falls under various categories. In virtue of being the breaking of a promise, for instance, it tends to be wrong; in virtue of being an instance of relieving distress it tends to be right. Tendency to be one's duty may be called a parti-resultant attribute, i.e. one which belongs to an act in virtue of some one component in its nature. *Being* one's duty is a toti-resultant attribute, one which belongs to an act in virtue of its whole nature and of nothing less than this.[7] This distinction between parti-resultant and toti-resultant attributes is one which we shall meet in another context also.[8]

Another instance of the same distinction may be found in the operation of natural laws. *Qua* subject to the force of gravitation towards some other body, each body tends to move in a particular direction with a particular velocity; but its actual movement depends on *all* the forces to which it is subject. It is only by recognizing this distinction that we can preserve the absoluteness of laws of nature, and only by recognizing a corresponding distinction that we can preserve the absoluteness of the general principles of morality. But an important difference between the two cases must be pointed out. When we say that in virtue of gravitation a body tends to move in a certain way, we are referring to a causal influence actually exercised on it by another body or other bodies. When we say that in virtue of being deliberately untrue a certain remark tends to be wrong, we are referring to no causal relation, to no relation that involves succession in time, but to such a relation as connects the various attributes of a mathematical figure. And if the word 'tendency' is thought to suggest too much a causal relation, it is better to talk of certain types of act as being *prima facie* right or wrong (or of different persons as having different and possibly conflicting claims upon us), than of their tending to be right or wrong.

[7] But cf. the qualification in p. 33, n. 2 [p. 186, n. 10 this volume].
[8] Cf. pp. 122–3.

Something should be said of the relation between our apprehension of the *prima facie* rightness of certain types of act and our mental attitude towards particular acts. It is proper to use the word 'apprehension' in the former case and not in the latter. That an act, *qua* fulfilling a promise, or *qua* effecting a just distribution of good, or *qua* returning services rendered, or *qua* promoting the good of others, or *qua* promoting the virtue or insight of the agent, is *prima facie* right, is self-evident; not in the sense that it is evident from the beginning of our lives, or as soon as we attend to the proposition for the first time, but in the sense that when we have reached sufficient mental maturity and have given sufficient attention to the proposition it is evident without any need of proof, or of evidence beyond itself. It is self-evident just as a mathematical axiom, or the validity of a form of inference, is evident. The moral order expressed in these propositions is just as much part of the fundamental nature of the universe (and, we may add, of any possible universe in which there were moral agents at all) as is the spatial or numerical structure expressed in the axioms of geometry or arithmetic. In our confidence that these propositions are true there is involved the same trust in our reason that is involved in our confidence in mathematics; and we should have no justification for trusting it in the latter sphere and distrusting it in the former. In both cases we are dealing with propositions that cannot be proved, but that just as certainly need no proof.

Some of these general principles of *prima facie* duty may appear to be open to criticism. It may be thought, for example, that the principle of returning good for good is a falling off from the Christian principle, generally and rightly recognized as expressing the highest morality, of returning good for evil. To this it may be replied that I do not suggest that there is a principle commanding us to return good for good and forbidding us to return good for evil, and that I do suggest that there is a positive duty to seek the good of all men. What I maintain is that an act in which good is returned for good is recognized as *specially* binding on us just because it is of that character, and that *ceteris paribus* any one would think it his duty to help his benefactors rather than his enemies, if he could not do both; just as it is generally recognized that *ceteris paribus* we should pay our debts rather than give our money in charity, when we cannot do both. A benefactor is not only a man, calling for our effort on his behalf on that ground, but also our benefactor, calling for our *special* effort on *that* ground.

Our judgements about our actual duty in concrete situations have none of the certainty that attaches to our recognition of the general principles of duty. A statement is certain, i.e. is an expression of knowledge, only in one or other of two cases: when it is either self-evident, or a valid conclusion from self-evident premisses. And our judgements about our particular duties have neither of these characters. (1) They are not self-evident. Where a possible act is seen to have two characteristics, in virtue of one of which it is *prima facie* right, and in virtue of the other *prima facie* wrong, we are (I think) well aware that we are not certain whether we ought or ought not to do it; that whether we do it or not, we are taking a moral risk. We come in the long run, after consideration, to think one duty more pressing than the other, but we do not feel certain that it is so. And though we do not always recognize that a possible act has two such characteristics, and though there *may* be cases in which it has not, we are never certain that any particular possible act has not, and therefore never certain that it is right, nor certain that it is wrong. For, to go no further in the analysis, it is enough to point out that any particular act will in all probability in the course of time contribute to the bringing about of good or of evil for many human beings, and thus have a *prima facie* rightness or wrongness of which we know nothing. (2) Again, our judgements about our particular duties are not logical conclusions from self-evident premisses. The only possible premisses would be the general principles stating their *prima facie* rightness or wrongness *qua* having the different characteristics they do have; and even if we could (as we cannot) apprehend the extent to which an act will tend on the one hand, for example, to bring about advantages for our benefactors, and on the other hand to bring about disadvantages for fellow men who are not our benefactors, there is no principle by which we can draw the conclusion that it is on the whole right or on the whole wrong. In this respect the judgement as to the rightness of a particular act is just like the judgement as to the beauty of a particular natural object or work of art. A poem is, for instance, in respect of certain qualities beautiful and in respect of certain others not beautiful; and our judgement as to the degree of beauty it possesses on the whole is never reached by logical reasoning from the apprehension of its particular beauties or particular defects. Both in this and in the moral case we have more or less probable opinions which are not logically justified conclusions from the general principles that are recognized as self-evident.

There is therefore much truth in the description of the right act as a fortunate act. If we cannot be certain that it is right, it is our good fortune if the act we do is the right act. This consideration does not, however, make the doing of our duty a mere matter of chance. There is a parallel here between the doing of duty and the doing of what will be to our personal advantage. We never *know* what act will in the long run be to our advantage. Yet it is certain that we are more likely in general to secure our advantage if we estimate to the best of our ability the probable tendencies of our actions in this respect, than if we act on caprice. And similarly we are more likely to do our duty if we reflect to the best of our ability on the *prima facie* rightness or wrongness of various possible acts in virtue of the characteristics we perceive them to have, than if we act without reflection. With this greater likelihood we must be content.

Many people would be inclined to say that the right act for me is not that whose general nature I have been describing, viz. that which if I were omniscient I should see to be my duty, but that which on all the evidence available to me I should think to be my duty. But suppose that from the state of partial knowledge in which I think act *A* to be my duty, I could pass to a state of perfect knowledge in which I saw act *B* to be my duty, should I not say 'act *B* was the right act for me to do'? I should no doubt add 'though I am not to be blamed for doing act *A*.' But in adding this, am I not passing from the question 'what is right' to the question 'what is morally good'? At the same time I am not making the *full* passage from the one notion to the other; for in order that the act should be morally good, or an act I am not to be blamed for doing, it must not merely be the act which it is reasonable for me to think my duty; it must also be done for that reason, or from some other morally good motive. Thus the conception of the right act as the act which it is reasonable for me to think my duty is an unsatisfactory compromise between the true notion of the right act and the notion of the morally good action.

The general principles of duty are obviously not self-evident from the beginning of our lives. How do they come to be so? The answer is, that they come to be self-evident to us just as mathematical axioms do. We find by experience that this couple of matches and that couple make four matches, that this couple of balls on a wire and that couple make four balls; and by reflection on these and similar discoveries we come to see that it is of the nature of two and two to make four. In a precisely similar way, we see the *prima facie* rightness of an act which would be the fulfilment of a particular promise, and of another which would be the fulfilment of another promise, and when we have reached sufficient maturity to think in general terms, we apprehend *prima facie* rightness to belong to the nature of any fulfilment of promise. What comes first in time is the apprehension of the self-evident *prima facie* rightness of an individual act of a particular type. From this we come by reflection to apprehend the self-evident general principle of *prima facie* duty. From this, too, perhaps along with the apprehension of the self-evident *prima facie* rightness of the same act in virtue of its having another characteristic as well, and perhaps in spite of the apprehension of its *prima facie* wrongness in virtue of its having some third characteristic, we come to believe something not self-evident at all, but an object of probable opinion, *viz.* that this particular act is (not *prima facie* but) actually right.

In this respect there is an important difference between rightness and mathematical properties. A triangle which is isosceles necessarily has two of its angles equal, whatever other characteristics the triangle may have—whatever, for instance, be its area, or the size of its third angle. The equality of the two angles is a parti-resultant attribute.[9] And the same is true of all mathematical attributes. It is true, I may add, of *prima facie* rightness. But no act is ever, in virtue of falling under some general description, necessarily actually right; its rightness depends on its whole nature[10] and not on any element in it. The reason is that no mathematical

---

[9] Cf. pp. 28 [p. 183 this volume], 122–3.
[10] To avoid complicating unduly the statement of the general view I am putting

object (no figure, for instance, or angle) ever has two characteristics that tend to give it opposite resultant characteristics, while moral acts often (as every one knows) and indeed always (as on reflection we must admit) have different characteristics that tend to make them at the same time *prima facie* right and *prima facie* wrong; there is probably no act, for instance, which does good to any one without doing harm to some one else, and *vice versa*.

Supposing it to be agreed, as I think on reflection it must, that no one *means* by 'right' just 'productive of the best possible consequences,' or 'optimific,' the attributes 'right' and 'optimific' might stand in either of two kinds of relation to each other. (1) They might be so related that we could apprehend a *priori*, either immediately or deductively, that any act that is optimific is right and any act that is right is optimific, as we can apprehend that any triangle that is equilateral is equiangular and *vice versa*. Professor Moore's view is, I think, that the coexistensiveness of 'right' and 'optimific' is apprehended immediately.[11] He rejects the possibility of any proof of it. Or (2) the two attributes might be such that the question whether they are invariably connected had to be answered by means of an inductive inquiry. Now at first sight it might seem as if the constant connexion of the two attributes could be immediately apprehended. It might seem absurd to suggest that it could be right for any one to do an act which would produce consequences less good than those which would be produced by some other act in his power. Yet a little thought will convince us that this is not absurd. The type of case in which it is easier to see that this is so is, perhaps, that in which one has made a promise. In such a case we all think that *prima facie* it is our duty to fulfil the promise irrespective of the precise goodness of the total consequences. And though we do not think it is necessarily our actual or absolute duty to do so, we are far from thinking that any, even the slightest, gain in the value of the total consequences will necessarily justify us in doing something else instead. Suppose, to simplify the case by abstraction, that the fulfilment of a promise to A would produce 1,000 units of good [12] for him, but that by doing some other act I could produce 1,001 units of good for B, to whom I have made no promise, the other consequences of the two acts being of equal value; should we really think it self-evident that it was our duty to do the second act and not the first? I think not. We

---

forward, I have here rather overstated it. Any act is the origination of a great variety of things many of which make no difference to its rightness or wrongness. But there are always many elements in its nature (i.e. in what it is the origination of) that make a difference to its rightness or wrongness, and no element in its nature can be dismissed without consideration as indifferent.

[11] *Ethics*, 181.

[12] I am assuming that good is objectively quantitative (cf. pp. 142–4), but not that we can accurately assign an exact quantitative measure to it. Since it is of a definite amount, we can make the *supposition* that its amount is so-and-so, though we cannot with any confidence *assert* that it is.

should, I fancy, hold that only a much greater disparity of value between the total consequences would justify us in failing to discharge our *prima facie* duty to *A*. After all, a promise is a promise, and is not to be treated so lightly as the theory we are examining would imply. What, exactly, a promise is, is not so easy to determine, but we are surely agreed that it constitutes a serious moral limitation to our freedom of action. To produce the 1,001 units of good for *B* rather than fulfil our promise to *A* would be to take, not perhaps our duty as philanthropists too seriously, but certainly our duty as makers of promises too lightly.

Or consider another phase of the same problem. If I have promised to confer on *A* a particular benefit containing 1,000 units of good, is it self-evident that if by doing some different act I could produce 1,001 units of good for *A* himself (the other consequences of the two acts being supposed equal in value), it would be right for me to do so? Again, I think not. Apart from my general *prima facie* duty to do *A* what good I can, I have another *prima facie* duty to do him the particular service I have promised to do him, and this is not to be set aside in consequence of a disparity of good of the order of 1,001 to 1,000, though a much greater disparity might justify me in so doing.

Or again, suppose that *A* is a very good and *B* a very bad man, should I then, even when I have made no promise, think it self-evidently right to produce 1,001 units of good for *B* rather than 1,000 for *A*? Surely not. I should be sensible of a *prima facie* duty of justice, i.e. of producing a distribution of goods in proportion to merit, which is not outweighed by such a slight disparity in the total goods to be produced.

Such instances—and they might easily be added to—make it clear that there is no self-evident connexion between the attributes 'right' and 'optimific.' The theory we are examining has a certain attractiveness when applied to our decision that a particular act is our duty (though I have tried to show that it does not agree with our actual moral judgements even here). But it is not even possible when applied to our recognition of *prima facie* duty. For if it were self-evident that the right coincides with the optimific, it should be self-evident that what is *prima facie* right is *prima facie* optimific. But whereas we are certain that keeping a promise is *prima facie* right, we are not certain that it is *prima facie* optimific (though we are perhaps certain that it is *prima facie* bonific). Our certainty that it is *prima facie* right depends not on its consequences but on its being the fulfilment of a promise. The theory we are examining involves too much difference between the evident ground of our conviction about *prima facie* duty and the alleged ground of our conviction about actual duty.

The coextensiveness of the right and the optimific is, then, not self-evident. And I can see no way of proving it deductively; nor, so far as I know, has any one tried to do so. There remains the question whether it can be established inductively. Such an inquiry, to be conclusive, would have to be very thorough and extensive. We should have to take a large variety of the acts which we, to the best of our ability, judge to be right. We should have to trace as far as possible their consequences, not only for the persons directly affected but also for those indirectly affected, and to these no limit can be set. To make our inquiry thoroughly conclusive, we should have to do what we cannot do, *viz.* trace these consequences into an unending future. And even to make it reasonably conclusive, we should have to trace them far into the future. It is clear that the most we could possibly say is that a large variety of typical acts that are judged right appear, so far as we can trace their consequences, to produce more good than any other acts possible to the agents in the circumstances. And such a result falls far short of proving the constant connexion of the two attributes. But it is surely clear that no inductive inquiry justifying even this result has ever been carried through. The advocates of utilitarian systems have been so much persuaded either of the identity or of the self-evident connexion of the attributes 'right' and 'optimific' (or 'felicific') that they have not attempted even such an inductive inquiry as is possible. And in view of the enormous complexity of the task and the inevitable inconclusiveness of the result, it is worth no one's while to make the attempt. What, after all, would be gained by it? If, as I have tried to show, for an act to be right and to be optimific are not the same thing, and an act's being optimific is not even the ground of its being right, then if we could ask ourselves (though the question is really unmeaning) which we ought to do, right acts because they are right or optimific acts because they are optimific, our answer must be 'the former.' If they are optimific as well as right, that is interesting but not morally important; if not, we still ought to do them (which is only another way of saying that they *are* the right acts), and the question whether they are optimific has no importance for moral theory.

There is one direction in which a fairly serious attempt has been made to show the connexion of the attributes 'right' and 'optimific.' One of the most evident facts of our moral consciousness is the sense which we have of the sanctity of promises, a sense which does not, on the face of it, involve the thought that one will be bringing more good into existence by fulfilling the promise than by breaking it. It is plain, I think, that in our normal thought we consider that the fact that we have made a promise is in itself sufficient to create a duty of keeping it, the sense of duty resting on remembrance of the past promise and not on thoughts of the future consequences of its fulfilment. Utilitarianism tries to show that this is not so, that the sanctity of promises rests on the good consequences of the fulfilment of them and the bad consequences of their non-fulfilment. It does so in this way: it points out that when you break a promise you not only fail to confer a certain advantage on your promisee but you diminish his confidence, and indirectly the confidence of others, in the fulfilment of promises. You thus strike a blow at one of the devices that have been found most useful in the relations between man and man—

the device on which, for example, the whole system of commercial credit rests—and you tend to bring about a state of things wherein each man, being entirely unable to rely on the keeping of promises by others, will have to do everything for himself, to the enormous impoverishment of human well-being.

To put the matter otherwise, utilitarians say that when a promise ought to be kept it is because the total good to be produced by keeping it is greater than the total good to be produced by breaking it, the former including as its main element the maintenance and strengthening of general mutual confidence, and the latter being greatly diminished by a weakening of this confidence. They say, in fact, that the case I put some pages back [13] never arises—the case in which by fulfilling a promise shall bring into being 1,000 units of good for my promisee, and by breaking it 1,001 units of good for some one else, the other effects of the two acts being of equal value. The other effects, they say, never are of equal value. By keeping my promise I am helping to strengthen the system of mutual confidence; by breaking it I am helping to weaken this; so that really the first act produces $1,000 + x$ units of good, and the second $1,001 - y$ units, and the difference between $+ x$ and $- y$ is enough to outweigh the slight superiority in the *immediate* effects of the second act. In answer to this it may be pointed out that there must be *some* amount of good that exceeds the difference between $+ x$ and $- y$ (i.e. exceeds $x + y$); say, $x + y + z$. Let us suppose the *immediate* good effects of the second act to be assessed not at 1,001 but at $1,000 + x + y + z$. Then its *net* good effects are $1,000 + x + z$, i.e. greater than those of the fulfilment of the promise; and the utilitarian is bound to say forthwith that the promise should be broken. Now, we may ask whether that is really the way we think about promises? Do we really think that the production of the slightest balance of good, no matter who will enjoy it, by the breach of a promise frees us from the obligation to keep our promise? We need not doubt that a system by which promises are made and kept is one that has great advantages for the general well-being. But that is not the whole truth. To make a promise is not merely to adapt an ingenious device for promoting the general well-being; it is to put oneself in a new relation to one person in particular, a relation which creates a specifically new *prima facie* duty to him, not reducible to the duty of promoting the general well-being of society. By all means let us try to foresee the net good effects of keeping one's promise and the net good effects of breaking it, but even if we assess the first at $1,000 + x$ and the second at $1,000 + x + z$, the question still remains whether it is not our duty to fulfil the promise. It may be suspected, too, that the effect of a single keeping or breaking of a promise in strengthening or weakening the fabric of mutual confidence is greatly exaggerated by the theory we are examining. And if we suppose two men dying together alone, do we think that the duty of one to fulfil before he dies a promise he has made to

[13] p. 34 [p. 187 this volume].

the other would be extinguished by the fact that neither act would have any effect on the general confidence? Any one who holds this may be suspected of not having reflected on what a promise is.

I conclude that the attributes 'right' and 'optimific' are not identical, and that we do not know either by intuition, by deduction, or by induction that they coincide in their application, still less that the latter is the foundation of the former. It must be added, however, that if we are ever under no special obligation such as that of fidelity to a promisee or of gratitude to a benefactor, we ought to do what will produce most good; and that even when we are under a special obligation the tendency of acts to promote general good is one of the main factors in determining whether they are right.

In what has preceded, a good deal of use has been made of 'what we really think' about moral questions; a certain theory has been rejected because it does not agree with what we really think. It might be said that this is in principle wrong; that we should not be content to expound what our present moral consciousness tells us but should aim at a criticism of our existing moral consciousness in the light of theory. Now I do not doubt that the moral consciousness of men has in detail undergone a good deal of modification as regards the things we think right, at the hands of moral theory. But if we are told, for instance, that we should give up our view that there is a special obligatoriness attaching to the keeping of promises because it is self-evident that the only duty is to produce as much good as possible, we have to ask ourselves whether we really, when we reflect, *are* convinced that this is self-evident, and whether we really *can* get rid of our view that promise-keeping has a bindingness independent of productiveness of maximum good. In my own experience I find that I cannot, in spite of a very genuine attempt to do so; and I venture to think that most people will find the same, and that just because they cannot lose the sense of special obligation, they cannot accept as self-evident, or even as true, the theory which would require them to do so. In fact it seems, on reflection, self-evident that a promise, simply as such, is something that *prima facie* ought to be kept, and it does *not*, on reflection, seem self-evident that production of maximum good is the only thing that makes an act obligatory. And to ask us to give up at the bidding of a theory our actual apprehension of what is right and what is wrong seems like asking people to repudiate their actual experience of beauty, at the bidding of a theory which says 'only that which satisfies such and such conditions can be beautiful.' If what I have called our actual apprehension is (as I would maintain that it is) truly an apprehension, i.e. an instance of knowledge, the request is nothing less than absurd.

I would maintain, in fact, that what we are apt to describe as 'what we think' about moral questions contains a considerable amount that we do not think but know, and that this forms the standard by reference to which the truth of any moral theory has to be tested, instead of having itself to be tested by reference to any theory. I hope that I have in what precedes indicated what in my view these elements of knowledge are that are involved in our ordinary moral consciousness.

It would be a mistake to found a natural science on 'what we really think,' i.e. on what reasonably thoughtful and well-educated people think about the subjects of the science before they have studied them scientifically. For such opinions are interpretations, and often misinterpretations, of sense-experience; and the man of science must appeal from these to sense-experience itself, which furnishes his real data. In ethics no such appeal is possible. We have no more direct way of access to the facts about rightness and goodness and about what things are right or good, than by thinking about them; the moral convictions of thoughtful and well-educated people are the data of ethics just as sense-perceptions are the data of a natural science. Just as some of the latter have to be rejected as illusory, so have some of the former; but as the latter are rejected only when they are in conflict with other more accurate sense-perceptions, the former are rejected only when they are in conflict with other convictions which stand better the test of reflection. The existing body of moral convictions of the best people is the cumulative product of the moral reflection of many generations, which has developed an extremely delicate power of appreciation of moral distinctions; and this the theorist cannot afford to treat with anything other than the greatest respect. The verdicts of the moral consciousness of the best people are the foundation on which he must build; though he must first compare them with one another and eliminate any contradictions they may contain.

It is worth while to try to state more definitely the nature of the acts that are right. We may try to state first what (if anything) is the universal nature of *all* acts that are right. It is obvious that any of the acts that we do has countless effects, directly or indirectly, on countless people, and the probability is that any act, however right it be, will have adverse effects (though these may be very trivial) on some innocent people. Similarly, any wrong act will probably have beneficial effects on some deserving people. Every act therefore, viewed in some aspects, will be *prima facie* right, and viewed in others, *prima facie* wrong, and right acts can be distinguished from wrong acts only as being those which, of all those possible for the agent in the circumstances, have the greatest balance of *prima facie* rightness, in those respects in which they are *prima facie* right, over their *prima facie* wrongness, in those respects in which they are *prima facie* wrong—*prima facie* rightness and wrongness being understood in the sense previously explained. For the estimation of the comparative stringency of these *prima facie* obligations no general rules can, so far as I can see, be laid down. We can only say that a great deal of stringency belongs to the duties of 'perfect obligation'—the duties of keeping our promises, of repairing wrongs we have done, and of returning the equivalent of services we have received. For the rest, ἐν τῇ αἰσθήσει ἡ κρίσις.[14] This sense of our particular duty in particular circumstances, preceded and informed by the fullest reflection we can bestow on the act in all its bearings, is highly fallible, but it is the only guide we have to our duty.

When we turn to consider the nature of individual right acts, the first point to which attention should be called is that any act may be correctly described in an indefinite, and in principle infinite, number of ways. An act is the production of a change in the state of affairs (if we ignore, for simplicity's sake, the comparatively few cases in which it is the maintenance of an existing state of affairs; cases which, I think, raise no special difficulty). Now the only changes we can *directly* produce are changes in our own bodies or in our own minds. But these are not, as such, what as a rule we think it our duty to produce. Consider some comparatively simple act, such as telling the truth or fulfilling a promise. In the first case what I produce directly is movements of my vocal organs. But what I think it my duty to produce is a true view in some one else's mind about some fact, and between my movement of my vocal organs and this result there intervenes a series of physical events and events in his mind. Again, in the second case, I may have promised, for instance, to return a book to a friend. I may be able, by a series of movements of my legs and hands, to place it in his hands. But what I am just as likely to do, and to think I have done my duty in doing, is to send it by a messenger or to hand it to his servant or to send it by post; and in each of these cases what I *do* directly is worthless in itself and is connected by a series of intermediate links with what I do think it is my duty to bring about, *viz.* his receiving what I have promised to return to him. This being so, it *seems* as if what I *do* has no obligatoriness in itself and as if one or other of three accounts should be given of the matter, each of which makes rightness not belong to what I do, considered in its own nature.

(1) One of them would be that what is obligatory is not *doing* anything in the natural sense of producing any change in the state of affairs, but *aiming at* something—at, for instance, my friend's reception of the book. But this account will not do. For (*a*) to aim at something is to act from a motive consisting of the wish to bring that thing about. But we have seen [15] that motive never forms part of the content of our duty; if anything is certain about morals, that, I think, is certain. And (*b*) if I have promised to return the book to my friend, I obviously do not fulfil my promise and do my duty merely by aiming at his receiving the book; I must see that he actually receives it. (2) A more plausible account is that which says I must do that which is likely to produce the result. But this account is open to the second of these objections, and probably also to the first. For in the first place, however likely my act may seem, even on careful

---

[14] 'The decision rests with perception.' Arist. *Nic. Eth.* 1109 b 23, 1126 b 4.
[15] pp. 5–6 [pp. 165–7 this volume].

consideration, and even however likely it may in fact be, to produce the result, if it does not produce it I have not done what I promised to do, i.e. have not done my duty. And secondly, when it is said that I ought to do what is likely to produce the result, what is *probably* meant is that I ought to do a certain thing as a result of the wish to produce a certain result, and of the thought that my act is likely to produce it; and this again introduces motive into the content of duty. (3) Much the most plausible of the three accounts is that which says, 'I ought to do that which will actually produce a certain result.' This escapes objection (*b*). Whether it escapes objection (*a*) or not depends on what exactly is meant. If it is meant that I ought to do a certain thing from the wish to produce a certain result and the thought that it will do so, the account is still open to objection (*a*). But if it is meant simply that I ought to do a certain thing, and that the reason why I ought to do it is that it will produce a certain result, objection (*a*) is avoided. Now this account in its second form is that which utilitarianism gives. It says what is right is certain acts, not certain acts motivated in a certain way; and it says that acts are never right by their own nature but by virtue of the goodness of their actual results. And this account is, I think, clearly nearer the truth than one which makes the rightness of an act depend on the goodness of either the *intended* or the *likely* results.

Nevertheless, this account appears not to be the true one. For it implies that what we consider right or our duty is what we do *directly*. It is this, e.g. the packing up and posting of the book, that derives its moral significance not from its own nature but from its consequences. But this is *not* what we should describe, strictly, as our duty; our duty is to fulfil our promise, i.e. to put the book into our friend's possession. This we consider obligatory in its own nature, just because it is a fulfilment of promise, and not because of *its* consequences. But, it might be replied by the utilitarian, I do not do this; I only do something that leads up to this, and what I do has no moral significance in itself but only because of its consequences. In answer to this, however, we may point out that a cause produces not only its immediate, but also its remote consequences, and the latter no less than the former. I, therefore, not only produce the immediate movements of parts of my body but also my friend's reception of the book, which results from these. Or, if this be objected to on the grounds that I can hardly be said to have produced my friend's reception of the book when I have packed and posted it, owing to the time that has still to elapse before he receives it, and that to say I have produced the result hardly does justice to the part played by the Post Office, we may at least say that I have *secured* my friend's reception of the book. What I do is as truly describable in this way as by saying that it is the packing and posting of a book. (It is equally truly describable in many other ways; e.g. I have provided a few moments' employment for Post Office officials. But this is irrelevant to the argument.) And if we ask ourselves whether it is *qua* the packing and posting of a book, or *qua* the securing of my friend's getting what I have promised to return to him, that my action is right, it is clear that it is in the second capacity that it is right; and in this capacity, the only capacity in which it is right, it is right by its own nature and not because of its consequences.

This account may no doubt be objected to, on the ground that we are ignoring the freedom of will of the other agents—the sorter and the postman, for instance—who are equally responsible for the result. Society, it may be said, is not like a machine, in which event follows event by rigorous necessity. Some one may, for instance, in the exercise of his freedom of will, steal the book on the way. But it is to be observed that I have excluded that case, and any similar case. I am dealing with the case in which I secure my friend's receiving the book; and if he does not receive it I have not secured his receiving it. If on the other hand the book reaches its destination, that alone shows that, the system of things being what it is, the trains by which the book travels and the railway lines along which it travels being such as they are and subject to the laws they are subject to, the postal officials who handle it being such as they are, having the motives they have and being subject to the psychological laws they are subject to, my posting the book was the one further thing which was sufficient to procure my friend's receiving it. If it had not been sufficient, the result would not have followed. The attainment of the result proves the sufficiency of the means. The objection in fact rests on the supposition that there can be unmotived action, i.e. an event without a cause, and may be refuted by reflection on the universality of the law of causation.

It is equally true that non-attainment of the result proves the insufficiency of the means. If the book had been destroyed in a railway accident or stolen by a dishonest postman, that would prove that my immediate act was not sufficient to produce the desired result. We get the curious consequence that however carelessly I pack or dispatch the book, if it comes to hand I have done my duty, and however carefully I have acted, if the book does not come to hand I have not done my duty. Success and failure are the only test, and a sufficient test, of the performance of duty. Of course, I should deserve more praise in the second case than in the first; but that is an entirely different question; we must not mix up the question of right and wrong with that of the morally good and the morally bad. And that our conclusion is not as strange as at first sight it might seem is shown by the fact that if the carelessly dispatched book comes to hand, it is not my duty to send another copy, while if the carefully dispatched book does not come to hand I must send another copy to replace it. In the first case I have not my duty still to do, which shows that I have done it; in the second I have it still to do, which shows that I have not done it.

We have reached the result that my act is right *qua* being an ensuring of one of the particular states of affairs of which it is an ensuring, *viz.*, in the case we have taken, of my friend's receiving the book I have promised to return to him. But this answer requires some correction; for it refers only to the *prima facie* rightness of my act. If to be a fulfilment of promise were a sufficient ground of the rightness of an act, all fulfilments of promises would be right, whereas it seems clear that there are cases in which some other *prima facie* duty overrides the *prima facie* duty of fulfilling a promise. The more correct answer would be that the ground of the actual rightness of the act is that, of all acts possible for the agent in the circumstances, it is that whose *prima facie* rightness in the respects in which it is *prima facie* right most outweighs its *prima facie* wrongness in any respects in which it is *prima facie* wrong. But since its *prima facie* rightness is mainly due to its being a fulfilment of promise, we may call its being so the salient element in the ground of its rightness.

Subject to this qualification, then, it is as being the production (or if we prefer the word, the securing or ensuring) of the reception by my friend of what I have promised him (or in other words as the fulfilment of my promise) that my act is right. It is not right as a packing and posting of a book. The packing and posting of the book is only incidentally right, right only because it is a fulfilment of promise, which is what is directly or essentially right.

Our duty, then, is not to do certain things which will produce certain results. Our acts, at any rate our acts of special obligation, are not right because they will produce certain results—which is the view common to all forms of utilitarianism. To say that is to say that in the case in question what is essentially right is to pack and post a book, whereas what is essentially right is to secure the possession by my friend of what I have promised to return to him. An act is not right because it, being one thing, produces good results different from itself; it is right because it is itself the production of a certain state of affairs. Such production is right in itself, apart from any consequence.

But, it might be said, this analysis applies only to acts of special obligation; the utilitarian account still holds good for the acts in which we are not under a special obligation to any person or set of persons but only under that of augmenting the general good. Now merely to have established that there *are* special obligations to do certain things irrespective of their consequences would be already to have made a considerable breach in the utilitarian walls; for according to utilitarianism there is no such thing, there is only the single obligation to promote the general good. But, further, on reflection it is clear that just as (in the case we have taken) my act is not only the packing and posting of a book but the fulfilling of a promise, and just as it is in the latter capacity and not in the former that it is my duty, so an act whereby I augment the general good is not only, let us say, the writing of a begging letter on behalf of a hospital, but the producing (or ensuring) of whatever good ensues therefrom, and it is in the latter capacity and not in the former that it is right, if it *is* right. That which is right is right not because it is an act, one thing, which will produce another thing, an increase of the general welfare, but because it is itself the producing of an increase in the general welfare. Or, to qualify this in the necessary way, its being the production of an increase in the general welfare is the salient element in the ground of its rightness. Just as before we were led to recognize the *prima facie* rightness of the fulfilment of promises, we are now led to recognize the *prima facie* rightness of promoting the general welfare. In both cases we have to recognize the *intrinsic* rightness of a certain type of act, not depending on its consequences but on its own nature.

APPENDIX I
RIGHTS

A general discussion of right or duty would hardly be complete without some discussion, even if only a brief one, of the closely related subject of rights. It is commonly said that rights and duties are correlative, and it is worth while to inquire whether and, if at all, in what sense this is true. The statement may stand for any one, or any combination, of the following logically independent statements:

(1) A right of A against B implies a duty of B to A.
(2) A duty of B to A implies a right of A against B.
(3) A right of A against B implies a duty of A to B.
(4) A duty of A to B implies a right of A against B.

What is asserted in (1) is that A's having a right to have a certain individual act done to him by B implies a duty for B to do *that* act to A; (2) asserts the converse implication; what is meant by (3) is that A's having a right to have a certain act done to him by B implies a duty for A to do *another* act to B, which act may be either a similar act (as where the right of having the truth told to one implies the duty of telling the truth) or a different sort of act (as where the right to obedience implies the duty of governing well); (4) asserts the converse implication.

Of these four propositions the first appears to be unquestionably true; a right in one being against another is a right to treat or be treated by that other in a certain way, and this plainly implies a duty for the other to behave in a certain way. But there is a certain consideration which throws doubt on the other three propositions. This arises from the fact that we have duties to animals and to infants. The latter case is complicated by the fact that infants, while they are not (so we commonly believe) actual moral agents, are potential moral agents, so that the duty of parents, for instance, to support them may be said to be counterbalanced by a duty which is not incumbent on the infants at the time but will be incumbent on them later, to obey and care for their parents. We had better therefore take the less complicated case of animals, which we commonly suppose not to be even potential moral agents.

It may of course be denied that we have duties to animals. The view held by some writers is that we have duties concerning animals but not to them, the theory being that we have a duty to behave humanely to our fellow men, and that we should behave humanely to animals simply for fear of creating a disposition in ourselves which will make us tend to be cruel to our fellow men. Professor D. G. Ritchie, for instance, implies that we have not a duty to animals except in a sense like that in which the owner of an historic house may be said to have a duty to the house.[16] Now the latter sense is, I suppose, purely metaphorical. We may in a fanciful mood think of a noble house as if it were a conscious being having feelings which we are bound to respect. But we do not really think that it has them. I suppose that the duty of the owner of an historic house is essentially a duty to his contemporaries and to posterity; and he may also think it is a duty to his ancestors. On the other hand, if we think we ought to behave in a certain way to animals, it is out of consideration primarily for *their* feelings that we think we ought to behave so; we do not think of them merely as a practising-ground for virtue. It is because we think their pain a bad thing that we think we should gratuitously cause it. And I suppose that to say we have a duty to so-and-so is the same thing as to say that we have a duty, grounded on facts relating to them, to behave in a certain way towards them.

Now if we have a duty to animals, and they have not a duty to us (which seems clear, since they are not moral agents), the first and last of our four propositions cannot both be true, since (4) implies that a duty of men to animals involves a right of men against animals, and (1) implies that this involves a duty of animals to men, and therefore (4) and (1) together imply that a duty of men to animals involves a duty of animals to men. And since the first proposition is clearly true, the fourth must be false; it cannot be true that a duty of A to B necessarily involves a right of A against B. Similarly, the second and third propositions cannot both be true; for (2) and (3) taken together imply that a duty of men to animals involves a duty of animals to men. But here it is not so clear which of the two propositions is true; for it is not clear whether we should say that though we have a duty to animals they have no right against us, or that though they have a right against us they have no duty to us. If we take the first view, we are implying that in order to have rights, just as much as in order to have duties, it is necessary to be a moral agent. If we take the second view, we are implying that while only moral agents have duties, the possession of a nature capable of feeling pleasure and pain is all that is needed in order to have rights. It is not at all clear which is the true view. On the whole, since we mean by a right something that can be justly claimed, we should probably say that animals have not rights, not because the claim to humane treatment would not be just if it were made, but because they cannot make it. But the doubt which we here find about the application of the term 'rights' is characteristic of the term. There are other

[16] *Natural Rights*, 108.

ways too in which its application is doubtful. Even if we hold that it is our duty not merely to do what is just to others but to promote their welfare beyond what justice requires, it is not at all clear that we should say they have a right to beneficent treatment over and above what is just. We have a tendency to think that not every duty incumbent on one person involves a right in another.

This characteristic of our way of thinking about rights has been fastened upon by theory. Green, for instance, divides the whole region of duty into three parts: (1) moral duties which involve no rights on the other side, (2) obligations involving such rights, both obligations and rights being included in the *jus naturae* and being such as *should* be legally recognized, (3) legal obligations involving legal rights on the other side.[17] He describes the rights in class (2)—what I will for brevity call moral rights—as sharing with legal rights the characteristic of depending for their existence on some form of general recognition. The recognition in the latter case consists in the making of a law; in the former it consists simply in a general state of public opinion. Now it is plainly wrong to describe either legal or moral rights as depending for their existence on their recognition, for to recognize a thing (in the sense in which 'recognize' is here used) is to recognize it as existing already. The promulgation of a law is not the recognition of a legal right, but the creation of it, though it may imply the recognition of an already existing moral right. And to make the existence of a *moral* right depend on its being recognized is equally mistaken. It would imply that slaves, for instance, acquired the moral right to be free only at the moment when a majority of mankind, or of some particular community, formed the opinion that they ought to be free, i.e. when the particular person whose conversion to this view changed a minority into a majority changed his mind. Such a view, of course, cannot be consistently maintained, and we find Green implying in successive sections that social recognition is indispensable to the existence of rights,[18] and that the slave has a right to citizenship though this right is not recognized by society.[19] In the latter passage we see the true Green, the passionate lover of liberty, reacting against the theory of the previous page. Some may think that slavery is not wrong; but every one will admit that there are certain forms of treatment of others which are wrong and which the sufferer has the right to have removed, whether this right is recognized by society or not.

There is, however, to be found in Green another view which is less clearly false. According to this, the existence of a right is made to depend

---

[17] *Principles of Political Obligation*, §§ 10, 11.

[18] 'A claim to which reality is given by social recognition, and thus implicitly a right' (§ 139). Cf. 'This recognition of a power, in some way or other, as that which should be, is always necessary to render it a right' (§ 23). 'Rights are made by recognition. There is no right "but thinking makes it so"' (§ 136).

[19] § 140 implies that the slave's right to citizenship is founded on his possessing a common human consciousness with the citizens of the state.

not on the recognition of *it* but on the recognition of a power in the person in question to seek an end common to all the citizens of a community.[20] This avoids the patent error of making the existence of a right depend on its being recognized to exist. Yet like the former view it makes a moral right depend not on the nature of a given person and his relations to his fellows, but on what people think about them, i.e. on what a majority of the community think about them. But though the existence of *legal* rights depends on the degree of enlightenment of the community, the existence of moral rights plainly does not, but on the nature and relations of the persons concerned.

Green's theory seems to have arisen as follows. He starts his historical survey with Hobbes and Spinoza, both of whom identify right with power. A *legal* right *may* be identified with a certain kind of power; it is the power of getting certain things not by one's own brute force but by the aid of the law. Green seems to have tried to get a theory of moral rights by making a similar amendment of the bare identification of right with power; and he accordingly identifies them with the power of getting certain things not by one's own brute force nor by the aid of the law but by the aid of public opinion; instead of saying, what is surely evident, that a moral right is not a power at all. Yet there are elements in his account which point to a truer theory; e.g. 'a "right" is an ideal attribution ("ideal" in the sense of not being sensibly verifiable).' [21] Now whether a given society recognizes a particular right is, I take it, sensibly verifiable in the sense in which Green here insists that a right is not. What is not sensibly verifiable is whether the society is justified in recognizing the right, and this depends on whether the right is there antecedently to society's recognition of it. Thus the insistence that a right is not sensibly verifiable points to an objective theory of rights; but unfortunately Green follows this clue no farther.

If we eliminate the possibility of holding that animals have rights, by saying that only that which has a moral nature can have a right, our main doubt with regard to the correlation of rights and duties is on the question whether there is a right to beneficence. It is obvious that a man has a right to just treatment, and it is commonly agreed that he has a right to have promises made to him fulfilled; it is less generally agreed that he has a right to beneficent treatment, even when it is admitted that it is our duty to treat him beneficently.

Some would even say that to treat others beneficently is to go beyond our duty. But probably this statement rests on a mere confusion. We usually oppose justice to *benevolence*. But while treating a man justly is commonly understood to mean doing certain things to him (paying our debts to him, and the like), irrespective of the spirit in which we do them, treating him benevolently obviously means doing certain things to him

[20] Cf. e.g. § § 25, 26.
[21] § 38.

from goodwill. And it is rightly felt that there is a great difference between the two things, and it is found natural to say that the one implies,
and the other does not, a right on the other side, and (by some people)
even to say that the one is a duty and the other is not. But if we will distinguish between doing what is just and doing it in the spirit of justice,
and between doing what is beneficent and doing it in the spirit of beneficence, then (in accordance with the principle that it is always acts, and
not acts from a certain motive, that are our duty) it is clear that it is not
our duty to act in the spirit of justice, any more than in the spirit of
beneficence, and that it *is* our duty to do what is beneficent, as it is our
duty to do what is just.

   If we are clear on this point, our main objection to saying that the
other person has a right to beneficence disappears. I do not say that our
whole objection disappears; for there hangs about the notion of a 'right'
the notion of its being not only something which one person should in
decency respect but also something which the other person can in decency
claim, and we feel that there is something indecent in the making of a
claim to beneficence.

   These doubts about the application of the term 'right' appear to
spring from the fact that 'right' (the noun) does not stand for a purely
moral notion. It began, I suppose, by standing for a legal notion, and its
usage has broadened out so as to include certain things that cannot be
claimed at law; but its usage has not yet broadened out so much as to
become completely correlative to duty. Once we start on the process of
broadening it out, however, there seems to be no secure resting-place short
of this.

   Returning now to the four propositions about the correlativity of
duties and rights, it seems that with regard to the second proposition, 'A
duty of B to A implies a right of A against B' (which has latterly been the
subject of our discussion), we should say (1) that this is not true when A
is not a moral agent, and (2) that it is true when A is a moral agent (even if
the duty be the duty of beneficent action). And since our only doubt
about the third proposition, 'A right of A against B implies a duty of A to
B,' arises from our doubt whether animals have not rights, if we agree that
animals have not rights we need not doubt the truth of this proposition.
It is this proposition, above all, that has been maintained by those who have
insisted on the correlativity of rights and duties; for this was maintained
essentially against the belief that men have 'natural rights' in a state of
nature in which they have no duties.

   A further problem, however, awaits us, *viz.* whether a failure to do
one's duty involves a corresponding loss of right. Or rather, as we have
found the meaning of 'rights' more doubtful than that of 'duties,' it will
be more profitable to omit any reference to rights, and put our question
in the form, 'if A fails in his duty to B, does that put an end to B's duty to
A?' In some cases we seem to be clear that this is so. If a tradesman sends

me goods inferior to those I chose in his shop, I am not morally, any more than legally, bound to pay him the full price; I may return the goods and pay nothing, or (with his consent) keep them and pay a lower price. And in general any duty arising out of a contract is cancelled by non-fulfilment of the corresponding duty on the other side. In other cases we are not so clear. It is not so generally agreed, for instance, that if *A* tells lies to *B*, *B* is justified in telling lies to *A*. Two blacks, we say in such a case, do not make a white. Yet the peculiar stringency of the duty of veracity seems to spring from an implicit understanding that language shall be used to convey the real opinions of the speakers, and it would seem that a failure to carry out the understanding on one side makes it no longer binding on the other; and we should have small patience with an habitual liar who insisted on strict veracity in others. It must be admitted that a man who has deceived me has destroyed what would have been the main reason for its being my duty to tell him the truth. But we should probably hesitate to say that by his breach of the implicit understanding my duty to tell him the truth has been entirely destroyed, as by the tradesman's breach of contract my duty to pay him has been destroyed. Various reasons help to account for this. For one thing, it is likely that by deceiving a liar I may indirectly deceive innocent people; for another, the consequences for my own character are likely to be particularly dangerous. But the main reason probably lies elsewhere. Before the contract was made between my tradesman and me, there was no duty incumbent on me of paying him this sum of money. I had a general duty to promote the good of all men, but there was no obvious reason for supposing that this could be best done by transferring this sum of money to him. But even before the implicit undertaking to tell the truth was established I had a duty not to tell lies, since to tell lies is *prima facie* to do a positive injury to another person. Since this duty does not rest on contract, it is not abolished by the breach of contract, and therefore while a person who has been deceived by another is justified in refusing to answer his questions, he is not justified in telling him lies. Yet that this forms only a small part of the stringency of the duty of truthfulness may be inferred from the leniency with which we should judge deceit, in a case in which no implicit undertaking to tell the truth has been established, e.g. when a civilized man deceives a savage whom he has just met for the first time, or *vice versa*, or when one of two savages belonging to different tribes deceives the other. Deceit is much more venial in such a case, because the offender has no reason to suppose that the other is not deceiving, or going to deceive, *him*.

Taking, then, the obvious division between duties arising out of contract and those that arise otherwise, we must say that while the former are cancelled by breach of the contract on the other side, the latter are not cancelled by the bad behaviour of the other person. It would also seem, from a consideration of our actual moral judgements, that the former type of duty is the more stringent of the two.

Now the distinction between the rights corresponding to duties that arise out of contract, and the rights corresponding to other duties, may be quite suitably expressed as a distinction between contractual and natural rights, and the notion of natural rights as a distinct class may thus be vindicated, if it be cut free from the belief which has been so often bound up with it, that there are rights in a state of nature, i.e. in a state in which there are no duties. Such a belief is made possible for Hobbes only by a complete confusion between rights and powers, amounting to an express identification of the two.

APPENDIX II
PUNISHMENT

In connexion with the discussion of rights it is proper to consider a question which has always interested and usually puzzled moralists, and which forms a crucial example for the testing of moral theories—the question of punishment. A utilitarian theory, whether of the hedonistic or of the 'ideal' kind, if it justifies punishment at all, is bound to justify it solely on the ground of the effects it produces. The suffering of pain by the person who is punished is thought to be in itself a bad thing, and the bringing of this bad thing into the world is held to need justification, and to receive it only from the fact that the effects are likely to be so much better than those that would follow his non-punishment as to outweigh the evil of his pain. The effects usually pointed to are those of deterrence and of reformation. In principle, then, the punishment of a guilty person is treated by utilitarians as not different in kind from the imposition of inconvenience, say by quarantine regulations, on innocent individuals for the good of the community. Or again, if a state found to be prevalent some injury to itself or to its members that had not been legislated against, and proceeded to punish the offenders, its action would in principle be justified by utilitarians in the same way as its punishment of offenders against the law is justified by them, *viz.* by the good of the community. No doubt the state would have greater difficulty in justifying its action, for such action would produce bad consequences which the punishment of law-breakers does not. But the difference would be only in degree. Nay more, a government which found some offence against the law prevalent, and in its inability to find the offenders punished innocent people on the strength of manufactured evidence, would still be able to justify its action on the same general principle as before.

Plain men, and even perhaps most people who have reflected on moral questions, are likely to revolt against a theory which involves such consequences, and to exclaim that there is all the difference in the world between such action and the punishment of offenders against the law. They feel the injustice of such action by the state, and are ready to say, in the words imputed to them by Mr. Bradley: 'Punishment is punishment, only when it is deserved. We pay the penalty because we owe it, and for no other reason; and if punishment is inflicted for any other reason whatever than because it is merited by wrong, it is a gross immorality, a crying injustice, an abominable crime, and not what it pretends to be. We may have regard for whatever considerations we please—our own convenience, the good of society, the benefit of the offender; we are fools, and worse, if we fail to do so. Having once the right to punish, we may modify the punishment according to the useful and the pleasant; but these are external to the matter, they cannot give us a right to punish, and nothing can do that but criminal desert.' [22]

There is one form of utilitarian view which differs in an important respect from that above ascribed to utilitarians. Professor Moore admits the possibility, which follows from his doctrine of organic unities, that punishment may not need to be justified merely by its *after*-effects. He points out [23] that it may well be the case that though crime is one bad thing and pain another, the union of the two in the same person may be a less evil than crime unpunished, and might even be a positive good. And to this extent, while remaining perfectly consistent with his own type of utilitarianism, he joins hands with intuitionists, most of whom, at any rate, would probably hold that the combination of crime and punishment is a lesser evil than unpunished crime.

Most intuitionists would perhaps take the view that there is a fundamental and underivative duty to reward the virtuous and to punish the vicious. I am inclined to diverge from this view. Two things seem to me to be clear: that we have a *prima facie* duty to do this, and that a state of affairs in which the good are happy and the bad unhappy is better than one in which the good are unhappy and the bad happy. Now if the first of these is an underivative fact, the two facts are logically unconnected. For it can be an underivative fact only if the intuitionist view is true, and if that view is true the superiority of the one state of affairs over the other cannot follow from the duty of producing it, since on the intuitionist view there are duties other than the duty of producing good. But an intuitionist may with propriety perform the reverse derivation; he may derive the *prima facie* duty of reward and punishment from the superiority of the state of affairs produced, since he may—and, as I think, must—admit that if a state of affairs is better than its alternatives there is a *prima facie* duty to produce it if we can. The duty of reward and punishment seems to me to be in this way derivative. It can be subsumed under the duty of producing as much good as we can; though it must be remembered that the good to be produced in this case is very different from the other goods we recognize (say virtue, knowledge, and pleasure), consisting as it does in a certain relative arrangement of virtue, vice, pleasure, and pain.

But if we hold that there is this duty, it must be admitted that it is one

[22] *Ethical Studies*, ed. 2, 26–7.
[23] *Principia Ethica*, 214.

which it is very difficult for us to see our way to performing, since we know so little about the degrees of virtue and vice, and of happiness and unhappiness, as they occur in our fellow men. And in particular there are two grave objections to holding that the principle of punishing the vicious, for the sake of doing so, is that on which the state should proceed in its bestowal of punishments.

(1) What we perceive to be good is a condition of things in which the total pleasure enjoyed by each person in his life as a whole is proportional to his virtue similarly taken as a whole. Now it is by no means clear that we should help to bring about this end by punishing particular offences in proportion to their moral badness. Any attempt to bring about such a state of affairs should take account of the whole character of the persons involved, as manifested in their life taken as a whole, and of the happiness enjoyed by them throughout their life taken as a whole, and it should similarly take account of the virtue taken as a whole, and of the happiness taken as a whole, of each of the other members of the community, and should seek to bring about the required adjustments. In the absence of such a view of the whole facts, the criminals that a retributive theory of state punishment would call on us to punish for the sake of doing so may well be persons who are more sinned against than sinning, and may be, quite apart from our intervention, already enjoying less happiness than a perfectly fair distribution would allow them. The offences which the state legislates against are only a small part of the wrong acts which are being done every day, and a system which punishes not all wrong acts, but only those which have been forbidden by law, and does not attempt to reward all good acts—such an occasional and almost haphazard system of intervention does not hold out any good hope of promoting the perfect proportionment of happiness to virtue. Nor would it be in the least practicable for the state to attempt the thorough review of the merit and the happiness of all its members, which alone would afford a good hope of securing this end.

(2) Even if it were practicable, it is by no means clear that it is the business of the state to aim at this end. Such a view belongs, I think, to an outworn view of the state, one which identifies the state with the whole organization of the community. In contrast to this, we have come to look upon the state as the organization of the community for a particular purpose, that of the protection of the most important rights of individuals, those without which a reasonably secure and comfortable life is impossible; and to leave the promotion of other good ends to the efforts of individuals and of other organizations, such as churches, trade unions, learned and artistic societies, clubs. Now it cannot, I think, be maintained that the apportionment of happiness to merit is one of the essential conditions to the living of a reasonably secure and comfortable life. Life has gone on for centuries being lived with reasonable security and comfort though states have never achieved or even attempted with any degree

of resolution to effect this apportionment. And in fact for the state to make such an attempt would seriously interfere with its discharge of its proper work. Its proper work is that of protecting rights. Now rights are (as we have seen) rights to be treated in certain ways and not to be treated in certain ways from certain motives; what the state has to take account of, therefore, is not morally bad actions, but wrong acts, and it has to take account of them in such a way as to diminish the chance of their repetition. And this attempt would only be interfered with if the state were at the same time trying to effect a proportionment of happiness to moral worth in its members. The latter task, involving as it would a complete review of the merit and happiness of all its members, would involve leaving the punishment for each offence undetermined by law, and to be determined in the light of all the circumstances of each case; and punishment so completely undetermined in advance would be quite ineffective as a protector of rights.

But to hold that the state has no duty of retributive punishment is not necessarily to adopt a utilitarian view of punishment. It seems possible to give an account of the matter which retains elements in punishment other than that of expediency, without asserting that the state has any duty properly defined as the duty of punishing moral guilt. The essential duty of the state is to protect the most fundamental rights of individuals. Now, rights of any human being are correlative to duties incumbent on the owner of rights, or, to put it otherwise, to rights owned by those against whom he has rights; and the main element in any one's right to life or liberty or property is extinguished by his failure to respect the corresponding right in others.[24] There is thus a distinction in kind which we all in fact recognize, but which utilitarianism cannot admit, between the punishment of a person who has invaded the rights of others and the infliction of pain or restraint on one who has not. The state ought, in its effort to maintain the rights of innocent persons, to take what steps are necessary to prevent violations of these rights; and the offender, by violating the life or liberty or property of another, has lost his own right to have his life, liberty, or property respected, so that the state has no *prima facie* duty to spare him, as it has a *prima facie* duty to spare the innocent. It is morally at liberty to injure him as he has injured others, or to inflict any lesser injury on him, or to spare him, exactly as consideration both of the good of the community and of his own good requires. If, on the other hand, a man has respected the rights of others, there is a strong and distinctive objection to the state's inflicting any penalty on him with a view to the good of the community or even to his own good. The interests of the society may sometimes be so deeply involved as to make it right to punish an innocent man 'that the whole nation perish not.' But then the *prima facie* duty of consulting the general interest has proved more obligatory than the

[24] Cf. pp. 54–5 [pp. 201–2 this volume].

perfectly distinct *prima facie* duty of respecting the rights of those who have respected the rights of others.

This is, I believe, how most thoughtful people feel about the affixing of penalties to the invasion of the rights of others. They may have lost any sense they or their ancestors had that the state should inflict retributive punishment for the sake of doing so, but they feel that there is nevertheless a difference of kind between the community's right to punish people for offences against others, and any right it may have to inconvenience or injure innocent people in the public interest. This arises simply from the fact that the state has a *prima facie* duty not to do the latter and no such duty not to do the former.

We can, I think, help ourselves towards an understanding of the problem by distinguishing two stages which are not usually kept apart in discussions of it. The infliction of punishment by the state does not, or should not, come like a bolt from the blue. It is preceded by the making of a law in which a penalty is affixed to a crime; or by the custom of the community and the decisions of judges a common law gradually grows up in which a penalty is so affixed. We must, I think, distinguish this stage, that of the affixing of the penalty, from that of its infliction, and we may ask on what principles the state or its officials should act at each stage.

At the earlier stage a large place must be left for considerations of expediency. We do not claim that laws should be made against all moral offences, or even against all offences by men against their neighbours. Legislators should consider such questions as whether a given law would be enforced if it were made, and whether a certain type of offence is important enough to make it worth while to set the elaborate machinery of the law at work against it, or is better left to be punished by the injured person or by public opinion. But even at this stage there is one respect in which the notion of justice, as something quite distinct from expediency, plays a part in our thoughts about the matter. We feel sure that if a law is framed against a certain type of offence the punishment should be proportional to the offence. However strong the temptation to commit a certain type of offence may be, and however severe the punishment would therefore have to be in order to be a successful deterrent, we feel certain that it is unjust that very severe penalties should be affixed to very slight offences. It is difficult, no doubt, to define the nature of the relation which the punishment should bear to the crime. We do not see any *direct* moral relation to exist between wrong-doing and suffering so that we may say directly, such and such an offence deserves so much suffering, neither more nor less. But we do think that the injury to be inflicted on the offender should be not much greater than that which he has inflicted on another. Ideally, from this point of view, it should be no greater. For he has lost his *prima facie* rights to life, liberty, or property, only in so far as these rested on an explicit or implicit undertaking to respect the corresponding rights in others, and in so far as he has failed to respect those rights. But laws must be stated in general terms, to cover a variety of cases, and they cannot in advance affix punishments which shall never be greater than the injury inflicted by the wrongdoer. We are therefore content with an approximation to what is precisely just. At the same time we recognize that this, while it is a *prima facie* duty, is not the only *prima facie* duty of the legislator; and that, as in the selection of offences to be legislated against, so in the fixing of the penalty, he must consider expediency, and may make the penalty more or less severe as it dictates. His action should, in fact, be guided by regard to the *prima facie* duty of injuring wrong-doers only to the extent that they have injured others, and also to the *prima facie* duty of promoting the general interest. And I think that we quite clearly recognize these as distinct and specifically different elements in the moral situation. To say this is not to adopt a compromise between the intuitionist and the utilitarian view; for it can fairly be plain that one of the duties we apprehend intuitively is that of promoting the general interest so far as we can.

When the law has been promulgated and an offence against it committed, a new set of considerations emerges. The administrator of the law has not to consider what is the just punishment for the offence, nor what is the expedient punishment, except when the law has allowed a scale of penalties within which he can choose. When that is the case, he has still to have regard to the same considerations as arose at the earlier stage. But that, when the penalty fixed by law is determinate, this and no other should be inflicted, and that, when a scale of penalties is allowed, no penalty above or below the scale should be inflicted, depends on a *prima facie* duty that did not come in at the earlier stage, *viz.* that of fidelity to promise. Directly, the law is not a promise: it is a threat to the guilty, and a threat is not a promise. The one is an undertaking to do or give to the promisee something mutually understood to be advantageous to him; the other, an announcement of intention to do to him something mutually understood to be disadvantageous to him. Punishment is sometimes justified on the ground that to fail to punish is to break faith with the offender. It is said that he has a right to be punished, and that not to punish him is not to treat him with due respect as a moral agent responsible for his actions, but as if he could not have helped doing them. This is, however, not a point of view likely to be adopted by a criminal who escapes punishment, and seems to be a somewhat artificial way of looking at the matter, and to ignore the difference between a threat and a promise.

But while the law is not a promise to the criminal, it is a promise to the injured person and his friends, and to society. It promises to the former, in certain cases, compensation, and always the satisfaction of knowing that the offender has not gone scot-free, and it promises to the latter this satisfaction and the degree of protection against further offences which punishment gives. At the same time the whole system of law is a promise to the members of the community that if they do not commit any of the prohibited acts they will not be punished.

Thus to our sense that *prima facie* the state has a right to punish the guilty, over and above the right which it has, in the last resort, of inflicting injury on any of its members when the public interest sufficiently demands it, there is added the sense that promises should *prima facie* be kept; and it is the combination of these considerations that accounts for the moral satisfaction that is felt by the community when the guilty are punished, and the moral indignation that is felt when the guilty are not punished, and still more when the innocent are. There may be cases in which the *prima facie* duty of punishing the guilty, and even that of not punishing the innocent, may have to give way to that of promoting the public interest. But these are not cases of a wider expediency overriding a narrower, but of one *prima facie* duty being more obligatory than two others different in kind from it and from one another.

Different Meanings of "Good" and "Ought" *

A. C. EWING

WE SHALL PASS in due course to another definition of "good" which is not open to the same objections as the definitions which I have discussed, but since "good" and "ought" are very ambiguous words it will be wise first to distinguish various senses in which they are used, and the present chapter will be devoted to this essential preliminary.

In the first place I must remind the reader (1) that, whether a naturalist view of ethics be right or not, it is certainly true that "good" is sometimes used in a purely naturalist, psychological sense to mean "pleasant." When I say "This pudding is good" I do not think I mean anything more than that I like it or find it pleasant, with the possible implication that most other people would do so too.

Similarly, (2), when I talk of somebody's good, I may only mean what will satisfy his desires.[1]

But I may also mean what is "really to his good," as when I say that it is not to a man's good to have everything that he wants, and the two meanings shade into each other so that it is often difficult to tell which is intended. This is because it is usually assumed that to have one's desires satisfied is for one's real good, provided they are not positively immoral desires. To say that something is for a man's good is to say that it will directly or indirectly result in a part of his life being better in some way (not necessarily hedonistically) than would otherwise be the case without a counterbalancing loss somewhere else in his life. If "better" is being used naturalistically, this will probably mean only that his desires will be more fully satisfied; but the word may also be used differently, and then it will fall under one of the other senses of "good" to be enumerated later.

It is clear also that "good" is very often, perhaps most often, used in an instrumental sense to signify "good as a means," which sense has, almost from time immemorial, been distinguished from "good-in-itself." But the term "instrumentally good" or "good as a means" is itself ambiguous. It may mean—and this gives another naturalist sense of "good"—(3) capable

[1] Vide Carritt, "An Ambiguity of the Word 'Good'," *Proceedings of the British Academy,* Vol. 23, 1937.

of doing a particular kind of thing efficiently, whether that thing be itself good, bad, or indifferent. A knife might still be a "good knife" even if it were never used for anything but the most atrocious murders.

(4) "*Good as a means*" may also mean "productive of something intrinsically good." In this sense we speak of pure water as good and impure water as bad. Pure water, while more efficient as a means of maintaining health than impure water, is far less efficient as a means of producing typhoid fever; but we look on typhoid fever as evil or necessarily accompanied by intrinsic evils, while we look on health, which is maintained by pure water, as intrinsically good, or necessarily or probably accompanied by what is intrinsically good, and therefore we speak of pure water as good and impure water as bad. The distinction between (3) and (4) is still clearer in the case of "bad." We may call somebody or something bad just because it is inefficient, or we may call it bad because it is all too efficient in producing intrinsically bad effects. For example, diseases and hurricanes are called in this sense bad, though not themselves intrinsically bad.

(5) "Good" may mean not "efficient in producing effects" but rather "efficiently produced." I think this is the most usual meaning of a "good book," a "good stroke at cricket," etc.

(6) It is obvious, however, that these senses (at least 4 and 5) presuppose a further, more primary sense of "good." This sense is commonly expressed by the terms "intrinsically good," "good-in-itself," "good as an end." There would be no point in being efficient if we could not thereby produce something that was good as an end and not only as a means.

But there is a point I wish to mention here. By calling a thing "intrinsically good" or "good-in-itself" I do not mean to commit myself to the view that it would necessarily be good in all contexts or could still be good if everything else in the universe were different. "Good-in-itself" has been used in this sense; but it need not imply this, as far as I can see. What I mean by "good-in-itself" is simply "good itself," in opposition to good as a means; that is, I mean that the thing called good really has the characteristic goodness in its primary sense, and is not merely called good because it produces something else which has the quality in question. As far as I can see, something might really have the characteristic goodness in some contexts and yet not have it in others, or have it only in a lower degree, as a poker is really hot when placed near the fire and not hot or not so hot when placed elsewhere.

Again, there is nothing to exclude a thing being both good in itself and good as a means in any ordinary sense of the latter term. The things that are intrinsically best themselves are also most likely to produce intrinsically good effects.

(7) Moore makes a distinction between "ultimately" and "intrinsically good." [2] Anything is intrinsically good, provided it contains elements which are good for their own sake, even if it also contains elements

[2] *Ethics*, pp. 73–5 [pp. 57–8 this volume; pp. 46–7 reset edition of *Ethics*].

which are quite indifferent, provided only the other elements do not actually counteract the value of the good part. Such a thing would still be good even if it existed alone, he says, and he therefore calls it intrinsically good; but he will call something ultimately good only if it has no parts which are not themselves intrinsically good, so this gives a seventh sense of "good," ultimately good. In the sixth sense a successful life or a long holiday might be described as good, but it could hardly be called good in the seventh sense because the best holiday and, still more, the best life will contain stretches which are indifferent in respect of value, or at any rate stretches which are unpleasant rather than pleasant and in which there are no other values realised adequate to counteract this unpleasantness.

It is not clear whether it is the sixth or the seventh sense of "good" which should in preference be regarded as indefinable. In the passage mentioned Moore defines the seventh in terms of the sixth sense—what is "ultimately good" is something intrinsically good which either has no parts or has parts which are all intrinsically good—so presumably he regarded the sixth sense as primary. It might be argued that it would be better to take the reverse course on the ground that it is the ultimately good parts belonging to it which make anything intrinsically good, but this does not agree with Moore's principle of organic unities according to which something in itself indifferent or even bad might increase the intrinsic goodness of the whole to which it belonged. Usually no distinction has been made between these two senses, but I think the term "intrinsically good" has generally been used to express the seventh rather than the sixth sense of good.

"Good" is also often used to mean "either instrumentally or intrinsically or ultimately good," where the speaker believes something is good in one of these senses but has not thought it necessary to ask which (as indeed it often is not for purposes of practice). But we should swell our list of meanings so far as to exhaust the patience of the reader if we assigned a separate heading for each such unprecise usage of "good."

(8) "Good" in sense (6) or sense (7) is not properly applied to characteristics. When "good" is applied to a characteristic of something it signifies not that the characteristic is intrinsically good itself, but that things which have the characteristic are in so far intrinsically good. Thus we get an eighth sense of "good," in which "good" means good-making, to use Broad's terminology. In this sense "good" is applied to qualities to signify that the quality in question makes the things which have it good in sense 6 or sense 7. For example, the statement that pleasure is good means that the quality of pleasantness makes what has it good.

(9) "Good" often means morally good. Obviously moral goodness is not the only kind of intrinsic goodness, and it may possibly be denied that it is a case of intrinsic goodness at all, yet the people who deny this would still use of it the term "good." But this must be a matter for further discussion. In the sense of "morally good," the term is applied both to men

and to actions, but it can hardly be applied to both in the same sense, so we now get both a ninth sense, "good" means "morally good" as applied to actions, and a tenth, "good" means "morally good" as applied to persons. No doubt "good" as applied to persons may also mean merely "efficient" (sense 3), for example, when we speak of a man as a good cricketer or a good philosopher, but it obviously sometimes stands for a more specifically moral quality.

Laird also introduces the concept of "dominant good" as of fundamental importance, meaning by this a good "which, irradiating its surroundings, dignifies whatever it touches";[3] but I am not sure that this is not better regarded as a description of a particular species of good thing than as a different sense of "good." Moore also points out that "good" is sometimes used to mean "adding to the value of many intrinsically good wholes."[4]

Another sense of "good" which is sometimes admitted is "typical of its species,"[5] but I think this is reducible to some of the other senses mentioned above. A thing is most commonly called a good specimen of its class because it is more efficient than the average member of the class in fulfilling certain ends, namely, those characteristic of the class or those for which that class of thing was made. It may also be called "a good specimen of the class" because it is a useful sample for the purposes of research. And, finally, it may be called a good specimen because it provides a certain aesthetic satisfaction, that is, something good in senses 6 and 7, for aesthetic satisfactions should be regarded as intrinsically valuable and not valuable merely in a naturalist sense.

Corresponding to the ten senses of "good" there are ten senses of "bad." "Bad" may mean (1) unpleasant; (2) contrary to what we desire; (3) inefficient in fulfilling certain purposes, whether these are themselves good, bad or indifferent; (4) productive of something intrinsically evil; (5) inefficiently made; (6) intrinsically bad, in Moore's sense as applied to particulars; (7) ultimately bad as applied to particulars; (8) as applied to qualities, such as to make what has it bad in the sixth or seventh sense; (9) morally bad as applied to actions; (10) morally bad as applied to persons. "Evil" is synonymous with "bad," except that it is not customarily used unless the degree of badness is very serious, and it could not, I think, correctly be applied to what was considered bad only in senses 1,2,3, or 5, except as a piece of "slang." It has therefore, unlike "bad," no purely naturalist sense at all.

The terms "good" and "bad" are thus extremely ambiguous, and in ethical discussion it is therefore most important to be clear in which sense we are using them. It is obvious, however, that sense 6 or sense 7 is fundamental and is of very special importance for philosophers. We

---

[3] *A Study in Moral Theory*, p. 46.
[4] *Ethics*, p. 250 [p. 154 reset edition].
[5] For the attempt to make this the main definition of good v. above, pp. 104–6.

have now come to the conclusion that in these senses at any rate "good" cannot be naturalistically defined. Of the other senses some are definable in terms of (6) or (7), others may be naturalistically defined. Senses 9 and 10 at least seem definable in terms of another non-naturalist ethical concept, ought. I shall now turn to the terms "ought," "right," "duty." It is obvious that these have a close relation to each other and that their chief application is to actions. They are not such ambiguous words as "good"; but there are at least three different usages of them in ethics which it is very important for the philosopher to distinguish. I shall explain the three different usages in the case of "ought." [6]

1. "The action we ought to do" may mean that action which is really preferable, taking everything into account. This would be the action which an omniscient and perfectly wise being would advise us to perform; but it is impossible for us to take everything into account, and it may even be doubted whether any action that ought to be done in this sense has ever in the whole of history been performed by a human being. For, whatever benefits I may produce by a certain expenditure of time or money, it seems in the highest degree likely that a being who knew all the circumstances and foresaw all the consequences could suggest some expenditure still more beneficial. For example, such a being would know the cure for cancer and would know how to prove to the medical profession that it was a cure. Now obviously to inform medical experts of the right cure and persuade them to adopt it, if I could do this, would be a more beneficial action than any which I am likely to perform during my life in the normal course and would be an action that ought to be carried out immediately to save life and suffering, so that whatever I do now such a being could advise me of something more beneficial to do instead; that is, take steps to bring about the adoption of the method of cure. It may be retorted that at any rate I know that I ought to pay my debts and this could not be altered even by the information of an omniscient being, but "pays a debt" is an incomplete description of an act. I am under an obligation to pay my debts; but I am not under an obligation to pay them this very moment, especially where there is some other pressing obligation, and hardly anybody would expect me to keep an appointment if, as in this case, the lives of many people depended on my missing it. Besides, even in the case of paying debts, such a being could probably suggest something in my manner of doing it which would have better effects than my present manner of doing it,[7] and could certainly suggest some mental state in re-

[6] In "Some of the Main Problems of Ethics," *Philosophy*, Vol. XXI, No. 79, pp. 110–11, Professor Broad distinguishes three senses of "right." The first and third respectively correspond to my first and second, but Broad's second ("formally right") does not correspond to my third. ["Some of the Main Problems of Ethics" is reprinted in Herbert Feigl and Wilfrid Sellars, eds., *Readings of Philosophical Analysis*, Appleton-Century-Crofts, Inc., 1949].

[7] I am not assuming that the consequences are the only factor in determining whether one action is preferable to another, but only that they are at least highly relevant to this question.

paying the debt preferable to the one actually experienced by me. It is highly doubtful whether the mental state of any human being is ever completely and absolutely ideal even for a moment. It seems to me therefore objectionable to take the present as the main sense of "ought," "right" or "duty," as is done, for example, by Moore in his *Ethics*,[8] at least when we are applying "ought" to actions regarded as a whole. It is surely desirable to use the word in a sense in which we can be confident that there are actions to which it applies. It is unsatisfactory to choose a meaning for the word which makes it necessary to say that probably no human being in the whole course of history has ever acted as he ought. On the other hand, there is plenty of scope for this sense of "ought" when not applied to actions regarded as a whole. We can use it of what have been called *prima facie* duties, and say that in the absence of a conflicting obligation we ought always to keep a promise in this sense of "ought." We can also say in this sense that we ought to prefer certain ends to certain others, for example that we ought to value justice rather than money, and that certain emotional attitudes are fitting or unfitting towards certain kinds of objects, for example, we ought to dislike cruelty, we ought to love good parents. For here the complications about consequences do not arise, it being rather a question of the intrinsic value of something, so that if we had made any mistake in such judgements it would be a mistake of value and not of fact. We are rightly so confident of the truth of many such judgements that we use the term "know" rather than "believe," and the objection that probably no human being has ever done as he ought is certainly not applicable here. I am convinced that I ought to dislike the unnecessary infliction of pain, and not only that relatively to the available evidence I ought to do so; and this is not contradicted by the fact that it might under certain circumstances be the least undesirable course for me to choose to do something which gave much pain, and even which by an unfortunate concatenation of circumstances encouraged people to take pleasure in the pain; for example, if I take steps to secure the punishment of a criminal.

2. "Ought," both in philosophy and in ordinary discussion, is also used in a sense in which not to do what one ought, or to do what one ought not to do, is always morally blameworthy. To say that I ought to do A in this sense is indeed not the same as saying that I believe I ought to do A, for the proposition that I ought to do what I believe I ought to do is synthetic, but it is, I think, synthetic *a priori*. This sense of the word is extremely important, but it obviously presupposes another sense. That is made clear by considering the principle that we always ought to do what we believe we ought. We may believe, for example, that the soldiers who fight against us in a war are acting wrongly in fighting, yet every reasonable person will admit that, as long as they really think they ought to fight, they ought "to obey their consciences" and fight. In general, it is clear that a person may make a mistake and decide that he ought to do A, though A is really

[8] p. 190 ff.

wrong. In that case he clearly ought to do A, therefore he ought to do what is wrong, that is, what he ought not to do. Self-contradiction can only be avoided if we suppose that "ought" is being used in two different senses here. Again, if there is no sense of "ought" in which it is false to say that we always ought to do what we think we ought, we could discover what we ought to do by mere introspection without considering anything else whatever. These paradoxes can only be met by recognising another sense of "ought" besides the sense in which not to do what one "ought" is always morally blameworthy, and we have seen that the first sense is not adequate. So a third sense is required.

3. "The action which I ought to perform" may mean the action which it is, humanly speaking, preferable to choose, though it may not in fact necessarily turn out best. It seems to me that this is the sense in which the term "ought" is most commonly employed. We should not usually say that a man had not done what he ought just because some unforeseeable accident had changed the consequences from good to bad. It would be a very unusual use of language to say that I had done something which I ought not to have done because a man whom I had invited to tea was run over and killed on his way to my house; and if I saw somebody about to drink a glass of prussic acid and refrained from warning him, it would hardly be said that I had done what I ought because it was a new variety of prussic acid just discovered which was harmless or the man had such an abnormal physiology that he could drink prussic acid with impunity, if I had no knowledge of this circumstance but believed that the drink would bring about his death. Likewise no one would say that I had acted wrongly or had not done my duty in the first case, or that I had acted rightly or had done my duty in the second. We rarely employ these terms in our first sense, but we do employ them in our third sense very frequently. A good example of the difficulties which arise from not making the distinction between the first sense and the third sense is provided by Professor Prichard in his paper on *Duty and Ignorance of Fact*.[8a]

We may explain the third sense further by saying that in this sense we ought to perform an act if in the light of the available evidence it seems the preferable act to choose. By "available evidence" I mean evidence which the agent either possesses already or could obtain without more trouble than is practicable or worth while, everything considered. The phrase is vague, but so is the common usage of words, especially words like "ought," and though it is difficult in borderline cases to say how much the agent could have been expected to foresee, it is easy enough to distinguish between some consequences which he could have been expected to foresee and some which he could not, and clear enough that he would be accused of not having done what he ought on account of the former but not on account of the latter. The definition is not intended to exclude cases

[8a] [*Proceedings of the British Academy*, Vol. 18, 1932. Also reprinted in H. A. Prichard, *Moral Obligation*, Oxford University Press, 1950.—Ed.]

where the only evidence of which he could be expected to take account is evidence which he actually had in mind when the emergency came or could obtain in the course of a very short time, for example in meeting a sudden attack, because immediate action of some sort was necessary.

I have not in all this attempted to give a definition of the different senses of "ought," but a rough explanation sufficient to distinguish them. The phrase I have used to explain the third sense of "ought," and perhaps also those used to explain the first and second senses, if taken as defining "ought," would be circular. For "preferable to choose" here really only means that the action is the one the agent *ought* to choose in preference to others. The first and the third alike depend directly on the same indefinable notion, as we shall see; with the second usage the question is a little more complicated.

A person who fails to do what he ought in the third sense is not necessarily morally to blame for this, since he may be honestly mistaken in the conclusions he drew from the evidence; but he will be either morally or intellectually to blame or both, that is he will have either willed more or less badly or reasoned more or less badly (including under this the omission of relevant points), or both. The difference between the three senses of "ought" may be illustrated in this way: If a motor knocks down and kills a man it is plain that the motorist ought not to have done what he did in the first sense of "ought," since it had unfortunate consequences (unless we argue that perhaps the death was a blessing in disguise); but it would be a matter for a court to decide whether he ought not to have done it in the third sense, with a view to determining whether damages were payable, while the question whether he did what he ought in the second sense would be considered by the court if it were a question of murder or manslaughter.

Corresponding to the three different senses of "ought" there are three different senses of "duty," "right," "wrong," which can easily be derived from the different senses of "ought," *mutatis mutandis*. Nor is the difference between the usage of the terms "ought," "right," "duty" of much philosophical importance. It does not at any rate point to a difference of fundamental concept at all. "The right action" is synonymous with the action which ought to be done, except that we should speak of God as doing what was right but should not apply to God the terms "duty" and "ought." This is because we do not admit the possibility of God's doing wrong. But "right" without the definite article has a wider significance. While an action which I ought to do or which it is my duty to do is always right, in the sense corresponding to the one of the three senses in which "ought" is being used in the given context, the converse does not hold. It is, for example, a right action to hand, with appropriate motives, a five-pound note to somebody to whom I owe five pounds, if I am not thereby violating any still more important obligation; but I cannot say that I ought to do this or that it is my duty to do this, because I should still be acting rightly if I handed him five pound notes instead, and two incompatible actions cannot both be duties. So we should say that I ought to pay the debt, but not that I ought to hand him a five-pound note. An act is thus right but not a duty, nor an act which we ought to do, where it is one of a number of alternative acts which are such that one ought to be done but there is no reason for preferring any one to any other of them. "Right," I think, means the same as "not wrong." We do not indeed usually use the term, "right," of indifferent acts, because we are not interested in these; but we should, if asked whether these were right or not right, admit that they were right. Ross, though he notes the distinction between "right" and "what ought to be done," in *The Right and the Good* [9] purposely chooses to use "right" as the adjective corresponding to "something that ought to be done"; but I do not intend to follow him in this, which, as he admits, is not the normal usage.

A "duty" is generally equivalent to an action or class of actions which ought to be done. But the term is not applied if (1) the main direct reason in favour of the action is its conduciveness to the agent's own pleasure, and if (2) the action is in accord with the inclinations and present mood of the agent. If one of these two conditions is fulfilled but not the other, the action may, I think, still be called a duty. In general, however, the term is reserved for occasions on which we wish very specially to emphasize the moral aspect of an act. We are reluctant to describe acts of slight importance too readily as duties, thus cheapening the notion. It would not, however, be correct to say that "duty" was limited to the second sense of "ought," since we certainly admit that it is possible to make a mistake about one's duty.

In so far as the rightness or obligatoriness of an action depends on its consequences at all, whether we ought to perform an action in the first sense of "ought" will depend on the actual consequences, whether we ought to do it in the second sense on the consequences we judge likely, whether we ought to do it in the third sense neither on the actual consequences, nor on the consequences we judge likely, but on the consequences that relatively to our data really are likely. For to say that something is likely or probable is not merely to make a statement about my own or anybody else's subjective state. It has often been supposed that it is,[10] because I may truly say that something is improbable and yet it may really happen, or again I may judge something to be probable at one time

[9] pp. 3-4 [pp. 163-166 this volume]. In *Foundations of Ethics* (p. 44) he expresses the view that according to the normal usage of "right" any right act must be "a fulfilment of at least one claim upon us." But suppose somebody asks—Is it morally right to read a particular, harmless novel on Sunday? Anybody but a fanatical sabbatarian would surely answer—Yes, it is right, though no one would hold that there was a moral claim on us to read the novel.

[10] See Prichard in "Duty and Ignorance of Fact." *Proceedings of the British Academy*, Vol. 18, 1932. Prichard's difficulties in this pamphlet seem to me to arise mainly from (a) ignoring the third sense of "right," (b) assuming that probability cannot be objective.

and improbable at another and yet neither of the judgements may be wrong. If a person in July, 1940, judged that Germany would probably win the war, he is not proved to have been wrong by the fact that she did not do so. But judgements of probability cannot really be judgements about the subjective state of the person judging, for they are not reached by introspection but by considering the objective situation, and I may make mistakes about estimating probability that are not mistakes about my subjective condition at all. If judgements of probability are judgements about one's own subjective state, it may be asked what they assert. They cannot be merely assertions about the degree of confidence with which the asserter entertains a proposition, if by "confidence" is meant confident feeling, because it is quite obvious that somebody, for example a sanguine gambler, may judge A to be less probable than B and yet feel more confident about A's happening than B, and it is still more obvious that he may feel a high degree of confidence concerning an event which he is quite wrong in judging probable at all. Nor can judgements of probability be merely assertions as to whether the assertor thinks something to be probable. The vicious circle is perfectly plain, and it is equally plain that a person may be mistaken in judging something probable and yet that it may be perfectly true that he thought it probable, indeed this must be true if he is even to make a mistake in judging the event probable. To be mistaken in judging it probable he must really judge it probable. Nor on a subjective view of probability do I see what possible sense could be given to statements attributing to an event a more or less definite degree of numerical probability. Some people have asserted that, when we judge an event probable, what we are really judging is that we shall act as if the event were going to occur; but owing to human folly or immorality people do not always act in accordance with their beliefs as to what is probable and, when I judge an event probable, I need not even anticipate that I will act in accord with my belief that it is probable. If I do anticipate this, it will only be because I have first concluded that the event is probable. After all it is surely quite clear that an event is not made probable, in any ordinary sense of the term, because we feel confident about it or think that it will happen or act as if it will.

Another objection is that, if we take a subjective view of probability, we shall have to say that all or most judgements of physical science or human history, since they are believed, or ought to be believed, by the person who makes them not to be quite certain but only probable, are or ought to be merely judgements about his state of mind at the time he makes them. Some philosophers have indeed held that all judgements, outside mathematics and formal logic, except those about one's own present state are uncertain; but surely they would not therefore be committed to saying that all these judgements are only about their own state of mind. That would commit them to solipsism. And if we do not go so far as these philosophers and admit that some judgements about physical objects and other human beings are certain, we still surely cannot say that, while the judgement that King George VI of England is alive at a particular date is about King George, the judgement that one of the Roman emperors was alive at a particular date, because it is only probable, only asserts that the man who makes it is in a certain state of mind now.

I therefore hold probability [11] to be an objective relation, whether definable or indefinable I need not discuss. This seems to me the only satisfactory way of reconciling (a), the fact that some events may truly be said, at different times, to be both probable and improbable, with (b), the fact that we can make mistakes about probability. The statement that A is probable is an incomplete statement like the statement that A is to the north or to the right, and there is no more difficulty in seeing how the statement that A is probable may be true in one case and false in another of the same event A than there is in seeing how the statement "Cambridge is to the north" may be true in London and false in Edinburgh. Nobody doubts on this ground that "Cambridge is to the north" can describe an objective fact. "A is probable" makes no sense unless it is understood in relation to certain data, namely those available at the time the judgement is made, and therefore it may be true at one time and false at another according to differences in the data. It is obvious that in the light of probabilities we can determine with relative ease and even sometimes with fair certainty what we ought to do in the third sense of "ought" where it would be quite impossible to determine what we ought to do in the first, and that this goes far to explain the confidence which we often feel in ethical judgements, despite the multiplicity of possible consequences.

I must add, however, that, while I generally prefer to use "ought" in my third sense rather than in my first sense, what I "ought" to do in my first sense is still highly relevant to ethics. For it is only because, if I find out what is right in my third sense and act accordingly, I am more likely to approximate to what is right in my first sense, that I ought to do what is right in my third sense at all. We only consider what we ought to do in the third sense as a means to this approximation. We may compare the case of most theoretical knowledge. Outside mathematics, formal logic, and simple observations and memories, we have in theoretical knowledge to content ourselves with finding out what is probably, not what is certainly, true, yet the value of finding out what is probably true only lies in the fact that it is the best way of approximating to the objectively true, which is not itself probable or improbable but actual. In the theoretical sphere, if we accept what is really most probable relatively to our data rather than rush to conclusions without due consideration, we may err but at any rate we are likely to get nearer the truth than if we do not act in this reasonable way. We can be confident at least that we shall be far more

[11] At least in the sense under discussion here.

often right, and that, where we err, we are likely to be less badly wrong and almost certain in most cases to have included some substantial truth in our error. The same applies in ethics. We cannot indeed hope to hit upon the absolutely best action to choose in any given situation, as in the realm of theory we cannot hope to hit upon the complete truth about any fact. But, as in the realm of theory we can arrive at some true propositions about something the nature of which is not wholly grasped, either scientifically or philosophically, so in the realm of ethics we may hope to make proper choices between alternatives and rightly prefer a to b, though we shall probably not think at all of the alternative action which it would be absolutely best to perform.

For what I have said about the first sense of "ought" should not suggest too extreme a scepticism. I do think that we can never be justified in believing a particular act to be the act which we ought to do in this sense of "ought"; but at least we can be sure that we are justified in believing it in the highest degree probable of many acts that they are much further than others from being what we ought to do in this sense. If the question is simply which to choose of a certain limited number of alternatives, there are many cases in which we can have at least a very well justified belief that it is right in my first sense to choose one kind of action rather than the others. For example, it is possible that, if I knocked somebody down because he criticised my philosophical arguments, it might by some indirect and unforeseeable concatenation of circumstances produce good effects which outbalanced the harm, but I should still be justified in strongly holding the opinion that it would be right even in my first sense of "right" to prefer to give a courteous answer; and this is unaffected by the fact that it is in the extremest degree unlikely that I should have hit upon the ideally and absolutely best way of treating the criticism. I can indeed not merely have a justifiable opinion, but know that, if I do knock the man down, I shall be committing an action that is very wrong in the first sense, as well as in the second and third senses, because even if owing to the strange concatenation of circumstances suggested it should turn out to be the right act *externally*, it is quite certain that, since I do not foresee these beneficent effects, I should not, if I did it, be acting in a right state of mind, and that is sufficient to prevent it from being right. But the most important point here is that the fact that the absoluely ideal action under the circumstances is not likely to occur to us need not make us sceptical as to our belief that certain actions under certain circumstances are preferable to certain others even in the first sense or that it is better to omit than to perform a certain action. The belief often does not amount to knowledge, but neither do many other beliefs on which the most timorous man is prepared to stake his life without a qualm; for example, that there is, in the absence of very special reasons for suspecting the contrary, no poison in his dinner. We may still go on fairly confidently with our moral judgements of preference. In no case may the ideal solution have occurred to us, but at least we may be confident that one particular solution is much better than another would be.

It may be objected that, when I talk about "ought" in the first and third usages, I am not really talking about anything moral at all. It is not my moral duty to choose rightly, though it is my moral duty to try to choose rightly, so you can only say that I *morally* ought to do something in the second sense of "ought," the sense according to which I am morally blameworthy if I do not do what I ought. However, whether I am talking about the specifically moral "ought" or not, I am talking about something which is extremely relevant to ethics and which is presupposed by the specifically moral sense of "ought." For I cannot decide what I ought to do in that sense without making up my mind what I ought to do in my third sense of "ought." I must first believe that an act is the preferable one to choose in view of the available data if I am to be morally bound to do it. Some philosophers have spoken as if the only proper sense of "ought" were the specifically moral sense.[12] But I do not know what the criterion of "proper" usage can be except the way in which educated people use a term, and it is quite certain that "ought" is very widely and constantly used in a sense which does not necessarily presuppose that it is morally wrong not to do what we ought. Indeed it seems to me that in ordinary conversation it is more commonly used in such a way than in the specifically moral sense, largely because people are shy of commenting to somebody else about his morals. "You ought to have seen this film," "You ought to have moved your queen," even "Hitler ought to have invaded England immediately after Dunkirk," are perfectly good English, and may be quite true statements even though it is not considered a moral duty to see a film, to make the right move in chess, and still less (by an Englishman) for Hitler to invade England. The third sense of "ought" cannot, however, be strictly described as a non-moral sense, nor for that matter can the first sense of "ought." For to say that A "ought" to do so-and-so in either of these senses entails that under certain (factual) conditions he ought to do it in the specifically moral sense of "ought." The proposition that a man "ought" to do n in the first sense entails that he will do n if he is adequately informed, wise and moral, and the proposition that a man "ought to do n" in the third sense entails that he will do n if he is wise and moral. Similarly the proposition that he ought not (in the third sense) to have done what he has done entails that he either has been unwise or has immorally neglected his duty. For I may fail to do what I "ought" in that sense for two reasons, (a) because of a defect of intelligence, (b) because of a defect of will. To say A ought in that sense of "ought" to have done something which he did not do is to say that his action was inadequate or harmful through a defect in him, but to leave open

---

[12] Ross seems to take this view about "ought," though he admits that "right" may legitimately be used in both senses (*Foundations of Ethics*, p. 55).

(as we very often must in judging others) the question whether the defect was one of intelligence or of will. It implies that he either acted immorally or made a mistake. We are using "ought" in a completely non-moral sense only where we do not attach moral significance to the act at all, as in a game, or where we are considering not whether the act is right or wrong on the whole, but only whether it is so as means to a given end, which, as in the Hitler example, may be bad.

This brings out the point that "ought" really covers two different concepts, the concept of fittingness [13] and the concept of moral obligation. If I ought to do something there must be a certain relation between the action and its environment such that the action is fitting, appropriate, suitable, and its omission unfitting, inappropriate, unsuitable. This in itself is, however, a different concept from the concept of a moral obligation which we must fulfil or be guilty of sin, yet the latter concept must always be based on the former. Sin cannot occur unless our act is inappropriate in some way to the situation or at least we believe it to be so. This is obviously true, though we generally express it by using some stronger word than "unfitting" or "inappropriate." Nobody would in ordinary conversation describe a brutal murder as "unfitting"; the murder would no doubt be unfitting, but the word is not felt to be strong enough. It is, however, very convenient for philosophical purposes to have a single word which covers all degrees, so I shall follow Broad in using "fitting" for this purpose, as a physicist in defiance of ordinary usage employs the word "heat" to cover temperatures far below zero. But this concept of fittingness by no means exhausts the significance of "ought." There is the further concept of strictly moral obligation. We feel that we are under binding laws which we cannot break without being ourselves evil in a more serious and quite different way from that in which pain is evil. We feel that it is not merely an interesting fact that A is an unfitting action in circumstances B, C, D, but one which has a claim to authority over us. This is not to define "moral obligation," but to clarify the distinction between it and mere fittingness. Even if it is held that we are morally obliged to do what is most fitting, it must be admitted that the two concepts are distinct. But it is not the case that we are always morally obliged to do what is most fitting. For, although A is really the most fitting action relatively to all the circumstances, or even to those which are known to the agent, he may through ignorance or misjudgement not be aware of this, and in that case he will not be under a moral obligation to do A. Further, we can apply the term "fitting" in regard to matters which are not subject to volition, while we cannot apply the term "morally obligatory" in that way. Finally, certain actions are fitting simply because they are conducive to the agent's happiness, yet it may at least be doubted whether this is a sufficient ground to make them morally obligatory, which at any rate proves the two concepts not to be identical, even if we should finally reject the doubt and

[13] This term is borrowed from Prof. Broad.

decide that they are morally obligatory after all. "Fittingness" stands for a relation between an action and its environment, moral obligation is something analogous to an imperative on the agent. So we have at least three different and apparently fundamental ethical concepts—goodness, fittingness, and moral obligation—the relations of which to explore.

It may be objected that the concept of moral obligation in so far as it goes beyond fittingness is theological, as has often been said to be the case with the allied concept of sin, and that therefore as long as we are dealing simply with ethics apart from any theological assumptions we ought not to introduce it. But it is certainly a part of the moral consciousness, if anything is, that we are under binding obligations, and if we took the notion away from ethics there would be little left of ethics. If this concept does necessarily involve theology, then we can argue from ethics to the existence of God. As I have tried to make clear earlier, we must in any case not reverse the argument and say that we must first believe in theology before we can rightly believe that we are under moral obligations. We are directly and certainly conscious of moral obligation, and if that is disputed there can be little ground for a theology which would re-establish ethics. If belief in a good God—and a God that was not good would assuredly provide no basis for ethics—is to be established by argument, the argument must already presuppose ethical concepts and propositions. On the other hand, if it is claimed that we can be immediately aware without argument of such a being independently of the ethical consciousness and deduce our ethics from the nature of the being thus intuited, we are basing the more certain on the less certain, since we are appealing to an intuition which is, at the best, less, not more, certain than are our clearest ethical intuitions. Even if belief in God were based exclusively not on our reason or intuition at all but on the revelation of Christ, we may reply that there would be little ground indeed for believing in the revelation if we did not assume at least that Christ was good, and we could not assume this without trusting to our own power of ethical discrimination. Even if theology be the *ratio essendi* of ethics, it is certainly not its *ratio cognoscendi*. In order to be aware that we are under moral obligations we need not first come to know or believe anything about God, even that there is a God. This will be the case even if it should turn out that some of the concepts of ethics—we have seen above [14] that this cannot be the case with all—cannot be analysed or at least grasped adequately without a reference to God.

My first and third senses of "ought" express fittingness, not merely fittingness for a particular end (as with Kant's "hypothetical imperatives"), though I do not deny that "ought" is also used in that sense, but fittingness in regard to the situation as a whole. But with the first sense the situation is viewed in abstraction from any imperfections in the agent's knowledge and beliefs, and with the third sense the situation is viewed in

[14] V. pp. 106 ff.

abstraction, not from all such imperfections, but from those due to his mistakes, negligence, or prejudice. The first and third senses give the act which of those possible is the most fitting if we take into account everything except the above circumstances. The second sense gives the action which is fitting in relation to the situation as the agent views it and at the same time the action which is morally obligatory. I think it to be a true synthetic *a priori* proposition that it is morally obligatory for an agent to do A where he thinks A the most fitting action in his power and where it is both possible for him to do and also possible for him not to do A. There would be serious difficulties and disputes about the definition of "possible," but these are beyond the scope of this book; and even the determinist would admit some sense of "possible" in which it is possible for a man to act differently from the way in which he actually does act. In order to decide which action is most fitting the agent cannot first take into account his belief as to which is most fitting, for this is not yet formed, therefore he must be asking himself which action he ought to do in my third sense of "ought," not in my second sense which already presupposes that he has made up his mind as to which act is the fitting one to do. Now suppose he is mistaken and acts according to his false belief. He can be said to have done what he morally ought to do, but he cannot be said to have done what he ought in the sense of what is most fitting to the situation. It might be argued that he has still done the most fitting, or the least unfitting, act in his power, for if he had done the act which was externally the most fitting, he would have done it from a bad motive or in a bad state of mind, and it therefore would not have been really the most fitting action. In such a situation, since there is no absolutely fitting action which he could do, the question is which is the least unfitting. But, bad as it is to do what one believes to be wrong, it may be on occasion less inappropriate to the situation that somebody should do this than that he should do a terribly harmful act which he erroneously thinks right. To make this clear by an example, let us suppose that on September 1, 1939, Hitler really thought it his duty to order the invasion of Poland. It would still have been less inappropriate to the situation that Hitler should have neglected to obey his conscience on this occasion, even through bad motives such as laziness or cowardice, than that he should have obeyed it with all the terrible effects in suffering and moral evil that the war brought in its wake. We cannot therefore say that it is always most fitting to do what one thinks most fitting, but one may still be able to say that it is always morally obligatory to do so. To keep the peace, even believing this to be wrong, would have been less unfitting than to break the peace believing it to be right. Yet the latter, and not the former, was Hitler's duty in my second sense of "duty," if he held that belief, though no doubt he violated his duty in all senses in getting into a state in which it was possible for him to hold (if he ever did hold) the belief. I think, therefore, that the second sense of "ought" differs from the other two in that to say something ought to be done in this sense is to make no statement about the real, as opposed to the believed, fittingness of the action. It also differs in that it can be applied only to actions. The first and third can also be applied to emotions or opinions, whereas it cannot be said that a person "ought" in my second sense to have an emotion or opinion, though it can be said that he ought (in this sense of "ought") to take steps to develop right emotions and opinions.

What is it that I ought to do in any or all the different senses of "ought"? Ought I to act from a certain motive, or is it only true that I ought to act or "set myself to act"? Ross has maintained that it is never the case that I ought to act from a certain motive, since "ought" implies "can" and it is not in my power to remove or alter a desire at once at the time I have it.[15] It is in my power to take steps which will affect the desires I shall feel at some future time, but this will be too late to influence the motive of the action I am doing now, though it may influence future motives. The same applies to the sense of duty as a motive, even if that is distinguished from any desire. Ross therefore held in *The Right and the Good* [16] that what we ought to do is only to produce certain results, so that if I return a book to a friend and it reaches him I shall have done what I ought, however bad my motives and however carelessly I packed it, while if it fails to reach him through an unforeseen accident I shall, however good my motives and however carefully I packed it, not have done what I ought. But before he published *Foundations of Ethics* Ross was convinced by some of the objections to this view, so then he substituted for it the view that what we ought to do is, not to produce a given result or perform a given physical act, but merely to set ourselves to do so. He, however, still maintained the view that it was not our duty to do, or to set ourselves to do, anything from a given motive, since our motives are not directly under the control of the will.[17] But it still seems paradoxical to say that I have done what I ought if I either give or "set myself" to persuade the board of examiners to give a candidate who deserves it a third-class mark not because I think he deserves it but because I dislike him, or if I set myself to pay my debts because I want to ingratiate myself with my creditor in order to obtain his help in robbing a third party. We must not indeed exaggerate the paradoxical character of what Ross is saying: he would admit that it is morally bad to do these things from such motives, and that I ought to try to reform myself so that on future occasions I shall have better motives. But, if I acted in the way mentioned, it would seem obvious to most people not only that I had done something morally bad but that I had done something wrong. They would admit that I had neglected my duty.

Yet Ross's argument must somehow be met if we are to maintain that it is ever a duty to act from a given motive. I thought at one time that I

[15] *The Right and the Good*, pp. 4–5 [pp. 165–6 this volume].
[16] Id., pp. 42 ff. [pp. 193 ff. this volume].
[17] V. *Foundation of Ethics*, Chap. VI.

could refute his argument by pointing out that "motive" is not equivalent just to "desire" but to "desire *qua* cause of an act." I then contended that, though it is impossible for me to remove a desire except by a somewhat lengthy process, I can still be said to be able to control my motives because I can prevent a desire from causing me to act and so from becoming a motive. But this oversimplifies the situation. If I can control my acts at all, it must indeed be possible for me sometimes at the moment of acting to prevent a certain desire from causing me to act. For I choose to put in a different way from that to which the desire points. But what about the case Ross has in mind where two different desires would each produce the same act? Supposing I perform the act, is it in my power at the time to decide which of the desires is to cause it? It is difficult to see how it could be, for it can only be caused by a past (though very recently past) state, not a present state, and I cannot now alter the past. Further, the act which I will is *ex hypothesi* the same whichever desire caused it, therefore it is difficult to see what difference there would be between choosing to act on one and choosing to act on the other except that I should feel differently, and it is generally admitted, as Ross urges, that my feelings cannot be changed immediately by an act of will but require for their alteration a longer process.

In order to deal with this question I think the best course is to ask: What then ought I to do if I believe that *n* is the right act but the state of my desires is such as to make me inclined to do *n* from a wrong motive? Clearly I ought to take special care in deciding whether *n* really is the right act, since there will be a great danger of my desires prejudicing me in the matter, and it may even for that reason be best to postpone acting. On these grounds Plato laid down the rule that we ought to avoid punishing somebody while we are angry. But postponement of a decision may some-times be disastrous. Suppose I am convinced after adequate consideration that *n* is right and that it would be foolish to wait longer before doing *n*, but suppose also that the bad motive is more clearly present in my mind than the good. (It cannot be alone present, otherwise I should not seriously ask the question what I ought to do at all.) Clearly it is now my duty to do *n*, and it will not be possible for me to prevent myself feeling a certain satisfaction at this for wrong reasons, but I can at least direct my attention to the aspects of the question which make the action my duty rather than to those which give me illicit satisfaction. Modern psychology has shown that it is best to recognise frankly that the less desirable tendency is present, but it is clearly also true that I ought not to rest in the enjoyment of this but recognise it as something to be fought against. At any rate it is clear that, although we cannot alter our desires at a moment's notice, we can control our attention and therefore our present state of mind to some ex-tent, so that there seems to me to be no adequate ground for saying that it can only be my duty to act, not to act in a certain state of mind. A state of mind in which I will to punish A but attend mainly to the pleasure I obtain from doing so or to the harm A has done *me* is radically different from a state of mind in which I will to punish A but direct my attention to the good reasons for doing so, even if I cannot now help feeling the pleasure (whatever I might have done earlier to avoid getting into this malevolent frame of mind). The morally important thing is, not how I feel, but how my will is directed. If it be objected that some time, however little, will elapse between my willing to attend and my actually attending, it may equally be said that some time will elapse between my willing to perform and my actually performing a physical act. If, as in Prichard's *Duty and Ignorance of Fact* and Ross's *Foundations of Ethics*, what a man ought to do is held to be simply to "set himself" to effect a certain change, this is already to admit that his duty is to change his state of mind in a certain way. So why not also admit a duty to change it in the way I suggest, since he would thereby, as Ross and Prichard both admit, make his action intrinsically better than it would otherwise be?

So the answer to the question whether it is our duty only to do something or to do it from a particular motive seems to depend on whether we mean by "motive" (1) a desire causing action or (2) circumstances relevant to the action on which our attention is fixed at the time of action. In the former case we perhaps cannot say that it is our duty at the time of action to act from one motive rather than another, for, since a cause must lie in the past, that would be saying that it was our duty to alter the past. But we can say that it is our duty to deflect our attention in such a way as to weaken the desire by attending to circumstances which would discourage rather than encourage it. In the latter case we can say that it is our duty at the time to act from a certain motive, as truly as we can say that it is our duty to act, or set ourselves to act, at all. It may be contended in regard to acting and acting from a given motive alike that they are duties which never refer to the present but always only to the (very) immediate future, since all causation takes time. The recognition that the exhortation to act from good motives is an exhortation not so much to cultivate certain feelings directly as to attend to certain features of the act and of its consequences in preference to others also enables one to reconcile the duty to act from good motives with a new line of argument introduced by Ross in *Foundations of Ethics*.[18] He says there: "When we ask what it is that makes an act my duty we are asking what is the *distinctive* feature of that act that makes it and not some other to be my duty. Now, *whichever* of two or more acts I decide to be my duty, I shall do it (if I carry out my intention) from the sense of duty. The motive will be the same whichever I do; the motive therefore can be no part of that which makes the one act my duty while the others are not, since the same motive will be the motive of whichever act I do. . . . What is it to which we in fact find ourselves attending when we are trying to discover our duty in some situation? Is it not clear that what we attend to is the nature of the possible acts, con-

[18] P. 123.

sidered apart from the motive from which we should do them—their tendency to affect the welfare of other people in this way or in that, their quality as fulfilments of promise or breaches of promise, and the like?" I certainly agree that, except for some indirect reason, consideration of my motives as desires does not help me to find out what is my duty. On the whole the objective features of an action are what we should consider, and the duty to act from a good motive, in so far as it can be contrasted with the duty of acting as such, seems to lie in attending to some of these rather than to others.

Ross also argues that, if it is my duty to do act A from the sense of duty, we must admit that it is my duty to do A from the sense that it is my duty to do A from the sense that it is my duty to do A and so on *ad infinitum*, thus involving a vicious infinite regress.[19] However, it seems to me that in the sentence "It is my duty to do A from a sense of duty" "duty" is usually being used in two different ways. Where it occurs first in the sentence, it is used in my second sense, that is, to mean that it is morally obligatory to act in a certain way; where it occurs for the second time, it is used in my third sense. The sentence then will mean that it is a moral obligation to do A because you believe A to be objectively fitting relatively to the available data, and therefore there will be no contradiction in saying that it is my duty to do A from the sense of duty, even though we mean by the latter the sense that it is our duty to do it *simpliciter* (not from a sense of duty), because "duty" means something different in the two cases. But even if it were held that I ought to act from a sense that it was morally obligatory (not merely from a sense that it was fitting) to act in this way, it would not necessarily follow that I ought to act from a sense that it was morally obligatory to act from a sense that it was morally obligatory to act in this way, still less from a sense that it was morally obligatory to act from a sense that it was morally obligatory to act from a sense that it was morally obligatory to act in this way. It may be doubted whether anybody has such a sense at all, and certainly nobody will have it but a philosopher! These conclusions, it seems to me, would only follow if we assumed that it was my duty always to do whatever I did from a sense of duty, and this Ross himself does not hold. If it is only my duty to do some of the things that I do from a sense of duty, it may well be my duty to do A from a sense of duty without its being also my duty to have this motive itself from a sense of duty and so on *ad infinitum*.

Ross's argument seems to depend also on supposing that there is a contradiction between saying that it is my duty to do A *simpliciter* and saying that it is my duty to do A from a sense of duty. But doing A is a genus of which the various species are doing A from the various kinds of possible motive, and if it is my duty to do an action which falls in one of the species it is *ipso facto* my duty to do an action which falls in the

[19] *The Right and the Good*, p. 5 [p. 166 this volume]; *Foundations of Ethics*, pp. 116 ff.

genus. The latter assertion, so far from contradicting the former, is entailed by it. There can be no contradiction in saying that I ought to do an action of genus A from the sense that it is my duty to do an action of this genus. It might after all be true both that I ought to pay a particular debt and that I ought to pay it from certain motives rather than from others. That the statement that I ought to pay the debt does not give a complete description of what I ought to do in this matter does not prevent it from being a true statement as far as it goes. However, as what I have said before suggests, the truth probably is, not that we ought to act from a sense of duty in the sense of our act being determined by the desire to do our duty, but in the sense that we ought to act with our attention directed to those characteristics of the act which make it a duty rather than to others. For example, in paying our debts we ought to attend rather to the fact that we owe the money than to the fact that we shall be summoned if we do not pay them, or shall make it easier for ourselves to obtain improper favours from our creditors if we do.

It follows that in all the senses of "ought" discussed what we ought to do is not merely to act, but to act in a certain state of mind or with a certain direction of attention. I therefore cannot agree with Ross's view in *The Right and the Good* [20] that what ought to be done is never morally good. It is morally good to act in the fitting way with my attention directed towards the right aspects of the act, especially where there is a temptation to do the opposite. And to do so is both fitting and, if I believe it to be the fitting course, obligatory. An immoral action, on the other hand, is from the nature of the case one not done with a right direction of attention, and so even if it turned out by accident to be in its external features the most beneficial act possible it would not be right. As regards mistakes I should say that if I mistakenly believe that *a* is my duty (in my first or my third sense), when *a* is really wrong, it is impossible for me to perform the right (fitting) action (in the sense in question), though it is possible for me to perform the morally obligatory act (second sense of "duty" or "right"). For if I do the act which I think right, it will for external reasons be unfitting, and if I perform the act which is really externally right I shall be performing it in a state of mind which is unfitting.

[20] p. 4 [p. 165 this volume].

A Suggested Non-Naturalistic Analysis of Good*

A. C. EWING

THIS ARTICLE is not intended to state what I positively believe to be true, but to make a suggestion which I think it well worth while working out. The suggestion is not altogether unfamiliar, but it has certain implications that seem to have been so far overlooked, or at any rate have never been developed. I do not think that it is the duty of a philosopher to confine himself in his publications to working out theories of the truth of which he is convinced, though no doubt when he is not convinced of the truth of what he is saying he ought to make the tentative character of his statements clear. It is part of a philosopher's work, as it is of a scientist's, to try out tentative hypotheses and examine their advantages and disadvantages, and I am trying this one out in public in the hope that it may suggest to someone else considerations which would confirm or refute the theory more decisively than I can do. Therefore in this article, when I refer to "my theory," I do not mean a theory which I accept, but a theory in which I am interested here, while in a state of indecision as to its acceptance or rejection. I shall mention openly the difficulties I feel most about it, and not merely give one side of the story.

It has been for some time a common amusement among philosophers to attempt an analysis of "good" which reduces it wholly to terms that are not themselves ethical, and it has often been assumed that the only alternative to this is to hold that "good" is unanalysable. This is not, however, the case. If we are to escape such an analysis we must indeed hold that at least one ethical term is unanalysable, but this one need not be "good," for good is not the only ethical term. "Good" might then be defined in terms of other ethical concepts, or, more probably, partly in psychological, partly in ethical terms. Such a definition, since it is partly ethical, even though also partly psychological, would not be open to the objections brought against "naturalism." No doubt the number of other ethical terms that could be claimed with the least plausibility to be thus

* Reprinted by kind permission of the author and the editor from *Mind*, 48, 1939. This essay was substantially incorporated in Ewing's *The Definition of Good*, The Macmillan Company, 1949, and is reprinted here with the publisher's permission.

fundamental is very limited. There seem to be three only—ought, right, duty—and these are so closely connected that a definition of "good" in terms of one could easily be turned into a definition in terms of either of the others. I wish in the present article to suggest a definition of this kind. It would, if adopted, cut away the ground beneath the feet of both sides in one of the chief controversies of modern ethics, that between those who hold and those who reject "ideal utilitarianism." It would also, I think, take away some of the apparent plausibility of naturalistic views of ethics.

But as a preliminary it is first necessary to say something about right, ought and duty, and distinguish two different usages of these terms. Firstly, the act that I ought to perform may mean that act of those physically in my power in a given situation which it would be preferable for me to choose in the light of the available evidence. "Available evidence" is here used to mean "evidence of which I am either aware or could become aware without more trouble and loss of time than is practicable under the circumstances." Some philosophers have used "ought" in a sense in which it is to be understood without this reservation,[1] but in ordinary speech we should usually admit that a man had done what he ought even if the act turned out unfortunately owing to some unforeseen consequence, provided the consequence was, humanly speaking, unforeseeable, or could not have been anticipated without obtaining expert advice that was not at the man's disposal. A man may fail to do what he ought in this sense for three reasons: (a) because he has made a mistake as to certain matters of fact or anticipated consequences, (b) because he has made certain wrong value judgments, (c) because, while recognising that he ought to do A, he wishes rather to do B and gives way to the temptation. In the first case it would generally be admitted that he was not *morally* to blame except in so far as the mistake was due to neglect to take adequate trouble in order to find out what he ought to do; but this admission would not prevent us from saying that he ought to have acted differently. We say this even where the only reason for performing the act was that it would give the agent pleasure, in which case we do not usually think of the agent as morally to blame if he knowingly neglects to do it, e.g. "you really ought to have seen this film," "you ought to have ordered clear soup—you know you never care much about thick." Turning to (c), we certainly should in most cases admit that the agent was morally to blame in some degree if he believed that he ought to perform the act in this sense and yet did not do it, though, as I have said, we should, rightly or wrongly, not be inclined to think this if the reason in favour of doing it were simply that it ministered to his own pleasure. In every other case I think we should. In case (b), i.e. where he acts wrongly through a mistake not about facts but about values, we should also be inclined to think him to blame morally, and

---

[1] e.g. Moore, *Ethics*, pp. 190 ff. [pp. 117 ff. reset edition].

not only intellectually, if we thought the error a big one and he was not insane or handicapped by a very bad education.

But that there are at least two different senses of "ought" seems to be shown by the now common-place paradox of ethics that a man ought always to do what he thinks his duty even if he is wrong in thinking it his duty, i.e. in thinking that he ought to do it. Obviously this statement would be absurd unless "ought" was being used in two different senses. In the one sense "the act I ought to perform" stands for the act which is most fitting or most desirable in view of the situation; in the other sense it stands for an act neglect to perform which would be morally bad. An act that a given person ought to perform in the first sense might clearly not be an act which he ought to perform in the second sense, namely, because he might have made a mistake as to the consequences of the act and therefore would not be morally to blame for omitting to do what he honestly thought harmful. We may even, as the above paradox shows, blame a person morally for not performing an act that we thought very wrong in the first sense, because he believed it to be right and therefore must have neglected to perform it out of bad motives, so that an act which a man ought not to do in the first sense may be an act that he positively ought to do in the second. E.g. I should think it wrong to subscribe to a loan for helping Japan to conquer China, but if a Japanese honestly thought it his duty to do this I should say that he would be morally to blame if he did not do it.

Note that these are not *definitions* of "ought": if so they would be circular, at least the first, for "preferable act to choose" cannot be understood without already presupposing the notion of "ought," and I think "morally good" (or bad) has to be defined in terms of the second sense of "ought." I think at least the first sense of "ought" unanalysable, but we may still make use of phrases which help the reader to distinguish it from the second. It is clear that the second presupposes the first in the sense that in order ever to do what I ought in the second sense I must have at least some belief about what I ought to do in the first sense; but this does not mean that it is analysable in terms of the first sense. I shall suggest later that it may be, but *prima facie* they are quite different. The notion involved in the first sense is that which Prof. Broad calls fittingness.

I have in this connection been using the term *act* in the same way as Sir David Ross to cover only the initiation of a change, and not its initiation from a certain motive, but I should hold against him that we are under an obligation not only to act, but to act from a right motive. In supporting his view he uses the argument that "ought" implies "can" and that, a motive being a desire, we cannot remove or alter it at the time, though we can voluntarily take steps which will tend to its increase or diminution at some future time.[2] To this I should reply that "motive" is not equivalent to "desire" but to desire quâ cause of an act, and if I can control my acts

2 *The Right and the Good*, p. 5 [p. 166 this volume].

at all it must sometimes be possible for me at the moment of acting to prevent a certain desire from causing me to act and so from becoming a motive, though it is impossible for me to remove the desire except by a gradual process. I thus at the moment of acting determine my motive. I cannot determine immediately what the desires are to be which accompany the act, at least in its initial phase, but I can determine which desire (or desires) is to act as motive. So, following Ross's terminology [3] in using "act" to stand for the initiation of change, and "action" for the initiating of it from a certain motive, I should hold in disagreement with him that we can apply the terms ought, right, duty, not only to acts but to actions.[3a]

In ordinary speech "right" is used in two senses closely corresponding to those of "ought." *The* right act is in fact synonymous with "the act I ought to perform," but right without the prefix *the* is most commonly used as equivalent to "not wrong." It is thus applied to acts which are permissible but not obligatory as well as to those which are obligatory in either of the senses of "ought." It can also be applied to any one of several alternative acts, where it is the case that I ought to do one of them but it does not matter which. "A wrong act" just means an act which ought not to be done, in one or both of the two senses of "ought." "A duty" (I am here referring to absolute, not *prima facie*, duty) is used most commonly to stand for an act which I ought to perform in the second sense. But, since we can talk about making a mistake as to one's duty, it is also used to stand for an act which I ought to perform in the first sense. However, the term is not usually applied to acts primarily directed towards our own pleasure, however innocent and rational the act be, or to relatively trivial acts, or to acts which there is no possible motive for omitting.

We shall now turn to "good." It is quite impossible to deny that the term is highly ambiguous, and we must be prepared to admit that it is sometimes used in a purely naturalistic, psychological sense. When I say "these strawberries are good" I probably do not mean anything more than that I like them or find them pleasant, and perhaps that most people would do so; when I say "this is a good knife" I probably do not mean anything more than that it is likely to be efficient in carrying out any of the purposes, good or bad, for which knives are primarily used in preference to other instruments. The question at issue between naturalist and non-naturalist is not whether "good" is *ever* used in a naturalistic sense, but whether it *always* is so used. But the sense of "good" which is usually being discussed when we ask whether "good" is or is not analysable is that usually distinguished from others by the use of the phrases "intrinsically good," "good as an end," "good-in-itself." It is this sense of "good" that Prof. Moore declares indefinable in *Principia Ethica*, and it is round this sense that the controversy has largely turned.

It is not indeed the only sense of good which the non-naturalist will

[3] p. 7 [p. 167 this volume].
[3a] [Cf. Ewing's more elaborate discussion of this point, pp. 226 ff. this volume.]

hold incapable of reduction to naturalistic terms; others are (1) productive of what is intrinsically good, (2) good-making [4] as applied to characteristics, while "good" in the primary sense mentioned above is applied only to particular existents, (3) morally good. But of these other senses (1) and (2) are definable in terms of "intrinsically good" as applied to particulars, and (3) is usually held to stand for either a particular species of intrinsic goodness or for intrinsic goodness as qualifying a particular class of objects. It has usually been assumed that, if goodness ever can reasonably be interpreted non-naturalistically, it must be so interpreted in the sense used by Prof. Moore, *intrinsically good*. This indeed would be disputed by Prof. Campbell, who gives a naturalistic definition of good in this sense, but refuses to give a naturalistic definition of "morally good." [5] He would, however, no doubt not regard the latter as indefinable, but define it in terms of ought in my second sense. At any rate, the definition of "good" I am going to propose now is intended as a definition of "good" in the intrinsic sense (1) above.

It is not necessary here to discuss Prof. Moore's arguments for the view that "good" is indefinable. What Moore is attacking is any attempt to define "good" wholly in non-ethical terms, and in this I agree with him, although I should not accept his arguments in *Principia Ethica* as they stand any more than he himself would do now. What I shall suggest is a definition of "good" partly in ethical and partly in psychological terms. Provided ethical terms are introduced at all, even though they do not make up the whole of the definition, this will save it from the charge of being naturalistic.

Now we may note that Moore has himself suggested a synonym for good as applied to an experience, i.e. "worth having for its own sake." [6] This is not necessarily inconsistent with the view that good is indefinable, for there might be various verbal phrases which could be properly used as synonyms in order to help people to see more clearly what was meant by a term without being themselves eligible as definitions of the term. It might be the case that "worth" in "worth having for its own sake" could itself only be defined in terms of good, so that the phrase would be quite useless as a definition of the latter, and yet the phrase might be appropriately used to help some people to become clearer as to what they meant by "good," and especially to distinguish the sense under discussion from other senses of "good." But I think in fact "worth having for its own sake" can be analysed in a way which does not make it a vicious circle to use the phrase as a definition of good; but before I propound the analysis, I should like the reader to consider carefully whether the phrase "an intrinsically good experience" is or is not the exact equivalent of "an experience worth

---

[4] To borrow Prof. Broad's term.

[5] "Moral and Non-moral Values," *Mind*, vol. xliv, no. 175, pp. 273 ff. [pp. 340 ff. this volume].

[6] *Proceedings of Arist. Soc.*, Suppl., vol. xi, pp. 122 ff.

having for its own sake." In this definition, unlike the naturalistic definitions, it seems clear both that the *definiens* and the *definiendum* are co-extensive, and that this is a necessary proposition. It seems clear that there could not be an experience which was intrinsically good that was not worth having for its own sake, or an experience which was worth having for its own sake that was not intrinsically good. This seems to be not merely a contingent fact but a logical necessity. Now it may well be the case that, say, AB entails and is entailed by C, and yet that AB is not a definition of C; consequently it is impossible strictly to prove that anything is a definition of anything else, and in the present case it is open to anybody to maintain that besides the characteristic expressed by the words "worth having for its own sake" there is another indefinable characteristic "good," if he thinks he can discern such a characteristic, which always necessarily accompanies but is different from the characteristic of being "worth having for its own sake." But I am not clear that I can discern any such characteristic, and I should point to the fact that when in ordinary conversation we wish to convey exactly the meaning of the term "intrinsically good" to a person not familiar with it we should most naturally use just the phrase in question. "Worth having for its own sake" seems to be in fact just the phrase which the man in the street would use when he wishes to express what the philosopher calls "intrinsically" as distinct from "instrumentally good."

But, while "worth having for its own sake" is equivalent to "intrinsically good" when applied to an experience, there is an objection to taking it as equivalent to "intrinsically good" without qualification. It is this: though it is often held that experiences are the only things which can be intrinsically good, we must not define "intrinsically good" in a way which would make it a verbal contradiction to say of anything but an experience that it was intrinsically good. To say that the State is good-in-itself or to say that beautiful objects are good in themselves may be wrong, but is not verbally self-contradictory. Now on the definition of "intrinsically good" suggested it would be meaningless, because experiences are the only kind of things that we can be said to "have" in the sense in which the term "have" is being used here,[7] though there is another sense or senses of "have" in which it is possible to have a State or to have beautiful objects. But this does not prevent the two phrases being exactly equivalent when they are applied to an experience.

What analysis are we to give of "worth having for its own sake?" Surely it means just "such that, in the absence of any positive reason against it, it ought to be chosen for its own sake." Thus we have a definition of "intrinsically good" in terms of "ought," and while the phrase "worth having for its own sake" can, without verbal contradiction, only be applied to experiences, the definition now given can be applied more widely if there are indeed things other than experiences which are intrinsically good in the

[7] As Moore points out (*ib.*, p. 124).

sense under discussion. But what is the sense of "ought" here? Not the second, because we are not necessarily thinking of moral obligation. If the experience is merely a pleasure of an innocent but not very elevated kind, most people would hold that I should not be *morally* to blame for deliberately neglecting to produce it in myself, and this, whether a right judgment or not, is certainly not verbally inconsistent with saying that the pleasure is intrinsically good. But it does seem clear that when I say that an experience is intrinsically good I am asserting that it is preferable to have it rather than not, that, other things being equal, I ought to choose it in the first sense of "ought." [8] Whether I should be morally to blame or not for declining to produce it when I could produce it without doing corresponding harm, at any rate it would be rational and desirable to choose to produce it, other things being equal.

I do not wish to insist on the word "choose," to which some people may object. It is always difficult to make ordinary terms serve the purposes of philosophical definition, and I can only use it to cover everything I want it to cover by using the term in a somewhat strained sense. "Produce" or "promote" would perhaps have been better terms. And I certainly do not wish to analyse the notion of choice here. What I meant by using the term is that "the good" means "what it is fitting to bring into existence for its own sake," or "what ought to be brought into existence, other things being equal"; but the important point I think is that "good" has been defined in terms of what Ross calls a pro-attitude. When something is good it is fitting that we should welcome it, rejoice in it if it exists, desire and seek it if it does not exist. I think that there is something vague and indeterminate about the use of almost all terms in ordinary speech, and therefore we cannot expect to analyse a common-sense proposition in a way which is both quite precise or definite and quite correct. Sometimes we may be thinking rather of the fact that we ought to welcome a thing when we call it good, sometimes rather of the fact that we ought to seek it, etc. But I think we can see quite clearly that the various attitudes I have mentioned have something in common which is opposite to the common element in condemning, shunning, fearing, regretting, etc. The former may well be called pro-attitudes, the latter anti-attitudes. The former are positive and favourable to their object, the latter negative and hostile. What is good is a suitable object of pro-attitudes, what is evil a suitable object of anti-attitudes. What is intrinsically good is a suitable object of a pro-attitude for its own sake.[9]

It might be suggested that I should have defined "good" in terms of desire rather than in terms of choice, i.e. as what ought to be desired for its own sake. I have not done so for the following reasons. (1) It seems to me that to say we ought to choose a thing because it ought to be desired for its own sake is to put the cart before the horse. It is in general

---

[8] v. above, p. 3 [p. 232 this volume].
[9] For a similar theory v. Osborne, *The Philosophy of Value*, pp. 93 ff.

only good to desire something for its own sake because it is worth having when we have got it. (2) If desire means a certain uneasy emotion, it is not the case that we ought to feel it towards whatever is good. The less we feel this emotion towards what we cannot obtain or bring about, however good that object may be, the better on the whole, since it will only make us less happy without doing any good; but if "desire" means something more than this uneasy emotion, it becomes a striving to pursue and bring about the existence of its object, and if so the definition in terms of desire merges into my definition. This is in fact what we mean when we use the term "desirable," a common synonym for "good"; we do not mean that we ought to feel a certain emotion towards what is described as desirable, but that this object is worth attaining.

Now if the analysis I have suggested be adopted, it has an important bearing on one of the chief controversies of recent years in this country on ethics, that between the "Ideal Utilitarians," who differ indeed from hedonistic utilitarians in holding that there are other goods besides pleasure but agree with them that we ought always to aim at producing the greatest amount of good and the least amount of evil, and those like Ross who think that there are independent "*prima facie* duties," i.e. that there are certain kinds of acts, e.g. promise-keeping, which carry with them an obligation not derivable from the good they produce or the evil they avert.

Now at the ordinary level the controversy between the two sides is very hard to solve. I think we must admit that the obligation, e.g. to keep promises, is not to be explained solely by the consequences of doing so; but this does not prove that we have a *prima facie* duty to keep promises over and above the duty to produce the greatest possible amount of good; for the Utilitarian, if he is not also a hedonist, can always retort that the act of keeping a promise is good-in-itself, or the act of breaking it bad. In that case the obligation would not be explained entirely by the consequences of the act, and yet it would be derivable from the obligation to produce the greatest good, as the Ideal Utilitarian maintains. For in the good produced by an action must be included not only the good lying in its consequences, but any intrinsic good that belongs to the action itself in its own right. The intrinsic good might indeed be outweighed in certain cases by the badness of the consequences, so that the Ideal Utilitarian could not admit the impossibility of cases arising which would make it a duty to break a promise or violate other *prima facie* duties. But neither does Ross. He holds that two *prima facie* duties may clash and that one has then to give way to the other. It might indeed be doubted whether the keeping of a promise is by itself intrinsically good, e.g., there does not seem to be any intrinsic value in my paying a bill as a matter of course, having no temptation to do otherwise; but it seems plain to me that to break a promise is intrinsically bad, and this evil should therefore be avoided even apart from its consequences; and, if the Utilitarian takes this line, it seems impossible to refute his theory at the usual level at which the controversy is conducted.

But if the suggested analysis of good is adopted the position is radically altered at once. For in that case to say that something is intrinsically good just means to say that I ought to choose it other things being equal, i.e. I have a *prima facie* duty to produce it, so that something like Ross's position becomes inevitable. There is no sense any longer in opposing to it Ideal Utilitarianism, for "good" is now no longer another concept from which we infer what we ought to do. An "intrinsic good" just means something which we have a *prima facie* duty to produce if we can, and to give a list of the different kinds of intrinsic goods is just to give a list of our *prima facie* obligations. It might indeed seem that the view suggested made the utilitarian principle that we ought always to produce the greatest good in our power a tautology, so that utilitarianism must be true; for "the greatest good" would then have to mean, it seems, "that which we ought to choose in preference to any other." But it would be a Pyrrhic victory, for the whole point of the utilitarian principle was that obligation is derivable from good, while the reverse is true if the suggested analysis of good be correct. The utilitarian would be guilty of a vicious circle if he insisted on deducing obligation from "good" and then accepted an analysis which made "good" itself definable in terms of what we ought to do. That it makes the principle that we ought always to produce the greatest good in our power necessarily true, seems to me the chief argument for Ideal Utilitarianism against Ross's view; for it seems hardly credible that it could ever be a duty deliberately to produce less good when we could produce more; but if the analysis I have suggested were adopted this principle would be accepted in a form which did not contradict the contentions of Ross. The antithesis between a view which based the "ought" or "the right" on the "good" and a view which based it on *prima facie* duties would then disappear. There would still be an antithesis between a view according to which what we ought to do depended entirely on consequences and a view according to which it depended partly on the intrinsic nature of the action; but the former view would seem very unreasonable, for surely we must take account of the intrinsic nature of an action before we decide whether we ought to do it.

It may be objected that there seem clearly to be cases where it is at the very least arguable that the act which I ought to do is not the act which, as far as we can tell, is likely to produce the greatest good, e.g. the case of stealing from a rich miser in order to give the money to a poor man who is deserving. It seems a perfectly intelligible and not self-contradictory position to admit on the one hand that I should do more good if I stole the money and gave it to the poor man, and yet that I still ought to refrain from stealing it. But I suggest that the distinction here is really between (*a*) what I ought to choose in abstraction from the only available means of producing it, (*b*) what I ought to choose to produce by these means.

Thus I ought to choose that A who is poor should have £100 rather than B who is rich, but I ought not to choose that he should have it through my stealing. We think it a greater good that A should have the £100, and other things being equal I ought to bring this about, if I can, in preference to the other state of affairs; but if I can only bring it about by stealing, other things are not equal. It is better that B should have the £100 and not A than that A should have the £100 obtained by stealing.

But now there arises a new complication. There is a sense in which it is sometimes right to speak of an action as intrinsically good. But, when people describe actions as intrinsically good, I do not think they are usually using the term in the same sense as when they use it, e.g., of pleasant experiences. We regard, e.g., a particular action of self-sacrifice as intrinsically good. Do we mean to say that it is fitting that the person who makes the sacrifice should choose it for its own sake quite apart from consequences? Surely not. That would lead to irrational asceticism. To sacrifice himself when it does no good to anyone is not something which a man ought to choose. The self-sacrificing action does not seem to be intrinsically good in the sense in which, e.g., innocent pleasures, aesthetic experience, personal affection, intellectual activity are held to be so. If it were, we ought to spend most of our time torturing ourselves in order to realise the admittedly very high intrinsic value of self-sacrifice. I suggest, however, that intrinsic goodness as applied to actions may still be analysed in terms of "ought" (in the first sense of the term), provided the psychological term of the analysis is different. I suggest that we usually mean by good actions simply actions that ought to be admired or approved, which is certainly not the usual meaning of "intrinsically good" in the other case. A pleasure, however innocent, is not something to be admired, though it is something to be liked and, other things being equal, pursued.

But we must add, I think, a qualification and say "morally admired." For we may also admire a cleverness which does not display moral qualities, though our admiration even for the cleverness is lessened if it displays immoral ones. Nor must we use "admired" or "approved" here to stand for "judged good," since in that case we should be guilty of a vicious circle. It must, in the analysis given, stand for an emotion or a state of mind tinged with emotional qualities. I do not wish to discuss the psychological question whether moral admiration is a single emotion or a class or a blend of emotion; but it does seem to me that there is something specific about this kind of admiration which distinguishes it from other kinds. And it is quite clear that there are certain actions to which this kind of feeling is the appropriate reaction, as sympathy is to suffering and certain aesthetic experiences to a great drama. There is, however, a curious point to note here in passing: with persons other than the agent himself the appropriate reaction is admiration, but with the agent himself it is not. A man should not admire himself for his moral virtues. In the opposite case moral disapproval is an appropriate emotion for both the agent and others, but moral disapproval of oneself feels very different from moral disapproval of another. For one thing it is, generally at least, an asthenic, while the latter is generally a sthenic emotion. If we are not willing to regard moral admiration as a specific emotion, we can still retain the principle of the definition but say that good actions in the moral sense are actions more or less admirable on account of their volitional quality, i.e. as showing a persistence of the will in face of what would be a great temptation to most people, and a direction of the will to good ends. Clever or beautiful pieces of work would also be fitting objects of admiration, but for a different reason.

There will then be at least two senses of "intrinsically good," but these, though different, will have two very important points in common: (*a*) they will both be analyses of "good" in terms of "ought" together with a psychological concept, (*b*) the latter will be in both cases that of a "pro-attitude," though the pro-attitude will be different. Admiration and choosing (or pursuing) have both in common something important which may be expressed by this term pro-attitude, they are both in a very definite sense favourable to the object towards which they are directed. That "intrinsically good" should be used in two different senses not clearly distinguished, when the senses have so much in common, is not to be wondered at. I had arrived at this distinction before hearing the paper of Sir David Ross at the International Congress of Philosophy [10] in 1937, but when I heard it this paper provided welcome confirmation of the point that there are two such different senses. He there uses the term "worthy object of interest" of objects which are said to be intrinsically good in the one sense, and the term "admirable" of those which are said to be intrinsically good in the other. This agrees substantially with the theory suggested by me except that he does not claim that the term "admirable" gives an *analysis* of what good means in the second sense of good, though he thinks that "worthy object of interest" does in the first.

I am not prepared to say that, when we speak of a moral action as good, we are never using "intrinsically good" in the first as opposed to the second sense, but in the majority of cases I think it is impossible to distinguish "intrinsically good" as thus applied from "morally admirable." I think this second sense is also our usual sense when we speak of a man's character or life as good, though we should grant that it could also be good in the first sense of the term. A good character or a morally good life is assuredly a worthy object of pursuit, and is so not merely for any hedonistic advantages it may have to oneself and others. But when we appraise particular actions as good I do not think this is what we are usually thinking of. We are rather thinking of their admirable qualities, and in some cases it is quite certain that actions we rightly admire are not actions which ought to be chosen except for the sake of their consequences.

It is irrelevant to object that we cannot say I ought to feel a certain emotion, such as admiration, because I cannot alter my emotions at a mo-

[10] *Travaux du IXe Congrès International de Philosophie*, xi, p. 78 ff.

ment's notice. Perhaps our second sense of ought is only applicable where the thing which it is said we ought to do could be brought about by an act of will on our part at the time, but we can certainly speak of the emotions a man ought to have in the sense of "the suitable emotions for him to have" (first sense of ought).

I have thus been using "ought" here in its wider sense, and not in the sense in which failure to do what one ought implies moral blameworthiness.[11] But this still leaves us with two unreduced ethical concepts, i.e. "ought" in its two different senses. However, there remains a possible way of defining one sense of "ought" in terms of the other together with a psychological concept. I suggest, namely, that we might analyse "A ought (second sense) to do this" as meaning "(1) A ought (first sense) to do this, and (2) if he does not do this he ought (first sense) to be in that respect an object of the emotion of moral disapproval," or perhaps as meaning simply (2) without (1).

I have not analysed the proposition as asserting that if he does this he will be a suitable object of moral admiration, because there are many acts which it would be wrong not to do but the doing of which does not call for admiration. It would be very wrong of me to cheat people by not paying my debts, yet I certainly under normal circumstances deserve no admiration for paying my debts, though I should be a suitable object of a condemnatory emotion if I did not do so. I am not at all certain that this account adequately brings out the full, specific nature of the ethical ought, but I put it forward as at least worth discussion.

If the analyses suggested be correct, we have succeeded in reducing the different fundamental ethical concepts to one, "ought" in the first sense given. This, I think, is in principle the same as to reduce them to what Prof. Broad calls the concept of *fittingness*.

Besides settling the issue between Ross's view and Ideal Utilitarianism, my theory has the advantage of being the minimum non-naturalistic theory of ethics, i.e. the theory other than naturalism which admits least in the way of non-natural concepts. For it only admits one unanalysable ethical concept; and as against the theories which hold "good" to be the only such unanalysable concept it has also an advantage in that it is even more difficult to deny that there is a relation of fittingness which is not definable in purely psychological terms than to deny that there is a quality of good which is not thus definable. In these days when naturalistic tendencies are so strong, it is more than ever worth while for a non-naturalist to ask— What is the maximum of concessions I can make without destroying my whole view of ethics? and for a naturalist to ask— Have I refuted all forms of non-naturalistic ethics or only some? (I include under the heading "naturalistic," theories which, while not admitting that ethical statements can be analysed wholly in psychological terms, reduce the additional element to a sort of emotional penumbra, or an expletive added for practical

----

[11] *v.* above, p. 3 [p. 233 this volume].

effect, e.g. the theory of Duncan-Jones.) It is a curious fact that the controversy between naturalists and their opponents has centred rather round "good" than round "ought," and I think that this was a mistake in tactics on the part of the latter. I do not think that a plausible naturalistic account of "good" can be given, but at least this is somewhat less difficult than to give a plausible naturalistic account of "ought." Once, however, we have accepted a non-naturalistic view of "ought," it is clearly only reasonable to suppose that there are non-naturalistic senses of good, because "good" in some of its uses at any rate can clearly be analysed in terms of "ought."

Now let us turn to the objections to the theory suggested. Most people will probably be left unsatisfied by it because they will feel that a theory like this gives no real explanation why I ought to do one thing rather than another while Utilitarianism at least does that. One must be careful not to state this objection wrongly. We must not express it by saying that the fact that something ought to be produced is not the reason why it is good; for my theory does not hold it to be the reason why it is good but identical with the fact that it is good. But my theory does leave the fact that we ought to do certain things unexplained, while utilitarianism explains it further by reference to the good. True, the Utilitarian, if asked to explain why certain things are good-in-themselves, cannot do so but just has to say that he sees them to be good; but at any rate he does carry the explanation one stage further back. And it does to many seem somehow more rational to take propositions such as "this is good" as ultimate and self-vindicating than to hold this view about propositions such as "this is what I ought to do." I seem to be left with nothing but a chaos of *prima facie* duties for none of which there is any reason beyond themselves, and thus to abandon the essential purpose of Ethics, which is to make coherent our ethical beliefs. It is true that the advantage of Utilitarianism relatively to my theory is much less than might seem at first sight, because unless he is a hedonist the utilitarian will have to admit an ultimate variety of intrinsic goods, and it might be argued that this is quite as bad as to admit an ultimate variety of *prima facie* duties. There is a good deal in this reply, but I cannot be at all satisfied with the position unless it is possible on principle to bring the *prima facie* duties into some kind of system.

Now there are different kinds of system. If we could deduce all ethical duties from a single principle, e.g. that I ought always to do what I could will everybody else to do, or from one single type of good, e.g. pleasure, we should have a system of a certain kind. Such systems in ethics seem to me impracticable. They either give only a pretence of explanation, because they leave outside any concrete idea of the good, which has to be smuggled in unnoticed if the system is to work; or they conflict with moral judgments which we see to be true. They do not do justice to the complexity of ethics.

But you may have a system of another kind. The systematic character of a body of beliefs may lie, not in the fact that they are all deducible from one and the same principle, but in the fact that, though no single one of the beliefs can occupy the exalted position of being premiss for all the rest, they are all logically related to each other so that you could not alter any one without contradicting others. It is a system of this sort that is envisaged in the coherence theory of truth. Could the propositions of ethics form a system of this kind? Clearly not in the full sense. For one could deny that it was, e.g., a *prima facie* duty not to lie, without contradicting any other of the *prima facie* duties. But there is still, I think, a sense in which they may be said to form a system. Although I could perhaps deny the existence of any one of the *prima facie* duties without contradicting the assertion of any of the others, they might still form a system in the sense that the different *prima facie* duties were so connected that to fulfil any one, on principle and in general harmonised with and forwarded the fulfilment of others; and this seems to be the case in fact. The utilitarians hold that it is generally a duty to tell the truth, keep promises, be just, make reparation for wrong one has done, treat our parents with love, look after our children in preference to those of other people, etc., but as is well known they all maintain that these are generally duties because they further other goods. The view that this is the only reason for their being duties has been challenged by non-utilitarians, but hardly the view that they do further other goods and on the whole make for the best state of society attainable all round. Now "further other goods" becomes on the view I have suggested "fulfil other *prima facie* duties." But, if the different *prima facie* duties play into each other's hands in this way, that may well serve as a confirmation that we are on the right lines in admitting them, so that we are not wholly dependent on intuition, but have also this test by consistency to use.

But what about the undoubted clashes between different *prima facie* duties that do occur at times? Surely I may be easily placed in a situation in which I have to break one of two promises because the two are incompatible with each other, or to neglect either my *prima facie* duty to a relative or my *prima facie* duty to the State? Is not this sufficient to show that the line of argument suggested is a cul-de-sac, and that the *prima facie* duties cannot possibly be regarded as constituting a system?

It may be retorted, however, that if we investigate these cases of clash we find that so far from refuting they support the view that the *prima facie* duties constitute a system in some sense like the one I suggested. Let us take one of the acutest possible clashes, that arising in the case of war. Suppose one's country has promised to help another country against aggression,[12] and that country is wrongfully attacked by a Power whose form of government we cannot help regarding as a tyranny which has deliberately and persistently set aside in theory and practice principles

[12] This was written before the crisis of last September, and is not intended to have any political reference.

of justice and liberty which we consider quite fundamental to civilisation. What are we to do? If we fight we are certainly violating *prima facie* duties by the killing and other evil practices which war involves. If we do not fight we are breaking our solemn word and letting a higher form of civilisation be overthrown by a lower, and injustice and wrong triumph over right. I do not propose to answer this question here, but *whichever* answer we give it should be clear that we are violating some *prima facie* duties. But this does not disprove; it on the contrary supports the view that the *prima facie* duties constitute a system. For why does this acute clash arise? Only because somebody has done wrong first. In every war at least one party is to blame. But, if the *prima facie* duties do form a system, surely the only thing to expect is that, if you violate one, you or someone else will be brought to a position in which others have to be violated, as, if you make a mistake in a proposition in the arithmetical system, this will lead to more contradictions. The occurrence of clashes as a resultant of violating one *prima facie* duty is thus not a contradiction, but a confirmation, of the view that the *prima facie* duties constitute a system. If they do constitute a system, clashes are just what one ought to expect under these circumstances; and most of the serious clashes which occur in fact are due to previous violations of duty on the part of some person. If I make two inconsistent promises I must break one, but then I have violated my duty already in making them: I may have to choose between lying and confessing to a crime the knowledge of which will bring great pain to those I love; but then I have already done wrong in committing the crime: I live in a social system in which I cannot give satisfactory opportunities to my family without grasping after material gain somewhat more zealously than is desirable; that is because the social system is morally evil in so far as, through being too competitive, it encourages selfishness and makes money too much the standard of success: one cannot overthrow a particular existing bad political or economic system rapidly without a violent revolution that will involve great misery and injustice; but that clash arises because the people who think they benefit by it are too much concerned for their own interests and too little for the welfare of others to let it be amended peaceably, and perhaps because the people who lose by it are not disciplined enough to avoid revolutionary excesses. We need not therefore, I think, confine ourselves to saying that the *prima facie* duties are known intuitively; we can add that they are confirmed by the fact that to further one on the whole furthers others, and to violate one involves sooner or later violating others. There is thus a sort of coherence test available in ethics after all.

But we must not go too far in this line of reply. All clashes cannot be explained in this way. Natural disasters, as well as wars and bad social systems, may cause clashes, e.g. there is the well-known case of lying in order to save an invalid from hearing bad news, or again a man might through an earthquake be placed in a position in which he had to choose between saving the life of his child and that of two other persons unknown to him.

So the most we can say is that in general and on principle the *prima facie* duties fit together. To fulfil one tends, of its intrinsic nature, to fulfil others, and to violate one tends to the violation of others.

Let us now consider further objections to our theory. The most serious perhaps is this. If "good" means "what ought to be chosen," "A is better than B" will presumably mean "A ought to be chosen in preference to B," and "this act produces the greatest good" will presumably mean "This act ought to be chosen in preference to any other alternative possible at the time." But if so it would seem to be a tautology to say that I ought, apart from ulterior consequences, always to choose my own greater good in preference to somebody else's lesser good, or the greater good of a total stranger in preference to my mother's lesser good; and these propositions, whether true or not, are certainly not tautologies. They have been maintained, e.g. by utilitarians, and they may even be tenable when one has allowed, in estimating the consequences, for the good effects of encouraging an unselfish spirit and family affection even at the cost of some loss of immediate good; but they would be hotly disputed, and to dispute them does not seem to be equivalent to the self-contradiction of asserting that the greater good is not greater. Therefore, since the theory proposed makes what is clearly a synthetic proposition into a tautology, it would seem that the theory must be mistaken. The objection would be still stronger if we had substituted "ought to be desired" for "ought to be chosen" as an analysis of good; for to say that I ought to desire the good of a stranger as much as the equal good of my mother is quite obviously false.

A person who maintains the analysis of "good" that I have suggested might avoid this objection by admitting the logical possibility that something, A, might be better than something else, B, relatively to one agent but not to another. He might still hold that whatever was good at all (in the sense under discussion) was good for all men, i.e. anyone ought to produce it if he could do so without sacrificing anything else worth producing—or producing anything else, e.g. lies, which ought to be avoided; but he would have to say also that, where the agent had to choose between producing one good thing and another good thing, it would not necessarily be the case that each agent ought to produce the same one. This involves the admission of a certain relativity into the conception of good. What is good relatively to me, though perhaps always also good relatively to you, is not necessarily equally good relatively to you. The innocent pleasure of a close relative of mine is relatively to any mind good, but it might still be better relatively to me than it is relatively to you, in this sense of good. This relativity contradicts any notion of intrinsic goodness hitherto propounded by people who took an objective view of ethics, as far as I know; but it may be right for all that and, although not easy about it in my own mind, I am not clear that it involves any of the objections brought against the ordinary types of ethical relativism or subjectivism. We must remember also that to say that A is better than B for me and not for you is not, on the analysis of "good" given, to say that it possesses one quality for me in itself and a contradictory quality for you, but simply that I ought to choose A rather than B and you B rather than A.

But there remains another way out. It may be said that what I ought to choose is not my mother's good but the production of my mother's good by myself. (I cannot indeed choose the former in abstraction from the latter.) Now the production of my mother's good by myself is a different thing from the production of my mother's good by a stranger, and therefore it might easily be the case that I ought to choose the production of my mother's good by myself in preference to the production of a stranger's equal good by myself, while the stranger's son ought to choose the production of his parent's good by himself in preference to the production of my parent's good by himself. To speak of the goods of the parents as equal means that, other things being equal, neither has more claim to pursuit than the other; but if I have a special relation involving obligation to one person which I have not to the other, other things are not equal, and it does not follow that because the goods of A and B are equally worth pursuit *per se*, therefore the whole—good of A + the pursuit and attainment of A's good by me—will be of equal value to the whole—good of B + the pursuit and attainment of B's good by me.

Ross denies that the pursuit of one's own pleasure is a *prima facie* duty, but I should not follow him here. I think that one ought, other things being equal, to do what makes for one's own pleasure, and that the contrary supposition is due to a confusion of the two senses of "ought" above mentioned. It is at any rate arguable that I am not morally to blame for neglecting my own pleasure unnecessarily; but even if this be so, it is unsuitable, unfitting, irrational that I should neglect it. I *ought* to do what furthers my own pleasure in my first, if not in my second, sense of "ought." If I were not under a *prima facie* obligation to do so, I should always be under an obligation to sacrifice any amount of my pleasure, however great, for any amount of somebody else's, however small, provided no other goods were at stake. For I certainly have a *prima facie* obligation to further the pleasure of others, and this could not be counteracted except by a contrary *prima facie* obligation to further my own. We need not therefore follow Ross in denying that pleasure is a good in the non-naturalistic sense in which, e.g., knowledge or love is a good, though it may be a lower kind of good.

If the analysis of good suggested were adopted, it would explain how it is that it has seemed likely to many people that "good" could be analysed naturalistically. The most popular naturalistic analyses of good are in terms of either desire or approval. Now in one sense good has been analysed by me as what ought to be chosen or pursued, and, while a case, though I do not think an adequate case, can no doubt be made out for the view that it would have been better to analyse it as what ought to be desired, pursuit is at any rate very closely connected with desire. And in the other sense treated, "good" has been analysed by me as what ought to be admired or approved. Now "ought" is a relational term, and we do not have a distinct perception of relations in the sense in which we have a distinct perception of qualities. We do not have a distinct idea of what it is like to perceive between-ness or of-ness, in the sense in which we have a distinct idea of what it is like to see colour or feel fear. And it has often been noticed that it has been one of the most common vices of philosophers to overlook the importance of relations. Now, if the view I have suggested is true, the naturalistic analyses take the concrete, more distinctly perceptible part of goodness but omit the relational element, and therefore, although people feel as if they had left something out, they, misled partly by the fact that "good" is an adjective, look for some other *quality* and cannot find it and then become more and more inclined to adopt the naturalistic view. But what they should have looked for is perhaps a relation. And they could hardly deny that there is such a relation as fittingness on which the concept of "ought" is based, the action which I ought to do being the action which fits the situation. It may also be noted that, while there is some uncertainty as to whether we can find any non-natural qualities other than good, it is very difficult even outside ethics to deny that there are non-natural relations, if we mean by "non-natural" what is not given by sense-perception or introspection. (I do not think "non-natural" a happy term as it suggests the miraculous, but I retain it as the one generally used by philosophers in this connection.) Entailment, probability, causality are cases of non-natural relations that seem to me quite impossible to explain away.

The naturalist will thus be right if he holds that "good" is connected very closely with desire, for what we pursue we desire. And he will also be right if he holds that moral good is very closely connected with the emotion of approval. The theory suggested would also explain how it is that our ability to make the right value judgments depends a good deal on our emotional disposition. For it is hardly to be expected that we should learn thoroughly what emotions it is fitting to feel on certain occasions without frequently feeling these emotions on suitable occasions.

It has been urged as a point in favour of naturalistic theories that they agree best with the way in which we learn the use of ethical words as children. For a very young child "bad" or "wrong" probably mean practically "what its nurse or parents disapprove of"; and it seems to learn the application of the words to acts by hearing them spoken, on the occasion of the acts, in tones or with gestures which express the emotion of disapproval, or by connecting the acts with punishments actual or threatened, punishment being in its very nature a mark of disapproval. (No doubt it can, and should be, shown that actions are wrong as far as possible by pointing out bad consequences and by the use of reasoning generally, but that of itself cannot teach the child the meaning of the words good, bad, right, wrong.) Now this is taken as evidence that "bad" or "wrong" means "disapproved," and similarly with "good," *mutatis mutandis*. But clearly if "bad" does not mean just what is disapproved (either by oneself or others) but what ought to be disapproved, this will equally well explain why the expression of approval or disapproval should be the natural and normal way of teaching a child what is meant by good or bad. For if "good," as applied to actions, means that towards which one ought to feel approval and "bad" that towards which one ought to feel disapproval, you must teach the child the meaning of the words by expressing to it the emotions of approval and disapproval on suitable occasions. (In so far as "good" means what we ought to pursue and "bad" what we ought to avoid, ethical education will consist in inducing the child by example and precept to pursue and avoid what it is suitable to pursue or avoid.) However I do not wish to lay much stress on this as an argument for the theory I have suggested, as against the theory that good is indefinable; but since some people are in fact influenced by this kind of argument in favour of a naturalistic theory I should like to point out that whatever weight it has equally supports my theory. But I must repeat that the whole of this article is of a very tentative character.

Ethical Intuitionism*

〽〜〜〽

P. F. STRAWSON

NORTH.—What is the trouble about moral facts? When someone denies that there is an objective moral order, or asserts that ethical propositions are pseudo-propositions, cannot I refute him (rather as Moore refuted those who denied the existence of the external world) by saying: "You know very well that Brown did wrong in beating his wife. You know very well that you ought to keep promises. You know very well that human affection is good and cruelty bad, that many actions are wrong and some are right"?

WEST.—Isn't the trouble about moral facts another case of trouble about knowing, about learning? We find out facts about the external world by looking and listening; about ourselves, by feeling; about other people, by looking and listening *and* feeling. When this is noticed, there arises a wish to say that the facts *are* what is seen, what is heard, what is felt; and, consequently, that moral facts fall into one of these classes. So those who have denied that there are "objective moral characteristics" have not wanted to deny that Brown's action was wrong or that keeping promises is right. They have wanted to point out that rightness and wrongness are a matter of what is felt in the heart, not of what is seen with the eyes or heard with the ears. They have wanted to emphasise the way in which "Promise-keeping is right" resembles "Going abroad is exciting," "Stories about mothers-in-law are comic," "Bombs are terrifying"; and differs from "Roses are red" and "Sea-water is salt." This does not prevent you from talking about the moral order, or the moral world, if you want to; but it warns you not to forget that the only access to the moral world is through remorse and approval and so on; just as the only access to the world of comedy is through laughter; and the only access to the coward's world is through fear.

NORTH.—I agree, of course, that we cannot see the goodness of something as we see its colour, or identify rightness by the sense of touch; though I think you should add that the senses are indispensable as a means of our becoming aware of those characteristics upon which moral characteristics depend. You may be partly right, too, in saying that access to the

* Reprinted by kind permission of the author and the editor from *Philosophy*, 24, 1949.

moral world is obtained through experience of the moral emotions; for it may be that only when our moral feelings have been strongly stirred do we first become clearly aware of the characteristics which evoke these feelings. But these feelings are not identical with that awareness. "Goodness" does not stand to "feeling approval," "guilt" to "feeling guilty," "obligation" to "feeling bound," as "excitingness" stands to "being excited" and "humorousness" to "feeling amused." To use the jargon for a moment: moral characteristics and relations are non-empirical, and awareness of them is neither sensory nor introspectual. It is a different kind of awareness, which the specialists call "intuition": and it is only empiricist prejudice which prevents your acknowledging its existence. Once acknowledged, it solves our problems: and we see that while "Promise-keeping is right" differs from "The sea is salt," this is not because it resembles "Detective-stories are exciting"; it differs from *both* in being the report neither of a sensible nor an introspectible experience, but of an intuition. We may, perhaps, know some moral characteristics mediately, through others. ("Obligation" is, perhaps, definable in terms of "goodness.") But at least one such characteristic —rightness or goodness—is unanalysable, and known by intuition alone. The fundamental cognitive situation in morals is that in which we intuit the rightness of a particular action or the goodness of a particular state of affairs. We see this moral characteristic as present in virtue of some other characteristics, themselves capable of being described in empirical terms, which the action or state of affairs possesses. (This is why I said that sense-perception is a necessary, though not a sufficient, condition of obtaining information about the moral order.) Our intuition, then, is not a bare intuition of the moral characteristic, but also the intuition of its dependence on some others: so that this fundamental situation yields us, by intuitive induction, knowledge of moral rules, generalisations regarding the right and the good, which we can apply in other cases, even when an actual intuition is lacking. So much do these rules become taken for granted, a part of our habitual moral life, that most of our everyday moral judgments involve merely an implicit reference to them [1]: a reference which becomes explicit only if the judgment is challenged or queried. Moral emotions, too, assume the character of habitual reactions. But emotions and judgments alike are grounded upon intuitions. Emotion may be the gatekeeper to the moral world; but intuition is the gate.

WEST.—Not so fast. I understand you to say that at least one fundamental moral characteristic—rightness or goodness—is unanalysable. Perhaps both are. The experts are divided. In any case, the fundamental characteristic (or characteristics) can be known only by intuitive awareness of its presence in some particular contemplated action or state of affairs. There is, then, a kind of analogy between the word "right" (or "good") and the name of some simple sensible characteristic such as "red." [2] Just

[1] Cf. D. Daiches Raphael, *The Moral Sense*, Chapters V and VI.
[2] Cf. G. E. Moore, *Principia Ethica*, p. 7 *et seq.* [pp. 70 ff. this volume].

as everybody who understands the word "red" has seen some red things, so everybody who understands the word "right" or the word "good" has intuited the character, rightness, in some actions, or the character, goodness, in some states of affairs; and nobody who has not intuited these characters understands the words "right" or "good." But this is not quite enough, is it? In order for me to know *now* the meaning of an indefinable word, it is not enough that a certain perceptual or intuitional event should have occurred at some particular point in my history; for I might not only have forgotten the details of that event; I might have forgotten what *kind* of an event it was; I might not know *now* what it would be like for such an event to occur. If the word "red" expresses an indefinable visual concept, then it is self-contradictory to say: "I know what the word 'red' means, but I can't remember ever *seeing* red and I don't know what it would be *like* to see red." Similarly, if the word "right," or the word "good," expresses an indefinable intuitive concept, then it is self-contradictory to say: "I know what the word 'right' or the word 'good' means, but I can't remember ever *intuiting* rightness or goodness, and I don't know what it would be *like* to intuit rightness or goodness." If your theory is true, then this statement is a contradiction.

But it is not at all obvious to me that it is a contradiction. I should be quite prepared to assert that I understood the words "right" and "good," but that I couldn't remember ever intuiting rightness or goodness and that I couldn't imagine what it would be like to do so. And I think it is quite certain that I am not alone in this, but that there are a large number of people who are to be presumed capable of accurate reporting of their own cognitive experience, and who would find nothing self-contradictory in saying what I say. And if this is so, you are presented with a choice of two possibilities. The first is that the words "right" and "good" have quite a different meaning for one set of people from the meaning which they have for another set. But neither of us believes this. The second is that the intuitionist theory is a mistake; that the phrase "intuitional event having a moral characteristic as its object (or a part of its object)" is a phrase which describes nothing at all; or describes misleadingly the kind of emotional experience we both admit. There is no third possibility. It is no good saying: "All people who succeed in learning the meaning of moral words do as a matter of fact have moral intuitions, but unfortunately many people are inclined to forget them, to be quite unable to remember what they are like." True, there would be nothing self-contradictory in saying this: but it would simply be a variant of the first possibility; for I cannot be said to know *now* the meaning of a word expressing an intuitive concept unless I know now what it would be like to intuit the characteristic of which it is a concept. The trouble with your intuitionist theory is that, if true, it should be a truism. There should be no doubt about the occurrence of the distinctive experience of intuiting rightness (or goodness), and about its being the only way to learn the meaning of the primary moral words; just as there is no doubt about the occurrence of seeing red (or blue), and about this being the only way to learn the meaning of the primary colour words. But there *is* doubt; and over against this doubt there rises a certainty: the certainty that we all know what it is to *feel* guilty, to *feel* bound, to *feel* approving.

NORTH.—What I have said *is* a truism; and that is its strength. It is not I who am inventing a mythical faculty, but you, irritated, perhaps, by the language of intuitionism, who are denying the obvious. When you said that you couldn't *imagine* what it would be like to have moral intuitions, isn't it clear that you wanted "intuiting a moral characteristic" to be like seeing a colour or hearing a sound? Naturally you couldn't *imagine* anything of the sort. But I have already pointed out that moral characteristics are dependent on others of which the presence *is* ascertainable by looking and listening. You do not intuit rightness or goodness independently of the other features of the situation. You intuit *that* an action is (or would be) right, a state of affairs good, *because* it has (or would have) certain other empirically ascertainable qualities. The total content of your intuition includes the "because" clause. Of course, our ordinary moral judgments register unreflective reactions. Nevertheless "This act is right (or this state of affairs is good) because it has P, Q, R"—where "P, Q, R" stands for such empirically ascertainable qualities—expresses the type of fundamental cognitive situation in ethics, of which our normal judgments are copies, mediated by habit, but ready, if challenged, to become explicit as their original. Consider what happens when someone dissents from your opinion. You produce reasons. And this is not a matter of accounting for an emotional condition; but of bringing evidence in support of a verdict.

WEST.—When the jury brings in a verdict of guilty on a charge of murder, they do so because the facts adduced in evidence are of the kind covered by the definition of "murder." When the chemical analyst concludes that the material submitted for analysis is a salt, he does so because it exhibits the defining properties of a salt. The evidence is the sort of thing that is *meant* by "murder," by "salt." But the fundamental moral word, or words, you say, cannot be defined; their concepts are unanalysable. So it cannot be in this way that the "because" clause of your ethical sentence functions as evidence. "X is a right action because it is a case of promise-keeping" does not work like "X is a salt because it is a compound of basic and acid radicals"; for, if "right" is indefinable, "X is right" does not *mean* "X is an act of promise-keeping or of relieving distress or of telling the truth or . . ."

When I say "It will be fine in the morning; for the evening sky is red," the evidence is of a different sort. For I might observe the fine morning without having noticed the state of the evening sky. But you have rightly stressed the point that there is no *independent* awareness of *moral* qualities: that they are always "seen" as dependent on those other features mentioned in the "because" clause. So it is not in this way, either, that the "because" clause of your ethical sentence functions as evidence. And there is no other way. Generally, we may say that whenever *q* is evidence for *p*, *either q* is the sort of thing we mean by "*p*" ("*p*" is definable in terms of "*q*") *or* we can have knowledge of the state of affairs described by "*p*" independently of knowledge of the state of affairs described by "*q*." But neither of these conditions is satisfied by the *q*, the "because" clause, of your ethical sentence.

The "because" clause, then, does not, as you said it did, constitute evidence for the ethical judgment. And this, it seems to me, should be a serious matter for you. For where is such evidence to be found? It is no good saying that, after all, the ethical judgments of other people (or your own at other times) may corroborate your own present judgment. They may agree with it; but their agreement strengthens the probability of your judgment only on the assumption that their moral intuitions tend on the whole to be correct. But the only possible evidence for the existence of a *tendency* to have correct intuitions is the correctness of *actual* intuitions. And it is precisely the correctness of actual intuitions for which we are seeking evidence, and failing to find it.

And evidence you must have, if your account of the matter is correct. You will scarcely say that ethical intuitions are infallible; for ethical disagreements may survive the resolution of factual disagreements. (You might, of course, say that *genuine* intuitions were infallible: then the problem becomes one of finding a criterion for distinguishing between the genuine ones and those false claimants that carry the same inner conviction.) So your use of the language of "unanalysable predicates ascribed in moral judgment to particular actions and states of affairs" leads to contradiction. For to call such a judgment "non-infallible" would be meaningless unless there were some way of checking it; of confirming or confuting it, by producing evidence for or against it. But I have just shown that your account of these judgments is incompatible with the possibility of producing evidence for or against them. So, if your account is true, these judgments are both corrigible and incorrigible; and this is absurd.

But the absurdity points to the solution. Of course these judgments are corrigible: but not in the way in which the diagnosis of a doctor is corrigible; rather in the way in which the musical taste of a child is corrigible. Correcting them is not a matter of *producing evidence* for them or their contraries, though it is (partly) a matter of *giving reasons* for them or their contraries. We say, warningly, that ethical judgments are corrigible, because ethical disagreement sometimes survives the resolution of factual disagreement. We say, encouragingly, that ethical judgments are corrigible, because the resolution of factual disagreement sometimes leads to the resolution of ethical disagreement. But the one kind of agreement leads (when it *does* lead) to the other, not in the way in which agreed evidence leads to an agreed conclusion, but in the way in which common experience leads to sympathy. The two kinds of agreement, the two kinds of judgment, are as different as chalk from cheese. Ordinary language can

accommodate the difference without strain: it is the pseudo-precise philosophical use of "judgment" which slurs over the difference and raises the
difficulty. Is it not clear, then, what people have meant when they said
that ethical disagreements were like disagreements in taste, in choice, in
practical attitude? [3] Of course, as you said, when we produce our reasons,
we are not often simply giving the causes of our emotional condition. But
neither are we producing evidence for a verdict, for a moral diagnosis.
We are using the facts to back our attitudes, to appeal to the capacity of
others to feel as we feel, to respond as we respond.

NORTH.—I think I see now what you have been leaving out all the
time. First, you accused me of inventing a mythical faculty to give us
ethical knowledge. Then, when I pointed out that ethical qualities are not
intuited out of all relation to other empirically ascertainable features of
actions and states of affairs, but are intuited as dependent upon these, you
twisted this dependence out of all recognition. You wanted to make it like
the causal dependence of a psychological disposition upon some empirical
feature of its object: as a child's fondness for strawberries depends upon
their sweetness. But the connection between wrongness and giving pain
to others is not an accident of our constitution; nor does its perception
require any special faculty—but *simply that which we use in all our
reasoning*. From the fact that an action involves inflicting needless pain
upon others, *it follows* necessarily that the action is wrong, just as, from
the fact that a triangle is equilateral, it follows necessarily that its angles
are equal. This is the kind of dependence that we intuit; not an analytic
dependence, but a synthetic entailment; and this is why the "because"
clause of my ethical sentence does, after all, constitute evidence for the
ascription of the moral characteristic.

I can anticipate the obvious objection. No moral rule, you will say,
no moral generalisation concerning the rightness of acts or the goodness
of conditions, holds without exception. It is always possible to envisage
circumstances in which the generalisation breaks down. Or, if the generalisation is so wide that no counter-example can be found, if it can be so interpreted as to cover every case, then it has become too wide: it has become
tautologous, like "It is always right to do that which will have the best
results on the whole," or intolerably vague, like "It is always right to treat
people as ends in themselves" or "The greatest good is the greatest general
welfare." It is plainly not with the help of such recipes as these that we find
out what is right, what is good, in a particular case. There are no criteria
for the meaning of "treating a man as an end," for "the greatest general
welfare," which do not presuppose the narrower criteria of rightness and
goodness of which I spoke and which seem always to have exceptions. All
this is true. But it calls only for a trifling amendment to those narrower
criteria. We cannot, for example, assert, as a necessary synthetic proposi-

[3] Cf. Charles Stevenson, *Ethics and Language*, Chapter 1. See also his paper "The
Emotive Meaning of Ethical Terms," [pp. 415 ff., this volume].

tion, "All acts of promise-keeping are right" or "All states of aesthetic enjoyment are good." But we *can* assert, as a necessary synthetic proposition, "All acts of promise-keeping *tend as such* to be right (or have *prima facie* rightness)" [4] or "All states of aesthetic enjoyment *tend as such* to be good." And we derive our knowledge of such general necessary connections from seeing, in particular cases, that the rightness of an action, the goodness of a state, *follows from* its being an action or state of a certain kind.

WEST.—Your "trifling amendment" is a destructive one. When we say of swans that they tend to be white, we are not ascribing a certain quality, namely "tending to be white," to each individual swan. We are saying that the number of swans which are white exceeds the number of those which are not, that if anything is a swan, the chances are that it will be white. When we say "Welshmen tend to be good singers," we mean that most Welshmen sing well; and when we say, of an *individual* Welshman, that *he* tends to sing well, we mean that he sings well more often than not. In all such cases, we are talking of a *class* of things or occasions or events; and saying, not that *all* members of the class have the property of *tending-to-have* a certain characteristic, but that *most* members of the class do in fact have that characteristic. Nobody would accept the claim that a sentence of the form "*Most* As are Bs" expresses a necessary proposition. Is the claim made more plausible by re-writing the proposition in the form "*All* As *tend to be* Bs"?

But, waiving this point, there remains the difficulty that the need for such an amendment to our moral generalisations is incompatible with the account you gave of the way in which we come to know both the moral characteristics of individual actions and states, and the moral generalisations themselves. You said that we intuited the moral characteristic as *following from* some empirically ascertainable features of the action or state. True, if we did so, we should have implicitly learnt a moral generalisation: but it would be one asserting *without qualification* the entailment of the moral characteristic by these other features of the case. In other words, and to take your instance, if it *ever* follows, from the fact that an act has the empirically ascertainable features described by the phrase "being an act of promise-keeping," that the act is right, then it *always* follows, from the fact that an act is of this kind, that it has this moral quality. If, then, it is true that we intuit moral characteristics as thus "following from" others, it is false that the implied generalisations require the "trifling amendment"; and if it is true that they require the amendment, it is false that we so intuit moral characteristics.[5]

[4] Ross, *Foundations of Ethics*, pp. 83–86; Broad, "Some of the Main Problems of Ethics," *Philosophy*, 1946, p. 117. [Reprinted in Herbert Feigl and Wilfrid Sellars, eds., *Reading in Philosophical Analysis*, Appleton-Century-Crofts, Inc., 1949.]

[5] One desperate expedient might occur to North. He might say that it is not the bare presence of the promise-keeping feature that entails the rightness of the act, but the presence of this feature, coupled with the absence of any features which would

And this is all that need be said of that rationalist superstition according to which a quasi-logical necessity binds moral predicates to others. "Le coeur a ses raisons, que la raison ne connaît pas": this is the whole truth of the matter: but your attention was so riveted to the first half of it that you forgot the second.

Looking for a logical nexus where there was none to be found, you overlooked the logical relations of the ethical words among themselves. And so you forgot what has often been pointed out: that for every expression containing the words "right" or "good," used in their ethical senses, it is always possible to find an expression with the same meaning, but containing, instead of these, the word "ought." The equivalences are various, and the variations subtle; but they are always to be found. For one to say, for example, "I know where the good lies, I know what the right course is; but I don't know the end I *ought* to aim at, the course I *ought* to follow" would be self-contradictory. "Right"-sentences, "good"-sentences are shorthand for "ought"-sentences. And this is enough in itself to explode the myth of unanalysable characteristics designated by the indefinable predicates, "right" and "good." For "ought" is a *relational* word; whereas "right" and "good" are *predicative*. The simplest sentences containing "ought" are syntactically more complicated than the simplest sentences containing "right" or "good." And hence, since the equivalences of meaning hold, the various ethical usages of "right" and "good" *are all definable:* variously definable in terms of "ought."

Of course this last consideration alone is not decisive against intuitionism. If this were all, you could still re-form the ranks: taking your stand on an intuited unanalysable non-natural *relation* of obligation, and admitting the definability of the ethical predicates in terms of this relation. But the objections I have already raised apply with equal force against this modified positon; and, in other ways, its weakness is more obvious.[6]

---

entail its wrongness. His general rules would then be, not of the form " '*x* has *φ*' entails '*x* is right,' " but of the form " '*x* has *φ* and *x* has no *ψ* such that "*x* has *ψ*" entails "*x* is wrong" ' entails '*x* is right.' " But the suggestion is inadmissible, since (i) the establishment of the general proposition "*x* has no *ψ*, etc." would require the enumeration of all those features which would make it wrong to keep a promise, and (ii) any rule of the form " '*x* has *ψ*' entails '*x* is wrong' " would require expansion in exactly the same way as the "right-making" rule; which would involve an infinite regress of such expansions. Besides having this *theoretical* defect, the suggested model is, of course, *practically* absurd.

[6] E.g. There was a certain plausibility in saying "My feeling morally obliged to pursue such a course (or end) presupposes my believing that it is right (or good)," and thence concluding that this belief cannot be "reduced to" the feeling which it arouses. (For examples of this sort of argument, see Ross, *op. cit.*, pp. 261–262, and Broad, *op. cit.*, p. 115.) But the weakness of the reasoning is more clearly exposed when the sentence is re-written as "My feeling morally obliged to pursue such a course presupposes my believing that I *am* morally obliged to pursue it." The point is that "presupposes" and "believing" are both ambiguous. If "presupposes" means "causally requires" and "believing" is used in its ordinary sense, then it is obviously false that the beliefs which *occasion* such a feeling invariably include some belief which would be correctly described in these terms. (Compare: "My feeling frightened presupposes my

NORTH.—Well, then, suppose we agree to bury intuitionism. What have you to offer in its place? Has any analysis of moral judgments in terms of feeling ever been suggested which was not monstrously paradoxical or artificial? Even the simplest ethical sentence obstinately resists translation: and not in the way in which "Life, like a dome of many-coloured glass, Stains the white radiance of eternity" resists translation. For the ethical language is not the language of the poets, but the language of all the world. Somehow justice must be done both to this irreducible element of significance in ethical sentences, and to the community of knowledge of their correct, their appropriate, use. Intuitionism, at any rate, was a way of attempting to do this.

WEST.—Yes, intuitionism was a way of attempting to do this. It started from the fact that thousands and thousands of people can say, with perfect propriety: "I know that this is right, that is good"; and ended, as we have seen, by making it inexplicable how anybody could ever say such a thing. This was because of a failure to notice that the whole sentence, including the "I know," and not just the last word in the subordinate clause, is a unit of the ethical language; and, following upon this failure, a feverish ransacking of the drawers of a Theory of Knowledge for an "I know" which would fit. (Do I, perhaps, work it out like the answer to a sum?)

The man who attempts to provide a translation sees more than this. He sees, at any rate, that the sentence must be treated as a unit. His error is to think that he can find a substitute, in a different language, which will serve the same purpose. So long as he confines himself to describing how, in what sort of circumstances, the sentence is used, he does valuable work. He errs when he talks as if to say how a sentence is used is the same as to use it. The man who says he can translate ethical sentences into feeling sentences makes the same sort of mistake as some who said they could (if they had time) translate material-object sentences into sentences about actual and possible sense-experiences. What they *mean*—the commentary they are making on the use of the ethical language or the material-object language—is correct. And it is precisely because the commentary would be incorrect as a translation that it is useful as a commentary. For it brings out the fact that the irreducibility of these languages arises from the systematic vagueness of the notation they use in comparison with that of the commentary-languages, and not from their being used to talk of, to describe, different things from those of which the commentary-languages talk. This descriptive vagueness is no defect: it is what makes these languages useful for the kinds of communication (and persuasion) for which they are

---

believing that I am frightened.") But the argument begins to have weight against the "analysability" of beliefs correctly so described only if they are invariably present as occasioning factors. If, on the other hand, "presupposes" means "logically requires," then "believing" might be used in a queer sense such that the sentence is *tautologically* true. But this result is secured only by defining "believing" (used in this sense) in terms of feeling (compare the sense in which "thinking *x* funny" means "being amused by *x*"): and this was precisely the result which North sought to avoid.

severally required. But by being mistaken for something more than it is, it leads to one kind of metaphysics: the metaphysics of substance (the thing-in-itself), or of intuited unanalysable ethical characteristics. And by being ignored altogether, it leads to another kind of metaphysics: the tough metaphysics of translation, the brutal suggestion that we could get along just as well without the ethical language. Neither metaphysics—neither the tender metaphysics of ultimacy, nor the tough metaphysics of reduction [7] —does justice to the facts: but the latter does them less injustice; for it doesn't seek to supplement them with a fairy-tale.

And so the alternative to intuitionism is not the provision of translations. For the communication and sharing of our moral experience, we must use the tools, the ethical language, we have. No sentences provided by the philosopher will take their place. His task is not to supply a new set of tools, but to describe what it is that is communicated and shared, and how the tools are used to do the work. And though the experience he describes is emotional experience, his descriptions are not like those of the psychologist. The psychologist is concerned with the relation of these experiences to others of a different sort; the philosopher is concerned with their relation to the ordinary use of ethical language. Of course, then, it would be absurd for the philosopher to deny that some actions are right (fair, legitimate, etc.) and others wrong (unfair, illegitimate, etc.), and that we know this; and absurd to claim that we can say what such sentences say without using such words. For this *is* the language we use in sharing and shaping our moral experience; and the occurrence of experience so shared, so shaped, is not brought into question.

We are in the position of the careful phenomenalist; who, for all his emphasis on sense-experience, neither denies that there is a table in the dining-room, nor claims to be able to assert this without using such words as "dining-room" and "table." A phenomenalism as careful as this has been said to forfeit the right to be called a "philosophical doctrine." [8] Then let the title be reserved for the productions of those who rest in myth or paradox, and fail to complete that journey, from the familiar to the familiar,[9] which is philosophical analysis.

[7] Cf. Wisdom, "Metaphysics and Verification," *Mind*, 1938.
[8] Hardie, "The Paradox of Phenomenalism," *Proceedings of the Aristotelian Society*, 1945-46, p. 150.
[9] Wisdom.

IV

THE NATURALISTIC REJOINDER

Hypostatic Ethics *

⟨⟨⟨⟨

GEORGE SANTAYANA

IF MR. RUSSELL, in his essay on "The Elements of Ethics," † had wished
to propitiate the unregenerate naturalist, before trying to convert him, he
could not have chosen a more skilful procedure; for he begins by telling us
that "what is called good conduct is conduct which is a means to other
things which are good on their own account; and hence . . . the study of
what is good or bad on its own account must be included in ethics." Two
consequences are involved in this: first, that ethics is concerned with the
economy of all values, and not with "moral" goods only, or with duty;
and second, that values may and do inhere in a great variety of things and
relations, all of which it is the part of wisdom to respect, and if possible to
establish. In this matter, according to our author, the general philosopher is
prone to one error and the professed moralist to another. "The philosopher,
bent on the construction of a system, is inclined to simplify the facts unduly
. . . and to twist them into a form in which they can all be deduced from
one or two general principles. The moralist, on the other hand, being
primarily concerned with conduct, tends to become absorbed in means,
to value the actions men ought to perform more than the ends which such
actions serve. . . . Hence most of what they value in this world would
have to be omitted by many moralists from any imagined heaven, because
there such things as self-denial and effort and courage and pity could find
no place. . . . Kant has the bad eminence of combining both errors in
the highest possible degree, since he holds that there is nothing good except
the virtuous will—a view which simplifies the good as much as any
philosopher could wish, and mistakes means for ends as completely as any
moralist could enjoin."

Those of us who are what Mr. Russell would call ethical sceptics will
be delighted at this way of clearing the ground; it opens before us the prospect of a moral philosophy that should estimate the various values of things
known and of things imaginable, showing what combinations of goods

* Excepted and reprinted by kind permission of the author and the publishers from
"The Philosophy of Bertrand Russell," *Winds of Doctrine*, pp. 138–154. J. M. Dent
and Sons, London, 1940 edition; New York, Charles Scribner's Sons. (First published,
1913.)
† [p. 1 ff. this volume.]

are possible in any one rational system, and (if fancy could stretch so far) what different rational systems would be possible in places and times remote enough from one another not to come into physical conflict. Such ethics, since it would express in reflection the dumb but actual interests of men, might have both influence and authority over them; two things which an alien and dogmatic ethics necessarily lacks. The joy of the ethical sceptic in Mr. Russell is destined, however, to be short-lived. Before proceeding to the expression of concrete ideals, he thinks it necessary to ask a preliminary and quite abstract question, to which his essay is chiefly devoted; namely, what is the right definition of the predicate "good," which we hope to apply in the sequel to such a variety of things? And he answers at once: The predicate "good" is indefinable. This answer he shows to be unavoidable, and so evidently unavoidable that we might perhaps have been absolved from asking the question; for, as he says, the so-called definitions of "good"—that it is pleasure, the desired, and so forth—are not definitions of the predicate "good," but designations of the things to which this predicate is applied by different persons. Pleasure, and its rivals, are not synonyms for the abstract quality "good," but names for classes of concrete facts that are supposed to possess that quality. From this correct, if somewhat trifling, observation, however, Mr. Russell, like Mr. Moore before him, evokes a portentous dogma. Not being able to define good, he hypostasises it. "Good and bad," he says, "are qualities which belong to objects independently of our opinions, just as much as round and square do; and when two people differ as to whether a thing is good, only one of them can be right, though it may be very hard to know which is right." "We cannot maintain that for me a thing ought to exist on its own account, while for you it ought not; that would merely mean that one of us is mistaken, since in fact everything either ought to exist, or ought not." Thus we are asked to believe that good attaches to things for no reason or cause, and according to no principles of distribution; that it must be found there by a sort of receptive exploration in each separate case; in other words, that it is an absolute, not a relative thing, a primary and not a secondary quality.

That the quality "good" is indefinable is one assertion, and obvious; but that the presence of this quality is unconditioned is another, and astonishing. My logic, I am well aware, is not very accurate or subtle; and I wish Mr. Russell had not left it to me to discover the connection between these two propositions. Green is an indefinable predicate, and the specific quality of it can be given only in intuition; but it is a quality that things acquire under certain conditions, so much so that the same bit of grass, at the same moment, may have it from one point of view and not from another. Right and left are indefinable; the difference could not be explained without being invoked in the explanation; yet everything that is to the right is not to the right on no condition, but obviously on the condition that some one is looking in a certain direction; and if some one else at the same time is looking in the opposite direction, what is truly to the right will be truly to the left also. If Mr. Russell thinks this is a contradiction, I understand why the universe does not please him. The contradiction would be real, undoubtedly, if we suggested that the *idea* of good was at any time or in any relation the *idea* of evil, or the *intuition* of right that of left, or the *quality* of green that of yellow; these disembodied essences are fixed by the intent that selects them, and in that ideal realm they can never have any relations except the dialectical ones implied in their nature, and these relations they must always retain. But the contradiction disappears when, instead of considering the qualities in themselves, we consider the things of which those qualities are aspects; for the qualities of things are not compacted by implication, but are conjoined irrationally by nature, as she will; and the same thing may be, and is, at once yellow and green, to the left and to the right, good and evil, many and one, large and small; and whatever verbal paradox there may be in this way of speaking (for from the point of view of nature it is natural enough) had been thoroughly explained and talked out by the time of Plato, who complained that people should still raise a difficulty so trite and exploded.[1] Indeed, while square is always square, and round round, a thing that is round may actually be square also, if we allow it to have a little body, and to be a cylinder.

But perhaps what suggests this hypostasis of good is rather the fact that what others find good, or what we ourselves have found good in moods with which we retain no sympathy, is sometimes pronounced by us to be bad; and far from inferring from this diversity of experience that the present good, like the others, corresponds to a particular attitude or interest of ours, and is dependent upon it, Mr. Russell and Mr. Moore infer instead that the presence of the good must be independent of all interests, attitudes, and opinions. They imagine that the truth of a proposition at-

---

[1] Plato, *Philebus*, 14, D. The dialectical element in this dialogue is evidently the basis of Mr. Russell's, as of Mr. Moore's, ethics; but they have not adopted the other elements in it, I mean the political and the theological. As to the political element, Plato everywhere conceives the good as the eligible in life, and refers it to human nature and to the pursuit of happiness—that happiness which Mr. Russell, in a rash moment, says is but a name which some people prefer to give to pleasure. Thus in the *Philebus* (11, D) the good looked for is declared to be "some state and disposition of the soul which has the property of making all men happy"; and later (66, D) the conclusion is that insight is better than pleasure "as an element in human life." As to the theological element, Plato, in hypostasising the good, does not hypostasise it as good, but as cause or power, which is, it seems to me, the sole category that justifies hypostasis, and logically involves it; for if things have a ground at all, that ground must exist before them and beyond them. Hence the whole Platonic and Christian scheme, in making the good independent of private will and opinion, by no means makes it independent of the direction of nature in general and of human nature in particular; for all things have been created with an innate predisposition towards the creative good, and are capable of finding happiness in nothing else. Obligation, in this system, remains internal and vital. Plato attributes a single vital direction and a single moral source to the cosmos. This is what determines and narrows the scope of the true good; for the true good is that relevant to nature. Plato would not have been a dogmatic moralist, had he not been a theist.

tributing a certain relative quality to an object contradicts the truth of another proposition, attributing to the same object an opposite relative quality. Thus if a man here and another man at the antipodes call opposite directions up, "only one of them can be right, though it may be very hard to know which is right."

To protect the belated innocence of this state of mind, Mr. Russell, so far as I can see, has only one argument, and one analogy. The argument is that "if this were not the case, we could not reason with a man as to what is right." "We do in fact hold that when one man approves of a certain act, while another disapproves, one of them is mistaken, which would not be the case with a mere emotion. If one man likes oysters and another dislikes them, we do not say that either of them is mistaken." In other words, we are to maintain our prejudices, however absurd, lest it should become unnecessary to quarrel about them! Truly the debating society has its idols, no less than the cave and the theatre. The analogy that comes to buttress somewhat this singular argument is the analogy between ethical propriety and physical or logical truth. An ethical proposition may be correct or incorrect, in a sense justifying argument, when it touches what is good as a means, that is, when it is not intrinsically ethical, but deals with causes and effects, or with matters of fact or necessity. But to speak of the truth of an ultimate good would be a false collocation of terms; an ultimate good is chosen, found, or aimed at; it is not opined. The ultimate intuitions on which ethics rests are not debatable, for they are not opinions we hazard but preferences we feel; and it can be neither correct nor incorrect to feel them. We may assert these preferences fiercely or with sweet reasonableness, and we may be more or less incapable of sympathising with the different preferences of others; about oysters we may be tolerant, like Mr. Russell, and about character intolerant; but that is already a great advance in enlightenment, since the majority of mankind have regarded as hateful in the highest degree any one who indulged in pork, or beans, or frogs' legs, or who had a weakness for anything called "unnatural"; for it is the things that offend their animal instincts that intense natures have always found to be, intrinsically and *par excellence*, abominations.

I am not sure whether Mr. Russell thinks he has disposed of this view where he discusses the proposition that the good is the desired and refutes it on the ground that "it is commonly admitted that there are bad desires; and when people speak of bad desires, they seem to mean desires for what is bad." Most people undoubtedly call desires bad when they are generically contrary to their own desires, and call objects that disgust them bad, even when other people covet them. This human weakness is not, however, a very high authority for a logician to appeal to, being too like the attitude of the German lady who said that Englishmen called a certain object *bread*, and Frenchmen called it *pain*, but that it really was *Brod*. Scholastic philosophy is inclined to this way of asserting itself; and Mr. Russell, though he candidly admits that there are ultimate differences of opinion about good and evil, would gladly minimise these differences, and thinks he triumphs when he feels that the prejudices of his readers will agree with his own; as if the constitutional unanimity of all human animals, supposing it existed, could tend to show that the good they agreed to recognise was independent of their constitution.

In a somewhat worthier sense, however, we may admit that there are desires for what is bad, since desire and will, in the proper psychological sense of these words, are incidental phases of consciousness, expressing but not constituting those natural relations that make one thing good for another. At the same time the words desire and will are often used, in a mythical or transcendental sense, for those material dispositions and instincts by which vital and moral units are constituted. It is in reference to such constitutional interests that things are "really" good or bad; interests which may not be fairly represented by any incidental conscious desire. No doubt any desire, however capricious, represents some momentary and partial interest, which lends to its objects a certain real and inalienable value; yet when we consider, as we do in human society, the interests of men, whom reflection and settled purposes have raised more or less to the ideal dignity of individuals, then passing fancies and passions may indeed have bad objects, and be bad themselves, in that they thwart the more comprehensive interests of the soul that entertains them. Food and poison are such only relatively, and in view of particular bodies, and the same material thing may be food and poison at once; the child, and even the doctor, may easily mistake one for the other. For the human system whiskey is truly more intoxicating than coffee, and the contrary opinion would be an error; but what a strange way of vindicating this real, though relative, distinction, to insist that whiskey is more intoxicating in itself, without reference to any animal; that it is pervaded, as it were, by an inherent intoxication, and stands dead drunk in its bottle! Yet just in this way Mr. Russell and Mr. Moore conceive things to be dead good and dead bad. It is such a view, rather than the naturalistic one, that renders reasoning and self-criticism impossible in morals; for wrong desires, and false opinions as to value, are conceivable only because a point of reference or criterion is available to prove them such. If no point of reference and no criterion were admitted to be relevant, nothing but physical stress could give to one assertion of value greater force than to another. The shouting moralist no doubt has his place, but not in philosophy.

That good is not an intrinsic or primary quality, but relative and adventitious, is clearly betrayed by Mr. Russell's own way of arguing, whenever he approaches some concrete ethical question. For instance, to show that the good is not pleasure, he can avowedly do nothing but appeal "to ethical judgments with which almost every one would agree." He repeats, in effect, Plato's argument about the life of the oyster, having pleasure with no knowledge. Imagine such mindless pleasure, as intense and prolonged as you please, and would you choose it? Is it your good? Here the British reader, like the blushing Greek youth, is expected to answer instinctively, No! It is an *argumentum ad hominem* (and there can be no other kind of argument in ethics); but the man who gives the required answer does so not because the answer is self-evident, which it is not, but because he is the required sort of man. He is shocked at the idea of resembling an oyster. Yet changeless pleasure, without memory or reflection, without the wearisome intermixture of arbitrary images, is just what the mystic, the voluptuary, and perhaps the oyster find to be good. Ideas, in their origin, are probably signals of alarm; and the distress which they marked in the beginning always clings to them in some measure, and causes many a soul, far more profound than that of the young Protarchus or of the British reader, to long for them to cease altogether. Such a radical hedonism is indeed inhuman; it undermines all conventional ambitions, and is not a possible foundation for political or artistic life. But that is all we can say against it. Our humanity cannot annul the incommensurable sorts of good that may be pursued in the world, though it cannot itself pursue them. The impossibility which people labour under of being satisfied with pure pleasure as a goal is due to their want of imagination, or rather to their being dominated by an imagination which is exclusively human.

The author's estrangement from reality reappears in his treatment of egoism, and most of all in his "Free Man's Worship." Egoism, he thinks, is untenable because "if I am right in thinking that my good is the only good, then every one else is mistaken unless he admits that my good, not his, is the only good." "Most people . . . would admit that it is better two people's desires should be satisfied than only one person's. . . . Then what is good is not good *for me* or *for you*, but is simply good." "It is, indeed, so evident that it is better to secure a greater good for *A* than a lesser good for *B*, that it is hard to find any still more evident principle by which to prove this. And if *A* happens to be some one else, and *B* to be myself, that cannot affect the question, since it is irrelevant to the general question who *A* and *B* may be." [1a] To the question, as the logician states it after transforming men into letters, it is certainly irrelevant; but it is not irrelevant to the case as it arises in nature. If two goods are somehow rightly pronounced to be equally good, no circumstance can render one better than the other. And if the locus in which the good is to arise is somehow pronounced to be indifferent, it will certainly be indifferent whether that good arises in me or in you. But how shall these two pronouncements be made? In practice, values cannot be compared save as represented or enacted in the private imagination of somebody: for we could not conceive that an alien good *was* a good (as Mr. Russell cannot conceive that the life of an ecstatic oyster is a good) unless we could sympathise with it in some way

[1a] These two passages are quoted from "The Elements of Ethics," [pp. 26–7 this volume].

in our own persons; and on the warmth which we felt in so representing
the alien good would hang our conviction that it was truly valuable, and
had worth in comparison with our own good. The voice of reason, bidding
us prefer the greater good, no matter who is to enjoy it, is also nothing but
the force of sympathy, bringing a remote existence before us vividly *sub
specie boni*. Capacity for such sympathy measures the capacity to recognise duty and therefore, in a moral sense, to have it. Doubtless it is conceivable that all wills should become co-operative, and that nature should
be ruled magically by an exact and universal sympathy; but this situation
must be actually attained in part, before it can be conceived or judged to
be an authoritative ideal. The tigers cannot regard it as such, for it would
suppress the tragic good called ferocity, which makes, in their eyes, the
chief glory of the universe. Therefore the inertia of nature, the ferocity of
beasts, the optimism of mystics, and the selfishness of men and nations
must all be accepted as conditions for the peculiar goods, essentially incommensurable, which they can generate severally. It is misplaced vehemence
to call them intrinsically detestable, because they do not (as they cannot)
generate or recognise the goods we prize.

In the real world, persons are not abstract egos, like *A* and *B*, so that
to benefit one is clearly as good as to benefit another. Indeed, abstract egos
could not be benefited, for they could not be modified at all, even if somehow they could be distinguished. It would be the qualities or objects distributed among them that would carry, wherever they went, each its inalienable cargo of value, like ships sailing from sea to sea. But it is quite vain
and artificial to imagine different goods charged with such absolute and
comparable weights; and actual egoism is not the thin and refutable thing
that Mr. Russell makes of it. What it really holds is that a given man,
oneself, and those akin to him, are qualitatively better than other beings;
that the things they prize are intrinsically better than the things prized by
others; and that therefore there is no injustice in treating these chosen
interests as supreme. The injustice, it is felt, would lie rather in not treating
things so unequal unequally. This feeling may, in many cases, amuse the
impartial observer, or make him indignant; yet it may, in every case,
according to Mr. Russell, be absolutely just. The refutation he gives of
egoism would not dissuade any fanatic from exterminating all his enemies
with a good conscience; it would merely encourage him to assert that what
he was ruthlessly establishing was the absolute good. Doubtless such conscientious tyrants would be wretched themselves, and compelled to make
sacrifices which would cost them dear; but that would only extend, as it
were, the pernicious egoism of that part of their being which they had
allowed to usurp a universal empire. The twang of intolerance and of self-
mutilation is not absent from the ethics of Mr. Russell and Mr. Moore,
even as it stands; and one trembles to think what it may become in the
mouths of their disciples. Intolerance itself is a form of egoism, and to
condemn egoism intolerantly is to share it.

I cannot help thinking that a consciousness of the relativity of values, if it became prevalent, would tend to render people more truly social than would a belief that things have intrinsic and unchangeable values, no matter what the attitude of any one to them may be. If we said that goods, including the right distribution of goods, are relative to specific natures, moral warfare would continue, but not with poisoned arrows. Our private sense of justice itself would be acknowledged to have but a relative authority, and while we could not have a higher duty than to follow it, we should seek to meet those whose aims were incompatible with it as we meet things physically inconvenient, without insulting them as if they were morally vile or logically contemptible. Real unselfishness consists in sharing the interests of others. Beyond the pale of actual unanimity the only possible unselfishness is chivalry—a recognition of the inward right and justification of our enemies fighting against us. This chivalry has long been practised in the battle-field without abolishing the causes of war; and it might conceivably be extended to all the conflicts of men with one another, and of the warring elements within each breast. Policy, hypnotisation, and even surgery may be practised without exorcisms or anathemas. When a man has decided on a course of action, it is a vain indulgence in expletives to declare that he is sure that course is absolutely right. His moral dogma expresses its natural origin all the more clearly the more hotly it is proclaimed; and ethical absolutism, being a mental grimace of passion, refutes what it says by what it is. Sweeter and more profound, to my sense, is the philosophy of Homer, whose every line seems to breathe the conviction that what is beautiful or precious has not thereby any right to existence; nothing has such a right; nor is it given us to condemn absolutely any force —god or man—that destroys what is beautiful or precious, for it has doubtless something beautiful or precious of its own to achieve.

The consequences of a hypostasis of the good are no less interesting than its causes. If the good were independent of nature, it might still be conceived as relevant to nature, by being its creator or mover; but Mr. Russell is not a theist after the manner of Socrates; his good is not a power. Nor would representing it to be such long help his case; for an ideal hypostasised into a cause achieves only a mythical independence. The least criticism discloses that it is natural laws, zoological species, and human ideals, that have been projected into the empyrean; and it is no marvel that the good should attract the world where the good, by definition, is whatever the world is aiming at. The hypostasis accomplished by Mr. Russell is more serious, and therefore more paradoxical. If I understand it, it may be expressed as follows: In the realm of eternal essences, before anything exists, there are certain essences that have this remarkable property, that they ought to exist, or at least that, if anything exists, it ought to conform to them. What exists, however, is deaf to this moral emphasis in the eternal; nature exists for no reason; and, indeed, why should she have subordinated her own arbitrariness to a good that is no less arbitrary? This good, however, is somehow good notwithstanding; so that there is an abysmal wrong in its not being obeyed. The world is, in principle, totally depraved; but as the good is not a power, there is no one to redeem the world. The saints are those who, imitating the impotent dogmatism on high, and despising their sinful natural propensities, keep asserting that certain things are in themselves good and others bad, and declaring to be detestable any other saint who dogmatises differently. In this system the Calvinistic God has lost his creative and punitive functions, but continues to decree groundlessly what is good and what evil, and to love the one and hate the other with an infinite love or hatred. Meanwhile the reprobate need not fear hell in the next world, but the elect are sure to find it here.

What shall we say of this strangely unreal and strangely personal religion? Is it a ghost of Calvinism, returned with none of its old force but with its old aspect of rigidity? Perhaps: but then, in losing its force, in abandoning its myths, and threats, and rhetoric, this religion has lost its deceptive sanctimony and hypocrisy; and in retaining its rigidity it has kept what made it noble and pathetic; for it is a clear dramatic expression of that human spirit—in this case a most pure and heroic spirit—which it strives so hard to dethrone. After all, the hypostasis of the good is only an unfortunate incident in a great accomplishment, which is the discernment of the good. I have dwelt chiefly on this incident, because in academic circles it is the abuses incidental to true philosophy that create controversy and form schools. Artificial systems, even when they prevail, after a while fatigue their adherents, without ever having convinced or refuted their opponents, and they fade out of existence not by being refuted in their turn, but simply by a tacit agreement to ignore their claims: so that the true insight they were based on is too often buried under them. The hypostasis of philosophical terms is an abuse incidental to the forthright, unchecked use of the intellect; it substitutes for things the limits and distinctions that divide them. So physics is corrupted by logic; but the logic that corrupts is perhaps correct, and when it is moral dialectic, it is more important than physics itself. Mr. Russell's ethics *is* ethics. When we mortals have once assumed the moral attitude, it is certain that an indefinable value accrues to some things as opposed to others, that these things are many, that combinations of them have values not belonging to their parts, and that these valuable things are far more specific than abstract pleasure, and far more diffused than one's personal life. What a pity if this pure morality, in detaching itself impetuously from the earth, whose bright satellite it might be, should fly into the abyss at a tangent, and leave us as much in the dark as before!

The Construction of Good *

JOHN DEWEY

WE SAW AT the outset of our discussion that insecurity generates the quest for certainty. Consequences issue from every experience, and they are the source of our interest in what is present. Absence of arts of regulation diverted the search for security into irrelevant modes of practice, into rite and cult; thought was devoted to discovery of omens rather than of signs of what is to occur. Gradually there was differentiation of two realms, one higher, consisting of the powers which determine human destiny in all important affairs. With this religion was concerned. The other consisted of the prosaic matters in which man relied upon his own skill and his matter-of-fact insight. Philosophy inherited the idea of this division. Meanwhile in Greece many of the arts had attained a state of development which raised them above a merely routine state; there were intimations of measure, order and regularity in materials dealt with which give intimations of underlying rationality. Because of the growth of mathematics, there arose also the ideal of a purely rational knowledge, intrinsically solid and worthy and the means by which the intimations of rationality within changing phenomena could be comprehended within science. For the intellectual class the stay and consolation, the warrant of certainty, provided by religion was henceforth found in intellectual demonstration of the reality of the objects of an ideal realm.

With the expansion of Christianity, ethico-religious traits came to dominate the purely rational ones. The ultimate authoritative standards for regulation of the dispositions and purposes of the human will were fused with those which satisfied the demands for necessary and universal truth. The authority of ultimate Being was, moreover, represented on earth by the Church; that which in its nature transcended intellect was made known by a revelation of which the Church was the interpreter and guardian. The system endured for centuries. While it endured, it provided an integration of belief and conduct for the western world. Unity of thought and practice extended down to every detail of the management of life; efficacy of its operation did not depend upon thought. It was guaranteed by the most powerful and authoritative of all social institutions.

Its seemingly solid foundation was, however, undermined by the conclusions of modern science. They effected, both in themselves and even more in the new interests and activities they generate, a breach between what man is concerned with here and now and the faith concerning ultimate reality which, in determining his ultimate and eternal destiny, had previously given regulation to his present life. The problem of restoring integration and coöperation between man's beliefs about the world in which he lives and his beliefs about the values and purposes that should direct his conduct is the deepest problem of modern life. It is the problem of any philosophy that is not isolated from that life.

The attention which has been given to the fact that in its experimental procedure science has surrendered the separation between knowing and doing has its source in the fact that there is now provided within a limited, specialized and technical field the possibility and earnest, as far as theory is concerned, of affecting the needed integration in the wider field of collective human experience. Philosophy is called upon to be the theory of the practice, through ideas sufficiently definite to be operative in experimental endeavor, by which the integration may be made secure in actual experience. Its central problem is the relation that exists between the beliefs about the nature of things due to natural science and beliefs about values— using that word to designate whatever is taken to have rightful authority in the direction of conduct. A philosophy which should take up this problem is struck first of all by the fact that beliefs about values are pretty much in the position in which beliefs about nature were before the scientific revolution. There is either a basic distrust of the capacity of experience to develop its own regulative standards, and an appeal to what philosophers call eternal values, in order to ensure regulation of belief and action; or there is acceptance of enjoyments actually experienced irrespective of the method or operation by which they are brought into existence. Complete bifurcation between rationalistic method and an empirical method has its final and most deeply human significance in the ways in which good and bad are thought of and acted for and upon.

As far as technical philosophy reflects this situation, there is division of theories of values into two kinds. On the one hand, goods and evils, in every region of life, as they are concretely experienced, are regarded as characteristic of an inferior order of Being—intrinsically inferior. Just because they are things of human experience, their worth must be estimated by reference to standards and ideals derived from ultimate reality. Their defects and perversion are attributed to the same fact; they are to be corrected and controlled through adoption of methods of conduct derived from loyalty to the requirements of Supreme Being. This philosophic formulation gets actuality and force from the fact that it is a rendering of the beliefs of men in general as far as they have come under the influence of institutional religion. Just as rational conceptions were once superimposed upon observed and temporal phenomena, so eternal values are superimposed upon experienced goods. In one case as in the other, the alternative is supposed to be confusion and lawlessness. Philosophers suppose these eternal values are known by reason; the mass of persons that they are divinely revealed.

Nevertheless, with the expansion of secular interests, temporal values have enormously multiplied; they absorb more and more attention and energy. The sense of transcendent values has become enfeebled; instead of permeating all things in life, it is more and more restricted to special times and acts. The authority of the church to declare and impose divine will and purpose has narrowed. Whatever men say and profess, their tendency in the presence of actual evils is to resort to natural and empirical means to remedy them. But in formal belief, the old doctrine of the inherently disturbed and unworthy character of the goods and standards of ordinary experience persists. This divergence between what men do and what they nominally profess is closely connected with the confusions and conflicts of modern thought.

It is not meant to assert that no attempts have been made to replace the older theory regarding the authority of immutable and transcendent values by conceptions more congruous with the practices of daily life. The contrary is the case. The utilitarian theory, to take one instance, has had great power. The idealistic school is the only one in contemporary philosophies, with the exception of one form of neo-realism, that makes much of the notion of a reality which is all one with ultimate moral and religious values. But this school is also the one most concerned with the conservation of "spiritual" life. Equally significant is the fact that empirical theories retain the notion that thought and judgment are concerned with values that are experienced independently of them. For these theories, emotional satisfactions occupy the same place that sensations hold in traditional empiricism. Values are constituted by liking and enjoyment; to be enjoyed and to be a value are two names for one and the same fact. Since science has extruded values from its objects, these empirical theories do everything possible to emphasize their purely subjective character of value. A psychological theory of desire and liking is supposed to cover the whole ground of the theory of values; in it, immediate feeling is the counterpart of immediate sensation.

I shall not object to this empirical theory as far as it connects the theory of values with concrete experiences of desire and satisfaction. The idea that there is such a connection is the only way known to me by which the pallid remoteness of the rationalistic theory, and the only too glaring presence of the institutional theory of transcendental values can be escaped. The objection is that the theory in question holds down value to objects *antecedently* enjoyed, apart from reference to the method by which they come into existence; it takes enjoyments which are casual because unregulated by intelligent operations to be values in and of themselves. Operational thinking needs to be applied to the judgment of values just as it has now finally been applied in conceptions of physical objects. Experimental empiricism in the field of ideas of good and bad is demanded to meet the conditions of the present situation.

The scientific revolution came about when material of direct and uncontrolled experience was taken as problematic; as supplying material to be transformed by reflective operations into known objects. The contrast between experienced and known objects was found to be a temporal one; namely, one between empirical subject-matters which were had or "given" prior to the acts of experimental variation and redisposition and those which succeeded these acts and issued from them. The notion of an act whether of sense or thought which supplied a valid measure of thought in immediate knowledge was discredited. Consequences of operations became the important thing. The suggestion almost imperatively follows that escape from the defects of transcendental absolutism is not to be had by setting up as values enjoyments that happen anyhow, but in defining value by enjoyments which are the consequences of intelligent action. Without the intervention of thought, enjoyments are not values but problematic goods, becoming values when they re-issue in a changed form from intelligent behavior. The fundamental trouble with the current empirical theory of values is that it merely formulates and justifies the socially prevailing habit of regarding enjoyments as they are actually experienced as values in and of themselves. It completely side-steps the question of regulation of these enjoyments. This issue involves nothing less than the problem of the directed reconstruction of economic, political and religious institutions.

There was seemingly a paradox involved in the notion that if we turned our backs upon the immediately perceived qualities of things, we should be enabled to form valid conceptions of objects, and that these conceptions could be used to bring about a more secure and more significant experience of them. But the method terminated in disclosing the connections or interactions upon which perceived objects, viewed as events, depend. Formal analogy suggests that we regard our direct and original experience of things liked and enjoyed as only *possibilities* of values to be achieved; that enjoyment becomes a value when we discover the relations upon which its presence depends. Such a causal and operational definition gives only a conception of a value, not a value itself. But the utilization of the conception in action results in an object having secure and significant value.

The formal statement may be given concrete content by pointing to the difference between the enjoyed and the enjoyable, the desired and the desirable, the satis*fying* and the satis*factory*. To say that something is enjoyed is to make a statement about a fact, something already in existence; it is not to judge the value of that fact. There is no difference between such a proposition and one which says that something is sweet or sour, red or black. It is just correct or incorrect and that is the end of the matter. But to call an object a value is to assert that it satisfies or fulfills certain conditions. Function and status in meeting conditions is a different matter from bare existence. The fact that something is desired only raises the *question* of its desirability; it does not settle it. Only a child in the degree of his immaturity thinks to settle the question of desirability by reiterated proclamation: "I want it, I want it, I want it." What is objected to in the current empirical theory of values is not connection of them with desire and enjoyment but failure to distinguish between enjoyments of radically different sorts. There are many common expressions in which the difference of the two kinds is clearly recognized. Take for example the difference between the ideas of "satisfying" and "satisfactory." To say that something satisfies is to report something as an isolated finality. To assert that it is satis*factory* is to define it in its connections and interactions. The fact that it pleases or is immediately congenial poses a problem to judgment. How shall the satisfaction be rated? Is it a value or is it not? Is it something to be prized and cherished, *to be* enjoyed? Not stern moralists alone but everyday experience informs us that finding satisfaction in a thing may be a warning, a summons to be on the lookout for consequences. To declare something satis*factory* is to assert that it meets specifiable conditions. It is, in effect, a judgment that the thing "will do." It involves a prediction; it contemplates a future in which the thing will continue to serve; it *will* do. It asserts a consequence the thing will actively institute; it will *do*. That it is satisfying is the content of a proposition of fact; that it is satisfactory is a judgment, an estimate, an appraisal. It denotes an attitude *to be* taken, that of striving to perpetuate and to make secure.

It is worth notice that besides the instances given, there are many other recognitions in ordinary speech of the distinction. The endings "able," "worthy" and "ful" are cases in point. Noted and notable, noteworthy; remarked and remarkable; advised and advisable; wondered at and wonderful; pleasing and beautiful; loved and lovable; blamed and blameable, blameworthy; objected to and objectionable; esteemed and estimable; admired and admirable; shamed and shameful; honored and honorable; approved and approvable, worthy of approbation, etc. The multiplication of words adds nothing to the force of the distinction. But it aids in conveying a sense of the fundamental character of the distinction; of the difference between mere report of an already existent fact and judgment as to the importance and need of bringing a fact into existence; or, if it is already there, of sustaining it in existence. The latter is a genuine practical judgment, and marks the only type of judgment that has to do with the direction of action. Whether or no we reserve the term "value" for the latter (as seems to me proper) is a minor matter; that the distinction be acknowledged as the key to understanding the relation of values to the direction of conduct is the important thing.

This element of direction by an idea of value applies to science as well as anywhere else. For in every scientific undertaking, there is passed a constant succession of estimates; such as "it is worth treating these facts as data or evidence; it is advisable to try this experiment; to make that observation; to entertain such and such a hypothesis; to perform this calculation," etc.

The word "taste" has perhaps got too completely associated with arbitrary liking to express the nature of judgments of value. But if the word be used in the sense of an appreciation at once cultivated and active, one may say that the formation of taste is the chief matter wherever values enter in, whether intellectual, esthetic or moral. Relatively immediate judgments, which we call tact or to which we give the name of intuition, do not precede reflective inquiry, but are the funded products of much thoughtful experience. Expertness of taste is at once the result and the reward of constant exercise of thinking. Instead of there being no disputing about tastes, they are the one thing worth disputing about, if by "dispute" is signified discussion involving reflective inquiry. Taste, if we use the word in its best sense, is the outcome of experience brought cumulatively to bear on the intelligent appreciation of the real worth of likings and enjoyments. There is nothing in which a person so completely reveals himself as in the things which he judges enjoyable and desirable. Such judgments are the sole alternative to the domination of belief by impulse, chance, blind habit and self-interest. The formation of a cultivated and effectively operative good judgment or taste with respect to what is esthetically admirable, intellectually acceptable and morally approvable is the supreme task set to human beings by the incidents of experience.

Propositions about what is or has been liked are of instrumental value in reaching judgments of value, in as far as the conditions and consequences of the thing liked are thought about. In themselves they make no claims; they put forth no demand upon subsequent attitudes and acts; they profess no authority to direct. If one likes a thing he likes it; that *is* a point about which there can be no dispute:—although it is not so easy to state just *what* is liked as is frequently assumed. A judgment about what is *to be* desired and enjoyed is, on the other hand, a claim on future action; it possesses *de jure* and not merely *de facto* quality. It is a matter of frequent experience that likings and enjoyments are of all kinds, and that many are such as reflective judgments condemn. By way of self-justification and "rationalization," an enjoyment creates a tendency to assert that the thing enjoyed is a value. This assertion of validity adds authority to the fact. It is a decision that the object has a right to exist and hence a claim upon action to further its existence.

The analogy between the status of the theory of values and the theory of ideas about natural objects before the rise of experimental inquiry may be carried further. The sensationalistic theory of the origin and test of thought evoked, by way of reaction, the transcendental theory of *a priori* ideas. For it failed utterly to account for objective connection, order and regularity in objects observed. Similarly, any doctrine that identifies the mere fact of being liked with the value of the object liked so fails to give direction to conduct when direction is needed that it automatically calls forth the assertion that there are values eternally in Being that are the standards of all judgments and the obligatory ends of all action. Without the introduction of operational thinking, we oscillate between a theory that, in order to save the objectivity of judgments of values, isolates them from experience and nature, and a theory that, in order to save their concrete and human significance, reduces them to mere statements about our own feelings.

Not even the most devoted adherents of the notion that enjoyment and value are equivalent facts would venture to assert that because we have once liked a thing we should go on liking it; they are compelled to introduce the idea that *some* tastes are to be cultivated. Logically, there is no ground for introducing the idea of cultivation; liking is liking, and one is as good as another. If enjoyments *are* values, the judgment of value cannot regulate the form which liking takes; it cannot regulate its own conditions. Desire and purpose, and hence action, are left without guidance, although the question of regulation of their formation is the supreme problem of practical life. Values (to sum up) may be connected inherently with liking, and yet not with *every* liking but only with those that judgment has approved, after examination of the relation upon which the object liked depends. A casual liking is one that happens without knowledge of how it occurs nor to what effect. The difference between it and one which is sought because of a judgment that it is worth having and is to be striven for, makes just the difference between enjoyments which are accidental and enjoyments that have value and hence a claim upon our attitude and conduct.

In any case, the alternative rationalistic theory does not afford the guidance for the sake of which eternal and immutable norms are appealed to. The scientist finds no help in determining the probable truth of some proposed theory by comparing it with a standard of absolute truth and immutable being. He has to rely upon definite operations undertaken under definite conditions—upon method. We can hardly imagine an architect getting aid in the construction of a building from an ideal at large, though we can understand his framing an ideal on the basis of knowledge of actual conditions and needs. Nor does the ideal of perfect beauty in antecedent Being give direction to a painter in producing a particular work of art. In morals, absolute perfection does not seem to be more than a generalized hypostatization of the recognition that there is a good to be sought, an obligation to be met—both being concrete matters. Nor is the defect in this respect merely negative. An examination of history would reveal, I am confident, that these general and remote schemes of value actually obtain a content definite enough and near enough to concrete situations as to afford guidance in action only by consecrating some institution or dogma already having social currency. Concreteness is gained, but it is by protecting from inquiry some accepted standard which perhaps is outworn and in need of criticism.

When theories of values do not afford intellectual assistance in framing ideas and beliefs about values that are adequate to direct action, the gap must be filled by other means. If intelligent method is lacking, prejudice, the pressure of immediate circumstance, self-interest and class-interest, traditional customs, institutions of accidental historic origin, are *not* lacking, and they tend to take the place of intelligence. Thus we are led to our main proposition: *Judgments about values are judgments about the conditions and the results of experienced objects; judgments about that which should regulate the formation of our desires, affections and enjoyments.* For whatever decides their formation will determine the main course of our conduct, personal and social.

If it sounds strange to hear that we should frame our judgments as to what has value by considering the connections in existence of what we like and enjoy, the reply is not far to seek. As long as we do not engage in this inquiry enjoyments (values if we choose to apply that term) are casual; they are given by "nature," not constructed by art. Like natural objects in their qualitative existence, they at most only supply material for elaboration in rational discourse. A *feeling* of good or excellence is as far removed from goodness in fact as a feeling that objects are intelligently thus and so is removed from their being actually so. To recognize that the truth of natural objects can be reached only by the greatest care in selecting and arranging directed operations, and then to suppose that values can be truly determined by the mere fact of liking seems to leave us in an incredible position. All the serious perplexities of life come back to the genuine difficulty of forming a judgment as to the values of the situation; they come back to a conflict of goods. Only dogmatism can suppose that serious moral conflict is between something clearly bad and something known to be good, and that uncertainty lies wholly in the will of the one choosing. Most conflicts of importance are conflicts between things which are or have been satisfying, not between good and evil. And to suppose that we can make a hierarchical table of values at large once for all, a kind of catalogue in which they are arranged in an order of ascending or descending worth, is to indulge in a gloss on our inability to frame intelligent judgments in the concrete. Or else it is to dignify customary choice and prejudice by a title of honor.

The alternative to definition, classification and systematization of satisfactions just as they happen to occur is judgment of them by means of the relations under which they occur. If we know the conditions under which the act of liking, of desire and enjoyment, takes place, we are in a position to know what are the consequences of that act. The difference between the desired and the desirable, admired and the admirable, becomes effective at just this point. Consider the difference between the proposition "That thing has been eaten," and the judgment "That thing is edible." The former statement involves no knowledge of any relation except the one stated; while we are able to judge of the edibility of anything only when we have a knowledge of its interactions with other things sufficient to enable us to foresee its probable effects when it is taken into the organism and produces effects there.

To assume that anything can be known in isolation from its connections with other things is to identify knowing with merely having some object before perception or in feeling, and is thus to lose the key to the traits that distinguish an object as known. It is futile, even silly, to suppose that some quality that is directly present constitutes the whole of the thing presenting the quality. It does not do so when the quality is that of being hot or fluid or heavy, and it does not when the quality is that of giving pleasure, or being enjoyed. Such qualities are, once more, effects, ends in the sense of closing termini of processes involving causal connections. They are something to be investigated, challenges to inquiry and judgment. The more connections and interactions we ascertain, the more we *know* the object in question. Thinking is search for these connections. Heat experienced as a consequence of directed operations has a meaning quite different from the heat that is casually experienced without knowledge of how it came about. The same is true of enjoyments. Enjoyments that issue from conduct directed by insight into relations have a meaning and a validity due to the way in which they are experienced. Such enjoyments are not repented of; they generate no after-taste of bitterness. Even in the midst of direct enjoyment, there is a sense of validity, of authorization, which intensifies the enjoyment. There is solicitude for perpetuation of the *object* having value which is radically different from mere anxiety to perpetuate the *feeling* of enjoyment.

Such statements as we have been making are, therefore, far from implying that there are values apart from things actually enjoyed as good. To find a thing enjoy*able* is, so to say, a *plus* enjoyment. We saw that it was foolish to treat the scientific object as a rival to or substitute for the perceived object, since the former is intermediate between uncertain and settled situations and those experienced under conditions of greater control. In the same way, judgment of the value of an object to be experienced is instrumental to appreciation of it when it is realized. But the notion that every object that happens to satisfy has an equal claim with every other to be a value is like supposing that every object of perception has the same cognitive force as every other. There is no knowledge without perception; but objects perceived are *known* only when they are determined as consequences of connective operations. There is no value except where there is satisfaction, but there have to be certain conditions fulfilled to transform a satisfaction into a value.

The time will come when it will be found passing strange that we of this age should take such pains to control by every means at command the formation of ideas of physical things, even those most remote from human concern, and yet are content with haphazard beliefs about the qualities of objects that regulate our deepest interests; that we are scrupulous as to methods of forming ideas of natural objects, and either dogmatic or else driven by immediate conditions in framing those about values. There is, by implication, if not explicitly, a prevalent notion that values are already well known and that all which is lacking is the will to cultivate them in the order of their worth. In fact the most profound lack is not the will to act upon goods already known but the will to know what they are.

It is not a dream that it is possible to exercise some degree of regulation of the occurrence of enjoyments which are of value. Realization of the possibility is exemplified, for example, in the technologies and arts of industrial life—that is, up to a definite limit. Men desired heat, light, and speed of transit and of communication beyond what nature provides of itself. These things have been attained not by lauding the enjoyment of these things and preaching their desirability, but by study of the conditions of their manifestation. Knowledge of relations having been obtained, ability to produce followed, and enjoyment ensued as a matter of course. It is, however, an old story that enjoyment of these things as goods is no warrant of their bringing only good in their train. As Plato was given to pointing out, the physician knows how to heal and the orator to persuade, but the ulterior knowledge of whether it is better for a man to be healed or to be persuaded to the orator's opinion remains unsettled. Here there appears the split between what are traditionally and conventionally called the values of the baser arts and the higher values of the truly personal and humane arts.

With respect to the former, there is no assumption that they can be had and enjoyed without definite operative knowledge. With respect to them it is also clear that the degree in which we value them is measurable by the pains taken to control the conditions of their occurrence. With respect to the latter, it is assumed that no one who is honest can be in doubt what they are; that by revelation, or conscience, or the instruction of others, or immediate feeling, they are clear beyond question. And instead of action in their behalf being taken to be a measure of the extent to which things *are* values to us, it is assumed that the difficulty is to persuade men to act upon what they already know to be good. Knowledge of conditions and consequences is regarded as wholly indifferent to judging what is of serious value, though it is useful in a prudential way in trying to actualize it. In consequence, the existence of values that are by common consent of a secondary and technical sort are under a fair degree of control, while those denominated supreme and imperative are subject to all the winds of impulse, custom and arbitrary authority.

This distinction between higher and lower types of value is itself something to be looked into. Why should there be a sharp division made between some goods as physical and material and others as ideal and "spiritual"? The question touches the whole dualism of the material and the ideal at its root. To denominate anything "matter" or "material" is not in truth to disparage it. It is, if the designation is correctly applied, a way of indicating that the thing in question is a condition or means of the existence of something else. And disparagement of effective means is practically synonymous with disregard of the things that are termed, in eulogistic fashion, ideal and spiritual. For the latter terms if they have any concrete application at all signify something which is a desirable consummation of conditions, a cherished fulfillment of means. The sharp separation between material and ideal good thus deprives the latter of the underpinning of effective support while it opens the way for treating things which should be employed as means as ends in themselves. For since men cannot after all live without some measure of possession of such matters as health and wealth, the latter things will be viewed as values and ends in isolation unless they are treated as integral constituents of the goods that are deemed supreme and final.

The relations that determine the occurrence of what human beings experience, especially when social connections are taken into account, are indefinitely wider and more complex than those that determine the events termed physical; the latter are the outcome of definite selective operations. This is the reason why we know something about remote objects like the stars better than we know significantly characteristic things about our own bodies and minds. We forget the infinite number of things we do not know about the stars, or rather that what we call a star is itself the product of the elimination, enforced and deliberate, of most of the traits that belong to an actual existence. The amount of knowledge we possess about stars would not seem very great or very important if it were carried over to human beings and exhausted our knowledge of them. It is inevitable that genuine knowledge of man and society should lag far behind physical knowledge.

But this difference is not a ground for making a sharp division between the two, nor does it account for the fact that we make so little use of the experimental method of forming our ideas and beliefs about the concerns of man in his characteristic social relations. For this separation religions and philosophies must admit some responsibility. They have erected a distinction between a narrower scope of relations and a wider and fuller one into a difference of kind, naming one kind material, and the other mental and moral. They have charged themselves gratuitously with the office of diffusing belief in the necessity of the division, and with instilling contempt for the material as something inferior in kind in its intrinsic nature and worth. Formal philosophies undergo evaporation of their technical solid contents; in a thinner and more viable form they find their way into the minds of those who know nothing of their original forms. When these diffuse and, so to say, airy emanations re-crystallize in the popular mind they form a hard deposit of opinion that alters slowly and with great difficulty.

What difference would it actually make in the arts of conduct, personal and social, if the experimental theory were adopted not as a mere theory, but as a part of the working equipment of habitual attitudes on the part of everyone? It would be impossible, even were time given, to answer the question in adequate detail, just as men could not foretell in advance the consequences for knowledge of adopting the experimental method. It is the nature of the method that it has to be tried. But there are generic lines of difference which, within the limits of time at disposal, may be sketched.

Change from forming ideas and judgments of value on the basis of conformity to antecedent objects, to constructing enjoyable objects directed by knowledge of consequences, is a change from looking to the past to looking to the future. I do not for a moment suppose that the experiences of the past, personal and social, are of no importance. For without them we should not be able to frame any ideas whatever of the conditions under which objects are enjoyed nor any estimate of the consequences of esteeming and liking them. But past experiences are significant in giving us intellectual instrumentalities of judging just these points. They are tools, not finalities. Reflection upon what we have liked and have enjoyed is a necessity. But it tells us nothing about the *value* of these things until enjoyments are themselves reflectively controlled, or, until, as they are recalled, we form the best judgment possible about what led us to like this sort of thing and what has issued from the fact that we liked it.

We are not, then, to get away from enjoyments experienced in the past and from recall of them, but from the notion that they are the arbiters of things to be further enjoyed. At present, the arbiter is found in the past, although there are many ways of interpreting what in the past is authoritative. Nominally, the most influential conception doubtless is that of a revelation once had or a perfect life once lived. Reliance upon precedent, upon institutions created in the past, especially in law, upon rules of morals that have come to us through unexamined customs, upon uncriticized tradition, are other forms of dependence. It is not for a moment suggested that we can get away from customs and established institutions. A mere break would doubtless result simply in chaos. But there is no danger of such a break. Mankind is too inertly conservative both by constitution and by education to give the idea of this danger actuality. What there is genuine danger of is that the force of new conditions will produce disruption externally and mechanically: this is an ever present danger. The prospect is increased, not mitigated, by that conservatism which insists upon the adequacy of old standards to meet new conditions. What is needed is intelligent examination of the consequences that are actually effected by inherited institutions and customs, in order that there may be intelligent consideration of the ways in which they are to be intentionally modified in behalf of generation of different consequences.

This is the significant meaning of transfer of experimental method from the technical field of physical experience to the wider field of human life. We trust the method in forming our beliefs about things not directly connected with human life. In effect, we distrust it in moral, political and economic affairs. In the fine arts, there are many signs of a change. In the past, such a change has often been an omen and precursor of changes in other human attitudes. But, generally speaking, the idea of actively adopting experimental method in social affairs, in the matters deemed of most enduring and ultimate worth, strikes most persons as a surrender of all standards and regulative authority. But in principle, experimental method does not signify random and aimless action; it implies direction by ideas and knowledge. The question at issue is a practical one. Are there in existence the ideas and the knowledge that permit experimental method to be effectively used in social interests and affairs?

Where will regulation come from if we surrender familiar and traditionally prized values as our directive standards? Very largely from the findings of the natural sciences. For one of the effects of the separation drawn between knowledge and action is to deprive scientific knowledge of its proper service as a guide of conduct—except once more in those technological fields which have been degraded to an inferior rank. Of course, the complexity of the conditions upon which objects of human and liberal value depend is a great obstacle, and it would be too optimistic to say that we have as yet enough knowledge of the scientific type to enable us to regulate our judgments of value very extensively. But we have more knowledge than we try to put to use, and until we try more systematically we shall not know what are the important gaps in our sciences judged from the point of view of their moral and humane use.

For moralists usually draw a sharp line between the field of the natural sciences and the conduct that is regarded as moral. But a moral that frames its judgments of value on the basis of consequences must depend in a most intimate manner upon the conclusions of science. For the knowledge of the relations between changes which enable us to connect things as antecedents and consequences *is* science. The narrow scope which moralists often give to morals, their isolation of some conduct as virtuous and vicious from other large ranges of conduct, those having to do with health and vigor, business, education, with all the affairs in which desires and affection are implicated, is perpetuated by this habit of exclusion of the subject-matter of natural science from a rôle in formation of moral standards and ideals. The same attitude operates in the other direction to keep natural science a technical specialty, and it works unconsciously to encourage its use exclusively in regions where it can be turned to personal and class advantage, as in war and trade.

Another great difference to be made by carrying the experimental habit into all matter of practice is that it cuts the roots of what is often called subjectivism, but which is better termed egoism. The subjective attitude is much more wide-spread than would be inferred from the philosophies which have that label attached. It is as rampant in realistic philosophies as in any others, sometimes even more so, although disguised from those who hold these philosophies under the cover of reverence for and enjoyment of ultimate values. For the implication of placing the standard of thought and knowledge in antecedent existence is that our thought makes no difference in what is significantly real. It then affects only our own attitude toward it.

This constant throwing of emphasis back upon a change made in ourselves instead of one made in the world in which we live seems to me the essence of what is objectionable in "subjectivism." Its taint hangs about even Platonic realism with its insistent evangelical dwelling upon the change made within the mind by contemplation of the realm of essence, and its depreciation of action as transient and all but sordid—a concession to the necessities of organic existence. All the theories which put conversion "of the eye of the soul" in the place of a conversion of natural and social objects that modifies goods actually experienced, is a retreat and escape from existence—and this retraction into self is, once more, the heart of subjective egoisms. The typical example is perhaps the other-worldliness found in religions whose chief concern is with the salvation of the personal soul. But other-worldliness is found as well in estheticism and in all seclusion within ivory towers.

It is not in the least implied that change in personal attitudes, in the disposition of the "subject," is not of great importance. Such change, on the contrary, is involved in any attempt to modify the conditions of the environment. But there is a radical difference between a change in the self that is cultivated and valued as an end, and one that is a means to alteration, through action, of objective conditions. The Aristotelian-medieval conviction that highest bliss is found in contemplative possession of ultimate Being presents an ideal attractive to some types of mind; it sets forth a refined sort of enjoyment. It is a doctrine congenial to minds that despair of the effort involved in creation of a better world of daily experience. It is, apart from theological attachments, a doctrine sure to recur when social conditions are so troubled as to make actual endeavor seem hopeless. But the subjectivism so externally marked in modern thought as compared with ancient is either a development of the old doctrine under new conditions or is of merely technical import. The medieval version of the doctrine at least had the active support of a great social institution by means of which man could be brought into the state of mind that prepared him for ultimate enjoyment of eternal Being. It had a certain solidity and depth which is lacking in modern theories that would attain the result by merely emotional or speculative procedures, or by any means not demanding a change in objective existence so as to render objects of value more empirically secure.

The nature in detail of the revolution that would be wrought by carrying into the region of values the principle now embodied in scientific practice cannot be told; to attempt it would violate the fundamental idea that we know only after we have acted and in consequences of the outcome of action. But it would surely effect a transfer of attention and energy from the subjective to the objective. Men would think of themselves as agents not as ends; ends would be found in experienced enjoyment of the fruits of a transforming activity. In as far as the subjectivity of modern thought represents a discovery of the part played by personal responses, organic and acquired, in the causal production of the qualities and values of objects, it marks the possibility of a decisive gain. It puts us in possession of some of the conditions that control the occurrence of experienced objects, and thereby it supplies us with an instrument of regulation. There is something querulous in the sweeping denial that things as experienced, as perceived and enjoyed, in any way depend upon interaction with human selves. The error of doctrines that have exploited the part played by personal and subjective reactions in determining what is perceived and enjoyed lies either in exaggerating this factor of constitution into the sole condition—as happens in subjective idealism—or else in treating it as a finality instead of, as with all knowledge, an instrument in direction of further action.

A third significant change that would issue from carrying over experimental method from physics to man concerns the import of standards, principles, rules. With the transfer, these, and all tenets and creeds about good and goods, would be recognized to be hypotheses. Instead of being rigidly fixed, they would be treated as intellectual instruments to be tested and confirmed—and altered—through consequences effected by acting upon them. They would lose all pretence of finality—the ulterior source of dogmatism. It is both astonishing and depressing that so much of the energy of mankind has gone into fighting for (with weapons of the flesh as well as of the spirit) the truths of creeds, religious, moral and political, as distinct from what has gone into effort to try creeds by putting them to the test of acting upon them. The change would do away with the intolerance and fanaticism that attend the notion that beliefs and judgments are capable of inherent truth and authority; inherent in the sense of being independent of what they lead to when used as directive principles. The transformation does not imply merely that men are responsible for acting upon what they profess to believe; that is an old doctrine. It goes much further. Any belief as such is tentative, hypothetical; it is not just to be acted upon, but is to be *framed* with reference to its office as a guide to action. Consequently, it should be the last thing in the world to be picked up casually and then clung to rigidly. When it is apprehended as a tool and only a tool, an instrumentality of direction, the same scrupulous attention will go to its formation as now goes into the making of instruments of precision in technical fields. Men, instead of being proud of accepting and asserting beliefs and "principles" on the ground of loyalty, will be as ashamed of that procedure as they would now be to confess their assent to a scientific theory out of reverence for Newton or Helmholz or whomever, without regard to evidence.

If one stops to consider the matter, is there not something strange in the fact that men should consider loyalty to "laws," principles, standards, ideals to be inherent virtue, accounted unto them for righteousness? It is as if they were making up for some secret sense of weakness by rigidity and intensity of insistent attachment. A moral law, like a law in physics, is not something to swear by and stick to at all hazards; it is a formula of the way to respond when specified conditions present themselves. Its soundness and pertinence are tested by what happens when it is acted upon. Its claim or authority rests finally upon the imperativeness of the situation that has to be dealt with, not upon its own intrinsic nature—as any tool achieves dignity in the measure of needs served by it. The idea that adherence to standards external to experienced objects is the only alternative to confusion and lawlessness was once held in science. But knowledge became steadily progressive when it was abandoned, and clews and tests found within concrete acts and objects were employed. The test of consequences is more exacting than that afforded by fixed general rules. In addition, it secures constant development, for when new acts are tried, new results are experienced, while the lauded immutability of eternal ideals and norms is in itself a denial of the possibility of development and improvement.

The various modifications that would result from adoption in social and humane subjects of the experimental way of thinking are perhaps summed up in saying that it would place *method and means* upon the level of importance that has, in the past, been imputed exclusively to ends. Means have been regarded as menial, and the useful as the servile. Means have been treated as poor relations to be endured, but not inherently welcome. The very meaning of the word "ideals" is significant of the divorce which has obtained between means and ends. "Ideals" are thought to be remote and inaccessible of attainment; they are too high and fine to be sullied by realization. They serve vaguely to arouse "aspiration," but they do not evoke and direct strivings for embodiment in actual existence. They hover in an indefinite way over the actual scene; they are expiring ghosts of a once significant kingdom of divine reality whose rule penetrated to every detail of life.

It is impossible to form a just estimate of the paralysis of effort that has been produced by indifference to means. Logically, it is truistic that lack of consideration for means signifies that so-called ends are not taken seriously. It is as if one professed devotion to painting pictures conjoined with contempt for canvas, brush and paints; or love of music on condition that no instruments, whether the voice or something external, be used to make sounds. The good workman in the arts is known by his respect for his tools and by his interest in perfecting his technique. The glorification in the arts of ends at the expense of means would be taken to be a sign of complete insincerity or even insanity. Ends separated from means are either sentimental indulgences or if they happen to exist are merely accidental. The ineffectiveness in action of "ideals" is due precisely to the supposition that means and ends are not on exactly the same level with respect to the attention and care they demand.

It is, however, much easier to point out the formal contradiction implied in ideals that are professed without equal regard for the instruments and techniques of their realization, than it is to appreciate the concrete ways in which belief in their separation has found its way into life and borne corrupt and poisonous fruits. The separation marks the form in which the traditional divorce of theory and practice has expressed itself in actual life. It accounts for the relative impotency of arts concerned with enduring human welfare. Sentimental attachment and subjective eulogy take the place of action. For there is no art without tools and instrumental agencies. But it also explains the fact that in actual behavior, energies devoted to matters nominally thought to be inferior, material and sordid, engross attention and interest. After a polite and pious deference has been paid to "ideals," men feel free to devote themselves to matters which are more immediate and pressing.

It is usual to condemn the amount of attention paid by people in general to material ease, comfort, wealth, and success gained by competition, on the ground that they give to mere means the attention that ought to be given to ends, or that they have taken for ends things which in reality are only means. Criticisms of the place which economic interest and action occupy in present life are full of complaints that men allow lower aims to usurp the place that belongs to higher and ideal values. The final source of the trouble is, however, that moral and spiritual "leaders" have propagated the notion that ideal ends may be cultivated in isolation from "material" means, as if means and material were not synonymous. While they condemn men for giving to means the thought and energy that ought to go to ends, the condemnation should go to them. For they have not taught their followers to think of material and economic activities as *really* means. They have been unwilling to frame their conception of the values that should be regulative of human conduct on the basis of the actual conditions and operations by which alone values can be actualized.

Practical needs are imminent; with the mass of mankind they are imperative. Moreover, speaking generally, men are formed to act rather than to theorize. Since the ideal ends are so remotely and accidentally connected with immediate and urgent conditions that need attention, after lip service is given to them, men naturally devote themselves to the latter. If a bird in the hand is worth two in a neighboring bush, an actuality in hand is worth, for the direction of conduct, many ideals that are so remote as to be invisible and inaccessible. Men hoist the banner of the ideal, and then march in the direction that concrete conditions suggest and reward.

Deliberate insincerity and hypocrisy are rare. But the notion that action and sentiment are inherently unified in the constitution of human nature has nothing to justify it. Integration is something to be achieved. Division of attitudes and responses, compartmentalizing of interests, is easily acquired. It goes deep just because the acquisition is unconscious, a matter of habitual adaptation to conditions. Theory separated from concrete doing and making is empty and futile; practice then becomes an immediate seizure of opportunities and enjoyments which conditions afford without the direction which theory—knowledge and ideas—has power to supply. The problem of the relation of theory and practice is not a problem of theory alone; it is that, but it is also the most practical problem of life. For it is the question of how intelligence may inform action, and how action may bear the fruit of increased insight into meaning: a clear view of the values that are worth while and of the means by which they are to be made secure in experienced objects. Construction of ideals in general and their sentimental glorification are easy; the responsibilities both of studious thought and of action are shirked. Persons having the advantage of positions of leisure and who find pleasure in abstract theorizing—a most delightful indulgence to those to whom it appeals—have a large measure of liability for a cultivated diffusion of ideals and aims that are separated from the conditions which are the means of actualization. Then other persons who find themselves in positions of social power and authority readily claim to be the bearers and defenders of ideal ends in church and state. They then use the prestige and authority their representative capacity as guardians of the highest ends confers on them to cover actions taken in behalf of the harshest and narrowest of material ends.

The present state of industrial life seems to give a fair index of the existing separation of means and ends. Isolation of economics from ideal ends, whether of morals or of organized social life, was proclaimed by Aristotle. Certain things, he said, are conditions of a worthy life, personal and social, but are not constituents of it. The economic life of man, concerned with satisfaction of wants, is of this nature. Men have wants and they must be satisfied. But they are only prerequisites of a good life, not intrinsic elements in it. Most philosophers have not been so frank nor perhaps so logical. But upon the whole, economics has been treated as on a lower level than either morals or politics. Yet the life which men, women and children actually lead, the opportunities open to them, the values they are capable of enjoying, their education, their share in all the things of art and science, are mainly determined by economic conditions. Hence we can hardly expect a moral system which ignores economic conditions to be other than remote and empty.

Industrial life is correspondingly brutalized by failure to equate it as the means by which social and cultural values are realized. That the economic life, thus exiled from the pale of higher values, takes revenge by declaring that it is the only social reality, and by means of the doctrine of materialistic determination of institutions and conduct in all fields, denies to deliberate morals and politics any share of causal regulation, is not surprising.

When economists were told that their subject-matter was merely material, they naturally thought they could be "scientific" only by excluding all reference to distinctively human values. Material wants, efforts to satisfy them, even the scientifically regulated technologies highly developed in industrial activity, are then taken to form a complete and closed field. If any reference to social ends and values is introduced it is by way of an external addition, mainly hortatory. That economic life largely determines the conditions under which mankind has access to concrete values may be recognized or it may not be. In either case, the notion that it is the means to be utilized in order to secure significant values as the common and shared possession of mankind is alien and inoperative. To many persons, the idea that the ends professed by morals are impotent save as they are connected with the working machinery of economic life seems like deflowering the purity of moral values and obligations.

The social and moral effects of the separation of theory and practice have been merely hinted at. They are so manifold and so pervasive that an adequate consideration of them would involve nothing less than a survey of the whole field of morals, economics and politics. It cannot be justly stated that these effects are in fact direct consequences of the quest for certainty by thought and knowledge isolated from action. For, as we have seen, this quest was itself a reflex product of actual conditions. But it may be truly asserted that this quest, undertaken in religion and philosophy, has had results which have reinforced the conditions which originally brought it about. Moreover, search for safety and consolation amid the perils of life by means other than intelligent action, by feeling and thought alone, began when actual means of control were lacking, when arts were undeveloped. It had then a relative historic justification that is now lacking. The primary problem for thinking which lays claim to be philosophic in its breadth and depth is to assist in bringing about a reconstruction of all beliefs rooted in a basic separation of knowledge and action; to develop a system of operative ideas congruous with present knowledge and with present facilities of control over natural events and energies.

We have noted more than once how modern philosophy has been absorbed in the problem of affecting an adjustment between the conclusions of natural science and the beliefs and values that have authority in the direction of life. The genuine and poignant issue does not reside where philosophers for the most part have placed it. It does not consist in accommodation to each other of two realms, one physical and the other ideal and spiritual, nor in the reconciliation of the "categories" of theoretical and practical reason. It is found in that isolation of executive means and ideal interests which has grown up under the influence of the separation of theory and practice. For this, by nature, involves the separation of the material and the spiritual. Its solution, therefore, can be found only in action wherein the phenomena of material and economic life are equated with the purposes that command the loyalties of affection and purpose, and in which ends and ideals are framed in terms of the possibilities of actually experienced situations. But while the solution cannot be found in "thought" alone, it can be furthered by thinking which is operative—which frames and defines ideas in terms of what may be done, and which uses the conclusions of science as instrumentalities. William James was well within the bounds of moderation when he said that looking forward instead of back-ward, looking to what the world and life might become instead of to what they have been, is an alteration in the "seat of authority."

It was incidentally remarked earlier in our discussion that the serious defect in the current empirical philosophy of values, the one which identi-fies them with things actually enjoyed irrespective of the conditions upon which they depend, is that it formulates and in so far consecrates the con-ditions of our present social experience. Throughout these chapters, primary attention has perforce been given to the methods and statements of philo-sophic theories. But these statements are technical and specialized in formu-lation only. In origin, content and import they are reflections of some condition or some phase of concrete human experience. Just as the theory of the separation of theory and practice has a practical origin and a mo-mentous practical consequence, so the empirical theory that values are identical with whatever men actually enjoy, no matter how or what, formulates an aspect, and an undesirable one, of the present social situation.

For while our discussion has given more attention to the other type of philosophical doctrine, that which holds that regulative and authori-tative standards are found in transcendent eternal values, it has not passed in silence over the fact that actually the greater part of the activities of the greater number of human beings is spent in effort to seize upon and hold onto such enjoyments as the actual scene permits. Their energies and their enjoyments are controlled in fact, but they are controlled by external con-ditions rather than by intelligent judgment and endeavor. If philosophies have any influence over the thoughts and acts of men, it is a serious matter that the most widely held empirical theory should in effect justify this state of things by identifying values with the objects of any interest as such. As long as the only theories of value placed before us for intellectual assent alternate between sending us to a realm of eternal and fixed values and sending us to enjoyments such as actually obtain, the formulation, even as only a theory, of an experimental empiricism which finds values to be identical with goods that are the fruit of intelligently directed activity has its measure of practical significance.

Value as Any Object of Any Interest[*][1]

R. B. PERRY

I. PRELIMINARY FORMULATION AND ARGUMENT

§ 49. *Exposition and Illustration.* It is characteristic of living mind to be *for* some things and *against* others. This polarity is not reducible to that between 'yes' and 'no' in the logical or in the purely cognitive sense, because one can say 'yes' with reluctance or be glad to say 'no.' To be 'for' or 'against' is to view with favor or disfavor; it is a bias of the subject toward or away from. It implies, as we shall see more clearly in the sequel, a tendency to create or conserve, or an opposite tendency to prevent or destroy. This duality appears in many forms, such as liking and disliking, desire and aversion, will and refusal, or seeking and avoiding. It is to this all-pervasive characteristic of the motor-affective life, this *state, act, attitude or disposition of favor or disfavor*, to which we propose to give the name of '*interest*.'[2]

This, then, we take to be the original source and constant feature of all value. That which is an object of interest is *eo ipso* invested with value.[3] Any object, whatever it be, acquires value when any interest, whatever it be, is taken in it; just as anything whatsoever becomes a target when anyone whosoever aims at it. In other words, Aristotle was fundamentally mistaken when he said, that as a thing's "apparent good" makes it an object of appetite, so its real good makes it the object of "rational desire."[4] By the same token Spinoza was fundamentally correct when he said that

[*] Excerpted and reprinted with the kind permission of the author and the publisher from *General Theory of Value*, Chapter V. The Harvard University Press, 1950. (Published originally in 1926 by Longmans, Green and Co.)

[1] Parts of the present chapter are reprinted from an article entitled "A Behavioristic View of Purpose," published in the *Journal of Philosophy*, Vol. XVIII, 1921.

[2] Cf. § 14. The term 'interest' has been employed for technical purposes by various psychologists, but by none, I think, in the precise sense in which it is employed here. W. Mitchell, in his *Structure and Growth of Mind*, 1907, defines interest as our "feeling towards" an object, or, as how the object "strikes or affects us" (p. 64); whereas I propose to use the term to embrace desire and disposition as well. G. F. Stout, in his *Groundwork of Psychology*, 1903, uses the term for organized and permanent forms of the emotional life, such as sentiments [pp. 221 ff.]. More commonly 'interest' is employed by psychology to mean *attention*.

[3] An object is valuable when *qualified* by an act of interest; relation to interest assuming, in the experience or judgment of value, the rôle of adjective.

[4] *Metaphysica*, XII, Ch. 7, trans. by W. D. Ross, 1072a.

"in no case do we strive for, wish for, long for, or desire anything because we deem it to be good, but on the other hand we deem a thing to be good, because we strive for it, wish for it, long for it, or desire it." [5]

The view may otherwise be formulated in the equation: x is valuable $=$ interest is taken in x. Value is thus a specific relation into which things possessing any ontological status whatsoever, whether real or imaginary, may enter with interested subjects.

This is value *simpliciter*,—value in the elementary, primordial and generic sense. It follows that any variation of interest or of its object will determine a variety of value; that any derivative of interest or its object will determine value in a derived sense; and that any condition of interest or its object will determine a conditional value. In short, interest being constitutive of value in the basic sense, theory of value will take this as its point of departure and centre of reference; and will classify and systematize values in terms of the different forms which interests and their objects may be found to assume.

This view has rarely found a perfectly clear and consistent expression. It is, however, essentially conveyed in an early work of Mr. George Santayana:

"Apart from ourselves, and our human bias, we can see in such a mechanical world no element of value whatever. On removing consciousness, we have removed the possibility of worth. But it is not only in the absence of all consciousness that value would be removed from the world; by a less violent abstraction from the totality of human experience, we might conceive beings of a purely intellectual cast, minds in which the transformations of nature were mirrored without any emotion. . . . No event would be repulsive, no situation terrible. . . . In this case, as completely as if consciousness were absent altogether, all value and excellence would be gone. . . . Values spring from the immediate and inexplicable reaction of vital impulse, and from the irrational part of our nature. . . . The ideal of rationality is itself as arbitrary, as much dependent on the needs of a finite organization, as any other ideal." [6]

A more recent statement, and one more explicitly in accord with the view here proposed, is the following:

"Anything is properly said to have value in case, and only in case, it is the object of the affective motor response which we call being *interested* in, positively or negatively. . . . The being liked, or disliked, of the object is its value. And since the being liked or disliked, is being the object of a motor-affective attitude in a subject, some sort of a subject is always requisite to there being value at all—not necessarily a *judging* subject, but a subject capable of at least motor-affective response. For the cat the cream has value, or better and more simply, the cat values the cream, or the warmth, or having her back

[5] *Ethics*, Part III, Prop. IX, Note, trans. by R. H. M. Elwes, 1901. It is, of course, possible to desire a thing because it is good, where its goodness consists in its being desired by other subjects, or by some other interest of the same subject. But *in the last analysis* good springs from desire and not desire from good.

[6] *The Sense of Beauty*, 1899, pp. 17-19. Cf. also William James: "*The essence of good is to satisfy demand*" (*Will to Believe*, etc., 1898, p. 201).

scratched, quite regardless of her probable inability to conceive cream or to make judgments concerning warmth." [7]

* * *

§ 52. *Summary of the Argument.* How is the view here proposed to be proved? What is the evidence upon which it rests?

In the first place, we have reached it by a process of systematic elimination. We have first examined and eliminated those views which affirm value to be indefinable, or to be definable independently of interest. If value cannot be successfully identified or defined without reference to interest, then we must incorporate interest into our definition. We have next examined those views which relate value to interest in some qualified and exclusive sense; first, those views which have proposed to qualify and limit the object of interest; second, those views which have proposed to qualify and limit the act or state of interest itself. The result has been to exhibit a variety of values all having the common generic character of being 'object-of-interest.' We have thus been led to define value as the peculiar relation between any interest and its object; or that special character of an object which consists in the fact that interest is taken in it. We are now justified in framing this hypothesis as a last remaining alternative. There is a certain presumption in favor of this remaining alternative not only because of the elimination of the others, but also because these have all betrayed a common tendency. They have not only through their failure left the field clear for our definition of value, but they have *pointed* to that definition and incidentally argued in its support.

A certain positive plausibility is given to this hypothesis by the fact that in order to create values where they did not exist before it seems to be sufficient to introduce an interest. The silence of the desert is without value, until some wanderer finds it lonely and terrifying; the cataract, until some human sensibility finds it sublime, or until it is harnessed to satisfy human needs. Natural substances or the by-products of manufacture are without value until a use is found for them, whereupon their value may increase to any degree of preciousness according to the eagerness with which they are coveted. There is no entity that can be named that does not, in the very naming of it, take on a certain value through the fact that it is selected by the cognitive purpose of some interested mind. As interests grow and expand, multiplying in number and extending their radius through experience and imagination, the store of cosmic values is enriched and diversified.

But it may be contended that such proof is redundant or verbal. It proves only that objects of interest appear whenever interest is taken in objects; or, it proves at most that what is added to a given situation when

---

[7] D. W. Prall, *A Study in the Theory of Value,* Univ. of California Publications in Philosophy, Vol. 3, No. 2, 1921, pp. 215, 227. The present writer is in essential agreement with the whole of this admirable monograph.

interests are introduced corresponds closely to what it is customary to *call* value. It does not add to our knowledge by demonstrating the existence of value where it was not suspected, or by resolving doubts as to what is *really* valuable.

This objection again brings to light the difference between the general definition of value and the solution of special questions of value. The doubts and perplexities of everyday life, as well as the limited theoretical problems of the several value-sciences, commonly assume a general definition of value, and turn upon some question of fact. Is this distant island worth annexing and defending? The answer depends upon the existence of mineral deposits or a good harbor, assuming that it is worth annexing if the satisfactions and utilities which it affords outweigh the sacrifices which it costs. Ought I to surrender my position for the sake of my scruples, or compromise temporarily in the hope of converting others to my way of thinking? The answer depends on certain probable trains of consequences following from each of the alternatives, assuming that the one or the other ought to be adopted in accordance with the principle of human happiness, broadly applied. Is recent American verse to be ranked as genuine poetry? The answer depends experimentally on the sort of feeling aroused in certain persons, such as the critic himself, by the prolonged and attentive reading of it, on the assumption that such a judgment of taste is decisive. Is the economic worth or the aesthetic superiority of a work of art dependent on its moral wholesomeness? The answer is assumed to depend on the record of transactions made in the market place, or the reported sentiments of connoisseurs.

Now the general definition of value does not directly answer any such question, because it does not ascertain the specific facts and probabilities upon which they turn. It concerns itself with the *assumption*, and must therefore always appear to deal with the obvious rather than with the questionable. Its proper task is to make these assumptions explicit and consistent. By so doing it will inevitably affect the solution of such special questions, since it will prescribe the terms or the principle of their solution. But it has to do with the use which is to be made of evidence, rather than with the uncovering of new facts.

It follows that there can be no conclusive proof of a general definition of value, short of its success in facilitating the solution of all special questions of value. Such a definition is *an experiment in generalization.* If we adopt the fact of interest as our centre of reference, and view other facts of the surrounding field *in that relation*—if, in short, we take life *interest-wise,* as it can, in fact, be taken—do the data and the perplexities denoted by 'good' and 'evil,' 'right' and 'wrong,' 'better' and 'worse,' or grouped within the special fields of morality, art, religion and kindred institutions, then fall into place and form a comprehensive system? It is evident that the only proof of which such a hypothesis is capable lies in its complete elaboration. In short the argument for the thesis submitted in the present study is cumulative, and cannot properly claim the assent of the reader until the last chapter is written.

II. REPLY TO THE CHARGE OF RELATIVISM

§ 53. *Relativism as an Epithet.* Although no conclusive proof of the present view is possible until it is completely elaborated, it has been supposed that there is a conclusive *disproof* which can be urged without further ado. To attribute value to any object of any interest is at once to expose oneself to the charge of *relativism*, whatever the psychological details, and however successful such a definition may prove for purposes of systematic generalization.

No one can afford to disregard this charge. Relativism is an epithet which implies disparagement, when, as is often the case, it implies nothing more. Even the respectable scientific authority which has pronounced in its favor has not saved the physical theory of relativity from being regarded as somewhat *risqué*,—as evidence of the corruption of the times or of the malicious influence of the Semitic mind. There is no man who would not rather be absolute than relative, even though he has not the faintest conception of the meaning of either term.

This sentiment is peculiarly strong in the field of values, and pre-eminently in the province of morals. Nothing could be more scandalous than these lines of Sir Richard Burton:

"There is no good, there is no bad, these be the whims of mortal will;
What works me weal that call I good, what harms and hurts I hold as ill.
They change with space, they shift with race, and in the veriest space of time,
Each vice has worn a virtue's crown, all good been banned as sin or crime." [8]

How much nobler and more edifying in tone are such utterances as these of Froude and Carlyle:

"The eternal truths and rights of things exist, fortunately, independent of our thoughts or wishes, fixed as mathematics, inherent in the nature of man and the world. They are no more to be trifled with than gravitation."
"What have men to do with interests? There is a right way and a wrong way. That is all we need think about it." [9]

Yet there can scarcely be more offence in the adjective 'relative' than there is in the substantive 'relation'; and when we investigate the world in which we live, we discover as a rule that what we took to be an absolute does as a matter of fact both stand in relations and comprise relations. In any case we shall be influenced only by such *theoretical* difficulties as may be urged against a relativistic theory of value, and not in the least by practical or sentimental objections.

§ 54. *Epistemological Relativism, or Scepticism.* There is unquestion-

[8] Quoted by L. Dickinson, *Meaning of Good*, 1907, p. 5.
[9] J. A. Froude, *Inaugural Lecture at St. Andrews*, 1869, p. 41; Letter of Carlyle to Froude, *Longman's Magazine*, 1892, p. 151.

ably one form of relativism which is theoretically objectionable. He who identifies the act of *cognizing* values with that act of the subject which *constitutes* them, or holds that values are both known and created in one and the same act, does imply the impossibility of knowing anything whatsoever about value, and thus belies any statements that he himself may make about it. This objection holds against certain philosophers who have identified value with interest, and it therefore behooves us to discover whether our own view is similarly objectionable.

Professor G. E. Moore distinguishes two forms in which this vicious relativism may be stated. In the first place, "it may be held that whenever any man asserts an action to be right or wrong, what he is asserting is merely that he *himself* has some particular feeling toward the action in question." [10] In this case the act of knowing or judging value, is construed as simply an expression of the judge's own interest. The following famous passage from Hobbes is a case in point:

"But whatsoever is the object of any man's appetite or desire, that is it which he for his part calleth 'good'; and the object of his hate and aversion, 'evil'; and of his contempt 'vile' and 'inconsiderable.' For these words of good, evil, and contemptible, are ever used with relation to the person that useth them: there being nothing simply and absolutely so; nor any common rule of good and evil, to be taken from the nature of the objects themselves." [11]

The *reductio ad absurdum* of such a view lies, as Professor Moore points out, in the fact that it would lead to the mutual irrelevance of all judgments in which the value-predicates are employed. If in affirming an act to be right or wrong, good or evil, a judge were always referring to *his own present feeling* about it, then no two judges could ever agree or disagree with one another, nor could the same judge ever reaffirm or correct his own past opinions.[12] In other words, on questions of value there could not be any such thing as judgment or opinion in the ordinary sense of these terms. This is not only contrary to fact, but it is inevitably contradicted by the very man who makes the assertion.

A second statement of this vicious relativism is the assertion "that when we judge an action to be right or wrong what we are asserting is merely that somebody or other thinks it to be right or wrong." Generalized and simplified, this assertion is to the effect that value consists in being thought to be valuable—"There is nothing either good or bad, but thinking makes it so." Now the fundamental difficulty with this view lies in the fact that one would then have nothing to think about. If a thing is valuable by virtue of being believed to be valuable, then when one believes a thing to be valuable, one believes that it is believed to be valuable, or one believes that it is believed to be believed to be valuable, and so on *ad infinitum*.[13]

---

[10] *Ethics*, Home University Library, p. 89 [p. 55 reset edition].
[11] *Leviathan*, Part I, Ch. VI.
[12] Cf. G. E. Moore, *op. cit.*, pp. 100–103 [pp. 62–3 reset edition].
[13] Cf. G. E. Moore, *op. cit.*, pp. 122–124 [pp. 76–7 reset edition].

In short, there can be no judgment about value, or about anything else, unless there is some content or object other than the act of judgment itself, —a judged as well as a judging.

It is this error or confusion which vitiates the work of Westermarck and others who, not content with a history of moral opinion, have attempted to *define* moral values in *terms* of moral opinion.[14] It is the characteristic and besetting error of all anthropological and sociological theories of value, which aim to be scientific or 'positive.'[15] What has been judged with unanimity to be good or evil by members of a social group, is a matter of record; and is thus a fact ascertainable by archaeological or historical methods, and with a precision and indubitableness peculiar to these methods. But such methodological preferences do not alter the fact that these judgments, if judgments at all, must have been *about* something; and in theory of value it is this *object*, and not the acts of judgment themselves, which is primarily in question. There are also recorded opinions about the stars, and anthropologists may and do investigate these opinions; but one does not therefore propose to substitute a history of astronomical opinions for astronomy.

Let us now inquire whether the view here proposed is guilty of a vicious or sceptical relativism in either or both of these two senses. In the first place, although defining value as relative to interest, we have not defined value as exclusively relative to the present interest of the judge. Thus if Caesar was ambitious when he waged war upon Pompey, the definition implies that power was in fact good, as being coveted by Caesar. But this fact may have been affirmed by Mark Antony, or afterwards denied by Caesar himself in his own defence. Value, therefore, lends itself to judgment in the ordinary sense,—to judgments which are true or false, and which may agree or disagree.

In the second place, having defined value as constituted by interests, such judgments have a content or object other than themselves. They may refer to the interest of the judge, or to any other interests, past or present, common or unique; but the interest that creates the value is always other than the judgment that cognizes it. Theory of value is not a history of opinion about values, but deals with that to which such opinion refers.

§ *55. The Argument from 'Intrinsic' Value.* Professor Moore has further weapons in his arsenal which he believes to be fatal not only to the particular forms of epistemological relativism just rejected, but in general to the view that "by calling a thing 'good' or 'bad' we merely mean that some being or beings have a certain mental attitude towards it"; or that "what we mean by calling a thing 'good' is that it is *desired*, or desired in

[14] E. Westermarck, *Origin and Development of Moral Ideas*, 1906, Vol. I, *passim.* Westermarck's confusion is largely due to the ambiguity of the term 'approval,' and the absence of any clear notion of judgment.

[15] For a general statement of this position, cf. L. Lévy-Bruhl, *La Morale et la Science des Mœurs*, 1910.

some particular way." [16] Since we have in effect maintained precisely this view, his objections are relevant and must be met.

He appeals, in the first place, to the fact that we may use the word 'good' without consciously meaning 'object of interest.' Judging by what the speaker has in mind, to say that the object is good is not the same as to say that some one is interested in it.[17] This type of argument would prove altogether too much if it proved anything. No definition has ever been formulated that is perfectly in keeping either with verbal usage or conscious meanings. For words may be mere echoes, and conscious meanings careless and obscure. The absurdity of the argument is especially evident in the case of complex entities, such as the exponents of the present view hold value to be. A complex entity is only summarily denoted in common discourse, and analysis will invariably reveal a structure which is not present to a mind which employs terms in a stereotyped sense. It would, for example, scarcely be urged that circularity is indefinable because one can judge an object to be circular without judging that all points on its perimeter are equi-distant from the centre. In the one case as in the other the nature of the predicate is revealed not in customary usage, but when doubt has arisen as to its applicability. Where the circularity of an object is in question one falls to measuring; and when its goodness is in question one falls to considering its relation to interests.

A much more serious objection is based upon the notion of *intrinsic* value. We judge a thing to be intrinsically good "where we judge, concerning a particular state of things that it would be worth while—would be 'a good thing'—that that state of things should exist, *even if nothing else were to exist besides*, either at the same time or afterwards." [18] If a thing derives value from its relation to an interest taken in it, it would seem impossible that anything whatsoever should possess value in itself. But in that case value would seem always to be borrowed, and never owned; value would shine by a reflected glory having no original source.

The question turns upon the fact that any predicate may be judged synthetically or analytically. Suppose that 'good' were to be regarded as a simple quality like yellow. It would then be possible to judge either synthetically, that the primrose was fair or yellow; or, analytically, that the fair, yellow primrose was fair or yellow. Only the fair, yellow primrose would be fair and yellow "even if nothing were to exist besides." But the logic of the situation is not in the least altered if a relational predicate is substituted for a simple quality; indeed it is quite possible to regard a quality as a monadic (a single term) relation. Tangential, for example, is a relational predicate; since a line is a tangent only by virtue of the peculiar relation of single-point contact with another line or surface. Let R^t represent this peculiar relation, and A, B, two lines. One can then judge either syntheti-

---

[16] *Op. cit.*, pp. 157 [p. 97 reset edition], 159 [pp. 98–9 reset edition.]

[17] This argument is applied primarily to the term 'right,' but is equally applicable to the term 'good.' Cf. *ibid.*, pp. 111 [p. 69 reset edition], 163 [p. 101 reset edition].

[18] *Ibid.*, p. 162 [p. 101 reset edition].

cally, that (A) R^t (B); or, analytically, that (A) R^t (B) is R^t. Similarly, let S represent an interested subject, O an object, and R^i the peculiar relation of interest, taken and received. We can then judge either synthetically, that (O) R^i (S); or, analytically that (O) R^i (S) is R^i. In other words, one can say either that O is desired by S, or that O-desired-by-S is a case of the general character 'desired.'

The situation is complicated, but not logically altered, by the fact that either O, or O's-being-desired-by-S^1, may be desired by S^2, and so stand in a second value-relation of the same type. In other words, as we have already seen, the question of value is peculiarly recurrent.[19] But value is intrinsic when it is independent of such ulterior interests. Similarly, the primrose as enjoyed is intrinsically good; the primrose as sought for the sake of such ulterior enjoyment, is instrumentally, conditionally, or otherwise extrinsically good. In other words, according to the present view an object unrelated to a subject cannot be good in itself, any more than, in Professor Moore's view,[20] an object can be good in itself without possessing the specific superadded quality 'good'; but an object-desired-for-itself, that is, any value of the variable function (O) R (S), can and does possess value in itself.[21]

The special case of the universe as a whole [22] furnishes a further and peculiarly instructive example. It is evident that by definition the universe as a whole cannot stand in relation to any desiring subject outside itself. In what sense, therefore, can it be said to possess value in accord with our definition? In the first place, it might, for certain familiar metaphysical reasons which are not here in question, be conceived as a single all-embracing interest. The total universe would be divided between a universal subject and a universal object, with a relation of will or love (perhaps of self-love) uniting the two. In that case the world in its unity would possess intrinsic value. Or, independently of such metaphysical speculation, the universe may be said to possess value in so far as loved or hated by its own members, taken severally. Or it may be said to contain value,[23] in that it embraces interests and their objects. Or it may be said to be an instrument of value, in that it provides the conditions by which interests and their objects may arise and be conserved. There is no cosmic paradox which can be urged against the definition of value in terms of the interest-relation which could not with equal force be urged against any other view of value, including the view that value is an indefinable quality. For if it be urged that

19 Cf. §§ 17 and 56.
20 As set forth above, § 15.
21 Even Professor Moore says (ibid., p. 167 [pp. 103–4 reset edition]): "I think it is true that no whole can be intrinsically good, unless it contains some feeling toward something as a part of itself." According to this view the 'something' and the 'feeling toward,' taken together, are 'good': there being three factors involved. In my view 'good' means the 'feeling toward,' or more precisely, 'the being felt toward.'
22 Cf. G. E. Moore, ibid., p. 58 [p. 37 reset edition].
23 And thus to be better than no universe at all, by the principle of 'inclusiveness.' Cf. Ch. XXII, Sect. III.

the universe so defined as to embrace all interests cannot be synthetically good through any interest taken in it, it can equally well be urged that the universe so defined as to embrace the indefinable quality 'good,' cannot be good through the super-addition of this quality.

We may safely conclude, therefore, that the definition of value herein proposed provides for intrinsic value in such intelligible senses as are provided for in any other theory of value.

§ 56. *The Charge of Circularity.* In criticising the view that value is a "relational attitude," Professor W. M. Urban argues that it involves "a definition in a circle."

"The value of an object consists, it is said, in its satisfaction of desire, or more broadly, fulfilment of interest. But it is always possible to raise further questions which show conclusively that the value concept is already presupposed. Is the interest itself worthy of being satisfied? Is the object worthy of being of interest? In other words, the fact of intrinsic value requires us to find the essence of value in something other than this type of relation." [24]

This expresses the most popular objection to the present view. The fact of desire is not accepted as final in most judgments of value. Objects of desire are held to be bad despite their being desired, and desires themselves are held to be bad whether or no they are satisfied. Vicious appetites, vulgar taste, o'erweening ambition, are the most notorious of evils. Indeed the general terms 'desire' and 'interest' have acquired a specific flavor of moral disrepute. Must we not conclude therefore that value, instead of flowing from interest, is an independent, if not antagonistic, principle by which interests and their objects are judged? Despite the strong appeal which this argument must make to common-sense, we shall find not only that it rests upon a confusion, but that the very facts to which it refers can be understood only by such a definition of value as is here proposed.

Let us consider, first, the relatively simple case in which *all* desire is condemned. The argument as presented by Schopenhauer and by other Occidental and Oriental advocates of the cult of apathy, is based upon the generalization that desire is doomed to defeat. Desire asks what in the very nature of the case it can never obtain. It asks for private advantage or special privilege in a world which is indifferent to such claims; or it perpetually begets new desires out of its own satisfaction, and is thus in a chronic state of bankruptcy. But why, then, condemn it? Pessimism is founded on a conception of evil, which in turn must be assumed to be the converse of good. There would be no reason for condemning the *futility* of desire as evil unless the *success* of desire were supposed to be good. This implication is more clearly evident in the Stoic cult of resignation. Thus Epictetus exhorts his followers to "demand not that events should happen as you wish; but wish them to happen as they do happen and you will go

24 "Value and Existence," *Jour. of Philos.*, Vol. XIII, 1916, pp. 452, 453.

on well." [25] There would be no meaning in such counsel if 'going on well' were not conceived as consisting in some sort of accord between events and what men wish.

Let us now consider those cases which arise not from disaccord between interests and their natural environments, but from disaccord between one interest and another. The same object may be liked or desired by one man, and disliked or avoided by another. Our definition requires us to attribute evil to the object as being disliked, *despite* the fact that it is liked. It may, then, be argued that liking cannot make an object good. Or it may be objected that our definition requires us to affirm that the same object is at one and the same time both evil and good, which is contradictory. But *is* it contradictory? The fact is, on the contrary, that a relational definition, such as that here proposed, is the only means of *avoiding* contradiction. It is not denied that the same object may be both liked and disliked; this is the very premise of the objection. If, then, good is *defined* as being liked, and evil as being disliked, it follows that the same object may *in this sense* be without contradiction both good and evil. A term may always possess relational attributes in opposite senses, provided such relations are sustained toward different terms. The same physical object may be both 'to the right of' and 'to the left of,' both 'above' and 'below'; the same man may be both friend and enemy, both agent and patient.

A yet more common case is that in which one interest is condemned because of being contrary to another interest. Such condemnation arises from the fact that interests conflict, so that the affirmation of one implies the negation of the other. This occurs in sheer struggle where both interests are upon the same plane. When two appetites require for their satisfaction the exclusive use of the same object, the desired object is *good* in relation to each appetite; while each appetite is *evil* in relation to the other, as tending to prevent its satisfaction.

But the case which has most deeply affected popular habits of thought, and which is mainly responsible for the prejudice against the present theory of value, is the case in which an interest or its object is morally condemned. Interests are deemed 'bad,' and not merely in the sense of being hostile to other rival interests of the same rank; they are deemed 'downright' bad, in a sense in which all judges, including the agent himself, are expected to agree.

The explanation of this case lies, however, in the fact that moral judgments are not concerned with value in the generic sense, but with a specific and complex *aspect* of it. They are concerned with organizations of values, whether in the personal or in the social life. They do not deal with interests *per se*, but with the relation of interests to the comprehensive purposes in which they are incorporated. From the moral point of view value *begins*

[25] *Ench*. VIII, translated in Bakewell's *Source Book in Ancient Philosophy*, 1907, p. 318.

with the bearing of a 'lower' interest upon a 'higher' interest. To quote Mr. Santayana,

"It is in reference to such constitutional interests that things are 'really' good or bad; interests which may not be fairly represented by any incidental conscious desire. No doubt any desire, however capricious, represents some momentary and partial interest, which lends to its objects a certain real and inalienable value; yet when we consider, as we do in human society, the interests of men, whom reflection and settled purposes have raised more or less to the ideal dignity of individuals, then passing fancies and passions may indeed have bad objects, and be bad themselves, in that they thwart the more comprehensive interests of the soul that entertains them." [26]

It is in this sense that appetites may be vicious in relation to health, or efficiency; that special inclinations or passions may corrupt character, or hinder a life-purpose; and that personal ambition may imperil the well-being of the nation, or of humanity at large. But while such values may be absolutes for the moral consciousness, it is the avowed purpose of a general theory of value to analyze and relate them. Theory of value takes all value for its province, even values which are too evident or ignoble for the judgments of common-sense. This does not imply any neglect of 'higher' values, but only the method of understanding the special case in terms of the generic type.

§ 57. *Realistic Basis of the Present Definition.* We have reached the general conclusion that while there *is* an epistemological relativism which is vicious and self-defeating, the relativity of values is not only logically innocuous but logically helpful and illuminating. The genuine logical difficulties that have attended the theory of value have arisen from a persistent unwillingness to accept the palpable fact that values *are* relative in different senses to different subjects. This unwillingness has taken the form of denying that values are relative to interests at all, or the form of affirming their exclusive relation to some one interest, or to some one type or class of interests. The really vicious relativism arises not from the recognition of relations, but from the *insufficient* recognition of relations. The error of the old geo-centric astronomy lay not in its affirmation of the relation of sun, moon and stars to the earth, but in the distorted perspective which under-emphasized or ignored other relations. The same defect has subsequently appeared in the Newtonian mechanics. The error of anthropocentrism lies not in affirming the relation of all things to man, but in an exaggeration of that relation. In all of these cases advancing enlightenment has generalized a relation which was previously thought to be unique.

The analogous case in theory of value is the affirmation in behalf of any subject that its interests constitute the only centre or point of reference for all values. The common and disreputable case is egoism where an agent

[26] G. Santayana, *Winds of Doctrine,* 1913, p. 146 [p. 267 this volume].

baldly asserts his own private interests. The more insidious case is that which enjoys among philosophers the highly reputable name of 'idealism.'

This form of relativism arises from the general thesis characteristic of all idealism that the cognitive act creates its objects. According to this thesis, when I know reality, I make it; and since there can be only one reality, what I thus make takes exclusive possession of the field. In making reality myself I must reject the work of others save in so far as it coincides with my own. What holds of objects of knowledge generally, holds of values in particular. Value is held to be relative to the subject's *judgment*. Since one is justified in claiming the assent of others to one's judgment, and must regard other and conflicting judgments as false, one may thus claim priority or exclusiveness for that system of values which centres in oneself. This view is viciously relativistic in that it imputes absoluteness to a limited and partial set of relations. The way of escape lies not in the denial of the relativity of value to interest, but in the *generalization* of that relation. Where all interests are viewed as equally constitutive of value, and none is viewed as exclusive or preëminent, then the relativism of values loses those characters of arbitrariness, contradictoriness and asymmetry, which make it morally and logically objectionable.

It has sometimes been supposed that a realistic theory of knowledge, such as is professed in the present study, implies that values shall be conceived as 'objective' in the sense of being independent of *any* relation to a subject. But such an inference is wholly gratuitous. A realistic theory of knowledge is a theory of *knowledge*, to the effect, namely, that *what* is known is independent as regards its existence and essential nature, of the *act* or *state* of knowledge. It is asserted that when the mountain, for example, is perceived by Mahomet, this relation is something super-added to the mountain; in such wise that the mountain can maintain its historic existence and its mountainous nature uninterruptedly, whether in the presence or in the absence of Mahomet's perception. But this thesis does not imply that only mountains or similar inanimate and insensible beings can exist or be perceived. Mahomet, for example, perceived his daughter Fatima and her love for Ali; he was doubtless aware of his own hopes and fears for the future of Islam. Realism contends only that love, hope and fear, like mountains, are independent of the acts of perception or judgment whereby they are known. There is not the slightest ground for imputing to realism the grotesque notion that there are no such things as acts or states of mind, or that such things cannot be known. If a realist entertained this grotesque notion he could not affirm anything about the act of knowledge itself, which is the central topic of his discourse. Because he seeks to avoid a philosophical psycho-mania, there is no reason to accuse him of psychophobia.

The view here opposed may properly be termed a biocentric or psycho-centric theory of value, in the sense that values are held to be functions of certain acts of living mind to which we have given the name of interest. Interests and their objects, or the complex facts, objects-of-interest, can be known like any other facts. But they do not have to obtain from anybody's knowledge of them, permission either to exist or to be what they are. No subject whatsoever, human or divine, has the power to make or unmake them by his own simple affirmation or denial. When value is defined in terms of these facts it possesses the same independence. A value acquires existence when an interest is generated, regardless of any knowledge about it. A value will cease to exist when its own sustaining interest is destroyed or altered; but it does not cease to exist simply because it is cognitively excommunicated. He who knows values, and takes account of them, profits from that knowledge through his better adaptation to the environment in which he lives; and he who ignores them, does so at his peril.

III. PROBLEMS AND METHODS

§ *58*. Assuming that value is a function of what may broadly be termed 'interest,' it becomes imperative to examine the fundamental or generic character of this phenomenon. What is that state, or attitude, or act, or process, which is characteristic of living things, which is unmistakably present in the motor-affective consciousness of man, and which shades away through instinct and reflex to the doubtful borderland of tropism? Both the vocabulary and the grammatical structure of common speech provide for the category of interest. There is something in our world to which they serve to call attention. What is it?

The fact that we have found it necessary to paraphrase interest as "the motor-affective life" indicates the complexity of the topic. If value in the generic sense is defined in terms of interest in the generic sense, then it is evident that the varieties of value must be understood in terms of the varieties of interest. These varieties, and the rival claims to which they give rise, have provoked most of the controversies of contemporary psychology. Some interests, called 'instincts,' are held to be innate, and others acquired. Some, called 'reflexes,' are held to be blind and automatic; others are held to be 'intelligent.' The expression, 'motor-affective,' as well as the traditional division of mind into thought, will, and feeling, suggests a duality between active and passive interests; or a duality between interests directed to an imagined or represented future, and those directed to an immediate present. Terms such as 'character' and 'disposition' testify to a type of interest which is latent or unconscious, and which manifests itself in its outward or ulterior effects, rather than in any present subjective state. The antithesis between 'impulse' and 'volition' implies that interest is qualified by the presence, in some degree, of the intellectual process. The difference between desire and aversion, pleasure and pain, or liking and disliking, indicates a peculiar polarity or opposition of interest. Finally, all of these modal differences imply corresponding standards of measurement, such as 'intensity' of feeling, or 'strength' of desire.

In undertaking to refine and amplify the meaning of interest, we are confronted at the outset by a choice of methods. There is a *prima facie* discontinuity between the field of mental states disclosed by introspection, and the field of organic phenomena in which the biologist and other physical scientists conduct their investigations; and if an observer commits himself initially to the former, it would seem that he can never escape its limits. We shall therefore look for interest in the open,—upon the plane and in the context of physical nature.

We cannot determine the rôle of introspective data in interest, unless we first take that view of the matter in which both consciousness and its physical context are taken into account. Behavior or conduct, broadly surveyed in all the dimensions that experience affords, can alone give us the proper perspective. Furthermore, we want if possible to discover what it is to *be* interested, not what it is merely to *feel* interested. What is implied in *being* favorably or unfavorably disposed to anything? It may be that it all comes to nothing more than a peculiar quality or arrangement among the data of introspection, but such a conclusion would be equivalent to an abandonment of the widespread notion that interest is a kind of determination of events. The really important claim made in behalf of interest is the claim that things happen *because* of interest. Are acts performed *on account* of ends? Is it proper to *explain* what takes place in human or animal life, or in the course of nature at large, by the categories of teleology? The most exhaustive introspective analysis of the motor-affective consciousness would leave this question unanswered, and to confine ourselves to the data which such analysis affords would be to prejudge it unfavorably.

For the first time since the moralists and theologians divided the soul from the body, man is beginning to find a place in nature without being stripped of his most distinctive characteristics. He has begun to move about on the surface of the planet while still retaining possession of his faculties. This achievement is due primarily to that general psychological tendency which has acquired the name of 'behaviorism,' from one of its particular and recent manifestations.[27]

Behaviorism, in the general sense, is simply a return to the original Aristotelian view that mind and body are related as activity and organ. The activities of mind, so construed, are observable and describable functions of the physical organism, continuous with those of life, and differing from them in pattern and complexity rather than in constituents. The so-called 'states' of mind, or 'contents of consciousness,' on the other hand, are identified with the environment of behavior, being mental only in so far as behavior selects and combines them. The result is to avoid construing either

[27] Summaries of this tendency, with bibliography, will be found in G. C. Dickinson, *Economic Motives*, 1922, Ch. VII; A. A. Roback, *Behaviorism and Psychology*, 1923. The best critical exposition is to be found in K. S. Lashley: "The Behavioristic Interpretation of Consciousness," *Psych. Rev.*, Vol. XXX, 1923.

the subjective or the objective aspect of mind in terms of a unique substance or quality.

It has been objected that this is to leave out 'consciousness.' But what is this 'consciousness' which we are under obligation to include—is it a datum or a theory? It was once said that psychology omitted the soul. And so it did, in so far as the term 'soul' was the name for a theory formulated in theology or "rational" psychology. But psychology never deliberately neglected any of the facts or problems lying within the field of the mental life of man; and as a result of omitting the older theory of the soul, it reached a very much better understanding of the actual mode of existence in question. No one would now think of conceiving the soul as a simple, indivisible and incorruptible static entity, or as a naked act of pure reason. In every philosophy the soul is now a process; or a flowing, and more or less complexly organized, experience. When, therefore, we say the soul is lost, what we really mean is that a theory is more or less obsolete, as a result of its having been successfully ignored. The soul as an existent fact having a nature and an explanation, is not lost, but found.

Now something of this same outcome may with reasonable safety be predicted in the case of 'consciousness.' If a behaviorist be enlightened he will have no intention of omitting any facts, but only of abandoning a theory which he believes has proved unsatisfactory. He does not abandon *consciousness*, but the introspective *theory* of consciousness; and in so far as the new theory is more successful than the old, consciousness as a group of facts, as something that exists and happens, will have been found and not lost.[28]

The limitations of the introspective theory of consciousness have been most flagrant in the region of the will and the affections; in other words, in that department of human nature with which theory of value is primarily concerned. The failure of introspection to give any satisfactory account of feeling, desire, will, and conation scarcely admits of doubt.

The dubious feelings of 'pleasantness' and 'unpleasantness,' which if they *are* a unique species of introspective data ought to be *indubitable,* are held by some to be simple sensations, by others to be fusions of organic sensations, and by others to be acts or 'attitudes' of liking or disliking. Desire, viewed introspectively, can never be anything but a combination of ideas and feelings. Exponents of the introspective method have seen the difficulty

[28] Whether this is or is not a "strict" behaviorism, is a matter of no consequence. I am concerned with the possibilities afforded by a program and a method, broadly conceived. It is too early, even if it were profitable, to discuss questions of orthodoxy and heresy. Most of the current criticisms of behaviorism are irrelevant to the position here taken. Thus Mr. C. D. Broad attacks the behaviorist who says "that all mental processes reduce without residue to the fact that the body is behaving in a certain specific way" (*The Mind and its Place in Nature*, 1925, p. 616). I agree that such a behaviorist (*i.e.,* one who denies or ignores the *content* of consciousness) deserves attack. Mr. Broad also defines the behaviorist as a "reductive materialist" (*ibid.,* p. 612); which fits *some* behaviorists, but not that general tendency of which I make bold to claim Mr. Broad himself as an adherent, in so far as he prefers to view mind as an "emergent characteristic" of the material world (*ibid.,* pp. 610, 650).

of accounting in these terms for actual dynamic differences: such as that between desiring a thing, and liking to think of it; or that between real desire, and the sham-desire characteristic of play and aesthetic detachment.[29] As to will, Münsterberg's reduction of this to such terms as "the perception of an attained effect whose idea has gone before" [30] perfectly illustrates the extent to which the method of introspection endeavors to make up the whole of will by piecing together its cognitive shreds and patches. It is evident that the distinctive feature of will lies in this "attained effect" (*erreichten Effektes*), which is the one element in the situation which cannot be defined in introspective terms.

Similarly, wherever accounts of *conation* preserve anything distinctive, they appear to incorporate something of the action of the physical organism. The basic antithesis of favor and disfavor, which is said to distinguish active feelings, is an echo of the antithesis between positive and negative bodily reactions. Thus Professor G. F. Stout speaks of a "mental striving," which "tends to realize itself," and of which the physiological correlate is "the tendency of a neural system to recover a relatively stable condition." What, one may fairly ask, is the common meaning of "tendency" on the mental and the physiological sides? Or is the latter, perhaps, the *real* tendency, and the former the feeling of it? [31] Professor William McDougall says that every instance of instinctive behavior involves "a striving *towards or away from*" an object; and that in all instinctive behavior there is "*a persistent striving towards the natural end of the process*," which is intensified by obstacles.[32] This account seems clearly to have been derived in the first instance from the organism's action on its environment, and irresistibly suggests that the subjective or introspective sense of striving is the consciousness *of* the stresses and strains incidental to this action.[33]

Almost every recent advance in the motor-affective field of the mental life has resulted from the more or less complete abandonment of the introspective method. The most notable general advance, an advance that has now been accepted by the social sciences as well as by popular opinion, is the rejection of the once-classic view that conduct is ruled by the selfish calculation of pleasure and pain. This theory of human motivation has been superseded by explanations in terms of reflex, instinct, imitation, the learning process, habit, or unconscious 'complex.' These and other allied conceptions, characteristic of what is known as "dynamic psychology," have come into

---

[29] An instructive example of the futility of attempting to reduce desire to introspective terms is afforded by the controversy within the school of Meinong on the relations of desire and feeling. Cf. Ch. Ehrenfels, *System der Werttheorie*, 1897, Vol. I, pp. 41, 248–251; A. Meinong, *Über Annahmen*, 1902, pp. 293–296; W. M. Urban, *Valuation*, 1909, pp. 35–37; and the writer's "Behavioristic View of Purpose," *Jour. of Philos.*, Vol. XVIII, 1921.

[30] H. Münsterberg, *Willenshandlung*, 1888, p. 88.

[31] *Analytical Psychology*, 1896, Vol. II, pp. 82, 83.

[32] *Social Psychology*, 1910, pp. 26, 27. The italics are mine.

[33] I do not deny the common opinion that the animistic view of nature results from a projection into external objects of the experience of conation, but I do affirm that what is so projected is mainly if not wholly the experience of organic action.

vogue as a result of attempts to describe the behavior of animals, children, men, and social groups; or the misbehavior of criminals, or crowds, or the insane. They do not imply the abandonment of introspection, but they do signify the fruitfulness of a new method in which mind is conceived as an organic rather than as a purely subjective entity. The history of psychology, the record both of its past failures and of its recent successes, thus abundantly justifies our provisional adoption of the objective method. In accord with this method we shall begin our study of interest by an examination of certain peculiarities of the biological organism.

The Nature of Goodness*

SIR DAVID ROSS

IT IS ROUND the question of the intrinsically good that the chief controversies about the nature of goodness or of value revolve. For most theories of value may be divided into those which treat it as a quality and those which treat it as a relation between that which has value and something else—which is usually but not always said to be some state of a mind, such as that of being pleased by the object or desiring it or approving of it or finding its desire satisfied by it. And it seems clear that any view which treats goodness as a relation between that which is good and something else denies that anything is intrinsically good, since by calling a thing intrinsically good we mean that it would be good even if nothing else existed. One of the advocates of a relational view of value, Professor Perry, seeks to maintain that a relational view does not involve the denial of intrinsic value, which he evidently thinks would be a consequence hostile if not fatal to his view. 'A . . . serious objection' to his theory, he says,[1] 'is based upon the nature of *intrinsic* value. We judge a thing to be intrinsically good "where we judge, concerning a particular state of things, that it would be worth while—would be 'a good thing'—that that state of things should exist, *even if nothing else were to exist besides*, either at the same time or afterwards." '[2] If a thing derives value from its relation to an interest taken in it, it would seem impossible that anything whatsoever should possess value in itself. But in that case value would seem always to be borrowed, and never owned; value would shine by a reflected glory having no original source.

'The question,' he continues, 'turns upon the fact that any predicate may be judged synthetically or analytically. Suppose that "good" were to be regarded as a simple quality like yellow. It would then be possible to judge either synthetically, that the primrose was fair or yellow; or, analytically, that the fair, yellow primrose was fair or yellow. Only the fair, yellow primrose would be fair and yellow "even if nothing were to exist besides." But the logic of the situation is not in the least altered if a relational

* Excerpted and reprinted by kind permission of the author and the publisher from *The Right and the Good*, pp. 75–104. The Clarendon Press, 1930.

[1] *A General Theory of Value*, 132 [p. 299 this volume].

[2] G. E. Moore, *Ethics*, 162 [p. 101 reset edition].

predicate is substituted for a simple quality; indeed it is quite possible to regard a quality as a monadic (a single term) relation. Tangential, for example, is a relational predicate; since a line is a tangent only by virtue of the peculiar relation of single-point contact with another line or surface. Let R^t represent this peculiar relation, and A, B, two lines. One can then judge either synthetically, that $(A)\ R^t(B)$; or, analytically, that $(A)\ R^t$ (B) is R^t. Similarly, let S represent an interested subject, O an object, and R^i the peculiar relation of interest taken and received. We can then judge either synthetically, that $(O)\ R^i\ (S)$; or, analytically, that $(O)\ R^i\ (S)$ is R^i. In other words, one can say either that O is desired by S, or that O-desired-by-S is a case of the general character "desired." '

I assume, as it seems necessary to assume in order to make the example relevant, that 'fair' here = 'beautiful,' and that beauty is taken as a species of goodness. Professor Perry is evidently taking 'yellow' to be a simple, non-relational quality, and holding 'good' to be a relational one, viz. = 'object of interest to some one' (loosely represented by 'desired-by-S'). I am in doubt about the meaning of 'only' in the sentence 'Only the fair, yellow primrose would be fair and yellow "even if nothing were to exist besides." ' (1) 'Only' may mean 'yet.' If so, Professor Perry is admitting that the fair yellow primrose would be yellow, and would be beautiful if beauty were a non-relational quality, even if there were nothing else in the world. And if this be so, that constitutes a vital difference between such attributes, which would attach to their subject even if there were nothing else in the world, and attributes such as 'desired-by-S,' which certainly would not attach to O unless S existed as well. (2) More probably, I think, 'only' means 'alone'; i.e. Professor Perry is saying that in contrast with the fair yellow primrose, the *primrose* would not be fair and yellow if nothing else were to exist, just as O would not be desired by S if S did not exist as well as O.

Now it is true that the primrose could not be fair or yellow if nothing but it existed. It could not be fair if its fairness did not exist, nor yellow if its yellowness did not. But it is equally true that the *fair yellow primrose* (which Professor Perry contrasts with the *primrose* in this respect) could not be fair or yellow if its fairness or its yellowness did not exist; and its fairness and its yellowness are quite as different from the fair yellow primrose as they are from the primrose, so that there is no difference between the primrose and the fair yellow primrose in this respect. But if yellowness, or fairness, is a non-relational quality of the primrose, the primrose might be yellow or fair though nothing but the primrose *and its attribute* of being yellow or fair existed. On the other hand, if goodness is a relational quality (say = object of interest to some one), nothing could be good unless, besides it and its attribute of 'being an object of interest to some one,' something else existed, viz. a person to whom it is an object of interest. The essential difference would remain, that non-relational attributes can be possessed by subjects though nothing but the subjects and the attributes exist; while relational attributes can be possessed by subjects only if something besides both the subjects and the attributes exists, *viz.* the things that form the other terms of the relations. Thus if the definition of an intrinsic attribute as one which its subject would possess if nothing other than the subject existed, be amended into the form 'an intrinsic attribute is one which the subject would possess even if nothing but the subject and the attribute existed,' it is evident that non-relational attributes are intrinsic and that relational attributes cannot be so. If 'good,' then, be defined as Professor Perry defines it, nothing can be intrinsically good. And his attempt to get over the difficulty of the apparent necessity (for a relational view of value) of denying that anything has intrinsic value, by means of the distinction between analytic and synthetic judgments, comes to nothing. 'O-desired-by-S' is not a different object which can truly be said to possess intrinsic value when it is denied that any O apart from being desired has intrinsic value. 'O-desired-by-S is good' is simply another way of saying 'any O has value not in itself but by virtue of the co-existence with it, and in a certain relation to it, of S.' And to say this is to deny intrinsic value to anything. And similarly any other view which identifies goodness with or makes it depend upon a relation between that which is good and something else, denies the existence of intrinsic value.

The theories which identify goodness with some relation are bound to think of this either (I) as a relation between that which is good and some or all of its elements, *or* (II) as a relation between some or all of its elements, *or* (III) as a relation between it or some or all of its elements and something else.

Out of the many theories about the nature of goodness, I am unable to think of any which belongs to type (I), and this type need not, perhaps, be examined. There have been theories of type (II), viz. those that identify the good with the harmonious or coherent. With reference to any such view, the question must first be asked whether it is meant (*a*) that goodness just is coherence, or (*b*) that what is good is good because it is coherent. Only the first of these views is strictly relevant here, where we are inquiring what goodness *is*. The second view does not answer this question; it leaves still open the question what is the nature of the attribute goodness which coherent things are said to have because they are coherent. Now the first view seems to be clearly false. It is surely clear that, however close a connexion there may be between coherence and goodness, we never *mean*, when we call a thing good, that it is coherent. If this were what we meant, 'the coherent, and only the coherent, is good' would be a mere tautology, since it would be equivalent to 'the coherent, and only the coherent, is coherent'; but it is evidently not a mere tautology, but a proposition which if true is very important. The theory then, if it is to have any plausibility, must be understood in the second form; and in this form it is no answer to the question we are asking, what is goodness.

It may be well, however, to offer some comments on the theory in its second form, even if this is not strictly relevant to the present stage of our inquiry. In the first place it may be remarked that any such theory seems to start with the presumption that there is some single attribute, other than goodness, that makes all good things good, and that the only question is what this attribute is. Now I agree that goodness is a consequential attribute; that anything that is good must be good either by virtue of its whole nature apart from its goodness, or by virtue of something in its nature other than goodness. This seems to me a very important fact about goodness, and one that marks it off from most other attributes.[3] But I cannot agree that the presumption is that there is any *one* characteristic by virtue of which all the things that are good are good. If conscientiousness and benevolence, for instance, are both good, it is just as likely, initially, that conscientiousness is good because it is conscientiousness, and benevolence good because it is benevolence. Still, this must not be assumed to be the case, any more than the opposite view must be assumed. We must be prepared to consider on its merits any suggested general ground of goodness. But when I ask myself whether conscientiousness, or benevolence, for instance, can be held to be good by virtue of the coherence of its elements, I have to ask what the supposed elements are, and in what respect they are supposed to cohere, and to these questions I find no clear answer given by those who hold the theory. It would be more plausible (though not, I think, true) to say that the goodness of conscientious or benevolent action depends on its coherence with something outside it, e.g. with the whole system of purposes of the agent, or of the society he lives in. But such a theory would belong not to type (II), which we are examining, but to type (III). Or again, suppose that one judges a particular pleasure to be good, is it not clear that even if most and possibly all pleasures are complex, it is not on account of its being a complex united by the relation of coherence, but on account of its having the felt character of pleasantness, that it is judged to be good?

When we turn to type (III), we find that the relation which is identified with goodness (or else held to be what makes good things good) is sometimes held to be necessarily a relation to a mind, while sometimes this limitation is not imposed. I take as a typical view of the latter kind one of which I owe my knowledge to an article by Professor Urban.[4] Professor Sheldon, as reported by Professor Urban, holds that value is 'fulfilment of any tendency whatever.' The essential objection to this theory seems to me to be this. Empty 'tendency' of any reference to the aims of conscious beings (which it is the special point of this theory to do), and what meaning is left for 'fulfilment of any tendency'? What is left is the notion of a thing's being under the influence of a certain force, and of its

[3] Cf. pp. 121–2.
[4] *Journal of Philosophy*, 1916, 454.

actually passing into the state it would pass into if acted on by that force alone. And who will say that this purely physical circumstance is either identical or even coextensive with value?

To this Professor Sheldon (as reported by Professor Urban) answers: 'Good is no doubt a different notion from fulfilment, and therefore appears to contain something not authorized in the content of the latter notion. But that is because good or value is the relation between the fulfilment (or furthering) and the tendency, a relation uniquely and sufficiently determined by the two.' [5] To this it seems to me enough to reply that this relation can exist, as much as anywhere else, in the case of bodies acted on by physical forces, where no one would dream of applying the notion of good or value. If we *must* have a relational theory of value, there seems to be much more plausibility in the 'psychological' than in the 'ontological' form of the theory.

The 'psychological' theories as a rule take the form of holding that a thing's being good means either (*A*) that some person or persons have some feeling towards it, or (*B*) that some person or persons think it to be good; and such views, or rather those of the first type, have some initial attractiveness. (*A*) Our judgements that certain things are good are in fact constantly accompanied by feelings towards them—feelings of pleasure, and of regret for their absence; and this fact is apt to lead to one or other of two views, or more often perhaps to a mixture of the two. One view is that by being objects of some such feeling (let us say, adopting Professor Perry's comprehensive phrase, by being 'objects of interest') things acquire a further character, that of value. The other is that to have value is just to be an object of interest, and nothing more. I am rather in doubt how to classify the view put forward in *A General Theory of Value* by Professor Perry himself. Passages could be found in his book to support the interpretation of him as holding the first view; e.g. those in which value is described as *dependent* on interest. But on the whole it seems pretty clear that it is the second view he wishes to maintain. 'The view,' he says,[6] 'may otherwise be formulated in the equation: x is valuable = interest is taken in x'; and immediately after, 'Value is thus a specific relation into which things possessing any ontological status whatsoever, whether real or imaginary, may enter with interested subjects'—i.e. the relation of being objects of interest to them. Again,[7] 'Thus the question' (the question to which he provides an answer) 'is the question, In what consists' (*not*, On what depends) 'value in the generic sense?'

If the *first* interpretation be the true one, there remain difficult questions to which he provides no answer. If value is something not consisting in, but depending on, being an object of interest, what is value itself, and what is the nature of the relation vaguely described as dependence? Is the

[5] Ib.
[6] *A General Theory of Value*, 116 [p. 293 this volume].
[7] *Ib.* 118

relation a causal one, or a logical one, and if neither of these, what is it? To these no answer is suggested. But these questions need not be pressed, for I fancy that Professor Perry would accept the *second* interpretation as the true account of his view.

On this second interpretation, the theory is that 'good' and 'object of interest' are just different ways of expressing exactly the same notion. But it is surely clear that this is not true. It is surely clear that when we call something good we are thinking of it as possessing in itself a certain attribute and are not thinking of it as necessarily having an interest taken in it. If when we attend to something we are impelled to describe it as good, it is surely not impossible to think that, though of course we can only discover its goodness by attending to it, it had its goodness before we attended to it and would have had it if we had not attended to it. And again it is evidently possible to think that some of the things in which an interest has been taken have nevertheless been bad. But if 'good' and 'object of interest' meant exactly the same, it would be impossible to think either of these two things which it clearly is possible to think. The view, therefore, that 'good' and 'object of interest' stand for the same notion must be given up. What the relational theory must maintain, if it is to be plausible, must be something different; it must be that whereas most people think that certain things have a characteristic, goodness, distinct from that of being objects of interest, nothing has any such characteristic. And then the question arises, what could have led mankind to form this quite superfluous notion to which nothing in reality corresponds? It is not as if the notion of goodness were a complex notion formed, like such notions as that of 'centaur,' by a play of fancy in which characteristics found separate in reality are imagined to coexist; for there are no characteristics of which 'good' can be said to be a compound. We may, however, not merely ask how the notion could have come into being if it were not the apprehension of a reality.[8] We may claim that we are directly aware that conscientious action, for example, has a value of its own, not identical with or even dependent upon our or any one else's taking an interest in it. Our reason informs us of this as surely as it informs us of anything, and to distrust reason here is in principle to distrust its power of ever knowing reality.

Another fatal objection to any theory which identifies good with being an object of interest, or of any particular type of feeling, becomes apparent when we ask by whom the interest or the feeling is supposed to be felt. Some answers escape some objections and others escape others, but each possible answer is exposed to at least one fatal objection of its own. This ground has been very fully covered by Professor Moore in an examination of the corresponding theories about 'right,'[9] and both in the case of 'right' and in the case of 'good' his line of argument seems to

[8] Cf. Cook Wilson's argument against the possibility of a fictitious 'simple idea,' *Statement and Inference*, ii. 511–21.

[9] *Ethics*, chs. 3 and 4.

me unanswerable. Theories of this type are divisible into those which identify goodness with the presence of some feeling (1) in at least one person, no matter who he is, (2) in the person who judges an object to be good, (3) in a majority of persons of some class or other—say persons belonging to a particular stage in the history of civilization, (4) in a majority of mankind, or (5) in all mankind. To (1) there seem to be four objections. (*a*) It surely can hardly be denied that, whatever feeling we select as the feeling involved—whether for instance this be taken to be pleasure, or approval—a man may doubt whether a certain thing is good, even when he does not doubt that some one or other has had such a feeling towards it. (*b*) If what I mean when I call something good is that some one or other has a certain feeling towards it, and if what any other person means when he calls it bad is that some one or other has an opposite feeling towards it, we should not be at variance, because both propositions might be true. Yet if anything is clear, it is that we do suppose ourselves to be making incompatible statements about the object. (*c*) If something, without changing its nature, at some moment aroused for the first time the feeling in question in some mind, we should clearly judge not that the object had then first become good, but that its goodness had then first been apprehended. And (*d*) it might be enough to ask whether any one finds it even possible to think that goodness could be brought into being by the feeling of *some one or other*, no matter how vicious or stupid or ignorant he might be. It seems clear that by goodness we mean something at any rate more objective than that.

To the theory in form (2) the primary objection is identical with objection (*b*) above. If all I mean by saying that an object is good were that it arouses a certain feeling in me, and all you mean by saying that it is not good, or is bad, were that it does not arouse that feeling, or arouses an opposite feeling, in you, we should not be at variance, for we might both be right. And objection (*c*) applies with just as much force to this theory as to the previous one.

To the theory in form (3) it may be objected (*a*) that it will follow that two people who claim to be representing the feelings of majorities of different sets of persons will never be at variance if they pronounce the same thing respectively good and bad. Yet it is clear that even when two men belong to different sets of persons, the feelings of a majority of which they would on this view be claiming to represent, they believe themselves to be making incompatible statements when they call something respectively good and bad. Clearly therefore what they claim to be expressing is not the feelings of different majorities. But further (*b*) it is surely plain that there are cases in which a man thinks something good, without thinking that there is a majority of any class of men who have a certain feeling towards it. Even if we think that a majority of persons at our own stage of civilization, for instance, would have feelings like ours if they attended to the object, we may feel sure that they have not attended to it and therefore have not the feeling in question towards it.

The theory in form (4) is not open to the *first* objection made to the previous theory. For any one who thought that a majority of mankind had a certain feeling towards an object *would* be at variance with any one who thought that they had not this feeling, or had an opposite feeling. But objection (*b*) to theory (3) applies with redoubled force to theory (4).

And finally, to theory (5) it applies with even greater force.

(B) The second and remaining type of what I may call purely subjective theories of good is that which holds that for me to think an object good is to think that (1) some one or other, or (2) I, or (3) a majority of some set of men, or (4) a majority of mankind, or (5) all mankind, *think* it good. It is unnecessary and would be tedious to examine these theories as fully as we have examined those of type (*A*). It is enough to point out that corresponding objections are equally fatal to them, and to add a new objection fatal to all theories of type (*B*).

The objections to A 1 apply equally to B 1
"   "   " A 2   "   "   " B 2
"   "   " A 3   "   "   " B 3
"   "   " A 4   "   "   " B 4
"   "   " A 5   "   "   " B 5

But apart from these objections to special forms of theory (*B*), the whole theory has one absurdity common to all its forms. It is perfectly evident that the meaning of 'X is good' cannot be identical with the meaning of 'some one (or I, or a majority of some class of men, &c.) thinks that X is good,' since it *is* identical with the meaning of only one element in the latter phrase. Or, to put the same objection otherwise, to say that S thinks X good leaves it an open question whether X *is* good. For opinion has the characteristic, which feeling has not, of being either true or false. If S thinks falsely that X is good, then X is not good; and if S thinks truly that X is good, then X's being good is neither identical with nor dependent on S's thinking it good. In fact, while theory (*A*) deserves the most serious consideration, and it is excessively hard to be sure whether one is right in rejecting it or may not have been guilty of some logical confusion, theory (*B*) may be rejected out of hand. Professor Perry, as one might expect, repudiates it with vigour.

I turn to a reconsideration of theory (*A*) in the light of Professor Perry's discussion. He divides all possible theories of value into four types, according to the view they take of the relation of value to interest, interest being identified 'with the motive-affective life; that is to say, with instinct, desire, feeling; these, and all their family of states, acts, and attitudes.' [10] 'There are four possible relations of value to interest. In the first place,

[10] *A General Theory of Value*, 27.

value may be, in its essential nature, quite irrelevant to interest. . . . In the second place, value may be held to be the character of an object which qualifies it to be an end; in other words, that which implies, evokes or regulates interest . . . In the third place, value may be assigned to the objects of certain duly qualified interests, such as the final, harmonious, absolute, or imperative interest. Finally, there is the simpler and more comprehensive view, that value in the generic sense attaches promiscuously to all objects of all interest.' [11]

I am not specially concerned with the two intermediate views, and agree with many of Professor Perry's criticisms of them. I am mainly interested in the first, which I believe to be true,[12] and in the fourth, which he believes to be true. He takes as a typical expression of the first view Professor Moore's remark 'my point is that "good" is a simple notion, just as "yellow" is a simple notion; that, just as you cannot, by any manner of means, explain to any one who does not already know it, what yellow is, so you cannot explain what good is'; and he treats this view as being best 'understood as an extension of that pan-objectivism which, having concluded that the so-called "secondary qualities," such as colour, have as good a title to extra-mental existence as the so-called primary qualities, such as figure, sees no reason why the so-called "tertiary" qualities, such as good, should not be assigned the same status.' [13]

There may be in some minds a connexion between a realistic view of the secondary qualities and an objective view of goodness, but it should be pointed out that there is no necessary connexion between the two views. For my own part, reflection on the facts of perception and of its illusions forces me to think that there is no such thing as objective colour, for example; I am driven to suppose that colour-sensation is a mental state which is not perception of colour. But colour-sensation [14] is an indubitable fact, and I can with a certain modification accept Professor Moore's comparison. I can say that goodness is a quality which can no more be defined in terms of anything other than itself, than can the quality of the sensation which we describe as being one of 'seeing yellow.' Whatever we may think about the objectivity of colour, there can, I imagine, be no doubt of the indefinability of the character of our sensation. Thus the adoption of this comparison is in no way bound up with an objective view of secondary qualities. Nor, again, do I think of goodness as 'extra-mental'; for while I do not think it is essentially *for* minds, I think it is essentially a quality *of* states of mind.

Professor Perry's first criticism of the objective view of good is that

[11] Ib.

[12] I think, of course, that a thing may arouse interest, and will arouse it in a well-constituted mind, *because of* its goodness. What I wish to deny is that its goodness either is or depends on its arousing interest.

[13] *A General Theory of Value*, 29.

[14] i.e. the experience which we habitually, whether rightly or (as I suggest) wrongly, describe as that of seeing colour.

'one who upholds this view of good must be prepared to point to a distinct *quale* which appears in that region which our value terms roughly indicate, and which is different from the object's shape and size, from the inter-relation of its parts, from its relation to other objects, or to a subject; and from all the other factors which belong to the same context, but are designated by words other than "good." The present writer, for one, finds no such residuum.' [15] The existence of such a residuum is just the point at issue. So far we have only the word of those who agree with Professor Moore that they do discern in certain things a unique quality which can only be expressed by the term 'goodness' or some synonym of 'goodness,' and the word of those who agree with Professor Perry that they do not; and so long as the question is considered on these lines, all that we can do is to invite others to contemplate, for instance, conscientious action, and try for themselves whether they do or do not discern such a quality in it. But Professor Perry is, of course, not content with his *ipse dixit*. He argues that if goodness were an indefinable quality like yellowness its presence, when it is present, should be equally self-evident; and he points to the hesitancy of Professor Moore's report as to what things are good, as showing that the presence of goodness is *not* equally self-evident with that of yellowness. Here he seems to be stressing too much the analogy which Professor Moore has alleged to exist between goodness and yellowness. The analogy exists only in respect to the indefinability of both. It is not argued that in other respects the two qualities are on all fours. In particular, the one is appre-hended (if apprehended at all) [16] by sense-perception, the other by in-telligence; and there is no reason to anticipate that what is discerned by the intelligence should be as easily discerned as what is discerned by sense-perception. But Professor Perry exaggerates the difference between the ease of discernment in the two cases. There is, he says, 'no serious difference of opinion as to the distribution of terms connoting empirical qualities. "Things wear them in public, and any passer-by may note them." ' [17] But does not yellow merge into green, and into orange, and are there not border-line cases in which it is extremely difficult to say whether what we have before us is yellow or green, or whether it is yellow or orange? And if there are things about whose goodness there is room for difference of opinion, are there not other things, such as conscientious action, whose goodness is matter of general agreement?

But I should not like to rest the case for the indefinability of goodness merely on this *argumentum ad hominem*. It seems to me more important to point out that the question whether the presence of a given quality in some particular thing is easily discerned has nothing to do with the question

---

[15] *A General Theory of Value*, 30.

[16] This caution seems necessary in view of the doubt I have expressed on p. 86 [p. 318 this volume] as to whether colour is something apprehended at all. The sentence in the text *without* the parenthesis would state the defence which I believe Professor Moore would make of his view.

[17] *A General Theory of Value*, 30.

whether the quality is indefinable. If two people differ, for instance, as to whether a particular action is good, their differing implies, no less than their agreeing would have done, that they mean by 'goodness' a definite quality; and their mere differing does not imply that that quality is *not* indefinable any more than their agreement would imply that it *is*. The questions of its definability and of its discernibility are different and not logically connected.

But if I attempt to vindicate Professor Moore's comparison of goodness with yellowness as being like it an indefinable quality, I do not wish (any more than I imagine he would) to be thought to suppose that it is a quality in other respects like yellowness. The most salient difference is that it is a quality which anything that has it can have only in virtue of having some other characteristic; as e.g. a conscientious act is good in virtue of being conscientious. This I express later by describing it as a consequential and not a fundamental quality.[18]

Professor Perry turns next to mention Professor Laird's presentment of the objective view. Professor Laird, he says, 'appeals to the fact that there is an immediate objectivity in the appreciation of beauty, or in the admiration of conduct. These are not mere subjective states *caused* by an object; they *present* the object, clothed in its quality of charm or moral worth.'[19] Professor Perry points out that there are many adjectives which we apply to objects, and which therefore *prima facie* might appear to stand for qualities of objects apart from any relation to persons, but which on examination turn out to refer simply to the existence of some such relation,—adjectives like 'coveted,' 'boresome,' 'tiresome,' 'hopeful'; and that on the other hand adjectives like 'red' resist all attempts to localize them in the subject and insist on being localized in the object. But it is surely unfair to argue from words like 'coveted,' 'boresome,' 'tiresome,' 'hopeful,' which by their very formation point to a relation between a subject and an object, and the word 'good,' which equally clearly points to nothing of the kind but to a quality resident in the object itself, independent of any subject's reaction to the object. As regards 'beautiful' I am, as I shall point out later,[20] inclined to agree that the fact that lies at the back of our predications of it *is* simply the power something has of producing a certain kind of emotion in us; and the frequent use of such words as 'charming,' 'delightful,' almost as synonyms of 'beautiful' may be held to lend this view some support. But it is surely a strange reversal of the natural order of thought to say that our admiring an action either is, or is what necessitates, its being good. We think of its goodness as what we admire in it, and as something it would have even if no one admired it, something that it has in itself. We could suppose, for instance, an action of self-denial which neither the doer nor any one else had ever admired. If now

[18] Cf. pp. 121–2.
[19] *A General Theory of Value*, 31.
[20] pp. 127–30.

some one were to become aware of it and admire it, he would surely pronounce that it had been good even when no one had been admiring it.

Professor Perry makes the further objection that the 'objective' theory derives all its plausibility from its exponents' being preoccupied with 'the aesthetic and contemplative values,' and that it precludes them from giving a comprehensive account of all values. 'The most serious defect of this type of theory is its failure to provide any systematic principle whatsoever. There are as many indefinable values as there are feeling attitudes, and since these are to be regarded as objective qualities rather than as modes of feeling, there is nothing to unite them, not even the principle of feeling. If "good" is a unique quality, then so are "pleasant," "bad," and "ought." There is no way of subsuming pleasant under good, or of defining the opposition of good and bad, or of subsuming both good and ought under a more general category such as value. If, on the other hand, value is defined in terms of interest, then the variability of interest seems to account for both the unity and the diversity of values.' [21] His assumption, then, is that there must be some single sense of 'valuable' in which the word is always used, and his contention is that a subjective theory alone will serve to assign such a single meaning and to show the relations between the various specific kinds of value. And under the heading of 'valuable' he includes both things which would not naturally be described as being valuable at all, and things which we can surely recognize to have value only in fundamentally different senses. Does any one really think that obligatoriness is a special form of being valuable? [22] Is it not a hasty assumption to assume that it is an instance of the same kind of thing of which moral goodness or beauty is another instance? And is it not clear that what we call economic values [23] are merely instrumental values, different in kind from the goodness of virtue or of pleasure? The assumption that there must be 'a general theory of value' applicable to value in all the senses of that word seems to me to be unjustified.

At the same time, I am inclined to agree with Professor Perry in one of his contentions, though not in what he (if I understand him aright) seeks to deduce from it. He is seeking to find a single thread of identity which unites all our *applications* of the word good, and to infer from this that the word 'good' has the single *meaning* which he assigns to it. Now when I consider the variety of meanings of 'good' indicated in the preceding chapter—the predicative and the attributive use, the meanings 'successful in his endeavour' and the 'useful,' the instrumental and the intrinsic sense—though I cannot agree that what we mean in all or any of these cases by 'X is good' is 'X is an object of interest to some one,' I am inclined to think that the only thread that connects our *application* of the word in all these senses—i.e. the only common fact that is present whenever we

[21] *A General Theory of Value*, 34.
[22] Ib.
[23] Ib.

use the term 'good'—is that in each case the *judger* has some feeling of approval or interest towards what he calls good. But this in no way proves that we are always using 'good' in the same *sense*. The *senses* 'intrinsically good' and 'useful' appear to me entirely different, though whether we use the word good in one or the other we have in both cases a feeling of approval or interest towards what we call good. What common thread there is, is one that connects not the various meanings of good, but our use of it in these various meanings. The attempt to find a common thread in our *application* of the term is not what I am chiefly interested in. What I am interested in, and what I cannot but think to be the more important question for philosophy, is whether there is not a sense of good in which it can be applied to things not as meaning that they are successful or useful members of a class, and not as meaning that they are instrumental to a good beyond themselves, but as meaning that they are good in themselves. And it is surely plain that when we state, for instance, that courage is good, this is what we mean—even if some one may maintain that we are mistaken in making this statement. I have tried to do some justice, briefly, to the other senses, in the preceding chapter, and from that point onwards I have been interested solely in this other and more fundamental sense of 'good.' And of this I feel pretty clear, that though our applications of it are always accompanied by an interest in what we thus call good, the existence of that interest is not what we assert when we so describe things.

Professor Perry turns next to consider in detail Professor Moore's argument for the indefinability of 'good.' He quotes the remark 'it would be absolutely meaningless to say that oranges were yellow, unless yellow did in the end mean just "yellow" and nothing else whatever—unless it were absolutely indefinable.' [24] And to this, taken alone, his objection is well founded. 'It is *not* meaningless,' he points out, 'to say that "the conception of substance is pre-historic," or that "the painting is post-impressionistic," or that "the argument is circular"; and yet in these cases the assigned predicates are definable.' [25] The statement 'oranges are yellow' certainly is meaningless unless 'yellow' has in this statement a single self-identical meaning. In a sense 'yellow' must mean yellow and nothing else whatever. But this does not show it to be indefinable. For if we could correctly define 'yellow' as, say, 'x which is y,' we should not be saying that 'yellow' means anything other than 'yellow,' for 'x which is y' would be just what yellow is. But, it might be said in support of the view that 'good' is obviously indefinable, there is a great difference between 'good' and such attributes as 'pre-historic,' 'post-impressionistic,' 'circular.' If a term is definable, i.e. stands for a certain complex,[26] we can use the term intelligently and in-

---

[24] G. E. Moore, *Principia Ethica*, 14 [p. 75 this volume].

[25] *A General Theory of Value*, 35.

[26] I should explain that I mean by a complex here a complex of elements co-ordinate in respect of universality, in distinction from another class of terms which *might* be called complex, and which are indefinable, viz. those that involve elements *not* co-ordinate in respect of universality, as 'red' involves both colour and redness. Cf. Cook Wilson, *Statement and Inference*, ii. 502–4.

telligibly only if we have the definition to some extent before our minds; and we have in fact at least rough definitions of such terms in our minds when we use them. On the other hand, the fact that we use the term 'good' intelligently and intelligibly without having any definition of it in our minds shows that it is indefinable.

Professor Moore uses an argument of somewhat the same type when he argues, against any attempt to define 'good,' that given any set of concepts not containing good, it is always possible to inquire whether a thing answering to this set of concepts is good.[27] Suppose some one claims that 'being-desired-by-anybody is being good,' this claim is met by the fact that even if we know that war is desired by some people, we may still doubt whether it is good.

Both of these arguments amount, I think, to saying that if 'good' stood for any complex (as on any relational theory it does), we ought, if we use the word intelligently, to have in our minds the notion of a definite relation between definite things. It seems to me clear that we have no such notion in our minds when we use the word in ordinary discourse.

But I cannot be sure that this entirely settles the question. For there seem to be cases in which we seek for the definition of a term and finally accept one as correct. The fact that we accept some definition as correct shows that the term did somehow stand for a complex of elements; yet the fact that we are for some time in doubt whether the term is analysable, and if so, what the correct analysis is, shows that this complex of elements was not distinctly present to our mind before, or during, the search for a definition. It appears as if we cannot avoid recognizing that there is such a thing as using a term which implicitly refers to a certain complex, while yet the complex is not explicitly present to our minds. And in principle this might, it seems, be true of 'good.' The absence of an explicit reference to a complex in our ordinary use of the term should therefore not be taken as necessarily implying that the term is indefinable, nor, in particular, as excluding the possibility of its standing for a relation. The method should, I think, rather be that of attending to any proposed definition that seems at all plausible. If it is the correct definition, what should happen is that after a certain amount of attention to it we should be able to say, 'yes, that is what I meant by "good" all along, though I was not clearly conscious till now that it was what I meant.' If on the other hand the result is that we feel clear that 'that was not what I meant by good,' the proposed definition must be rejected. If, after we have examined all the definitions that possess any initial plausibility, we have found this negative result in every case, we may feel fairly confident that 'good' is indefinable. And there is no initial presumption that it is definable. For it seems clear that there could be no complex entities unless there were some simple ones; and, in a universe so various as the universe is, there is no reason to suppose that the simple entities are few in number.

[27] *Principia Ethica*, 15 [p. 76 this volume].

In the process of criticizing proposed definitions of a term, there are two moments. Perhaps the most obvious ground for rejection of a definition is that we are able to point to things of which the term is predicable but the definition not, or *vice versa*. And any one will be able without difficulty to think of definitions of 'good' that have been proposed, which come to grief on one or other of these two objections. But even when the denotations of the term and of the definition coincide (or when we cannot be sure that they do not), we can often see that a proposed definition does not express what we *mean* by the term to be defined. It would be on this ground, for example, that we should reject a definition of 'equilateral triangle' as 'triangle with all its angles equal.' And it is on this ground that most of the proposed definitions of 'good' can be rejected—many of the metaphysical definitions, such as those which identify goodness with comprehensiveness or with reality; and many of the psychological definitions, such as those which identify it with being productive of pleasure or with being an object of desire. The point is not that the proposed definition is not seen at first sight to be true, or that it needs inquiry, but that it does not survive inquiry.

Professor Perry's own criticism of Professor Moore takes the following form. Suppose that 'good' be defined as 'desired by some one.' This definition is disproved, says Professor Moore, by the fact that even if war is desired by some one, it is still possible to inquire whether war is good. Professor Perry seems to admit this as fatal to the proposed definition, for he proposes to substitute for it what he evidently thinks of as a different definition, 'good in some sense = desired by some one.' And he endeavours to turn the edge of Professor Moore's objection by saying that the correctness of *this* definition is quite compatible with our still being able to inquire (as we evidently can) whether war, if it is good in this sense, is also good in some other sense, e.g. desired by all men, or obligatory, or beautiful.[28]

This seems to me strangely to miss the point. No one would, I suppose, dream of objecting to the equating of 'good in some sense' with 'desired by some one' on the ground that war though desired by some persons is not desired by every one, or not beautiful, or not obligatory. The objections are (1) that, even though desired by some persons, war is not in any sense good (though there may be elements in it that are good), and (2) that, even if it were in some sense good, what would be *meant* by calling it good is most certainly not that it is desired by some one.

Professor Perry further tries to base an argument for the relativity of good to the interests of individuals, on the fact 'that the question may be submitted once again to each individual judge.' 'If when a given object *a* is already acknowledged to be good the question of its goodness is nevertheless put to a subject *M*, the question is assumed to refer to the special sense of good which is relative to *M*.'[29] This would surely be a nonsensical

28 *A General Theory of Value*, 36–7.
29 Ib. 37.

procedure. If the goodness of *a* is already 'acknowledged,' i.e. admitted by both the persons involved, there is *no* sense in the one asking the other whether the object is good; and anything that the other may say such as 'I desire it' or 'I don't desire it' has *no* relevance to the question whether it is good, which has already *ex hypothesi* been settled in the affirmative.

The advocates of the view he is criticizing are, Professor Perry points out, anxious to secure for 'good' a meaning which shall 'provide judgments of value with a common object which will determine their truth or falsity.' And for this purpose, he insists, 'an interest is as good an object as any other. The fact that *M* takes an interest in *a*, consists in a relation of *a* to *M*; but this fact itself is not relative to *M*'s judgment about it, or to the judgment of any other subject.' [30] There is, in fact, a great difference between a view which makes the goodness of an object depend on a subject's judgement that it is good, and one which makes it depend on his interest in it. The former view is one that will not stand a moment's examination; the latter is one that does provide judgements of value with some reality to judge about, and that therefore requires serious consideration. But while it provides for our judgements of value an object independent of our judgements, it fails to do justice to what is also implied in our judgements of value, that when one person says an object is good and another says it is not, they are contradicting one another. For if *M* only meant 'I take an interest in *a*' and *N* only meant 'I do not,' they would *not* be contradicting each other.

Professor Perry sometimes, for brevity, uses as equivalent to 'good' 'enjoyed by a subject,' and sometimes 'desired by a subject.' Neither of these phrases does full justice to his theory. His theory is that to be good is to be an object of *interest*, and interest is thought of as covering both desire and enjoyment; i.e. the goodness of some things consists in their being enjoyed, that of others in their being desired, and that of others, perhaps, in their being both enjoyed and desired (though this, as we shall see, is impossible). Now so long as we say (as he is apt to say) that 'the goodness of the primrose consists in its being desired,' [31] the theory seems at first sight attractive enough. But obviously it is only a rough and ready description of my desire to say I desire a primrose. What I desire is to be seeing it or smelling it or possessing it. As soon as we describe definitely what it is that we desire, we see that it is something which does not yet exist. There are no doubt cases in which we desire to go on doing what we are doing, or being in the same sort of state that we are in. But even if I desire, for instance, to go on looking at a primrose, what I desire is not the looking which is taking place at present, but the looking which I wish to take place in the immediate future. The object of desire is always something non-existent. If it be said that it exists as a possibility, we must reply that that

[30] Ib. 38.
[31] Cf. *A General Theory of Value*, 133 [p. 300 this volume].

is an inexact way of saying that the possibility of it exists, which means that though it does not exist, the nature of some or all of the things that do exist is not incompatible with its coming into existence.

It is plain that in so far as goodness were either identical with or dependent upon being desired, nothing could both exist and be good. Now I suppose that we are all convinced both that some things that exist now are good, and that things of certain kinds, which may come into existence in the future, will be good if and when they exist; and I suppose that apart from these convictions we should have little or no interest in the topic of 'good,' and ethics in particular would go by the board. Yet in so far as the theory identifies the good with the desired, it denies both these convictions. But it might be replied that the goodness of existent things consists in their being enjoyed, and the goodness of non-existent things in their being desired. I must take leave, however, to doubt whether we can say of a non-existent thing that it *is* good. However much one were convinced that conscientiousness, for example, is good, and that A might *become* conscientious, no one would say 'A's conscientiousness is good' if he were convinced that A is not in fact conscientious. But, our opponent might reply, we can say of *kinds* of thing that they are good even if we are not convinced that any instances of these kinds exist. We might say 'perfectly conscientious action is good,' even if (as Kant suggests) we are not convinced that there has ever been such an action. But that is only a short-hand way of saying that without being sure that such an action ever has existed, we can be sure that *if* any existed it would be good. Hypothetical goodness presupposes hypothetical existence just as actual goodness presupposes actual existence. And if so, being good can never be identical with being desired, or even compatible with it.

The relation in which the primrose stands to desire is not that of being desired but that of exciting desire. This is a relation in which existing things *can* stand to desire, and the theory might be transmuted into the form, 'the good is that which excites desire.' But the excitants of desire fall into two classes. There are things our experience of which is such as to make us desire to remain in our existing relation to them, or to get into some closer relation to them, and to others like them; and there are things our experience of which is such as to make us desire to get away from them. Things of the second class are just as decidedly excitants of some desires as things of the first class are of others. And obviously one main sub-class (if not the whole) of the second class consists of things that cause pain. Thus if 'good' meant 'excitant of desire' we should be led to the conclusion that things that cause pain are, as such, an important class of goods. This conclusion would evidently not be accepted, and therefore the theory would have to be modified into the form 'the good is that which excites the desire to maintain our relations with it, or to get into closer relations with it, and with others of its kind'—what we may, for short, call 'positive desire.'

Now, on the face of it, some of the things that excite positive desire [32] do so because they are judged to be good. *Prima facie* one would say that if the consciousness of a good disposition in oneself or the contemplation of it in another leads me to wish to maintain and develop that sort of disposition, it is not because I feel it to be pleasant but because I judge it to be good. But this alternative is not open to Professor Perry, for, in basing our taking an interest in the thing on our thinking it good, it would involve the giving up of his main thesis, that a thing's being good either is or is based upon our taking an interest in it. All that is left for him therefore is to identify what is good with that which by virtue of the pleasure it causes excites desire for a closer relation with it and with other things like it. What is good, then, for him is that which excites pleasure and thereby excites such a desire. And though he includes both these elements in his formula, the fact of exciting pleasure is evidently the root fact of which the other is a mere consequence.

Not only, however, is pleasantness the fundamental and tendency to excite desire only a consequential element in goodness, according to the theory in the form in which it seems necessary to restate it, but it is far more plausible to put forward pleasantness, than to put forward this tendency, as the essence of goodness. If we say 'that which produces so-and-so is, as doing so, good,' we are evidently implying that what is produced is intrinsically good, and what produces it instrumentally good. And it is plausible enough to say 'pleasure is intrinsically good, and what produces it instrumentally good'; there is a pretty general agreement that pleasure, whether it is the good or not, is at least good. But there is no general agreement that desire, or even positive desire, is good. If we take the moral standpoint we must say that some desires are good and others bad, and that when desires are good they are good not because they are desires but because they are the sort of desires they are. And if we take the hedonistic standpoint, we must say that desires are good or bad (which will mean 'pleasant or unpleasant') not in virtue of being desires but mainly (I suppose) in virtue of their being supposed to be likely or unlikely to be fulfilled. Desire (even positive desire) thus not being a thing necessarily good in itself, there is no reason why, in general, things that excite desire (or positive desire) should be good. So long as we thought of things as objects of desire, it was perhaps not unplausible to say that objects of desire are good even when the desire is not; but if we recast the theory in the form in which we have found it necessary to recast it, and say the good is that which excites positive desire, i.e. which is to it as cause to effect, there is no reason (obvious or alleged) why, positive desires not being always good, their excitants should nevertheless always be so.

The most favourable way, then, of presenting the theory we are exam-

---

[32] Desire, of course, not for them to exist but for us to be in some new relation to them or to continue to be in the same relation to them.

ining is to exclude from it the reference to desire and to reduce it to the form 'what is good is that which produces pleasure.'[33] But no one would in fact say that everything which produces pleasure is good unless he thought pleasure itself good;[34] and the theory emerges in the final form 'pleasure, and pleasure alone, is good by its own nature; and what produces pleasure, and only what produces pleasure, is good because it produces something good.' The heart of the theory, then, in spite of all it has said by way of attack on ordinary notions of intrinsic good, is that there is one thing, and one thing only, that is intrinsically good, *viz.* pleasure. The theory when reduced to its simple terms seems to be our old friend, hedonism. After all the able refutations of hedonism that have been published in recent years, it seems to me unnecessary to tread once more on this rather hackneyed ground, and I suppose that Professor Perry would agree that hedonism is untenable, and claim that his own theory is tenable only in virtue of elements that distinguish it from hedonism. But these elements are, if I am not mistaken, among the least tenable elements in his theory.

There is, however, one more point of view from which the theory may be examined. Professor Perry describes 'the most popular' objection to it as being that 'the fact of desire is not accepted as final in most judgments of value. Objects of desire are held to be bad in spite of their being desired, and desires themselves are held to be bad whether or no they are satisfied.'[35] I need not consider (a) one form of this objection with which I have no sympathy—the view of Schopenhauer and others that *all* desire is bad; that is an extravagance of quietism for which there is little to be said. (b) The first real difficulty to which the theory is exposed is that named next by Professor Perry, *viz.* the fact that 'the same object may be liked or desired by one man, and disliked or avoided by another.'[36] This fact, taken with the identification of 'good' with 'object of interest,' leads to the conclusion that the same thing may be both good and bad. On the face of it, this result is paradoxical, and all but self-contradictory; but he claims that 'a relational definition, such as that here proposed, is the only means of *avoiding* contradiction.'[37] The claim is an odd one: by identifying good with object of interest we get into the paradox of calling the same thing good and bad (a paradox which an absolute theory at least escapes, whatever be its other merits or demerits); and then we triumphantly get out

[33] This is ambiguous, since it may mean ' "good" means "productive of pleasure," ' or 'what is good is good because it produces pleasure'; i.e. the ambiguity involved in the theory from the start (cf. pp. 80–1 [pp. 314–15 this volume]) still remains.

[34] And inferred from this that what produces it is good. But it is surely plain that it does *not* follow from a thing's being good that what produces it is good, in the same sense of 'good.' It must be admitted that we often call 'good' things that are merely useful, but then 'good' is being used improperly. Where I use the phrase 'instrumentally good.' I use it to indicate this common but loose sense of 'good.'

[35] *A General Theory of Value*, 134 [p. 301 this volume].

[36] Ib. 135 [p. 302 this volume].

[37] Ib. 136 [p. 302 this volume].

of the difficulty by saying, 'Oh, but good only means good for one person, and bad only means bad for another person, so that there is no paradox.'

Is it not clear that when we assert the goodness of anything we do assert something which we believe to be incompatible with the same thing's being bad? We may describe a thing as 'both good and bad,' but such language is not strict. (i) We may mean that the thing contains some elements that are good and some that are bad, but then *that* is the right way of putting the matter, and 'the thing is both good and bad' is only a loose way of putting it. It is implied in our thought on the subject both that if we push our analysis far enough we shall find some elements that are simply good and others that are simply bad, *and* that the whole is not both good and bad but is either on the whole good or on the whole bad. (ii) It may be suggested that, without thinking of a thing as consisting of good and bad elements, we may judge it to be good from one point of view and bad from another—that a state of mind, say, may be morally good and intellectually bad. But this turns out to be reducible to the former case, in which analysis reveals a good and a bad element. If we take a temporal section of the history of a mind, however short be the section there will be elements in it of knowledge and opinion which have a certain value, and actions or dispositions to act which have a certain value (positive or negative). The whole state of mind, then, cannot be judged from the moral point of view, nor from the intellectual, but some elements in it from the one and some from the other. And each such element will have a goodness that is incompatible with its being bad, or a badness that is incompatible with its being good; and the whole state of mind will have a degree of goodness or *else* a degree of badness, which can be assessed only from a point of view in which we transcend both the moral and the intellectual point of view.

(*c*) 'The case which has most deeply affected popular habits of thought, and which is mainly responsible for the prejudice against the present theory of value,' says Professor Perry, 'is the case in which an interest or its object is morally condemned.' [88] It is certainly an obvious objection to the theory that all objects of interest are good, that in point of fact we do judge to be bad many things in which nevertheless some one or other takes or has taken an interest. Professor Perry's answer to this objection is to urge that in such a case we are performing a *moral* judgement, and that 'moral judgments are not concerned with value in the generic sense, but with a specific and complex *aspect* of it. . . . They do not deal with interests *per se*, but with the relation of interests to the complex purposes in which they are incorporated.' [89]

In answer to this it is important to point out that the term 'moral judgement' contains a serious ambiguity. There are three types of judgement which have by various writers been termed moral judgements. These

[88] Ib. 136 [p. 302 this volume].
[89] Ib. 136-7 [p. 302 this volume].

are (i) the judgements in which an act is pronounced to be right or wrong; (ii) the judgements in which an action or disposition is judged to be morally good, or bad, or indifferent, i.e. to have (or fail to have) the kind of goodness or badness that only dispositions and actions can have; (iii) the judgements in which something is said to be good or bad or indifferent *sans phrase*. The first two may be said to be departmental judgements, in the sense that each of them is applicable only to one class of objects, the first to acts considered apart from their motives, the second to dispositions and actions considered in respect of their motives. Judgements of the third class are not in any way departmental; they may be made about anything in the whole world. It can be said of some things—I suggest, as at any rate an adumbration of the things of which it can be said, virtue, knowledge and well-grounded opinion, and pleasure [40]—that they are good; of others —vice, badly grounded opinion, and pain—that they are bad; and of other things that they are indifferent, i.e. considered in themselves, though many of them may be instrumental to good or to evil. In making such judgements we are not adopting a *narrowly* ethical standpoint; we are saying for instance that wisdom and pleasure are good, though they are not morally good. We are taking the most commanding point of view that can be taken with regard to the value of the things in the universe. Yet this is a point of view which a moral philosopher should, in part of his inquiry, adopt, since ethics is the study of that which we ought to do, and of what is involved in its being what we ought to do, and since what we ought to do depends to a large extent (though, as I have urged, not entirely) on the goodness or the badness of the things we can in our acts bring into being.

It would, however, be a mistake to spend time in arguing the question whether the theory of good in general belongs to ethics or to metaphysics. The other two types of judgement belong exclusively to ethics. Goodness in general runs out beyond the strict scope of ethics, if ethics be the philosophical study of good conduct; for some of the things that are good are neither conduct nor dispositions to conduct. But the study of the meaning of good in general, and of the types of thing that are good, is either a part of ethics, or a part of metaphysics to which the study of purely ethical problems inevitably leads us: which it is, depends on how we define ethics and metaphysics. Neither ethics nor metaphysics is a study to which definite limits have hitherto been set, or one, probably, to which they can profitably be set. The only way, perhaps, in which we could prescribe a quite rigid programme for metaphysics would be by saying that it is the study of the characteristics possessed in common by everything that is; and from this point of view the theory of goodness would have to be pronounced not to be part of metaphysics. But whether we widen our notion of metaphysics to make it include the theory of all very widely distributed characteristics (among which goodness and badness are included), or treat the study of

---

[40] To avoid making my statement too complicated, I omit a further kind of good which will be mentioned later, cf. p. 138.

value as a part of ethics, or recognize an intermediate science of axiology (or theory of value) less wide than metaphysics and wider than ethics, is a question the discussion of which does not lead us any distance at all towards understanding the facts.

We must return, however, to the objection Professor Perry is at the moment considering, and to his answer to it. The objection is that many of the things in which people find pleasure and which they desire are nevertheless bad. His answer is that they are not bad in general but only bad from the ethical standpoint. And our answer to that is that while there is what may be called a narrowly ethical standpoint from which we judge such and such an action to be vicious or morally bad, there is also a more commanding standpoint from which we view the agent's total state of mind at the time and judge that in spite of any elements of pleasure-value it may contain it is on the whole a bad thing, a thing for whose occurrence the world is the worse. This is not the narrowly ethical standpoint, for it is the same standpoint from which we judge that the occurrence of a pain is, considered apart from its accompaniments, a bad thing, though a pain is not morally bad. Now if from this, which is the most commanding standpoint, we say that many states of mind in which their owners have taken interest and found pleasure are nevertheless bad, 'good' cannot be identical with 'object of interest.'

My general conclusion is that Professor Perry's arguments have not succeeded either in refuting the view that goodness is an intrinsic quality of certain things, or in defending from attack the view that it is identical with being an object of interest to some mind.[41]

[41] I may refer here to the weighty final chapter of Meinong's last treatment of the problem of value, in his *Zur Grundlegung der allgemeinen Werttheorie*. It is remarkable that though he approaches the problem from the side of the subjective act of valuation, and of the analysis of this, he concludes that there are 'unpersonal goods,' in the sense that there are goods which are not essentially for a subject at all, though they are in a subject (cf. p. 147 of his work). This is exactly the position I wish to establish.

*　　*　　*

Value and Obligation
In Dewey and Lewis*

MORTON G. WHITE

THE APPEARANCE of Professor C. I. Lewis' *Analysis of Knowledge and Valuation*, with its forthright defense of the thesis that all statements of value are empirical, presents an opportunity to examine the present state of pragmatic value theory and ethics. In particular it presents an opportunity to compare Lewis' views with those of Dewey on the relation between value and obligation. The third book of Lewis' *Analysis* presents a carefully worked out doctrine which closely resembles the one Dewey outlines in the tenth chapter of *The Quest for Certainty*,† but these doctrines exhibit a great difference as well. The agreement and difference may be summarized by saying that whereas both Lewis and Dewey defend a view according to which value statements are empirical, Lewis, unlike Dewey, makes a distinction between value statements and ethical statements, according to which the latter are not empirical. The purpose of this article is to make some critical observations on this entire problem.

Dewey's central concern in this area is to distinguish between the *desirable* and the *desired* in a way that guarantees a clear distinction between what he calls "de jure" statements and what he calls "merely factual" statements; a *de jure* statement asserts the desirability of an object whereas a merely *de facto* statement asserts that it is desired. I do not think he makes this distinction successfully, and I will try to show why in the first part of this article.[1] Lewis, in spite of the similarity between his position and Dewey's, avoids what I think is Dewey's error, but the manner in which he avoids it creates a problem for his theory of knowledge. In passing I will compare the difficulties facing Dewey's theory with those which have been pointed out by almost all critics of Mill's notorious analogy between the desirable and the visible. The difficulties are more alike than is usually supposed.

* Reprinted by kind permission of the author and the editors from *The Philosophical Review*, 58, 1949.

† [This chapter is printed pp. 272 ff. this volume.]

[1] This problem has been discussed by C. L. Stevenson from another point of view. See his *Ethics and Language*, pp. 253–264.

Dewey is anxious to distinguish between the satisfying and the satisfactory, the enjoyed and the enjoyable, the desired and the desirable. Most of us would agree that the last of these pairs of concepts illustrates an important difference—indeed the most important difference in the theory of the subject. Dewey objects to what he calls an "empirical theory of values," according to which values are constituted by liking and enjoyment, so that "to be enjoyed and to be a value are two names for one and the same fact." [2] But although he denies this theory he maintains that there is a connection between value and being desired, for he says: "I shall not object to this empirical theory so far as it connects the theory of values with concrete experiences of desire and satisfaction. The idea that there is such a connection is the only way known to me by which the pallid remoteness of the rationalistic theory, and the only too glaring presence of the institutional theory of transcendental values can be escaped." [3] But this is not the only condition he sets upon the solution of the problem. In connecting the desirable (value) with the desired he must connect them in such a way as to show clearly that whereas the statement "a is desired now" is merely a statement of fact, the statement "a is desirable" is a factual statement which also has a "*de jure* quality." The problem, then, is to give an analysis of "*a* is desirable" when it is construed as meaning *a ought to be desired*, which will render it an empirical statement, a statement which conveys empirical knowledge. What I will argue here is not that this is impossible in general, but rather that Dewey's particular method of solving the problem as set forth in the tenth chapter of *The Quest for Certainty* does not accomplish this difficult task.

The relation between the desirable and the desired is not expressed so as to make me wholly confident of my interpretation, but in many passages Dewey seems to suggest that it resembles the connection between what Lewis calls "Value in Objects" and the immediate experience of satisfaction. "As a first approximation," Lewis says, "we might say that attributing value to an existent, *O*, means that under circumstances, *C*, *O* will or would, lead to satisfaction in the experience of somebody, *S*." [4] For purposes of this discussion Lewis' first approximation will suffice. Now it seems to me that there are many occasions on which Dewey speaks as though

[2] *The Quest for Certainty*, p. 258 [p. 274 this volume].

[3] *Ibid.*, p. 258. It should be pointed out that my chief criticisms of Dewey are not affected by the conclusions of his controversy with Professor P. B. Rice in *The Journal of Philosophy*, XL (1943). For there Dewey reiterates his belief that there is a connection between value and satisfaction. What I am concerned with here is this *connection* rather than the nature of satisfaction. For this reason I do not consider Dewey's views on introspection and the subjective: they are not relevant in my opinion. If I were to enter this vexed problem no doubt important differences would turn up between Dewey and Lewis, but no difference of that sort would interfere with their maintaining the agreement I discuss in the present article. Nor do I foresee any alteration of Dewey's views on satisfaction which might affect my remarks on his theory of the connection between satisfaction and value.

[4] *An Analysis of Knowledge and Valuation*, p. 512.

he holds this kind of theory of objective value. For example: "A *feeling* of good or excellence is as far removed from goodness in fact as a feeling that objects are intellectually thus and so is removed from their being actually so." [5] Many statements of this kind lead me to believe that Dewey's view of the relation between what is desirable and what is desired identifies it with the relation which holds between the objective property of being red and the appearance of red. It would seem that according to Dewey we cannot infer validly that an object has value simply on the basis of enjoying it casually, without having instituted tests analogous to those which are instituted by the careful investigator of the objective color of something. And it would appear that according to Dewey only an object which satisfies us under conditions which are analogous to the normal conditions involved in testing colors, has value in his sense. Although there are other passages which present difficulties for this interpretation I believe there is considerable evidence for holding that it does render Dewey's meaning in some places. This interpretation has the virtue of helping us understand a number of statements which would otherwise be vague. We can understand more easily now (or at least the writer can) what Dewey means when he says that a judgment of value involves a prediction; it also makes clear his analogy between statements of what is immediately satisfying and statements which report immediate "havings" in the perception of colors; it clarifies to a degree the following passage:

To assume that anything can be known in isolation from its connections with other things is to identify knowing with merely having some object before perception or in feeling, and is thus to lose the key to the traits that distinguish an object as known. It is futile, even silly, to suppose that some quality that is directly present constitutes the whole of the thing presenting the quality. It does not do so when the quality is that of being hot or fluid or heavy, and it does not when the quality is that of giving pleasure, or being enjoyed. Such qualities are . . . effects, ends in the sense of closing termini of processes involving causal connections. They are something to be investigated, challenges to inquiry and judgment. The more connections and interactions we ascertain, the more we *know* the object in question. Thinking is search for these connections. Heat experienced as a consequence of directed operations has a meaning quite different from the heat that is casually experienced without knowledge of how it came about. The same is true of enjoyments.[6]

It seems reasonable to conclude that Dewey construes both "desirable" and "value" as disposition-predicates, and in so doing thinks he has reduced "desirable" (in the sense of "ought to be desired") to empirical terms. Lewis analyzes "value in objects" in this way but refrains from concluding that he has simultaneously taken care of "desirable" in the sense of "ought to be desired." I will treat the relations between Dewey's views and those of Lewis after I have considered the connection between Dewey's views and those of John Stuart Mill.

[5] Dewey, *op. cit.*, p. 265 [p. 279 this volume].
[6] *Ibid.*, p. 267 [p. 280 this volume].

The relation between Mill's views and Dewey's may be seen more clearly if we begin by comparing the different respects in which "soluble" and "objectively red" are disposition-predicates. To say that a is soluble is to say that a is capable of being dissolved. When we say that a is soluble we mean that there are [7] conditions under which a dissolves. But when we say that a is objectively red we don't mean simply that a has the capacity to appear red, although it is true that if a is objectively red it does have the capacity to appear red. The point is that whereas being objectively red implies having the capacity to appear red, the converse is not true. Obviously, many things which are not objectively red (probably all things) have the capacity to appear red; there are conditions under which they will appear red. For this reason "a is objectively red" is not even materially equivalent to "There are conditions under which a appears red." This difference between "soluble" and "objectively red" is reflected in another way. Because "a is soluble" means that a can be dissolved, we feel justified in inferring "a is soluble" from "a is dissolved," on the ground of the maxim that whatever is actual is possible. But clearly we don't feel justified in inferring "a is objectively red" from "a appears red." And the reason for this is now obvious: "a is objectively red" is roughly synonymous with "a looks red under normal conditions," and so the mere fact that it appears red without specification of the conditions merely justifies our concluding that a has the capacity to appear red, not that it *is* red. This difference between "soluble" and "objectively red" may be summarized by pointing out that although everything that dissolves is soluble, not everything that appears red is objectively red. Let us see how this is related to the views of Dewey and Mill on the *desirable*.

According to Mill an assertion to the effect that a is desirable can be proved by showing that a is desired.[8] I shall understand him to mean that "a is desired" logically implies "a is desirable," though he may not have been using the word "proof" in this strict sense. This, of course, puts "desirable" in the same category as "soluble" in one respect. Now Dewey, if I understand him, holds that this is not true. Dewey believes, and I agree with him, that some things that are now desired are not desirable. Consequently one of the conditions we impose on our definition of "desirable" is that "a is desired now" does not entail "a is desirable." Now when "desirable" is construed as a disposition-predicate like "objectively red" rather than like "soluble," it does satisfy this condition. For, as we have seen, "a appears red" does not entail "a is objectively red," and therefore, if "a is desirable" is synonymous with "a is desired under normal conditions," "a is desirable" will not be entailed by "a is desired." It is this latter circumstance which creates some of Dewey's difficulties. He sees, correctly in my opinion, that one relation between the desirable (what ought to be

[7] The phrase "there are" is construed tenselessly.

[8] *Utilitarianism*, ch. IV, par. 4. Mill says that it can be proved *only* in this way, but I am not concerned with this more extensive claim.

desired) and the desired is preserved by this mode of construing the desirable. It allows him to prove that "*a* is desired" does not logically imply "*a* is desirable." But although one of the necessary conditions for a definition of "desirable" is that "*a* is desired" does not entail "*a* is desirable," this is not sufficient. Dewey, I believe, has been misled into supposing that it is sufficient, and for this reason thinks that he has adequately defined "desirable" in what he calls its "*de jure*" sense. Dewey, I suggest, has been misled by the "able" ending of "desirable" into supposing that it is wholly analyzable as an object disposition-predicate. In this respect his error resembles that of Mill. Mill, however, makes the more obvious error of thinking that "desirable" is like "soluble," whereas Dewey makes the more subtle one of thinking it is a disposition-predicate like "objectively red."

I am not concerned here with the general question of whether "desirable," in the sense of "ought to be desired," can be analyzed so that statements like "*a* is desirable" are shown to convey empirical knowledge. I am merely interested in pointing out that the particular empirical or naturalistic interpretation which Dewey gives in the tenth chapter of *The Quest for Certainty* is defective in a subtle way; I am not concerned to criticize all of Dewey's writings on this theme, but I am not aware of any that supplements the view expressed in *The Quest for Certainty* in a way that obviates the difficulties in it. My chief criticism depends on the fact that the relation between "desirable" and "desired" is allegedly identical with that between "objectively red" and "appears red." But "*a* appears red" and "*a* is objectively red" do not differ in any way which would allow us to say that the first has a merely "*de facto*" quality, whereas the second has a "*de jure*" quality, to use Dewey's language. The fact that *a* is objectively red, to put it in another language, is no more *normative* than the fact that *a* appears red now. And since the fact that *a* is desirable (as Dewey construes it) is related to the fact that *a* is desired in precisely the way that the fact that *a* is objectively red is related to the fact that *a* appears red, it would follow that "*a* is desirable" is no more normative than "*a* is desired." I conclude that Dewey has defined "value" and "desirable" in an interesting way, but that he has not succeeded in construing "desirable" in the sense of "ought to be desired," as he thinks he has. I do not see how the statement "*a* is desired under normal conditions" can be taken as synonymous with "*a* ought to be desired" without taking "*a* appears red under normal conditions" as synonymous with "*a* ought to appear red," but I feel that this consequence is absurd, and hence fatal for Dewey's view.

Some philosophers who share my opinion on this might conclude that *any* so-called naturalistic definition of "ought to be desired" is refuted by an argument which is similar to the one I have offered above. But I am not convinced of this, and I want to repeat that my argument is directed solely against one naturalistic proposal. Some of the difficulties involved in a blanket rejection of the naturalistic program for analyzing "ought to be desired" appear in Lewis' work, I think, and so I turn now to his views on this question.

Lewis is convinced of the impossibility of a purely empirical analysis of the right, the just, that which ought to be. So far as I can gather, he agrees with Dewey in construing objective value as a potentiality of objects whose realization takes place in immediate experience, in immediate satisfactions, but does not go on to construe value so defined as identical with *desirable* in any way that confers *"de jure"* status on judgments of value. Dewey does, and it is here that my difficulties with Dewey arise. But Dewey does so because he is anxious to proceed to some analysis of "desirable" in the *"de jure"* sense which will result in construing it as an empirical predicate. Lewis does not even attempt this because he holds that judgments of what ought to be, in particular judgments of what ought to be desired, are matters of ethics rather than of value. "The problem which delimits the field of ethics is not that of the empirically good or valuable but that of the right and morally imperative. To be sure, there is essential connection between rightness of action and goodness in that which this action is intended to effect. At least, it is with this general conception that rightness of action derives from value in the end, with which we should agree. But just at this point we should be careful that we do not illicitly connect the right and the good, before ever we have distinguished them." [9] Here we see plainly the gap between Lewis and Dewey, but it is here that new problems arise.

Lewis holds: "Valuation is always a matter of empirical knowledge. But what is right and just, can never be determined by empirical facts alone." [10] But if this is juxtaposed with Lewis' belief that there are only two kinds of knowledge—knowledge of empirical propositions and knowledge of analytic propositions—we find it difficult to see how he will classify ethical knowledge—knowledge of what is just, what is right, what ought to be. He has cut himself off from regarding ethical knowledge as empirical by definition of what is ethical. Can he regard all true ethical propositions as analytic? To be sure Lewis regards *some* ethical propositions as analytic, e.g., "No rule of action is right except one which is right in all instances, and therefore right for everyone." But it is not at all clear that he is willing to call *every* true proposition which involves the notion of *right* analytic, e.g., *it was not right of Brutus to stab Caesar*. At any rate it does not follow from the fact that some principles of ethics are analytic that all ethical propositions are. *No rule of action may be right except one which is right in all instances* may be an analytic proposition for Lewis, but clearly the fact that it is analytic does not imply that the proposition, *Truth-telling is right*, is analytic. We may regard the proposition that all men are animals as analytic and yet maintain that the proposition that Jones is a man is synthetic. I point this out only because some readers of Lewis have con-

[9] Lewis, *op. cit.*, p. 552.
[10] *Ibid.*, p. 554.

cluded from the fact that he cites one ethical proposition as analytic (the one quoted above) that he holds that *all* true ethical propositions are analytic.

But if he refuses to take this alternative (which does not seem defensible), what other alternatives are there? One is to surrender the view that all knowledge is exclusively and exhaustively divisible into the analytic and the empirical. But he seems to hold to this too confidently for us to expect that he will choose this course. Can he, then, face Russell's conclusion that "knowledge" of ethical propositions is not knowledge at all? Several things he says suggest that he rejects this alternative. The problem is one that is immensely perplexing and is precisely the problem which leads Stevenson to *his* position,[11] I think. We must observe, therefore, how Lewis' concluding remarks about the nonempirical character of ethical propositions (as distinct from value propositions) bring him closer to a position which he attacks in value theory. "The denial to value-apprehensions in general of the character of truth or falsity and of knowledge" is a denial which he describes as "one of the strangest aberrations ever to visit the mind of man." [12] But I should say that after showing successfully that value propositions *do* express empirical knowledge, he formulates a position in ethics which is closer in motivation to that of the "emotivists" than he thinks. For he has simply postponed to ethics the problem that has troubled them in what he calls theory of value. In denying that ethical statements convey empirical knowledge he joins with those who deny to apprehensions of what is right (as distinct from what has value) the character of empirical truth or falsity and of empirical knowledge. To be sure he does not go on to treat judgments of right in the positive manner of the emotivists. But he does join with them in denying that ethical propositions are to be settled by appeal to factual considerations alone. Indeed, I might remark here that it is not clear whether Lewis means to divorce ethical judgments from *all* appeal to fact or whether he means merely to say that more than factual considerations enter into a determination of what is right. But clearly if he argues that more than factual considerations enter, thereby implying that they do enter, he must show what *other* considerations must be added.

The resulting situation in the ethics and value-theory of contemporary pragmatism may be summarized as follows. Dewey is anxious to analyze statements of the form "*a* is desirable" so that they are seen to be empirical. He does this by construing the property of being desirable as a disposition by analogy with objective characteristics like red as distinct from phenomenal appearances of red. This, I have argued, does not clarify or define "desirable" in the sense of "ought to be desired." Lewis has elaborated this same theory with great success but avoids identifying what they both call value (in objects) with what ought to be desired. Lewis holds that what

---

[11] *Op. cit.*
[12] Lewis, *op. cit.*, pp. 365–366.

is right and what ought to be, and hence what ought to be desired, is not a matter of value but of ethics, and ethics does not depend on empirical knowledge alone. But Lewis has also divided knowledge into the analytic and the empirical and has excluded anything like the synthetic a priori. How, then, will he classify and analyze propositions concerning what is right and just without making them all trivially analytic and without appealing to something like the synthetic a priori? We must await Lewis' further considerations before judging their likely success, but at this moment it is not improper to point to what seems like an insurmountable task in the light of his epistemological commitments. The writer must admit that he is as puzzled about the problem as anyone, and that it is for this reason that he raises the whole issue. The disagreement between Dewey and Lewis on this question deserves notice as representing an important cleavage, on these questions, in American pragmatism, for Lewis has called himself a conceptual pragmatist on other occasions. Evidently pragmatism is united on the subject of value but not on obligation or justice. Dewey, in spite of a valiant attempt, has not given us a naturalistic account of obligation, and Lewis foresakes the task as impossible. We may safely say, therefore, that pragmatism is still without a solution of the fundamental problem of ethics.[13]

[13] I am indebted to Professor Nelson Goodman for helping me clarify some of my ideas on the difference between "soluble" and "objectively red." Robert M. Browning's interesting article, "On Professor Lewis's Distinction between Ethics and Valuation" (*Ethics,* LIX [1949], 95–111), came to my attention after my article had been prepared for publication.

Moral and Non-Moral Values: A Study in the First Principles of Axiology [*]

C. A. CAMPBELL

I

It would, I suppose, be pretty generally agreed that the fundamental cleavage within value-philosophy at the present day is between those who hold that goodness (or value) is a simple unanalysable—and hence indefinable—*quality* which certain things possess, and those who hold that it consists in a *relation* of some kind between the things of which value is predicated and some mind or minds. As labels will be convenient for views of which we shall have much to say in the sequel, let us call these two schools of thought the 'Objectivist' and the 'Subjectivist' respectively.

Of these schools, the Objectivist is, of course, by far the more recent —dating virtually from the publication of *Principia Ethica* some thirty years ago. And I do not think it unfair to suggest that its considerable authority has been due much less to its own positive merits than to certain apparently irremediable defects in the Subjectivist theories which seem to offer the only plausible alternatives. Its authority can hardly be accounted for by the logical arguments which appeared to Dr. Moore in 1903 to prove irresistibly that goodness could only be a simple quality: for these arguments have not, as a rule, been found satisfactory even by those who are most sympathetic with the general trend of the theory, and they are not now, one learns,[1] acceptable to Dr. Moore himself. Nor is the doctrine qualified to attract adherents by any power of affording an intelligent comprehension of the vast and varied panorama of value-judgments disclosed to us by the student of comparative cultures: for this is just what any view of value which denies the relevance of subjective interests is singularly incompetent to do. Indeed, the advantage of Subjectivism with respect to this important requirement of a sound value-theory is at once so great and so evident that only the presence of very grave counter-balancing disabilities seems able to explain the preference accorded in so many quarters to the claims of the Objectivist type of theory.

[*] Reprinted by kind permission of the author and the editor from *Mind*, 44, 1935.
[1] *Proceedings of the Aristotelian Society*, Supplementary Vol. XI., p. 127.

It must be admitted, however, that very grave difficulties do beset the path of the Subjectivist. Two, I think, are outstanding, and are constantly being adduced by critics as manifestly fatal to the pretensions of Subjectivism. Let me state them very briefly.

(1) If what we mean when we predicate goodness of X is that X is liked (or desired, approved, etc.) by some mind or minds, then goodness must be something of a highly contingent character. It must, apparently, be something that comes into being and passes away not only (as is natural enough) through changes in the nature of X, but also on account merely of changes in certain conscious states. And it is very difficult to believe that this is what we do in fact mean, at least in our more considered and unqualified value-judgments. When we assert that knowledge is good, or that beauty is good, surely we do not mean that knowledge and beauty own this character only if and when certain conscious states are directed towards them? Is it not evident that we regard the goodness of each of these 'goods' as possessed of the same kind of permanence as the nature of the thing itself, and not as something which fluctuates with the fluctuation of any person's, or group of persons', feelings towards the thing?

(2) Among conventionally accepted good things there is one whose goodness we feel it quite peculiarly repugnant to identify with any relation to subjective interests. I refer to moral virtue. In the case of other good things—such as knowledge—we at least do not feel that there is anything inherently absurd in enquiring whether the goodness we attribute to the thing may not be derivable from its being an object of interest to some subject or subjects (or from its being a means to the attainment of some such object of interest). However difficult it may be to devise a formula which avoids the difficulty alluded to under (1), we at least recognise nothing crassly incongruous in undertaking the attempt. But the case of moral virtue appears to fall into quite a different category. When a man in defiance of strong temptations rises to what he recognises to be his duty, it seems merely inept to suggest that his dutiful act derives the value which we all regard it as possessing from any subjective feelings that are entertained towards it by any one. We seem to see quite clearly that we need pay no attention to the presence or absence of any subjective feelings whatsoever in order to know that the act has value. Whether or not the act may have some *further* value in virtue of a relation to subjective feelings, we may here be content to leave as an open question. But it can only be by confusion that we fail to distinguish the 'supplementary' value which the act may possess on *this* account from the value which it possesses simply and solely in virtue of its being the kind of act that it is, i.e., an act of duty.

Now I do not believe, for reasons which I shall later explain, that the former of these difficulties is really insuperable. But I confess that the latter difficulty does seem to me fatal to any purely Subjectivist theory of value. It is, I think, quite hopeless to seek to identify the value we attribute to moral virtue with any relation to anything that can legitimately be called a subjective interest. Indeed, the simple appeal to reflect upon our own value-responses to moral virtue seems to me to be by far the most effective weapon in the whole armoury of the critics of Subjectivism, and it has probably been responsible for making more converts to the general Objectivist stand-point than all other arguments put together. It is very noticeable—and, as I shall attempt to show, highly significant—how frequently it recurs at critical junctures in the pages of Dr. W. D. Ross's recent important work.[2] I cite here only a single typical passage, from the chapter on 'the Nature of Goodness.' 'We may claim,' writes Dr. Ross, 'that we are directly aware that conscientious action, for example, has a value of its own, not identical with or even dependent upon our or any one else's taking an interest in it. Our reason informs us of this as surely as it informs us of anything, and to distrust reason here is in principle to distrust its power of ever knowing reality.'[3] It is a claim, I think, whose cogency will strike home to almost every reader. But note how immeasurably it would be weakened in its effect if, instead of the *moral* value of 'conscientiousness,' we were to insert some non-moral value—even one of the so-called 'intrinsic' values like 'knowledge.' It is possible that, if we were to substitute 'knowledge,' we should still feel an *inclination* to assert that this good 'has a value of its own, not identical with or even dependent upon our or any one else's taking an interest in it.' But I doubt if there is one of us who would go so far as to contend that 'our reason informs us of this as surely as it informs us of anything, and to distrust reason here is in principle to distrust its power of ever knowing reality.' The strength of the case against Subjectivism depends, I think, far more than is generally recognised upon the special instance of the value we apprehend in moral virtue.

Still, a single argument, if it be sound, is enough to establish any position: and I am willing to admit, on the strength of the argument we have been considering, that an adequate theory of value is not possible on purely Subjectivist lines. But before we acquiesce in a thorough-going and general rejection of Subjectivism, there is one alternative which, as it seems to me, we ought to explore with a great deal of care. Is it absolutely necessary, I want to ask, that we should extend to the meaning of value or goodness generally those characteristics which we find ourselves forced to apply to it in the case of moral virtue? Is it quite certain that we mean the same thing by 'good' when we judge that moral virtue is good as we do when we judge that knowledge is good—or indeed as we do in any other of those instances (the crucial ones, of course, for the determination of the ultimate nature of value) in which we predicate goodness in an apparently 'absolute' sense? If this is *not* so, then it may remain possible to give a Subjectivist account of value in respect of non-moral values, even while we recognise that such an account is definitely false in respect of moral values: a consummation which would deliver us from the embarrassment, which presses

[2] *The Right and the Good.*
[3] *Ibid.,* p. 82 [p. 315 this volume].

so sorely upon the Objectivist school, of holding a theory of value which leaves in outer darkness by far the larger proportion of the value-judgments of mankind.

I hope that the reader will not dismiss this alternative too hastily as savouring of mere convenient eclecticism. It has, I believe, a much more solid base. Indeed it is, in my opinion (which I shall endeavour to substantiate in this paper), the one view capable of introducing coherence into the general theory of value. I believe that the chief source of the confusion which envelops current value philosophy lies precisely in the failure to recognise that there is an absolutely vital distinction of kind between our value-reaction to the value of moral virtue and our value-reaction to any other value whatsoever.

To explain my thesis in more formal terms, what I am going to argue is that a subjectivist definition of value is valid, *save only* in the single case of the value which inheres in moral virtue. How exactly we are to understand the meaning of value in the latter connection, and what is the nature of the identity or analogy between it and value in the former connection which leads us to employ the same term 'value,' or 'goodness,' in respect of both, are questions which must engage our attention at some later stage. But our chief preoccupation will be with the meaning of value in the former connection; and our chief problem in the effort to vindicate a subjectivist interpretation of 'non-moral' values will be to devise a formula in terms of subjective feelings which will escape, along with other difficulties, the major difficulty alluded to at the outset of this paper.

2

It is perhaps desirable, before we settle to the task of constructing a subjectivist formula for non-moral values, to say something more of a general character in support of the uniqueness of the value which we attribute to moral virtue. Let us begin by trying to give to the difference in kind which we allege, at least the status of an initial probability: for the reader who is already persuaded that this alleged difference at least *may* have a foundation in fact, is likely to explore with considerably greater sympathy the hypothesis that a subjectivist interpretation is valid for non-moral values.

One piece of evidence in support of the validity of the distinction has already been referred to, and I shall develop it only briefly. I quoted[4] a passage from Dr. Ross which purported to show that the value which we accord to conscientious action cannot be given a subjectivist interpretation, and I invited the reader to observe the effect upon the argument of substituting for conscientious action some non-moral value. If we carefully examine our value-reactions in the two cases, it seems to me that the difference between them is very marked, and highly important. We feel, so Dr.

[4] p. 275 [p. 342 this volume].

Ross contends, completely certain that conscientious action has value irrespective of any subjective interest in it—a value to which subjective liking and disliking are merely irrelevant. I think that very few persons, if any, would maintain that a value like beauty (or, as I should prefer to express it, aesthetic experience) evokes a corresponding assurance. The habit of mind, engendered by a long tradition, which tempts us to take it as established verity that Truth, Beauty and Goodness are a sort of holy trinity of 'intrinsic' values may, and only too probably will, predispose us to believe in objectivity in this value-realm also. But we surely cannot pretend that we here enjoy anything even approximating to *certitude*. We should not stake the very validity of our reason upon the objectivity of this value. The difference in our attitudes is very easy to understand if the distinction I am contending for is *bene fundatum*. It is not easy to explain on any other hypothesis.

Further evidence may be derived from considering a problem which has evidently very much exercised the author of *The Right and the Good*— the problem of the commensurability of values. If we suppose that the goodness, possessed by moral virtue on the one hand, and by non-moral good on the other hand, is goodness in the same sense of goodness, then presumably it should be possible, since goodness admits of a more and less, to measure the goodness of virtue against the goodness of the other goods in at least a rough and ready, approximate fashion. Yet in actual truth it seems impossible to dissent from Dr. Ross's own considered judgment that the goodness of virtue is really incommensurable with the goodness of any of the other 'intrinsic goods.' Critical examination of our own value-responses strongly suggests that we decline to accept any amount, however large, of a good like knowledge as exceeding in value the very smallest amount of moral virtue. 'When I ask myself,' says Dr. Ross, 'whether any increase in knowledge, however great, is worth having at the cost of a wilful failure to do my duty or of a deterioration of character, I can only answer in the negative.' [5] And this is surely a correct answer. For my own part, I should say that the very question has about it an unreal, artificial flavour. It is the kind of question which no one could seriously put to himself save in a mood of half-conscious sophistry, or else—as here —under the influence of a philosophical motive which demands the explicit examination of even the most remotely possible alternatives. I am not myself aware of any philosopher, with the possible exception of Dr. Moore— who in theory assigns to moral virtue a very modest degree of value— likely to return an affirmative answer to the question, and it seems fair to take the negative answer as possessing a pretty high measure of certainty.

Now if the goodness of virtue is really felt to be incommensurable with the goodness of other good things, can we still hold that we are meaning by 'goodness' the same thing in both cases? Dr. Ross tries to evade the difficulty, which his own candour has so clearly exposed, by suggesting

[5] *The Right and the Good*, p. 152.

that 'virtue belongs to a higher order of value, beginning at a point higher on the scale of value than that which (the others) ever reach.'[6] But I feel very doubtful whether this supposed relationship will bear examination. If it is really the *same scale* to which they belong—and this condition seems to be necessary if they are to be defended as 'good' in the same sense—two difficulties emerge. In the first place, since it does not seem possible to set any assignable limit to the amount imaginable of goods like knowledge and pleasure, must we not say that at *some* point the goodness possessed by these goods equals the goodness possessed by the minimal amount of virtue? And, in the second place, ought we not to feel that with increasing amounts of knowledge and pleasure we are continuously *getting nearer to* the degree of goodness which the minimal amount of virtue possesses? I think that if the values do indeed belong, as Dr. Ross says they do, to the *same scale of value*, an affirmative answer to both of these questions is logically entailed. Yet it seems to me in the last degree doubtful whether an affirmative answer can be supported by the actual responses of our value-consciousness, and I imagine that Dr. Ross's own recognition of the peculiar claims of moral value must make him extremely reluctant to accept that answer himself.

Now the difficulties, it should be noticed, which beset the attempt to measure the value of virtue against the value of other goods, are precisely what one would expect if the thesis that I am to defend in this paper is a sound one. If virtue is a value not just of a *higher order* but in a *different category*, if it is, in fact, the one thing which has a value independent of all relation to subjective interests, then little wonder that we are aware of an inherent impropriety in seeking to apply a common yard-stick to it and other goods.

3

It is rather more than time, however, that we passed on to our main task. Our real problem still awaits us, *viz.*, to justify the contention that all value-judgments other than those referring to moral virtue involve an essential reference to human liking.[7] Let me say a word or two, first of all, about the method I propose to adopt.

Naturally, I shall not attempt to deal explicitly with every variety of value-judgment. Our main concern must be with those judgments which are especially appealed to by the Objectivists as furnishing indubitable instances of the apprehension of a value which is not reducible to subjectivist terms. There is, indeed, no list common to all the Objectivists;

---

6 *The Right and the Good*, p. 150. In the context the statement relates only to the non-moral value of 'pleasure,' but the sequel makes it clear that Dr. Ross intends his view to apply to other non-moral values also.

7 I shall explain shortly why, in my judgment, 'liking' is to be preferred in this connection to 'interest' or 'desire,' or any other term that Subjectivist axiologists have proposed.

but the claims of knowledge and æsthetic experience (Truth and Beauty, in popular parlance) have received such wide-spread acknowledgment that it is certain that no Subjectivist theory has any hope of acceptance which cannot make clear the disguised relationship to human liking which obtains in their case. If we can find a formula in terms of human liking which can be regarded as representing fairly what is really meant by goodness or value in the value-judgments directed upon these crucial instances, it will probably be agreed that we have surmounted by far the greatest obstacle to the vindication of our general thesis.

Now the formula which I shall venture to put forward is, as might be expected from the nature of the case, of a somewhat intricate character. The one thing abundantly certain is that no simple formula—such as 'liked by the person judging,' or 'liked by the majority of the community'—has the faintest chance of withstanding criticism. But, because of its complexity, our formula, if stated baldly at this juncture, would convey very little meaning indeed. I propose, therefore, to lead up to it gradually by undertaking a systematic examination of the nature and growth of our value-consciousness in so far forth as that value-consciousness *is* rooted in human liking.

For the sake of clearness, let me outline very briefly in advance the main stages through which we shall pass on the way to our goal.

I shall start from what appears to me to be the most rudimentary expression of 'subjective value-consciousness'—if I may so entitle the value-consciousness that is rooted in human liking—*viz.*, that which is ingredient in simple private liking and which manifests itself in the concept 'good-for-self.' I shall then endeavour to show how, by an entirely natural development, incited by the growing recognition of certain distinctions which force themselves upon an intelligent subject of experience, that value-consciousness comes eventually to identify with 'good for self' only objects of its liking *which are qualified in a highly specific way*. I next turn to consider the reaction of our value-consciousness to the recognition (in practice, of course, present from the start) that other persons also have likes and dislikes, and that there are also likes and dislikes which may be said to be inherent in our common human nature as such. This leads us to see that our value-consciousness (still operating on the basis solely of human likes and dislikes) will naturally take a vital interest not only in the concept 'good for self,' but also in the concept 'good for man,' and that what it means by 'good for man' is an object of liking to human nature qualified in a specific way parallel to that which we found to be involved in the developed concept 'good for self.' We then observe that the formula to which we have been led in considering the true meaning of 'good for man' is one which, if applied to the matter of experience, must issue in a list of goods which bears a remarkable resemblance to that which is currently supposed to represent goods that are intrinsic and objective, goods without any relational qualification. This discovery suggests the possibility that the concept which controls our recognition of the so-called intrinsic goods is really the concept 'good for man.' An explanation will, of course, require to be given of how it is that the relational qualification—good *for man*—if it controls our thoughts, does not appear in our speech. If we really mean 'good for man,' why do we say just 'good'? This difficulty, however, proves to be superficial. Further difficulties are also considered and rejected, and the final conclusion come to that our real meaning when we seem to be asserting intrinsic goodness of such goods as knowledge, æsthetic emotion, etc., is that they are specifically qualified objects of liking to human nature.

4

We start, then, from the experience of simple private liking. That which we like, we 'put a value upon,' as the common phrase has it. It is, to be sure, only a value-*for-self*, not a value *in itself*. For the value which we attach to the thing merely in so far forth as it is an object of our liking is certainly not regarded by us as a value 'in the nature of things,' nor even as a value for anyone besides the person liking. But it certainly *is* regarded as a *value*. It is possible to dispute the relevance of the term 'value' here, only if we quite arbitrarily, and indeed perversely, decide that the term 'value' is to be used as the equivalent of the term 'objective value.' There seems no excuse whatever for such a usage, which can hardly be so much as intelligibly formulated to oneself without drawing a distinction in thought between objective and subjective value; a distinction which, if admitted, at once makes nonsense of the proposed identification of 'value' with 'objective value.'

I take it, then, to be indisputable that there is a fundamental manifestation of value-consciousness which is the consciousness of 'value-for-self.' But before we go any further, a word must be said about the choice of 'liking' as the basis of that consciousness. That the interruption may be as brief as possible, I shall do little more than tabulate the chief grounds (as I see them) for preferring 'liking' to certain other terms that have from time to time been suggested in a subjectivist interest.

If we compare 'liking' first of all with 'desire,' the advantage of the former term is two-fold.

(1) We often ascribe value to an object (or state, activity, etc.) understood to be already in existence, and which we therefore—since desire is always for something conceived as not yet existing—cannot be said to desire. Perhaps it will be said that desire *is* present in such cases, in that we desire the continuance in existence of the object. But clearly that desire is posterior to the consciousness of the value of the object. It is because we value the object, 'like' its existence, that we desire the continuance of its existence. 'Liking' is to be preferred, then, in that, unlike 'desire,' it applies indifferently to the existent and the non-existent, just as valuing does.

(2) Desire, as ordinarily understood, is always an *actual* state of mind,

whereas there are certainly value-*dispositions*. It is awkward, if not impossible, to say that a person desires an object if he does not have a present conscious attitude towards it. Yet he may certainly be said to value an object under these conditions. We may legitimately say that X values exercise, even if we know that while we say it X is in bed asleep. In this respect too, then, 'liking' shows its superiority to 'desire.' For 'likes and dislikes' signify conative dispositions quite as much as they do present mental states.

The claims of 'pleasure' to be the basis of value-consciousness have some *prima facie* strength. But a fatal objection is that we can certainly feel pleasure without being conscious of an object which we are pleased with, or at, whereas value-consciousness is essentially transitive, implying an object which is evaluated. Our chosen term, liking, obviously possesses the same transitive implication. It might be suggested, perhaps, that 'being pleased with' is the basic state. But 'being pleased with' seems to be just a longer way of saying 'liking.'

Mr. Perry's term 'interest'—to take note of one further possibility—does not lie open to any of the above objections. It is transitive, it can refer to dispositions, and it is applicable both to the existent and the non-existent. On the other hand, the use to which this term has been put in the science of Psychology has left it with associations misleading in the present connection, and it has not the natural power, which the term 'liking' possesses, to suggest that favouring attitude of the subject mind which is absolutely fundamental. Moreover, it is a disadvantage that the term 'interest' is applied indifferently to the psychical state and to the object of the psychical state. And, finally, it would be inconvenient to be precluded from using the term 'interest' when we wished to signify that cognitive attentiveness which the term is commonly used to signify.

'Liking,' then, seems on the whole to be the best term to express the basic element in the consciousness of value-for-self. We must now take up our task of tracing the manner in which the concept of value-for-self acquires for the reflective consciousness a much more specific meaning than mere 'objective of self's liking,' owing to the recognition of certain distinctions within objects of liking. I shall set out these distinctions in logical rather than historical order, beginning with the most simple and working towards the more complex.

The first distinction is the very elementary one between objects liked *more* and objects liked *less*. This distinction need not detain us. It introduces, in its crudest form, the distinction between major and minor values-for-self, corresponding to objects of major and minor liking respectively. It ought not, in strictness, to have any effect in modifying the meaning of the concept 'value-for-self'; although I shall have to point out later that it is not altogether certain that it does not in fact have some slight modifying influence.

The next distinction has greater importance. There are some objects that we like for themselves, others that we like only because they help in the attainment of objects liked for themselves. Recognition of this distinction leads us to make a distinction between *end* values-for-self and *instrumental* values-for-self, corresponding to objects of independent and dependent liking respectively. And with the emergence of this distinction the meaning of 'value-for-self' does begin to undergo definite modification. Since it is from end values that instrumental values derive all the value that they possess for us, it will be natural to recognise that it is only end values that have a direct claim to the title 'value.' In so far as this distinction is active in the mind, therefore, there will be a tendency to identify value-for-self not with object of *any* liking of the self, but with object of an *independent* liking of the self.

Our next distinction, one which has very important consequences, arises within the field of end values. It rests upon recognition of the fact that some end values have *also* instrumental value, being conducive to the attainment of certain other things liked for themselves, while other end values have from the same point of view a definite *dis*value. Thus ends like health and knowledge may be liked for themselves, but liked *further* because seen to contribute usefully to the attainment of many other liked things, whereas a good many things liked for themselves, e.g., idleness and gluttony, have quite obviously an opposite tendency. We may perhaps express the situation that arises by saying that end values fall roughly into two classes, according as their main tendency is to co-operate with or to obstruct the end values of the self as a whole.

Now the 'co-operative' end values, if we may so christen them, will certainly be accorded a much higher status as values-for-self than the 'obstructive' end values. But the precise nature of this 'higher status' is something which we must determine with a good deal of care, for in truth we meet here with a very important development in the meaning of the concept 'value-for-self.' There is no question, indeed, of any modification in principle of the original equation 'value-for-self' = 'liked by self.' But a complexity now reveals itself within the meaning of 'liked by *self*' which reacts profoundly upon the meaning of 'value-for-self.' For it now appears that 'liked by self' may mean either, on the one hand, to be an object of liking to the self as a whole, to the self as the unitary centre of its several likings—as in varying degrees is the case with what we have called the 'co-operative' end values—or it may mean, on the other hand, to be an object of liking to the self only in some very partial aspect of its being, and so inimical to the self's other likings as to be more properly called an object of *disliking* to the self as a whole—as in the case of the 'obstructive' end values. Now it can hardly be denied, I think, that it is in the former of these two conceptions of itself, i.e., in its being as the unitary centre of manifold likings, that the self recognises its essential selfhood to consist. Accordingly, it will be only those objects of liking which are harmonious, if not positively at least negatively, with the self's likings as a whole, objects which belong to the class of co-operative end values, or, at the least, of neutral end values, which will now be accepted by the self as genuinely representing what is 'liked by *self*'; and it is they alone which will now be recognised as 'values-for-self.' It is evident that when this distinction has become operative in the mind many things previously regarded as values-for-self will present themselves quite definitely in the light of *dis*values: because, though in one sense still 'liked by self,' in a more profound sense of 'self' they are in antagonism to what is 'liked by self.'

The distinction which is now engaging us concerns our ultimate purpose so closely that I may be excused if, in spite of the limited space at my disposal, I dwell for a little upon its general principle. The general principle is, I think, neither obscure nor seriously debatable. The essence of the matter is just this, that as self-consciousness develops, and the self becomes conscious of itself as the unitary centre of manifold likings, the meaning of 'object of liking to self,' and consequently of 'value to self,' becomes deepened, and in a manner transformed. Whatever is now regarded as good or valuable for the self has got to be something that respects the systematic manifoldness that belongs to the nature of a self. 'Good-for-self' will now mean object not merely of an independent liking, but of an independent and *integral* liking of the self—an 'integral' liking being definable as one which is substantially consistent with the likings of the self as a whole.

We must note now, but more briefly, a further modification of the meaning of value-for-self which arises at the same level of reflective self-consciousness as that which we have just considered. At this same level, the self will become explicitly conscious of its perduring identity, conscious of itself as a relatively *abiding* subject. For a self which so understands its self-hood, an object of liking will tend to be regarded as fully deserving the title of object of the *self's* liking only in so far as the liking in question is of a relatively permanent and not a merely ephemeral character. It would appear, therefore, that the epithet 'relatively permanent' ought to be added to the epithets 'integral' and 'independent' in order to denote accurately the kind of object of liking which is on this developed plane of experience identified with 'value-for-self.'

There is just one other distinction which must, I think, add its quota of meaning to the concept 'value-for-self.' The immediately preceding determinations rested upon the self's consciousness of a distinction between a relatively real and a relatively unreal expression of self-hood. But self-consciousness leads to the recognition of a further distinction within self-hood, the distinction of the self as it is from the self as it is capable of becoming. We become aware of the self containing within itself possibilities of desirable development in a multitude of directions. Now when we consider the significance of this manifestation of our self-consciousness in its relation to the self's likings, we can see that the self will recognise (1) that there are many things which it does not now like, but which it is in principle possible for it to *come* to like; and (2) that among these things there are some which there is good reason to suppose that it is *worth while* coming to like, since we can even now see their nature to be such that the liking of them is in a high degree integral, and relatively permanent, as well as independent. Thus a person might very well have no present liking for scientific pursuits, or for music, but at the same time, because fully realising their fulfilment of the conditions required for a high degree of value-for-self to any self which does like them, he might *want* to like them. What will be the attitude of the value-consciousness towards such objects of prospective but unawakened liking, objects which it does not now like but would only, as it were, *like* to like? On the whole, it seems probable that their relation to the likings of the ideally developed self will bring them recognition as values-for-self in some sense. Just how much the concept of value-for-self must be modified thereby it is not easy to determine, and it is fortunate that, as will become apparent later, this particular modification has not the importance of its predecessors for the fulfilment of our ultimate purpose.

Now we have so far been studying only that branch of our value-consciousness which is connected with the self's consciousness of its *own* likes and dislikes. But man's life is lived in a social medium, and it is very certain that every self is aware that the other selves with whom it is in contact have their likes and dislikes also. To be conscious of a value-for-self relative to one's own likings is thus in principle to be conscious also of a value-for-others relative to others' likings. It must further become apparent at no very advanced level of reflection that likes and dislikes show a considerable amount of variation as between different persons, and that accordingly things which are values for A and B may very well be disvalues for the differently constituted persons C and D. But what must especially engage the attention of man as a member of a social group, of a body organised for a substantially common purpose, is not the values which are private to the individuals A and B and C and D, but the values that are *common* to all of them; the values which are values for *man*, rather than for this man or that man. Doubtless the 'manhood' or 'common human nature' to which reference is thus made will in early communities be interpreted exclusively in terms of the common human nature of the members of that community. But it is clear that this is a stage destined to be superseded with the advance of civilisation. The growing sense of an universal human kinship can hardly fail to bring in its train a conscious interest in a human nature common to all men, and a consequent interest in the concept of a good which is good relatively not merely to the likings of this or that man, nor even to the likings of the typical man of this or that community, but rather good relatively to the likings of man as such, to the likings inherent in the common constitution of human nature.

It is, I think, altogether to be expected that when men have become 'kind-conscious' the concept of 'value for man as such' should evoke a very particular interest. Unlike the concept of value-for-self, it is conspicuously a concept of common interest, and thus an appropriate subject for the mutual interchange of ideas. What is good for the individual A is of great interest to A, but not as a rule of very much interest to individuals B, C and D. But what is good for man as man, in virtue of the common human nature shared by A, B, C and D alike, is a topic of interest to them all, a topic upon which they may pool their powers and their knowledge to mutual advantage. We might perhaps put it this way, that mankind will have little interest in 'subjective' goods *except* where the 'subject' in question is the human self as such.

I think we may regard it as natural, then, that just as our value-consciousness is interested in value-for-self, conceived on the basis of the self's likes and dislikes, so also it should be interested in value-for-man, conceived on the basis of the likes and dislikes inherent in human nature as such. And it seems fairly obvious that substantially the same distinctions whose recognition sharpens, and at the same time gives depth to, the meaning of good-for-self are equally applicable to the conception of good-for-man. The distinctions of major from minor likings, of independent from dependent likings, of integral from partial likings, and of relatively permanent from sporadic likings, all retain their significance when it is the conative constitution of the human self as such, rather than of the individual historic self, that is under consideration: and in a way strictly analogous to that already discussed in the case of good-for-self, the appreciation of these distinctions must issue in the recognition of good-for-man as equivalent not to *any* object of liking to human nature, but rather to 'object of an independent, integral, and relatively permanent liking of human nature.' Thus—to take a simple illustration which may help to elucidate the somewhat arid formula—knowledge would naturally come to be regarded as a good-for-man on the ground that man is so constituted that he has a liking for it which is entertained towards the object for itself, is compatible with his liking nature as a whole, and is relatively enduring.

One distinction appealed to in the determination of the meaning of good-for-self is, however, not here in point, *viz.*, the distinction of present from prospective likings. It is not in point, because the meaning which human nature has for us at any time defines itself, as a matter of course, in terms of all that human nature has ever revealed itself to be, in its most ideally advanced quite as much as in its elementary manifestations. Accordingly, since the most developed human likings of which we have any conception will enter into what we mean by human nature, there will be no room here for a contrast between present and unawakened likings, appropriate as that distinction is to the case of a developing historic self.

As to the distinction of major from minor liking, it is not at first sight obvious whether the epithet 'major' ought not to be added to the qualifications of liking necessary to make an object of liking equivalent to 'good,' both in the case of good-for-self and in the case of good-for-man. Strictly, I do not think it ought to appear. On the other hand, it seems clear that if anyone were attempting to draw up a list of 'goods-for-man' (to confine ourselves to this issue), he would probably not be satisfied to include in the list an object liked for itself, liked integrally, and liked in a relatively permanent way, if it should happen that it was not *also* liked *much*. Perhaps, however, the explanation is really a very simple one, just the fact that any attempt to draw up a list of goods will tend naturally to limit its field to the major representatives of the class. On the whole, I think we should say that the question of major or minor liking has no bearing on the *meaning* of goodness, but has a good deal of influence in determining what things we select as typical examples of 'goods.'

We have reached the point, then, of seeing the meaning of good-for-man, for a developed consciousness, to be an 'object of an independent, integral, and relatively permanent liking of human nature.' I do not mean, of course, that these several determining characters are explicitly present in the minds of all persons who use, even significantly use, the concept 'good-for-man.' But I do maintain that this formula expresses the meaning of the concept which we must suppose to have been operative in men's minds throughout the gradual process of determining what things are good for man, if that process has been a work of intelligence at all. This is the meaning, I believe, which has underlain and guided, whether explicitly recognised or not, the unsystematic reflections of the value-consciousness of generations of men, reflections which have resulted in the now traditional acceptance by the civilised world of a more or less definite set of things as pre-eminently 'goods-for-man.'

But *are* there certain things that have received this public and traditional endorsement? The phrase 'good-for-man' is not a common phrase in ordinary discourse, and the critic may very reasonably ask what kind of value-judgment I have in mind when I speak of the value-consciousness of mankind having found expression in the endorsement of a definitive set of things as good-for-man. I answer—and here we come to the kernel of the matter—that the kind of judgment I have in mind is precisely the kind of judgment which is commonly supposed by the Objectivist to assert a good simple and unqualified, an 'intrinsic' good. When goodness is predicated of such things as knowledge or æsthetic experience, the Objectivist holds that we are using, or may be using, the term goodness in an absolutely simple, unrelational, unanalysable sense. I contend against this that the apparent simplicity is never a real simplicity; that actually there underlies the predication of goodness in all such cases the conception of a certain relationship between the things and the emotional nature of man as we know it, a relationship which is indispensable to the recognition of the things as good; and that this relationship is precisely expressed by saying that the things are objects of independent, integral, and relatively permanent liking to human nature.

This then is our hypothesis. And before considering the evidence in its favour it will be well to deal at once with an obvious objection. If people really mean 'good-for-man' in these judgments, why do they say just 'good'? The objection is, I think, less formidable than it appears. It seems appropriate, on reflection, that the relational qualification should tend to drop out where the relativity in question is to our common human nature. In the case of a quality which (as we claim to be the case with goodness) is naturally thought of as relative to persons in some sense, it will be necessary to add a relational phrase only where a *special* relativity to some *special* person or persons is intended. If *no* relativity is indicated, the natural presumption will be that the quality is relative not to any special party, but just to our common human nature. Hence the *omission* of the relational qualification may be said in such cases to serve exactly the same purpose as would be served by its *inclusion*. We might perhaps imagine a parallel case, to illustrate our point, in respect of colour-judgments. Even if we all believed, as many people do believe, that red is red only for man, we should continue to say 'this is red,' not 'this is red-for-man.' We should only feel the need of appending a relational qualification if the relativity was to an *individual:* as, e.g., a colour-blind person who was aware of his peculiarity might say 'this is red *to me.*' The omission of a relational qualification would imply that the relativity was merely to our common sensitive organisation.

Passing from this difficulty which meets us at the threshold, let us now consider the positive evidence that the formula I have reiterated does represent, in the sense of making fully explicit, what is really meant by good when that term is predicated in an ostensibly unqualified sense. The first and the chief point to which I wish to call attention is that the so-called 'intrinsic' goods of the Objectivist are precisely the kind of things that would come to be called just 'good' if our theory of the meaning given to goodness is correct. If goodness means the quality of being an object of independent, integral and relatively permanent liking to human nature, then the particular group of things which tradition has called just 'good,' and which the Objectivist declares therefore to be intrinsically good, is exactly the group of things that we should expect. Truth and Beauty, for example, in their more philosophical dress as knowledge and æsthetic experience, fall into line at once. Each has in a pre-eminent degree the characteristic of being an object of independent, integral, relatively permanent,—and we may properly add here, major—liking of human nature. And the same thing may be said of such goods as health and friendship, on whose behalf the common value-consciousness of mankind has also made high, though less high, claims. Pleasure, I agree, occupies a somewhat equivocal position for our formula. It is an object of human liking, of major liking, of independent liking, and of relatively permanent liking. But whether or not it is an object of *integral* liking, a liking consistent with the liking nature as a whole, depends entirely upon what *kind* of pleasure it is. But then is not this equivocal position of pleasure for our formula precisely the kind of position it occupies for the value-consciousness of mankind also? The general attitude towards pleasure would probably be expressed fairly enough by saying that it is regarded as good in so far as it is not seriously obstructive of other values. But if so, that would admirably fit in with our formula. For it would mean that wherever the pleasure was of such a kind that it could be an object of integral liking to man it would be a good; and if not of such a kind, not good. But that is just what would be maintained if our formula were operative.

Now this applicability of our formula to the so-called intrinsic goods is not, indeed, conclusive *proof* that our formula expresses what is really meant in these contexts by goodness. Nevertheless, I think we may say that if this is *not* what is meant by goodness, then the applicability of the formula is a very odd coincidence indeed. Actually, I think we are entitled to go further. I think we are entitled to say that the onus of proof now lies upon the Objectivist. For consider just where we stand. Our account started from a value-experience, admittedly subjectivist, which all must concede to be actual, and it proceeded from that basis to show, without any appeal to other than well-recognised psychical and other factors, how man would eventually come to pronounce as 'good,' without explicit relational qualification, whatever was an object of independent, integral, and relatively permanent liking to human nature. We then found that the very things which are in *fact* pronounced to be good in this way—the so-called 'intrinsic goods'—possess all the characteristics of our formula. The Objectivist, on the other hand, has to appeal to an unique kind of perception whose claim to be something real is still, at best, *sub judice,* and whose strangely erratic behaviour even among its best friends is something of a scandal. Moreover, as was hinted earlier, the Objectivist is powerless to explain why so many mutually contradictory things have been called good in the same apparently unqualified way by different peoples in different ages—a phenomenon which is easily explicable on our view, since we can recognise the vast difference which different conditions of life and different levels of mental development must make to the things that are conceived to be objects of integral, independent and relatively permanent liking to human nature. It seems to me, therefore, that the onus of proof now lies upon the Objectivist, our present theory being one of greater *prima facie* probability. And I propose to devote most of what time remains to repelling objections to our theory, rather than to seeking for further positive support.

5

It will not, I think, present itself as a very serious objection to anyone that our formula is certainly not explicitly present in the minds of most of those who predicate goodness (in the context we have been considering). It seems fairly clear that a formula can accurately represent what persons really mean by good even though they have no recognisable version of the formula before them. In ordinary discourse we are very seldom indeed conscious of the full definitory meaning of the complex terms that we use;

and yet, in so far as we are using the terms intelligently, that meaning is operative in and controlling our usage. I am glad here to be able to enlist the authority of Dr. Ross. 'It appears,' he writes, 'as if we cannot avoid recognising that there is such a thing as using a term which implicitly refers to a certain complex, while yet the complex is not explicitly present to our minds. And in principle this might, it seems, be true of good.' [8] After all, even in philosophical discourse, the valuable maxim 'define your terms' has to be applied with something less than absolute rigour if the argument is to advance at a tolerable pace at all.

But by what test, it may fairly be asked, are we to determine whether any particular complex, not explicitly before our minds when we use a term, is in fact implicitly present? Again I am well content with Dr. Ross's answer. 'If it is the correct definition,' he holds, 'what should happen is that after a certain amount of attention to it we should be able to say "Yes, that is what I meant by 'good' all along, though I was not clearly conscious till now that it *was* what I meant." ' [9] The process of criticising proposed definitions, he adds, has two moments. A definition of a term must be rejected if (*a*) we are able to point to things of which the term is predicable and the definition not, or *vice versa;* or if (*b*) even when the denotations of the term and of the definition coincide (or when we cannot be sure that they do not), we can 'see that a proposed definition does not express what we *mean* by the term to be defined.' [10] This seems to me to be a valid and valuable statement of the situation, and I should make no objection whatever to the application of such a test to the formula I have put forward as representing the meaning of 'good' in the value-judgments which 'at the first look' predicate intrinsic goodness. I am well aware, of course, that in Dr. Ross's judgment the application of the test proves fatal to *all* relational definitions of the nature of goodness. But while fully agreeing that it is fatal to the relational definitions which Dr. Ross actually cites, and which he appears to have alone before his mind, I must point out that our particular variety of relational definition does not appear in Dr. Ross's list at all—either explicitly or implicitly.

It will be worth our while, however, to consider with some care Dr. Ross's criticism of relational definitions of goodness, or at least of the subjectivist group of relational definitions. For, while we are claiming exemption for our own particular formula, it is evident that Dr. Ross intends his criticism to have an exhaustive reference. On pages 80–83 [10a] he furnishes what, I take it, he regards as a systematic classification of those theories of the nature of goodness which make goodness depend upon a relation to subjective or psychological factors. He arranges them under two main heads, *A* and *B*. *A* consists of those theories which hold that a thing's being good means that some person has, or some persons have, some

---

[8] *The Right and the Good*, p. 93 [p. 323 this volume].
[9] *Ibid.*
[10] *Ibid.*
[10a] [pp. 314 ff. this volume].

kind of *feeling* towards it, *B* of those theories which hold that what is meant is rather that some person *thinks*, or some persons *think*, the thing to be good. Upon the second group, *B*, Dr. Ross wastes few words; and, being in perfect accord with all that he says, I propose to waste even fewer by making no further reference to this type of theory. But we must follow Dr. Ross into his sub-division of group *A*, to which our own theory would most naturally belong, and which Dr. Ross allows to possess a much greater *prima facie* plausibility than the other group. The sub-division adopted will be best explained in its author's own words. 'Theories of this type,' he says, 'are divisible into those which identify goodness with the presence of some feeling (1) in at least one person, no matter who he is, (2) in the person who judges an object to be good, (3) in a majority of persons of some class or other—say persons belonging to a particular stage in the history of civilisation, (4) in a majority of mankind, or (5) in all mankind.' [11]

Now of course the most conspicuous feature of Dr. Ross's classification from our point of view is that it omits altogether the particular variety of type *A* which seems to ourselves to offer the true definition. For it need scarcely be pointed out that being an object of liking to human nature is by no means identical with being an object of liking either to all mankind or to a majority of all mankind—while much less is it identical with any of the other suggested formulæ. Yet there is surely nothing unintelligible, or even strained, about the concept 'object of liking to *human nature*.' There are appropriate objects of liking to human nature just as there are appropriate objects to cat nature or dog nature. Cat nature is so constituted as to like stalking its prey and to dislike immersion in water. What is the difficulty about saying that human nature is so constituted as to like and dislike certain specific things also? Indeed, aren't we saying that kind of thing almost every day of our lives? And aren't our psychologists busily engaged at this very time in trying to ascertain just what the basic likes and dislikes of human nature are? And wasn't it the chief aim of the Greek moralist to determine what mode of life human nature was so constituted as in the end, and on the whole, to like best?

I hope, then, that no one will retort against me that while Tom, Dick or Harry can have likings, it is not possible to assign likings to what is not a person but an abstraction, *viz.*, human nature. If we are to take that view in earnest, then we ought likewise to insist, I presume, that *instincts* cannot intelligibly be assigned to human nature either, since, strictly speaking, it is only an actual living creature that can have an instinct. But I fancy that the critic would wish neither to forbid other people to speak, nor himself to refrain from speaking, of 'the instincts of human nature.' In neither case is there any real difficulty about the meaning that is intended. Just as there are instincts which men have in virtue of their common human nature, so too there are likings which men have, or tend to come to have, in virtue of their common human nature.

[11] *The Right and the Good*, pp. 82–83 [p. 316 this volume].

But perhaps the best analogy for our usage is provided by the usage of the Greek philosophers in their search after man's *summum bonum*. Who is the 'man' whose *summum bonum* is sought? Not surely any particular man, but just 'man as such,' the exemplar of our common human nature. The Greek moralist works with a *type man*, constituted by the conative, emotional, and intellectual proclivities believed to be common to human nature, sets him in a natural and social environment which, though inevitably relative to the age and place of the moralist, is made as little specific as possible, and seeks to determine what mode of life will afford the fullest satisfaction to a being so constituted and so conditioned. It is not anything essentially dissimilar, in my judgment, that mass opinion has been doing in the long process of constructing its list of 'goods for man.' The chief difference is due to the simple fact that in the one case the process is undertaken with scientific thoroughness and method, and in the other case not. That is why mass opinion is content with a set of pre-eminent *goods*, and does not concern itself with the deeper, and to ethical science vitally important, question of the relation of these goods to one another within the unity of *the good*. But so far as the concept of 'human nature' is concerned, the procedure seems fundamentally the same; and there seems no more difficulty in applying the concept in one case than in the other.

I must claim, then, that the subjectivist definition of good which I have placed before you is not to be put out of court on the score of being unintelligible, and I must insist that Dr. Ross's criticism of subjectivist theories is not exhaustive of the type so long as the classification upon which it is based ignores this particular variety. It *might* be the case, indeed, that the exclusion of it was only formal. That is, it might be the case that some of Dr. Ross's criticisms of the theories on his list are capable of being adapted, with more or less trifling modifications, to the destruction of our theory too. It is therefore of first-rate importance to observe that this is not even remotely the case—as anyone may assure himself by even a cursory inspection of the relevant pages of Dr. Ross's book.[12] His criticisms simply do not touch our theory at all. And this is not really surprising. For in spite of superficial resemblances, there is one highly important difference between our theory and any of those which Dr. Ross considers. Each of Dr. Ross's theories makes the goodness of a thing depend upon the feelings (we may say, for convenience, the 'likings') of *some definitive existing person or persons*. Now it is extremely easy to show, as Dr. Ross does clearly show, that when we say 'X is good' we are not, as these theories would imply, meaning to assign to X a quality so impermanent that its coming to belong to X, and its ceasing to belong to X, are contingent upon the mere shift of favour on the part of some particular person or persons. There is undoubtedly an implication of permanence and 'objectivity' about our more 'absolute' value-judgments which belies any such description. But if

[12] *The Right and the Good*, pp. 83–84 [pp. 316–17 this volume].

goodness is made relative, as we make it, to the likings not of definitive persons but of human nature as such, this implication is saved. If what we mean when (in these value-judgments) we say 'X is good' is that X is related in a certain way to the liking nature of *man*, we are not implying, nor indeed even allowing, that X's possession of goodness is at the mercy of the changing likes and dislikes of any persons whatsoever.

I want to turn next—and, I may add, finally—to a difficulty of quite a different kind. It would, naturally, be a crushing objection to our theory, as to any other relational theory of the nature of goodness, if the Objectivist were able to exhibit to us *just one thing* (other, of course, than moral virtue) whose goodness is beyond question underived from relationship to subjective liking or to anything else. Has this ever been achieved? I am going to argue here that no Objectivist has even come near to achieving it. There are, of course, in the writings of all Objectivist axiologists chapters ostensibly directed to 'proving' some selected list of 'intrinsic' values. But close inspection will, I think, reveal a fatal flaw in these arguments. What we find in them is, as a rule, a very cogent demonstration that certain things are good irrespective of any relation to other *goods*, but it is merely *taken for granted*, on the basis of a prior attempted refutation in principle of subjectivist accounts of the nature of goodness, that these things are good irrespective of any relation to subjective feelings *also*. Hence if the prior 'refutation' be itself fallacious (as we have seen reason to believe must be maintained in Dr. Ross's case), the proof of the intrinsic value of particular good things will be fundamentally defective.

I shall illustrate once again by a reference to Dr. Ross's stimulating book. In his short chapter upon 'What things are good' Dr. Ross claims to be offering considerations which will assist the reader to apprehend virtue and knowledge and certain other things as each having a value absolutely in and for itself. What the reader in fact finds is that his arguments are one and all designed to demonstrate that the goodness of each of these goods is independent of any relationship to other goods, but that nothing whatsoever is done to show that the goodness in question is independent of a relationship to subjective feelings. The latter question is not, I think, affected one way or the other by a single word in the whole chapter. We may take the thoroughly typical argument whereby Dr. Ross seeks to persuade us of the intrinsic value of knowledge. He ask us [13] to 'suppose two states of the universe equal in respect of virtue and of pleasure and of the allocation of pleasure to the virtuous, but such that the persons in the one have a far greater understanding of the nature and laws of the universe than those in the other. Can any one doubt,' he goes on, 'that the first would be a *better* state of the universe?' Dr. Ross expects, and rightly expects, that this question will receive an affirmative answer. But I must point out that an affirmative answer does not carry with it a recognition of *intrinsic* value in knowledge. Dr. Ross has so constructed his hypothetical

[13] *The Right and the Good*, p. 139.

situation that an affirmative answer certainly entails the recognition that knowledge has a value which is not dependent upon a relationship to other *goods*. But, so far as his argument here is concerned, it must remain an entirely open question whether the value recognised is an 'objective' quality, or whether, on the other hand, it is dependent upon a relationship to subjective factors—such as, e.g., the likings of human nature. The terms of Dr. Ross's argument are such that no light at all can be shed upon this crucial issue.

How, one might ask, would Dr. Ross's argument require to be supplemented in order to become relevant to the question of the *objectivity* of the value of knowledge? It would, I think, be formally satisfactory if, in being invited to appraise the relative value of these two states of the universe, we were at the same time instructed to rule out from our minds all considerations arising from our familiarity with human likes and dislikes. Thus we should be obliged to suppose, for the sake of the argument, that there is no native impulse of curiosity in man which makes him come to like knowing for its own sake. If, fulfilling these conditions, we were to proceed to put to ourselves Dr. Ross's question, an affirmative answer *would*, I think, imply the recognition of a strictly 'intrinsic' value in knowledge.

But *should* we then be able to return an affirmative answer? It is a matter which each must decide for himself by personal experiment, but I feel convinced that, if the experiment be performed with due observance of the conditions, only a negative answer will be found possible. No legitimate ground remains, I believe, for judging the first state of the universe to be the better. Old emotional habits, like old cognitive habits, die hard, and there is undoubtedly a great mass of prepossessions to be broken through before one can hope to return a fair answer. But I must leave the experiment with the reader, pausing only to draw attention to two pitfalls which seem especially liable to engulf the unwary. (1) We know that knowledge, even if it were not itself liked, would still be instrumental to a host of things that are liked, and this makes it difficult for us not to think of the state of the universe with knowledge as the 'better' state. But it is clear that the terms of the hypothesis make this consideration irrelevant. Reference to other goods, whether as 'objects of liking' or in any other sense, is definitely ruled out. (2) A good many of us are more deeply influenced than we are apt to realise by an inherited religious tradition which leads us to think of our faculties as given to us by God for use and development, so that it is in accord with the Will of God, and so far 'good,' that they should be exercised to the full. On this ground alone there is a powerful disposition in most of us to regard a state of the universe in which the faculty of knowledge finds active expression as better than a state in which it does not. Evidently, however, we are not, in making this judgment, recognising knowledge to be something 'good in itself.' We are merely recognising respect for the gifts of God, or obedience to the Divine Will, to be a duty.[14]

It appears to me, then, that Dr. Ross totally fails to demonstrate the objective goodness of his 'intrinsic goods,' and I am not able to conceive any other method likely to yield a different result. Dr. Moore's attempt fails for exactly the same reason as Dr. Ross's. His argument in Chapter VI of *Principia Ethica* depends essentially upon a prior supposed refutation of relational theories of the meaning of good in Chapter I; and, as we noted earlier, Dr. Moore is himself the latest recruit to the ranks of those who find the reasoning of Chapter I fallacious. I do not find, therefore, in Dr. Moore's attempted demonstration of intrinsic goods anything which places in serious jeopardy the central contention of this paper—the contention that there is nothing whatsoever, with the single exception of moral virtue, which does not derive its goodness from a relationship to subjective liking.

6

It is more than time that this paper drew to its belated close. Nevertheless, I must add just a very few brief words upon a matter alluded to at an early stage of the paper, if I am to round off my theory with any pretence of completeness at all. It has been an implication of my argument that when we predicate value of morally virtuous conduct we mean something rather radically different by the term value from what we mean when we predicate value of anything else whatsoever. In the latter applications the meaning always involves an essential relation to human liking. In the former application no such reference is involved. Yet there clearly must be some common factor in the two meanings. Otherwise, why use the same term 'good' or 'valuable' in both cases? What is this common factor? What is the analogy between the usages which justifies us in employing common terms?

The correct answer, I think, is that all usages of the term 'good' signify at least this common feature in that to which goodness is attributed, *viz.*, that it is the object of what may perhaps least misleadingly be called a *pro*-attitude: just as that to which badness is attributed is always the object of a *contra*-attitude. An object of liking is quite obviously the object of a *pro*-attitude. But it is equally obvious, when we reflect upon it, that morally

---

[14] It must be admitted that it is extremely difficult, in an ideal experiment such as that which we are here called upon to perform, to prevent one's value-judgments from being affected by the cross-currents of moral and religious duty. Many, perhaps most, educated persons, even apart from religious considerations, believe it to be their duty to develop their capacity for knowledge. On that account the conception of 'knowledge' is closely associated in their minds with the conception of 'goodness.' But clearly the effort has got to be made to abstract from the influence of this connection, if we are seeking to discover, by the device of experiment upon our value-responses, whether knowledge is good simply *as such*, in and by itself, as the Objectivist claims that it is.

virtuous conduct is likewise the object of a *pro*-attitude. The latter *pro*-attitude is certainly not the same kind of *pro*-attitude as is entertained towards an object of mere liking. But a *pro*-attitude it undoubtedly is. The identity and the difference can probably be made most plainly apparent by reflecting upon the value-judgments ingredient in any simple case of so-called 'moral temptation,' in which the course we believe that we ought to follow is recognised to be incompatible with the course that we like best. Our mental attitudes towards the two courses are conspicuously different, but both of them are beyond question *pro*-attitudes. Indeed, if they were not, there could be no consciousness of inner conflict. It is equally certain, on the one hand, that the morally right course does not appeal to our mere 'liking,' and, on the other hand, that it does *appeal* to us. Its appeal is such, indeed, that it may be made by us the motive of our act, and thus be adopted as our 'end' in preference to that which we 'like best.'

If this is true, it appears that what we mean ultimately when we predicate goodness of moral virtue is that it is an object of approval or favour to the moral consciousness. Does this then imply, it may perhaps be asked, that even the goodness of moral virtue is in the last resort 'subjective,' consisting in a certain relationship to a state of consciousness? It is, I think, partly a question of the use of words. Most people, however, would probably agree that the moral consciousness, though it must be *in* a subject, is yet not 'subjective' in the same sense as desires and likings are 'subjective.' But I cannot now embark upon the long and arduous task of defining the true status within the self—much less within the whole scheme of things—of the moral consciousness. A fully adequate theory of value could not, I am sure, be dispensed from this obligation. But the pretensions of the present paper are more modest. I am content if I have established a *prima facie* case for the view that the meaning of value as applied to all the so-called intrinsic values with the exception of moral virtue involves an essential relationship to human liking.

Some Reflections on Moral-Sense Theories
in Ethics *

C. D. BROAD

DURING THE Long Vacation of 1944 I spent such time as I could spare from my other duties in reading with some care Richard Price's book *A Review of the Principal Questions and Difficulties in Morals*. This was first published in 1758, and it reached a third edition in 1787. Price died soon afterwards, *viz.*, in 1791. Until Ross published his book *The Right and the Good* in 1930 there existed, so far as I know, no statement and defence of what may be called the "rationalistic" type of ethical theory comparable in merit to Price's. Price was thoroughly well acquainted with the works of other great English philosophers and moralists, such as Locke, Berkeley, Hume and Butler, and he developes his own views in conscious opposition to those of Hutcheson, the founder of the so-called "moral-sense" type of ethical theory.

I had thought at one time of writing a critical account of Price's doctrines. But, when I began to do so, I soon found that it would be more profitable to treat independently and in modern terminology some of the questions with which Price was mainly concerned. Therefore my further references to Price will be only occasional and incidental; but I wish to make it plain that his book is the background of my paper, and that reading the former was the stimulus to writing the latter.

The topic with which I shall be primarily concerned may be called the "epistemology of moral judgments." This subject is of considerable interest in itself, and I think that it has been very inadequately treated by most writers on ethics. But it is important also for another reason. Questions of epistemology and of logical analysis are interconnected, and the answer which we give to a question of the one kind may have an important bearing on that which we should be inclined to give to a question of the other kind, e.g., I should be prepared to argue that, if ethical terms, such as *right* and *good*, are simple and non-naturalistic or are complex and contain a non-naturalistic constituent, then the concepts of them must be wholly or partly *a priori*. On the same hypothesis I should be prepared to argue that

* Reprinted by kind permission of the author and the editors from the *Proceedings of the Aristotelian Society*, 45, 1944–5.

such judgments as "Any act of promise-keeping tends as such to be right" must be synthetic and *a priori*. Now it is a well-known and plausible epistemological theory that there are no *a priori* concepts and no synthetic *a priori* judgments. If I am right, anyone who feels no doubt about this epistemological theory can safely reject the analysis of moral judgments which makes them contain non-naturalistic constituents. On the other hand, anyone who feels bound to accept that analysis of moral judgments will have to reject this epistemological theory.

In the discussion which follows I shall confine myself to the concepts *right* and *wrong*, in the specifically moral sense, and to judgments in which they occur as predicates. I think that most of what I say could be transferred *mutatis mutandis* to the concepts *morally good* and *evil* and to judgments in which they occur.

As Price points out, the words "right" and "wrong" are used in at least two different senses. This is made obvious by the fact that the sentence "It is always right for a person to do what he honestly believes to be right, and wrong for him to do what he honestly believes to be wrong," is intelligible and would generally be admitted to be in some sense true. The two senses in which "right" and "wrong" occur in this sentence may be described as the "subjective" and the "material." An act is subjectively right if the consequences which the agent *expects* it to have are such as he *thinks* would be materially right in the situation as he *believes* it to be. We shall be concerned here only with material rightness and wrongness. Let us call sentences in which the words "right" or "wrong," used in the material sense, occur as predicates "deontic sentences." An example would be "Any act of promise-breaking tends as such to be wrong."

I shall first distinguish certain alternative analyses which have been proposed for the situations expressed by deontic sentences, and then I shall consider certain alternative theories which might be held concerning deontic knowledge or belief. In the course of the discussion I shall try to bring out the relations between the two sets of theories.

(1) *Alternative Analyses of Deontic Sentences*—When a person utters such a sentence as "That act is right" he seems *prima facie* to be expressing a judgment, and in that judgment he seems *prima facie* to be ascribing to a subject a predicate which has no reference to his own or other men's sensations, emotions, desires, or opinions. But we know that such appearances may be misleading. Such sentences as "This food is nice" and "That thing is yellow" are of the same grammatical form as "That act is right." Yet everyone would hold that the predicate of the first refers to the speaker's sensations of taste, and many people would hold that the predicate of the second refers to the visual sensations of human beings. So the first question to be asked is this. Do sentences like "That act is right" express judgments at all? If not, what do they express?"

As is well known, there is a theory that such sentences do not really express judgments at all. It has been held that they express only certain emotions felt by the speaker, or certain desires of his, or certain commands. I shall call this the "Interjectional Theory." Price does not consider this extreme view. If it had been put to him, he would probably have regarded it as too fantastically absurd to be taken seriously. It is, indeed, the kind of theory which can be swallowed only after one has undergone a long and elaborate process of "conditioning" which was not available in the eighteenth century.

Suppose that the Interjectional Theory is rejected. Suppose we hold that deontic sentences do express judgments of *some* kind, and that at any rate the fact that they are in the indicative mood is not misleading. The next suggestion is that the judgments which they express are really about certain human experiences, certain sensations or emotions or desires. I shall call this the "Subjective Theory." I shall now point out that it may take a great number of different forms, and shall try to classify them.

The factor common to all forms of the Subjective Theory is that there is a peculiar kind of experience which human beings are liable to have when they contemplate certain acts, e.g., acts of promise-keeping or of treachery, just as there is a peculiar kind of experience which they have when they look at certain objects, e.g., at snow or at soot. I propose to call this at present by the intentionally vague name "moral feeling." I use this term because it covers both sensation and emotion. Since deontic judgments take the two opposite forms "That is right" and "That is wrong," it must be assumed that moral feeling takes two opposite forms. There are analogies to this both in sensation and emotion. There are the opposed temperature-sensations of hotness and coldness, and there are the opposed non-moral emotions of love and hate. I shall speak of the "pro-form" and the "anti-form" of moral feeling, and will assume that the former is associated with judgments of rightness and the latter with those of wrongness. The first division of Subjective Theories is into *Sensational* and *Emotional*, according to whether moral feeling is held to be analogous to sensation and moral judgment to be analogous judgments of sense-perception, or whether the feeling is held to be a form of emotion and the judgments to be concerned with that emotion.

The next division of Subjective Theories is into what I will call the "Intra-subjective" and the "Trans-subjective" varieties. According to the first of these a person who judges that so-and-so is right is asserting something about *his own* moral pro-feelings only. He is not saying anything about the moral feelings of other men. According to the second variety such a person is asserting something about all men, or most men, or a certain restricted class of men, and not only about himself.

Lastly, each of these two varieties of the Subjective Theory can be subdivided into what I call an "Occurrent" and a "Dispositional" form. On the occurrent form of the intra-subjective variety of the subjective theory a person who says that so-and-so is right is asserting only that at this moment he is having a moral pro-emotion towards so-and-so. On the occurrent form of the trans-subjective variety of the theory he is asserting that all or most members of a certain class of men, e.g., most members of the *Athenæum*, are at present having a moral pro-emotion towards so-and-so. On the dispositional form of the intra-subjective variety of the theory he is asserting that he has a disposition to feel a moral pro-emotion whenever he contemplates so-and-so or other acts like it. He may not be feeling such an emotion at the moment when he is saying that so-and-so is bright. He might not be actually witnessing or thinking of such an act at the time; or, if he were, he might be in some special occurrent state, such as anger or jealousy, which is inhibiting or reversing his disposition to feel moral pro-emotion. On the dispositional form of the trans-subjective variety of the theory he is asserting that all or most men or all or most members of a certain class of men have a disposition to feel moral pro-emotion when they contemplate so-and-so or other acts like it. He might have strong reason to believe this even if he lacked that disposition himself. I have, e.g., strong reason to believe that most men have a disposition to like the taste and smell of apples, though I personally loathe them.

It appears then that there are at least eight possible species of the Subjective Theory, according as it is (i) sensational or emotional, (ii) intra-subjective or trans-subjective, or (iii) occurrent or dispositional. There are two remarks that I would make at this point.

(i) Even on the occurrent intra-subjective form of the theory such a statement as "That act is wrong" could be questioned without accusing the speaker of lying about his own feelings at the time. But this could happen only in one way. The speaker might be mistaken about the kind of feeling which he is having when contemplating this act. He might think that he is having a moral anti-feeling when really he is having what Sidgwick calls a "feeling of quasi-moral repugnance." I have no doubt that such mistakes are often made by people, e.g., about their own feelings towards abnormal sexual desires and practices. (ii) I am inclined to think that the only form of the theory that is worth serious consideration is the trans-subjective dispositional form of it. But I should admit that it is not unplausible to hold that *sometimes* when a person says that so-and-so is right or that it is wrong he may be talking only of his own disposition to have a moral pro-feeling or anti-feeling when he contemplates such acts.

So far I have spoken only of singular deontic judgments, i.e., those of the form "That act is right (or is wrong)." But there are also universal deontic judgments, such as "Any act of promise-keeping tends as such to be right" or "Any act of deliberate deception tends as such to be wrong." How would the Subjective Theory deal with the latter? Let us take, e.g., the trans-subjective dispositional form of the subjective theory and consider how it would deal with "Any act of promise-keeping tends as such to be right." It would say that this is equivalent to "Any person contemplating an act which he believed to be one of promise-keeping would tend to have a moral pro-feeling in so far as he confined his attention to that aspect of the act." No doubt this might require various qualifications, e.g., we might have to substitute "any *normal* person" for "any person" in order to allow for moral lunatics, and we might have to add "provided he were in a normal state at the time" in order to allow for the possibility of his disposition to have a moral pro-feeling being inhibited or reversed if he were in a state of rage or of jealousy. But the general principle is clear enough.

Next let us suppose that all forms of the Subjective Theory are dismissed. We should then have to accept some form of what I will call the "Objective Theory." According to this a deontic judgment ascribes to an act a certain quality or relation or relational property which has no reference to the feelings or desires or opinions of the speaker or of anyone else concerning that act. Such judgments would be significant and might be true even if no human being had ever had moral feelings of any kind.

No doubt the Objective Theory might take many different forms. But for our purpose the most important principle of division is the following. Let us describe an "ethical sentence" by enumeration as any sentence in which the words "right" or "wrong," "ought" or "ought not," "morally good" or "morally evil" or mere dictionary equivalents of them occur. Now, if the words "right" and "wrong" denote opposite forms of a certain objective characteristic, the following possibilities are open about that characteristic. (i) It may be simple and therefore indefinable, as, e.g., the quality of sensible yellowness and the relation of temporal precedence are. (ii) It may be complex and therefore definable. If so, it may be definable (*a*) only by means of ethical sentences or (*b*) without the use of such sentences. The following alleged definitions of "right" would illustrate these two possibilities. The first would be exemplified if "right" could be defined only as "what it is *fitting* to approve" or only as "what is conducive to *morally good* experiences." The second would be exemplified if "right" were definable as "conducive to social stability" or as "productive of a balance of *pleasant* experiences." I propose to give the name "naturalistic" to (i) all forms of the Subjective Theory, and (ii) any form of the Objective Theory which holds that "right" and "wrong" are definable without the use of ethical sentences. I shall give the name "non-naturalistic" to any form of the Objective Theory which holds that "right" and "wrong" are either indefinable or definable only by means of ethical sentences. For the present purpose it is not important to consider whether this use of "naturalistic" and "non-naturalistic" agrees exactly either in extension or in intension with Professor Moore's usage.

Before leaving this topic there is one further remark to be made. I think it is fair to say that most competent persons who have reflected on this subject in recent years would agree that the only alternatives worth serious consideration are some form of either (*a*) the Interjectional Theory, or (*b*) the dispositional variety of the Subjective Theory, or (*c*) the non-naturalistic variety of the Objective Theory. Perhaps I should add that under the head of "competent persons" in this connexion I do not include the eminent natural scientists who from time to time take a holiday from their professional labours in order to instruct us in ethical theory.

(2) *Alternative Epistemological Theories of Deontic Cognition.*—I shall begin by considering singular deontic judgments, i.e., ones of the form: "That act is right (or is wrong)." Presumably those moralists who hold a Moral Sense Theory intend at least to assert that these judgments are analogous in certain important respects to judgments of sense-perception, such as "That thing is yellow."

Now the first thing to notice is that two very different accounts may be given of such judgments as "That thing is yellow." These may be described as the Naïvely Realistic Account and the Dispositional Account. I will now explain these terms.

(i) I think that the plain man in his plainer moments uncritically takes for granted that the very same sensible quality of yellowness which is presented to him when he looks at a bit of gold in white light literally pervades the surface of that bit of gold, not only when he is looking at it in white light, but also and in precisely the same sense when no one is looking at it and when it is in the dark. He believes that looking at the thing and its being illuminated by white light serve only to *reveal* to him the yellowness which has been there all the time in precisely the form in which it is now presented to him. This is what I call the "Naïvely Realistic Interpretation." Price seems to have thought that this, or something like it, is what plain men believe. He also thought that this belief is not only mistaken, but can be seen to be internally inconsistent by anyone who reflects carefully on the natures of sensible yellowness and of material objects. I must confess that I cannot see this myself.

(ii) A person who makes the judgment "That thing is yellow" may be expressing *only* his belief that it would present a yellow appearance to any normal human being who might at any time view it in white light. No doubt a person who accepts the Naïvely Realistic Interpretation also believes this conditional proposition. But this belief is certainly not the whole of what he expresses by saying "That thing is yellow," and it might not even be a part of it. It might be for him only a very obvious and immediate consequence of what he expresses by that statement. I give the name "Dispositional Account" to the view that the whole meaning of such judgments as "That thing is yellow" is a conditional proposition of the kind which I have just enunciated.

The next point to notice is this. If a person believes that a certain thing would present a yellow appearance to any normal human being who should at any time view it in white light, he does not generally accept this conditional proposition as an ultimate fact. He generally amplifies it as follows. He ascribes to the thing a certain intrinsic property, and he ascribes to each human being a certain other intrinsic property correlated with the former. Let us call these respectively the "objective" and the "subjective correlate" in the perception of yellowness. It is held that when and only when a certain relationship is set up between a human being and this thing the subjective correlate in the person and the objective correlate in the thing together cause the thing to present a yellow appearance to the person.

This is common ground to the holders of the Naïvely Realistic and of the Dispositional Account. But there is a profound difference between them in point of detail. On the Naïvely Realistic Interpretation the objective correlate just is that quality of sensible yellowness which, according to that theory, is spread out over the surface of the thing ready to be presented whenever the appropriate revelatory conditions are fulfilled. The subjective correlate just is the power of prehending the yellowness of yellow things when such conditions are fulfilled. That power is activated whenever a person who possesses it stands in a certain bodily and mental relation to a thing which possesses yellowness.

On the Dispositional Interpretation the objective correlate is generally held to be a certain kind of minute structure and internal agitation in a thing which is not itself literally and non-dispositionally coloured. Again, the subjective correlate is not now the power of prehending the objective correlate. We have no such power. It is the capacity to have sensations of a certain kind, called "sensations of yellowness"; and these are not prehensions of a quality of yellowness inherent in the thing perceived. There is no such quality. That power is activated whenever a person who possesses it stands in a certain bodily and mental relation to a thing which has this peculiar kind of minute structure and internal agitation.

I do not think that anyone who accepted the dispositional interpretation would give the name "yellowness" to that minute structure and internal agitation of a colourless object which, according to him, is the objective correlate of sensations of yellow. He would confine the name "yellow" to (a) the peculiar sensible quality of certain sensations, e.g., those which he has when he looks at the yolk of an egg in white light, and (b) the dispositional property which certain things have of giving rise to such sensations in a normal human observer when he views them in white light. If he were wise, he would distinguish these two usages of the word as "sensible" and "physical" yellowness; or he might prefer the more general phrases "occurrent" and "dispositional" yellowness. To the minute structure and internal agitation which are the objective correlate of the perception of things as yellow we might give the name "physical correlate of yellowness."

We can now see that the Moral Sense Theory of singular deontic judgments might take two entirely different forms, viz., a naïvely realistic one and a dispositional one. Both would start from the common ground that there is a peculiar kind of experience which human beings are liable to have when they contemplate certain acts, and that this can take either of two opposite forms, viz., a pro-form and an anti-form. Both would hold that this experience is of the nature of feeling, where "feeling" is used to include both sensation and emotion as distinguished from thought. From this common basis they diverge as follows:

The naïvely realistic form of the Moral Sense Theory would take moral feeling to be like what visual sensation is supposed to be on the naïvely realistic view of visual perception. When a person contemplates a certain act and has a moral pro-feeling in doing so that feeling either is or involves a prehension by him of a certain characteristic, viz., rightness, in the act; and that characteristic belongs literally and non-dispositionally to the act quite independently of whether anyone happens to contemplate it or to have a moral pro-feeling when doing so. (I have used the alternative phrase "is or involves a prehension" rather than the simpler phrase "is a prehension" because it might well be held that a moral feeling is never *just* a prehension of the objective rightness or wrongness of a contemplated act, but is always such a prehension qualified by a certain kind of emotional tone.)

I am fairly certain that the adherents of the Moral Sense Theory did not interpret it in this way; for they did not, I think, put a naïvely realistic interpretation on visual sense-perception. But some of them may quite likely have thought that plain men mistakenly put this interpretation both on such judgments as "That act is right" and on such judgments as "That thing is yellow." On the other hand, I suspect that Professor Moore, when he compared intrinsic goodness with yellowness in *Principia Ethica,* was tacitly assuming something like the naïvely realistic interpretation of both such judgments.

The dispositional form of the Moral Sense Theory would take moral feeling to be either (*a*) a special kind of emotion or (*b*) a sensation analogous to those of taste or smell and not to those of sight. I suppose that hardly anyone would put a naïvely realistic interpretation on such perceptual judgments as "That is bitter" even if he were inclined to put such an interpretation on judgments like "That is yellow."

Starting from this basis the theory might take the dispositional form in one or other of its main varieties. The feature common to all of them would be that the moral feeling which a person has when he contemplates an act neither is nor involves a prehension by him of an independent non-dispositional characteristic of rightness inherent in that act. On the trans-subjective variety of this theory a person who says that an act is right means, roughly speaking, no more than that any normal person who should contemplate this act when he was in a normal condition would have a moral pro-feeling. On the intra-subjective variety of the theory the speaker would mean the same kind of thing with "he himself" substituted for "any normal person." I have little doubt that most upholders of the Moral Sense Theory meant to assert the trans-subjective variety of the dispositional form of it. But they did not always make this clear to their readers, and perhaps they were not always clear about it themselves.

It is perhaps worth remarking that the Moral Sense Theory might conceivably take the occurrent intra-subjective form. It might allege that, when a person calls an act right, all that he means is that his present contemplation of it is accompanied by a moral pro-feeling. I think that this form of the theory is so obviously inadequate that supporters of the Moral Sense doctrine can hardly have meant to assert it. But some of them may have incautiously made statements which would suggest that this is what they meant, and their opponents may sometimes have found it convenient to seize upon these as readily assailable Aunt Sallies. It seems to me that the only two forms of the Moral Sense Theory that are worth serious consideration are the naïvely realistic form and the trans-subjective variety of the dispositional form. I shall now consider them in turn.

(2.1) *Naïvely Realistic Form of the Moral Sense Theory*. The only kinds of sense-perception which can with any plausibility be interpreted in a naïvely realistic way are visual and tactual perception. Therefore the naïvely realistic form of the Moral Sense Theory will have very little to recommend it if singular deontic judgments differ from judgments of visual and tactual perception in just those respects which make a naïvely realistic interpretation of the latter plausible. It seems to me that the relevant differences are profound and that the analogies are superficial.

(i) In stating the Moral Sense Theory I have so far used the intentionally vague phrase "having a moral pro-feeling or anti-feeling when one *contemplates* an action." If singular deontic judgments are to be analogous to judgments of visual or tactual sense-perception, this must be held to be analogous to having a sensation of yellowness when one *looks at* the yolk of an egg or having a sensation of coldness and hardness when one *touches* a block of ice. Is there any such analogy?

We must begin by distinguishing two cases, viz. (*a*) where one person makes a deontic judgment about an act done by another, and (*b*) where he makes such a judgment about an act done by himself.

(*a*) One person never can perceive the act of another, if by "act" we mean something to which moral predicates can be applied. He can perceive only some bit of overt behaviour on the part of another, e.g., writing a cheque and handing it over to a third person. That bit of overt behaviour may be an act of forgery or of paying a debt or of subscribing to a charity or of bribing an official. As a subject of moral predicates it is a different act according to the different intentions with which it is done. Now one person can contemplate another's intentions only in the sense of making them objects of *thought* and never in that of *perceiving* them.

I think that this suffices to wreck the Moral Sense Theory in its naïvely realistic form as applied to singular deontic judgments made by one person about the acts of another. Even if a naïvely realistic account of such judgments as "That thing is yellow" were acceptable, there would be no analogy between them and such judgments as "That act is right" when the judger and the agent are different. For "that thing," e.g., a certain bit of gold, is perceived by the person who makes the judgment that it is yellow.

The thing is *perceived;* it is perceived *as yellow;* and the sensation of yellow-ness is an *essential constituent* of the perception of the thing. The naïvely realistic account of the situation is that the percipient is acquainted with the surface of the thing, and that the latter reveals to the percipient through his sensation of yellow that objective non-dispositional quality of yellow-ness which it possesses independently of human observers and their sensa-tions. This account is here *prima facie* highly plausible. But "that act," if done by another, is not perceived except as a bit of overt behaviour. In respect of those characteristics which make it a possible subject for moral predicates it can only be *conceived.* The moral feeling, even if it be a sensa-tion and not an emotion only, is not an essential constituent of the percep-tion of the act as a bit of overt behaviour; only visual sensations are essen-tial constituents of that perception. And finally the relation of the moral pro-feeling or anti-feeling to the *conception* of the act as, e.g., one of debt-paying or one of bribery cannot possibly be like the relation of a sensation to a perception of which it is a constituent, e.g., the relation of a sensation of yellowness to the visual perception of a thing as yellow.

(*b*) When a deontic judgment is passed by a person on one of his own acts the above criticism does not hold. In performing an act a person is or may be directly aware of his own intentions. He knows it directly as an act of intended bribery or forgery or debt-paying or whatever it may be, and not merely as a bit of overt behaviour of a certain kind. Similarly, in retrospection a person generally knows by personal memory what were his intentions in his own past acts. No doubt introspective self-perception and personal memory are very different in important respects from sense-perceptions. But they agree with it, and differ from one's awareness of the experiences of another person in being ostensibly instances of direct acquaintance with particulars. It seems to me then that, if the Moral Sense Theory in its naïvely realistic form is to be defended, it must be confined in the first instance to deontic judgments made by a person about his own acts. We might suppose that he derives his notions of rightness and wrong-ness from perceiving those characteristics in certain of his own acts by means of moral sensations. Once he has acquired the notions in this way he can proceed to apply them to the acts of other persons; although he can-not perceive these and therefore cannot perceive their rightness or wrong-ness, but can have only conceptual cognition about them.

Now I think that there is a very serious objection to this view. It is certain that I have moral pro-feelings and anti-feelings *both* when I intro-spect or remember certain acts of my own and when I conceptually cog-nise the similar acts of other persons. Now I cannot detect any relevant difference between my moral feelings in the two cases. But, as we have seen, it is impossible in the latter case to hold that there is any analogy to visual sense-perception as interpreted by the naïvely realistic theory. It is impossible to hold here that the moral feeling is a state of acquaintance with an objective characteristic of rightness or wrongness in the cognised act. Therefore it seems unreasonable to suppose that the precisely similar moral feelings which one has when introspectively perceiving or remembering one's own acts is susceptible of a naïvely realistic interpretation.

I pass now to another profound *prima facie* difference between singular deontic judgments and judgments of visual or tactual perception. If I judge that a certain act is right or that it is wrong, it is always sensible for anyone to raise the question "What *makes* it right or *makes* it wrong?" The answer that we expect to such a question is the mention of some non-ethical characteristic of the act, e.g., that it is an act of promise-keeping, of giving a false answer to a question, and so on. Let us call these "right-inclining" and "wrong-inclining" characteristics. Now the connexion between the presence of any of these non-ethical characteristics and the tendency of an act to be right or to be wrong seems to be necessary and self-evident, not causal and contingent. (I say the "*tendency* to be right or to be wrong" and not just "rightness" or "wrongness" for a reason which will be familiar to all readers of Ross's ethical writings. One and the same act may be, e.g., an act of truth-telling and one of betrayal. It is not self-evident that such an act is resultantly right or resultantly wrong. But it might well be held to be self-evident that it tends to be right in respect of being an act of truth-telling and to be wrong in respect of being one of betrayal, and that it would be right if it had no wrong-inclining characteristic and would be wrong if it had no right-inclining characteristic. These points were made clearly enough by Price, but have since been made much more clearly by Ross.)

Now the fact which I have just mentioned is relevant to both forms of the Moral Sense Theory, but for the present we are concerned only with the naïvely realistic form of it. If I look at a thing and judge it to be yellow, it is not particularly sensible to ask "What makes it yellow?" The question is sensible only if it is interpreted causally, e.g., in some cases the answer might be that it contains saffron. And a more ultimate answer would be that it has such and such a minute structure and internal agitation. Now on the naïvely realistic theory the thing is pervaded literally and non-dispositionally by an inherent quality of yellowness; and there is no self-evident necessity for all things which have a certain kind of minute structure and internal agitation and only such things to be pervaded by yellowness. It is simply a contingent general connexion between two sets of properties of a material thing, viz., certain geometrical and kinematic properties, on the one hand, and a certain objective colour, on the other. The connexion between being an act of promise-breaking and tending to be wrong does not seem to be in the least like this.

It is worth while to remark before leaving this topic that, even if our cognition of the rightness or wrongness of acts were analogous to visual or tactual perception interpreted in the naïvely realistic way, it is quite certain that our cognition of right-inclining and wrong-inclining characteristics is not. Such characteristics as being an intentional breach of promise, an intentional return of a borrowed article, and so on, are highly complex relational properties. They can be cognised only *conceptually*; it is non-sensical to suggest that they could be cognised by anything analogous to sense-perception or to introspective self-perception.

On the other hand, the fact, if it be a fact, that the connexion between certain non-ethical characteristics and the tendency to be right is necessary and self-evident is not in itself a reason for denying that rightness and wrongness are cognised by something analogous to sensation interpreted in a naïvely realistic way. For the connexion between having shape and having size is necessary and self-evident, and yet both these characteristics are cognised by visual sense-perception.

I think that the upshot of this discussion is that there is little to be said for and much to be said against the Moral Sense Theory in its naïvely realistic form as applied to deontic judgments. We can therefore pass to the Dispositional Form of the theory.

(2.2) *Dispositional Form of the Moral Sense Theory.*—I do not think that we shall be unfair to the theory if we confine our attention to the trans-subjective variety of it and if we assume that moral feeling is of the nature of emotion rather than sensation.

I shall begin with some general remarks about emotion. (i) An emotion, e.g., an experience of fearing or hating, as distinct from an emotional mood, such as a state of apprehension or of crossness, is always directed to a cognised object. This may be real or hallucinatory, e.g., one may be afraid of a real man who is pointing a revolver at one or of an hallucinatory appearance of such a man in a dream. Again, if the object be real, it may be correctly or more or less incorrectly cognised, e.g., one may be afraid of a real physical object which one sees when crossing a field in twilight and takes to be a man pointing a revolver at one, and this object may really be a harmless scarecrow.

(ii) We must distinguish between what I will call "mediated" and "unmediated" emotions. Sometimes when a person feels a certain emotion towards a certain object he has an experience which may be described as feeling that emotion towards that object *in respect of* certain characteristics which he believes (rightly or wrongly) that it possesses. In that case I shall say that his emotion is *mediated* by this belief about the characteristics of the object, and I shall call these characteristics the "mediating characteristics" of the emotion. Often, however, the emotion is not felt in respect of any characteristic which the experient believes the object to have. In that case I shall say that the emotion is *unmediated*. If I am angry with a person, e.g., I may feel this anger in respect of some fault which I believe (rightly or wrongly) that he has committed. But I may feel angry with a person, and still more obviously I may dislike him, just directly and, as we say, "for no assignable reason." This is an example of an *unmediated* emotion.

(iii) Presumably every occurrence of any emotion, whether mediated or unmediated, has a *total cause*. In many cases, no doubt, an essential factor in that cause is the presence of certain characteristics in the object.

I will call these "evoking characteristics." In the case of a mediated emotion the evoking and the mediating characteristics may be, and no doubt often are, wholly or partly the same. But very often they must be different; for the object often does not really have the characteristics which the experient believes it to have and in respect of which he feels his emotion towards it.

(iv) It is commonly held that certain kinds of emotion are in some sense "appropriate to" objects which have certain characteristics, and that they are "inappropriate to" objects which lack these or which have certain others, e.g., fear is held to be appropriate only to objects which are dangerous. Again, it is held that for a given degree of dangerousness there is, within fairly narrow limits, a fitting degree of fear. To fear objects which are not really dangerous is described as "irrational"; and to fear intensely objects which are only slightly dangerous is described as "inordinate."

It is a well-known fact that if a person begins by feeling an unmediated emotion towards an object he is very liable to go on to ascribe to that object such characteristics as would make the emotion appropriate and to ascribe to those characteristics such a degree as would make his emotion ordinate. A very familiar example of this is provided by persons who are jealous of others. Lastly, if a person feels a mediated emotion towards an object in respect of a characteristic to which that emotion is inappropriate, he is very liable to divert his attention from this fact and to ascribe to the object another characteristic in respect of which the emotion would be appropriate. These tendencies, which have been perfectly familiar to playwrights, preachers and plain men throughout the ages, have been hailed as great discoveries of modern psychology under the name of "rationalisation."

We are now in a position to consider the trans-subjective dispositional form of the Moral Sense Theory. In essence the theory is that such judgments as "That act is right (or is wrong)" are analogous to such judgments as "That food is nice (or is nasty)." The correct analysis of them is some variant on the formula "That act would evoke a moral pro-emotion (or anti-emotion) in any human being who might at any time contemplate it." There might have to be qualifications about the individual being "normal" and being "in a normal state," but we need not trouble about them at present.

Now this form of the theory does avoid the first objection which I made against the naïvely realistic form of it. It does not have to assume that one person literally has knowledge by acquaintance of the intentions of another. It does not have to assume that the experience of having a moral feeling when contemplating an act of one's own is fundamentally different in kind from that of having a moral feeling when contemplating a similar act of another person. For we can and do have emotions towards objects which are cognised only conceptually, and we can and do feel such emotions in respect of characteristics whose presence is only conceived and not perceived.

It seems to me that the main difficulties of the theory can be summed up in the following three questions: (i) Can it deal with the fact that judgments like "That act is right" seem always to be grounded upon the supposed presence in the act of some non-ethical right-inclining characteristic, such as being the fulfilment of a promise? (ii) If so, can it deal with the further fact that the connexion between a right-inclining characteristic and the rightness which it tends to convey seems to be necessary and synthetic? And (iii) can it deal with the fact that it seems not only intelligible but also true to say that moral pro-emotion is felt towards an act in respect of the characteristic of *rightness* and moral anti-emotion in respect of the characteristic of *wrongness?* I shall take these three questions in turn.

(i) I think that a fairly plausible answer, so far as it goes, can be made to the first question. We shall have to say that the right-inclining characteristic which is the ground of the judgment "That act is right" just is the mediating characteristic of the moral pro-emotion which is felt towards such acts. To say that every moral judgment is founded upon some non-ethical characteristic of the act which is its subject will be equivalent to saying that every moral emotion is a mediated emotion. Such characteristics as being an act of promise-keeping will be mediating characteristics for moral pro-emotion; such characteristics as being an act of lying or of deliberate cruelty will be mediating characteristics of moral anti-emotion.

It should be noticed that the theory can account quite plausibly for the facts which Ross describes under the head of his distinction between "*prima facie* duties" and "a duty proper." (I prefer to use the phrases "components of obligation" and "resultant obligation.") An act is known or believed to have various characteristics, e.g., to be an act of truth-telling, a breach of confidence, and an optimific act. The first and the third of these features give rise to components of obligation of various degrees of urgency towards doing it; the second gives rise to a component of a certain degree of urgency against doing it. According to circumstances the resultant obligation may be to do it or to avoid doing it. Now it is a perfectly familiar fact that an object may have several characteristics, and that it may call forth an emotion of one kind in respect of some of them and an emotion of the opposite kind in respect of others; so that the emotion towards the object as a whole may be predominantly of the opposite kind. The present theory would say that we tend to feel a moral pro-emotion of a certain strength towards the act in respect of its being one of truth-telling and in respect of its being optimific; that we tend to feel a moral anti-emotion of a certain strength towards it as being a breach of confidence; and that our moral emotion towards it as a whole is the resultant of these two tendencies, and may be either predominantly *pro* or predominantly *anti* according to circumstances.

(ii) The second question is much harder. It is alleged, e.g., that the proposition "Any act of promise-keeping tends as such to be right, and any act of promise-breaking tends as such to be wrong" is necessary, self-evident, and synthetic. On the present theory of deontic judgments this would be equivalent to something like the following proposition: "It is necessary, self-evident and synthetic that any human being who should contemplate an act which he believed to be one of promise-keeping would tend to feel a moral pro-emotion towards it, and that he would tend to feel a moral anti-emotion towards any act which he believed to be one of promise-breaking."

Now it might be objected that the latter statement is certainly false. It is a purely contingent fact that human beings have a disposition to feel moral emotions at all. They might have been as devoid of them as they are of a disposition to have special sensations in presence of magnets. Moreover, granted that they do have such an emotional disposition, it is a purely contingent fact that moral emotions are mediated in the particular ways in which they are. It is quite conceivable that the belief that an act is one of promise-keeping should have mediated a moral *anti*-emotion, and that the belief that it is one of promise-breaking should have mediated a moral *pro*-emotion; just as it is conceivable that men should have liked the taste of castor oil and disliked that of sugar. In that case, on the present theory, promise-breaking would have tended to be right and promise-keeping to be wrong; just as castor oil would have been nice and sugar nasty.

So the objection comes to this. If the present form of the Moral Sense Theory were true, certain propositions which are in fact necessary and knowable *a priori* would have been contingent and knowable only empirically. Therefore the theory is false. I am sure that this is the most important of Price's objections to the Moral Sense Theory, though I have developed it in my own way. What are we to say about it?

It is plain that there are only two lines of defence open to the present form of the Moral Sense Theory. (*a*) One is to argue that propositions like "Any act of promise-keeping tends as such to be right" are *not* necessary. (*b*) The other is to argue that propositions like "Any human being who should contemplate an act which he believed to be one of promise-keeping would tend to feel a moral pro-emotion towards it" are *not* contingent. Let us consider the two alternatives in turn:

(*a*) I think that this line of argument would divide into two parts, which might be called the "offensive" and the "defensive." The offensive part would take the opposite view as a hypothesis and try to show that it is untenable. The defensive part would try to explain why certain propositions which are in fact empirical and contingent appear to many people to be *a priori* and necessary.

(*a, a*) The offensive part may be put as follows: What precisely do our opponents maintain? If we may take Price as their ablest representative, they seem to assert something like the following doctrine. Suppose that a person reflects, e.g., on the situation of being asked a question and on the notions of responding to it by a true answer and responding to it by a false answer. Then he will find it self-evident that the former kind of response has a certain relation of "moral fittingness" and that the latter has an opposite relation of "moral unfittingness" to such a situation. This relation of moral fittingness or unfittingness is held to be unique and unanalysable. And the process of recognising that it necessarily holds between certain kinds of response and certain kinds of situation is held to be analogous to that of recognising that certain mathematical terms, e.g., stand in certain mathematical relations.

Now the objection which will be made by supporters of the Moral Sense Theory is twofold. It will be said that the doctrine just enunciated involves *a priori* concepts and synthetic *a priori* judgments, and that neither of these is admissible. We will take these two points in order.

If there is a simple unanalysable relation of moral fittingness or unfittingness, it is certainly not manifested to us by any of our senses. We literally *see* that one coloured patch is surrounded by another; we literally *hear* that two notes, sounded together or in very close succession, concord or discord with each other; and so on. In such cases we presumably derive our ideas of the relation of *surrounding* and the relation of *concording or discording* by comparison and abstraction from such sensibly presented instances of terms standing in these relations. It is plain that we do not acquire the idea of moral fittingness or unfittingness in this way. Nor do we derive the idea from instances of terms presented to us by introspection as standing in that relationship. Introspection presents us with certain of our own experiences as standing in certain temporal relations, e.g., as being in the same specious present and partly overlapping in time, and so on. Again, since the relation of moral fittingness or unfittingness is held to be simple and unanalysable, the idea of it cannot be one which we have constructed in thought from elements presented separately or in different contexts by sensation or introspection or both. (The idea of the complex relationship of a colonel to the subordinate officers of his regiment, e.g., is no doubt reached in some such way as this.) But it is held by many philosophers to be a fundamental epistemological principle that every idea is either derived by abstraction from instances presented in sensation or introspection or is an intellectual construction from elements so derived. If this principle be admitted, it is impossible that we should have any conception of the relations of moral fittingness and unfittingness as described by such moralists as Price.

For my part I attach very little weight to this argument. I can see nothing self-evident in what I will call for short "Hume's Epistemological Principle," and I am not aware that any conclusive empirical evidence has been adduced for it. It seems to me to be simply a useful goad to disturb our dogmatic slumbers, and a useful guide to follow until it begins to tempt us to ignore some facts and to distort others. I am inclined to think that the concepts of Cause and of Substance are *a priori* or contain *a priori* elements; at any rate I have never seen any satisfactory account of them in accordance with Hume's Principle.

The second point in the offensive part of the argument is this: Suppose, if possible, that "right" and "wrong" are simple unanalysable notions, as Price, e.g., held them to be. Then any proposition which asserts a connexion between some non-ethical characteristic, such as promise-keeping, and tendency to be right must be synthetic. Now a proposition may be synthetic and contingent or analytic and necessary, but it is an admitted general principle that no proposition can be both synthetic and necessary. Therefore the combined doctrine that "right" and "wrong" are unique unanalysable notions and that such propositions as "Any act of promise-keeping tends as such to be right" are necessary must be false.

Such an argument would have different effects on different persons. Suppose that *A* and *B* are both quite convinced up to a certain moment of the truth of a certain general principle, and suppose that at that moment *C* brings to their notice an apparent counter-instance. If each is to be self-consistent, *something* will have to give way in each of them. But it need not be the same something. *A* may remain completely certain of the general principle; he will then have to maintain that the instance is only apparently contrary to it and explain why it seems to be so. *B* may find it impossible to doubt that the instance is contrary; he will then be forced to give up the general principle and explain why it seemed evident. These are the two extreme possibilities. Between them are numberless possible intermediate alternatives, where the person concerned is led to feel *some* doubt of the unqualified truth of the principle and *some* doubt whether the apparent counter-instance really conflicts with it. Speaking for myself, I occupy one of these intermediate positions. As for Price, he would have been completely unmoved by this kind of argument. For he held, in full knowledge of Hume's doctrine and in conscious opposition to it, that there are plenty of synthetic necessary facts in other departments beside that of morals. For these reasons I think that it is rather futile to rely on a general argument of this kind.

(*a*, *β*) The defensive part of the argument might take the following line. Civilised men throughout human history have been assiduously conditioned in infancy and youth by parents, nurses, schoolmasters, etc., to feel moral pro-emotions towards acts of certain kinds and to feel moral anti-emotions towards acts of certain other kinds. Moreover, if we consider what kinds of acts are the objects of moral pro-emotions and what kinds are the objects of moral anti-emotions we notice the following facts about them. The former are acts whose performance by most people on most occasions when they are relevant is essential to the stability and efficient working of any society. The latter are acts which, if done on many occasions and by many people, would be utterly destructive to any society. On the other hand, the former are acts which an individual is often strongly tempted to omit, and the latter are acts which he is often strongly tempted to commit. This is either because we have strong natural impulses moving us to omit the former and to commit the latter, or because the attractive consequences of the former and the repellent consequences of the latter are often remote, collateral, and secondary. It follows that any group of men in which, from no matter what cause, a strong pro-emotion had become associated with acts of the first kind and a strong anti-emotion with acts of the second kind would be likely to win in the struggle for existence with other groups in which no such emotions existed or in which they were differently directed. Therefore it is likely that most of the members of all societies which now exist would be descendants of persons in whom strong moral pro-emotions had become attached to acts of the first kind and strong anti-emotions to acts of the second kind. And most existing societies will be historically and culturally continuous with societies in which such emotions had become attached to such acts. These causes, it might be argued, conspire to produce so strong an association between such emotions and such acts in most members of every existing society that the connexion between the emotion and the act seems to each individual to be necessary.

No doubt this line of argument will produce different effects on different persons. For my own part I am inclined to attach a good deal of weight to it.

(*b*) I pass now to the second kind of defence which might be made for the dispositional form of the Moral Sense Theory. This is to contend that the proposition about human emotional dispositions which, according to the theory, is equivalent to "Any act of promise-keeping tends as such to be right" *is* necessary. It might be thought that this contention is so palpably absurd as not to be worth putting forward. But I believe that a case can be made for it, and I propose to make it.

We must begin by noting that the proposition which is equivalent to "Any act of promise-keeping tends as such to be right" could not with any plausibility be taken to be the crude unqualified proposition "Any human being has a disposition to feel a moral pro-emotion whenever he contemplates an act which he believes to be one of promise-keeping." So far from being necessary the latter proposition is not even true. To make it true it will have to be qualified somewhat as follows. We must substitute for it the proposition "Any *normal* human being has a disposition to feel a moral pro-emotion towards any act which he believes to be one of promise-keeping if he contemplates it when he is in a *normal* state."

Now it might be argued that, when the proposition is thus qualified, it *is* necessary. For, it might be said, it has then become *analytic*. It is part of the definition of a "normal" human being that he has a disposition to feel moral emotion, and that he will feel that emotion in its pro-form towards acts which he believes to be ones of promise-keeping, of truth-telling, of beneficence, and so on. And it is part of the definition of "being in a normal state" that when one is in such a state this moral-emotional disposition will not be inhibited altogether or excited in abnormal ways.

No doubt the immediate answer which an opponent of the Moral Sense Theory would make to this contention is the following: He would say that such propositions as "Any act of promise-keeping tends as such to be right" are not only necessary but *synthetic*. The defender of the dispositional form of the Moral Sense Theory has shown that, on his analysis, they would be necessary only at the cost of showing that they would be *analytic*. This answer is correct so far as it goes, but I think that the defender of the Moral Sense Theory could rebut it as follows.

The fact is that it is often by no means easy to say whether a proposition is analytic or not. The analytic propositions of real life are not like the trivial examples in logic-books, such as "All Negroes are black" or "All right angles are angles." The following are much better worth considering, e.g., "The sun rises in the east," "A freely suspended magnet sets itself with its axis pointing north and south," and "Pure water boils at 100° C. under a pressure of 76 centimetres of mercury." The first of these is analytic if "east" and "west" are defined by means of the sun, and synthetic if they are defined by means of the magnetic or the gyroscopic compass. The second is analytic if "north" and "south" are defined by means of the magnetic compass, and synthetic if they are defined by means of the sun or the gyroscopic compass. The third might be taken as a definition of '100° C.' But if that term were defined in some other way, e.g., thermodynamically, as on Lord Kelvin's absolute scale, it might be regarded as an analytic proposition about *pure water*. For an important element in the definition of "pure water" is that it has a certain boiling-point under certain standard conditions.

Two important points emerge from these examples. The first is that the same type-sentence may express both an analytic and a synthetic proposition, and that a person who uses several tokens of this type even in a single discourse may sometimes be expressing the analytical and sometimes the synthetic proposition. The former is necessary and the latter is contingent. It would not be surprising if a person should sometimes become confused in such cases and think that every token of this type expresses *one and the same proposition* which is *both* synthetic and necessary.

The second point is this. Such an analytic proposition as "Pure water boils at 100° C. under a pressure of 76 centimetres of mercury" has at the back of it a whole system of interconnected empirical generalisations, apart from which it would never have been worth anyone's while to formulate it. It would take me far too long even to begin to state a few of these empirical generalisations. It will suffice to say that they are all represented in the various qualifications which make the proposition "Pure water boils at 100° C. under a pressure of 76 centimetres of mercury" analytic.

Now it might be suggested that facts like these throw some light on the alleged synthetic necessity of such propositions as "Any act of promise-keeping tends as such to be right," and on the claim of defenders of the dispositional form of the Moral Sense Theory that the equivalent propositions about human emotional dispositions are necessary because analytic.

The proposition "Any act of promise-keeping would tend to call forth a moral pro-emotion in any *normal* human being who might contemplate it when in a *normal* state" is obviously rather like the proposition "Any sample of *pure* water boils at 100° C. under the *normal* atmospheric pressure, i.e., 76 centimetres of mercury." Just as the latter is analytic, but is founded on a whole mass of interconnected empirical generalisations, so is the former. I will now try to justify this statement.

It is an empirical fact that the vast majority of men have a disposition to feel moral emotions, and that the minority who lack it differ in many other ways from the majority of their fellows. It is an empirical fact that there is very substantial agreement among men in the kinds of act which call forth moral pro-emotion and in the kinds which call forth moral anti-emotion. The small minority of men who habitually feel moral pro-emotion where most of their fellows feel moral anti-emotion, or *vice versa*, are generally found to be odd and abnormal in many other ways. There is, in fact, so high a degree of positive association between moral and non-moral normality that it would make very little difference in practice whether we defined a "normal" man solely by reference to his moral dispositions or solely by reference to his non-moral dispositions, or by reference to a mixture of both. But the proposition that any normal human being would tend to feel a moral pro-emotion towards any act which he believed to be one of promise-keeping would be synthetic if one defined "normality" solely by reference to non-moral dispositions, whilst it might well be analytic if one defined it wholly or partly in terms of moral dispositions.

Again, there is a very high degree of positive association between the tendencies to feel moral pro-emotion towards acts of promise-keeping, of truth-telling, of beneficence, etc.; and there is perhaps an even stronger degree of positive association between the tendencies to feel moral anti-emotion towards acts of treachery, of unfairness, of cruelty, etc. Therefore it would make little practical difference which of these mediating characteristics was included and which was omitted from the definition of "normality." Now, if the tendency to feel moral pro-emotion towards any act which is believed to be one of promise-keeping were included in the definition of "normality," the proposition that any normal man would tend to feel such an emotion towards such acts would be analytic; whilst, if this were omitted and "normality" were defined by reference to some of the other mediating characteristics of moral emotion, this proposition would be synthetic.

It therefore seems likely that, if the analysis which the dispositional form of the Moral Sense Theory offers for such propositions as "Any act of promise-keeping tends as such to be right" were correct, a sentence of this type might often express a proposition which is analytic and necessary and might as often express one that is synthetic and contingent. If so, it is not unlikely that a confusion should arise and that it should be thought that *every* such sentence expresses one and the same proposition which is *both* necessary and synthetic.

It remains to say something of the qualification "when in a normal state," which has to be added to make the statement universally true, and which at the same time makes it more nearly analytic. It may be compared to the qualifications about the water being pure and the barometric pressure being normal in my example about boiling-point.

At the back of this qualification lie certain negative and certain positive empirical facts. It is found that a person who generally does feel moral pro-emotions towards acts of certain kinds and moral anti-emotions towards acts of certain other kinds will on some occasions not do so. He may feel no moral emotion; or perhaps on very exceptional occasions the normal form of his moral emotion may be reversed. These are the negative facts. The positive facts are certain empirical generalisations about the kinds of occurrent conditions under which such inhibitions or reversals of moral emotion tend to take place. "Being in a normal state" is then defined in terms of the absence of such conditions, e.g., not being angry with or jealous of or frightened by the agent whose act is being contemplated. Now, although one has at the back of one's mind a fairly adequate but rather confused idea of these negative conditions, only one or two of them will be explicitly before one's mind on any particular occasion when one uses the expression "in a normal state." According as one or another is in the foreground on a given occasion the same sentence may express an analytic or a synthetic proposition.

I suggest, then, that defenders of the dispositional form of the Moral Sense Theory might attempt in some such ways as these to rebut the objection that, whilst propositions like "Any act of promise-keeping tends as such to be right" are *necessary and synthetic*, the propositions which it asserts to be their equivalents are either *contingent or analytic*.

(iii) The third difficulty which the Moral Sense Theory, in the form of it which we are considering, has to meet is this. It might be alleged that the mediating characteristics in respect of which a person feels moral pro-emotion or anti-emotion towards an act which he contemplates are the supposed *rightness* or *wrongness* of the act. Suppose, e.g., that a person feels a moral anti-emotion when he contemplates an act which he believes to be one of promise-breaking. Then, it might be said, he does so only in so far as he believes promise-breaking to be wrong. Suppose that he believed the act to be one of promise-breaking but did not believe that such acts tend to be wrong. Then, it might be alleged, there is no reason to think that he would feel a moral anti-emotion towards it.

Let us begin by considering what view a Rationalist, like Price, would take on this question of the mediating characteristics of moral emotion. I think that the following is a fair statement of his position. It is a necessary proposition that any rational being who contemplated an act which he believed to be one of promise-breaking would tend to feel towards it a moral anti-emotion. But, though true and necessary, it is not self-evident. It is a logical consequence of two more fundamental propositions, each of which is self-evident. They are these: (a) It is self-evident to any rational being that any act of promise-breaking tends as such to be wrong. (b) It is self-evident that any rational being who contemplated an act which he believed to be wrong would feel towards it a moral anti-emotion.

We have already considered what the supporters of the Moral Sense Theory might say about the first of these propositions. What are we to say about the second? It seems to me that everything depends here on how much we put into the connotation of the phrase "rational being." On a narrower interpretation of that phrase proposition (b) is synthetic but contingent, on a certain wider interpretation that proposition becomes necessary but analytic. Sometimes the one interpretation and sometimes the other is at the back of one's mind without one realising the fluctuation, and so one is inclined to think that proposition (b) is both necessary and synthetic.

A "rational being," on the narrowest interpretation, means roughly one who is capable of comparing, abstracting, and forming general notions; who is capable of seeing necessary connexions and disconnexions between terms and between propositions; and who has the power of making inferences, both deductive and inductive. I call this the "narrowest" interpretation, because it takes account only of cognitive characteristics and leaves out emotional and conative ones. The next stage in widening it would be to include in the definition of a "rational being" what I will call "purely intellectual" emotions and conations, e.g., intellectual curiosity, taking pleasure in neat arguments and displeasure in clumsy ones, desire for consistency in one's beliefs, and desire to apportion the strength of one's beliefs to the weight of the evidence.

Let us say that a person who had the cognitive, conative and emotional dispositions which I have just enumerated would be rational "in the ethically neutral sense." Suppose that Price were correct in thinking that moral fittingness and unfittingness are relations which hold of necessity between certain types of response and certain types of situation. Then a person who was rational in the ethically neutral sense would in principle be capable of having ideas of right and wrong and of making moral judgments. (I say "in principle" because (a) he would, by definition, have the *general* capacity to see necessary connexions between terms and between propositions, whilst (b) it might happen that his insight in this particular department was lacking, as that of some rational beings is in the department of mathematical relations.) But, so far as I can see, there would not be the slightest inconsistency in supposing that a being who was rational in the ethically neutral sense, and did in fact have the ideas of right and wrong and make moral judgments, was completely devoid of specifically moral emotion and conation. The fact that he knew or believed A to be right and B to be wrong might arouse in him neither moral pro-emotion towards the former nor moral anti-emotion towards the latter, and it might not evoke in him the slightest desire to do A or to avoid doing B or *vice versa*. I cannot see any *logical* impossibility in the existence of such a being; whether it would involve a conflict with some of the *de facto* laws of psychology I do not know.

Now the vast majority of the beings whom we know to be rational in the ethically neutral sense do in fact feel moral pro-emotion towards acts which they believe to be right and moral anti-emotion towards those which they believe to be wrong, and they are in fact to some extent attracted towards doing the former and repelled from doing the latter. Moreover, it is *logically* impossible that these specifically moral emotions and desires should exist in a being who was not rational in the ethically neutral sense; for their characteristic objects can be presented only by a process of reflective thinking. The wider interpretation of the phrase "rational being" includes these specifically moral conative and emotional characteristics in addition to those which constitute the definition of "rational" in the ethically neutral sense. It is, of course, logically impossible that a person who is rational in this widest sense should fail to feel moral pro-emotion towards what he believes to be right and moral anti-emotion towards what he believes to be wrong. But this is a merely analytical proposition. It is synthetic and contingent that a person who is rational in the ethically neutral sense should be so in the wider ethical sense also. But the fact that rationality in the ethically neutral sense is almost invariably accompanied in our experience by the additional features which convert it into ethical rationality and the fact that the latter logically entail the former produce a confusion in our minds. We are thus led to think that the proposition that any rational being would feel a moral pro-emotion towards any act which he believed to be right and a moral anti-emotion towards any that he believed to be wrong is both necessary and synthetic.

So much for the Rationalist account of moral emotion and its mediation by the characteristics of rightness and wrongness. What can the Moral Sense Theory, in its trans-subjective dispositional form, make of the alleged facts?

On the face of it this theory is presented with the following difficulty. Suppose that we try to combine the alleged fact that rightness and wrongness are the mediating characteristics for moral emotion with the analysis of moral judgments given by the theory in question. Then we seem to be committed to the following proposition: "A person will tend to feel a moral anti-emotion towards an act which he believes to be one of promise-breaking so far and only so far as he believes that most persons when in a normal condition would feel such an emotion in contemplating such an act." Now this has a *prima facie* appearance of circularity; and, even if it be neither logically nor causally circular, it certainly does not seem very plausible.

The first remark that I have to make is that the objection just stated rests on a premiss which is plausible but false. It tacitly assumes that, if the correct analysis of the proposition "S is P" is "S is p_1-and-p_2," then anyone who is believing the former proposition is *ipso facto* believing the latter. Now there may be some sense of "believe" in which this is true; but there certainly is an important sense in which it is false. It is quite obvious that a number of persons who accept different and incompatible analyses of a proposition may all believe it; and therefore there must be a sense in which some at least of them believe it without *ipso facto* believing the proposition which is its correct analysis. This is particularly obvious in the present case. Nearly everyone believes that acts of promise-breaking tend as such to be wrong; but some of these persons think that wrongness is a simple characteristic, others think that it can be analysed in one way, and others think that it can be analysed in various other ways. So, even if the correct analysis of "X is wrong" is "Any normal person who should contemplate such an act as X when in a normal state would feel a moral anti-emotion towards it," it does not follow that the correct analysis of "A believes that X is wrong" is "A believes that any normal person who should contemplate such an act as X when in a normal state would feel a moral anti-emotion towards it." So it is not fair to say that the Moral Sense Theory must hold that anyone who feels a moral anti-emotion towards an act in respect of his belief that it is wrong is *ipso facto* feeling that emotion in respect of his belief that any normal person who would feel such an emotion if he were to contemplate such an act while in a normal state.

I suppose that this argument would be generally admitted as applied to the case of a person who did not accept, or did positively reject, the analysis of moral judgments proposed by the Moral Sense Theory. But it might be said that it will not apply to the case of a person who accepts that analysis. I think, however, that even this could be questioned. A person may have assented to a certain analysis of a proposition when the question of its analysis and the arguments *pro* and *con* were before his mind. He may continue to accept it, in the *dispositional* sense that he *would* assent to it again at any time when the question was raised for him. But during the intervals he may often have the experience of believing the proposition without thinking of the analysis of it which he has accepted. Therefore it seems to me that even an adherent of the Moral Sense Theory might often feel a moral anti-emotion towards an act in respect of his belief that it is wrong without *ipso facto* feeling that emotion in respect of the belief that it has those characteristics which he holds to be the correct analysis of "being wrong."

So much for the dialectics of the matter. But what is really happening when a person is said to feel a moral pro-emotion or anti-emotion towards an act in respect of his belief that it is right or that it is wrong? We must begin by distinguishing what I will call "first-hand" and "second-hand" emotion. Suppose that a certain word has been very often used in connexion with objects towards which a certain kind of emotion has been felt and that it has seldom or never been used except on such occasions. Then this word may come to act as a stimulus calling forth this kind of emotion. When the emotion is evoked in this way I call it "second-hand."

Now there is no doubt that a great deal of moral emotion is, in this sense, second-hand. And there is no doubt that the words which have come by association to act as evokers of second-hand moral emotion are the words "right" and "wrong." When a person is said to feel a moral emotion towards an act in respect of his belief that it is right or that it is wrong what is really happening is very often the following. He knows or believes that acts of this kind are commonly *called* "right" or called "wrong." He repeats these words *sotto voce* to himself or has auditory images of them when he thinks of the act in question; and by association they evoke a second-hand moral pro-emotion or anti-emotion towards the act. Plainly there is nothing in this to cause difficulty to the supporters of the Moral Sense Theory.

But of course this does not cover the whole field. There *is* first-hand moral emotion; indeed, if no one had ever felt a first-hand emotion of a given kind, it is difficult to believe that anyone could now feel a second-hand emotion of that kind. What is happening when a person is said to be feeling a *first-hand* moral emotion towards an act in respect of his belief that it is right or that it is wrong? I can give only a very tentative answer to this question, based on my own imperfect introspection of a kind of situation with which I am not very familiar.

It *seems* to me that in such cases I do not first recognise or think that I recognise a quality or relation of rightness or wrongness in the act, and *then* begin to feel a moral pro-emotion or anti-emotion towards it in respect of this knowledge or belief. What I seem to do is to consider the act and its probable consequences under various familiar headings. "Would it do more harm than good? Would it be deceitful? Should I be showing ingratitude to a benefactor if I were to do it? Should I be shifting onto another person's shoulders a burden or a responsibility which I do not care to bear for myself?" In respect of each of these aspects of the act and its consequences I have a tendency to feel towards the act a certain kind of moral emotion of a certain degree of intensity. These emotional dispositions were largely built up in me by my parents, schoolmasters, friends and colleagues; and I know that in the main they correspond with those of other persons of my own nation and class. It seems to me that I call the act "right" or "wrong" in accordance with my final moral-emotional reaction to it, after viewing it under all these various aspects, and after trying to allow for any permanent or temporary emotional peculiarities in myself which may make my emotional reaction eccentric or unbalanced. By the time that this has happened the features which I had distinguished and had viewed and reacted to separately have fallen into the background and are again fused. They are the real mediating characteristics of my moral pro-emotion or anti-emotion; but I now use the omnibus words "right" or "wrong" to cover them all, and say that I feel that emotion towards the act in respect of my belief that it is right or that it is wrong.

V

THE EMOTIVE THEORY

A Suggestion about Value[*][1]

〰〰

W. H. F. BARNES

VALUE JUDGEMENTS in their origin are not strictly judgements at all. They are exclamations expressive of approval. This is to be distinguished from the theory that the value judgement, "A is good," states that I approve A. The theory that I am now putting forward maintains that "A is good," is a form of words expressive of my approval. To take an illustration:—When I say "I have a pain," that sentence states the occurrence of a certain feeling in me: when I shout "Oh!" in a certain way that is expressive of the occurrence in me of a certain feeling. We must seek then for the origin of value judgements in the expressions of approval, delight, and affection, which children utter when confronted with certain experiences.

If all so-called value judgements are, in principle, expressions of approval, then they will only possess meaning in so far as the society in which they are used is agreed on what things it approves. And then "good" and "value" will be terms which have meaning only by referring to the actual nature of the thing, not to any non-natural quality it possesses. Meanwhile it is worth while mentioning that many controversies arising out of value judgements *are* settled by saying, "I like it and you don't, and that's the end of the matter." We are content to adopt this solution of the difficulty on matters such as food and drink, though even here we admit the existence of epicures and connoisseurs. Why are we not content to accept the same solution on all matters where value is concerned?

The reason we are not so content seems to lie in the fact that the action of one man dictated by his approval of something is frequently incompatible with the action of another man dictated by his approval of something. Life in a society leads us continually to transfer our approval to different objects. Reflection upon that life leads to still further modifications. It is this opposition between the approval of one man and that of others which lies at the bottom of controversies about value. If I maintain "A is good" against the contention "A is bad," my attempt to prove the truth of my statement is not really what it pretends to be. I point out details in A which are the object of my approval. By so doing I hope that

* Reprinted by kind permission of the author and the editor from *Analysis*, 1, 1933.
[1] This note is an extract from a paper of which the main topic was Hartmann's Ethics. The paper was read before the Jowett Society on November 8th, 1933.

my opponent, when he becomes aware of these, will approve A: and so be ready to say "A is good." But what I have done is not really to gain his assent to a proposition but to change his attitude from one of disapproval to one of approval towards A. All attempts to persuade others of the truth of value judgements are thus really attempts to make others approve the things we approve.

Critique of Ethics *

~

A. J. AYER

THERE IS STILL one objection to be met before we can claim to have justified our view that all synthetic propositions are empirical hypotheses. This objection is based on the common supposition that our speculative knowledge is of two distinct kinds—that which relates to questions of empirical fact, and that which relates to questions of value. It will be said that "statements of value" are genuine synthetic propositions, but that they cannot with any show of justice be represented as hypotheses, which are used to predict the course of our sensations; and, accordingly, that the existence of ethics and æsthetics as branches of speculative knowledge presents an insuperable objection to our radical empiricist thesis.

In face of this objection, it is our business to give an account of "judgements of value" which is both satisfactory in itself and consistent with our general empiricist principles. We shall set ourselves to show that in so far as statements of value are significant, they are ordinary "scientific" statements; and that in so far as they are not scientific, they are not in the literal sense significant, but are simply expressions of emotion which can be neither true nor false. In maintaining this view, we may confine ourselves for the present to the case of ethical statements. What is said about them will be found to apply, *mutatis mutandis,* to the case of æsthetic statements also.

The ordinary system of ethics, as elaborated in the works of ethical philosophers, is very far from being a homogeneous whole. Not only is it apt to contain pieces of metaphysics, and analyses of non-ethical concepts: its actual ethical contents are themselves of very different kinds. We may divide them, indeed, into four main classes. There are, first of all, propositions which express definitions of ethical terms, or judgements about the legitimacy or possibility of certain definitions. Secondly, there are propositions describing the phenomena of moral experience, and their causes. Thirdly, there are exhortations to moral virtue. And, lastly, there are actual ethical judgements. It is unfortunately the case that the distinction between these four classes, plain as it is, is commonly ignored by ethical philosophers; with the result that it is often very difficult to tell

* Excerpted and reprinted by kind permission of the author and the publisher from *Language, Truth and Logic,* Chapter VI. Victor Gollancz, Ltd., 1936.

from their works what it is that they are seeking to discover or prove.

In fact, it is easy to see that only the first of our four classes, namely that which comprises the propositions relating to the definitions of ethical terms, can be said to constitute ethical philosophy. The propositions which describe the phenomena of moral experience, and their causes, must be assigned to the science of psychology, or sociology. The exhortations to moral virtue are not propositions at all, but ejaculations or commands which are designed to provoke the reader to action of a certain sort. Accordingly, they do not belong to any branch of philosophy or science. As for the expressions of ethical judgements, we have not yet determined how they should be classified. But inasmuch as they are certainly neither definitions nor comments upon definitions, nor quotations, we may say decisively that they do not belong to ethical philosophy. A strictly philosophical treatise on ethics should therefore make no ethical pronouncements. But it should, by giving an analysis of ethical terms, show what is the category to which all such pronouncements belong. And this is what we are now about to do.

A question which is often discussed by ethical philosophers is whether it is possible to find definitions which would reduce all ethical terms to one or two fundamental terms. But this question, though it undeniably belongs to ethical philosophy, is not relevant to our present enquiry. We are not now concerned to discover which term, within the sphere of ethical terms, is to be taken as fundamental; whether, for example, "good" can be defined in terms of "right" or "right" in terms of "good," or both in terms of "value." What we are interested in is the possibility of reducing the whole sphere of ethical terms to non-ethical terms. We are enquiring whether statements of ethical value can be translated into statements of empirical fact.

That they can be so translated is the contention of those ethical philosophers who are commonly called subjectivists, and of those who are known as utilitarians. For the utilitarian defines the rightness of actions, and the goodness of ends, in terms of the pleasure, or happiness, or satisfaction, to which they give rise; the subjectivist, in terms of the feelings of approval which a certain person, or group of people, has towards them. Each of these types of definition makes moral judgements into a sub-class of psychological or sociological judgements; and for this reason they are very attractive to us. For, if either was correct, it would follow that ethical assertions were not generically different from the factual assertions which are ordinarily contrasted with them; and the account which we have already given of empirical hypotheses would apply to them also.

Nevertheless we shall not adopt either a subjectivist or a utilitarian analysis of ethical terms. We reject the subjectivist view that to call an action right, or a thing good, is to say that it is generally approved of, because it is not self-contradictory to assert that some actions which are generally approved of are not right, or that some things which are generally approved of are not good. And we reject the alternative subjectivist view that a man who asserts that a certain action is right, or that a certain thing is good, is saying that he himself approves of it, on the ground that a man who confessed that he sometimes approved of what was bad or wrong would not be contradicting himself. And a similar argument is fatal to utilitarianism. We cannot agree that to call an action right is to say that of all the actions possible in the circumstances it would cause, or be likely to cause, the greatest happiness, or the greatest balance of pleasure over pain, or the greatest balance of satisfied over unsatisfied desire, because we find that it is not self-contradictory to say that it is sometimes wrong to perform the action which would actually or probably cause the greatest happiness, or the greatest balance of pleasure over pain, or of satisfied over unsatisfied desire. And since it is not self-contradictory to say that some pleasant things are not good, or that some bad things are desired, it cannot be the case that the sentence "x is good" is equivalent to "x is pleasant," or to "x is desired." And to every other variant of utilitarianism with which I am acquainted the same objection can be made. And therefore we should, I think, conclude that the validity of ethical judgements is not determined by the felicific tendencies of actions, any more than by the nature of people's feelings; but that it must be regarded as "absolute" or "intrinsic," and not empirically calculable.

If we say this, we are not, of course, denying that it is possible to invent a language in which all ethical symbols are definable in non-ethical terms, or even that it is desirable to invent such a language and adopt it in place of our own; what we are denying is that the suggested reduction of ethical to non-ethical statements is consistent with the conventions of our actual language. That is, we reject utilitarianism and subjectivism, not as proposals to replace our existing ethical notions by new ones, but as analyses of our existing ethical notions. Our contention is simply that, in our language, sentences which contain normative ethical symbols are not equivalent to sentences which express psychological propositions, or indeed empirical propositions of any kind.

It is advisable here to make it plain that it is only normative ethical symbols, and not descriptive ethical symbols, that are held by us to be indefinable in factual terms. There is a danger of confusing these two types of symbols, because they are commonly constituted by signs of the same sensible form. Thus a complex sign of the form "x is wrong" may constitute a sentence which expresses a moral judgement concerning a certain type of conduct, or it may constitute a sentence which states that a certain type of conduct is repugnant to the moral sense of a particular society. In the latter case, the symbol "wrong" is a descriptive ethical symbol, and the sentence in which it occurs expresses an ordinary sociological proposition; in the former case, the symbol "wrong" is a normative ethical symbol, and the sentence in which it occurs does not, we maintain, express an empirical proposition at all. It is only with normative ethics that we are at present concerned; so that whenever ethical symbols are used in the course of this argument without qualification, they are always to be interpreted as symbols of the normative type.

In admitting that normative ethical concepts are irreducible to empirical concepts, we seem to be leaving the way clear for the "absolutist" view of ethics—that is, the view that statements of value are not controlled by observation, as ordinary empirical propositions are, but only by a mysterious "intellectual intuition." A feature of this theory, which is seldom recognized by its advocates, is that it makes statements of value unverifiable. For it is notorious that what seems intuitively certain to one person may seem doubtful, or even false, to another. So that unless it is possible to provide some criterion by which one may decide between conflicting intuitions, a mere appeal to intuition is worthless as a test of a proposition's validity. But in the case of moral judgements, no such criterion can be given. Some moralists claim to settle the matter by saying that they "know" that their own moral judgements are correct. But such an assertion is of purely psychological interest, and has not the slightest tendency to prove the validity of any moral judgement. For dissentient moralists may equally well "know" that their ethical views are correct. And, as far as subjective certainty goes, there will be nothing to choose between them. When such differences of opinion arise in connection with an ordinary empirical proposition, one may attempt to resolve them by referring to, or actually carrying out, some relevant empirical test. But with regard to ethical statements, there is, on the "absolutist" or "intuitionist" theory, no relevant empirical test. We are therefore justified in saying that on this theory ethical statements are held to be unverifiable. They are, of course, also held to be genuine synthetic propositions.

Considering the use which we have made of the principle that a synthetic proposition is significant only if it is empirically verifiable, it is clear that the acceptance of an "absolutist" theory of ethics would undermine the whole of our main argument. And as we have already rejected the "naturalistic" theories which are commonly supposed to provide the only alternative to "absolutism" in ethics, we seem to have reached a difficult position. We shall meet the difficulty by showing that the correct treatment of ethical statements is afforded by a third theory, which is wholly compatible with our radical empiricism.

We begin by admitting that the fundamental ethical concepts are unanalysable, inasmuch as there is no criterion by which one can test the validity of the judgements in which they occur. So far we are in agreement with the absolutists. But, unlike the absolutists, we are able to give an explanation of this fact about ethical concepts. We say that the reason why they are unanalysable is that they are mere pseudo-concepts. The presence of an ethical symbol in a proposition adds nothing to its factual content. Thus if I say to someone, "You acted wrongly in stealing that money," I am not stating anything more than if I had simply said, "You stole that money." In adding that this action is wrong I am not making any further statement about it. I am simply evincing my moral disapproval of it. It is as if I had said, "You stole that money," in a peculiar tone of horror, or written it with the addition of some special exclamation marks. The tone, or the exclamation marks, adds nothing to the literal meaning of the sentence. It merely serves to show that the expression of it is attended by certain feelings in the speaker.

If now I generalise my previous statement and say, "Stealing money is wrong," I produce a sentence which has no factual meaning—that is, expresses no proposition which can be either true or false. It is as if I had written "Stealing money!!"—where the shape and thickness of the exclamation marks show, by a suitable convention, that a special sort of moral disapproval is the feeling which is being expressed. It is clear that there is nothing said here which can be true or false. Another man may disagree with me about the wrongness of stealing, in a sense that he may not have the same feelings about stealing as I have, and he may quarrel with me on account of my moral sentiments. But he cannot, strictly speaking, contradict me. For in saying that a certain type of action is right or wrong, I am not making any factual statement, not even a statement about my own state of mind. I am merely expressing certain moral sentiments. And the man who is ostensibly contradicting me is merely expressing his moral sentiments. So that there is plainly no sense in asking which of us is in the right. For neither of us is asserting a genuine proposition.

What we have just been saying about the symbol "wrong" applies to all normative ethical symbols. Sometimes they occur in sentences which record ordinary empirical facts besides expressing ethical feeling about those facts: sometimes they occur in sentences which simply express ethical feeling about a certain type of action, or situation, without making any statement of fact. But in every case in which one would commonly be said to be making an ethical judgment, the function of the relevant ethical word is purely "emotive." It is used to express feeling about certain objects, but not to make any assertion about them.

It is worth mentioning that ethical terms do not serve only to express feeling. They are calculated also to arouse feeling, and so to stimulate action. Indeed some of them are used in such a way as to give the sentences in which they occur the effect of commands. Thus the sentence "It is your duty to tell the truth" may be regarded both as the expression of a certain sort of ethical feeling about truthfulness and as the expression of the command "Tell the truth." The sentence "You ought to tell the truth" also involves the command "Tell the truth," but here the tone of the command is less emphatic. In the sentence "It is good to tell the truth" the command has become little more than a suggestion. And thus the "meaning" of the word "good," in its ethical usage, is differentiated from that of the word "duty" or the word "ought." In fact we may define the meaning of the various ethical words in terms both of the different feelings they are ordinarily taken to express, and also the different responses which they are calculated to provoke.

We can now see why it is impossible to find a criterion for determining the validity of ethical judgements. It is not because they have an "absolute" validity which is mysteriously independent of ordinary sense-experience, but because they have no objective validity whatsoever. If a sentence makes no statement at all, there is obviously no sense in asking whether what it says is true or false. And we have seen that sentences which simply express moral judgements do not say anything. They are pure expressions of feeling and as such do not come under the category of truth and falsehood. They are unverifiable for the same reason as a cry of pain or a word of command is unverifiable—because they do not express genuine propositions.

Thus, although our theory of ethics might fairly be said to be radically subjectivist, it differs in a very important respect from the orthodox subjectivist theory. For the orthodox subjectivist does not deny, as we do, that the sentences of a moralizer express genuine propositions. All he denies is that they express propositions of a unique non-empirical character. His own view is that they express propositions about the speaker's feelings. If this were so, ethical judgements clearly would be capable of being true or false. They would be true if the speaker had the relevant feelings, and false if he had not. And this is a matter which is, in principle, empirically verifiable. Furthermore they could be significantly contradicted. For if I say, "Tolerance is a virtue," and someone answers, "You don't approve of it," he would, on the ordinary subjectivist theory, be contradicting me. On our theory, he would not be contradicting me, because, in saying that tolerance was a virtue, I should not be making any statement about my own feelings or about anything else. I should simply be evincing my feelings, which is not at all the same thing as saying that I have them.

The distinction between the expression of feeling and the assertion of feeling is complicated by the fact that the assertion that one has a certain feeling often accompanies the expression of that feeling, and is then, indeed, a factor in the expression of that feeling. Thus I may simultaneously express boredom and say that I am bored, and in that case my utterance of the words, "I am bored," is one of the circumstances which make it true to say that I am expressing or evincing boredom. But I can express boredom without actually saying that I am bored. I can express it by my tone and gestures, while making a statement about something wholly unconnected with it, or by an ejaculation, or without uttering any words at all. So that even if the assertion that one has a certain feeling always involves the expression of that feeling, the expression of a feeling assuredly does not always involve the assertion that one has it. And this is the important point to grasp in considering the distinction between our theory and the ordinary subjectivist theory. For whereas the subjectivist holds that ethical statements actually assert the existence of certain feelings, we hold that ethical statements are expressions and excitants of feeling which do not necessarily involve any assertions.

We have already remarked that the main objection to the ordinary subjectivist theory is that the validity of ethical judgements is not determined by the nature of their author's feelings. And this is an objection which our theory escapes. For it does not imply that the existence of any feelings is a necessary and sufficient condition of the validity of an ethical judgement. It implies, on the contrary, that ethical judgements have no validity.

There is, however, a celebrated argument against subjectivist theories which our theory does not escape. It has been pointed out by Moore that if ethical statements were simply statements about the speaker's feelings, it would be impossible to argue about questions of value.[1] To take a typical example: if a man said that thrift was a virtue, and another replied that it was a vice, they would not, on this theory, be disputing with one another. One would be saying that he approved of thrift, and the other that he didn't; and there is no reason why both these statements should not be true. Now Moore held it to be obvious that we do dispute about questions of value, and accordingly concluded that the particular form of subjectivism which he was discussing was false.

It is plain that the conclusion that it is impossible to dispute about questions of value follows from our theory also. For as we hold that such sentences as "Thrift is a virtue" and "Thrift is a vice" do not express propositions at all, we clearly cannot hold that they express incompatible propositions. We must therefore admit that if Moore's argument really refutes the ordinary subjectivist theory, it also refutes ours. But, in fact, we deny that it does refute even the ordinary subjectivist theory. For we hold that one really never does dispute about questions of value.

This may seem, at first sight, to be a very paradoxical assertion. For we certainly do engage in disputes which are ordinarily regarded as disputes about questions of value. But, in all such cases, we find, if we consider the matter closely, that the dispute is not really about a question of value, but about a question of fact. When someone disagrees with us about the moral value of a certain action or type of action, we do admittedly resort to argument in order to win him over to our way of thinking. But we do not attempt to show by our arguments that he has the "wrong" ethical feeling towards a situation whose nature he has correctly apprehended. What we attempt to show is that he is mistaken about the facts of the case. We argue that he has misconceived the agent's motive: or that he has misjudged the effects of the action, or its probable effects in view of the agent's knowledge; or that he has failed to take into account the special circumstances in which the agent was placed. Or else we employ more general arguments about the effects which actions of a certain type tend to produce, or the qualities which are usually manifested in their performance. We do

[1] Cf. *Philosophical Studies*, "The Nature of Moral Philosophy."

this in the hope that we have only to get our opponent to agree with us about the nature of the empirical facts for him to adopt the same moral attitude towards them as we do. And as the people with whom we argue have generally received the same moral education as ourselves, and live in the same social order, our expectation is usually justified. But if our opponent happens to have undergone a different process of moral "conditioning" from ourselves, so that, even when he acknowledges all the facts, he still disagrees with us about the moral value of the actions under discussion, then we abandon the attempt to convince him by argument. We say that it is impossible to argue with him because he has a distorted or undeveloped moral sense; which signifies merely that he employs a different set of values from our own. We feel that our own system of values is superior, and therefore speak in such derogatory terms of his. But we cannot bring forward any arguments to show that our system is superior. For our judgement that it is so is itself a judgement of value, and accordingly outside the scope of argument. It is because argument fails us when we come to deal with pure questions of value, as distinct from questions of fact, that we finally resort to mere abuse.

In short, we find that argument is possible on moral questions only if some system of values is presupposed. If our opponent concurs with us in expressing moral disapproval of all actions of a given type *t*, then we may get him to condemn a particular action A, by bringing forward arguments to show that A is of type *t*. For the question whether A does or does not belong to that type is a plain question of fact. Given that a man has certain moral principles, we argue that he must, in order to be consistent, react morally to certain things in a certain way. What we do not and cannot argue about is the validity of these moral principles. We merely praise or condemn them in the light of our own feelings.

If anyone doubts the accuracy of this account of moral disputes, let him try to construct even an imaginary argument on a question of value which does not reduce itself to an argument about a question of logic or about an empirical matter of fact. I am confident that he will not succeed in producing a single example. And if that is the case, he must allow that its involving the impossibility of purely ethical arguments is not, as Moore thought, a ground of objection to our theory, but rather a point in favour of it.

Having upheld our theory against the only criticism which appeared to threaten it, we may now use it to define the nature of all ethical enquiries. We find that ethical philosophy consists simply in saying that ethical concepts are pseudo-concepts and therefore unanalysable. The further task of describing the different feelings that the different ethical terms are used to express, and the different reactions that they customarily provoke, is a task for the psychologist. There cannot be such a thing as ethical science, if by ethical science one means the elaboration of a "true" system of morals. For we have seen that, as ethical judgements are mere expressions of feeling, there can be no way of determining the validity of any ethical system, and, indeed, no sense in asking whether any such system is true. All that one may legitimately enquire in this connection is, What are the moral habits of a given person or group of people, and what causes them to have precisely those habits and feelings? And this enquiry falls wholly within the scope of the existing social sciences.

It appears, then, that ethics, as a branch of knowledge, is nothing more than a department of psychology and sociology. And in case anyone thinks that we are overlooking the existence of casuistry, we may remark that casuistry is not a science, but is a purely analytical investigation of the structure of a given moral system. In other words, it is an exercise in formal logic.

When one comes to pursue the psychological enquiries which constitute ethical science, one is immediately enabled to account for the Kantian and hedonistic theories of morals. For one finds that one of the chief causes of moral behaviour is fear, both conscious and unconscious, of a god's displeasure, and fear of the enmity of society. And this, indeed, is the reason why moral precepts present themselves to some people as "categorical" commands. And one finds, also, that the moral code of a society is partly determined by the beliefs of that society concerning the conditions of its own happiness—or, in other words, that a society tends to encourage or discourage a given type of conduct by the use of moral sanctions according as it appears to promote or detract from the contentment of the society as a whole. And this is the reason why altruism is recommended in most moral codes and egotism condemned. It is from the observation of this connection between morality and happiness that hedonistic or eudæmonistic theories of morals ultimately spring, just as the moral theory of Kant is based on the fact, previously explained, that moral precepts have for some people the force of inexorable commands. As each of these theories ignores the fact which lies at the root of the other, both may be criticized as being one-sided; but this is not the main objection to either of them. Their essential defect is that they treat propositions which refer to the causes and attributes of our ethical feelings as if they were definitions of ethical concepts. And thus they fail to recognise that ethical concepts are pseudo-concepts and consequently indefinable.

As we have already said, our conclusions about the nature of ethics apply to æsthetics also. Æsthetic terms are used in exactly the same way as ethical terms. Such æsthetic words as "beautiful" and "hideous" are employed, as ethical words are employed, not to make statements of fact, but simply to express certain feelings and evoke a certain response. It follows, as in ethics, that there is no sense in attributing objective validity to æsthetic judgements, and no possibility of arguing about questions of value in æsthetics, but only about questions of fact. A scientific treatment of æsthetics would show us what in general were the causes of æsthetic feeling, why various societies produced and admired the works of art they did, why taste varies as it does within a given society, and so forth. And these are ordinary psychological or sociological questions. They have, of course, little or nothing to do with æsthetic criticism as we understand it. But that is because the purpose of æsthetic criticism is not so much to give knowledge as to communicate emotion. The critic, by calling attention to certain features of the work under review, and expressing his own feelings about them, endeavours to make us share his attitude towards the work as a whole. The only relevant propositions that he formulates are propositions describing the nature of the work. And these are plain records of fact. We conclude, therefore, that there is nothing in æsthetics, any more than there is in ethics, to justify the view that it embodies a unique type of knowledge.

It should now be clear that the only information which we can legitimately derive from the study of our æsthetic and moral experiences is information about our own mental and physical make-up. We take note of these experiences as providing data for our psychological and sociological generalisations. And this is the only way in which they serve to increase our knowledge. It follows that any attempt to make our use of ethical and æsthetic concepts the basis of a metaphysical theory concerning the existence of a world of values, as distinct from the world of facts, involves a false analysis of these concepts. Our own analysis has shown that the phenomena of moral experience cannot fairly be used to support any rationalist or metaphysical doctrine whatsoever. In particular, they cannot, as Kant hoped, be used to establish the existence of a transcendent god.

*　　*　　*

Critique of Ayer [*]

〽〜〜

SIR DAVID ROSS

. . . THERE IS ONE of the arguments put forward by the positivists which seems to me to provide, when reflected on, an argument in favour not only of the view that our ethical judgments are genuine judgments, but of the view that there are fundamental ethical judgments for which general agreement may be claimed. Mr. Ayer remarks [1] that, while his theory escapes many of the objections brought against subjectivistic theories in ethics, there is one which it does not escape. This is the argument [2] that such theories would make it impossible to argue about questions of value, which nevertheless we undoubtedly do. He admits that his own theory also would make it impossible to argue about questions of value; as he holds that such sentences as "thrift is a virtue" and "thrift is a vice" do not express propositions at all, he clearly cannot hold that they express incompatible propositions. If, then, he is to resist the argument in question, he must simply deny that in fact we ever do dispute about questions of value; for if we did dispute about things which on his theory we cannot dispute about, his theory would clearly be untrue. He boldly adopts the course to which he is logically forced, and denies that we ever do dispute about questions of value. And he justifies this by saying that apparent disputes about questions of value are really disputes about questions of fact . . . [At this point Sir David quotes about two hundred words from Ayer's *Language, Truth and Logic*, pp. 163–6 (1936 edition), reprinted on pp. 399 ff. of the present volume.—Ed.] . . . It is perfectly true that, when we differ on a question of right or wrong, or of goodness or badness, it is by consideration of questions of fact—of the precise nature of the consequences or of the probable consequences, or of the motives involved —that we try to remove the difference of opinion on the moral question. And in doing so we betray the conviction that if we could get down to agreement about the facts of the case, we should find ourselves in agreement on the moral question; or in other words, that though we may differ in our moral judgments on some complicated case, we agree in our funda-

---

[*] Excerpted and reprinted by kind permission of the author and the publisher from *The Foundations of Ethics*, pp. 38–41. The Clarendon Press, 1939.
[1] *Language, Truth, and Logic*, p. 163 (1936 edition) [p. 399 this volume].
[2] Professor Moore's argument, in *Philosophical Studies*, 333–4.

mental judgments as to what kinds of consequences ought to be aimed at and what kinds of motive are good. The more Mr. Ayer emphasizes this element in our discussion of moral questions, the more he pays tribute to the strength of this conviction; for unless we thought that if we could agree on the factual nature of the act we should probably agree on its rightness or wrongness, there would be no point in trying to reach agreement about its factual nature. And in the great majority of cases we find this confidence confirmed, by finding that we agree in our moral judgements when we agree about the facts. But no doubt we sometimes fail to find agreement even then. We do not find, however, as Mr. Ayer claims, that no subject of dispute remains. We find, indeed, that there is no room for further *argument;* when we have come to some premiss which to us seems axiomatic, and which the other person denies, we can argue no further. But we do not find that all *difference of opinion* has vanished, and that we are left only with different feelings, one liking certain consequences or motives and another disliking them. We find ourselves still saying "this is good," and the person with whom we are speaking still saying "this is bad." And it is not by showing that *argument* ceases, but by showing that *difference of opinion* ceases, that Mr. Ayer could escape from Professor Moore's argument.

But indeed our adoption of the very practice which Mr. Ayer here describes is enough to refute his account of the nature of what are commonly called ethical judgments. He denies that they are judgments; he says they are mere expressions of liking or dislike. If that were all they are, why argue at all? What should we be trying to prove? Is *A* arguing to prove that he likes the given act, and *B* to prove that he dislikes it? Clearly not. *A* does not doubt that *B* dislikes it, nor *B* that *A* likes it; and if they did doubt, they would adopt quite different means of convincing one another, e.g. *A* by consistently seeking to do similar acts and *B* by consistently avoiding them. What they are attempting to do by the process Mr. Ayer describes is to convince each other that the liking, or the dislike, is justified, in other words that the act has a character that *deserves* to be liked or disliked, is good or is bad.

Moral Positivism and Moral Aestheticism[*]

E. F. CARRITT

MR. AYER, in *Language, Truth and Logic* (p. 161 [†]), says: "Sentences which simply express moral judgments do not say anything. They are pure expressions of feeling and as such do not come under the category of truth and falsehood . . . Aesthetic terms are used in exactly the same way as ethical terms."

This, I think, is one instance of a tendency to confuse the facts of moral and aesthetic experience which has been disastrous for both ethics and aesthetics. Its direct parentage is confessedly to be found in Hume, with his famous saying that "Morality is more properly felt than judged of," by which I suppose he means that what we call moral judgments would more properly be described as statements about or expressions of feeling. Butler, when controverting such views in the *Preface* to the Sermons, traces the confusion back to Shaftesbury, with the aphorism that "Beauty and Good (which in the context seems to mean moral goodness) are still the same" (*The Moralists*, Pt. III, ii, 67). Butler says: "The not taking into consideration the authority (i.e. obligation) which is implied in the idea of reflex approbation or disapprobation seems a material deficiency in Lord Shaftesbury's *Inquiry Concerning Virtue* (Bk. I, Pt. III, § iii; *Characteristics*, ii, p. 69). . . . Take in then that authority and obligation which is a constituent part of this reflex approbation, and it will undeniably follow, though a man should doubt of everything else, yet, that he would still remain under the nearest and most certain obligation to the practice of virtue." I want first to consider the view, surely a paradox in terms, that "moral judgments or the sentences expressing them do not say anything." For those who hold this cannot be expected to listen patiently to a discussion whether moral judgments say something (as Hume thought) about feelings or about some other facts, and if the latter whether they are ever true. If it can be shown that this view of Mr. Ayer is groundless and that moral judgments do assert something, it would be possible to go on to argue next that what they assert is not a state of mind of their maker or of anybody else, and lastly that they can be true. Indeed, if Mr. Ayer's view that "moral

* Excerpted and reprinted by kind permission of the author and the editor from *Philosophy*, 13, 1938.
† [p. 398 this volume.]

judgments assert nothing" can be refuted, we should have already converted at least him to the view that they assert something other than the existence of feelings. For he tells us that he was at first attracted by the view that moral judgments are really statements about somebody's state of feeling, and only when he saw this view to be clearly untenable, resorted to his own paradox as the sole remaining escape from what he calls "an absolutist view of ethics which would undermine the whole of his main argument" (*ibid.*, pp. 156–7 *). And if it can be shown not only that moral judgments assert something, but that what they assert is (as Mr. Ayer agrees) no state of anybody's mind, but rather a fact independent of anybody's thought or feeling about it, we might finally maintain that there is no reason to doubt that such assertions are sometimes true. Aesthetic judgments, assertions, i.e. that things are beautiful, also, I think, generally *mean* to attribute to the thing a quality independent of anybody's thoughts or feelings. But so far as they do assert this, there are reasons for thinking that perhaps none of them are true in the sense in which they are thus meant. But whether these reasons for denying the truth of aesthetic judgments, except as statements of feeling, are sound or no, they do not apply to moral judgments. Mr. Ayer at least would not pretend to show that moral judgments are false. It was just because his general theory would not allow him to hold any opinion about their truth or falsehood as regards independent facts that he was attracted by the view that they only asserted a state of mind, and when he found that untenable was driven to assert that they assert nothing. The steps of my argument then should be to show:

(1) That moral judgments, as the word judgment implies, assert something.
(2) That what they assert is not the existence of a feeling in myself or others, but, as they profess, a fact which is not a feeling.
(3) That once granted moral judgments do assert such a fact, there are no more valid reasons for doubting the possibility of their truth than that of other types of judgment, the motive for doing so being not any consideration of their own nature, but the desire to support a peculiar view of truth. And, in particular, we should try to show that certain arguments against the truth of any judgment which asserts beauty to belong to things independently of any feelings about them do not apply to moral judgments.

The first point, then, is that moral judgments assert something.

I

Mr. Ayer says (p. 158 †): "If I say to someone 'you acted wrongly in taking [1] that money, I am not stating anything more than if I had simply said, 'you took that money.' In adding that this action is wrong I am not making any further statement about it. I am simply evincing my moral

---

* [p. 396 this volume.]
† [pp. 396–7 this volume.]
[1] He says "stealing." I have substituted "taking" as he is clearly not entitled to a dyslogistic word.

disapproval of it. It is as if I had said 'you took that money' in a peculiar tone of horror, or written it with some special exclamation marks. The tone or the exclamation marks adds nothing to the literal meaning of the sentence. It merely serves to show that the expression of it is attended by certain feelings in the speaker. If now I generalize my previous statement and say 'Taking money is (in certain circumstances) wrong,' I produce a statement which has no factual meaning, that is, expresses no proposition which can be true or false. It is as if I had written 'Taking money!!' with two notes of exclamation to show, by a suitable convention, that a special sort of moral disapproval is the feeling which is being expressed." But let us take Mr. Ayer's language in this passage seriously. He says that if I say "you acted wrongly in taking that money" instead of saying "you took that money," the only difference (which he will not allow to be a difference of meaning) is that I *evince* moral disapproval, and again, he says that the sentence "stealing money is wrong" *shows* "by a *suitable convention* [2] that a special sort of moral disapproval is the feeling which is being expressed." But the evincing a feeling, or showing to others that I have a feeling, may be a voluntary act. And when I "adopt a suitable convention" for doing so, it certainly is. I clearly may tell or show a man, or evince to a man, that I feel disgust at what he is doing, though in fact I do not feel any, and he may believe me and alter his conduct in consequence. Evidently Mr. Ayer does not really think that to say "you ought not to take this money" is a mere involuntary symptom of disgust, as sweating may be of pain; it is a deliberate attempt to *show* or convince my audience of something by a *suitable verbal expression*, i.e. to *tell* them something, true or false. And what Mr. Ayer really, for all his protests, has said is that it tells them that I am feeling a certain disapproval or, as he says, that "a special sort of disapproval *is* the feeling that is being expressed." But unfortunately Mr. Ayer clearly recognizes that the two sentences, "I feel a special sort of moral disapproval for stealing" and "Men ought not to steal," cannot be substituted for one another, since he says that Professor Moore has pointed out there is no contradiction in asserting that stealing is wrong and that I do not have any feeling of disapproval against it, or, as I should prefer to put it, it is a perfectly intelligible question whether an act for which I feel moral disapproval is in fact one I ought not to do.

Just because Mr. Ayer had been convinced by Professor Moore on this point, he has to find some other account of what the statement "stealing is wrong" means. And he only sees two alternatives. He must either admit that when we say "taking such money is wrong" we mean (however mistakenly) that a man ought not to take such money, or he must resort to saying that we mean to assert nothing whatever, but are involuntarily symptomizing horror. It is hard to see how he can avoid the first course. For he grants that people do *think* that they have obligations, or, in his own Kantian language, "Moral precepts *present themselves to some people*

[2] My italics throughout.

as categorical commands" (p. 169 *), and "they have for some people *the force of* inexorable commands," where he cannot be using the word "command" literally, since moral judgments may apply to myself or to a third person or to past time. So when such people say they have a duty they in fact mean (however mistakenly) just what they say; yet Mr. Ayer argues that nevertheless the sentence they pronounce cannot mean what he allows they want it to mean. In the same way he says (p. 20) that a scientific sentence may be a pseudo-proposition (i.e. unmeaning) to one person, but not to another, since on him it may have the effect of making him believe *its* truth (p. 84) or at least assume its truth. But in that case what is "it"? We cannot either assume or believe the truth of a sentence which means nothing. For instance, Mr. Ayer says the sentence "*p* is a law of nature" may give rise to "a belief in a certain orderliness of nature." Yet he apparently holds that such beliefs, like moral beliefs, owing to a mysterious "rule which determines the literal significance of language," are incapable of being significantly expressed or stated to exist. I am at a loss about the nature of this rule or who issued it, or why it is called a rule rather than a fact. It can hardly be of the type "*Ought* in English means much the same as *Sollen* in German" or *Ought* means the opposite of *ought not*." So I am driven to fear that it was issued by Mr. Ayer, and that it is precisely the type of "rule" whose validity he is claiming to vindicate, such as "*Ought* means nothing." "*Law of nature* means nothing." If then "there are laws of nature (or obligations)" and "there are no laws of nature (or obligations)" are both unmeaning, they are not contradictory.

We are led to the curious conclusion that there are a large number of beliefs commonly held but incapable of being formulated in any sentence, and, by a strange coincidence, also a large number of sentences commonly supposed to formulate just those beliefs, but really incapable of meaning or asserting anything. It is a cruel law which debars these potential employers and potential employees from mutual accommodation. Again, if such sentences as "There are laws of nature" or "One ought to keep a promise" cannot mean what those who use them mean them to mean, namely, what Mr. Ayer admits they in fact believe, how did he come to know, or convey to us, what these beliefs are? He tells us men believe there are laws of nature and obligations, but "there are laws of nature (and obligations)" is an unmeaning sentence. Perhaps he remembers that he once held these beliefs and that, when he held them, he "evinced" the fact by certain unmeaning sentences which he then thought asserted what he believed. So he now conjectures that those who utter similar unmeaning sentences hold similar beliefs; and he hopes that when he tells us that "some men believe they have obligations," although "they have obligations" means nothing, we, too, shall recognize the meaningless sentence as a symptom of a belief which cannot be expressed.

* [p. 401 this volume.]

But, as I said before, though we cannot sweat in order to prove that we are in pain, we can always utter these symptomatic noises and so "by a *suitable* linguistic *convention*" induce others to believe *something*, either, for instance, that we have obligations or that we think we have. Of course, the fact is that when Mr. Ayer says such sentences as "stealing is wrong" have no meaning, he does not mean by his statement what other people would mean by it, or understand him to mean by it. Indeed, he tells us that he means by it that the sentence "stealing is wrong" cannot be translated into sentences which refer to sense-contents," or, in his other words, "it cannot be indicated how the proposition expressed by the sentence could be empirically verified." So that all he means when he says "stealing is wrong means nothing" is that it does not mean that the obligation has any sensible qualities such as colour, smell, taste, sound, or shape. And this would be true of some sentences which, I suppose, he would admit to express genuine propositions, if only about the speaker's state of mind, such as "I never understood that before" or "unverifiable sentences are meaningless." The view really implies, though Mr. Ayer would not admit it, that what a sentence means to assert is the possibility of obtaining sense-data which might verify or refute "it." But what then is "it"? Not surely, unmeaning sounds, for they cannot be verified or refuted. "It" must be the belief which the sentence means to assert and which another sentence may assert is verifiable in a certain way. If a belief, and therefore the sentence which expresses it, are about sensible things, then the sense-perception of those things might tend to refute or to verify that belief and sentence. But a belief cannot be that it is itself verifiable, and the same simple sentence cannot both assert what is believed and also how the belief can be verified. Yet surely the belief itself must be capable of being expressed and the sentence which expresses it must have a meaning. If a conjuror says, "There is a mouse in that box, but by the time you open it it will have disappeared without traces," he may be lying, but he is not making unmeaning sounds or even evincing feelings, and some people may believe him. That the sentences usually called moral judgments are not mere ejaculations which would be incapable of truth or of contradiction and are not even merely statements about the speaker's own feelings, is, I think, satisfactorily shown by Hume (*Enquiry*, IX, 1). "When a man denominates another, his *enemy*, his *rival*, his *antagonist*, his *adversary*, he is understood to speak the language of self-love, and to express sentiments, peculiar to himself, and arising from his particular circumstances and situation. But when he bestows on any man the epithets of *vicious* or *odious* or *depraved*, he then speaks another language, and expresses sentiments, in which he expects all his audience are to concur with him. He must here, therefore, depart from his private and particular situation, and must choose a point of view, common to him with others; he must move some universal principle of the human frame, and touch a string to which all mankind have an accord and symphony. If he means, therefore, to express *that this man possesses qualities, whose tendency is pernicious to society,* he has chosen this common point of view, and has touched the principle of humanity, in which every man, in some degree, concurs." Hume plainly thinks that if I say X ought not to have taken that money from Z, I can be contradicted, and that not merely by saying "I doubt if you really feel the disgust which such noises usually express," or even by saying "Hurrah for X," but rather by saying, "In taking that money from Z, X behaved in a beneficent way, and *therefore* in a way universally or generally agreeable to human contemplation." Indeed, the suggestion that so-called moral judgments assert nothing is so palpably false that I wonder Mr. Ayer did not try rather to bring them under his theory as what he calls tautologies. At least one type of moral judgment, "I ought to keep my promise," seems to be of the kind to which he should on his own theory give that name. It is indisputable that men use the expression "I promise," and I do not see how, when they do so, it could be maintained that they are either lying or deceived. For, of course, to say "you don't intend to keep your promise" is not to say "you don't promise." And other people understand what we mean when we promise and often alter their behaviour in consequence. Yet it is hard to see what a promise is if it is not, as Hume said, "binding oneself to the performance of an action." A man could not without self-contradiction make a promise while explaining that he was under no obligation to keep it. Possibly this is what Kant really *meant* when he said that to will universal promise-breaking involved a contradiction. If he did, we should have to suppose, that by his phrase "willing universal promise-breaking is contradictory" (a phrase I have never understood) he meant "denying the obligation to keep a promise which you have made is contradictory." Curiously enough, Hobbes seems to have held this view (*Leviathan*, XIV): "When a man hath abandoned, or granted away his Right, then is he said to be OBLIGED, or BOUND, not to hinder those, to whom such Right is granted, or abandoned, from the benefit of it: and that he *Ought*, and it is his DUTY, not to make voyd that voluntary act of his own: and that such hindrance is INJUSTICE, and INJURY, as being *sine jure*; the Right being before renounced, or transferred. So that *Injury*, or *Injustice*, in the controversies of the world, is somewhat like to that, which in the disputations of Scholars is called *Absurdity*. For as it is there called an Absurdity to contradict what one maintained in the Beginning; so in the world, it is called Injustice and Injury, voluntarily to undo that, which from the Beginning he hath voluntarily done."

II

To come now to my second point. If we agree with Hume that Mr. Ayer is wrong in saying that moral judgments assert nothing, we must agree with Mr. Ayer that Hume is wrong in saying that what they assert is the prevalence among mankind of a certain pleasure or distaste, arising from sympathy, in the contemplation of human dispositions and of the acts in which they issue. Just as I think Hume satisfactorily refutes Mr. Ayer's view, so I think Mr. Ayer satisfactorily refutes this of Hume.

*　　*　　*

III

It now remains to ask whether there is reason to think that all judgments thus asserting obligations must be false because on reflection we see that what we took for obligation is in fact a feeling. The answer seems to be that there is no such reason apart from the *dogma* that no judgments are true, or that there is no reason to think them so, unless they either could be sensibly verified or merely "state our intention to use language in a certain way."

The chief *argument* that moral judgments must be untrue is derived from a false analogy drawn between them and aesthetic judgments, which are assumed to be untrue if intended to assert an objective beauty. But just as I think the view that so-called moral judgments are meant to state the feelings of those who make them or of others is false, so I think the view that on reflection we see that consequently they are untrue, and that we must substitute for them judgments which do state the feelings of ourselves or others about actions is also false. And this latter false view, I believe, is closely connected with the venerable failure to distinguish moral and aesthetic experience.

*　　*　　*

A moral judgment (e.g. that I ought to pay this money) means something and can be significantly contradicted. But it is not contradicted by denying that I or the majority of people take any pleasure in contemplating the payment. The creditor's claim cannot vary with sympathies, or debts could be cancelled by propaganda. The judgment "he acted morally" no doubt generally *implies* a feeling of approbation, but it *states* that he did what he did because he believed it his duty; and this belief was not about feelings but about obligation.

It is by no means so clear that judgments like "The Alps are beautiful" or "Pope's Odyssey is less beautiful than that of Voss" truly assert any real quality of things other than their relation to human feelings. It is not clear that the Alps always had a quality of beauty though everybody had so far loathed the horrid sight, nor that the second statement could be consistent with asserting that everybody who knew both preferred Pope. And whatever our decision on the point may be, it is a significant fact that what by reflection becomes clearer about the moral judgments becomes less clear about the aesthetic.

*　　*　　*

It must be allowed, as the Provost of Oriel [3] points out, that we commonly *mean* by "beauty" (as we do by "pleasant" though not by "strange") a quality belonging to an object apart from relation to minds; but I agree with him that, on reflection, we see that the things called beautiful or pleasant may not have any common character (as "surprising" things have not) except the power to produce in some persons a particular kind of experience. "The actual occurrence of the enjoyment depends on conditions in the experient as well as conditions in the object." So if one man calls the object beautiful and another ugly, both are wrong if they are asserting it has either independent quality; both may be right if they only mean that it is capable of exciting genuine aesthetic enjoyment and repulsion in different persons.

This view is not inconsistent with Kant's claim that we *demand*, though we do not find, universal agreement with our aesthetic judgments—if only the object could, as it never can, have precisely the same emotional significance to all men. Nor is it inconsistent with the distinction of good and bad taste. Bad taste is the incapacity or narrowly limited capacity for pure aesthetic experiences. A man who enjoys contemplating nothing which does not soothe or profit or edify him, or gratify his pride or malice or appetites and affections, has bad taste. He may use the word beautiful, but he has few or no aesthetic experiences. The more capacity a man has for pure aesthetic experiences the better his taste, whatever the objects which arouse them.

Similarly a man is more *moral* (as distinct from being naturally virtuous on the one hand and correctly behaved on the other) the more moral experiences he has; that is to say, the more acts he does because he believes them to be his duty. The character of what he does in no way affects his morality. There are no acts moral or immoral in themselves apart from the agent's beliefs about his obligations. It is perhaps this analogy between morality and good taste which has contributed to the confusion of moral and aesthetic judgments. But the vital difference for which I have been contending remains. Moral judgments are of two kinds: "That act was done because the agent thought it his duty," and "A given situation involves an obligation on rational beings to act in a certain way." Both types of judgment seem to be true or false whatever people may think or feel about the acts in question. At least none of the arguments which we have been considering, as tending to show that what is called beauty is a subjective state, seem to apply to obligations. Obligations are not secondary qualities, nor indeed qualities of things at all. They arise out of the relations of persons, and there is nothing of whose reality we are more certain than persons. Kant, indeed, held that obligations or, as he oddly called them, the moral law, are the one kind of facts about which, and on the ground of which, we could make synthetic judgments *a priori* that could be true not only of what he calls phenomenal reality but of things in themselves.

[3] Ross, *The Right and the Good*, p. 128 n.

Nor is Price less emphatic in his condemnation of the "moral sense school."

One may have the pure moral experience in robbing the rich Peter to feed the starving Paul, and another in like situation might have it in resisting the temptation. And this difference may be due, like tastes in scenery, to their environment or upbringing. But once convince them that they have no duties to their neighbours and they could have no moral experience at all. On the other hand, Coleridge does not seem from his *Ode to Dejection* to have valued aesthetic experience less for being convinced that beauty lives in seeming.

Hitherto, for brevity and clearness, I have used the words obligation and duty in a general and popular sense. But certain objections, which might be suggested by the last paragraph, require to be met, and I believe can be met, by a more careful distinction. I do not feel these objections to be serious for my main point, but no doubt they have contributed to make plausible the view that obligation is a misnomer for peculiar feelings of pleasure in contemplating certain acts and characters. To begin with, obligations are in one sense mind-dependent in that they would not exist if there were no minds. They are not physical things, nor the relations of physical things or of animals to one another, if our idea of animal consciousness is correct. They arise out of the relations of persons to one another or to other sentient beings. Secondly, there is also a sense in which they depend upon feelings, or rather presuppose that the beings in question have feelings and desires. As Hume pointed out, if all sentient creatures were secure of satisfaction for all their desires, or if they had no desires at all, at least most of our more obvious duties would disappear. I do not see, for instance, how it would be possible to owe anybody anything. At any rate, *what* we ought to do for people must largely depend upon their feelings and wants, and these will to some extent depend upon their beliefs. But since in fact there are sentient beings, some of whom are rational persons, in various relations to one another, the obligations which arise out of these relations are facts whatever anybody may feel or think about them. Thirdly, there is a more subtle sense in which our obligations might be said to depend upon our beliefs. It seems that a man cannot be morally bound to do what is impossible for him. It cannot be a surgeon's duty to give anaesthetics if none are procurable or to fly to the patient's aid if there is no aircraft. But what makes it impossible to do something may be our ignorance. Nothing else prevented our ancestors from supplying surgeons with morphia and planes. It seems more natural to say that it is our duty to give a man the dose which, after the best inquiry, we think most likely to cure him than that it is our duty to cure him. Perhaps we may say that the duties to which situations give rise are always duties to *try* to alter or maintain those situations. There is nothing subjective about this. A little more puzzling is the fact that our duties depend upon our beliefs about the situation. If I believe a man is ill, it may be my duty to try to cure him though in fact he is shamming. So, strictly, our duties would be to try to maintain or alter situations which we believe to exist; and one element in all situations which we should try to alter would be our conscious ignorance of other elements in our situation the knowledge of which might give rise to obligations. And here, too, there seems nothing subjective about the obligation. It is true that when I remind a man of a debt I am more apt to say "You owe me" or "You ought to pay me" than "I can tell you something which will make you owe me." But I should not say, "You ought to have paid me though you did not know of the debt"; rather perhaps, "You ought to have been more careful to remember." We should certainly be prepared to say that I never ceased to have a right to be paid, and it has been suggested that it would be convenient to speak of "responsibilities" or "claims upon me," of which I may be ignorant and which, when I become aware of them (in the absence of any stronger conflicting claims), give rise to duties. In none of the situations described does my duty depend upon my belief that it is my duty (which would be absurd) or upon my feeling about the situation or the change in question. There is nothing here analogous to the doubt if beauty does not depend on thoughts and feelings. None of these considerations seem to me to make it at all plausible that, when we speak of an obligation to do something, all that is true is that we or others have a particular feeling about acts of the kind. Nor can I think of any other arguments directed to that end.

My conclusion is that our moral and aesthetic judgments differ fundamentally in this: It is at least very questionable if, on reflection, we can believe that things have what we call beauty whether anybody is affected aesthetically by them or not. All that may be true is that some or all things are capable, under certain conditions, of affecting persons in that way, as they may also be capable of affecting them with surprise or pleasure. And if this were true we should have no less reason to enjoy our aesthetic experiences or to distinguish them from other experiences or to value them in proportion to their purity. On the other hand, reflection on our moral judgments more and more convinces me that the relations in which we stand to our fellows are in objective fact grounds of real obligation. And if we could really cease to believe this, and be persuaded that when something is called our duty all that is true is that some people have certain feelings about it, the moral experience would become impossible for us. If we really sometimes are under obligations, there is goodness in acting from the belief that we are so on a given occasion; if not, not. And it seems to me undeniable that there is. But the goodness of aesthetic experience does not depend upon beauty being a quality of objects.

The Emotive Meaning of Ethical Terms *

C. L. STEVENSON

I

ETHICAL QUESTIONS first arise in the form "Is so and so good?" or "Is this alternative better than that?" These questions are difficult partly because we don't quite know what we are seeking. We are asking, "Is there a needle in that haystack?" without even knowing just what a needle is. So the first thing to do is to examine the questions themselves. We must try to make them clearer, either by defining the terms in which they are expressed, or by any other method that is available.

The present paper is concerned wholly with this preliminary step of making ethical questions clear. In order to help answer the question "Is X good?" we must *substitute* for it a question which is free from ambiguity and confusion.

It is obvious that in substituting a clearer question we must not introduce some utterly different kind of question. It won't do (to take an extreme instance of a prevalent fallacy) to substitute for "Is X good?" the question "Is X pink with yellow trimmings?" and then point out how easy the question really is. This would beg the original question, not help answer it. On the other hand, we must not expect the substituted question to be strictly "identical" with the original one. The original question may embody hypostatization, anthropomorphism, vagueness, and all the other ills to which our ordinary discourse is subject. If our substituted question is to be clearer, it must remove these ills. The questions will be identical only in the sense that a child is identical with the man he later becomes. Hence we must not demand that the substitution strike us, on immediate introspection, as making no change in meaning.

Just how, then, must the substituted question be related to the original? Let us assume (inaccurately) that it must result from replacing "good" by some set of terms which define it. The question then resolves itself to this: How must the defined meaning of "good" be related to its original meaning?

I answer that it must be *relevant*. A defined meaning will be called "relevant" to the original meaning under these circumstances: Those who

* Reprinted by kind permission of the author and the editor from *Mind*, 46, 1937.

have understood the definition must be able to say all that they then want to say by using the term in the defined way. They must never have occasion to use the term in the old, unclear sense. (If a person did have to go on using the word in the old sense, then to this extent his meaning would not be clarified, and the philosophical task would not be completed.) It frequently happens that a word is used so confusedly and ambiguously that we must give it *several* defined meanings, rather than one. In this case only the whole set of defined meanings will be called "relevant," and any one of them will be called "partially relevant." This is not a rigorous treatment of *relevance*, by any means; but it will serve for the present purposes.

Let us now turn to our particular task—that of giving a relevant definition of "good." Let us first examine some of the ways in which others have attempted to do this.

The word "good" has often been defined in terms of *approval*, or similar psychological attitudes. We may take as typical examples: "good" means *desired by me* (Hobbes); and "good" means *approved by most people* (Hume, in effect).* It will be convenient to refer to definitions of this sort as "interest theories," following Mr. R. B. Perry, although neither "interest" nor "theory" is used in the most usual way.

Are definitions of this sort relevant?

It is idle to deny their *partial* relevance. The most superficial inquiry will reveal that "good" is exceedingly ambiguous. To maintain that "good" is *never* used in Hobbes's sense, and never in Hume's, is only to manifest an insensitivity to the complexities of language. We must recognize, perhaps, not only these senses, but a variety of similar ones, differing both with regard to the kind of interest in question, and with regard to the people who are said to have the interest.

But this is a minor matter. The essential question is not whether interest theories are *partially* relevant, but whether they are *wholly* relevant. This is the only point for intelligent dispute. Briefly: Granted that some senses of "good" may relevantly be defined in terms of interest, is there some *other* sense which is *not* relevantly so defined? We must give this question careful attention. For it is quite possible that when philosophers (and many others) have found the question "Is X good?" so difficult, they have been grasping for this *other* sense of "good," and not any sense relevantly defined in terms of interest. If we insist on defining "good" in terms of interest, and answer the question when thus interpreted, we may be begging *their* question entirely. Of course this *other* sense of "good" may not exist, or it may be a complete confusion; but that is what we must discover.

Now many have maintained that interest theories are *far* from being completely relevant. They have argued that such theories neglect the very

* [The author has asked us, in republishing this paper, to add the note which follows: For a more adequate treatment of Hume's views see my *Ethics and Language* (Yale University Press, 1944), Chap. XII, Sect. 5. In the present paper the references to Hume are to be taken as references to the general *family* of definitions of which Hume's is typical; but Hume's own definition is somewhat different from any that is here specifically stated. Perhaps the same should be said of Hobbes.]

sense of "good" which is most vital. And certainly, their arguments are not without plausibility.

Only . . . what *is* this "vital" sense of "good"? The answers have been so vague, and so beset with difficulties, that one can scarcely determine.

There are certain requirements, however, with which this "vital" sense has been expected to comply—requirements which appeal strongly to our common sense. It will be helpful to summarize these, showing how they exclude the interest theories:

In the first place, we must be able sensibly to *disagree* about whether something is "good." This condition rules out Hobbes's definition. For consider the following argument: "This is good." "That isn't so; it's not good." As translated by Hobbes, this becomes: "I desire this." "That isn't so, for *I* don't." The speakers are not contradicting one another, and think they are, only because of an elementary confusion in the use of pronouns. The definition, "good" means *desired by my community*, is also excluded, for how could people from different communities disagree? [1]

In the second place, "goodness" must have, so to speak, a magnetism. A person who recognizes X to be "good" must *ipso facto* acquire a stronger tendency to act in its favour than he otherwise would have had. This rules out the Humian type of definition. For according to Hume, to recognize that something is "good" is simply to recognize that the majority approve of it. Clearly, a man may see that the majority approve of X without having, himself, a stronger tendency to favour it. This requirement excludes any attempt to define "good" in terms of the interest of people *other* than the speaker. [2]

In the third place, the "goodness" of anything must not be verifiable solely by use of the scientific method. "Ethics must not be psychology." This restriction rules out all of the traditional interest theories, without exception. It is so sweeping a restriction that we must examine its plausibility. What are the methodological implications of interest theories which are here rejected?

According to Hobbes's definition, a person can prove his ethical judgments, with finality, by showing that he is not making an introspective error about his desires. According to Hume's definition, one may prove ethical judgments (roughly speaking) by taking a vote. *This* use of the empirical method, at any rate, seems highly remote from what we usually accept as proof, and reflects on the complete relevance of the definitions which imply it.

But aren't there more complicated interest theories which are immune from such methodological implications? No, for the same factors appear; they are only put off for a while. Consider, for example, the definition: "X is good" means *most people would approve of X if they knew its nature and consequences*. How, according to this definition, could we prove that a certain X was good? We should first have to find out, empirically, just

[1] See G. E. Moore's *Philosophical Studies*, pp. 332–334.
[2] See G. C. Field's *Moral Theory*, pp. 52, 56–57.

what X was like, and what its consequences would be. To this extent the empirical method, as required by the definition, seems beyond intelligent objection. But what remains? We should next have to discover whether most people would approve of the sort of thing we had discovered X to be. This couldn't be determined by popular vote—but only because it would be too difficult to explain to the voters, beforehand, what the nature and consequences of X really were. Apart from this, voting would be a pertinent method. We are again reduced to counting noses, as a *perfectly final* appeal.

Now we need not scorn voting entirely. A man who rejected interest theories as irrelevant might readily make the following statement: "If I believed that X would be approved by the majority, when they knew all about it, I should be strongly *led* to say that X was good." But he would continue: "*Need* I say that X was good, under the circumstances? Wouldn't my acceptance of the alleged 'final proof' result simply from my being democratic? What about the more aristocratic people? They would simply say that the approval of most people, even when they knew all about the object of their approval, simply had nothing to do with the goodness of anything, and they would probably add a few remarks about the low state of people's interests." It would indeed seem, from these considerations, that the definition we have been considering has presupposed democratic ideals from the start; it has dressed up democratic propaganda in the guise of a definition.

The omnipotence of the empirical method, as implied by interest theories and others, may be shown unacceptable in a somewhat different way. Mr. G. E. Moore's familiar objection about the open question is chiefly pertinent in this regard. No matter what set of scientifically knowable properties a thing may have (says Moore, in effect), you will find, on careful introspection, that it is an open question to ask whether anything having these properties is *good*. It is difficult to believe that this recurrent question is a totally confused one, or that it seems open only because of the ambiguity of "good." Rather, we must be using some sense of "good" which is not definable, relevantly, in terms of anything scientifically knowable. That is, the scientific method is not sufficient for ethics.[3]

These, then, are the requirements with which the "vital" sense of "good" is expected to comply: (1) goodness must be a topic for intelligent disagreement; (2) it must be "magnetic"; and (3) it must not be discoverable solely through the scientific method.

II

Let us now turn to my own analysis of ethical judgments. First let me present my position dogmatically, showing to what extent I vary from tradition.

[3] See G. E. Moore's *Principia Ethica*, chap. i [pp. 66 ff. this volume]. I am simply trying to preserve the spirit of Moore's objection, and not the exact form of it.

I believe that the three requirements, given alone, are perfectly sensible; that there is some *one* sense of "good" which satisfies all three requirements; and that no traditional interest theory satisfies them all. But this does not imply that "good" must be explained in terms of a Platonic Idea, or of a Categorical Imperative, or of an unique, unanalyzable property. On the contrary, the three requirements can be met by a *kind* of interest theory. *But we must give up a presupposition which all the traditional interest theories have made.*

Traditional interest theories hold that ethical statements are *descriptive* of the existing state of interests—that they simply *give information* about interests. (More accurately, ethical judgments are said to describe what the state of interests is, was, or will be, or to indicate what the state of interests *would* be under specified circumstances.) It is this emphasis on description, on information, which leads to their incomplete relevance. Doubtless there is always *some* element of description in ethical judgments, but this is by no means all. Their major use is not to indicate facts, but to *create an influence*. Instead of merely describing people's interests, they *change* or *intensify* them. They *recommend* an interest in an object, rather than state that the interest already exists.

For instance: When you tell a man that he oughtn't to steal, your object isn't merely to let him know that people disapprove of stealing. You are attempting, rather, to get *him* to disapprove of it. Your ethical judgment has a quasi-imperative force which, operating through suggestion, and intensified by your tone of voice, readily permits you to begin to *influence*, to *modify*, his interests. If in the end you do not succeed in getting *him* to disapprove of stealing, you will feel that you've failed to convince him that stealing is wrong. You will continue to feel this, even though he fully acknowledges that you disapprove of it, and that almost everyone else does. When you point out to him the consequences of his actions—consequences which you suspect he already disapproves of—these *reasons* which support your ethical judgment are simply a means of facilitating your influence. If you think you can change his interests by making vivid to him how others will disapprove of him, you will do so; otherwise not. So the consideration about other people's interest is just an additional means you may employ, in order to move him, and is not a part of the ethical judgment itself. Your ethical judgment doesn't merely describe interests to him, it directs his very interests. The difference between the traditional interest theories and my view is like the difference between describing a desert and irrigating it.

Another example: A munition maker declares that war is a good thing. If he merely meant that he approved of it, he would not have to insist so strongly, nor grow so excited in his argument. People would be quite easily convinced that he approved of it. If he merely meant that most people approved of war, or that most people would approve of it if they knew the consequences, he would have to yield his point if it were proved that this wasn't so. But he wouldn't do this, nor does consistency require it. He is not *describing* the state of people's approval; he is trying to *change* it by his influence. If he found that few people approved of war, he might insist all the more strongly that it was good, for there would be more changing to be done.

This example illustrates how "good" may be used for what most of us would call bad purposes. Such cases are as pertinent as any others. I am not indicating the *good* way of using "good." I am not influencing people, but am describing the way this influence sometimes goes on. If the reader wishes to say that the munition maker's influence is bad—that is, if the reader wishes to awaken people's disapproval of the man, and to make him disapprove of his own actions—I should at another time be willing to join in this undertaking. But this is not the present concern. I am not using ethical terms, but am indicating how they *are* used. The munition maker, in his use of "good," illustrates the persuasive character of the word just as well as does the unselfish man who, eager to encourage in each of us a desire for the happiness of all, contends that the supreme good is peace.

Thus ethical terms are *instruments* used in the complicated interplay and readjustment of human interests. This can be seen plainly from more general observations. People from widely separated communities have different moral attitudes. Why? To a great extent because they have been subject to different social influences. Now clearly this influence doesn't operate through sticks and stones alone; words play a great part. People praise one another, to encourage certain inclinations, and blame one another, to discourage others. Those of forceful personalities issue commands which weaker people, for complicated instinctive reasons, find it difficult to disobey, quite apart from fears of consequences. Further influence is brought to bear by writers and orators. Thus social influence is exerted, to an enormous extent, by means that have nothing to do with physical force or material reward. The ethical terms facilitate such influence. Being suited for use in *suggestion*, they are a means by which men's attitudes may be led this way or that. The reason, then, that we find a greater similarity in the moral attitudes of one community than in those of different communities is largely this: ethical judgments propagate themselves. One man says "This is good"; this may influence the approval of another person, who then makes the same ethical judgment, which in turn influences another person, and so on. In the end, by a process of mutual influence, people take up more or less the same attitudes. Between people of widely separated communities, of course, the influence is less strong; hence different communities have different attitudes.

These remarks will serve to give a general idea of my point of view. We must now go into more detail. There are several questions which must be answered: How does an ethical sentence acquire its power of influencing people—why is it suited to suggestion? Again, what has this influence to do with the *meaning* of ethical terms? And finally, do these considerations really lead us to a sense of "good" which meets the requirements mentioned in the preceding section?

Let us deal first with the question about *meaning*. This is far from an easy question, so we must enter into a preliminary inquiry about meaning in general. Although a seeming digression, this will prove indispensable.

III

Broadly speaking, there are two different *purposes* which lead us to use language. On the one hand we use words (as in science) to record, clarify, and communicate *beliefs*. On the other hand we use words to give vent to our feelings (interjections), or to create moods (poetry), or to incite people to actions or attitudes (oratory).

The first use of words I shall call "descriptive"; the second, "dynamic." Note that the distinction depends solely upon the *purpose* of the *speaker*.

When a person says "Hydrogen is the lightest known gas," his purpose *may* be simply to lead the hearer to believe this, or to believe that the speaker believes it. In that case the words are used descriptively. When a person cuts himself and says "Damn," his purpose is not ordinarily to record, clarify, or communicate any belief. The word is used dynamically. The two ways of using words, however, are by no means mutually exclusive. This is obvious from the fact that our purposes are often complex. Thus when one says "I want you to close the door," part of his purpose, ordinarily, is to lead the hearer to believe that he has this want. To that extent the words are used descriptively. But the major part of one's purpose is to lead the hearer to *satisfy* the want. To that extent the words are used dynamically.

It very frequently happens that the same sentence may have a dynamic use on one occasion, and may not have a dynamic use on another; and that it may have different dynamic uses on different occasions. For instance: A man says to a visiting neighbour, "I am loaded down with work." His purpose may be to let the neighbour know how life is going with him. This would *not* be a dynamic use of words. He may make the remark, however, in order to drop a hint. This *would* be dynamic usage (as well as descriptive). Again, he may make the remark to arouse the neighbour's sympathy. This would be a *different* dynamic usage from that of hinting.

Or again, when we say to a man, "Of course you won't make those mistakes any more," we *may* simply be making a prediction. But we are more likely to be using "suggestion," in order to encourage him and hence *keep* him from making mistakes. The first use would be descriptive; the second, mainly dynamic.

From these examples it will be clear that we can't determine whether words are used dynamically or not, merely by reading the dictionary— even assuming that everyone is faithful to dictionary meanings. Indeed, to know whether a person is using a word dynamically, we must note his tone of voice, his gestures, the general circumstances under which he is speaking, and so on.

We must now proceed to an important question: What has the dynamic use of words to do with their *meaning?* One thing is clear—we must not define "meaning" in a way that would make meaning vary with dynamic usage. If we did, we should have no use for the term. All that we could say about such "meaning" would be that it is very complicated, and subject to constant change. So we must certainly distinguish between the dynamic use of words and their meaning.

It doesn't follow, however, that we must define "meaning" in some non-psychological fashion. We must simply restrict the psychological field. Instead of identifying meaning with *all* the psychological causes and effects that attend a word's utterance, we must identify it with those that it has a *tendency* (causal property, dispositional property) to be connected with. The tendency must be a particular kind, moreover. It must exist for all who speak the language; it must be persistent; and must be realizable more or less independently of determinate circumstances attending the word's utterance. There will be further restrictions dealing with the inter-relation of words in different contexts. Moreover, we must include, under the psychological responses which the words tend to produce, not only immediately introspectable experiences, but *dispositions* to react in a given way with appropriate stimuli. I hope to go into these matters in a subse-quent paper. Suffice it now to say that I think "meaning" may be thus de-fined in a way to include "propositional" meaning as an important kind. Now a word may *tend* to have causal relations which in fact it sometimes doesn't; and it may sometimes have causal relations which it *doesn't tend* to have. And since the tendency of words which constitutes their meaning must be of a particular kind, and may include, as responses, dispositions to reactions, of which any of *several* immediate experiences may be a sign, then there is nothing surprising in the fact that words have a permanent meaning, in spite of the fact that the immediately introspectable experiences which attend their usage are so highly varied.

When "meaning" is defined in this way, meaning will not include dynamic use. For although words are sometimes accompanied by dynamic purposes, they do not *tend* to be accompanied by them in the way above mentioned. E.g., there is no tendency realizable independently of the determinate circumstances under which the words are uttered.

There will be a kind of meaning, however, in the sense above defined, which has an intimate relation to dynamic usage. I refer to "emotive" meaning (in a sense roughly like that employed by Ogden and Richards).[4] The emotive meaning of a word is a tendency of a word, arising through the history of its usage, to produce (result from) *affective* responses in

---

[4] See *The Meaning of Meaning*, by C. K. Ogden and I. A. Richards. On p. 125, second edition, there is a passage on ethics which was the source of the ideas embodied in this paper.

people. It is the immediate aura of feeling which hovers about a word. Such tendencies to produce affective responses cling to words very tenaciously. It would be difficult, for instance, to express merriment by using the interjection "alas." Because of the persistence of such affective tendencies (among other reasons) it becomes feasible to classify them as "meanings."

Just *what* is the relation between emotive meaning and the dynamic use of words? Let us take an example. Suppose that a man is talking with a group of people which includes Miss Jones, aged 59. He refers to her, without thinking, as an "old maid." Now even if his purposes are perfectly innocent—even if he is using the words purely descriptively—Miss Jones won't think so. She will think he is encouraging the others to have contempt for her, and will draw in her skirts, defensively. The man might have done better if instead of saying "old maid" he had said "elderly spinster." The latter words could have been put to the same descriptive use, and would not so readily have caused suspicions about the dynamic use.

"Old maid" and "elderly spinster" differ, to be sure, only in emotive meaning. From the example it will be clear that certain words, because of their emotive meaning, are suited to a certain kind of dynamic use—so well suited, in fact, that the hearer is likely to be misled when we use them in any other way. The more pronounced a word's emotive meaning is, the less likely people are to use it purely descriptively. Some words are suited to encourage people, some to discourage them, some to quiet them, and so on.

Even in these cases, of course, the dynamic purposes are not to be identified with any sort of meaning; for the emotive meaning accompanies a word much more persistently than do the dynamic purposes. But there is an important contingent relation between emotive meaning and dynamic purpose: the former assists the latter. Hence if we define emotively laden terms in a way that neglects their emotive meaning, we are likely to be confusing. *We lead people to think that the terms defined are used dynamically less often than they are.*

IV

Let us now apply these remarks in defining "good." This word may be used morally or non-morally. I shall deal with the non-moral usage almost entirely, but only because it is simpler. The main points of the analysis will apply equally well to either usage.

As a preliminary definition, let us take an inaccurate approximation. It may be more misleading than helpful, but will do to begin with. Roughly, then, the sentence "X is good" means *We like X.* ("We" includes the hearer or hearers.)

At first glance this definition sounds absurd. If used, we should expect to find the following sort of conversation: A. "This is good." B. "But I *don't* like it. What led you to believe that I did?" The unnaturalness of B's reply, judged by ordinary word-usage, would seem to cast doubt on the relevance of my definition.

B's unnaturalness, however, lies simply in this: he is assuming that "We like it" (as would occur implicitly in the use of "good") is being used descriptively. This won't do. When "We like it" is to take the place of "This is good," the former sentence must be used not purely descriptively, but dynamically. More specifically, it must be used to promote a very subtle (and for the non-moral sense in question, a very easily resisted) kind of *suggestion*. To the extent that "we" refers to the hearer, it must have the dynamic use, essential to suggestion, of leading the hearer to *make* true what is said, rather than merely to believe it. And to the extent that "we" refers to the speaker, the sentence must have not only the descriptive use of indicating belief about the speaker's interest, but the quasi-interjectory, dynamic function of giving direct expression to the interest. (This immediate expression of feelings assists in the process of suggestion. It is difficult to disapprove in the face of another's enthusiasm.)

For an example of a case where "We like this" is used in the dynamic way that "This is good" is used, consider the case of a mother who says to her several children, "One thing is certain, *we all like to be neat.*" If she really believed this, she wouldn't bother to say so. But she is not using the words descriptively. She is *encouraging* the children to like neatness. By telling them that they like neatness, she will lead them to *make* her statement true, so to speak. If, instead of saying "We all like to be neat" in this way, she had said "It's a good thing to be neat," the effect would have been approximately the same.

But these remarks are still misleading. Even when "We like it" is used for suggestion, it isn't quite like "This is good." The latter is more subtle. With such a sentence as "This is a good book," for example, it would be practically impossible to use instead "We like this book." When the latter is used, it must be accompanied by so exaggerated an intonation, to prevent its becoming confused with a descriptive statement, that the force of suggestion becomes stronger, and ludicrously more overt, than when "good" is used.

The definition is inadequate, further, in that the definiens has been restricted to dynamic usage. Having said that dynamic usage was different from meaning, I should not have to mention it in giving the *meaning* of "good."

It is in connection with this last point that we must return to emotive meaning. The word "good" has a pleasing emotive meaning which fits it especially for the dynamic use of suggesting favourable interest. But the sentence "We like it" has no such emotive meaning. Hence my definition has neglected emotive meaning entirely. Now to neglect emotive meaning is likely to lead to endless confusions, as we shall presently see; so I have sought to make up for the inadequacy of the definition by letting the restriction about dynamic usage take the place of emotive meaning. What I should do, of course, is to find a definiens whose emotive meaning, like that of "good," simply does *lead* to dynamic usage.

Why didn't I do this? I answer that it isn't possible, if the definition is to afford us increased clarity. No two words, in the first place, have quite the same emotive meaning. The most we can hope for is a rough approximation. But if we seek for such an approximation for "good," we shall find nothing more than synonyms, such as "desirable" or "valuable"; and these are profitless because they do not clear up the connection between "good" and favourable interest. If we reject such synonyms, in favour of non-ethical terms, we shall be highly misleading. For instance: "This is good" has something like the meaning of "I *do* like this; do so as well." But this is certainly not accurate. For the imperative makes an appeal to the conscious efforts of the hearer. Of course he can't like something just by trying. He must be led to like it through suggestion. Hence an ethical sentence differs from an imperative in that it enables one to make changes in a much more subtle, less fully conscious way. Note that the ethical sentence centres the hearer's attention not on his interests, but on the object of interest, and thereby facilitates suggestion. Because of its subtlety, moreover, an ethical sentence readily permits counter-suggestion, and leads to the give and take situation which is so characteristic of arguments about values.

Strictly speaking, then, it is impossible to define "good" in terms of favourable interest if emotive meaning is not to be distorted. Yet it is possible to say that "This is good" is *about* the favourable interest of the speaker and the hearer or hearers, and that it has a pleasing emotive meaning which fits the words for use in suggestion. This is a rough description of meaning, not a definition. But it serves the same clarifying function that a definition ordinarily does; and that, after all, is enough.

A word must be added about the moral use of "good." This differs from the above in that it is about a different kind of interest. Instead of being about what the hearer and speaker *like*, it is about a stronger sort of approval. When a person *likes* something, he is pleased when it prospers, and disappointed when it doesn't. When a person *morally approves* of something, he experiences a rich feeling of security when it prospers, and is indignant, or "shocked" when it doesn't. These are rough and inaccurate examples of the many factors which one would have to mention in distinguishing the two kinds of interest. In the moral usage, as well as in the non-moral, "good" has an emotive meaning which adapts it to suggestion.

And now, are these considerations of any importance? Why do I stress emotive meanings in this fashion? Does the omission of them really lead people into errors? I think, indeed, that the errors resulting from such omissions are enormous. In order to see this, however, we must return to the restrictions, mentioned in section I, with which the "vital" sense of "good" has been expected to comply.

V

The first restriction, it will be remembered, had to do with disagreement. Now there is clearly some sense in which people disagree on ethical points; but we must not rashly assume that all disagreement is modelled after the sort that occurs in the natural sciences. We must distinguish between "disagreement in belief" (typical of the sciences) and "disagreement in interest." Disagreement in belief occurs when A believes p and B disbelieves it. Disagreement in interest occurs when A has a favourable interest in X, when B has an unfavourable one in it, and when neither is content to let the other's interest remain unchanged.

Let me give an example of disagreement in interest. A. "Let's go to a cinema to-night." B. "I don't want to do that. Let's go to the symphony." A continues to insist on the cinema, B on the symphony. This is disagreement in a perfectly conventional sense. They can't agree on where they want to go, and each is trying to redirect the other's interest. (Note that imperatives are used in the example.)

It is disagreement in *interest* which takes places in ethics. When C says "This is good," and D says "No, it's bad," we have a case of suggestion and counter-suggestion. Each man is trying to redirect the other's interest. There obviously need be no domineering, since each may be willing to give ear to the other's influence; but each is trying to move the other none the less. It is in this sense that they disagree. Those who argue that certain interest theories make no provision for disagreement have been misled, I believe, simply because the traditional theories, in leaving out emotive meaning, give the impression that ethical judgments are used descriptively only; and of course when judgments are used purely descriptively, the only disagreement that can arise is disagreement *in belief*. Such disagreement may be disagreement in belief *about* interests; but this is not the same as disagreement *in* interest. My definition doesn't provide for disagreement in belief about interests, any more than does Hobbes's; but that is no matter, for there is no reason to believe, at least on common-sense grounds, that this kind of disagreement exists. There is only disagreement *in* interest. (We shall see in a moment that disagreement in interest does not remove ethics from sober argument—that this kind of disagreement may often be resolved through empirical means.)

The second restriction, about "magnetism," or the connection between goodness and actions, requires only a word. This rules out *only* those interest theories which do *not* include the interest of the speaker, in defining "good." My account does include the speaker's interest; hence is immune.

The third restriction, about the empirical method, may be met in a way that springs naturally from the above account of disagreement. Let us put the question in this way: When two people disagree over an ethical matter, can they completely resolve the disagreement through empirical considerations, assuming that each applies the empirical method exhaustively, consistently, and without error?

I answer that sometimes they can, and sometimes they cannot; and that at any rate, even when they can, the relation between empirical knowledge and ethical judgments is quite different from the one which traditional interest theories seem to imply.

This can best be seen from an analogy. Let's return to the example where A and B couldn't agree on a cinema or a symphony. The example differed from an ethical argument in that imperatives were used, rather than ethical judgments; but was analogous to the extent that each person was endeavouring to modify the other's interest. Now how would these people argue the case, assuming that they were too intelligent just to shout at one another?

Clearly, they would give "reasons" to support their imperatives. A might say, "But you know, Garbo is at the Bijou." His hope is that B, who admires Garbo, will acquire a desire to go to the cinema when he knows what play will be there. B may counter, "But Toscanini is guest conductor to-night, in an all-Beethoven programme." And so on. Each supports his imperative ("*Let's* do so and so") by reasons which may be empirically established.

To generalize from this: disagreement in interest may be rooted in disagreement in belief. That is to say, people who disagree in interest would often cease to do so if they knew the precise nature and consequences of the object of their interest. To this extent disagreement in interest may be resolved by securing agreement in belief, which in turn may be secured empirically.

This generalization holds for ethics. If A and B, instead of using imperatives, had said, respectively, "It would be *better* to go to the cinema," and "It would be better to go to the symphony," the reasons which they would advance would be roughly the same. They would each give a more thorough account of the object of interest, with the purpose of completing the redirection of interest which was begun by the suggestive force of the ethical sentence. On the whole, of course, the suggestive force of the ethical statement merely exerts enough pressure to start such trains of reasons, since the reasons are much more essential in resolving disagreement in interest than the persuasive effect of the ethical judgment itself.

Thus the empirical method is relevant to ethics simply because our knowledge of the world is a determining factor to our interests. But note that empirical facts are not inductive grounds from which the ethical judgment problematically follows. (This is what traditional interest theories imply.) If someone said "Close the door," and added the reason "We'll catch cold," the latter would scarcely be called an inductive ground of the former. Now imperatives are related to the reasons which support them in the same way that ethical judgments are related to reasons.

Is the empirical method *sufficient* for attaining ethical agreement?

Clearly not. For empirical knowledge resolves disagreement in interest only to the extent that such disagreement is rooted in disagreement in belief. Not all disagreement in interest is of this sort. For instance: A is of a sympathetic nature, and B isn't. They are arguing about whether a public dole would be good. Suppose that they discovered all the consequences of the dole. Isn't it possible, even so, that A will say that it's good, and B that it's bad? The disagreement in interest may arise not from limited factual knowledge, but simply from A's sympathy and B's coldness. Or again, suppose, in the above argument, that A was poor and unemployed, and that B was rich. Here again the disagreement might not be due to different factual knowledge. It would be due to the different social positions of the men, together with their predominant self-interest.

When ethical disagreement is not rooted in disagreement in belief, is there *any* method by which it may be settled? If one means by "method" a *rational* method, then there is no method. But in any case there is a "way." Let's consider the above example, again, where disagreement was due to A's sympathy and B's coldness. Must they end by saying, "Well, it's just a matter of our having different temperaments"? Not necessarily. A, for instance, may try to *change* the temperament of his opponent. He may pour out his enthusiasms in such a moving way—present the sufferings of the poor with such appeal—that he will lead his opponent to see life through different eyes. He may build up, by the contagion of his feelings, an influence which will modify B's temperament, and create in him a sympathy for the poor which didn't previously exist. This is often the only way to obtain ethical agreement, if there is any way at all. It is persuasive, not empirical or rational; but that is no reason for neglecting it. There is no reason to scorn it, either, for it is only by such means that our personalities are able to grow, through our contact with others.

The point I wish to stress, however, is simply that the empirical method is instrumental to ethical agreement only to the extent that disagreement in interest is rooted in disagreement in belief. There is little reason to believe that all disagreement is of this sort. Hence the empirical method is not sufficient for ethics. In any case, ethics is not psychology, since psychology doesn't endeavour to *direct* our interests; it discovers facts about the ways in which interests are or can be directed, but that's quite another matter.

To summarize this section: my analysis of ethical judgments meets the three requirements for the "vital" sense of "good" that were mentioned in section I. The traditional interest theories fail to meet these requirements simply because they neglect emotive meaning. This neglect leads them to neglect dynamic usage, and the sort of disagreement that results from such usage, together with the method of resolving the disagreement. I may add that my analysis answers Moore's objection about the open question. Whatever scientifically knowable properties a thing may have, it *is* always open to question whether a thing having these (enumerated) qualities is good. For to ask whether it is good is to ask for *influence*. And whatever

I may know about an object, I can still ask, quite pertinently, to be influenced with regard to my interest in it.

VI

And now, have I really pointed out the "vital" sense of "good"?

I suppose that many will still say "No," claiming that I have simply failed to set down *enough* requirements which this sense must meet, and that my analysis, like all others given in terms of interest, is a way of begging the issue. They will say: "When we ask 'Is X good?' we don't want mere influence, mere advice. We decidedly don't want to be influenced through persuasion, nor are we fully content when the influence is supported by a wide scientific knowledge of X. The answer to our question will, of course, modify our interests. But this is only because an unique sort of *truth* will be revealed to us—a truth which must be apprehended *a priori*. We want our interests to be guided by this truth, and by nothing else. To substitute for such a truth mere emotive meaning and suggestion is to conceal from us the very object of our search."

I can only answer that I do not understand. What is this truth to be *about*? For I recollect no Platonic Idea, nor do I know what to *try* to recollect. I find no indefinable property, nor do I know what to look for. And the "self-evident" deliverances of reason, which so many philosophers have claimed, seem, on examination, to be deliverances of their respective reasons only (if of anyone's) and not of mine.

I strongly suspect, indeed, that any sense of "good" which is expected both to unite itself in synthetic *a priori* fashion with other concepts, and to influence interests as well, is really a great confusion. I extract from this meaning the power of influence alone, which I find the only intelligible part. If the rest is confusion, however, then it certainly deserves more than the shrug of one's shoulders. What I should like to do is to *account* for the confusion—to examine the psychological needs which have given rise to it, and to show how these needs may be satisfied in another way. This is *the* problem, if confusion is to be stopped at its source. But it is an enormous problem, and my reflections on it, which are at present worked out only roughly, must be reserved until some later time.

I may add that if "X is good" is essentially a vehicle for suggestion, it is scarcely a statement which philosophers, any more than many other men, are called upon to make. To the extent that ethics predicates the ethical terms of anything, rather than explains their meaning, it ceases to be a reflective study. Ethical statements are social instruments. They are used in a co-operative enterprise in which we are mutually adjusting ourselves to the interests of others. Philosophers have a part in this, as do all men, but not the major part.

The Emotive Theory of Values *

꒰꒰꒱꒱

A. J. AYER

THE EMOTIVE THEORY of values, which is developed in the sixth chapter of this book, has provoked a fair amount of criticism; but I find that this criticism has been directed more often against the positivistic principles on which the theory has been assumed to depend than against the theory itself.[1] Now I do not deny that in putting forward this theory I was concerned with maintaining the general consistency of my position; but it is not the only ethical theory that would have satisfied this requirement, nor does it actually entail any of the non-ethical statements which form the remainder of my argument. Consequently, even if it could be shown that these other statements were invalid, this would not in itself refute the emotive analysis of ethical judgements; and in fact I believe this analysis to be valid on its own account.

Having said this, I must acknowledge that the theory is here presented in a very summary way, and that it needs to be supported by a more detailed analysis of specimen ethical judgements than I make any attempt to give.[2] Thus, among other things, I fail to bring out the point that the common objects of moral approval or disapproval are not particular actions so much as classes of actions; by which I mean that if an action is labelled right or wrong, or good or bad, as the case may be, it is because it is thought to be an action of a certain type. And this point seems to me important, because I think that what seems to be an ethical judgement is very often a factual classification of an action as belonging to some class of actions by which a certain moral attitude on the part of the speaker is habitually aroused. Thus, a man who is a convinced utilitarian may simply mean by calling an action right that it tends to promote, or more probably that it is the sort of action that tends to promote, the general

---

* Excerpted and reprinted by kind permission of the author and the publisher from the Introduction to the second edition of *Language, Truth and Logic*, pp. 20–22. Victor Gollancz, Ltd., 1946.

[1] *Cf.* Sir W. David Ross, *The Foundations of Ethics*, pp. 30–41 [reprinted in part, pp. 403–4 this volume].

[2] I understand that this deficiency has been made good by C. L. Stevenson in his book, *Ethics and Language*, but the book was published in America and I have not yet been able to obtain it. There is a review of it by Austin Duncan-Jones in *Mind*, October, 1945, and a good indication of Stevenson's line of argument is to be found in his articles on "The Emotive Meaning of Ethical Terms," *Mind*, 1937, "Ethical Judgements and Avoidability," *Mind*, 1938, and "Persuasive Definitions," *Mind*, 1938. [The first two of these three essays are included in the present volume.—Ed.]

happiness; and in that case the validity of his statement becomes an empirical matter of fact. Similarly, a man who bases his ethical upon his religious views may actually mean by calling an action right or wrong that it is the sort of action that is enjoined or forbidden by some ecclesiastical authority; and this also may be empirically verified. Now in these cases the form of words by which the factual statement is expressed is the same as that which would be used to express a normative statement; and this may to some extent explain why statements which are recognized to be normative are nevertheless often thought to be factual. Moreover, a great many ethical statements contain, as a factual element, some description of the action, or the situation, to which the ethical term in question is being applied. But although there may be a number of cases in which this ethical term is itself to be understood descriptively, I do not think that this is always so. I think that there are many statements in which an ethical term is used in a purely normative way, and it is to statements of this kind that the emotive theory of ethics is intended to apply.

The objection that if the emotive theory was correct it would be impossible for one person to contradict another on a question of value is here met by the answer that what seem to be disputes about questions of value are really disputes about questions of fact. I should, however, have made it clear that it does not follow from this that two persons cannot significantly disagree about a question of value, or that it is idle for them to attempt to convince one another. For a consideration of any dispute about a matter of taste will show that there can be disagreement without formal contradiction, and that in order to alter another man's opinions, in the sense of getting him to change his attitude, it is not necessary to contradict anything that he asserts. Thus, if one wishes to affect another person in such a way as to bring his sentiments on a given point into accordance with one's own, there are various ways in which one may proceed. One may, for example, call his attention to certain facts that one supposes him to have overlooked; and, as I have already remarked, I believe that much of what passes for ethical discussion is a proceeding of this type. It is, however, also possible to influence other people by a suitable choice of emotive language; and this is the practical justification for the use of normative expressions of value. At the same time, it must be admitted that if the other person persists in maintaining his contrary attitude, without however disputing any of the relevant facts, a point is reached at which the discussion can go no further. And in that case there is no sense in asking which of the conflicting views is true. For, since the expression of a value judgement is not a proposition, the question of truth or falsehood does not here arise.

A Reply to My Critics (Excerpt) *

〰〰

G. E. MOORE

. . . I PROPOSE THEREFORE to begin by discussing this view of Mr. Stevenson's.

Consider the sentence "It was right of Brutus to stab Caesar" or the sentence "Brutus' action in stabbing Caesar was right" or the sentence "When Brutus stabbed Caesar, he was acting rightly"—three sentences which seem all to have much the same meaning. Mr. Stevenson thinks (p. 80) that the definition " 'It was right of Brutus to stab Caesar' has the same meaning as 'I now approve of Brutus' stabbing of Caesar, which was occurring' " gives, *if amended in a particular way*, at least *one* "typically ethical" sense of these sentences. But he adds that he only thinks it does this "as closely as the vagueness of ordinary usage will allow." I take it that by the last clause he means that the sense which his amended definition would give to these sentences is more precise than any with which they would actually be used by any one who was using them in a way that was in accordance with ordinary usage; but he thinks that, though more precise, it *approaches* at least *one* sense in which such a person might use them. He thinks moreover that the sense which it approaches is a "typically ethical" one; but in saying that his amended definition gives (approximately) at least *one* "typically ethical" sense, he is allowing that there may possibly be other "typically ethical" senses, equally in accordance with ordinary usage, which it does not give even approximately; and allowing also that there may possibly be other senses, equally in accordance with ordinary usage, which are not "typically ethical" and which also his amended definition does not give even approximately. This is a generous allowance of possible senses, all of them in accordance with ordinary usage, with which these simple sentences might be used. But perhaps it is not too generous; and, guarded and limited as Mr. Stevenson's statement is, I think it is sufficient to raise important questions.

It would seem that, before we can discuss whether Mr. Stevenson is right in this guarded statement, we ought to know what his amended definition is. And he professes to give it on p. 84. He says that his amendment

* Excerpted and reprinted from pp. 536–547 of *The Philosophy of G. E. Moore* (1942) by kind permission of the author and the editor and publisher of the Library of Living Philosophers.

is a very simple one, and possibly it may be; but it is certainly not a simple matter to discover from what he says on this page, what the amendment he has in mind is. Let us, for the sake of brevity, call the sentence "It was right of Brutus to stab Caesar" "the *definiendum*," and the sentence "I now approve of Brutus' stabbing of Caesar, which was occurring" "the *definiens*." The original definition stated that the *definiendum*, when used in the particular sense (approximating to an ordinary one) which Mr. Stevenson wants to "give" us, has the same meaning as the *definiens*. This definition, Mr. Stevenson now says, does not, *as it stands*, give us the sense he means, but must be amended. And it is obvious, from what he says, that the required amendment will have something to do with "emotive meaning": it will either mention the conception "emotive meaning" itself, or will mention some particular emotive meaning which a sentence might have. In order to help us to see what the required amendment (or, as he now calls it, "qualification") is, Mr. Stevenson tells us: " 'Right,' 'wrong,' and the other ethical terms, all have a stronger emotive meaning than any purely psychological terms." By this, I take it, he means to imply that the *definiendum* has a stronger emotive meaning than the *definiens*. And then he adds: "This emotive meaning is not preserved by" the original definition "and must be separately mentioned." And here, I take it, by "*must* be separately mentioned" he means "must" in the amended definition —in any definition which is to "give" the sense of the *definiendum* he wants to give. These two sentences are, I think, all the help he gives us. Well now, using this help, what *is* the amended definition? Does it merely say: The *definiendum* (when used in the sense in question) has the same meaning as the *definiens*, but it has an emotive meaning which the *definiens* lacks? Or does it say: It has the same meaning, but it has a *stronger* emotive meaning than the *definiens*? If either of these is all, it certainly does not *give* us any sense whatever of the *definiendum* over and above what the *definiens* gives; it only tells us something *about* a possible sense. Or would it be a statement, which mentioned some particular emotive meaning, and said: The *definiendum* (when used in the sense in question) has the same meaning as the *definiens*, but it has also *this* emotive meaning which the *definiens* lacks? Or would it mention *both* some particular emotive meaning, *and* some particular degree of strength in which a sentence might have that emotive meaning, and say: The *definiendum* (when used in the sense in question) has the same meaning as the *definiens*, but it has *this* emotive meaning in a degree of strength above *this* degree, whereas the *definiens* only has it in a degree of strength below *this* degree? In these two cases, the amended definition really would give us a sense of the *definiendum*; but it is certain that Mr. Stevenson has not given us any amendment of this sort. Perhaps there are other alternatives besides these four: how on earth are we to tell which Mr. Stevenson means? The bare fact is that he has not given us *any* sense whatever of the *definiendum* over and above what the *definiens* gives, nor any amended definition which gives such a sense. But nevertheless I think it is possible to gather from what he says that he holds the following views. Let us, in analogy with a way in which Mr. Stevenson himself uses the word "cognitive" and also in analogy with the way in which he uses the phrase "emotive meaning," distinguish between the "cognitive meaning" of a sentence and its "emotive meaning." I think we can then say Mr. Stevenson thinks that the *definiendum*, when used in the sense he has in mind, has exactly the same "cognitive meaning" as the *definiens*, but nevertheless has not the same *sense*, because it has a different "emotive meaning." But what does this mean? How are we using the term "cognitive meaning"? I think this can be explained as follows. Some sentences can (in accordance with ordinary usage) be used in such a way that a person who is so using them can be said to be *making an assertion* by their means. E.g., our *definiendum*, the sentence "It was right of Brutus to stab Caesar," can be used in such a way that the person who so uses it can be correctly said to be asserting that it *was* right of Brutus to stab Caesar. But, sometimes at least, when a sentence is used in such a way that the person who uses it is making an assertion by its means, he is asserting something which might conceivably be true or false—something such that it is logically possible that it should be true or should be false. Let us say that a sentence has "cognitive meaning," if and only if it is both true that it can be used to make an assertion, and also that anyone who was so using it would be asserting something which might be true or might be false; and let us say that a sentence, *p*, has *the same cognitive meaning* as another, *q*, if and only if both *p* and *q* have cognitive meaning, and also, *so far as* anybody who used *p* to make an assertion was asserting something which might be true or might be false, he would have been asserting exactly the same if he had used *q* instead. If so, then the view I am attributing to Mr. Stevenson is that if a person were using our *definiendum* to make an assertion, and were using it in the sense Mr. Stevenson has in mind, then so far as he was asserting anything which might be true or might be false, he might have asserted exactly the same by using the *definiens* instead, but that, if he had done this, he would *not* have been using the *definiens* in the same *sense* in which he actually used the *definiendum*, and would not therefore have been asserting that it was right of Brutus to stab Caesar, in the sense Mr. Stevenson means. In short, Mr. Stevenson is holding that there is at least one "typically ethical" sense in which a man may assert that it was right of Brutus to stab Caesar, which is such that, though the only assertion which might be true or false that he is making will be that he himself, at the moment of speaking, "approves of Brutus' stabbing of Caesar, which was occurring," yet from the mere fact that he is making this assertion it will not follow that he is asserting that Brutus' action was right, in the sense in question: that he is doing so will only follow from the *conjunction* of the fact that he is asserting that he "approves of Brutus' stabbing of Caesar which was occurring," with the fact that he is using words which have a certain emotive meaning (*what* emotive meaning, Mr. Stevenson has not told us). There is, Mr.

Stevenson seems to imply, at least one type of ethical assertion such that an assertion of that type is distinguished from a possible assertion, which would not be ethical at all, not by the fact that it asserts anything which might be true or false, which the other would not assert, but simply by its "emotive meaning."

Mr. Stevenson holds, then, if I understand him rightly, that there is at least one "typically ethical" sense in which a man might assert that it was right of Brutus to stab Caesar, which is such that (1) the man *would* be asserting that he, at the time of speaking, approved of this action of Brutus' and (2) would *not* be asserting anything, which might conceivably be true or false, *except* this or, possibly also, things entailed by it, as, for instance, that Brutus did stab Caesar. And I think he is right in supposing that, limited as this statement is, it is inconsistent with what I have stated or implied in my ethical writings. I have, I think, implied that there is *no* "typically ethical" sense in which a man might assert this, of which *both* these two things are true; and I have also implied, I think, that there is no "typically ethical" sense of which *either* is true. I will say something separately about each of these two separate contentions of Mr. Stevenson's.

(1) I am still inclined to think that there is no "typically ethical" sense of "It was right of Brutus to stab Caesar," such that a man, who asserted that it was right in that sense, would, as a rule, be *asserting* that he approved of this action of Brutus'. I think there certainly is a "typically ethical" sense such that a man who asserted that Brutus' action was right in that sense would be *implying* that at the time of speaking he approved of it, or did not disapprove, or at least had some kind of mental "attitude" towards it. (I do not think Mr. Stevenson means to insist on the word "approve" as expressing quite accurately what he means: I think the essence of his view is only that there is *some* kind of "attitude," such that a man would be asserting, if he used the words in the sense Mr. Stevenson means, that he had, at the time of speaking, that attitude towards it.) But I think that, as a rule at all events, a man would only be *implying* this, in a sense in which to say that he *implies* it, is *not* to say that he *asserts* it nor yet that it *follows* from anything which he does assert. I think that the sense of "imply" in question is similar to that in which, when a man asserts anything which might be true or false, he *implies* that he himself, at the time of speaking, believes or knows the thing in question—a sense in which he *implies* this, even if he is lying. If, for instance, I assert, on a particular day, that I went to the pictures the preceding Tuesday, I *imply*, by asserting this, that, at the time of speaking, I believe or know that I did, though I do not *say* that I believe or know it. But in this case, it is quite clear that this, which I *imply*, is no part of what I *assert;* since, if it were, then in order to discover whether I did go to the pictures that Tuesday, a man would need to discover whether, when I said I did, I believed or knew that I did, which is clearly not the case. And it is also clear that from what I assert, namely that I went to the pictures that Tuesday, it does not *follow* that I believe or know that I did, when I say

so: for it might have been the case that I did go, and yet that I did not, when I spoke, either believe or know that I did. Similarly, I think that, if a person were to assert that it was right of Brutus to stab Caesar, though he would be *implying* that, at the time of speaking, he approved, or had some similar attitude towards, this action of Brutus', yet he would *not* be *asserting* this that he would be implying, nor would this follow from anything, possibly true or false, which he was asserting. He would be implying, *by saying* that Brutus' action was right, that he approved of it; but he would not be *saying* that he did, nor would anything that he said (if anything) *imply* (in the sense of "entail") that he did approve of it: just as, if I say that I went to the pictures last Tuesday, I *imply by saying* so that I believe or know that I did, but I do not *say* that I believe or know this, nor does *what* I say, namely that I went to the pictures, *imply* (in the sense of "entail") that I do believe or know it. I think Mr. Stevenson's apparent confidence that, in at least one "typically ethical" sense, a man who asserted that it was right of Brutus to stab Caesar, would be *asserting* that he approved of this action, may be partly due to his having never thought of this alternative that he might be only *implying* it. But I think it may also be partly due to his shrinking from the paradox which would be involved in saying that, even where it can quite properly be said that a man is *asserting* that Brutus' action was right, yet he may be asserting *nothing whatever that could possibly be true or false*—that his words have absolutely no *cognitive* meaning—except, perhaps, that Brutus did stab Caesar. This paradox, however, is, I think, no greater than paradoxes which Mr. Stevenson is willing to accept, and I think that very possibly it may be true. So far as I can understand it, I think Mr. Stevenson's actual view is that sometimes, when a man *asserts* that it was right of Brutus to stab Caesar, the sense of his words is (roughly) much the same as if he had said "I approve of Brutus' action: do approve of it too!" the former clause giving the *cognitive* meaning, the latter the *emotive*. But why should he not say instead, that the sense of the man's words is *merely* "Do approve of Brutus' stabbing of Caesar!"—an imperative, which has absolutely no *cognitive* meaning, in the sense I have tried to explain? If this were so, the man might perfectly well be *implying* that he approved of Brutus' action, though he would not be *saying* so, and would be asserting nothing whatever, that might be true or false, except, perhaps, that Brutus did stab Caesar. It certainly seems queer—paradoxical—that it should be correct to say that the man was *asserting* that Brutus' action was right, when the only meaning his words had was this imperative. But may it not, nevertheless, actually be the case? It seems to me more likely that it is the case, than that Mr. Stevenson's actual view is true.

There seems to me to be nothing mysterious about this sense of "imply," in which if you assert that you went to the pictures last Tuesday, you *imply*, though you don't *assert*, that you believe or know that you did; and in which, if you assert that Brutus' action was right, you *imply*, but don't *assert*, that you approve of Brutus' action. In the first case, that you do imply this proposition about your present attitude, although it is not implied by (i.e., does not follow from) *what* you assert, simply arises from the fact, which we all learn by experience, that in the immense majority of cases a man who makes such an assertion as this does believe or know what he asserts: lying, though common enough, is vastly exceptional. And this is why to say such a thing as "I went to the pictures last Tuesday, but I don't believe that I did" is a perfectly absurd thing to say, although *what* is asserted is something which is perfectly possible logically: it is perfectly possible that you did go to the pictures and yet you do not believe that you did; the proposition that you did does not "imply" that you believe you did—that you believe you did does not *follow from* the fact that you did. And of course, also, from the fact that you say that you did, it does not follow that you believe that you did: you might be lying. But nevertheless your saying that you did, does *imply* (in another sense) that you believe you did; and this is why "I went, but I don't believe I did" is an absurd thing to say. Similarly the fact that, if you assert that it was right of Brutus to stab Caesar, you *imply* that you approve of or have some such attitude to this action of Brutus', simply arises from the fact, which we have all learnt by experience, that a man who makes this kind of assertion does in the vast majority of cases approve of the action which he asserts to be right. Hence, if we hear a man assert that the action was right, we should all take it that, unless he is lying, he does, at the time of speaking, approve, although he has *not* asserted that he does.

(2) Let us next consider the second part of Mr. Stevenson's view: namely the part which asserts that in some "typically ethical" cases, a man who asserts that it was right of Brutus to stab Caesar, is not asserting anything that might conceivably be true or false, *except* that he approves of Brutus' action, and possibly also that Brutus did stab Caesar. By this I mean a view which is merely negative: which does *not* assert that there are any cases in which such a man *is* asserting that he approves of Brutus' action; but which only asserts that there are cases in which he is *not* asserting anything *else*, leaving perfectly open the possibility that in all such cases he is not asserting *anything at all*, which could conceivably be true or false. Mr. Stevenson, of course, does not express any belief that there are any cases in which such a man, using the *definiendum* in a "typically ethical" sense, would not be asserting *anything at all*, which might conceivably be true or false. But he does imply that, if you consider all propositions, other than the propositions (1) that he now approves of Brutus' action and (2) that Brutus did stab Caesar and (3) the conjunction of these two, then there are cases in which such a man is not asserting any single one of these *other* propositions. This is the view of his I want now to consider.

It certainly is inconsistent with views which I have expressed or implied. I have certainly implied that in all cases in which a man were to assert in a "typically ethical" sense that it was right of Brutus to stab Caesar, he would be asserting something, capable of truth or falsity (some proposition, that is) which both (a) is not identical with any of the three propositions just mentioned, (b) does not follow from (3), and (c) is also a proposition from which (1) does not follow: some proposition, therefore, which might have been true, even if he had not approved of Brutus' action, and which may be false, even though he does approve of it—which is, in short, completely independent logically of the proposition that he does approve of the action.

What are we to say about these two incompatible views—the second part of Mr. Stevenson's view, and the view, implied in my writings, which I have just formulated?

I think I ought, first of all, to make as clear as I can what my present personal attitude to them is. I certainly think that this second part of Mr. Stevenson's view *may* be true: that is to say, I certainly think that I don't *know* that it is not true. But this is not all. I certainly have some inclination to think that it *is* true, and that therefore my own former view is false. And, thinking as I do, that the first part of Mr. Stevenson's view is false, this means that I have some inclination to think that there is at least *one* "typically ethical" sense of the sentence "It was right of Brutus to stab Caesar," such that a man who used this sentence in that sense and used it in such a way that he could be properly said to be *asserting* that this action of Brutus' was right, would nevertheless not be asserting anything at all that could conceivably be true or false, except, perhaps, that Brutus did stab Caesar: nothing, that is, *about* Brutus' action except simply that it occurred. And, going far beyond Mr. Stevenson's cautious assertion, I have a very strong inclination to think that, *if* there is at least *one* "typically ethical" sense of which these things are true, then of *all* "typically ethical" senses these things are true. So that I have some inclination to think that in *any* "typically ethical" sense in which a man might assert that Brutus' action was right, he would be asserting nothing whatever which could conceivably be true or false, except, perhaps, that Brutus' action occurred —no more than, if he said, "Please, shut the door." I certainly have *some* inclination to think all this, and that therefore not merely the contradictory, but the contrary, of my former view is true. But then, on the other hand, I also still have *some* inclination to think that my former view *is* true. And, if you ask me to which of these incompatible views I have the *stronger* inclination, I can only answer that I simply do not know whether I am any more strongly inclined to take the one than to take the other.—I think this is at least an honest statement of my present attitude.

Secondly, I want to call attention to the fact that, so far as I can discover, Mr. Stevenson neither gives nor attempts to give any reason whatever for thinking that his view is true. He asserts that it *may* be true, i.e., that he does not know that it's not, and that he *thinks* it is true; but, so far as I can see, he gives absolutely no positive arguments in its favour: he is only concerned ˙with showing that certain arguments which might be used against it are inconclusive. Perhaps, he *could* give some positive reasons for thinking that it is true. But, so far as I am concerned, though, as I say, I have some inclination to think it is true, and even do not know whether I have not as much inclination to think so as to think that my former view is so, I can give no positive reasons in its favour.

But now, how about reasons for thinking that Mr. Stevenson's view is false and my former one true? I can give at least one reason for this, namely that it *seems as if* whenever one man, using "right" in a "typically ethical" sense, asserts that a particular action was right, then, if another, using "right" in the same sense, asserts that it was not, they are making assertions which are logically incompatible. If this, which seems to be the case, really were the case, it would follow that Mr. Stevenson's view is false. But, of course, from the fact that it *seems* to be the case, it does not follow that it really is the case; and Mr. Stevenson suggests that it seems to be the case, not because it really is the case, but because, when such a thing happens, the two men, if both are sincere, really are *differing in attitude* towards the action in question, and we mistake this difference of attitude for the holding of logically incompatible opinions. He even says, in one place (p. 82), that he thinks I was led falsely to affirm that two such men really are holding logically incompatible opinions, because I "could not understand how people could differ or disagree in any sense" without holding logically incompatible opinions.

Now I think that as regards this suggestion as to how I was led to affirm that two such men are holding logically incompatible opinions, Mr. Stevenson has certainly not hit the right nail on the head. I think that, even when I wrote *Principia Ethica*, I was quite capable of understanding that, if one member of a party, A, says "Let's play poker," and another, B, says "No; let's listen to a record," A and B can be quite properly said to be disagreeing. What is true, I think, is that, when I wrote the *Ethics*, it simply had not occurred to me that in the case of our two men, who assert sincerely, in a "typically ethical" sense of "right," and both in the same sense, the one that Brutus' action was right, the other that it was not, the disagreement between them might possibly be merely of that sort. Now that Mr. Stevenson has suggested that it may, I do feel uncertain whether it is not merely of that sort: that is to say, I feel uncertain whether they are holding incompatible opinions: and therefore I completely agree with Mr. Stevenson that, when I used the argument "Two such men can't be merely asserting the one that he approves of Brutus' action, the other that he does not, because, if so, their assertions would not be logically incompatible," this argument was inconclusive. It is inconclusive, because it is not certain that their assertions are logically incompatible. I even go further, I feel some inclination to think that those two men are *not* making incompatible assertions: that their disagreement *is* merely a disagreement in attitude, like that between the man who says "Let's play poker" and the other who says "No; let's listen to a record": and I do not know that I am not *as much* inclined to think this as to think that they are making incompatible assertions. But I certainly still have *some* inclination to think that my old view was true and that they *are* making incompatible assertions. And I think that the mere fact that they *seem to be* is *a* reason in its favour, though, of course, not a conclusive one. As for Mr. Stevenson's cautious view that, in at least *one* "typically ethical" case, they are merely disagreeing in attitude and not making logically incompatible assertions, he, of course, gives no reason whatever for thinking it true, and I can see none, though I am perhaps as much inclined to think it is true, as to think that my old view is. How on earth is it to be settled whether they *are* making incompatible assertions or not? There are hosts of cases where we do know for certain that people *are* making incompatible assertions; and hosts of cases where we know for certain that they are not, as, for instance, if one man merely asserts "I approve of Brutus' action" and the other merely asserts "I don't approve of it." Why should there be this doubt in the case of ethical assertions? And how is it to be removed?

I think, therefore, that Mr. Stevenson has certainly not *shewn* that my old view was wrong; and he has not even *shewn* that this particular argument which I used for it is not conclusive. I agree with him that it is not conclusive. But he has not *shewn* that it is not; since he has simply asserted that in at least one "typically ethical" case two such men *may* be merely differing in attitude and not holding incompatible opinions: he has not shewn even that they *may*, i.e., that it is not certain that they aren't, far less that it is ever the case that they *are*. . . .

*   *   *

VI

THE PSYCHOLOGY OF CONDUCT AND THE CONCEPT OF OBLIGATION

Mill and the Hedonistic Principle[*]

ᵐᵐᵐ

G. E. MOORE

39. I propose, then, to begin by an examination of Mill's *Utilitarianism*. That is a book which contains an admirably clear and fair discussion of many ethical principles and methods. Mill exposes not a few simple mistakes which are very likely to be made by those who approach ethical problems without much previous reflection. But what I am concerned with is the mistakes which Mill himself appears to have made, and these only so far as they concern the Hedonistic principle. Let me repeat what that principle is. It is, I said, that pleasure is the only thing at which we ought to aim, the only thing that is good as an end and for its own sake. And now let us turn to Mill and see whether he accepts this description of the question at issue. 'Pleasure,' he says at the outset, 'and freedom from pain, are the only things desirable as ends' (p. 10[1]); and again, at the end of his argument, 'To think of an object as desirable (unless for the sake of its consequences) and to think of it as pleasant are one and the same thing' (p. 58). These statements, taken together, and apart from certain confusions which are obvious in them, seem to imply the principle I have stated; and if I succeed in shewing that Mill's reasons for them do not prove them, it must at least be admitted that I have not been fighting with shadows or demolishing a man of straw.

It will be observed that Mill adds 'absence of pain' to 'pleasure' in his first statement, though not in his second. There is, in this, a confusion, with which, however, we need not deal. I shall talk of 'pleasure' alone, for the sake of conciseness; but all my arguments will apply *à fortiori* to 'absence of pain': it is easy to make the necessary substitutions.

Mill holds, then, that 'happiness is desirable, and *the only thing desirable*,[2] as an end; all other things being only desirable as means to that end' (p. 52). Happiness he has already defined as 'pleasure, and the absence of pain' (p. 10); he does not pretend that this is more than an arbitrary verbal definition; and, as *such*, I have not a word to say against it. His principle, then, is 'pleasure is the only thing desirable,' if I may be allowed, when I

---

[*] Excerpted and reprinted by kind permission of the author and the publisher from *Principia Ethica*, pp. 64–74. The Cambridge University Press, 1903.
[1] My references are to the 13th edition, 1897.
[2] My italics.

444 PSYCHOLOGY AND OBLIGATION

say 'pleasure,' to include in that word (so far as necessary) absence of pain. And now what are his reasons for holding that principle to be true? He has already told us (p. 6) that 'Questions of ultimate ends are not amenable to direct proof. Whatever can be proved to be good, must be so by being shewn to be a means to something *admitted to be good without proof*.' With this, I perfectly agree: indeed the chief object of my first chapter was to shew that this is so. Anything which is good as an end must be admitted to be good without proof. We are agreed so far. Mill even uses the same examples which I used in my second chapter. 'How,' he says, 'is it possible to prove that health is good?' 'What proof is it possible to give that pleasure is good?' Well, in Chapter IV, in which he deals with the proof of his Utilitarian principle, Mill repeats the above statement in these words: 'It has already,' he says, 'been remarked, that questions of ultimate ends do not admit of proof, in the ordinary acceptation of the term' (p. 52). 'Questions about ends,' he goes on in this same passage, 'are, in other words, questions what things are desirable.' I am quoting these repetitions, because they make it plain what otherwise might have been doubted, that Mill is using the words 'desirable' or 'desirable as an end' as absolutely and precisely equivalent to the words 'good as an end.' We are, then, now to hear, what reasons he advances for this doctrine that pleasure alone is good as an end.

40. 'Questions about ends,' he says (pp. 52-3), 'are, in other words, questions what things are desirable. The utilitarian doctrine is, that happiness is desirable, and the only thing desirable, as an end; all other things being only desirable as means to that end. What ought to be required of this doctrine—what conditions is it requisite that the doctrine should fulfil—to make good its claim to be believed?

'The only proof capable of being given that a thing is visible, is that people actually see it. The only proof that a sound is audible, is that people hear it; and so of the other sources of our experience. In like manner, I apprehend, the sole evidence it is possible to produce that anything is desirable, is that people do actually desire it. If the end which the utilitarian doctrine proposes to itself were not, in theory and in practice, acknowledged to be an end, nothing could ever convince any person that it was so. No reason can be given why the general happiness is desirable, except that each person, so far as he believes it to be attainable, desires his own happiness. This, however, being the fact, we have not only all the proof which the case admits of, but all which it is possible to require, that happiness is a good: that each person's happiness is a good to that person, and the general happiness, therefore, a good to the aggregate of all persons. Happiness has made out its title as *one* of the ends of conduct, and consequently one of the criteria of morality.'

There, that is enough. That is my first point. Mill has made as naïve and artless a use of the naturalistic fallacy as anybody could desire. 'Good,' he tells us, means 'desirable,' and you can only find out what is desirable by seeking to find out what is actually desired. This is, of course, only one step towards the proof of Hedonism; for it may be, as Mill goes on to say, that other things beside pleasure are desired. Whether or not pleasure is the only thing desired is, as Mill himself admits (p. 58), a psychological question, to which we shall presently proceed. The important step for Ethics is this one just taken, the step which pretends to prove that 'good' means 'desired.'

Well, the fallacy in this step is so obvious, that it is quite wonderful how Mill failed to see it. The fact is that 'desirable' does not mean 'able to be desired' as 'visible' means 'able to be seen.' The desirable means simply what *ought* to be desired or *deserves* to be desired; just as the detestable means not what can be but what ought to be detested and the damnable what deserves to be damned. Mill has, then, smuggled in, under cover of the word 'desirable,' the very notion about which he ought to be quite clear. 'Desirable' does indeed mean 'what it is good to desire'; but when this is understood, it is no longer plausible to say that our only test of *that*, is what is actually desired. Is it merely a tautology when the Prayer Book talks of *good* desires? Are not *bad* desires also possible? Nay, we find Mill himself talking of a 'better and nobler object of desire' (p. 10), as if, after all, what is desired were not *ipso facto* good, and good in proportion to the amount it is desired. Moreover, if the desired is *ipso facto* the good; then the good is *ipso facto* the motive of our actions, and there can be no question of finding motives for doing it, as Mill is at such pains to do. If Mill's explanation of 'desirable' be *true*, then his statement (p. 26) that the rule of action may be *confounded* with the motive of it is untrue: for the motive of action will then be according to him *ipso facto* its rule; there can be no distinction between the two, and therefore no confusion, and thus he has contradicted himself flatly. These are specimens of the contradictions, which, as I have tried to shew, must always follow from the use of the naturalistic fallacy; and I hope I need now say no more about the matter.

41. Well, then, the first step by which Mill has attempted to establish his Hedonism is simply fallacious. He has attempted to establish the identity of the good with the desired, by confusing the proper sense of 'desirable,' in which it denotes that which it is good to desire, with the sense which it would bear, if it were analogous to such words as 'visible.' If 'desirable' is to be identical with 'good,' then it must bear one sense; and if it is to be identical with 'desired,' then it must bear quite another sense. And yet to Mill's contention that the desired is necessarily good, it is quite essential that these two senses of 'desirable' should be the same. If he holds they are the same, then he has contradicted himself elsewhere; if he holds they are not the same, then the first step in his proof of Hedonism is absolutely worthless.

But now we must deal with the second step. Having proved, as he thinks, that the good means the desired, Mill recognises that, if he is further to maintain that pleasure alone is good, he must prove that pleasure alone is really desired. This doctrine that 'pleasure alone is the object of all our desires' is the doctrine which Prof. Sidgwick has called Psychological Hedonism: and it is a doctrine which most eminent psychologists are now agreed in rejecting. But it is a necessary step in the proof of any such Naturalistic Hedonism as Mill's; and it is so commonly held, by people not expert either in psychology or in philosophy, that I wish to treat it at some length. It will be seen that Mill does not hold it in this bare form. He admits that other things than pleasure are desired; and this admission is at once a contradiction of his Hedonism. One of the shifts by which he seeks to evade this contradiction we shall afterwards consider. But some may think that no such shifts are needed: they may say of Mill, what Callicles says of Polus in the *Gorgias* [3], that he has made this fatal admission through a most unworthy fear of appearing paradoxical; that they, on the other hand, will have the courage of their convictions, and will not be ashamed to go to any lengths of paradox, in defence of what they hold to be the truth.

42. Well, then, we are supposing it held that pleasure is the object of all desire, that it is the universal end of all human activity. Now I suppose it will not be denied that people are commonly said to desire other things: for instance, we usually talk of desiring food and drink, of desiring money, approbation, fame. The question, then, must be of what is meant by desire, and by the object of desire. There is obviously asserted some sort of necessary or universal relation between something which is called desire, and another thing which is called pleasure. The question is of what sort this relation is; whether in conjunction with the naturalistic fallacy above mentioned, it will justify Hedonism. Now I am not prepared to deny that there is some universal relation between pleasure and desire; but I hope to shew, that, if there is, it is of such sort as will rather make against than for Hedonism. It is urged that pleasure is always the object of desire, and I am ready to admit that pleasure is always, in part at least, the *cause* of desire. But this distinction is very important. Both views might be expressed in the same language; both might be said to hold that whenever we desire, we always desire *because of* some pleasure: if I asked my supposed Hedonist, 'Why do you desire that?' he might answer, quite consistently with his contention, 'Because there is pleasure there,' and if he asked me the same question, I might answer, equally consistently with my contention, 'Because there is pleasure here.' Only our two answers would not mean the same thing. It is this use of the same language to denote quite different facts, which I believe to be the chief cause why Psychological Hedonism is so often held, just as it was also the cause of Mill's naturalistic fallacy.

Let us try to analyse the psychological state which is called 'desire.' That name is usually confined to a state of mind in which the idea of some

[3] 481 C—487 B.

object or event, not yet existing, is present to us. Suppose, for instance, I am desiring a glass of port wine. I have the idea of drinking such a glass before my mind, although I am not yet drinking it. Well, how does pleasure enter into this relation? My theory is that it enters in, in this way. The *idea* of the drinking causes a feeling of pleasure in my mind, which helps to produce that state of incipient activity, which is called 'desire.' It is, therefore, because of a pleasure, which I already have—the pleasure excited by a mere idea—that I desire the wine, which I have not. And I am ready to admit that a pleasure of this kind, an actual pleasure, is always among the causes of every desire, and not only of every desire, but of every mental activity, whether conscious or sub-conscious. I am ready to *admit* this, I say: I cannot vouch that it is the true psychological doctrine; but, at all events, it is not *primâ facie* quite absurd. And now, what is the other doctrine, the doctrine which I am supposing held, and which is at all events essential to Mill's argument? It is this. That when I desire the wine, it is not the wine which I desire but the pleasure which I expect to get from it. In other words, the doctrine is that the idea of a pleasure *not actual* is always necessary to cause desire; whereas my doctrine was that the *actual* pleasure caused by the idea of something else was always necessary to cause desire. It is these two different theories which I suppose the Psychological Hedonists to confuse: the confusion is, as Mr. Bradley puts it [4], between 'a pleasant thought' and 'the thought of a pleasure.' It is in fact only where the latter, the 'thought of a pleasure,' is present, that pleasure can be said to be the *object* of desire, or the *motive* to action. On the other hand, when only a pleasant thought is present, as, I admit, *may* always be the case, then it is the object of the thought—that which we are thinking about—which is the object of desire and the motive to action; and the pleasure, which that thought excites, may, indeed, cause our desire or move us to action, but it is not our end or object nor our motive.

Well, I hope this distinction is sufficiently clear. Now let us see how it bears upon Ethical Hedonism. I assume it to be perfectly obvious that the idea of the object of desire is not always and only the idea of a pleasure. In the first place, plainly, we are not always conscious of expecting pleasure, when we desire a thing. We may be only conscious of the thing which we desire, and may be impelled to make for it at once, without any calculation as to whether it will bring us pleasure or pain. And, in the second place, even when we do expect pleasure, it can certainly be very rarely pleasure *only* which we desire. For instance, granted that, when I desire my glass of port wine, I have also an idea of the pleasure I expect from it, plainly that pleasure cannot be the only object of my desire; the port wine must be included in my object, else I might be led by my desire to take wormwood instead of wine. If the desire were directed *solely* towards the pleasure, it could not lead me to take the wine; if it is to take a definite direction, it is absolutely necessary that the idea of the object, from which

[4] *Ethical Studies*, p. 232.

the pleasure is expected, should also be present and should control my activity. The theory then that what is desired is always and only pleasure must break down: it is impossible to prove that pleasure alone is good, by that line of argument. But, if we substitute for this theory, that other, possibly true, theory, that pleasure is always the cause of desire, then all the plausibility of our ethical doctrine that pleasure alone is good straightway disappears. For in this case, pleasure is not what I desire, it is not what I want: it is something which I already have, before I can want anything. And can any one feel inclined to maintain, that that which I already have, while I am still desiring something else, is always and alone the good?

43. But now let us return to consider another of Mill's arguments for his position that 'happiness is the sole end of human action.' Mill admits, as I have said, that pleasure is not the only thing we actually desire. 'The desire of virtue,' he says, 'is not as universal, but it is as authentic a fact, as the desire of happiness.' [5] And again, 'Money is, in many cases, desired in and for itself.' [6] These admissions are, of course, in naked and glaring contradiction with his argument that pleasure is the only thing desirable, because it is the only thing desired. How then does Mill even attempt to avoid this contradiction? His chief argument seems to be that 'virtue,' 'money' and other such objects, when they are thus desired in and for themselves, are desired only as 'a part of happiness.' [7] Now what does this mean? Happiness, as we saw, has been defined by Mill, as 'pleasure and the absence of pain.' Does Mill mean to say that 'money,' these actual coins, which he admits to be desired in and for themselves, are a part either of pleasure or of the absence of pain? Will he maintain that those coins themselves are in my mind, and actually a part of my pleasant feelings? If this is to be said, all words are useless: nothing can possibly be distinguished from anything else; if these two things are not distinct, what on earth is? We shall hear next that this table is really and truly the same thing as this room; that a cab-horse is in fact indistinguishable from St. Paul's Cathedral; that this book of Mill's which I hold in my hand, because it was his pleasure to produce it, is now and at this moment a part of the happiness which he felt many years ago and which has so long ceased to be. Pray consider a moment what this contemptible nonsense really means. 'Money,' says Mill, 'is only desirable as a means to happiness.' Perhaps so; but what then? 'Why,' says Mill, 'money is undoubtedly desired for its own sake.' 'Yes, go on,' say we. 'Well,' says Mill, 'if money is desired for its own sake, it must be desirable as an end-in-itself: I have said so myself.' 'Oh,' say we, 'but you also said just now that it was only desirable as a means.' 'I own I did,' says Mill, 'but I will try to patch up matters, by saying that what is only a means to an end, is the same thing as a part of that end. I daresay the public won't notice.' And the public haven't noticed. Yet this is cer-

[5] p. 53.
[6] p. 55.
[7] pp. 56–7.

tainly what Mill has done. He has broken down the distinction between means and ends, upon the precise observance of which his Hedonism rests. And he has been compelled to do this, because he has failed to distinguish 'end' in the sense of what is desirable, from 'end' in the sense of what is desired: a distinction which, nevertheless, both the present argument and his whole book presupposes. This is a consequence of the naturalistic fallacy.

44. Mill, then, has nothing better to say for himself than this. His two fundamental propositions are, in his own words, 'that to think of an object as desirable (unless for the sake of its consequences), and to think of it as pleasant, are one and the same thing; and that to desire anything except in proportion as the idea of it is pleasant, is a physical and metaphysical impossibility.' [8] Both of these statements are, we have seen, merely supported by fallacies. The first seems to rest on the naturalistic fallacy; the second rests partly on this, partly on the fallacy of confusing ends and means, and partly on the fallacy of confusing a pleasant thought with the thought of a pleasure. His very language shews this. For that the idea of a thing is pleasant, in his second clause, is obviously meant to be the same fact which he denotes by 'thinking of it as pleasant,' in his first.

Accordingly, Mill's arguments for the proposition that pleasure is the sole good, and our refutation of those arguments, may be summed up as follows:

First of all, he takes 'the desirable,' which he uses as a synonym for 'the good,' to *mean* what *can* be desired. The test, again, of what can be desired, is, according to him, what actually is desired: if, therefore, he says, we can find some one thing which is always and alone desired, that thing will necessarily be the only thing that is desirable, the only thing that is good as an end. In this argument the naturalistic fallacy is plainly involved. That fallacy, I explained, consists in the contention that good *means* nothing but some simple or complex notion, that can be defined in terms of natural qualities. In Mill's case, good is thus supposed to *mean* simply what is desired; and what is desired is something which can thus be defined in natural terms. Mill tells us that we ought to desire something (an ethical proposition), because we actually do desire it; but if his contention that 'I ought to desire' means nothing but 'I do desire' were true, then he is only entitled to say, 'We do desire so and so, because we do desire it'; and that is not an ethical proposition at all; it is a mere tautology. The whole object of Mill's book is to help us to discover what we ought to do; but, in fact, by attempting to define the meaning of this 'ought,' he has completely debarred himself from ever fulfilling that object: he has confined himself to telling us what we do do.

Mill's first argument then is that, because good means desired, therefore the desired is good; but having thus arrived at an ethical conclusion, by denying that any ethical conclusion is possible, he still needs another argu-

[8] p. 58.

ment to make his conclusion a basis for Hedonism. He has to prove that we always do desire pleasure or freedom from pain, and that we never desire anything else whatever. This second doctrine, which Professor Sidgwick has called Psychological Hedonism, I accordingly discussed. I pointed out how obviously untrue it is that we never desire anything but pleasure; and how there is not a shadow of ground for saying even that, whenever we desire anything, we always desire pleasure *as well as* that thing. I attributed the obstinate belief in these untruths partly to a confusion between the cause of desire and the object of desire. It may, I said, be true that desire can never occur unless it be preceded by some *actual* pleasure; but even if this is true, it obviously gives no ground for saying that the object of desire is always some *future* pleasure. By the object of desire is meant that, of which the idea causes desire in us; it is some pleasure, which we anticipate, some pleasure which we have not got, which is the object of desire, whenever we do desire pleasure. And any actual pleasure, which may be excited by the idea of this anticipated pleasure, is obviously not the same pleasure as that anticipated pleasure, of which only the idea is actual. This actual pleasure is not what we want; what we want is always something which we have not got; and to say that pleasure always causes us to want is quite a different thing from saying that what we want is always pleasure.

Finally, we saw, Mill admits all this. He insists that we do *actually* desire other things than pleasure, and yet he says we do *really* desire nothing else. He tries to explain away this contradiction, by confusing together two notions, which he has before carefully distinguished—the notions of means and of end. He now says that a means to an end is the same thing as a part of that end. To this last fallacy special attention should be given, as our ultimate decision with regard to Hedonism will largely turn upon it.

*   *   *

Bishop Butler's Conception of Human Nature[*]

C. D. BROAD

. . . WE CAN NOW consider in greater detail how Butler supposes human nature to be constituted. In all men he distinguishes four kinds of propensities or springs of action: (1) There are what he calls "particular passions or affections." These are what we should call impulses to or aversions from particular kinds of objects. Hunger, sexual desire, anger, envy, sympathy, etc., would be examples of these. It is obvious that some of them mainly benefit the agent and that others mainly benefit other people. But we cannot reduce the former to self-love or the latter to benevolence. We shall go more fully into this very important doctrine of Butler's later. (2) There is the general principle of cool self-love. By this Butler means the tendency to seek the maximum happiness for ourselves over the whole course of our lives. It is essentially a rational calculating principle which leads us to check particular impulses and to co-ordinate them with each other in such a way as to maximise our total happiness in the long run. (3) There is the general principle of benevolence. This, again, is a rational calculating principle, which must be sharply distinguished from a mere impulsive sympathy with people whom we see in distress. It is the principle which makes us try to maximise the general happiness according to a rational scheme and without regard to persons. I think it would be fair to say that the ideal of the Charity Organisation Society is benevolence in Butler's sense. (4) There is the principle of Conscience which is supreme over all the rest in authority. In ideal human nature conscience is supreme over self-love and benevolence; i.e., it determines how far each of these principles is to be carried. Self-love and benevolence in their turn are superior to the particular impulses; i.e., they determine when and to what extent each shall be gratified. In any actual man self-love may overpower conscience and so spread itself at the expense of benevolence. We then get the coolly selfish man. Or benevolence may overpower conscience and exercise itself at the expense of proper prudence. This happens when a man neglects self-culture and all reasonable care for his health and happiness in order to work for the general welfare. Butler holds that both these excesses are wrong. We do not indeed, as a rule, blame the latter as

[*] Excerpted and reprinted by kind permission of the author and the publishers from *Five Types of Ethical Theory*, pp. 60–83. Harcourt, Brace and Co., 1930.

much as the former. But we do blame it to some extent on calm reflection. We blame the imprudently benevolent man less than the coolly selfish man, partly because his fault is an uncommon one, and partly because it may be beneficial to society to have some men who are too benevolent when there are so many who are not benevolent enough. Butler does not mention this last reason; but I have no doubt that he would have accepted it, since he holds that the faulty behaviour of individuals is often overruled by Providence for the general good.

Particular impulse, again, may be too strong for self-love or for benevolence or for both. E.g., revenge often leads people to actions which are inconsistent with both benevolence and self-love, and ill-regulated sympathy may have the same effect. In the latter case we have the man who gives excessively to undeserving cases which happen to move his emotions, and who equally violates prudence by the extent of his gifts and benevolence by his neglect of more deserving but less spectacular cases. Butler makes the profoundly true remark that there is far too little self-love in the world; what we need is not *less self-love* but *more benevolence*. Self-love is continually overcome by particular impulses like pride, envy, anger, etc., and this is disastrous both to the happiness of the individual and to the welfare of society at large. Self-love is not indeed an adequate principle of action. But it is at least rational and coherent so far as it goes; and, if people really acted on it consistently, taking due account of the pleasures of sympathy and gratitude, and weighing them against those of pride, anger, and lust, their external actions would not differ greatly from those which benevolence would dictate. This seems to me to be perfectly true. Those actions which are most disastrous to others are nearly always such as no person who was clear-sightedly aiming at the maximum amount of happiness for himself would dream of doing. We have an almost perfect example of Butler's contention in the action of France towards Germany since the war of 1914 to 1918. It has been admirably adapted to producing the maximum inconvenience for both parties, and, if the French had acted simply from enlightened self-interest instead of malice and blind fear, they and all other nations would now be far better off.

The ideal human nature, then, consists of particular impulses duly subordinated, to self-love and benevolence, and of these general principles in turn duly subordinated to the supreme principle of conscience. This seems to me to be perfectly correct so far as it goes; and I will now consider in rather more detail each of these constituents of human nature.

1. *Particular Impulses.*—Butler's first task is to show that these cannot be reduced to self-love, as many people have thought before and since his time. It is easy to see that he is right. The object of self-love is one's own maximum happiness over the whole course of one's life. The object of hunger is food; the object of revenge is to give pain to someone who we think has injured us; the object of sympathy is to give another man pleas-

ure. Each of these particular impulses has its own particular object, whilst self-love has a general object, *viz.*, one's own maximum happiness. Again, these particular impulses often conflict with self-love, and this is equally true of those which we are inclined to praise and those which we are inclined to blame. Nor is this simply a question of intellectual mistakes about what will make us happy. A man under the influence of a strong particular impulse, such as rage or parental affection, will often do things which he knows at the time to be imprudent.

In a footnote Butler takes as an example Hobbes's definition of "pity" as "fear felt for oneself at the sight of another's distress." His refutation is so short and so annihilating that I will give the substance of it as a model of philosophical reasoning. He points out (*a*) that, on this definition, a sympathetic man is *ipso facto* a man who is nervous about his own safety, and the more sympathetic he is the more cowardly he will be. This is obviously contrary to fact. (*b*) We admire people for being sympathetic to distress; we have not the least tendency to admire them for being nervously anxious about their own safety. If Hobbes were right admiration for sympathy would involve admiration for timidity. (*c*) Hobbes mentions the fact that we tend specially to sympathise with the troubles of our friends, and he tries to account for it. But, on Hobbes's definition, this would mean that we feel particularly nervous for ourselves when we see a friend in distress. Now, in the first place, it may be doubted whether we do feel any more nervous for ourselves when we see a friend in distress than when we see a stranger in the same situation. On the other hand, it is quite certain that we do feel more sympathy for the distress of a friend than for that of a stranger. Hence it is impossible that sympathy can be what Hobbes says that it is. Butler himself holds that when we see a man in distress our state of mind may be a mixture of three states. One is genuine sympathy, i.e., a direct impulse to relieve his pain. Another is thankfulness at the contrast between our good fortune and his ill luck. A third is the feeling of anxiety about our own future described by Hobbes. These three may be present in varying proportions, and some of them may be wholly absent in a particular case. But it is only the first that any plain man means by "sympathy" or "pity." Butler makes a very true observation about this theory of Hobbes. He says that it is the kind of mistake which no one but a philosopher would make. Hobbes has a general philosophical theory that all action must necessarily be selfish; and so he has to force sympathy, which is an apparent exception, into accord with this theory. He thus comes into open conflict with common-sense. But, although common-sense here happens to be right and the philosopher to be wrong, I should say that this is no reason to prefer common-sense to philosophy. Common-sense would *feel* that Hobbes is wrong, but it would be quite unable to say *why* he is wrong. It would have to content itself with calling him names. The only cure for bad philosophy is better philosophy; a mere return to common-sense is no remedy.

We can now leave Hobbes to his fate, and return to the general question of the relation of our particular impulses to self-love. Why should it seem plausible to reduce particular impulses, like hunger and revenge and sympathy, to self-love? The plausibility arises, as Butler points out, from two confusions. (i) We confuse the ownership of an impulse with its object. All our impulses, no matter what their objects may be, are *ours*. They all *belong to* the self. This is as true of sympathy, which is directed to others, as of hunger, which is directed to modifying a state of oneself. (ii) Again, the satisfaction of any impulse is *my* satisfaction. *I* get the pleasure of satisfied desire equally whether the desire which I indulge be covetousness or malice or pity. So it is true that all impulses *belong to* a self, and that the carrying out of any impulse as such *gives pleasure to* that self. But it is not true that all impulses have for their objects states of the self whose impulses they are. And it is not true that the object of any of them is the general happiness of the self who owns them. Neither sympathy nor malice is directed to producing the happiness of the self who owns these impulses. One is directed to producing happiness in another person, and the other is directed to producing misery in another person. Thus there is no essential contrariety between any impulse and self-love. The satisfaction of any of my impulses as such gives me pleasure, and this is a factor in that total happiness of myself at which self-love aims. And self-love can gain its end only by allowing the various special impulses to pass into action. On the other hand, no impulse can be identified with self-love. The relation of particular impulses to self-love is that of means to end, or of raw materials to finished product.

All this is true and very important. But to make it quite satisfactory it is necessary, I think, to draw some distinctions which Butler does not. (i) We must distinguish between those pleasures which consist in the fulfilment of pre-existing desires and those which do not. Certain sensations are intrinsically pleasant, e.g., the smell of violets or the taste of sugar. Others are intrinsically unpleasant, e.g., the smell of sulphuretted hydrogen or the feel of a burn. We must therefore distinguish between intrinsic pleasures and pains and the pleasures and pains of satisfied or frustrated impulse. All fulfilment of impulse is pleasant for the moment at least; and all prolonged frustration of impulse is unpleasant. This kind of pleasure and pain is quite independent of the object of the impulse. Now these two kinds of pleasure and pain can be combined in various ways. Suppose I am hungry and eat some specially nice food. I have then both the intrinsically pleasant sensation of taste and also the pleasure of satisfying my hunger. A shipwrecked sailor who found some putrid meat or dined off the cabin-boy would enjoy the pleasure of satisfying his hunger accompanied by intrinsically unpleasant sensations of taste. A *bon-vivant* towards the end of a long dinner might get an intrinsically pleasant sensation of taste from his savoury although he was no longer hungry and therefore did not get the pleasures of satisfying his hunger.

(ii) I think that we must distinguish between the object of an impulse, its exciting cause, what will in fact satisfy it, and the collateral effects of satisfying it. Butler lumps together hunger and sympathy, and says that the object of one is food and the object of the other is the distresses of our fellow-men. Now, in the first place, the word "hunger" is ambiguous. It may mean certain organic sensations which are generally caused by lack of food. Or it may mean an impulse to eat which generally accompanies these. Butler evidently uses the word in the latter sense. But, even in this sense, it seems to me inaccurate to say that the object of hunger is food. It would be equally true to say that the object of a butcher going to market is food; but he may not be hungry. The object or aim of hunger is *to eat food*. The object of the butcher is to buy it as cheaply and sell it as dearly as possible. In fact the object of an impulse is never, strictly speaking, a thing or person; it is always to change or to preserve some state of a thing or person. So much for the object or aim of an impulse.

Now, as we eat, the impulse of hunger is gradually satisfied, and this is pleasant. If we are continually prevented from eating when we are hungry this continued frustration of the impulse is unpleasant. Lastly, the process of satisfying our hunger has the collateral effect of producing sensations of taste which may be intrinsically pleasant or unpleasant according to the nature of the food and the tastes of the eater. I would say then that the exciting cause of the impulse of hunger is lack of food, accompanied in general by certain characteristic organic sensations; that its aim or object is the eating of food; that its collateral effects are sensations of taste; and that it is accompanied by satisfaction or dissatisfaction according to whether we get food or are unable to do so. Now let us consider pity from the same points of view. The exciting cause is the sight of another person, particularly a friend or relation, in distress. The aim or object of it is to relieve the distress. The collateral effects of its exercise are the gradual relief of the distress, feelings of gratitude in the sufferer's mind, and so on. Lastly, in so far as we are able to exercise the impulse, there is a pleasant feeling of satisfaction in our minds; and, in so far as we are prevented from doing so, there is an unpleasant feeling of frustration.

Now, in considering the relations between the various particular impulses and the general principles of self-love and benevolence, it is very important to bear these distinctions in mind. Butler says that some particular impulses are more closely connected with self-love and others with benevolence. He gives examples, but he does not carry the analysis further. We can now state the whole case much more fully and clearly. (*a*) Some impulses have their exciting causes in the agent, some in inanimate objects, and some in other persons. Hunger is excited by one's own lack of food and the organic sensations which accompany it; covetousness may be excited by the sight of a book or a picture; pity is excited by another man's distress. (*b*) Some impulses aim at producing results within the agent himself; some aim at producing results in other men; and some aim at effecting changes in inanimate objects. Thus hunger aims at one's own eating; pity aims at the relief of another man's distress; and blind rage may aim at smashing plates or furniture. (c) The collateral effects of satisfying an impulse may be in the agent, or in others, or in both. Probably there are always collateral effects in the agent himself, and nearly always in other men too. But sometimes the collateral effects in the agent predominate, and sometimes those produced in other men are much more important. The collateral effects of satisfying hunger are, under ordinary circumstances, almost wholly confined to the agent. The collateral effects of the exercise of pity are mostly in the sufferer and the spectators, though there are always some in the agent. The collateral effects of ambition are divided pretty equally between self and others. Lastly, (d), the pleasures of satisfied impulse and the pains of frustrated impulse are naturally confined to the owner of the impulse.

It is evident that those particular impulses which aim at producing or maintaining states of the agent himself, and those whose collateral effects are mainly confined to the agent, will be of most interest to self-love. Hunger is a typical example. Those impulses which aim at producing or altering or maintaining states in other men, and whose collateral effects are mainly confined to others, will be of most interest to benevolence. Sympathy and resentment are typical examples. There will be some impulses which almost equally concern self-love and benevolence. For it may be that they aim at producing a certain state in others, but that their collateral effects are mainly in the agent; or conversely. Anger against those whom we cannot hurt is aimed against them but mainly affects ourselves. The question where the exciting cause of the impulse is situated is not of much importance for our present purpose, though it is likely that most impulses whose exciting causes are within the agent also aim at producing changes in his own state. The pleasures of satisfaction and the pains of frustration concern self-love alone, since they can be felt only by the agent.

It is important to notice that actions which were originally done from particular impulses may come to be done from self-love or from benevolence. As babies we eat and drink simply because we are hungry or thirsty. But in course of time we find that the satisfaction of hunger and thirst is pleasant, and also that the collateral sensations of eating certain foods and drinking certain wines are intrinsically pleasant. Self-love may then induce us to take a great deal of exercise so as to make ourselves thoroughly hungry and thirsty, and may then make us go to a restaurant and choose just those dishes and wines which we know will give intrinsically pleasant sensations in addition to the agreeable experience of satisfying our hunger and thirst. Again, a boy may play cricket simply because he likes it; but, when he grows older, he may devote his half-holidays to playing cricket with boy scouts from benevolence, although he is no longer specially keen on the game, and although he could enjoy himself more in other ways.

It sounds to us odd when Butler says that ambition and hunger are just as disinterested as pity and malice. He is perfectly right, in his own sense of "disinterested," and it is a very important sense. It is true that neither ambition nor hunger aims at one's own happiness. The object of one is power over others, the object of the other is to eat food. True, the satisfaction of either is *my* satisfaction; but so too is the satisfaction of pity or malice. If by "disinterested" you mean "not done with the motive of maximising one's own happiness on the whole," it is quite clear that hunger and ambition can lead only to disinterested actions. The appearance of paradox in Butler's statements is explained by the distinctions which we have drawn. It *is* true that ambition and hunger are more closely connected with self-love than are pity and malice. For they do aim at the production and modification of states of ourselves, although they do not aim at our own greatest happiness; whereas pity and malice aim at producing and modifying states of other men, and the collateral effects of their exercise are also largely confined to others. Thus both Butler and common-sense are here right, and the apparent difference between them is removed by clearly stating certain distinctions which are liable to be overlooked.

2. *Self-love and Benevolence.*—We can now deal in detail with the two general principles of self-love and benevolence. Butler seems to me to be clearer about the former than about the latter. I have assumed throughout that he regards benevolence as a general principle which impels us to maximise the happiness of humanity without regard to persons, just as he certainly regards self-love as a general principle leading us to maximise our own total happiness. I think that this is what he does mean. But he sometimes tends to drop benevolence, as a general principle co-ordinate with self-love, rather out of sight, and to talk of it as if it were just one of the particular impulses. Thus he says in the *First Sermon* that benevolence undoubtedly exists and is compatible with self-love, but the examples which he gives are in fact particular impulses which aim at the benefit of some particular person, e.g., paternal and filial affection. He says that, if you grant that paternal and filial affection exist, you must grant that benevolence exists. This is a mistake. He might as well say that, if you grant that hunger exists, you must grant that self-love exists. Really paternal affection is just as much a particular impulse as hunger, and it can no more be identified with benevolence than hunger can be identified with self-love. I think that he makes such apparent mistakes partly because he is anxious to show that benevolence is, as such, no more contrary to self-love than is any of the particular impulses. He shows, e.g., that to gratify the principle of benevolence gives just as much pleasure to the agent as to gratify any particular impulse, such as hunger or revenge. It is true that excessive indulgence in benevolence may conflict with self-love; but so, as he points out, may excessive indulgence of any particular impulse, such as thirst or anger. In fact benevolence is related to self-love in exactly the same way as any particular impulse is related to self-love. So far he is perfectly right.

But this identity of relation seems sometimes to blind Butler to the intrinsic difference between benevolence, which is a general principle, and the particular impulses which aim at producing happiness in certain particular men or classes of men, e.g., patriotism or paternal affection.

I think that there is undoubtedly a general principle of benevolence; and I think that Butler held this too, though he does not always make this clear. The main business of benevolence is to control and organise those impulses which aim at producing changes in others, or whose collateral effects are mainly in others. Thus it has to do with pity, resentment, paternal affection, and so on. The main business of self-love is to control and organise those impulses which aim at producing states in oneself, or whose collateral effects are largely in oneself. From the point of view of self-love benevolence is simply one impulse among others, like hunger, resentment, etc. But it is equally true that, from the point of view of benevolence, self-love is only one impulse among others. The prudent person may need to check his excessive benevolence towards mankind in general, just as he has to check blind anger or a tendency to over-eating. The benevolent person may need to check his excessive prudence, just as he has to check the special impulse to lose his temper.

There are, however, two respects in which self-love and benevolence seem to me to be not perfectly on a level. Conscience approves both of self-love and of benevolence in their proper degrees. But I think it is clear that conscience rates benevolence higher than self-love. It would hold that it is possible, though not easy, to have too much benevolence, but that you could quite easily have too much self-love, though in fact most people have too little. Again, from a purely psychological point of view, self-love and benevolence are not quite co-ordinate. The putting into action of *any* tendency, including benevolence, is as such pleasant to the agent, and so ministers in its degree to self-love. But the putting into action of our conative tendencies is not as such a source of happiness to others. Others may be affected either pleasurably or painfully according to the nature of the impulse which I exercise. But I get a certain amount of pleasure from the mere fact that I am doing what I want to do, quite apart from whether the object of the action is my own happiness or whether its collateral consequences are pleasant sensations in myself. Thus no action of mine can be *completely* hostile to self-love, though the collateral results of the action may be so unpleasant for me that cool self-love would not on the whole sanction it. But the gratification of many impulses may be completely hostile to benevolence. If I lose my temper and blindly strike a man, self-love gets something out of the transaction, *viz.*, the momentary feeling of satisfaction at fulfilling an impulse, even though the remoter consequences may be so unpleasant for me that cool self-love would have prevented the action. But benevolence gets nothing out of the transaction at all; it is wholly hostile to it.

As we have said, Butler holds that pure self-love and pure benevolence would lead to very much the same external actions, because the collateral results of most actions really make about as much for the happiness of the agent as for that of others. In this connexion he makes two profoundly true and important observations. (i) If you want to make yourself as happy as possible it is fatal to keep this object constantly before your mind. The happiest people are those who are pretty fully occupied with some activity which they feel to be honourable and useful and which they perform with reasonable success. The most wretched lives are led by men who have nothing to do but think of their own happiness and scheme for it. Happiness which is deliberately sought generally turns out to be disappointing, and the self-conscious egoist divides his time between wanting what he has not and not wanting what he has. (ii) The second point which Butler makes is that the common opinion that there is an inevitable conflict between self-love and benevolence is a fallacy based on the common confusion between enjoyment itself and the means of enjoyment. If I have a certain sum of money, it is evident that the more I spend on myself the less I shall have to spend on others, and conversely. It therefore looks at first sight as if self-love and benevolence must necessarily conflict. But, as Butler says, money and other kinds of property are not themselves happiness; they are only material objects which produce happiness by being used in certain ways. Now it is certain that both spending money on myself and spending it on others may give me happiness. If I already spend a good deal on myself it is quite likely that I shall gain more happiness by spending some of it on others than I shall lose by spending that much less on myself. This is certainly true; and the confusion between happiness and the means to happiness, which Butler here explains, is constantly made. The miser illustrates the typical and exaggerated form of this mistake; but nearly every one makes it to some extent.

I think there is only one point in Butler's theory of the substantial identity of the conduct dictated by self-love and by benevolence which needs criticism. It assumes an isolated purely selfish man in a society of people who are ruled by benevolence as well as by self-love and who have organised their social life accordingly. In such a case it certainly would pay this individual to act very much as the principle of benevolence would dictate. It is not so clear that it would pay to act in this way in a community of men who were all quite devoid of benevolence. All that we can say is that every one in such a society, if it could exist at all, would probably be very miserable; but whether one of them would be rendered less miserable by performing externally benevolent actions it is difficult to say. But, if we suppose Butler to mean that, taking men as they are, and taking the institutions which such men have made for themselves, enlightened self-interest would dictate a line of conduct not very different from that which benevolence would dictate, he seems to be right.

This fact, of course, makes it always difficult to say how far any particular action has been due to benevolence and how far to self-love. What is certain is that both principles exist, and that very few actions are due to one without any admixture of the other. Sometimes we can see pretty clearly which principle has predominated, but this is as far as we can safely go. Exactly the same difficulty arises as Butler points out, over self-love and the particular impulses. It is often impossible to say whether a certain course of action was due to self-love or to a particular impulse for power or money. All that we know for certain is that both principles exist and that they mix in all proportions. Sometimes the onlookers can tell more accurately than the agent what principle predominated, because they are less likely to be biased.

3. *Conscience.*—We come now to Butler's supreme principle of conscience. According to him this has two aspects, a purely cognitive and an authoritative. In addition, I think we must say that it is an active principle; i.e., that it really does cause, check, and modify actions. In its cognitive aspect it is a principle of reflection. Its subject-matter is the actions, characters, and intentions of men. But it reflects on these from a particular point of view. In one sense we are reflecting on our actions when we merely recall them in memory and note that some turned out fortunately and others unfortunately. But we should not call such reflection an act of conscience, but only an act of retrospection. The peculiarity of conscience is that it reflects on actions from the point of view of their rightness or wrongness. The very fact that we use words like "right," "wrong," "duty," etc., shows that there is an intellectual faculty within us which recognises the terms denoted by these names. Otherwise such words would be as meaningless to us as the words "black" and "white" to a man born blind. We clearly distinguish between a right action and one that happened to turn out fortunately. And we clearly distinguish between a wrong action and one that happened to turn out unfortunately. Again, we distinguish between mere unintentional hurt and deliberate injury. Conscience is indifferent to the former and condemns the latter. Finally, conscience recognises a certain appropriateness between wrong-doing and pain and between right-doing and happiness; i.e., it recognises the fact of merit or desert. If we see a man being hurt we judge the situation quite differently according to whether we think that he is innocent or that he is being punished for some wrong act.

So we may say that conscience, on its cognitive side, is a faculty which reflects on characters, actions, and intentions, with a special view to their goodness or badness, rightness or wrongness. And it further judges that pain is appropriate to wrong-doing, and happiness to right-doing. Lastly, we must add that it does not judge of actions or intentions in isolation, but judges them in reference to the ideal nature of the agent. The ideal nature of a child or a lunatic is different from that of a sane grown man, and so conscience takes a different view of the same action when performed by one or the other. Butler apparently assumes that, although the ideal nature of a child or a lunatic is different from that of a sane grown man, the ideal nature of all mature men is identical. No doubt we have to assume this in practice; but it seems hardly likely to be strictly true. It is hard to draw a perfectly sharp line between maturity and immaturity, or between sanity and insanity.

By saying that conscience has supreme authority Butler means that we regard the pronouncements of conscience, not simply as interesting or uninteresting statements of fact, and not simply as reasons to be balanced against others, but as *conclusive* reasons for or against doing the actions about which it pronounces. The fact that conscience pronounces an act to be wrong is admittedly one motive against doing it. But so too is the fact that self-love condemns it as imprudent, or that benevolence condemns it as likely to diminish the general happiness. Thus far conscience, self-love, and benevolence are all on a level. They are all capable of providing motives for acting or abstaining from action. The difference lies in their respective *authority*, i.e., in the relative strength which they *ought* to have and which they *would* have in an ideal human being. If self-love and benevolence conflict over some proposed course of action there is nothing in the nature of either which gives it authority over the other. Sometimes it will be right for self-love to give way to benevolence, and sometimes it will be right for benevolence to give way to self-love. But conscience is not in this position. In an ideal man conscience would not simply take turns with benevolence and self-love. If benevolence or self-love conflict with conscience it is always they, and never it, which should give way; and, if they conflict with each other, it is conscience, and it alone, which has the right to decide between them. In any actual man conscience is often overpowered by self-love or benevolence, just as they are often overpowered by particular impulses. But we recognise the *moral right* of conscience to be supreme, even when we find that it lacks the necessary *psychological power*.

I do not think that Butler means to say that every trivial detail of our lives must be solemnly debated before the tribunal of conscience. Just as the man whose aim is to secure his own maximum happiness best secures that end by not constantly thinking about it, so I should say that the man who wants always to act conscientiously will often do best by not making this his explicit motive. So long as our actions are those which conscience would approve, if we carefully considered the question, the supremacy of conscience is preserved, even though we have acted from immediate impulse or self-love or benevolence. Conscience, e.g., approves of a due measure of parental affection; but it is much better for this affection to be felt spontaneously than to be imposed on a parent by conscience as a duty. In fact the main function of conscience is regulative. The materials both of good and of evil are supplied by the particular impulses. These are organised in the first instance by self-love and benevolence, and these in turn are co-ordinated and regulated by conscience. In a well-bred and well-trained man a great deal of this organisation has become habitual, and in ninety-nine cases out of a hundred he does the right things without having to think whether or why they are right. It is only in the hundredth specially perplexing or specially alluring situation that an explicit appeal to conscience has to be made.

It remains to say something about two rather curious and difficult points in Butler's theory. (1) Although he constantly asserts the supremacy of conscience, yet there are one or two passages in which he seems to make self-love co-ordinate with it. In one place he actually says that no action is consistent with human nature if it violates *either* reasonable self-love or conscience. In another famous passage he seems to admit that, if we reflect coolly, we can justify no course of action which will be contrary to our happiness. The former passage I cannot explain away; it seems to be simply an inconsistency. But the latter occurs in the course of an argument in which he is trying to prove to an objector that there is no real conflict between conscience and enlightened self-love. I think it is clear from the context that he is not here asserting his own view, but is simply making a hypothetical concession to an imaginary opponent. He goes on to argue thus. Even if you grant that it can never be right to go against your own greatest happiness, yet you ought to obey conscience in cases of apparent conflict between it and self-love. For it is very difficult to tell what will make for your own greatest happiness even in this life, and it is always possible that there is another life after this. On the other hand, the dictates of conscience are often quite clear. Thus we can be far more certain about what is right than what is to our own ultimate interest; and therefore, in an apparent conflict between the two, conscience should be followed since we cannot be sure that this is not really to our own interest.

So Butler would probably answer that the question whether conscience is superior to self-love or co-ordinate with it is of merely academic interest. I do not think that this answer can be accepted. In the first place, as moralists we want to know what *should be* the relative positions of conscience and self-love. And it is no answer to this question to say that it is not practically important. Secondly, we may grant all that Butler says about the extreme uncertainty as to what is to our own ultimate interest. But the deliveries of conscience are by no means so certain and unambiguous in most cases as Butler makes out. And even if they were, it is not obvious why they should be assumed to be likely to be a better guide to our own interest than the best opinion that we could reach by reflecting directly on that subject.

(2) The other doubtful point is Butler's view about the value of happiness. In one place he says that it is manifest that nothing can be of consequence to mankind or to any creature but happiness. And he goes on to assert that all common virtues and vices can be traced up to benevolence and the lack of it. Finally, in the same sermon he says that benevolence

seems in the strictest sense to include all that is good and worthy. Now, if these statements be accepted at their face-value, Butler was a Utilitarian; i.e., he thought that happiness is the only intrinsic good and that virtue consists in promoting happiness. But it is to be noted that these remarks occur in the sermon on the *Love of our Neighbour*, where he is specially concerned to recommend benevolence to people who were sadly lacking in it. And even here he adds a footnote in which he distinctly says that there are certain actions and dispositions which are approved altogether apart from their probable effect on general happiness. He asserts this still more strongly in the *Dissertation on Virtue*, which is a later and more formal work. So I think it is clear that his considered opinion is against Utilitarianism.

But in both these works he seems to take the interesting view that God may be a Utilitarian, though this is no reason for our being so. It may be that God's sole ultimate motive is to maximise the total amount of happiness in the universe. But, even if this be the only thing of which he approves as an end, he has so made us that we directly approve of other tendencies beside benevolence, e.g., justice and truth-telling. And he has provided us with the faculty of conscience, which tells us that it is our duty to act in accordance with these principles no matter whether such action seems to us likely to increase the general happiness or not. It is quite possible that God may have given us this direct approval of truth-telling and justice, not because he directly approves of them, but because he knows that it will in fact make for the greatest happiness on the whole if we act justly and speak the truth regardless of the apparent consequences to ourselves and others. If so, that is his business and not ours. Our business is to act in accordance with our consciences, and only to promote the general happiness by such means as conscience approves, even though we may think that we could promote it more in certain cases by lying or partiality. If God does overrule our conscientious actions in such a way that they do make for the greatest possible happiness even when they seem to us unlikely to have that effect, so much the better. It makes no difference to our duty whether this be so or not.

It is of course plain that Butler leaves undiscussed many questions with which any complete treatise on Ethics ought to deal. We should like to know whether there is any feature common and peculiar to right actions, which we could use as a criterion of rightness and wrongness. And we should like to know how, when the same conscience at different times, or different consciences at the same time, seem to issue conflicting orders, we are to tell which is genuine and which is spurious. To such questions Butler does not attempt to give an answer, whilst the Utilitarians on the one hand and Kant on the other do give their respective very different answers to it. But, though his system is incomplete, it does seem to contain the prolegomena to any system of ethics that can claim to do justice to the facts of moral experience.

Remarks on Psychological Hedonism *

卅〜卅

C. D. BROAD

. . . WE CAN NOW deal with the question whether Psychological Hedonism be itself true. Let us begin with certain undoubted facts which
must be admitted. The belief that a future experience will be pleasant
is *pro tanto* a motive for trying to get it, and the belief that it will be painful is *pro tanto* a motive for trying to avoid it. Again, the felt pleasantness
of a present pleasant experience is *pro tanto* a motive for trying to make
it last, whilst the felt painfulness of a present experience is *pro tanto* a
motive for trying to make it stop. The question is whether the expected
pleasantness of a future experience is the only feature in it which can make
us want to get it, whether the felt pleasantness of a present experience is the
only feature in it which can make us want to prolong it, whether the expected painfulness of a future experience is the only feature in it which
can make us want to avoid it, and whether the felt painfulness of a present
experience is the only feature in it which can make us want to get rid of it.

I must begin with one explanatory remark which is necessary if the
above proposition is to be taken as a perfectly accurate statement of Psychological Hedonism. No sane Psychological Hedonist would deny that
a pleasure which is believed to be longer and less intense may be preferred
for its greater duration to one which is believed to be shorter and more
intense. Nor would he deny that a nearer and less intense pleasure may be
preferred for its greater nearness to a more intense but remoter pleasure.
And this implies that duration and remoteness are in some sense factors
which affect our desires as well as pleasantness and painfulness. This complication may be dealt with as follows. There are certain determinable
characteristics which every event, as such, must have. Date of beginning
and duration are examples. There are others which an event may or may
not have. Pleasantness, colour, and so on, are examples. Let us for the present
call them respectively "categorial" and "non-categorial" determinable
characteristics of events. Then the accurate statement of Psychological
Hedonism would be as follows. No non-categorial characteristic of a
present or prospective experience can move our desires for or against it
except its hedonic quality; but, granted that it has hedonic quality, the

* Excerpted and reprinted by kind ·permission of the author and the publishers
from *Five Types of Ethical Theory*, pp. 184–192. Harcourt, Brace and Co., 1930.

effect on our desires is determined jointly by the determinate form of
this and by the determinate forms of its categorial characteristics.

Now, so far as I am aware, no argument has ever been given for Psychological Hedonism except an obviously fallacious one which Mill produces in his *Utilitarianism*. He says there that "to desire" anything and
"to find" that thing "pleasant" are just two different ways of stating the
same fact. Yet he also appeals to careful introspection in support of Psychological Hedonism. Sidgwick points out that, if Mill's statement were
true, there would be no more need of introspection to decide in favour of
the doctrine than there is need for introspection to decide that "to be rich"
and "to be wealthy" are two different expressions for the same fact. But,
as he also points out, Mill is deceived by a verbal ambiguity. There is a
sense of "please" in English in which the two phrases "X pleases me" and
"I desire X" stand for the same fact. But the verb "to please" and the phrase
"to be pleasant" are not equivalent in English. In the sense in which "X
pleases me" is equivalent to "I desire X" it is not equivalent to "I find X
pleasant." If I decide to be martyred rather than to live in comfort at
the expense of concealing my opinions, there is a sense in which martyrdom
must "please me" more than living in comfort under these conditions.
But it certainly does not follow *ex vi termini* that I believe that martyrdom
will be "more pleasant" than a comfortable life of external conformity.
I do not think that "pleasantness" can be defined, or even described unambiguously by reference to its relations to desire. But I think we can give
a fairly satisfactory ostensive definition of it as that characteristic which
is common to the experience of smelling roses, of tasting chocolate, of
requited affection, and so on, and which is opposed to the characteristic
which is common to the experiences of smelling sulphuretted hydrogen,
of hearing a squeaky slate-pencil, of being hurt, of unrequited affection,
and so on. And it is certainly not self-evident that I can desire *only* experiences which have the characteristic thus ostensively defined.

I think that there is no doubt that Psychological Hedonism has been
rendered plausible by another confusion. The experience of having a desire
fulfilled is always *pro tanto* and for the moment pleasant. So, whenever I
desire anything, I foresee that if I get it I shall have the pleasure of fulfilled
desire. It is easy to slip from this into the view that my motive for desiring
X is the pleasure of fulfilled desire which I foresee that I shall enjoy if I
get X. It is clear that this will not do. I have no reason to anticipate the
pleasure of fulfilled desire on getting X unless I already desire X itself. It
is evident then that there must be *some* desires which are not for the
pleasures of fulfilled desire. Let us call them "primary desires," and the
others "secondary." Butler has abundantly shown that there must be some
primary desires. But, as Sidgwick rightly points out, he has gone to extremes
in the matter which are not logically justified. The fact that there must
be primary desires is quite compatible with Psychological Hedonism, since
it is quite compatible with the view that all primary desires are for primary

pleasures, i.e., for pleasures of taste, touch, smell, etc., as distinct from the pleasures of fulfilled desire. Still, introspection shows that this is not in fact so. The ordinary man at most times plainly desires quite directly to eat when he is hungry. In so doing he incidentally gets primary pleasures of taste and the secondary pleasure of fulfilled desire. Eventually he may become a *gourmand*. He will then eat because he desires the pleasures of taste, and he may even make himself hungry in order to enjoy the pleasures of fulfilled desire.

There is a special form of Psychological Hedonism of which Locke is the main exponent. This holds that all desire can be reduced to the desire to remove pain or uneasiness. The one conative experience is aversion to present pain, not desire for future pleasure. The position is as follows. When I am said to desire some future state X this means that the contemplation by me of my non-possession of X is painful. I feel an aversion to this pain and try to remove it by trying to get X. Since in the case of some things the contemplation of my non-possession of them is painful, whilst in the case of others it is neutral or pleasant, the question would still have to be raised as to why there are these differences. Perhaps the theory under discussion should not be counted as a form of Psychological Hedonism unless it holds that my awareness of the absence of X is painful if and only if I believe that the possession of X would be pleasant. This is in fact Locke's view, though he adds the proviso that my uneasiness at the absence of X is not necessarily proportional to the pleasure which I believe I should get from the possession of X. We will therefore take the theory in this form.

As regards the first part of the theory Sidgwick points out that desire is not usually a painful experience, unless it be very intense and be continually frustrated. No doubt desire is an unrestful state, in the sense that it tends to make us change our present condition. It shares this characteristic with genuine pain. But the difference is profound. When I feel aversion to a present pain I simply try to get rid of it. When I feel the unrest of desire for a certain object I do not simply try to get rid of the uneasiness; I try to get that particular object. I could often get rid of the feeling far more easily by diverting my attention from the object than by the tedious and uncertain process of trying to gain possession of it. As regards the second part of the theory, it seems plain on inspection that I may feel uneasiness at the absence of some contemplated object for other reasons than that I believe that the possession of it would be pleasant. I might feel uncomfortable at the fact that I am selfish, and desire to be less selfish, without for a moment believing that I should be happier if I were more unselfish.

The Psychological Hedonist, at this stage, has two more lines of defence: (*a*) He may say that we unwittingly desire things only in respect of their hedonic qualities, but that we deceive ourselves and think that we desire some things directly or in respect of other qualities. It is plain that this assertion cannot be proved; and, unless there be some positive reason to accept Psychological Hedonism, there is not the faintest reason to believe it. (*b*) He may say that our desires were originally determined wholly and solely by the hedonic qualities of objects; but that now, by association and other causes, we have come to desire certain things directly or for other reasons. The case of the miser who has come by association to desire money for itself, though he originally desired it only for its use, is commonly quoted in support of this view. Mill, in his *Utilitarianism*, deals with the disinterested love of virtue on these lines. Sidgwick makes the following important observations on this contention. In the first place it must be sharply distinguished from the doctrine that the original *causes* of all our desires were previous pleasant and painful experiences. The question is what were the original *objects* and *motives* of desire, not what kind of previous experiences may have *produced* our present desires. Secondly, the important question for ethics is what we desire here and now, not what we may have desired in infancy or in that pre-natal state about which the Psycho-analysts, who appear to be as familiar with the inside of their mother's womb as with the back of their own hands, have so much to tell us. If Ethical Hedonism be the true doctrine of the good, it is no excuse for the miser or the disinterested lover of virtue that they were sound Utilitarians while they were still trailing clouds of glory behind them. Lastly, such observations as we can make on young children point in exactly the opposite direction. They seem to be much more liable to desire things directly and for no reason than grown people. No doubt, as we go further back it becomes harder to distinguish between self-regarding and other impulses. But there is no ground for identifying the vague matrix out of which both grow with one rather than with the other.

I think that we may accept Sidgwick's argument here, subject to one explanation. It may well be the case that what very young children desire is on the whole what will in fact give them immediate pleasure, and that what they shun is what will in fact give them immediate pain; though there are plenty of exceptions even to this. But there is no ground to suppose that they think of the former things as likely to be pleasant, and desire them *for that reason*; or that they think of the latter things as likely to be painful, and shun them *for that reason*. It is unlikely that they have the experience of desiring and shunning for a reason at all at the early stages. And, if this be so, their experiences are irrelevant to Psychological Hedonism, which is essentially a theory about the reasons or motives of desire.

(2, 3) Psychological Hedonism is now refuted, and the confusions which have made it plausible have been cleared up. It remains to notice a few important general facts about the relations of pleasure and desire and of pain and aversion. (*a*) Just as we distinguish between the pleasure of fulfilled desire and other pleasures, such as the smell of roses, so we must distinguish between the pain of frustrated desire and other pains, such as being burnt. And just as there are secondary desires for the pleasures of fulfilled desire, so there are secondary aversions for the pain of frustrated desire. Secondary aversions presuppose the existence of primary aversions, and it is logically possible that all primary aversions might be directed to pains. But inspection shows that this is not in fact the case. (*b*) Among those pleasures which do not consist in the experience of fulfilled desire a distinction must be drawn between passive pleasures, such as the experience of smelling a rose, and the pleasures of pursuit. A great part of human happiness consists in the experience of pursuing some desired object and successfully overcoming difficulties in doing so. The relations of this kind of pleasure to desire are somewhat complicated. The pleasure of pursuit will not be enjoyed unless we start with at least some faint desire for the pursued end. But the intensity of the pleasure of pursuit may be out of all proportion to the initial intensity of the desire for the end. As the pursuit goes on the desire to attain the end grows in intensity, and so, if we attain it, we may have enjoyed not only the pleasure of pursuit but also the pleasure of fulfilling a desire which has become very strong. All these facts are illustrated by the playing of games, and it is often prudent to try to create a desire for an end in order to enjoy the pleasures of pursuit. As Sidgwick points out, too great a concentration on the thought of the pleasure to be gained by pursuing an end will diminish the desire for the end and thus diminish the pleasure of pursuit. If you want to get most pleasure from pursuing X you will do best to try to forget that this is your object and to concentrate directly on aiming at X. This fact he calls "the Paradox of Hedonism."

It seems to me that the facts which have been describing have a most important bearing on the question of Optimism and Pessimism. If this question be discussed, as it generally is, simply with regard to the prospects of human happiness or misery in this life, and account be taken only of passive pleasures and pains and the pleasures and pains of fulfilled or frustrated desire, it is difficult to justify anything but a most gloomy answer to it. But it is possibly to take a much more cheerful view if we include, as we ought to do, the pleasures of pursuit. From a hedonistic standpoint, it seems to me that in human affairs the means generally have to justify the end; that ends are inferior carrots dangled before our noses to make us exercise those activities from which we gain most of our pleasures; and that the secret of a tolerably happy life may be summed up in a parody of Hegel's famous epigram about the Infinite End,* *viz.*, "the attainment of the Infinite End just consists in preserving the illusion that there is an End to be attained."

* *Die Vollführung des unendlichen Zwecks ist so nur die Täuschung aufzuheben, als ob er noch nicht vollführt sei.*

Duty and Interest (Excerpt) *

H. A. PRICHARD

IN SEEKING A SUBJECT for an inaugural lecture, I have tried to find one which, without raising too technical issues, is near enough to every one to be of general interest and yet would be considered by philosophers still sufficiently controversial to deserve consideration. This subject I hope I have found in the relation between duty and interest. The topic is, of course, well worn. Nevertheless anyone who considers it closely will find that it has not the simple and straightforward character which at first sight it appears to possess.

A general but not very critical familiarity with the literature of Moral Philosophy might well lead to the remark that much of it is occupied with attempts either to prove that there is a necessary connexion between duty and interest or in certain cases even to exhibit the connexion as something self-evident. And the remark, even if not strictly accurate, plainly has some truth in it. It might be said in support that Plato's treatment of justice in the *Republic* is obviously such an attempt, and that even Aristotle in the *Ethics* tries to do the same thing, disguised and weak though his attempt may be. As modern instances, Butler and Hutcheson might be cited; and to these might be added not only Kant, in whom we should perhaps least expect to find such a proof, but also Green.

When we read the attempts referred to we naturally cannot help in a way wishing them to succeed; and we might express our wish in the form that we should all like to be able to believe that honesty is the best policy. At the same time we also cannot help feeling that somehow they are out of place, so that the real question is not so much whether they are successful, but whether they ought ever to have been made. And my object is to try to justify our feeling of dissatisfaction by considering what these attempts really amount to, and more especially what they amount to in view of the ideas which have prompted them. For this purpose, the views of Plato, Butler, and Green, may, I think, be taken as representative, and I propose to concentrate attention on them.

One preliminary remark is necessary. It must not be assumed that

* Prichard's inaugural lecture on becoming White's Professor of Moral Philosophy in 1928, pp. 3-29. Excerpted and reprinted by kind permission of the Oxford University Press.

what are thus grouped together as attempts either to prove or to exhibit the self-evidence of a connexion between duty and interest are properly described by this phrase, or even that they are all attempts to do one and the same thing. And in particular I shall try to show that the attempts so described really consist of endeavours, based on mutually inconsistent presuppositions, to do one or another of three different things.

On a casual acquaintance with the *Republic*, we should probably say without hesitation that, apart from its general metaphysics, what it is concerned with is justice and injustice, and that, with regard to justice and injustice, its main argument is an elaborate attempt, continued to the end of the book, to show in detail that if we look below the surface and consider what just actions really consist in and also the nature of the soul, and, to a minor degree, the nature of the world in which we have to act, it will become obvious, in spite of appearance to the contrary, that it is by acting justly that we shall really gain or become happy.

Further, if we were to ask ourselves, 'What are Plato's words for right and wrong?'—and plainly the question is fair—we should have in the end to give as the true answer what at first would strike us as a paradox. We should have to allow that Plato's words for right and wrong are not to be found in such words as χρῆ or δεῖ and their contraries, as in χρῆ δίκαιον εἶναι or ὄντινα τρόπον χρῆ ζῆν, where the subject is implied by the context to be τὸν μέλλοντα μακάριον ἔσεσθαι, but in δίκαιον and ἄδικον themselves. When he says of some action that it is δίκαιον, that is his way of saying that it is right, or a duty, or an act which we are morally bound to do. When he says that it is ἄδικον, that is his way of saying that it is wrong. And in the sense in which we use the terms 'justice' and 'injustice,' it is less accurate to describe what Plato is discussing as justice and injustice than as right and wrong. Our previous statement, therefore, might be put in the form that Plato is mainly occupied in the *Republic* with attempting to show it is by doing our duty, or what we are morally bound to do, that we shall become happy.

This is the account of his object which we are more particularly inclined to give if we chiefly have in mind what Socrates in the fourth Book is made to offer as the solution of the main problem. But this solution is preceded by an elaborate statement of the problem itself, put into the mouth of Glaucon and Adeimantus; and if we consider this statement closely, we find ourselves forced to make a substantial revision of this account of Plato's object. Glaucon and Adeimantus make it quite clear that whatever it is that they are asking Socrates to show about what they refer to as justice, their object in doing so is to obtain a refutation of what may be called the Sophistic theory of morality. Consequently, if we judge by what Glaucon and Adeimantus say, whatever Plato is trying to prove must be something which Plato would consider as affording a refutation of the Sophistic theory. But what is this theory as represented by Plato? It almost goes without saying that in the first instance men's attitude towards matters of right and wrong is an unquestioning one. However they have come to do so, and in particular whether their doing so is due to teaching or not, they think, and think without having any doubt, that certain actions are right and that certain others are wrong. No doubt in special cases, they may be doubtful; but, as regards some actions, they have no doubt at all, though to say this is not the same as to say that they are certain. But there comes a time when men are stirred out of this unquestioning frame of mind; and in particular the Sophists, as Plato represents them, were thus stirred by the reflection that the actions which men in ordinary life thought right, such as paying a debt, helping a friend, obeying the government, however they differed in other respects, at least agreed in bringing directly a definite loss to the agent. This reflection led them to wonder whether men were right in thinking these actions duties, i.e. whether they thought so truly. Then, having failed to find indirect advantages of these actions which would more than compensate for the direct loss, i.e. such advantages as are found in what we call prudent actions, they drew the conclusion that these actions cannot really be duties at all, and that therefore what may roughly be described as the moral convictions which they and others held in ordinary life were one gigantic mistake or illusion. Finally, they clinched this conclusion by offering something which they represented as an account of the origin of justice, but which is really an account of how they and others came to make the mistake of thinking these actions just, i.e. right.

This is the theory which on Plato's own showing he wants to refute. It is a theory about certain actions, and, on his own showing, what he has to maintain is the opposite theory about these same actions. But how, if our language is to be accurate, should these actions be referred to? Should they be referred to as *just*, i.e. right, actions, or should they be referred to as those actions which in ordinary life we *think* just, i.e. right? The difference, though at first it may seem unimportant, is really vital. In the unquestioning attitude of ordinary life we must either be *knowing* that certain actions are right or not knowing that they are right, but doing something else for which '*thinking* them right' is perhaps the least unsatisfactory phrase. There is no possibility of what might be suggested as a third alternative, *viz.* that our activity is one of thinking, which in instances where we are thinking truly is also one of knowing. For, as Plato realized, to think truly is not to know, and to discover that in some particular case we were thinking truly is not to discover that in doing so we were knowing. Moreover, when we are what is described as reflecting on the activity involved in our unquestioning attitude of mind, we are inevitably thinking of it as having a certain definite character, and, in so thinking of it, we must inevitably be implying either that the activity is one of knowing or that it is not. For we must think of this attitude either as one of thinking, or as one of knowing, and if we think of it as one of thinking, we imply that it is not one of knowing, and *vice versa*. In fact, however we think of the activity, we are committed one way or the other. Now the Sophists clearly implied that this unquestioning attitude is one of thinking and not one of knowing; for it would not have been sense to maintain that those actions which in ordinary life we know to be right are really not right. Their theory, then, must be expressed by saying that those actions which in ordinary life we think, and so do not know, to be right are not really right. Consequently Plato also, since he regards this as the theory to be refuted, is implying that in ordinary life we think, and do not know, that certain actions are right, and that, to this extent, he agrees with the Sophists. And for this reason, if we are to state accurately the problem which he is setting himself, we must represent it as referring not to *just* actions but to those actions which he and others in ordinary life *think* just.

It is clear then that when Plato states through the medium of Glaucon and Adeimantus the problem which he has to solve, he is guilty of an inaccuracy, which, though it may easily escape notice, is important. For Glaucon and Adeimantus persistently refer to the actions of which they ask Socrates to reconsider the profitableness as just and unjust actions, whereas they should have referred to them as the actions which men in ordinary life think just and unjust.

I shall now take it as established that when we judge from Plato's own statement of his problem, worked out as it is by reference to the Sophists, we have to allow that he is presupposing that ordinarily we do not know but think that certain actions are right and that he is thinking of his task as that of having to vindicate the truth of these thoughts against the Sophists' objection. And this is what must be really meant when it is said that Plato's object is to vindicate *morality* against the Sophistic view of it, for here 'morality' can only be a loose phrase for our ordinary moral thoughts or convictions.

Glaucon and Adeimantus, however, do not simply ask Socrates to refute the Sophistic view; they ask him to do so in a particular way, which they imply to be the only way possible, *viz.* by showing that if we go deeper than the Sophists and consider not merely the gains and losses of which they take account, *viz.* gains and losses really due to the reputation for doing what men think just and unjust, but also those which these actions directly bring to the man's own soul, it will become obvious that it is by doing what we think just that we shall really gain. And so far as the rest of the *Republic* is an attempt to satisfy this request, this must be what it is an attempt to show.

Now on a first reading of the *Republic*, it is not likely to strike us that there is anything peculiar or unnatural about this part of the request. Just because Plato takes for granted that this is the only way to refute the Sophists, we are apt in reading him to do the same, especially as our attention is likely to be fully taken up by the effort to follow Plato's thought. But if we can manage to consider Plato's endeavour to refute the Sophists with detachment, what strikes us most is not his dissent from their view concerning the comparative profitableness of the actions which men think just and unjust—great, of course, as his dissent is—but the identity of principle underlying the position of both. The Sophists in reaching their conclusion were presupposing that for an action to be really just, it must be advantageous; for it was solely on this ground that they concluded that what we ordinarily think just is not really just. And what in the end most strikes us is that at no stage in the *Republic* does Plato take the line, or even suggest as a possibility, that the very presupposition of the Sophists' arguments is false, and that therefore the question whether some action which men think just will be profitable to the agent has really nothing to do with the question whether it is right, so that Thrasymachus may enlarge as much as he pleases on the losses incurred by doing the actions we think just without getting any nearer to showing that it is a mere mistake to think them just. Plato, on the contrary, instead of urging that the Sophistic contention that men lose by doing what they think just is simply irrelevant to the question whether these actions are just, throughout treats this contention with the utmost seriousness; and he implies that unless the Sophists can be met on their own ground by being shown that, in spite of appearances to the contrary, these actions will really be for the good of the agent, their conclusion that men's moral convictions are mere conventions must be allowed to stand. He therefore, equally with the Sophists, is implying that it is impossible for any action to be really just, i.e. a duty, unless it is for the advantage of the agent.

This presupposition, however, as soon as we consider it, strikes us as a paradox. For though we may find ourselves quite unable to state what it is that does render an action a duty, we ordinarily think that, whatever it is, it is not conduciveness to our advantage; and we also think that though an action which is a duty may be advantageous it need not be so. And while we may not be surprised to find the presupposition in the Sophists, whose moral convictions are represented as at least shallow, we are surprised to find it in Plato, whose moral earnestness is that of a prophet. At first, no doubt, we may try to mitigate our surprise by emphasizing the superior character of the advantages which Plato had in mind. But to do this does not really help. For after all, whatever be meant by the 'superiority' of the advantages of which Plato was thinking, it is simply as advantages that Plato uses them to show that the actions from which they follow are right.

Yet the presupposition cannot simply be dismissed as obviously untrue. For one thing, any view of Plato's is entitled to respect. For another, there appear to be moments in which we find the presupposition in ourselves. There appear to be moments in which, feeling acutely the weight of our responsibilities, we say to ourselves, 'Why *should* I do all these actions, since after all it is others and not I who will gain by doing them?'

Moreover, there at least seems to be the same presupposition in the mind of those preachers whose method of exhortation consists in appeal to rewards. When, for instance, they commend a certain mode of life on the ground that it will bring about a peace of mind which the pursuit of worldly things cannot yield, they appear to be giving a resulting gain as the reason why we ought to do certain actions, and therefore to be implying that in general it is advantageousness to ourselves which renders an action one which we are bound to do. In fact the only difference between the view of such preachers and that of the Sophists seems to be that the former, in view of their theological beliefs, think that the various actions which we think right will have certain specific rewards the existence of which the Sophists would deny. And the identity of principle underlying their view becomes obvious if the preacher goes on to maintain, as some have done, that if he were to cease to believe in heaven, he would cease to believe in right and wrong. Again, among philosophers, Plato is far from being alone in presupposing that an action, to be right, must be for the good or advantage of the agent. To go no further afield than a commentator on Plato, we may cite Cook Wilson, whose claim to respect no one in Oxford will deny, and who was, to my mind, one of the acutest of thinkers. In lecturing on the *Republic* he used to insist that when men begin to reflect on morality they not only demand, but also have the right to demand, that any action which is right must justify its claim to be right by being shown to be for their own good; and he used to maintain that Plato took the right and only way of justifying our moral convictions, by showing that the actions which we think right are for the good of the society of which we are members, and that at the same time the good of that society *is* our good, as becomes obvious when the nature of our good is properly understood.

Moreover Plato, if he has been rightly interpreted, does not stand alone among the historical philosophers in presupposing the existence of a necessary connexion between duty and interest. At least Butler, whose thoughtfulness is incontestable, is with him. In fact in this matter he seems at first sight only distinguished from Plato by going further. In a well-known passage in the eleventh *Sermon*, after stating that religion always addresses itself to self-love when reason presides in a man, he says: 'Let it be allowed, though virtue or moral rectitude does indeed consist in affection to and pursuit of what is right and good, as such; yet that when we sit down in a cool hour, we can neither justify to ourselves this or any other pursuit, till we are convinced that it will be for our happiness, or at least not contrary to it.'

Here, if we take the phrase 'justify an action to ourselves' in its natural sense of come to know that we ought to do the action by apprehending a reason why we ought to do it, we seem to have to allow that Butler is maintaining that in the last resort there is one, and only one, reason why we ought to do anything whatever, *viz.* the conduciveness of the action to our happiness or advantage. And if this is right, Butler is not simply presupposing but definitely asserting a necessary connexion between duty and interest, and going further than Plato by maintaining that it is actually conduciveness to the agent's interest which renders an action right.

Nevertheless, when we seriously face the view that unless an action be advantageous, it cannot really be a duty, we are forced both to abandon it and also to allow that even if it were true, it would not enable us to vindicate the truth of our ordinary moral convictions.

It is easy to see that if we persist in maintaining that an action, to be right, must be advantageous, we cannot stop short of maintaining that it is precisely advantageousness and nothing else which renders an action right. It is impossible to rest in the intermediate position that, though it is something other than advantageousness which renders an action right, nevertheless an action cannot really be right unless it be advantageous. For if it be held that an action is rendered a duty by the possession of some other characteristic, then the only chance of showing that a right action must necessarily be advantageous must consist either in showing that actions having this other characteristic must necessarily be advantageous or in showing that the very fact that we are bound to do some action, irrespectively of what renders us bound to do it, necessitates that we shall gain by doing it. But the former alternative is not possible. By 'an action' in this context must be meant an activity by which a man brings certain things about. And if the characteristic of an action which renders it right does not consist in its bringing about an advantage to the agent, which we may symbolize by 'an X,' it must consist in bringing about something of a different kind, which we may symbolize by 'a Y,' say, for the sake of argument, an advantage to a friend, or an improvement in someone's character. There can, however, be no means of showing that when we bring about something of one kind, e.g. a Y, we must necessarily bring about something of a different kind, e.g. an X. The nature of an action as being the bringing about a Y cannot require, i.e. necessitate, it to be also the bringing about an X, i.e. to have an X as its consequence; and whether bringing about a Y in any particular case will bring about an X will depend not only on the nature of the act as being the bringing about a Y, but also on the nature of the agent and of the special circumstances in which the act is done. It may be objected that we could avoid the necessity of having to admit this on one condition, *viz.* that we knew the existence of a Divine Being who would intervene, where necessary, with rewards. But this knowledge would give the required conclusion only on one condition, *viz.* that this knowledge was really the knowledge that the fact of being bound to do some action itself necessitated the existence of such a Being as a consequence. For if it were the knowledge of the existence of such a Being based on other grounds, it would not enable us to know that the very fact that some action was the bringing about a Y *itself* necessitated that it would also be the bringing about an X, i.e. some advantage to the agent. No doubt if we could successfully maintain not only that an action's being the bringing about a Y necessitated its being a duty, but also that an action's being a duty necessitated as a consequence the existence of a Being who would reward it, we could show that an action's being the bringing about a Y necessitated its being rewarded. But to maintain this is really to fall back on the second alternative; and this alternative will, on consideration, turn out no more tenable than the first. It cannot successfully be maintained that the very fact that some action is a duty necessitates, not that the agent will *deserve* to gain—a conclusion which it is of course easy to draw, but that he *will* gain, unless it can be shown that this very fact necessitates, as a consequence, the existence of a being who will, if necessary, reward it. And this obviously cannot be done.

No doubt Kant maintained, and thought it possible to prove, not indeed that the obligation to do *any* action, but that the obligation to do a *certain* action, involves as a consequence that men will gain by carrying out their obligations.[1] In effect he assumed that we know that one of our duties is to endeavour to advance the realization of the highest good, *viz.* a state of affairs in which men both act morally, i.e. do what they think right, purely from the thought that it is right, and at the same time attain the happiness which in consequence they deserve. And he maintained that from this knowledge we can conclude *first* that the realization of the highest good must be possible, i.e. that so far as we succeed in making ourselves and others more moral, we and others will become proportionately happier; and *second* that, therefore, since the realization of this consequence requires, as the cause of the world in which we have to act, a supreme intelligent will which renders the world such as to cause happiness in proportion to morality, there must be such a cause. But his argument, although it has a certain plausibility, involves an inversion. If, as he rightly implied, an action can only be a duty if we *can* do it, and if we can only even in a slight degree advance a state of affairs in which a certain degree of morality is combined with a corresponding degree of happiness, *provided* there be such a supreme cause of nature, it will be impossible to know, as he assumed that we do, that to advance this state of affairs is a duty, *until* we know that there is such a supreme cause. So far, therefore, from the connexion which he thought to exist between right action and happiness being demonstrable from our knowledge of the duty in question, knowledge of the duty, if attainable at all, will itself require independent knowledge of the connexion.

We are therefore forced to allow that in order to maintain that for an action to be right, it must be advantageous, we have to maintain that advantageousness is what renders an action right. But this is obviously something which no one is going to maintain, if he considers it seriously. For he will be involved in maintaining not only that it is a duty to do whatever is for our advantage, but that this is our only duty. And the fatal objection to maintaining this is simply that no one actually thinks it.

Moreover, as it is easy to see, if we were to maintain this, our doing so, so far from helping us, would render it impossible for us to vindicate the truth of our ordinary moral convictions. For wherever in ordinary life

[1] Kant, *Critique of Practical Reason* (Bk. II, ii. § 5) [Abbott's Translation, pp. 220–9.]

we think of some particular action as a duty, we are not simply thinking of it as right, but also thinking of its rightness as constituted by the possession of some definite characteristic other than that of being advantageous to the agent. For we think of the action as a particular action *of a certain kind*, the nature of which is indicated by general words contained in the phrase by which we refer to the action, e.g. *'fulfilling* the *promise* which we made to X yesterday,' or *'looking after* our *parents.'* And we do not think of the action as right *blindly*, i.e. irrespectively of the special character which we think the act to possess; rather we think of it as being right in virtue of possessing a particular characteristic of the kind indicated by the phrase by which we refer to it. Thus in thinking of our keeping our promise to X as a duty, we are thinking of the action as rendered a duty by its being the keeping of our promise. This is obvious because we should never, for instance, think of using as an illustration of an action which we think right, telling X what we think of him, or meeting him in London, even though we thought that if we thought of these actions in certain other aspects we should think them right. Consequently if we were to maintain that conduciveness to the agent's advantage is what renders an action right, we should have to allow that any of our ordinary moral convictions, so far from being capable of vindication, is simply a mistake, as being really the conviction that some particular action is rendered a duty by its possession of some characteristic which is not that of being advantageous.

The general moral is obvious. Certain arguments, which would ordinarily be referred to as arguments designed to prove that doing what is right will be for the good of the agent, turn out to be attempts to prove that the actions which in ordinary life we think right will be for the good of the agent. There is really no need to consider in detail whether these arguments are successful; for even if they are successful, they will do nothing to prove what they are intended to prove, *viz.* that the moral convictions of our ordinary life are true. Further the attempts arise simply out of a presupposition which on reflection anyone is bound to abandon, *viz.* that conduciveness to personal advantage is what renders an action a duty. What Plato should have said to the Sophists is: 'You may be right in maintaining that in our ordinary unquestioning frame of mind we do not know, but only think, that certain actions are right. These thoughts or convictions may or may not be true. But they cannot be false for the reason which you give. You do nothing whatever to show that they are false by urging that the actions in question are disadvantageous; and I should do nothing to show that they are true, if I were to show that these actions are after all advantageous. Your real mistake lies in presupposing throughout that advantageousness is what renders an action a duty. If you will only reflect you will abandon this presupposition altogether, and then you yourself will withdraw your arguments.'

I next propose to contend that there is also to be found both in Plato and Butler, besides this attempt to show that actions which we *think* right will be for our good, another attempt which neither of them distinguishes from it and which *is* accurately described as an attempt to prove that *right* actions will be for our good. I also propose to ask what is the idea which led them to make the attempt, and to consider whether it is tenable.

When Plato raises the question 'What is justice?' he does not mean by the question 'What do we *mean* by the terms 'justice' and 'just,' or, in our language, 'duty' and 'right'?,' as we might ask 'What do we *mean* by the term 'optimism,' or again, by the phrase 'living thing'?' And as a matter of fact if he had meant this, he would have been raising what was only verbally, and not really, a question at all, in that any attempt to ask it would have implied that the answer was already known and that therefore there was nothing to ask. He means 'What is the characteristic the possession of which by an action necessitates that the action is just, i.e. an act which it is our duty, or which we ought, to do?' In short he means 'What renders a just or right action, just or right?'

Now this question really means 'What is the characteristic common to particular just acts which renders them just?' And for anyone even to *ask* this question is to imply that he already *knows* what particular actions are just. For even to *ask* 'What is the character common to certain things?' is to imply that we already *know* what the things are of which we are wanting to find the common character. Equally, of course, any attempt to *answer* the question has the same implication. For such an attempt can only consist in considering the particular actions which we know to be just and attempting to discover what is the characteristic common to them all, the vague apprehension of which has led us to apprehend them to be just. Plato therefore, both in representing Socrates as raising with his hearers the question 'What is justice?' and also in representing them all as attempting to answer it, is implying, whether he is aware that he is doing so or not, that they all know what particular acts are, and what particular acts are not, just. If on the contrary what he had presupposed was that the members of the dialogue think, instead of knowing, that certain actions are just, his question—whether he had expressed it thus or not—would really have been, not 'What *is* justice?,' but 'What do we *think* that justice is?'; or, more clearly, not 'What renders an act just?' but 'What do we think renders an act just?' But in that case an answer, whatever its character, would have thrown no light on the question 'What is justice?'; and apart from this, he is plainly not asking 'What do we *think* that justice is?.'

As has been pointed out, however, the view which Plato attributes to the Sophists presupposes that ordinary mankind, which of course includes the members of the dialogue, only thinks and does not know that certain actions are just. Therefore, when Plato introduces this view as requiring refutation and, in doing so, represents the members of the dialogue as not questioning the presupposition, he ought in consistency to have made someone point out that in view of the acceptance of this presupposition Socrates' original question 'What is justice?' required to be amended to the question 'What do we think that justice is?.' But Plato does not do so. In the present context the significant fact is that even after he has introduced the view of the Sophists he still represents the question to be answered as being 'What is justice?,' and therefore still implies that the members of the dialogue know what is just in particular. Even in making Glaucon and Adeimantus ask Socrates to refute the Sophists, what he, inconsistently, makes them ask Socrates to exhibit the nature of is not the acts which men think just but just acts. And when Plato in the fourth book goes on to give Socrates' answer, which, of course, is intended to express the truth, he in the same way represents Socrates as offering, and the others as accepting, an account of the nature of *just* acts, *viz.* that they consist in conferring those benefits on society which a man's nature renders him best suited to confer, and then makes Socrates argue in detail that it is *just* action which will be profitable. In doing so he is of course implying, inconsistently with the implication of his treatment of the Sophists' view, that the members of the dialogue, and therefore also mankind in ordinary life, *know* what is just in particular. For in the end the statement 'Justice is conferring certain benefits on society' can only mean that conferring these benefits is the characteristic the vague apprehension of which in certain actions leads us to know or apprehend them to be just; and the acceptance of this statement by the members of the dialogue must be understood as expressing their recognition that this characteristic is the common character of the particular acts which they already know to be just.

It therefore must be allowed that, although to do so is inconsistent with his view of the way in which the Sophistic theory has to be refuted, Plato is in the fourth book (and of course the same admission must be made about the eighth and ninth) endeavouring to prove that *just*, i.e. *right*, action, will be for the good or advantage of the agent.

Given that this is what Plato wants to prove in the fourth book, the general nature of what he conceives to be the proof is obvious. His idea is that if we start with the knowledge of what right actions consist in, *viz.*, to put it shortly, serving the state, and then consider what the effects of these and other actions will be by taking into account not only the circumstances in which we are placed, but also the various desires of the human soul and the varying amounts of satisfaction to which the realization of these objects will give rise, it will be obvious that it is by doing what is right that, at any rate in the long run, we shall become happy.

Now a particular proof of this kind, such as Plato's, naturally provokes two comments. The first is that there is no need to consider its success in detail, since we know on general grounds that it must fail. For it can only be shown that actions characterized by being the bringing about things of one kind, in this case benefits to society, will always have as their consequence things of another kind, in this case elements of happiness in the agent, provided that we can prove, as Plato makes no attempt to do, the existence of a Being who will intervene to introduce suitable rewards where they are needed. The second is that though the establishment of this conclusion, whether with or without the help of theological arguments, would be of the greatest benefit to us, since we should all be better off if we knew it to be true, yet it differs from the establishment of the corresponding conclusion against the Sophists in that it would throw no light whatever on the question 'What is our duty in detail, and why?' And this second comment naturally raises the question which seems to be the important one to ask in this connexion, *viz.* '*Why* did Plato think it important to prove that right action would benefit the agent?'

The explanation obviously cannot be simply, or even mainly, that the combination in Plato of a desire to do what is right and of a desire to become happy led him to try to satisfy himself that by doing what is right he would be, so to say, having it both ways. The main explanation must lie in a quite different direction. There is no escaping the conclusion that when Plato sets himself to consider not what *should*, but what *actually does* as a matter of fact, lead a man to act, when he is acting deliberately, and not merely in consequence of an impulse, he answers 'The desire for some good to himself and that only.' In other words we have to allow that, according to Plato, a man pursues whatever he pursues simply as a good to himself, i.e. really as something which will give him satisfaction, or, as perhaps we ought to say, as an element in what will render him happy. In the *Republic* this view comes to light in the sixth book. He there speaks of τὸ ἀγαθόν as that which every soul pursues and for the sake of which it does all it does, divining that it is something but being perplexed and unable to grasp adequately what it is; and he goes on to say of things that are good (τὰ ἀγαθά) that while many are ready to do and to obtain and to be what only *seems* just, even if it is not, no one is content with obtaining what *seems* good, but endeavours to obtain what is *really* good. It might be objected that these statements do not bear out the view which is attributed to Plato, since Plato certainly did not mean by an ἀγαθόν a source of satisfaction or happiness to oneself. But to this the answer is that wherever Plato uses the term ἀγαθά (goods) elsewhere in the *Republic* and in other dialogues, such as the *Philebus*, the context always shows that he means by a good a good to oneself, and, this being so, he must really be meaning by an ἀγαθόν, a source of satisfaction, or perhaps, more generally, a source of happiness. The view, however, emerges most clearly in the *Gorgias*, where Plato, in order to show that rhetoricians and tyrants do not do what they really wish to do, maintains that in all actions alike, and even when we kill a man or despoil him of his goods, we do what we do because we think it will be better for us to do so.

Now if we grant, as we must, that Plato thought this, we can find in the admission a natural explanation of Plato's desire to prove that just action will be advantageous. For plainly he passionately wanted men to do what is right, and if he thought that it was only desire of some good to themselves which moved them in all deliberate action, it would be natural, and indeed necessary, for him to think that if men are to be induced to do what is just, the only way to induce them is to convince them that thereby they will gain or become better off.

In Butler also we are driven to find the same attempt to prove that right action will benefit the agent, and to give the same explanation. The proper interpretation of the most important part of the statement quoted from Butler is not very easy to discover. What he says is that when we sit down in a cool hour we can neither justify to ourselves the pursuit of what is *right* and *good*, as such, or any other pursuit, till we are convinced that it will be for our happiness or at least not against it. Here a puzzle arises from the fact that whereas by referring to certain of the actions which we have to justify to ourselves as the pursuit of what is *right*, he inevitably implies that we already *know* them to be right, yet by speaking of our having to justify them to ourselves, i.e. apparently to prove to ourselves that they are right, he seems to imply that we do *not* know them to be right. The interpretation given earlier evaded the puzzle by tacitly assuming that Butler was using the term 'right' loosely for what we think, and so do not know, to be right. But it may well be asked whether the assumption was justified. And if we consider the statement in reference to the *Sermons* generally, we seem bound to conclude that Butler was really maintaining two different, and indeed inconsistent, doctrines without realizing their difference, the one involving that the word 'right' is here used strictly, and the other involving that it is not. When Kant contrasts the two kinds of statement containing the word 'ought' which he designated as Categorical and Hypothetical Imperatives, he implies, although he does not expressly state, that the term 'ought' is being used in the two kinds of statement in radically different senses. In a Categorical Imperative, he implies, 'ought' has the ordinary moral sense in which it is co-extensive with 'duty,' and 'morally bound.' In a Hypothetical Imperative it has the purely non-moral sense of proper in respect of being the thing which is conducive to our purpose, whether that purpose be the object of some special desire which is moving us, e.g. as when we wash in order to become clean, or whether it be our happiness, as when we make friends in order to become happy. Corresponding to these two senses of the term 'ought,' there will be two senses of 'justifying a certain action,' the one moral and the other not. We may mean by the phrase proving to ourselves that it is a duty to do the action, or we may mean proving to ourselves that the act is the proper one to do in respect of its being the act which will lead to the realization of our purpose.

Now if we understand Butler's word 'right' to be a loose phrase for what in ordinary life we *think* to be right, we can understand him to be using 'justify' in the moral sense of 'justify,' without having to admit that he is involved in contradiction. We can understand him to be saying that in order to know that some action which we ordinarily think to be right is right, we must first prove to ourselves that it will be for our happiness, or at least not against it; and we shall then be representing him as explicitly maintaining what the Sophists and Plato, in seeking to refute them, presupposed. On the other hand if we understand Butler to be using the term 'right' strictly, we can only avoid attributing to him the self-contradictory view already referred to by understanding him to be using the term 'justify' in the non-moral sense. For while he would be involved in contradiction if he maintained that even where we knew that some action is right, we still need to prove to ourselves that we ought in the moral sense to do it, he would not be so involved, if he maintained instead that what we still need is to prove to ourselves that we ought to do it in the non-moral sense. Now the general drift of what Butler says of conscience, and especially his statement that it carries its own authority with it, implies that he considered that in ordinary life we *know* and do not *think* that certain actions are right; and if we judge by this, we must understand Butler to be here using 'right' strictly, and to be maintaining that even when we know that we morally ought to do something, we still need to know that we ought to do it in the non-moral sense of its being conducive to our purpose, and that therefore, since our happiness is our purpose, we still need to know that it will conduce to our happiness. But if we think that this is what Butler is maintaining, we have to allow that the explanation of his maintaining it can only be the same as that given with regard to Plato. For if we ask '*Why*, according to Butler, when we already know that doing some action is a duty, do we still require to know that we ought to do the action in the non-moral sense of 'ought'?,' the answer can only be 'Because otherwise we shall not do the action.' And the implication will be that when, to use Butler's phrase, we sit down in a cool hour, i.e. when we are not under the influence of impulses, the only thing we desire, and therefore the only purpose we have, is our own happiness, and that therefore we shall do whatever we do only in order that we may become happy. The general drift of his *Sermons*, however, and more especially his statement that it is manifest that nothing can be of consequence to mankind or any creature but happiness shows that Butler actually thought this. We have therefore to attribute to Butler side by side with the view already attributed to him, and undistinguished from it, a view which is inconsistent with it and is really the second view already attributed to Plato, *viz.* that even though we know certain actions to be right, we must have it proved to us that they will be for our good or happiness, since otherwise, as we act only from desire of our own happiness, we shall not do them.

I propose now to take it as established (1) that both Plato and Butler in a certain vein of thought are really endeavouring to prove that right actions, in the strict sense of 'right actions,' will be for the agent's advantage; (2) that their reason for doing so lies in the conviction that even where we know some action to be right, we shall not do it unless we think that it will be for our advantage; and (3) that behind this conviction lies the conviction of which it is really a corollary, *viz.* the conviction that desire for some good to oneself is the only motive of deliberate action.

But are these convictions true? For if it can be shown that they are not, then at least Plato and Butler's reason for trying to prove the advantageousness of right action will have disappeared.

The conviction that even where we know some action to be right, we shall not do it unless we think we shall be the better off for doing it, of course, strikes us as a paradox. At first no doubt we are apt to mis-state the paradox. We are apt to say that the conviction, implying as it does that we only act out of self-interest, really implies that it is impossible for us to do anything which we ought to do at all, since if we did some action out of self-interest we could not have done anything which was a duty. But to say this is to make the mistake of thinking that the motive with which we do an action can possibly have something to do with its rightness or wrongness. To be morally bound is to be morally bound to *do* something, i.e. to bring something about; and even if it be only from the lowest of motives that we have brought about something which we ought to have brought about, we have still done something which we ought to have done. The fact that I have given A credit in order to spite his rival B, or again, in order to secure future favours from A, has, as we see when we reflect, no bearing whatever on the question whether I ought to have given A credit. The real paradox inherent in the conviction lies in its implication that there is no such thing as moral goodness. If I give A credit solely to obtain future favours, and even if I gave him credit either thinking or knowing that I ought to do so, but in no way directly or indirectly influenced by my either so thinking or knowing, then even though it has to be allowed that I did something which I was morally bound to do, it has to be admitted that there was no moral goodness whatever about my action. And the conviction in question is really what is ordinarily called the doctrine that morality needs a sanction, i.e. really the doctrine that, to stimulate a man into doing some action, it is not merely insufficient but even useless to convince him that he is morally bound to do it, and that, instead, we have to appeal to his desire to become better off.

Now we are apt to smile in a superior way when in reading Mill we find him taking for granted that morality needs a sanction, but we cannot afford to do so when we find Butler, and still more when we find Plato, really doing the same thing. Moreover when Plato and Butler maintain the doctrine that lies at the back of this conviction, viz. the doctrine that we always aim at, i.e. act from the desire of, some good to ourselves, they are in the best of company. Aristotle is practically only repeating the statement quoted from the sixth book of the *Republic* when he says in the first sentence of the *Ethics*, that every deliberate action seems to aim at something good, and that therefore the good has rightly been declared to be that at which all things aim. For this to become obvious it is only necessary to consider what meaning must be attributed to the term ἀγαθόν in the early chapters of the *Ethics*. Again, to take a modern instance, Green says: 'The motive in every imputable act for which the agent is conscious on reflection that he is answerable, is a desire for personal good in some form or other. . . . It is superfluous to add good to *himself*, for anything conceived as good in such a way that the agent acts for the sake of it, must be conceived as *his own* good, though he may conceive it as his own good only on account of his interest in others, and in spite of any amount of suffering on his own part incidental to its attainment.' [2] Moreover the doctrine seems plausible enough, if we ask ourselves in a purely general way 'How are we to be led into doing something?.' For the natural answer is: 'Only by thinking of some state of affairs which it is in my power to bring about and by which I shall become better off than I am now'; and the answer implies that only in this way shall we come to desire to do an action, and that, unless we desire to do it, we shall not do it.

Nevertheless it seems difficult, and indeed in the end impossible, to think that the doctrine will stand the test of instances. It seems impossible to allow that in what would usually be called disinterested actions, whether they be good or bad, there is not at least some element of disinterestedness. It strikes us as absurd to think that in what would be called a benevolent action, we are not moved at least in part by the desire that someone else shall be better off and also by the desire to *make* him better off, even though we may also necessarily have, and be influenced by, the desire to have the satisfaction of thinking that he is better off and that we have made him so. It seems equally absurd to maintain that where we are said to treat someone maliciously, we are not moved in part by the desire of his unhappiness and also partly by the desire to *make* him unhappy. Again when we are said to be pursuing scientific studies without a practical aim, it seems mere distortion of the facts to say that we are moved solely by the desire to have the satisfaction of knowing some particular thing and not, at least in part, by the desire to know it. And we seem driven to make a similar admission when we consider actions in which we are said to have acted conscientiously.

In this connexion it should be noted that the doctrine under consideration, *viz.* that our motive in doing any action is desire for some good to ourselves to which we think the action will lead, has two negative implications. The first is that the thought, or, alternatively, the knowledge, that some action is right has no influence on us in acting, i.e. that the thought, or the knowledge, that an action is a duty can neither be our motive nor even an element in our motive. The existence of this implication is obvious, since if our motive is held to be the desire for a certain good to ourselves, it is implied that the thought that the action is a duty, though present, is neither what moves us, nor an element in what moves us, to do the action. The second implication is that there is no such thing as a *desire* to do what is right, or more fully, a desire to do some action in virtue of its being a duty. The existence of this second implication is also obvious, since if

[2] *Prolegomena to Ethics*, §§ 91–2.

such a desire were allowed to exist, there would be no reason for maintaining that when we do some action which we think to be a duty, our motive is necessarily the desire for a certain good to ourselves. The truth of the doctrine could therefore be contested in one of two alternative ways. We might either deny the truth of the former implication; or, again, we might deny the truth of the latter. The former is, of course, the line taken by Kant, at any rate in a qualified form. He maintained in effect that the mere thought that an action is a duty, apart from a desire to do what we ought to do—a desire the existence of which he refused to admit—is at any rate in certain instances the motive, or at least an element in the motive, of an action. No doubt he insisted that the existence of this fact gave rise to a problem, and a problem which only vindication of freedom of the will could resolve; but he maintained that the problem was soluble, and that therefore he was entitled to insist on this fact. Now this method of refutation has adherents and at first sight it is attractive. For it seems mere wild paradox to maintain that in no case in which we do what we think of as right, do we ever in any degree do it *because* we think it right; and to say that we do some action *because* we think it right seems to imply that the thought that it is right is our motive. Again the statement seems natural that where we are said to have acted thus, we obviously did not want to do what we did but acted against our desires or inclinations. Nevertheless we are, I think, on further reflection bound to abandon this view. For one reason, to appeal to a consideration of which the full elucidation and vindication would take too long, the view involves that where we are said to have done some action because we thought it right, though we had a motive for what we did, we had no purpose in doing it. For we really mean by our purpose in doing some action that the *desire* of which for its own sake leads us to do the action. Again, if we face the purely general question 'Can we really do anything whatever unless in some respect or other we desire to do it?' we have to answer 'No.' But if we allow this, then we have to allow that the obvious way to endeavour to meet Plato's view is to maintain the existence of a desire to do what is right. And it does not seem difficult to do so with success. For we obviously are referring to a fact when we speak of someone as possessing a sense of duty and, again, a strong sense of duty. And if we consider what we are thinking of in these individuals whom we think of as possessing it, we find we cannot exclude from it a desire to do what is a duty, as such, or for its own sake, or, more simply, a desire to do what is a duty. In fact it is hard to resist the conclusion that Kant himself would have taken this line instead of the extreme line which he did, had he not had the fixed idea that all desire is for enjoyment. But if we think this—as it seems we must—we, of course, have no need to admit the truth of Plato's reason for trying to prove that right actions must be advantageous. For if we admit the existence of a desire to do what is right, there is no longer any reason for maintaining as a general thesis that in any case in which a man knows some action to be right, he must, if he is to be led to do it, be convinced that he will gain by doing it. For we shall be able to maintain that his desire to do what is right, if strong enough, will lead him to do the action in spite of any aversion from doing it which he may feel on account of its disadvantages.

It may be objected that if we maintain the existence of a desire to do what is right, we shall become involved in an insoluble difficulty. For we shall also have to allow that we have a desire to become well off or happy, and that therefore men have two radically different desires, i.e. desires the object of which are completely incommensurable. We shall therefore be implying that in those instances—which of course must exist—in which a man has either to do what is right or to do what is for his happiness he can have no means of choosing which he shall do, since there can be no comparable characteristic of the two alternative actions which will enable him to choose to do the one rather than, or in preference to, the other. But to this objection there is an answer which, even if it be at first paradoxical, is in the end irresistible, *viz.* that in connexion with such instances it is wholly inappropriate to speak of a *choice*. A choice is, no doubt, necessarily a choice between comparable alternatives, e.g. between an afternoon's enjoyment on the river and an afternoon's enjoyment at a cinema. But it is purely arbitrary to maintain that wherever we have two alternative courses of action before us we have necessarily to *choose* between them. Thus a man contemplating retirement may be offered a new post. He may, on thinking it over, be unable to resist the conclusion that it is a duty on his part to accept it and equally convinced that if he accepts it, he will lose in happiness. He will either accept from his desire to do what is right in spite of his aversion from doing what will bring himself a loss of happiness, or he will refuse from his desire of happiness, in spite of his aversion from doing what is wrong. But whichever he does, though he will have *decided* to do what he does, he will not have *chosen* to do it, i.e. chosen to do it in preference to doing the alternative action.

For the reasons given I shall treat it as established that, though there is to be found in Plato and Butler what is really an attempt to prove that right action is advantageous, the question of its success or failure can be ignored, since the attempt is based on a fundamental mistake about actual human nature.

*   *   *

A Criticism of Kant[*]

G. C. FIELD

. . . KANT, THEN, has not succeeded in the task he set himself. He thought that the nature of goodness or rightness could be derived from the conception of a rational being. If, as we have seen to be the case, his attempt thus to derive it was unsuccessful, the reason must be sought in one or both of two possible directions. On the one hand, it may be that he had not really understood what was involved in the nature of a rational being. On the other, he may have been mistaken in thinking that it was connected in this way with the conception of goodness or rightness. It would be well, perhaps, if we want to see which alternative to accept, to examine the conception of a rational being a little more closely.

A rational being, of course, is a being endowed with reason. But what is reason? Whatever else it is, it is in the first place a cognitive faculty of the conscious being, it is something in us which enables us to know something. We shall probably best distinguish it from other cognitive faculties by the kind of object that we know by it. Kant would say, for instance, that reason was that which enabled us to know universal and necessary truths. But however we distinguish it, the important point is that it is a form of knowing. As applied to actions, it tells us facts about the actions, it tells us the kind of action each one is. And we are here face to face with the crucial question, "Can reason be practical?" Or, in other words, "Can a knowledge of the nature of an action by itself move us to take that action?" Kant thought that it could: it is essential to his whole position. And if he is wrong in this, we have discovered the fundamental fallacy of his theory.

Let us try to realize the point of view of those who would hold that on this fundamental point Kant was wrong. We may, to begin with, set against Kant's view the dictum of Aristotle. The intellect by itself moves nothing, has no motive force. Or, in other words, the mere knowing that an action, or anything else, is of such-and-such a kind cannot possibly move us to act.

The point is of such vital importance that we must elaborate this point of view a little further. In the elementary stages of reflection, it might

* Excerpted and reprinted by kind permission of the author and the publisher from *Moral Theory*, pp. 46–51. Methuen and Co., Ltd., 1921.

seem to us that this was obviously at variance with certain observable facts. We may say that the would-be criminal knows that if he commits a murder, he will be hanged. This knowledge is enough to make him refrain from doing so, however much he may want to. I know, when I am ill, that a certain medicine will make me well, and therefore I take it, however unpleasant it may be. Here we have cases of knowledge moving us to action. The argument is really a very superficial one, and only worth mentioning because it helps to illustrate and emphasize the view against which it is directed. For the point is, of course, that it is not the mere knowledge that moves us to action at all. If the criminal did not mind being hanged, if I am absolutely indifferent whether I get well or not, then the knowledge would have no effect on our action one way or another. The reason why the knowledge moves us to action is that it is the knowledge that that particular kind of action will have an effect that we want or desire. But the bare knowledge that a particular action is of a certain kind or will have a certain effect has no influence on us unless we have an interest in that effect or that kind of action, unless, that is, we have some feeling towards it. In short, action of any kind will not take place without the presence of a desire or some element of feeling or emotion. So that if we were pure reason without any desire or feelings, we should not, as Kant thought, act in a particular way, but we should simply not act at all.[1]

If this is true, Kant's fallacy lies in thinking that just the bare knowledge that an action is of a certain kind is sufficient to move us to do that action. Why that may sound plausible, at first hearing, is that when we speak of the kind of action we are apt to include in the meaning of that phrase the effect the action has on us: thus, for instance, we may speak of pleasant and unpleasant actions as being different kinds of actions, though the difference lies not necessarily at all in the actions themselves but simply in the effect they have on us. But Kant, of course, is careful to avoid this confusion. When he speaks of the kind of action, he means simply what the action is in itself, apart from its effects on us or any relation to our feelings.

In the light of this, we can get a clearer view of the place of reason in action and the real meaning of reasonable action. Practical reason will mean for us what it meant for Aristotle, who first used the phrase: that is, the ability to discover what will be the best means to an end which we want to attain. The essence of unreasonable action will lie in doing something which will defeat our own ends: for instance, in doing something in obedience to an immediate desire which will hinder the attainment of

---

[1] We might express this in Kantian terms by saying that the reason cannot be free in his sense. If our reason acts, it acts according to certain laws of its own nature, no doubt. But to start it acting it needs an efficient cause, just as much as natural objects do, in this case, some form of desire or feeling. So far, therefore, is reason from supplying a possible motive for action, that it cannot itself act without a previous desire or feeling to set it in motion.

something else which we really want more. Practical reason will really be the capacity of finding means to ends.

We can apply the same consideration to the meaning of the term "ends." In that connexion we may recall the passage where Kant argues that all rational beings must be ends in themselves, because each one regards himself as an end. And as they are all rational beings, what holds of one must hold of the others. So that they must all be ends in themselves. However ready we may be to accept the valuable practical consequences that Kant draws from the principle we should probably all feel that the argument as it stands is singularly unconvincing. And, in the light of the above consideration, we begin to see the reason for that. For it becomes clearer that the argument really rests on a confusion about the sort of fact that being an end really is. Being an end is not, in our ordinary use of the term, a fact about things like being a human being or being green or being a triangle, a fact about the thing itself, a fact which belongs to the thing in its own right. Being an end is not really a fact about the thing at all. My end in ordinary speech means my object or purpose, what I am aiming at or trying to get at or want or desire. It is made an end by being wanted, and if I cease to want it it ceases to be my end. If no one wants it any longer, it ceases to be an end at all. That is, there is strictly no such thing as an end in itself unless we are going to attach an entirely new meaning to the word. Being an end implies some relation to the desires or purposes of some conscious being: and a thing is made an end by this relation. It follows, then, that nothing can be just an end: it could only be an end for someone, the purpose or desire of some conscious being. And there would, of course, be nothing self-contradictory in the view that each conscious being might have a different end, or that the same thing might be an end for one being and not for another.

The same consideration would apply, surely, to a conception like that of value. We should ask whether value must not be value for someone, whether we do not find that, if we are to think of value at all, we must think of it as essentially related to our feelings or the feelings of some conscious being or beings. This, at any rate, is our ordinary use of it. And ultimately we shall begin to ask ourselves whether we may not be finally forced to say the same of a wider conception like that of good. If we are, we shall have to say that our conception of good necessarily contains in itself a reference to some conscious being. We shall not be able to allow any such ideas as that of good, which was just good and not good for some being. Good would be found to be essentially related to and in some way dependent on the wishes or desires or feelings of some conscious being.

The Kantian would, of course, object here that Kant had already considered the claims of the desires and feelings and given reasons for rejecting them. In the first place, he had argued that to make goodness depend on desires or feelings, would make it something uncertain and fluctuating, because some people might desire a thing and others not, or the same person might desire it at one time and not at another. This is certainly a weighty objection, and will have to be considered at length later. Here it will suffice to suggest a possible line on which it might be met: that is, if we developed the idea of some end which every conscious being, by its very nature, must and would desire, if it only realized what it was. We shall meet with this conception later. In the second place he had argued that such a view would make what we desired not good in itself but only as a means to an end. Here we can only say that Kant, doubtless largely under the influence of a faulty psychology, seems to fail to realize the possibility or the true meaning of anything being desired purely for its own sake. Finally it would be argued that such a view would not give us a thing good in itself, because its goodness would depend upon something else outside of it, namely, our desire of or feeling towards it. This we should readily admit. And we should reply that we do not and cannot recognize the existence or possibility of any such thing as good in itself in that sense, out of all relation to anything else. It simply has no meaning for us. And if it had, it would make goodness something of no interest or importance to us, and of no possible influence upon our actions.

With this, we really return to the point from which Kant started. We shall remember that one of the assumptions on which he seemed to base his theory was that which was expressed by saying that if a thing is really good, it must be good in itself. If that appealed to us at first as a reasonable statement of our own ordinary ideas, it was only because we had not yet realized what it really meant. When we did realize this, instead of accepting it as a correct starting-point, we should be more inclined to describe it as the fundamental fallacy of Kant, as indeed of many other writers. Goodness, we should say now, is not a quality which belongs to things in themselves, quite apart from their effect on or their relation to us [2] or some conscious being. If it were, it could only be related to us as an object of cognition. And if it were simply an object of cognition, something that we merely knew without having any feeling towards it, it could not move us to action, or indeed be of any practical interest or importance to us at all.

There are many other objections to Kant's view. But if the argument has been correct, we have found his fundamental fallacy in the false assumptions from which he starts. They are really two in number. He starts from the assumption that what is good must be good in itself, apart from all relations to anything else. And in consequence of this he is forced to assume that the mere intellectual apprehension of the fact is sufficient to move us to action. The other assumptions which we have ascribed to him

[2] Of course, in a sense, as we have seen, Kant does make goodness related to us, because it is an essential quality of rational beings. But that merely means that we, in so far as we are rational, are the things which have this quality. It is obviously a very different thing from asserting that goodness itself consists in a relation to us or to any conscious being. And nothing short of this will satisfy the above criticism.

follow from these two or are different forms which they take. But, if our argument has been at all correct, we must maintain against this that the simple intellectual apprehension, the bare knowledge of anything can never move us to action. And consequently his idea of a good in itself is incompatible with one of the most deeply recognized characteristics of the moral fact, namely, that it is somehow a reason for action.

"Ought" and Motivation *

W. D. FALK

I WANT TO CONSIDER an argument put forward by the late Professor Prichard in his lecture on *Duty and Interest,*** as it raises issues of wider interest. The argument occurs in the second half of his lecture where Prichard attributes to popular moralists and philosophers a view which to him seems paradoxical. The view has been widely held and is well exemplified by Bishop Butler; whether it should also be attributed to Plato I shall not be concerned to discuss.

The problem is briefly this. Moralists in the past have been preoccupied with showing that a person who does his duty will, in doing so, also advance his personal good. This would be understandable if they thought that only acts which advance someone's good could be duties, for then we could never know we ought to do an act unless we were convinced of its good consequences for ourselves. But there are moralists, like Bishop Butler, who, as Prichard agrees, consider this view as obviously false. They grant we can have duties on other grounds than that an act would promote our own good, e.g. on the ground that an act will be one of beneficence or of keeping faith; but in spite of this, they remain worried by the problem of a necessary connection between duty and personal good. Thus Butler finds it necessary to supplement his conviction of the irreducible authority of conscience by an attempt to prove that whenever conscience bids us do some act on its own account and regardless of our own good, in fact, and contrary to appearances, our own good will always be served, or at least not be harmed, by our doing it. Now according to Prichard these attempts to prove a connection between duty and personal good where the duty itself is not thought to depend on this connection seem paradoxical: we cannot but view them with the suspicion that "the real question is not so much whether they are successful, but whether they ought ever to have been made"; and I myself share this feeling. But why should they never have been made? Prichard's answer to this question, an answer accepted by Sir David Ross in the *Foundations of Ethics,* is my reason for returning to the problem, for I feel it still does not meet the real point. The trouble, I think,

* Reprinted by kind permission of the author and the editors from the *Proceedings of the Aristotelian Society*, 48, 1947–8.
** [Reprinted in part pp. 469 ff. this volume.]

does not lie principally in the psychological errors of his opponents as alleged by Prichard: it lies deeper, in a persistent uncertainty shared by moralists and ordinary men about the relation to motivation of the very use of such words as "ought," "duty," "obligation."

According to Prichard the exponents of a connection between duty and interest in the above sense are concerned to meet a perplexity of ordinary life. They must be judged by their success in meeting it. People commonly take it for granted that, when it is their duty to do some act, they have also a reason or motive for doing it, in some sense even an especially stringent one. But for many there comes a time, particularly when some personal interest seems at stake, when they feel troubled by doubt or in need of re-assurance; and in this mood they turn to the moralist with a request: "Exhibit to me," they say in effect, "the reason or motive sufficient, even at cost to myself, to induce me to do what I ought, but don't want to do; for though I grant the duty, I see no such reason, and maybe there is none, or none sufficiently strong; and no one can do anything unless he has a sufficient reason for doing it, and knows what it is!" Here what is asked for is a "justification" in terms of motive for them doing some act whose moral obligatoriness is not questioned and the psychological possibility of moral conduct is made dependent on its success. How is the moralist to deal with this? He may either deny the legitimacy of the request—by denying that moral conduct requires a reason or motive sufficient or otherwise—or else he must show how it can be satisfied. The search for a connection between duty and interest is an attempt to do the latter. It is granted that the questioner has a real axe to grind: that when he has a duty it is still an open question whether he will also have a motive; but he is told that the facts, psychological and otherwise, will be found to dispel his doubts. It so happens that when he ought to do an act he will also, and in spite of contrary appearances, always be promoting his own good by doing it, and his own good is in fact what he desires to promote. He is therefore always in error when, while acknowledging a duty, he pleads absence of a motive.

But, tempting as this reply has seemed to many, Prichard's misgivings are justified. For if this were the only answer the connection between duty and motivation would be much looser than we commonly expect it to be. If the questioner were overlooking no more than a connection between duty and self interest, some may be right in denying that they had a motive sufficient for doing what they ought, since even if general, the connection could not be proved necessary; and in fact the exceptions would be likely to prove to be the rule.

But the chances of success apart, the reply seems altogether out of place, since it rests on the assumption that moral conduct can have none but interested motives. It implies that "morality needs a sanction"; that "to stimulate a man into doing some action it is not merely insufficient, but useless to convince him that he is morally bound to do it, and that, instead, we have to appeal to his desire to be better off." But, in fact, we believe that morality needs no external sanction: that the very thought that we morally ought to do some act is sufficient without reference to any ulterior motive to provide us with a reason for doing it; and we consider that strictly moral, i.e. morally good conduct is activated by no other motive than that provided by this thought. The reply offered by the exponents of a connection between duty and interest therefore fails altogether to meet what must be the questioner's fundamental error.

In what then does his error consist? According to Prichard, in a psychological oversight, a failure to notice within himself the existence of disinterested desires, and among them a desire to do acts simply because he ought to do them. The exponents of a connection between duty and interest fail to refer him to this, because they are themselves blinded by a psychological dogma, the belief that a person's own good is the one and only rational motive to action. But once the psychological facts are recognized for what they are, no difficulty remains in dealing with the request for a motive where a duty is acknowledged in a way that will account for our ordinary moral convictions. This is how Prichard summarizes his conclusion: "For, if we admit the existence of a desire to do what is right, there is no longer any reason for maintaining as a general thesis that in any case in which a man knows some action to be right, he must, if he is to be led to do it, be convinced that he will gain by doing it. For we shall be able to maintain that his desire to do what is right, if strong enough, will lead him to do the action in spite of any aversion from doing it, which he may feel on account of its disadvantages." *

The strength of this view lies in that it can explain how the man who acknowledges a duty to do some act may be provided with a motive for doing it, even at cost to himself, purely by the conviction that he ought to do it. To this extent, Prichard seems to account for our ordinary convictions more adequately than the rival doctrine. All the same, I think, he still does so to a far smaller extent than may at first sight appear. In fact, I shall argue that if, as he contends, a psychological oversight is all that accounts for the questioner's doubt of a motive for acting as he ought, some persistent features of our ordinary moral convictions, far from having been accounted for, will have to be discarded.

But before turning to these difficulties, some consideration must be given to what the demand for a motive or reason, as a condition of anyone's ability to act, amounts to. Among the confusions attending the use of words like "motive" and "reason" one arises from the habit of speaking of both thoughts and desires as motives for actions. The motive is described as being constituted by an impelling thought *or* desire. According to Prichard, there is here a distinction without a difference, as a motivating thought implies a purpose which it motivates, and a purpose is what someone desires to attain. The point, he says, needs stressing on account of a

* [pp. 485–6 this volume.]

and "desiring," introduced by Kant.
, according to Kant, we ha   e thought that we ought to do some
act a motive for doing it: but, "having a motive" does not here entail
"having a desire"; and when we act from the motive, we shall do so with
the aid of an effort of will and against desire or inclination rather than
from them. It seems plain to Prichard that Kant is here drawing an artificial
distinction, presumably under the influence of his conviction that desire
is always for some pleasurable experience, which would exclude the possibility of a desire for doing one's duty for its own sake. But the difficulty
disappears with the abandonment of the latter view. We shall then say, with
Kant, that we have in the thought that we ought to do some act a motive
for doing it, and equate this with saying that we possess a desire to do our
duty for its own sake or a "sense of duty." To convince a man that he has a
motive for doing his duty must therefore consist in convincing him that he
desires to do it; and when he comes to act, under the influence of this
motive he will be acting from desire pure and simple as he would under the
influence of any other motive.

But, whatever the merits of Kant's contribution, the problems involved
here are more complex than Prichard presents them. For we use "having a
motive" in different senses, and in neither of them, though for different
reasons, does it seem appropriate to equate "having a motive" with
"desiring." In order to avoid misunderstandings, I must here state what I
take a "reason" or "motive" to mean. In the sense relevant to this discussion,
a reason or motive is a moving or impelling thought, the thought of that for
the sake, or in view of which, some act is done; and I myself see no intelligible alternative to saying that it "moves" or "impels" in the sense that
it functions as a cause of actions, in the conventional sense of cause as an
antecedent implying a consequent by a rule of invariable connection. I
should therefore, describe a motive as a *causa rationis*, a mental antecedent
which, when attended to by a person, and in otherwise comparable conditions, will invariably be followed by an orientation of his organism towards the action thought of, in a way which, except for the intervention of
distractions, counter-motives and physical impediments, will terminate in
the action itself. Such a thought may be said to constitute simply a reason
or motive, if, when attended to by itself alone, it thus causally implies
action; and a sufficient reason or motive when, in addition, it persists in doing so even in view of opposing motives in the situation. Now, that someone has a motive may be used in either an *occurrent* or a *dispositional* sense;
for "he is being impelled (or caused) by the thought of some act to do
it," or "he would, if he dwelt on it, be impelled (or caused) by the thought
of some act to do it." The motive may be his either actually or potentially
and reflectively so. The differences between these two uses are considerable,
and each is differently related to "desiring." In the first use there is a connection, though none as close as Prichard presents it. Actually "to have a
motive to do some act" and "desiring to do it" would here mean the same

if "desiring" were used simply for "̶ ̶ ̶ ̶ ̶ ̶ ̶ ̶ ̶ ̶ ̶ ̶ ̶ ̶ ̶ ̶
is used not for "being," but for "f̶ ̶ ̶ ̶ ̶ impelled. But to say we
impelled to do some act functions (so it seems to me) as a composite statement, asserting that we are impelled and that we have perceptual evidence
of our being so, evidence derived from sensations which we take to arise,
under the influence of a motivating thought, from the orientation of our
organism towards an overt action. To say that someone desires to do some
act would therefore go beyond saying that he had a motive or was impelled,
even if, whenever anyone were impelled to action, he also felt desire; but
in fact people are often impelled to act under the influence of a motivating
thought without noticing any desire at all.[1] There is no harm if in ordinary
speech we refer to desires as well as impelling thoughts as the motives or
causes of actions: but consistently, not even impulses, let alone desires,
should be called causes, since our having an impulse is not the cause of our
acting, but the very fact of our being caused to act; and in referring to desires in this way we are confounding in parts at least our perception of the
operation of a law of motivation with the operation of this law itself.

But if, in the occurrent sense, there is at least a close connection between "having a motive" and "desiring," in the dispositional sense there is
none whatever. Here a person is said to have a motive when the thought of
some act (either as such, or as having some property or effect) is *capable* of
inducing him to do it; and that someone would be made to do some act if he
dwelt on the thought of it in no way entails that he is being made, or desires,
to do it. On the contrary, while dispositionally he may have the stronger
reason for doing one act, another may be all that he is desiring. Prichard
entirely ignores this latter use though it is the one that bears primarily on
his argument. There would be no point in making the questioner realise
that he had a "sense of duty" in the occurrent sense: that he thought he
desired only his own good but that really he desired to do his duty. For in
the occurrent sense, for someone to have a motive strong enough for
doing some act is for him to be subject to the operation of a law implying
action; and a law cannot be said to depend for its operation on anyone's
knowledge that it is operating. The questioner's failure to realise that, in the
occurrent sense, he had a motive could no more prevent him from acting
under its influence than the realization that he had it could assist him.[2] In
fact, it is in the dispositional sense only that it makes sense for people to
claim that their ability to do some act depends both on their *having* sufficient cause for doing it, and their *realizing* that they have it and in what it
consists. For a sufficient reason which exists dispositionally only will not
actually function as a cause as long as the thought that constitutes it is not

[1] In fact, the incidence of felt impulse, or desire, seems to depend on the extent
to which the passage of motives into action is obstructed by psychological or physical
impediments. We feel desire in proportion as our impulses are in difficulties.

[2] We cannot occurrently have a motive without knowing it in the sense that we
are acquainted with the thought that moves us, but this is not to say that we shall also
know *that* it is moving us.

being dwelt upon; and if anyone wanted to make it function as a cause, he would first have to realize that he had it and what it was. He would then, in the knowledge of the reason which dispositionally he has for doing the act, have a means for inducing himself to do it.

Instead of refusing to follow Kant, Prichard should therefore have agreed with him to the extent that the man who does not desire to act as he ought, and on this account questions his ability to do so, could still be shown that in the very thought that he ought to do the act, he had dispositionally a motive for doing it, so that if he tried he would induce himself to do it. Moreover Prichard should have acknowledged that if a man induced himself to act under the influence of such a motive he would not be acting simply from desire, or inclination, as the motive thought would here not function as a cause unless the agent had enabled it to do so.

I shall now turn to the difficulties which I said attach to Prichard's solution of the questioner's doubt. Here it is noteworthy that, sharply as Prichard censures his opponents, he agrees with them on one underlying assumption. Like them he holds that the man who while granting a duty doubts he has also a motive has a real axe to grind: there is no convincing him that he has a motive except by considerations additional to those which already convince him that he has the duty. The case of the exponents of a connection between duty and interest plainly rests on this assumption, but, only less obviously, so does Prichard's. For by convincing a man that he has a duty we are not on Prichard's view providing him with a motive in the sense that to convince him of the first consists in convincing him of the second, or of anything that necessarily entails the second. We are doing so in the sense only that in a suitably constituted person, the conviction of duty, when he attends to it, will incidentally also function as a motive, while itself being the conviction of something else, of what exactly Prichard never states, but presumably of some non-psychological fact inherent in the situation confronting the agent. Correspondingly when we speak of morally good conduct, we cannot on this view strictly say that it consists in actions conditioned solely by the fact that it was our duty to do them. For what would be moving us to action would not be a motive implicit in the very fact of duty itself; but a motive constituted by the thought that we had the duty, and existing apart from and additionally to the fact of duty. The point is candidly admitted by Ross, "An act's being our duty," he says, "is never the reason why we do it," for "I did the act simply because it was my duty" is elliptical. It really stands for saying "I did the act because I knew, or thought it to be my duty, and because I desired to do it, as being my duty, more than I desired to do any other act." [3]

This being so, it should be allowed that Prichard shares his opponent's view that morality needs a sanction, admittedly a more respectable one. For we imply that morality needs a sanction whenever we say that merely on account of the fact that we ought to do some act we have not yet any

[3] *Foundations of Ethics*, p. 227.

incentive sufficient for doing it; and that, whether we shall have the latter or not, will depend on conditions distinct from and additional to the former. It is merely a corollary of this, though an important one, that on Prichard's view no less than, say, on Butler's our doing what we ought to do needs a "justification" additional to that which we express by saying that we morally ought to do it. For there is a sense in which we may be said to justify to ourselves some act which, on some grounds, we are averse from doing by seeking to assure ourselves of a reason sufficient for doing it. In ordinary speech, we are seeking, in this sense, a justification when we ask with respect to some act "is there, when I come to think of it, any real need for my doing it at all, or one strong enough, considering the cost?," using here "is there any real need" for "is there any reason, at least potentially and reflectively, sufficiently compelling to make me do it?" To ask this sort of question, even when we grant that an act would be morally justified, being the one we morally ought to do, must on Prichard's view be permissible without involving the questioner in any absurdity; for no answer to a question of this sort would as yet be entailed by the questioner's conviction that he morally ought to do the act. Indeed far from being absurd it would be pertinent for people to ask this question; for on occasions when they do not actually desire, or desire sufficiently, to do some act which they grant they morally ought to do, or when they find themselves in a reflective state of mind, their very capacity to act morally will depend on the answer to it. Rather than object to Butler, Prichard should therefore have agreed with him on the principle that "in a cool hour" we will not be able, when our own good seems at stake, to do what we grant we morally ought to do, unless we can find in addition some "non-moral" justification of our doing it. He should consistently have objected only to Butler's insistence on seeking this justification in an interested rather than a disinterested motive. Nor finally does Prichard, any more than Butler, show that the attempt to prove a "real need" for moral conduct must always succeed. There may always be some who can maintain without absurdity and as a plain matter of fact that, though admittedly they are morally bound to do some act, at the same time there is no real need or sufficient reason whatever for them to do it. Hence whether the questioner is in error or not is not a question that affords of a general answer. The question is an open one, and each case has to be treated on its merits.

In a way all this seems plausible enough. The suggestion that we can refer the questioner, sometimes at least, to the thought of duty itself as a motive accords with our ordinary moral convictions, more so, at any rate, than the view that we can refer him to none but interested considerations; and the conclusion seems unavoidable that whether we shall be able to do so must turn on a question of psychological fact. But somehow, if its implications are considered, Prichard's solution still falls short of expectations: it makes the connection between duty and motivation less close than sometimes at least we are wont to view it. For it is a fact about ordinary

moral thinking that no less persistent than the conviction that morality
needs some sanction is its opposite, that it needs no sanction whatever: that
somehow the very fact of a duty entails all the motive required for doing
the act; and anyone who, rightly or wrongly, adheres to this conviction
will take exception to Prichard's solution. He will object to the question
of motive being made separate from and additional to that of duty: to its
being treated, when a person is said to have a duty, not as a foregone
conclusion, but as an open question, turning on a benevolent dispensation
of providence in the shape of a singular psychological disposition. Certainly
Kant, whose freedom from vulgar errors Prichard holds in such esteem,
would not have countenanced this solution. To Kant the very existence of
a duty was inseparable from the existence of a motive and anyone who had
a duty would, solely on this account and at whatever cost to himself, induce
himself to do it if he tried. And if we consider the implications of the opposite view, it is only tempting to sympathize with Kant. It seems paradoxical that moral conduct should require more than one kind of justification: that having first convinced someone that regardless of cost to himself
he was morally bound to do some act we should then be called upon to
convince him as well that he had some and some sufficiently strong reason
for doing this same act. "You have made me realize that I ought, now
convince me that I really need to" seems a spurious request, inviting the
retort "if you really were convinced of the first, you would not seriously
doubt the second." And even supposing we granted that to morally justify
an act and to justify the same act in terms of motive were distinct, we
would still be hankering after a necessary and not merely a contingent connection between the two. We would feel it was paradoxical for anyone
ever to be right in saying that, though regardless of some personal sacrifice
he ought to do some act, because of the sacrifice and in spite of the duty,
he, though others might, had no manner of sufficient reason for doing it.
We should readily grant him a lack of motive only in the occurrent sense:
that he may have a duty without actually having any, or any strong enough,
impulse or desire to do the act. At the back of these hesitations lies the
conviction that, if anyone has a duty, that he has it is inseparable from the
existence of some real check on his freedom to act otherwise; a conviction
which entails that the connection between duty and motivation is too close
to be merely contingent. Whether and how this conviction can be sustained
is another matter; but plainly Prichard does not account for it.

Some reflection of these unacknowledged difficulties in Prichard's
position is found in his failure to deal convincingly with a problem which,
he points out, may be said to present him with an "insoluble difficulty." If
doing our duty, he says,* depends on a special desire, then someone may hesitate between the desire to do one act because it is his duty, and another because it would be for his own good. Such conflict, we normally resolve by
means of a choice, resting on our eliciting a preference between the alterna-

* [p. 486 this volume.]

tives; but to do the same with the conflict between the act we ought and the act it would be for our interest to do feels inappropriate. Prichard seeks to explain this by saying that in the case of duty and personal good the objects of the conflicting desires are incommensurable, there being "no comparable characteristic of the two alternative actions which will enable us to choose to do the one rather than, or in preference to, the other"; and he concludes that the way of resolving conflict does here consist, paradoxical as it may seem, in a "deciding" that is *sui generis* and in no way rests on choice. But this argument is unconvincing. No doubt the objects of the conflicting desires are here incommensurable, but so are the objects of other desires (as of the desire to spare myself pain, and the desire to preserve my life) between which we allow choice to be possible; and in fact there is logically no reason why choice should depend on the commensurability of the objects between which we are undecided. For if choice rests on the eliciting of a preference between two incompatible courses of action, there is logically no reason why, if put to the test, the thought of one act should not prove impelling by comparison even to the exclusion of the other act, even though, why it did so, was inexplicable and not dependent on any common quality which the one act possessed in greater measure than the other (e.g. that the one should give more enjoyment than the other); and therefore, if it were for no other than the reason put forward by Prichard, there would logically be no bar whatever to our treating the conflict between duty and interest as an open question to be solved, one way or another, by eliciting a preference between them. Nor otherwise, is it clear by what means a person should here seek by "decision" to escape from the dilemma of irresolution. The only alternative, apart from random choice as by tossing a coin, would it seems be for him to wait for the one motive to get the better of the other on its own; but though with luck we sometimes come to be decided in this way, we could hardly here be said to have decided, in the sense of our having made any active contribution towards it. But none of this is to say that our feeling of inappropriateness of a choice between duty and interest must be groundless. On the contrary, this feeling would be justified on one assumption not considered by Prichard: on the assumption referred to before that our very thinking that we ought to do some act already entails that, by comparison, we have a stronger reason in the circumstances for doing it than any other. For it would then follow that whenever we acknowledged one act to be our duty, whether by comparison we had a stronger reason for doing this act or another conducing to our own good, would, ex hypothesi, be no longer an open question. Our indecision would here be of a special irrational kind: it would persist although the means for rationally resolving it were already at hand; and to pretend that the resolution of indecision still here depended on our making a rational choice would imply the absurdity of treating as open a question to which, whenever we asked it, we implicitly acknowledged that we knew the answer already. But if this is the explanation, and logically no other seems possible, it is plain why Prichard cannot offer it. For he is not prepared to hold that the sense of duty, even dispositionally, must always be everyone's strongest motive.

The nature of Prichard's dilemma will now be clear. He must on his premises present the conflict between duty and interest as an open question, so that consistently it should allow of resolution by way of rational choice in the same manner as the conflict between any other alternative actions. At the same time, he cannot resist the feeling that a rational choice would here be spurious, a feeling however which has no justification except on an assumption which, though a persistent ingredient of ordinary moral thinking, he is nowhere prepared to make. He is caught up at this point by the intrusion of a view of the connection between duty and motivation whose implications he cannot either accommodate or entirely reject. And the dilemma seems a real one. For neither position can be easily surrendered, neither that morality needs some additional psychological sanction, nor that what sanction it requires, it necessarily carries with it, and short of surrendering the one or the other there seems no getting away from the dilemma.

A problem like this does not arise without some deep seated confusion, and my object in the remainder of this paper will be to trace this confusion to its source. I shall suggest it has its origin in uncertainties and contradictions in the common use of words like "ought" or "duty," in an unnoticed juxtaposition of meanings each of which entails a different relation to motivation; and I shall try to bring out these ambiguities of language, and the confusions of thought that underlie them.

What Prichard supposes words like "ought" or "duty" to be used for cannot be clearly stated as he considers them unanalyzable. But this much is beyond doubt, that he holds them to refer to some non-psychological objective fact, a special feature of the situation confronting an agent. His general outlook at any rate is in line with similar contemporary views, such as Broad's or Ross's, according to which "someone ought" or "has a duty" means that an act of his and the "situation" would in some way be complementary to one another, so that we can say either an act of his is "called for" or "required" by the situation or would be "fitting" to the situation. Views like these seem the modern descendants of traditional views of a more full-blooded but in essentials similar kind: that a person's subjection to moral law consists in his subjection to demands to do or to forebear made on him by a deity, or society, or a confused mixture of these; and that his actions would be right or wrong in proportion as they conformed to this standard. For, whatever their differences, there is this much in common between all such views. They presuppose, not unnaturally, that when someone "ought" or "has a duty" he is subject to some manner of demand, made on him without regard to his desires; and they imply that this demand issues essentially from outside the agent: that, whether made by a deity or society, or the "situation" (if this means anything), it has an objective existence of its own depending in no way on anything peculiar to the agent's psychological constitution. Now, the view that morality needs some sanction is a traditional associate of all views of this kind and indeed their natural corollary. If "I ought" means "I am from outside myself demanded to do some act," whether by the will of another, or more impersonally by the "situation," there will then be no necessary connection for anyone between having the duty and being under any manner of real compulsion to do the act. For no one really need do any act merely because it is demanded of him, whether by a deity or society or the "situation," but only if, in addition, he finds within himself a motive sufficient for satisfying the demand. Inevitably therefore, at least in a "cool hour," moral conduct will require a two-fold justification: people will want to be assured not only that some act is their duty, but also that they really need to do it: and only the latter, and not merely that the act is their duty, would constitute an incentive for doing it. Thus, the problem would in some manner be solved if the claimant could be shown to demand only acts conducing on balance to the agent's own good, either in this life or in the next, or to some social good which the agent has at heart; or else we must postulate, as Prichard does, an endowment of human beings with a singular love for complying merely for its own sake with the demands on them of some external claimant strong enough, if need be, to overrule all concern for human good.[4] But also, whether people will be capable of such a desire, and if so sufficiently, must here remain an open question. For to say that the thought of any act can function as a motive is to assign to it a causal property which only experience can tell whether it will have. But provided the externalist view of "ought" or "duty" is consistently adhered to, we should not hesitate to accept this implication; and if we still feel that the claim of duty must necessarily be an over-riding one, but have on other grounds no reasons to support this feeling, it should be dismissed as a prejudice, founded most likely on a wishful expectation of a pre-established harmony between the existence of moral demands and of reasons for people to comply with them.

I should add that for Butler morality needs a sanction for somewhat different reasons, for according to him a duty does not consist in a demand on people of some external claimant, but of a demand arising from within their psychological constitution. People have duties because the thoughts of some acts will, if they contemplate the nature of these acts, raise an affection towards, or away from them, which by its "authority" is superior to all competing impulses in the situation. A duty therefore is here not a demand dissociated from any human end or purpose; on the contrary, that someone has a duty does here entail that he has some motive, or that the act

---

[4] For *ex hypothesi* the motive for the act which is one's duty must here be thought as independent of any relation to human good, and, in case of conflict, as its rival, since to any extent to which the latter were thought to matter, the act would no longer be done for a purely moral reason.

is an end for him. But it does not entail that the motive will be a sufficiently strong one, for Butler insists that the moral impulse derives its authority from a superiority in quality or kind, and not essentially in strength. To this extent the moral compulsion is divorced, as before, from people's natural capacity to do the act, and in consequence, at this point, the problem of a sanction must once again rise. The person who thus ought to do an act, even at apparent cost to himself, may rightly ask for a reason strong enough to induce him to do it; and there is here no other remedy but to explain away the conflict between duty and personal good as illusory. But once more, if Butler's use of "ought" or "duty" is strictly adhered to, there are no grounds on which to reject this implication merely because we should like to think of the claim of duty as necessarily overriding. If a duty can only be thought of as constituted by a "higher" but not necessarily dispositionally stronger compulsion to action there is no ground on which we can deny it assistance from being "at least not contrary" to our "lower" nature.

What then does explain the persistence of the conviction that all these accounts fall short of expectations? It is, I think, that we apply to them, without noticing, a standard foreign to them, but implicit in still another use of "ought" or "duty" which may be called the purely formal motivation sense. For there is a habit of speech according to which, when a person asks "need I really, or have I, if only dispositionally, a sufficiently strong reason for doing this act?", he might as well have said "should I or ought I really to do it?", the latter expression being in fact the more colloquial. This substitution could have been made whenever the previous discussion turned on the justification by motive of a person doing some act which he granted he morally ought to do. For we could also have presented him as asking "why should I, or ought I to do the act which I morally ought to do?"; and if he had been using the second "ought" in say some externalist sense he would not have been asking a spurious question. He would have been using the first "ought" in a motivation sense as referring to the question of whether, at least dispositionally, there was some sufficient motive or compulsion for him to do the act which he morally ought to do. In fact, whenever in any externalist sense a person ought to do some act, the further question of whether in the motivation sense he ought to do this same act can still always be asked; but equally, the latter question could be asked by anyone who had no use for duties in the externalist sense at all: who did not believe in a deity to make demands, who found the objective requirements of the "situation" too nebulous an expression to be meaningful, and who refused to call the demands on him of society moral imperatives. For even he might still wonder whether some act which he actually did not desire (say assisting another in need), or which he was actually averse to on account of its implications (say some personal sacrifice) was not one which, on its own account and in spite of all, he had dispositionally an over-riding reason for doing; and his natural way of expressing this puzzlement would be to ask whether, though he did not want to, he ought not to do it. Now, this motivation use of "ought" is important for our problem, for it would have all the implications demanded by the expectation of a necessary connection between ought and motivation. The "ought" here would express nothing other than a certain relation between a person's dispositional and occurrent motives: that though occurrently he had no impulse or desire to do an act or none sufficiently strong, dispositionally he was under an effective and over-riding compulsion to do it. A duty here would potentially carry with it all the sanction required for doing the act; and the need for postulating a special disposition to be moved to acts on account of their being duties would have disappeared. Nor would we here allow that the questioner who while acknowledging a duty requested in addition a motive had a real axe to grind, even if his own good was at stake. His very request would be absurd, since what he was overlooking was not some matter of psychological fact, but the logical implications of his saying that he had a duty. What might be called the "purist" view of the connection of "ought" with motivation would be justified, but only because of the special meaning assigned to the term. It is worth remembering that Kant who insisted most on the purist view of the connection insisted also on a use of "ought" in a purely formal motivation sense. Modern deontologists overlook that Kant would have rejected off-hand their view of duty as an objective requirement of the situation, as he did reject the view of duty as consisting of the demands of a deity, or of some inward compulsion of a special quality. For he objected to anything being called a moral imperative with regard to which a person could still ask whether the act required of him was one which, in a motivation sense, he really ought to do, i.e. in Kant's language, whether the act was one which rationally a person would be necessarily and unconditionally determined to will; and he insisted on "ought" or "duty" being used for nothing but the very fact itself that rationally a person would thus be made to will an act. Kant's very definition of "ought" therefore makes it a tautology that anyone who has a duty has, on this account alone, a reason, though not necessarily an impulse or desire, sufficient for doing the act; and Kant thus dispenses with a "sense of duty" in the shape of any singular and contingent psychological disposition.

But while such a use of "ought" would explain the purist view of its connection with motivation, before any conclusions can be drawn from this use it requires further clarification, as of all uses of "ought" this one has been explored least. Kant alone has attempted to give an account of it; and though this account deserves closer attention than it commonly receives, it is notoriously difficult and not free from faults. What is more, there is a deep-seated prejudice among contemporary moralists, hardened into the dogma of the "naturalistic fallacy," which commits them to disregard this use as *a fortiori* irrelevant to any discussion of "ought" in a moral or normative sense. For, in what I have called the motivation sense, "ought" statements would be about a certain kind of psychological fact, about the person who ought having dispositionally, though not occurrently, a compelling motive for doing an act; and, so it is laid down, no moral or normative statement can be analyzed without residue into any kind of statement of psychological fact. This is the view of those who regard moral or normative statements as being about some objective requirement of the situation, but also the view of their positivist critics. Professor Stevenson, in *Ethics and Language*, is emphatic on this point. The alternative to saying that normative language is about some "supersensible" fact cannot be that it is about some psychological fact, but must be, in so far as it is normative, that it is not about any fact at all. Thus we have the further complication that of the one use of "ought" which could explain the habit of connecting it necessarily with motivation, contemporary moralists are agreed that, if they were to grant it at all, it would have no significance within moral or normative discourse.

This is not the place to deal fully with this situation, but in order to conclude my argument, I shall show that the motivation use of "ought" bears at least a sufficient resemblance to what ordinary usage expects of a normative term for it to qualify for entrance in the general competition for recognition. It would probably be agreed, as a general characteristic of normative language, that it can function, in a manner peculiar to itself, in the direction of people's volitional attitudes and actions; and by this standard, beliefs, arguments, and enquiries about dispositional as opposed to people's "occurrent" motives, and among them about "ought" in the motivation sense, should be granted their places in any unprejudiced consideration of normative discourse, as they are prominent among the tools employed either when we seek to change other peoples' behaviour, or try to direct our own. In fact the denial of this seems to me the chief weakness of a writer otherwise as observant as Stevenson. For his contention that normative language *expresses* imperatives intended to function in the direction of conduct, but is in no way *about* imperatives capable of functioning in this manner, is bound up with the other contention that the arguments or enquiries employed in discourse concerned with the direction of volitional attitudes, are never *about* these attitudes, dispositional or otherwise, but only about non-psychological matters of fact, like the properties or effects of some course of action. But though all this applies sometimes, to contend it applies always is an over-simplification. The case of personal deliberation, where a person seeks escape from the dilemma of conflicting desires, alone bears this out. For we often organize our release from indecision by seeking an answer to a question such as "Should I do x rather than y?," "Which of the two would I prefer?," "Which by comparison would I want more?"; and the enquiry which answers a question of this kind, like the question itself, is about, not indeed an occurrent psychological state, but a dispositional one, our own state of motivation as it would be on condition that we had carried out some further mental operations. Among these no doubt, the articulation of our beliefs about the competing acts would take first place, but to clarify our beliefs concerning them would neither be one with the primary enquiry we are carrying out, nor often be the only consideration relevant to it. For often even the fullest clarification of the properties of competing acts will leave us only more tantalized than before; and decision will then depend on some further mental operation, on eliciting a preference between the alternatives in the light of the properties attributed to them, an operation which will also yield the answer to the original question. Even without fuller analysis this will serve to illustrate how personal deliberation may involve a specific enquiry into a hypothetical psychological state whose function it is to aid a practical decision. Correspondingly, statements concerning the likely outcome of such an enquiry may play a part in interpersonal discourse intended to effect change in the attitudes of others. A may say to B whom he considers to be undecided, "I think by comparison you would prefer x to y," inviting him thereby to go through the mental operations, which, if fulfilled, A thinks would prove his statement true. A would here be trying to change B's attitudes with the aid of a statement about B's dispositional attitudes, and with a view to converting B not to a change of attitude desired by A himself, but to one appropriate to B. A's statement would here be a quasi-normative statement, on account not of its emotive, but of its descriptive meaning.

I am calling such statements and enquiries quasi-normative in order to stress that, thought they essentially function in the direction of volitional attitudes, they are not about any "ought," but an hypothetical "want." But this only seems to confirm that no normative significance should be attached to "ought" statements in the motivation sense. For they have been described as being about someone having dispositionally a reason for doing an act, and, it may seem, any such statement, even if about an overridingly strong reason, can as well be said to be about what someone would want, or want most. Unless, therefore, "ought" statements can be distinguished, as a species of statements about dispositional motives, from statements about merely dispositional "wants," the objections to allowing them to be called normative would seem justified. Prichard once objected on this very ground to Kant's hypothetical "ought," as it would express no more than that someone would want to do one thing for the sake of another he desired, and thus could not properly be called an "ought" at all. Nevertheless, ordinary speech insists here on saying "ought" rather than "want." Someone who is divided in his feelings towards some act tends to ask "would I on the whole want it or not?," but someone undecided about adopting the means for some end will not ask "what would I want?," but "what ought I to do?" He will say that as he wants to get to London by 10.30 he will, even if it means rising early, have to take the 8.40, and not that on the whole he will want to take it: that if he wills the end, he must will, and not merely would will the means. A statement like this is also about a dispositional motive: it says of a person that he would want an act, but it adds that he also must, or would have to, want it. What this addition consists in has proved an elusive question, but I think Kant does here offer a clue when he says that any "ought" (whether "hypothetical" or "categorical") expresses a rationally necessary or objective determination of a person's will—though I shall not insist that in taking from Kant what I think is the correct clue I am interpreting him correctly. I take him to call "necessary" what no trying will alter, or what is invariable, and "rationally necessary" or "objective" what would not be altered or varied by reason, or by mental operations. A rationally necessary or objective willing in the case of the hypothetical "ought" would then be a willing, or an impulse to action, which a person would have if he both acquainted himself with the facts (with what end he desires, and the means to and implications of attaining it) and tested his reactions to them, *and* which he would have necessarily, i.e. unalterably by any repetition of these mental operations. Someone who thinks he would *have* to do some act will therefore think (and plainly no more than a probability judgment would here apply) he has dispositionally a reason for doing it that can satisfy some further test: the test of all the operations capable of affecting his attitude towards the act having been carried to an ideal limit, thus exhibiting to him an "objective" attitude, likely to be most adapted both to the realities of his situation and his own dispositions. The conception of such a test is not itself an abstraction from any psychological fact, but is the product of reflection on the range of our capacity to control, by means of mental operations, our volitional attitudes, an *ideal construction* developed from procedures familiar to us from experience; and the reasons why we should sometimes wish to apply this test are not far to seek. We habitually do so when we think there is, or might be, a threat of opposition between our occurrent and dispositional motives, as when, on their own account, we do not desire, or are averse, from adopting the means to some desired end. We then wish to be assured that the dispositional reason is at least one from which even further enquiry would not help us to escape; and it is also in this very situation that we view that we have such a reason as an "ought" or imperative, as what we apprehend in it is an ideally inescapable check on our freedom to act otherwise. A motivation "ought" thus expresses the reasonableness of a course of action for someone who is not actually feeling reasonable about it. According to Kant there is a further division within the motivation "ought" into a conditional and an unconditional or absolute "ought": but, though Kant is right here in principle, I do not think the division can be made to turn on the distinction between empirical and *a priori*. The crucial point is simply that not every motivation "ought" does as yet express a completely conclusive reason for doing an act. If an act must dispositionally be willed only on account of some other end which is desired, whether it also must or can be so willed in every respect would still be an open question; for it may still apply that this end itself need not or could not, on consideration, be willed, either on its own account, or on account of the implications of pursuing it in a given situation. A conclusive reason would be one with regard to which no further question could be asked: which was thought rationally unavoidable on account of the act itself (or on account of some other end thought rationally unavoidable in itself), and rationally, in the given circumstances, unavoidably stronger than all opposing motives.[5] An "ought" embodying such a reason would be "absolute" in the sense that, in relation to given circumstances, it was *formally complete;* and it is when such an "ought" is identified with a moral "ought" or duty that the connection of duty with sufficient motivation becomes logically necessary.

Enough has been said to show that there is a case for the purely formal motivation use of "ought," and that an analysis of normative language interested in its function in the directing of volitional attitudes is too narrowly conceived if it ignores statements and enquiries about it. Writers like Stevenson are, no doubt, right that "you ought" is often used to express a speaker's recommendation to another to change his attitudes to those favoured by the speaker himself; and argument here, as there is no normative assertion to prove or to disprove, can amount only to "support" of the speaker's aim by *any* change of belief in the hearer suitable to the speaker's purpose. In fact, this use most likely marks the beginnings of normative language, as it still permeates our habits of speech in the "ought" we first hear in childhood, or in that of social convention, or of political or commercial propaganda. But where A's "you ought" *expresses* his subjective recommendation, or command to B, "I ought" for B *states* the fact that he is so recommended or commanded. The use of "ought" for a requirement from outside is only the reverse of its subjective recommendation use. But surely some, when they reach mental maturity, become resistant to the appeal of this "ought" and the reasoning that "supports" it. They oppose to it the question whether, in the motivation sense, they really ought to do what another expresses to be his wish. They are interested in other people's emotive noises to the extent only to which perchance they might also embody an objectively valid recommendation for them. In fact, in dealing with them, if someone wanted to influence their volitional attitudes, he would most likely fare better if rather than express, and support, a subjective recommendation he did, from the start, state, and try to prove, an objective one. For any one familiar with the objective motivation use of normative language is apt to resent its subjective recommendation use in relation to himself; as he will be tempted to regard an analysis of normative language in terms of the latter alone to be about its abuse rather than its use, meaning by "abuse" here more than a subjective recommendation against using it.

I can now conclude my argument. Our problem arose from Prichard's

[5] I have discussed this use more fully in "Morals without Faith," *Philosophy*, April, 1944, and in "Morality and Nature," *The Australasian Journal of Philosophy*, September, 1950.

failure fully to justify the conviction that the thought that an act is a duty provides a motive for doing it. Prichard cannot on his view of "ought" allow for more than a contingent connection between "ought" and motive, while he makes claims which implicitly presuppose a necessary one; and in this confusion he reflects a pervading tendency of ordinary moral thinking. People very commonly combine a view of "ought" as a requirement from outside, or an inner compulsion of a special quality, with adherence to a purist view of its connection with motivation, not so much as long as they view the moral law as the demand of a deity or of social convention, but once they think of it as somehow objectively grounded in the nature of things. They tend to sympathize with the questioner's request for a motive, but they will not be satisfied with any merely contingent answer, even if shown that no other is available on their premises. The explanation of this confusion must be in an ambiguity in their use of moral language. There would not be so common an insistence on the purist view of the connection of duty with motivation, if, whatever people profess, they never used "ought" in the purely formal motivation sense; and the chances are that in the moment of moral doubt and decision they are thinking in these terms. When called upon to decide here and now which act to do they consider which act they have from within themselves the most conclusive reason for doing; and they then no longer think of being morally bound as an external requirement, but as an ideally inescapable inner entanglement, a dictate of conscience. But the confusions here are deep-seated. Historically, what most likely was first called a moral injunction or prohibition was some external demand complied with habitually. The habit of reasoned choice grows more slowly, and even where reasoned choice rather than habit operates, its nature and range remain imperfectly understood. The external and internal uses of "ought" remain undifferentiated, and are imperceptibly juxtaposed and confused. There may be an unnoticed switch from the use of "ought" from the one to the other, from a divine command, or requirement of others, to a dictate of conscience, or, when the more sophisticated speak the language of objective "claims," an alternation between a nebulous externalist and an internalist interpretation of one and the same thing. In fact the purist view of the connection of "ought" with motivation nearly always makes its appearance, if only by the acceptance of some of its implications, as in the conviction that morally good conduct is open to anyone who acknowledges a duty; but by force of habit, and perhaps for fear of its empiricist and subjectivist implications, this view is constantly blended with some externalist and non-psychological conception of "ought." Plainly, confusions like these must give rise to the dilemma indicated before, a dilemma which is as much Prichard's as it is common to ordinary moral thinking, except where moral scepticism has cut the knot. The exponents of a necessary connection between duty and interest, people feel, try wrongly to placate the questioner, but no satisfactory vindication of this feeling is forthcoming. For what kind of answer is appropriate to the questioner's doubt depends on the meaning attached to his admission that he ought to do the act. On an externalist view of "ought" his request is legitimate and in need of some factual answer; on a purely formal motivation view his very request is absurd; and where both views are confusedly held no answer can satisfy. There is no saying whether morality needs a sanction or not as long as there is confusion about what to call a moral duty.

Nor, once the confusions have been uncovered, can the matter rest here; for we cannot avowedly use "moral ought" both for an external and an internal state of affairs, as if a man might have one but not another sort of moral duty in respect of the same act. In using moral language we mean to denote something that, when known, can conclusively serve to direct what we do, and we cannot obey two masters. Analysis therefore reveals not so much a failure to distinguish between normative facts of different kinds, confusedly referred to by the same name; but ultimately a lack of clarity and decision about what fact would most nearly correspond to our intentions in the use of moral language, and which words like "ought" and "duty" should be made to denote. Nor could a person, aware of a capacity of reasoned choice and intent on using it, easily agree to a use of these words for any demand on him that still left him to ask whether he also had a formally sufficient reason for doing the act; and the only use of them free from this shortcoming would be for the very fact itself that he had such a reason. The present stalemate in ethics between an obscurantist objectivism and an avowed scepticism rests on a failure squarely to face this issue.

Obligation and Motivation[*]

〜〜〜〜

WILFRID SELLARS

I

THE FOLLOWING paragraphs will be devoted to a somewhat schematic discussion of the significance of the word "ought" in such distinctively ethical sentences as "I ought to do X (in circumstances C)" and "One ought to do X (in circumstances C)." The frame is provided by the thesis, formulated here without spit and polish, that to be aware of a property is to have "in one's mind" a token of an expression which designates that property. If the expression is a simple one, in that it is not compounded out of other expressions, then the awareness is a simple or unstructured awareness; otherwise a complex or structured awareness.

Thus, one can be aware of circularity by tokening the simple expression "circle" or by tokening the complex expression "closed plane curve with a constant degree of curvature." The former would constitute a simple awareness of what, after all, is a complex property. The latter would be a structured awareness of this same property, though the complexity of the awareness would be far from doing justice to the complexity of the property. Now, an unstructured awareness of a complex property may be mistaken, by philosophers, for the awareness of a simple property. This can occur even where the expression tokened by the simple awareness is paired in ordinary usage with a complex expression as neatly as "circularity" might be supposed to be paired with "closed plane curve . . ." Here the philosopher speaks of supervening Gestalt properties, e.g., of an unanalysable *circularity* which rides piggy-back on *closed-plane-curve-with-constant-degree-of-curvaturehood*. The mistake, however, is much more likely to be made where common usage contains no such unambiguous correlation.

Before applying these tools to "I ought to do X," let us try them out on "I want to do X." (For the sake of brevity, the phrase "in circumstances C" will be omitted but understood.) Consider Jones who is tokening this sentence "in his mind" and who therefore has an unstructured awareness of whatever it is that is meant by "want (to do)." Now if Jones has been sufficiently corrupted by philosophy, it is not beyond the bounds of prob-

* The first part of this essay is reprinted by kind permission of the editors from *Philosophical Studies*, 2, 1951.

ability that he would reply to the question "What kind of situation is described by the above sentence?" by saying, "It asserts an ultimate and unanalyzable relation of *want* to obtain between *myself* and *the doing of X by me*." From here he might go on to wonder how there could be a relation between himself and an action which might remain a mere possibility. This might lead him to interesting metaphysical discoveries.

Let us refrain, however, from following Jones along this path. As a matter of fact we took French leave at the beginning of his remarks with an unexpressed comment to the effect that Jones was misled by a superficial grammatical resemblance between "(I) (want) (to do X)" and "(I) (eat) (apples)." If we were challenged to show that this resemblance is indeed superficial, and that Jones was indeed misled, we should surely reply by offering an *analysis* of sentences of the form "Y wants to do X." As a first attempt we might suggest "Y finds the thought of doing X attractive," following this with "Y's thought of doing X tends to evoke the doing of X." Though these are drastic oversimplifications, they do indicate the essential features of a successful analysis.

As our next step we might claim that the sentence "Y's thought of doing X tends to evoke the doing of X" is to be understood in terms of a tendency of tokens "in Y's mind" of the expression "Y doing X" to evoke the doing of X by Y. I suspect, however, that we should hesitate to speak of this step as an analysis. But would such a hesitation be, after all, warranted? The term "analysis," having as its core the notion of explicit definition (usually definition in *usu*) seems clearly to cover the following gamut of cases: (1) The definition reflects an antecedent mutual substitutability in ordinary usage of expressions having a clear-cut and unambiguous sense. (2) The definition would reflect such a mutual substitutability only if ordinary usage were focused and fixed. (3) The definition would reflect such a mutual substitutability only if ordinary usage were enriched by a new set of expressions.

To this last category belongs the analysis of material objects in terms of the micro-particles of modern physics. Analyses of both the latter two types are actually proposals for reform. The second urges a better use of materials already at hand; the third requests the introduction of new materials together with a demotion of words already in current use from the status, in effect, of primitive terms to that of defined terms. A basement is proposed for an already existing house. Where in this scale do the above analyses of "Y wants to do X" belong? It is reasonably certain that none of them belongs in the immediate neighborhood of (1). The two analyses in terms of "the thought of doing X" would seem to belong in the neighborhood of (2); as for the analysis in terms of tokens of the expression "Y doing X," its place in the scale could be determined only after a far more protracted discussion.

In an earlier paragraph we pointed out that insofar as he tokens "in his mind" the simple expression "want (to do)," Jones has an unstructured awareness of whatever it is that is meant by this term. Let us now agree to say that "want (to do)" means that which would be mentioned by a successful analysis of "Y wants to do X." Assuming, then, that the above analyses are in the right direction, the term in question means a dispositional complex, and we can say that Jones has an unstructured awareness of a dispositional complex involving the thought of his doing an action, and the doing of the action. On the whole, philosophers have been fairly successful in avoiding the mistake of treating *wanting* (*to do*) as a simple relation obtaining between agents and actions. The materials for a successful analysis have been sufficiently close at hand to keep all but a determined few from falling into this trap.

Let us now suppose that Jones has a token "in his mind" of the sentence "I ought to do X," and, therefore, has an unstructed awareness of whatever it is that is meant by "ought." This time we should by no means be surprised to find Jones claiming that this sentence asserts an ultimate and unanalyzable relation of *ought* to obtain between *himself* and *his doing of* X. Nor would we be surprised to find him modifying and refining the metaphysics of oughtness as new perplexities occurred to him. Now it is my intention to defend an analysis of "ought (to do)" which has a fundamental kinship with the account above of "want (to do)." The parallel is easily stated. "Ought" as used in "I ought to do X" refers to a type of motivation, to a dispositional complex involving the thought of doing X and the doing of X. Yet it is the differences that must be stressed, for our moral consciousness finds all the difference in the world between merely wanting to do something and being morally obligated to do it.

Let me begin by putting my finger on the heart of the matter, though this involves an oversimplification which must later be made good. In wanting to do X (in circumstances C) it is the thought of *oneself doing* X (*in circumstances C*) which tends to evoke the doing of X in circumstances believed to be C. On the other hand, when I truly say "I *ought* to do X in circumstances C," it is the thought of *myself doing* X (*in circumstances C*) as an instance of *everybody doing X* (*in circumstances C*) which tends to evoke the doing of X in circumstances believed to be C. Let us call the content of the thought which tends to evoke action, the *logos* or "formula" of the motive-tendency. (To simplify our account, we shall suppose that any restriction on the class of agents in the formula of an ought is included in the "circumstances.") Then, the formula in the case of *want* (*to do*) concerns only the agent, the action, and the circumstances, whereas in the case of *I ought* (*to do*) the formula has a major premise which concerns the doing of X by all agents in circumstances C.

Impartiality has often (e.g. by Westermark) been found to constitute the essence of moral attitudes and motivations. However, it has almost as often been sadly misconstrued. According to the usual account, if Jones responds with approval to all situations of kind S regardless of who participates in S, his approval is *ipso facto* to be called impartial. Impartiality is thus conceived to be an "external" property of a feeling of approval, a matter of its being an instance of a uniformity. According to our account, on the other hand, the impartiality of an attitude, emotion or motive is a matter of the logical structure of its *logos,* and is therefore "intrinsic." The distinction between these two conceptions of impartiality corresponds to Kant's distinction between action *in accordance with* a rule, and action *because of* a rule.[1]

It will be noticed that I have gone out of my way to emphasize the autobiographical form "I ought to do X." I have done this deliberately as I wish to claim that this is the form through which alone "ought" can be understood. "You ought . . ." is not related to "I ought . . ." as "You eat . . ." is to "I eat . . ." (Or shall we say it is not *merely* related to it in this manner? The following remarks will explain this hesitation.) Note that in the analysans given above for "I ought to do X," the word "ought" does not occur in the statement of the formula of the motive-tendency. We conceived its major premise (and our account of ethical motivation will shortly become even more Aristotelian [2]) to be *All agents in circumstances C do X,* not . . . *ought to do X!* Instead of being a mere application of "Everybody ought to do X," "I ought to do X" is the *fons et origo* of "Everybody ought to do X." It is because "Everybody doing X (in circumstances C)" plays a motivational role in my conduct that there is such a significant sentence as "Everybody ought to do X." In other words, "I *ought* to do X" rests on "Everybody *doing* X," and "*Everybody* ought to do X" rests on "*I* ought to do X."

Yet we must hasten to add that in another sense, "I ought to do X" rests on "Everybody ought to do X." It is, indeed, an oversimplification to say that "I ought to do X" is an autobiographical sentence attributing to

---

[1] For a discussion of this and related topics, see my "Language, Rules and Behavior," in *John Dewey: Philosopher of Science and Freedom,* a volume of essays edited by Sidney Hook, and published by the Dial Press, New York, 1950.

[2] "The one opinion is universal, the other is concerned with the particular facts, and here we come to something within the sphere of perception; when a single opinion results from the two, the soul must in one type of case [Translator's note: i.e. in scientific reasoning] affirm the conclusion, while in the case of opinions concerned with production it must immediately act (e.g. if 'everything sweet ought to be tasted,' and 'this is sweet,' in the sense of being one of the particular sweet things, the man who can act and is not prevented must at the same time actually act accordingly). When, then, the universal opinion is present in us forbidding us to taste, and there is also the opinion that 'everything sweet is pleasant,' and that 'this is sweet' (now this is the opinion that is active [Translator's note: i.e. determines action]), and when appetite happens to be present in us, the one opinion bids us avoid the subject, but appetite leads us towards it (for it can move each of our bodily parts); so that it turns out that a man behaves incontinently under the influence (in a sense) of a rule and an opinion, and of one not contrary in itself, but only incidentally—for the appetite is contrary, not the opinion—to the right rule." Aristotle, *Nicomachean Ethics,* Bk. VII; Ch. 3, 1147a25–1147b2, translated by Sir David Ross and quoted from *The Basic Works of Aristotle,* edited by Richard McKeon, and published by Random House, New York, 1941. I have emphasized the kinship of my analysis with Kant's moral philosophy in "Language, Rules and Behavior," printed in *John Dewey: Philosopher of Science and Freedom,* cited in footnote 1 above.

myself a tendency to be moved to action by a syllogism whose major premise has the form *Everybody does do X in circumstances C.* For the truth of the matter is that the word "ought," which as far as our analysis has gone stands for the motivational force of a syllogistic formula whose major premise is of this form, has stolen a syntatical disguise which can be said to embody the mistake of thinking of *ought* not only as a unique relation between myself and an action, but one which is objective and independent of me in that it holds between *me* and *my doing X* because it holds between *everybody* and *their doing X*. To assume this disguise, which is an essential condition of moral consciousness, the word "ought" worms its way into the expression of the formula of the motive, and the formula becomes the familiar moral syllogism *Everybody ought to do X in C, I am in C, therefore I ought to do X.* To put the matter in a paradox: the *mistake* of thinking of *ought* as a *sui generis* relation is essential to the *correct* use of the word "ought."

II

We are now in a position to reformulate our thesis in a somewhat more systematic manner. Our basic line of thought was that "I ought" resembles "I want" in being the vehicle of our consciousness of a certain mode of motivation. This led to the suggestion that "ought" is to be analysed (in some sense of "analysis") in terms of a tendency to be moved by a syllogistic *logos*. Yet when we attempted to give a plausible analysis along these lines, we soon ran into a serious difficulty. For we saw that to be the *logos* of ethical motivation, the major premise of the *logos* must contain a term with the force of "ought." Can this appearance of circularity be overcome?

In discussing this point, let me begin by pointing out that whereas the definiendum of our proposed analysis of *I ought to do X in C* contains the word "ought," the definiens contains the expression ". . . the thought of . . . ought . . ." If we put this in terms of linguistic tokens rather than thoughts, we notice that whereas the definiendum *uses* the word "ought," the definiens *mentions* it. *I ought to do X in C* = Df *tokens of "Everybody ought to do X in C, and I am in C" tend to evoke my doing X in C.*

But does this really enable us to escape the charge of circularity? Clearly it does so only if we find it possible to characterize the tokens of ". . . ought . . ." *mentioned* by the definiens, without *using* the word "ought," at least in the sense in which it is used in the definiendum. This, I believe, can be done. The point is bound up with our previous claim that there is a sense in which "Everybody ought to do X in C" is prior to "I ought to do X in C," even though in another sense "Everybody ought . . ." would be completely lacking in significance unless I were able honestly to say "I ought . . ."

The fact of the matter is that the word "ought" plays at least four intimately related roles. In its minimal and, as such, incomplete role, it is the central term in the "language of norms," a mode of discourse which presupposes, but is irreducible to, the "language of fact." The term "ought" has a characteristic syntax by which it is related to other normative expressions, as well as to logical and descriptive categories. It is this role of "ought" which Prichard, Ross and other "deontological intuitionists" have ferreted out and made the core of their theory of morals. Their mistake, almost inevitable in view of their rationalistic background, was to suppose that it is merely by grasping the conceptual logic of the "language of norms" that we become conscious of having obligations.

Now, "I ought to do X in C" illustrates this minimal role of the word "ought." It is a statement in the normative mode of discourse, and *as such* is incapable of analysis in terms of factual discourse. Yet, if the only significance possessed by "I ought to do X in C" were that which it derives from being an application of "Everybody ought to do X in C," both these statements would be empty husks, interesting only because of their unique logical grammar. The crucial fact is that while we are learning to use the word "ought" in accordance with its grammar, we are also acquiring tendencies to be moved to act by moral syllogisms in which this term appears. It is by virtue of this involvement in motivation that the "language of norms" gains "application." This involvement may be compared to the way in which factual language gains application through the process misdescribed as "ostensive definition." This is the *second* of the four roles mentioned above.

Now, if we can honestly say "I ought to do X in C," and are not "mistaken," then we must have the tendency to be moved by the corresponding moral syllogism. Furthermore, if we made use of the familiar distinction between a *symptom* or *expression* of a state of mind, and a *mention* of a state of mind, we can safely say that "I ought to do X in C" is normally the *expression* of a motivational tendency. This is its *third* role.

But "I ought to do X in C" is also a *mention* of the motivational tendency in question. As such it is capable of analysis (though in which sense of "analysis" it is by no means easy to say) in descriptive terms along the lines we have suggested. This is the *fourth* role.

It should be noticed that of the four roles distinguished in this paper, only the first and fourth concern the conceptual meaning of "ought." Notice also that by virtue of these two roles, the word "ought" in "I ought to do X in C" has *two* logical grammars. Indeed, this one word embodies two distinguishable concepts which differ in their degrees of clarity and articulation. The first is the concept of *obligation;* the second might be called, in the light of the idiom, "I feel obligated to . . . ," the concept of *feeling obligated.*

At the end of the first section of this paper, I was moved to put its thesis in the form of a paradox, namely, "the mistake of thinking of *ought* as a *sui generis* relation is essential to the correct use of the word 'ought.' " It should be clear by now that to think of *obligation* is indeed to think of a *sui generis* connection between acts and agents. Thus, strictly speaking, it is not true to say that a mistake is involved in the correct use of the word "ought." It is, however, a mistake to assume that because there is such a thing as *thinking of a sui generis connection between acts and agents* (which thinking is just the use of the "language of norms"), there must be a sub-class of facts called obligations, so that a description of the world would be incomplete unless it mentioned *obligations*. It is rather the concept of *feeling obligated* that is required by a complete description of the world, and this is an analysable concept of empirical psychology. Now, it may be argued that the above mistake is a philosopher's mistake, and not a mistake of the plain man. I am strongly inclined to think, however, that the mistake is part and parcel of common-sense moral consciousness, and that the in-tuitionist does little more than dress it up in technical language. If so, this would justify the paradox on which we have been commenting. But I do not wish to press the point.

I shall conclude with three brief remarks. (1) If the main contention of this paper is sound, we can run with the "naturalists" (the psychology of *feeling obligated* can be developed in purely descriptive terms), while hunting with the "intuitionists" (in a perfectly legitimate sense, the con-cept of *obligation* is ultimate and irreducible). (2) The four roles of "ought" distinguished in the course of the argument are not intended to constitute an exhaustive list. For a perceptive treatment of additional roles played by the "language of norms," as well as of practical discourse in general, the reader is referred to C. L. Stevenson's *Ethics and Language.**
(3) The normative mode of discourse has as its characteristic sentence not "If anybody is in C, then he ought to do X" (which would raise questions as to the nature of the implicative relation), but rather a sentence of a unique type which we may perhaps represent by the form "Ought(anyone, X, C)." For this reason one is tempted to speak of *ought* as a 'category' or a 'modality.' But to explore the pros and cons of either classification would take us to the growing edge of metaphysics.

* [See also his paper on "The Emotive Meaning of Ethical Terms," reprinted in this volume.]

Evaluation and Obligation: Two Functions of Judgments in the Language of Conduct*

H. D. AIKEN

I

IT IS NOT the purpose of this paper to undertake still another, almost certainly unconvincing, analysis of so-called "ethical terms." I have no clear idea, and I have a shrewd suspicion that my colleagues have no clear idea, of either the scope or the meaning of this expression. My own view, which I shall not now attempt to defend, is that in some contexts *any* term may function ethically—"pleasure" as well as "good" or "right" —and that in other contexts any item may function non-ethically—"good" and "right" as well as "pleasure." In any case I am persuaded that exclusive preoccupation with the definitions of such individual words as "good," "right," and "duty" is largely responsible for the barrenness and triviality of so many recent works in ethical theory. I intend no invidious comparison in mentioning A. C. Ewing's *The Definition of Good* as the most recent and hence the most conspicuous example of the futility of most contemporary analytical ethics—the naturalists have done no better. No positive result has been achieved which has withstood the attacks of destructive criticism. None has won acceptance purely on intellectual grounds. Among naturalists and intuitionists alike, even the illusion of such a result has been achieved by obvious and egregious *petitio principii*, and the same is true of the proponents of the emotive theory. Indeed, it is not too much to say that in the present state of ethical theory, while we know that most, if not all, of the arguments which have been proposed in support of each theory are either fallacious or inconclusive, we do not in the least know whether any of the current theories is true or even probable. One can, of course, throw out an ethical theory on the ground that it conflicts with one's favorite theory of meaning or knowledge. I myself am sympathetic to such wholesale removals. But this leaves one no better off than before with respect to the remaining alternatives.

If, however, the arguments employed by analysts in defense of their

* Reprinted with the kind permission of the author and the editors from *The Journal of Philosophy*, 47, 1950.

theories are inconclusive, this is by no means their primary flaw. Usually they are stated in so unguarded a form that it is quite possible to draw conclusions from them which are wholly at odds with those intended by their authors. Consider the many "imaginative experiments," the "open question" and "elimination" arguments, the appeals to "hard cases," and the appeals to our "language sense" or "intuition": in nearly all instances that I have examined it is possible to construe them, not as proofs of what we mean, but as so many unconscious expressions of and appeals to individual attitudes and sentiments. No one who has pondered Moore's "beautiful world" argument, or James's "lost soul," or Mill's "happy pig," or Savery's "agonized oyster," or Lewis's recent refutation of the emotive theory—to mention only those which first come to mind—can have failed to notice that such arguments are far more obviously indicative of the feelings of their esteemed authors than of the characteristic meanings of the terms upon which they are intended to shed light. Apart from any other consideration, therefore, I think it not at all extravagant to say that in ethics the chances of confusing analysis with expression or persuasion are so pervasive, and their removal so well-nigh impossible, that the very significance of the arguments themselves remains at the least an open question.

And this is not all: there are other still more fundamental difficulties, inherent in the very conceptions and methods of analysis that now prevail. In the first place, there is no clear or established notion of what an "analysis" of ethical terms or judgments should accomplish. Is it to inform us concerning the actual meanings of such expressions as employed in common speech? Is it to prescribe what we would mean or ought to mean if we were clear instead of vague? Or is it to change our meanings so that they will conform to the canons, say, of the new empiricism or of liberal democracy? Examination of the literature reveals no unequivocal or sustained answer to these questions.

But even if we should waive these points and agree for the nonce that the primary purpose of analytical ethics is to determine the conventional meanings of ethical terms, many vexatious and imponderable questions remain. Consider, for example, the almost universal use of last-ditch appeals to "intuition" or, which comes to the same thing, our "sense of language." What are these but the contemporary semantical hangover of the discredited rational intuitionism of the seventeenth century, with all its antique gear of "clear and distinct ideas," its "self-evident truths," and its dogmatic appeals to the "light of reason"? The domain has been radically circumscribed, but the technique is no different nor any more capable of compelling agreement. The elect have long since recognized the futility of intuitionism in the sphere of statements of fact. Yet even the most uncompromising empiricists appear not to scruple at the revelations of in-
however, that the disclosures of "language sense" are at least as corrigible
tuition in the sphere of so-called "analytic"truth. Is it not quite apparent,

as those of the "natural light"? And, more important, is it not evident that statements asserting sameness of meaning between two expressions in ordinary language are nothing more than factual statements concerning the similarity of two classes of human sign-responses? In short, are not *all* questions concerning the meanings of statements in ordinary language wholly empirical? For my part, at any rate until some reliable and applicable behavioral criterion of synonymy has been established, all propositions asserting the intensional equivalence of two expressions in common speech must be regarded merely as speculative hypotheses.

In ethics, the problem of analysis is further complicated by the fact that such terms as "good" and "ought" are both extremely flexible and vague. It would appear, therefore, that any attempt to determine *the* unique and "characteristically ethical" sense which these and only these terms share in common is precluded at the outset. Moreover, the predicaments in which ethical terms are employed vary so greatly that the notion of a "characteristically ethical" use of them is no less obscure than the meaning which they reputedly have in that use. We can not assert with any show of reason that "good" in its characteristically ethical use does or does not mean the same thing as "pleasant" unless it is clear what that use is. But this is precisely what is most unclear. On the contrary, there appear to be many different predicaments which are more or less appropriately called "ethical," and in all of them such words as "good" and "ought" are correctly used.

Recent investigations also indicate that not merely the meanings of ethical terms, but also the modes in which they mean, are plural and variable. In short, the language of ethics is probably flexible and vague in several dimensions at once. But if the current methods of analysis are inadequate to determine the descriptive meanings of ethical terms, they are still more helpless to cope with the purely empirical problems of emotive meaning. At present, therefore, the whole issue of emotive meaning in ethics remains in its purely speculative phase; it will remain so until adequate experimental techniques of content analysis can be applied to them.

II

I see little hope of, at present, advancing our understanding of the problems of ethics by analyzing the common meanings of individual words such as "right" or "good." I propose, therefore, to adopt a completely different approach to what seems to me to be the only useful task of ethical theory, namely, the analysis of the language of conduct in general, or, as it used to be called, "practical reason." What I shall attempt to explain in the following pages are the functions and relations of two fundamental but non-exclusive types of judgment in practical discourse. The prevailing misconceptions concerning them, in my opinion, are very largely responsible for much of the endless and futile controversy in contemporary ethics.

When they are removed I suspect that much of the present interest in the correct analysis of particular ethical terms will disappear.

Let me emphasize at the outset that as I conceive them, there is no one set of terms in ordinary language by means of which either of these modes of judgment is exclusively or correctly expressed. On the contrary, both are expressible in a wide variety of ways, many of which are not usually thought of as distinctively "ethical." If their analysis belongs to the domain of ethical theory, this has nothing to do with the particular terms in which they happen to be formulated, but only with the fact that they are involved in nearly every deliberation or discourse concerned with the ends of conduct.

I shall speak of these two types or functions (it is immaterial which they are called) of judgment as (*a*) judgments of "evaluation" or "appraisal," and (*b*) judgments of "obligation." In the present section I shall confine myself primarily to the former, and in later sections to the latter.

By a judgment of "evaluation" or "appraisal," then, I *mean* any judgment whatever that identifies, describes, or compares actual or potential satisfactions, the objects in commerce with which satisfactions are consummated, or the causes by means of which satisfactions and their objects are realized. In preliminary elucidation of this definition let me at once make clear what I do *not* mean by the expression "satisfaction." [1] I explicitly do not mean either "object of interest" or "realization of object of interest." The reason for this is empirical. The occurrence of satisfactions is dependent in the last analysis not upon achieving results that we think we want, but upon actualizing consummatory behavior patterns which, in many instances, occur without any preparatory or anticipatory activity whatever. Satisfactions are recurrent termini or "ends" of action; they are not, as such, "ends-in-view," "objects of interest," or "goal objects"; nor are they realizations of the latter. This is not meant to imply, of course, that we may not deliberately direct conduct toward consummatory acts which result in satisfaction. But it does mean that there is no necessary connection between the objectives toward which interests *happen* to be directed and the behavior patterns in which the needs underlying them are satisfied. From the standpoint of the satisfactions which determine well-being, the function of goals or ends-in-view is no less instrumental and no less tentative and provisional than any other instrument employed in conduct. In short, whatever may be the correct analysis of those intentional objects which we call "goals" or "foreplans," it is clear that what we normally mean by the achievement of a plan, or by the realization of an object of interest is, tragically enough, quite a different thing from satisfaction, even though the achievement of goal-objects sometimes does result in the satisfaction of their governing propensities or needs. The contours of ordinary speech reflect this fact in

---

[1] For the present, "satisfaction" will be taken as a primitive term.

many ways. For example, it is perfectly permissible to say that a man's purpose or goal is realized after he is dead. But it would be nonsense to speak of dead men's satisfactions. And conversely, it is quite proper to speak of accidental enjoyment of pleasures as satisfactions even though we are unaware of any desire for them.

The subject-matter of statements of evaluation or appraisal (however expressed) supplies us with a basis for differentiating the several principal modes of what I call "value." [2] As here conceived the primary value-fact is satisfaction itself. Upon it, therefore, all other modes of value and all ascriptions of value to objects ultimately depend. By "intrinsic value," then, I here mean simply "satisfaction." All other states of affairs, whether they be merely antecedent causes of satisfactions or the immediate objects of satisfactions, are "extrinsic values." Most value-predications, however, have to do with value of the latter sort, since it is with them that deliberation and choice are more directly concerned. It is therefore essential to distinguish between several types of extrinsic value according to the relations in which they stand to satisfaction.

Events or activities which determine satisfactions or their objects are called "instrumental values." These in turn may be of two sorts, according as they are events occurring independently of human choice or volition or else states of affairs which may be affected or instituted by some human decision. For practical purposes, of course, a great many forces at work in nature, of great importance to human well-being, lie beyond the range of relevant appraisal and deliberation. Effective evaluations, capable of guiding conduct, are solely concerned with those instrumental values lying within the range of human control or adaptation. Hence, if it should be asked what theoretical interest such a distinction can have for value-theory, since from an objective standpoint all appraisals of instrumental value are on a par and must deal with the same general type of relation, namely, that of cause and effect, the reply is simply that the primary interest of any theory of valuation is the discrimination and clarification of judgments which are necessary to the practical decisions which determine conduct. I agree with Dewey that "no difference can be more important than that which concerns the nature of the subject-matter of deliberation." [3] This being so, theories of valuation which leave that subject-matter wholly indeterminate or blur it indiscriminately into that of physics, psychology, or general social science merely as such, would be *ipso facto* irrelevant.

Within the domain of extrinsic values an even more basic distinction must be drawn between instrumentalities as such and "objects" of intrinsic value, which I shall call "inherent values." This distinction, which C. I. Lewis has recently brought into prominence for the first time, is

---

[2] Let me remind the reader that I do not intend this as an analysis of the common meanings of "value."

[3] Dewey, *Human Nature and Conduct*, p. 201 (Modern Library Ed.).

necessary for a proper understanding of intrinsic value itself. Without it naturalistic theories of value run into the snarls which, for example, Ross has shown to be latent in Perry's version of the interest theory.[4] By "inherent value" I mean any state of affairs or "object" in immediate commerce with which satisfactions occur.

This conception of inherent value differs perhaps from that of Lewis, in that, according to my definition, inherent values may be valuable for one person alone. In two obvious senses the "objectivity" of inherent values may be granted. In the first place, I agree with Lewis that objects may possess inherent value "independently of any relation to a subject," [5] if by this is meant 'independently of any relation to the judgment of a subject." Clearly inherent values may occur which are not so judged, and in this respect Protagorean relativism is simply a logical blunder. Secondly, I agree that values which are predicated "in the mode of simple potentiality" may be regarded as "in" the object independently of any relation to a subject, just as solubility may be regarded as "in" salt even though there be no water to dissolve it. So far as I can see, however, this does not at all imply that there are no inherent values which are not inherently valuable for a "normal" or perhaps "discriminating" person. In short, as I conceive them, inherent values may be either normal or eccentric, either common to the "normal" satisfactions of the many or peculiar to exotic enjoyments of the few. From the standpoint of moral deliberation, normal inherent values are perhaps more important than those which are fugitive or odd, and from the standpoint of esthetic education, the inherent values of the connoisseur are more central than those of the vulgarian. Nevertheless, it seems to me a serious error to limit the conception of inherent value in general to those objects which would be capable of affording satisfaction either to any normal person or to any peculiarly qualified one. But in any event, the intersubjective verifiability of values is one thing, the common value of what is so verified is another. It will be useful, of course, to have value categories which will refer to and clarify the important notions of normal or common value and of connoisseur value. This may be accomplished, however, without denying the status of inherent value to those objects which are enjoyed by or enjoyable to only a single human being.

Observance of the distinction between "inherent" and "intrinsic" value is necessary for several reasons. Previous naturalistic value theories have generally defined intrinsic or primary value in terms of the "object" in which interest, satisfaction, or pleasure is taken. This is an error. In the first place, by defining value in terms of satisfaction itself, we avoid the paradox of ascribing value to something intrinsically in virtue of a relation between it and something else. If intrinsic value is attributed to objects of satisfaction or interest, then, according to the usual view of

[4] Ross, W. D., *The Right and the Good*, pp. 75–81.
[5] Lewis, *An Analysis of Knowledge and Valuation*, p. 520.

the matter, it is the object itself which is thought of as possessing the value, even though, as Perry puts it, it is interest which "confers" the value upon the object. But it is both offensive and confusing to say that objects are intrinsically valuable, i.e., in their own right, and yet that they are so only because something else bestows value upon them. On the present view, intrinsic value is identified squarely with satisfaction itself; values which are "conferred" or "bestowed" remain by definition derivative and extrinsic.

Secondly, the present conception of intrinsic value is morally preferable, since it avoids the "fetishism of objects"—the naturalistic counterpart of the "formalism" of Kant's ethics. For obvious reasons the immediate focus of practical reason must be directed toward the causes and the objects from which our satisfactions take rise. Nevertheless, to forget the end for the sake of which alone such causes or objects are worthy to exist is to run the risk of substituting achievement as an end in itself without regard to the human well-being from which achievement derives its inherent value.

Thirdly, in accordance with the present definitions of intrinsic and inherent value, the subjective focus of all significant predications of value is not begrudgingly acknowledged, but candidly and explicitly avowed. Indeed, from the present standpoint, this is regarded as a merit rather than a defect to be softened or glossed over for what are usually spurious moral reasons. Those naturalists who wish to save values from the supposed evils of "subjectivism" seem to me thoroughly quixotic when they admit that there would be no value whatever if there were no human beings capable of "conferring" it and at the same time seek to weaken the implications of this by a verbal trick. The only "objectivity" which is worth salvaging from the bankruptcy of objectivism in axiology is the empirical validity of value-judgments and the factual relevance of ascriptions of instrumental and inherent value to human well-being. Without these minimal commitments to objectivity, deliberation would indeed degenerate into whimsey and choice into mere impulse. But defense of the objectivity of evaluations would be pointless if not directed toward states of affairs which determine the individual enjoyments of actual human beings.

Fourthly, it is conceivable that there may be satisfactions which have no "objects." According to those theories which identify intrinsic value with the "object" such experiences would have no status as values, and, hence, would not, even in principle, fall within the subject-matter of evaluation. But if satisfaction is to be regarded as the source of all values which are imputed to objects, and if, therefore, such values are to be regarded as values only in a derivative or extrinsic sense, it seems arbitrary to deny value to objectless satisfactions. Moreover, if we do not wish to accept a definition of intrinsic value which would exclude from the domain of value any state of affairs which a benevolent spectator would approve, and if, as I believe, such satisfactions would clearly fall within the realm of his approval, the more inclusive or weaker definition of value in terms of satisfaction itself is obviously preferable to one which restricts value to objects of satisfaction.

The present view also has important implications regarding the status and rôle of interests in relation to evaluation.

Perhaps the basic error of interest theories of value is due to a confusion concerning the bearing of interest upon happiness. It has been implicitly assumed, I think, by Perry and others that getting what you desire is, in principle, constitutive of well-being. And it is precisely because of this assumption that value has been defined by them in terms of "object of interest." But clearly the relation between an object of interest or even its achievement and the satisfaction of the governing propensity which actuates an interest is an *external*, not an internal, relation. There is no guarantee whatever that the realization or achievement of objects of interest will automatically result in the satisfactions upon which well-being depends.

If this is so, it would appear that interest theories involve us in a violent functional inversion of ends and means, and require us to regard as a final and inviolable value-fact *any* goal-object to which the organism happens to direct its energies, however ill-suited it may be to satisfy the organism's wants. From a moral standpoint, moreover, such theories require us to regard achievement as such as an end in itself and the ultimate desideratum of the moral life the widest possible realization or even the creation of goals, no matter how pointless they may be from the standpoint of happiness. On such a view, the possibility that such ends-in-view may be indifferently satisfying or even positively painful is simply beside the point.

The interest theory thus makes it impossible to treat every interest, even apart from its bearing upon other interests, as a merely tentative foreplan whose right to be realized is always problematic. And it reduces the function of evaluation ultimately to a comparison of intensities of interest, preferences between interests, or numbers of interests; other things being equal, therefore, the more inclusive interest, or the preferred, or the more intense interest is *ipso facto* the more desirable. On the present view, however, the important distinction between the desirable and the desired may be preserved intact, and the desirability of any interest, including the good-will itself, remains subject to relevant criticism and evaluation.

Now in healthy organisms, whose expectations or anticipatory sets are usually based upon experience of objects which have been found to be inherently valuable, objects of interest may to some extent be regarded as *prima facie* signs or criteria of intrinsic value. But it must be borne in mind that the amount of effort expended in the realization of goal-objects bears no constant relation to the amount of satisfaction which may be found in their achievement. Hence, even among healthy organisms, the intensity or extent of any given interest is an inadequate criterion of the amount of intrinsic value to which it may lead.

For most of us, it remains problematic whether any given interest should be regarded even as an index of inherent value. And for many it is unfortunately the case that precisely the reverse is true. Under the stresses which in greater or lesser degree affect the lives of most human beings in civilized society, purposive behavior often tends to be fragmented or deflected toward goal-objects whose significance, from the standpoint of their satisfaction-value, is almost wholly substitutive and symbolic. Potentially, of course, the capacity to adopt substitute goals has its beneficent aspect. Nevertheless, it is evident that most substitute goals are pursued by necessity, rather than deliberately selected with a view to their adequacy to satisfy wants. By the nature of the case, such goals can provide hardly more than token satisfaction of their governing needs.

It must be understood that the preceding remarks are not intended as a *refutation* of the interest theory of "good." I have attempted merely to show the consequences which follow from this theory, and to indicate why I have chosen to define "value" in terms of satisfaction. Most proponents of interest theories—and here I have in mind particularly Dewey and Perry—have insisted, in season and out, upon the cognitive meaningfulness and verifiability of value-judgments. But the motive for distinguishing sharply between evaluations and decisions and for preserving the cognitive integrity of value-judgments seems to me to lose most of its point when value is identified with volition. In the end, it is primarily because of the enormous disparity between the *de facto* goals of human life and the objects which are suitable to the satisfaction of our needs that I am unwilling to accept either a purely emotive or an interest theory of value. Any interest appears to the organism obsessed with it at the time as preëminently important; it is only upon reflection that we come at last to recognize the vanity of human wishes and the futility of a life which achieves its ends-in-view without any quickening satisfaction in the result. Were it not for this fact, I for my part would see no point whatever to the defense of practical reason.

III

As a transition to the second main topic of the paper, I should like to consider briefly certain consequences of the preceding discussion from the standpoint of the normative functions of judgments of evaluation.

Now, according to the conception of human motivation which has won the widest degree of acceptance among contemporary psychologists and psychiatrists, all human behavior tends, on the whole, toward the satisfaction of organic and psychogenic wants or needs. Other things being equal, therefore, there is a tendency to reinstate those objects as goals which in the past have proved to some degree satisfactory. This is not taken to imply that such objects are always the best suited to satisfy their respective needs, or that organisms do not frequently become fixated upon goals which possess merely token satisfaction-value. It does mean, however, that among healthy organisms, not acting under stress, empirically tested evaluations will tend to have some normative appeal or urgency. This, I take it, is a matter of empirical fact.

But it is of the utmost importance, both to a proper grasp of the present doctrine and to an understanding of the problems involved in the normative use of appraisals, to realize that there is nothing inevitable in this. Unquestionably the most serious theoretical error of any axiology which accepts, even in principle, the type of value theory propounded in these pages is the assumption that evaluations are *ipso facto* normative. Nor is this error in the least relieved by acceptance of an interest rather than a satisfaction theory. The price to be paid—and, for my part, gladly paid—for a theory of valuation which identifies value descriptively with satisfaction (or interest) and which treats appraisals as bona fide empirical judgments is the recognition that the normative function of "ethical" or "practical" judgments and their appraisive or evaluative function can not be reduced to the same thing.

This consideration makes possible for the first time a clear understanding of the meanings of "justification" in ethics. There are at least two entirely different meanings of this notion, the confusion of which has had disastrous effects, both practically and theoretically. In one sense, an activity is said to be "justified" when it is shown to be conducive to the satisfaction of wants or the realization of human well-being. In this sense, any evaluation which truly states that an action is conducive to satisfaction will so far provide a justification of that action. Such a justification may be wholly "objective," and with respect to it considerations of normative appeal are quite irrelevant. But "justification" has another, wholly different, sense. In this sense, an activity is said to be justified only when and in so far as it ultimately succeeds in actively arousing our interest or in compelling our approval. So understood, any statement may be regarded as "justifying" an act when it succeeds in provoking interest in the act, *no matter how irrelevant it may be from the standpoint of rational appraisal.*

It follows from this that even in principle there is no process of analysis or dialectical manipulation by means of which we can deduce norms from values or normative statements from mere appraisals of value. Logically, therefore, the conformity of normative standards and the motives which they express to values that have been empirically certified by the methods of inquiry appropriate to the "science of man" is an accident. In principle, we may one day be able to predict that under certain circumstances such a conformity would occur, and, of course, it would be desirable, from a humanistic point of view, to create a cultural and social environment favorable to the existence of such circumstances. But however constant the relation between our norms and values might become, it would remain a psychological causal relation whose existence could be determined only by observation.

Thus the normative justification of values and evaluative justification of the decisions and choices which determine norms are two different things which can never be reduced to a single mode of validation. The former type of justification remains a justification *to* interest; the latter type remains a justification *of* interest. The former, in the last analysis, is incitive and rhetorical in method, even when it appears "rational" and proceeds by appeals to logic and evidence; the latter in no way differs, save its way of selecting and organizing its subject-matter, from the empirical methods which are employed in the "justification" of statements in psychology or the social sciences.

IV

In the light of the previous discussion, what remains to be said concerning what I have called "statements of obligation" may be put briefly. From the standpoint of the controversies now raging over the emotive theory, it is perhaps the most important part of the present paper, since, in one sense, it implies that this controversy is secondary and not fundamental to the question of norms. My purpose will be to show that no matter how "value" or "right" or "duty" may be defined, and no matter what conception we may have of the relations of cognition to interest—whether we agree with Hume and Perry and Stevenson that "reason is the slave of the passions" or with Kant that there is an autonomous rational moral will —there is no way whatever of deriving the obligatoriness or imperativeness of any statement, ethical or otherwise, from an analysis of its descriptive meaning. From my standpoint, moreover, disagreements in attitude and disagreements in belief are absolutely on a par in this respect: neither of them can be resolved simply by an appeal to the facts. Questions of belief are no less normative than questions of attitude, and "irrational" or "persuasive" methods are as common to the one as they are to the other.

I shall define "judgment of obligation" to mean any judgment, in whatever form or language it may be expressed, and whatever may be its subject-matter, which functions normatively, i.e., which functions as a determinant of attitude in the broadest sense.[6] As I understood this notion, therefore, questions of grammatical form, mood, or nomenclature are wholly secondary. Statements in the indicative or in the subjunctive mood, as well as those which are grammatically in the imperative, may function normatively as statements of obligation. The same is true also of ordinary statements of fact which contain no terms that would be construed by some writers as "ethical." But if this is true, I think it is obvious why, from the standpoint of the theory of norms and the language of conduct, the ques-

---

[6] It is clear that "judgment of obligation," as here employed, is not synonymous with "judgment containing the word 'ought.'"

tion as to the meanings of certain particular terms which have come to be called "ethical" should be regarded as a *mere incident* in the general theory of valuation and obligation. And if, as I am convinced, the fundamental characteristic of ethical statements that has always eluded a descriptivistic analysis is their characteristic of being "obligatory" or "binding," then I think there can be little doubt that the only peculiar problem which they present to the ethical theorist is the differentiation of the peculiar types of attitude called "moral" to which they make appeal. Conversely, if it is just this peculiar attitude or "sense" to which the moral obligatoriness of statements must finally be referred, and if it is implausible to suppose that just "ethical" terms and no other are sufficient to evoke such an attitude, then I think that the third sentence of this paper is so far evident: "in the proper context, any term whatever may function ethically."

In order to indicate the wide scope of what is here included under the rubric of obligation judgments, and as a means of amplifying my view that the question of emotive meaning as such is incidental to the fundamental problem of the relations of the normative use to the descriptive (including the evaluative) use of language, I propose to consider briefly certain aspects of the relation of description to belief itself. Afterwards I will consider certain functions of descriptive language in relation to attitudes generally.

Let me begin by stating the fundamental distinctions upon which the ensuing remarks are premised. The first distinction to be drawn is that between understanding a statement and believing it. Pragmatic theories of knowledge and meaning have tended to blur this distinction, just to the extent that they have identified, without sufficient qualification, understanding the meaning of a statement and the expectation or anticipatory set which, if followed through, would lead to or be verified by an appropriate state of affairs. I think it is clear, however, that *some* distinction must be drawn between the act of apprehending the meaning of a statement, and the attitude of acceptance in virtue of which we believe the statement to be true. We must, in short, account somehow for the phenomenon of supposition. Otherwise I do not see how we could account for inquiry or how it would be possible first to accept and then to reject the same statement. There is not space to discuss the matter fully here, but I think that any theory of descriptive meaning which does not permit (*a*) the same statement to be believed or disbelieved, and (*b*) the attitude of doubt, is so far incompetent. Whether adequate behavioral criteria of such distinctions is possible remains to be seen.

The second distinction to be drawn is between what may be called the logical or evidential reasons which make a proposition true or probable and the psychological "reasons" or causes which determine us to believe or accept it. Confusion of the two has recently led to considerable misapprehension as to the nature of disagreement and agreement in belief and the differences between the methods of resolving disagreements in belief and those employed in resolving disagreements in attitude. If I am correct in maintaining that belief is an attitude, and if the resolution of *all* disagreements in attitude depends upon psychological causes and not merely the citation of logical reasons or empirical evidence capable of demonstrating the truth or probability of statements, then the "methods" to be employed in forming or transforming beliefs are so far no less psychological than those employed in transforming other attitudes.

The third distinction has to do with the difference between the function of a statement in describing fact and its function in discourse as a means of communicating and evoking belief. When I assert in the course of an argument that "the moon is not made of green cheese" I am saying something which is true. But I am also expressing my belief that it is true and pragmatically implying to you that I do so believe it. In the context, my statement itself may be regarded, *prima facie*, as a natural sign or symptom of *my* belief. And I also am expressing something which is put forward for you to accept or believe. In short, my statement, in the context of discourse, carries with it, so to speak, a "belief claim," which is no less real because it remains pragmatically implied. In short when *A* and *B* disagree over a given proposition, their contrary utterances have something like the following force:

> *A* : *X* is true; I accept *X*; please do so also.
> *B* : *X* is false; I do not accept *X*; please do not also.

The illustration is doubtless crude and incomplete. It does serve to illustrate, however, that in the normal course of disagreement in belief, statements which are unquestionably descriptive and are so intended also function incitively. And it also brings out the point that there is some element of obligatoriness implicit in nearly all statements whose descriptive function is never doubted. In short, statements of fact generally function at once as descriptions and as prods which prescribe what we are to believe.

Notice, however, that the belief-claim or obligatoriness of such statements is not contained in their descriptive meaning. To perceive that it is there requires understanding of the purpose of human discourse generally and of the pragmatic context in which such discourse occurs. Observe, also, that the logical connections holding between statements are of an entirely different order from the psychological connections holding between statements and attitudes of belief or disbelief which they incite. If this is so, the obligation to believe a given statement, for whatever "reason" there may be to accept it, can never be more than pragmatically inferred from what it says.

Because of this, the same points which have previously been made concerning "justification" in the sphere of valuation have their precise analogues with respect to the "justification" of ordinary statements of fact. The justification of statements of fact to a believer is one thing. And the justification of the truth or logical validity of a belief is quite another. One may justify the truth or probability of a given statement so adequately as to leave no "reasonable" grounds for doubting it—indeed, this is probably tautological. It nevertheless does not follow that there is any obligation to accept it unless one is committed to the enterprise of "rational belief." And, in fact, there are unfortunately a great many, even among the philosophically eminent, who have simply rejected such an obligation. For them any such "rational" justification would be simply beside the point. There is a sense, indeed, in which any theory of knowledge must inevitably beg the question in precisely the same way in which any proposed system of ideals also begs the question, namely, of our willingness to accept and stand by the consequences of such criteria of validity as it may prescribe. But it is always open to any individual to make the sort of reply which Richard Price made to the empirical arguments against the necessary moral truths of ethical intuitionism:

> I do not at all care what follows from Mr. Hume's assertion, that all our ideas are either impressions, or copies of impressions; or from Mr. Locke's assertion that they are all deducible from sensation and reflexion.—The first of these assertions is, I think, destitute of all proof; supposes, when applied in this as well as many other cases, the point in question. . . .[6]

It has been said that there is nothing to do with a "moral idiot," if he is dangerous, but "shoot him." The ferocity of such a remark should not blind us to the profound truth implicit in it. The *same* truth is implicit in the view that there is no purely rational means of compelling belief, and that any obligation to abide by the canons of rational inquiry presupposes not merely that one is capable of making the necessary discriminations but also that he is committed to the business of adjusting his beliefs to meet the exigencies involved in the application of such canons.

Consideration of the limits and conditions of justification and obligation in the domain of belief is instructive since it reveals the cardinal point of the present analysis, namely, that so long as you direct analysis to the purely descriptive content of a given statement, its obligatoriness will escape you, and this regardless of the particular type of obligation involved. On this point, the difference between the obligations of rational inquiry and those of morality are quite irrelevant. It may be, as G. E. Moore suggested, that a "pragmatic implication" is "contained" in every descriptive assertion; but this will always fall outside of the descriptive meaning of any statement which is analytically equivalent to it.

The question whether the normative aspects of judgments of obligation are to be counted as a distinctive mode of "meaning," as Stevenson and others have maintained, is perhaps less important than I once considered it to be. I am still inclined to agree with Professor Black's contention that it is seriously misleading to speak of a response to inscriptions or vocables which in no sense involves the relation of "designation" or "standing for" as a species of meaning. But the question of terminology is of less importance

[6] Selby-Bigge, *British Moralists*, Vol. II, p. 123.

than what we understand by it. If, therefore, we should decide to limit "meaning" to that which a sign designates, and if we should then choose to say that the normative function of statements, although pragmatically implied by them (to an observer) is not a mode of meaning, we should still bear in mind that nothing is fundamentally altered by this decision. Obligation and description and *a fortiori* obligation and evaluation belong to different dimensions of conduct.

In so far, then, as ethical judgments *determine* what *ought* to be done by us and not merely state or indicate *what* we ought to do, there is clearly *a* sense—whether it is the "characteristically ethical" sense of Moore and his followers is no matter—in which such judgments can never be exhaustively translated in terms of *any* descriptive definition. In this sense, perhaps, "good" and "right" and "ought" may well be unanalyzable, although not because they are simple as Moore at one time supposed. Perhaps, after all, this *is* the sense of "ethical terms" which is brought out by the "open question" argument.

In any case, I shall dub as the "intellectualistic fallacy" any attempt to reduce the normative or obligatory aspect of judgments—and here I mean *all* judgments and not those conventionally referred to as ethical or value judgments—to their descriptive meaning. And this applies not only to those theories which, like Perry's, attempt to reduce value to "natural" properties or relations but also to Moore's or Ewing's which do not. It makes no difference whatever, whether "good" is simple or complex, natural or non-natural, a function of interest or the color blue, if it is conceived as being analyzable or designative in the descriptive mode of meaning, its normative function so far remains unaccounted for.

Now at one time it appeared to me that the fundamental reason for this is due to the fact, if it be such, that cognition without passion is incapable of motivating the will. The classic text for this position is to be found in Hume's *Treatise:* "Since morals . . . have an influence on the actions and affections, it *follows* that they cannot be deriv'd from reason, because reason alone, *as we have already prov'd,* can never have any such influence." [7] A similar view of human motivation, I believe, lies at the base of the emotive theory. It is evident, however, that Hume rests his case upon a particular empirical hypothesis concerning motivation, and in so far his theory, and in general any emotive theory, of obligation stands or falls with the truth of the hypothesis. Moreover, since a great many able thinkers have, for good or bad reasons, rejected this doctrine, any philosopher who chooses to reject the emotive theory can, with a certain show of authority and perhaps even of plausibility, argue that a purely "rational" account of at least moral obligation is possible, and that Hume and his followers have simply begged the point at issue.

I believe that this "out" is not available to the rationalists. Even if the Humean theory of motivation is false, they can derive no comfort whatever

[7] Hume, *Treatise of Human Nature,* p. 457, italics mine.

from the fact. What I have called the "intellectualistic fallacy," as I now see, does not depend on any special theory of motivation. It would remain a fallacy, even if there were a perfect correlation between "knowing the good" and "aiming at it," even, in short, if there were such a thing as practical reason, i.e., a cognitive faculty which, apart from any natural desire, is capable of activating the will. The reason, I think, is clear: the relation between cognition and motivation, on any theory of motivation whatever, is a causal, not a logical, relation. There would, therefore, always be a logical possibility that the cognition of good would not cause us to favor it. Hence, at best one can never do more than "pragmatically infer" that any statement, whatever it means descriptively and however reasonable it may be from the standpoint of some ideal of conduct, is normative or that it will exert its normative effect in one particular way rather than some other. Hence also the obligatoriness of moral judgments, if this is to be regarded as their characteristic and salient trait or—if one prefers—"meaning," can never be deduced from their descriptive meaning—if they have such a meaning.

VII

MORAL FREEDOM, GUILT, AND RESPONSIBILITY

Free Will and Responsibility[*]

~~~

A. K. STOUT

I

THE VERY MEANING of the term *free will* is often identified with a
certain theory about it. It is taken for granted that if our volitions are
free they must in some way be cut loose from the causal order of the universe. This view rests on the assumption that if they fall within the causal
order they must be determined for us by conditions extraneous to ourselves,
such as heredity and environment; thus they would not be free, nor would
we be morally responsible for them. I reject it because it presupposes that
within the causal order we are merely effects and not also agents, distinct
from all other agents and exercising a causality distinctively our own; and
this assumption seems to me gratuitous and false. In our voluntary conduct,
so far as it is voluntary, it is we who determine in favour of this or that
alternative, not something else which determines for us. But how can this
be so if what we are and what we will are determined by past events and
by our present environment? I suggest that the difficulty is due to a failure
to distinguish between two quite different meanings of "determination."
One is *compulsion* and the other logical *correlation*.

In saying that in voluntary decision it is we who choose and not something else which chooses for us, I mean by the term *voluntary decision*
only the actual process of making up our minds, including no factors other
than those actually at work in that process, and excluding any of its more
or less remote conditions. Since these factors (e.g., emotions, sentiments,
desires, beliefs, etc.) are not extraneous conditions, but belong to ourselves
as experiencing individuals, volitions which they contribute to determine
are so far determined by us, and not by something external to us. On the
other hand, such conditions as past events and present environment, taken
apart from our knowledge of or belief about them and our interest in them,
are not actually operative in the process of coming to a voluntary decision.
It is therefore nonsense to say that they *compel* or in any way actuate us
to will this rather than that, or that they take the decision out of our hands
and make it for us. But, of course, we cannot deny that there is a sense in

[*] Reprinted by kind permission of the author and the editors from the *Proceedings
of the Aristotelian Society*, 37, 1936–7.

which they may be said to *determine* what we will—a sense other than that of *compel;* to do so would be to deny that volitions fall within the causal order of the universe. When we say that past events, which may have happened long before we were born, determine what we now are and will, we are using the term "determine" in the sense of "are logically correlated with"—a sense in which it is irrelevant to the nature and freedom of voluntary choice. The past events, having ceased to exist, cannot be actually operative in the living present. Each successive stage in the train of past events is causally active, but ceases to be so as it ceases to exist, when its successor in turn begins to act. But between the final term (or any term) of the series and its most remote antecedent there is a relation independent of the lapse of time, which I call logical correlation. When we say that events of the distant past determine our present volition, we can only mean that if they had been different we should have been correspondingly different and therefore should have willed otherwise. But it is equally true to say that if we were different from what we are and therefore willed differently there must have been a corresponding difference in the course of past events. Neither side exercises compulsion on the other. My ancestors no more force me to will what I will than I force them to will what they willed. They and I enter into the causal order on equal terms, not only as effects but also as causes; we are alike causes of what is to come.

I will put the point in another way. Suppose that I came into the world just as I am now, without any antecedent conditions, as a going concern. Granted that I had the nature which in fact I have, the absence of past conditions would make no difference to the freedom of my volitions. In either case they would flow from my nature, and so be mine. They would flow from it no more and no less if I started ready made, as it were, than they would if it had been determined by a long train of conditions extending indefinitely into the past.

Here I must leave this side of the question, in spite of the inadequacy of my treatment of it, since my main purpose in this paper is to try to sketch a view of free will which, without removing volition from the causal order, will satisfy ethical needs and in particular enable us to give a tenable account of moral responsibility.

II

What do we mean by "free" when we say that the will is or is not free? I suggest that, to begin with, we may agree that volition is free so far as it really proceeds from the self which is said to will, and is not imposed upon it by conditions external to it. If we can accept this as a preliminary definition to be made more precise as we go on, our main problem will be found to concern the relation of volition to motives.

If motives are regarded as something extraneous to the self, determining it to will this or that, then a volition determined by motives is not free. Those who hold this view of the relation between motives and self, and yet maintain the freedom of the will, have to assume a pure or noumenal self behind the play of motives and undetermined by them. They assert that this pure ego intervenes from behind the scenes to decide in favour of one alternative rather than another, either without any reference to motives, or by strengthening one against others. But even if it is thought of as reinforcing a relatively weak motive, it cannot on this view of the relation of motives to self do so because it is attracted by some motives and repelled by others; for this very attraction and repulsion would themselves be motives and therefore extraneous to the self and determining it. Such liberty would be only what is called liberty of indifference. There are two main objections to this view. (1) It separates the volition from the causal order of nature. (2) It seems to exclude moral responsibility. If there is nothing in the nature of the self as a voluntary agent which determines it to decide in one way rather than another, the decision cannot properly be attributed to it; it does not really decide. It has no inducement to intervene in favour of one course rather than another. Where the connexion, between it and its so-called decision ought to come in, there is a gap. Since it is not really the author of the volition, it cannot be held responsible for it.

If we reject this view the only way of saving free will is to deny that determination by motives and determination by the self are in principle opposed and mutually exclusive. Action from motives, we must maintain, is free action inasmuch as the motives belong to the nature of the self and are not external forces acting upon it. I do not mean by this that the self which wills is identical with this or that special motive or group of motives *taken separately*—not even with that which in the end prevails as the motive for the voluntary decision. The self is rather the complex whole within which alone the several motives can exist at all and interact with each other. It is only as related to each other within the unity of the self that the motives are motives for a self at all. This unity of the self on the conative side is best exemplified in the process of deliberating, or making up one's mind, which issues in voluntary decision. Here there are ordinarily several motives at work in interaction with each other, but we are badly misinterpreting the process if we regard these as having each a quite separate and independent existence, so that the outcome of their interaction is merely a mechanical resultant. On the contrary, throughout the process the way in which each of the different motives works is determined more or less by the unity of the whole process within which they are factors; and the tendency of the self in the whole process is towards its own satisfaction as a whole.[1] And as the whole process varies in passing through successive and fluctuating stages, the relative values of the several motives also vary continuously.[2]

[1] What Green would call "personal good" or "the satisfaction of the self as a whole" rather than of this or that motive.

[2] I have here been adapting and applying to the conative side of our nature the principles of Gestalt Psychology which have yielded such brilliant results, experimentally verified, in the field of sense-perception.

III

So far we have taken a free volition to mean a volition proceeding from the self which is said to will. But there is a further condition which must be fulfilled by any volition for which freedom as ordinarily understood can be claimed. In saying that a man wills freely, part at least of what is ordinarily meant is that he could have willed otherwise. What, then, is meant by the statement "I was free in doing this because I might have done otherwise?" In every other case, whenever we say that something might not have happened, we mean that there are certain conditions of a general character which leave open the alternatives of the event's happening or not happening. We do not mean that if all the conditions had been present unchanged in their complete determinateness and particularity the issue could have been other than it is. The sun might be shining to-day, though it is actually raining. This means that from what we know of the general weather conditions the sun might be shining; it does not mean that if all the weather conditions are as they actually are the sun might be shining. If all the relevant conditions are present, then the event happens; if any are absent, then the event is impossible. Is free will an exception to this general rule? We have no right to assume that it is without very strong reason. If we can give a satisfactory account of it on the assumption that here too possibility is relative to given conditions, and not absolute, this account of it is to be preferred.

Now, there are at least three meanings which can be given to the phrase "I might have acted otherwise," corresponding to three different senses in which an act may be said to proceed from the self.

(1) We may mean that external circumstances are such as to leave open alternatives, and that it depends on our will which alternatives shall be realized. In this sense Socrates might have escaped from prison; the means of escape were provided, and whether he would or would not actually escape depended only on himself—on his own voluntary decision. Though this seems to be always part of what we mean by free agency, we may dismiss it here as irrelevant to our present problem, which is to determine the nature of free volition itself, not of our power to give effect to a voluntary decision once formed.

(2) There is another sense of freedom in which it means freedom to form a voluntary decision, not freedom to carry it out. It is this freedom which seems to be denied by those who say that a man's volition is determined by his previous mental history and his present character, together with the given situation. Yet in the process of deciding on one alternative rather than another we feel that the issue is not determined by our previous mental history and present character. Whatever these may have been we still ourselves have to determine what our action shall be. Consciousness

of freedom in this sense seems an indubitable fact and, what is more, it is present just as much in those who hold that decision depends on our past mental history as in those who do not. But what precisely do we mean when in forming a decision we assert that it is not pre-determined by our past history and present character? We mean that it is not so determined independently of the actual process of making up our minds on the practical question before us. A man in making up his mind how he is going to act does not and cannot do so by reflecting on his previous mental history and what he knows of his own character. He has to go through the process of coming to a decision before he knows what that decision is going to be. He cannot predict (as someone else might try to predict about him) by any considerations about his own character and past mental history what the decision is going to be. Even if he admits that the decision *will* be an outcome of his character as brought to bear on the practical issue, yet he does not know what his character in this regard is till he has developed it through the actual process of deliberating and deciding. He is right, therefore, in saying that apart from this process and its result his voluntary decision is not predetermined. And he cannot, of course, analyse the process itself before it takes place, so as to see how its successive stages necessarily lead up to each other and to the result. He has only the general presumption that what he shall decide is dependent on the process of deciding. But from the nature of the case this may have one or other of various alternative results. Hence it is clear that in *this* sense he is bound to recognize that he may decide in favour either of one alternative or the other. Indeed, he could not deliberate at all if he did not recognize this.

This is a very essential part, if not the whole, of the reason why in the process of willing we may adopt one or other of two alternative courses, and why in retrospect we say that we might have adopted one or other of them. But I think there is still something more to be said.

(3) We may say that we were free to do otherwise in the sense that the self from which the decision proceeded is only a partial and imperfect and transitory phase of a fuller self—a self more coherent or more comprehensive, or both. It is the more fully developed self which we recognize as the true self or real self. This may sound mysterious, but its meaning is really contained in the expression "the appeal from Philip drunk to Philip sober." Philip drunk is a relatively disintegrated self. The decision he comes to expresses only a partial and fragmentary side of his nature. Philip sober therefore disowns the decision. He says he was not himself when he made it. Wherever there is genuine remorse or repentance, the wider and fuller self rejects the act of the partial and imperfect self, and freedom is relatively absent—there is on the contrary what is called bondage to passion and impulse.

It is important to distinguish these last two meanings of freedom, or two senses in which a volition may be said to proceed from the self, since the common failure to do so is responsible for some confusion. When freedom is asserted in one of the two senses it is apt to be questioned and tested as if it were meant in the other.

IV

I shall now consider more fully the second and third senses of free will which I have pointed out, so as to connect them with moral responsibility. In the second a voluntary decision is free merely because it proceeds from the self as it is at the time the decision is made, and not from any external conditions. If a man signs a document or discloses the name of an accomplice only under threat of immediate death he would ordinarily be said to act under compulsion. Yet he does actually prefer to sign than to be shot. The choice is his own and is in this sense free. It is not as if his hand had been forced to make the movement of signing, or as if he had signed under the influence of hypnotic suggestion or had been deceived about the nature of the document.

Freedom so understood belongs equally to all volitions just because they are volitions. They would not be volitions at all if they did not proceed from the self as it is at the time. Hence this conception of freedom admits of no degrees. If we keep strictly to it, the man who signs the document under threat of death is just as free as if he had triumphed over the threat and chosen to die rather than sign. When we say, as we commonly do, that he acts under compulsion, we must be using some other conception of freedom. The inadequacy of this general freedom common to all volitions as such becomes evident when we consider the connexion of freedom with moral responsibility. A man is held to be responsible for what he wills only so far as he is free in willing it. And since there are various degrees in which he may be held responsible for the same act, it follows that there must be correspondingly various degrees of freedom. But there are no degrees in the freedom which belongs to every volition as such. Some other conception of freedom is therefore needed if we are to account for the varying degrees of responsibility.

I urge that the third meaning of freedom, and no other, can enable us to do this. Freedom in this sense consists in the degree in which the volition of the moment proceeds from and expresses the self as a whole. Now, the self may be a whole in very varying degrees. It would be so completely if all its more special and limited tendencies were subordinated to more general and comprehensive interests and tendencies within a systematic plan of life, so that whatever it willed in detail it willed only as a contribution to this plan. Further, the unity of the plan would have to be maintained throughout the life-history of the individual, whatever new interests might arise as his experience changed and developed. There would have to be complete comprehensiveness as well as complete coherence. This conception of the self as a perfect whole represents an ideal which

can never be realized by "such beings as we are in such a world as ours"—
not even by Wordsworth's "Happy Warrior." Considered as a regulative
idea in the Kantian sense it no doubt has value for ethical theory. But I want
to make it clear that it is not this that I mean when I speak of the self as a
whole. I am not concerned with the perfect freedom of an ideally perfect
self, but only with the relative freedom within the reach of our actual, imperfect selves. In particular, I am concerned with the degree of unity and
comprehensiveness which may characterise a self at the time at which it is
forming a voluntary decision.

There are plainly great differences in this respect between different
individuals and between different stages in the life of the same individual.
The various forms and degrees of insanity are simply various forms and
degrees of the disintegration of the self; to these correspond various forms
and degrees of moral and even legal responsibility and irresponsibility. Except in extreme cases responsibility does not cease altogether; praise and
blame, reward and punishment have their place even in a lunatic asylum.
A child, as compared with an adult, is a creature of impulse, living mentally
from hand to mouth; but this is only an early stage of the process through
which his mental life develops in unity and comprehensiveness. As between
adults, again, there are great differences. Some are almost as much at the
mercy of passing impulses as the child, while others possess remarkable
consistency and self-control. Further, a high development in certain directions may go along with a very low development in others. Thus an artist
who is devoted to his art and has a high sense of responsibility in all that
concerns it may be remarkably lax in money matters, spending or giving
away on impulse whatever comes to him, whether he has earned or borrowed it. The business man who has no sympathy with him as an artist condemns him too harshly, while those who have this sympathy may excuse
him too completely on the ground that he has no sense of the value of
money. It is such lopsidedness of mental development which makes it hard
to judge of men like Napoleon.

So far I have been considering freedom as depending on the degree
in which the self is a whole—the degree in which its mental life on the
conative side is organized. But free will also depends on the degree in which
the self as a whole (in whatever degree it may be a whole) comes into play
in each particular volition. Let us return to the case of the man who chooses
dishonour, by signing a document or betraying his comrade, rather than
immediate death, although under less urgent pressure he would have made
a different choice, and although he afterwards feels keen and persistent remorse for what he has done, so that perhaps if he were again faced with
a similar situation he would unhesitatingly choose to die. We must admit
that he does at the moment actually choose to sign. But he is held to be
choosing under compulsion and therefore to be in a high degree excusable.
It is felt that to defy the threat of immediate death is more than can reasonably be expected of normal human nature. And since the compulsion is

not, strictly speaking, physical, it affects the will itself. In some sense the man is willing against his will.

But in what sense? The theory of the motiveless intervention of a pure ego or noumenal self on the side of the decision he actually makes, independent of the actual interplay of motives, does not help us to answer this question. For the pure ego would be equally present and equally capable of intervening in all volitions; it cannot, then, account for one volition's being more free than another. Those who hold this view therefore express it by such sweeping and unqualified general statements as "the will is free." If we reject this view there seems to be only one explanation of how a man can will against his will. The volition of the moment is more or less opposed to the permanent trend of the will; the self of the moment is more or less in conflict with the self as a whole. In our example, the present fear, owing to its intensity and suddenness, more or less completely prevents the man from bringing to bear those motives and considerations, expressive of the more permanent trend of his will, which would or might have led him to make the opposite choice. To this extent he fails to realize the implications of what he is doing; and the more complete the failure, the less free is the voluntary act and the less the moral responsibility. He would have been freer and more responsible if instead of being threatened with immediate death he had been allowed time for deliberation. He would have been freer still if the threat had been only a loss of money or if, instead of a threat, the inducement had been a bribe of "a ribbon to stick in his coat" or thirty pieces of silver to put in his purse. If, on the other hand, he chooses death rather than dishonour, his choice is in an exceptionally high degree free, in the sense that it must proceed from a highly developed self which is fully brought to bear on the issue before him.[3] The more excusable the opposite choice would have been, the more the actual choice is felt to be worth admiring approval. Thus we can see that an excuse, however strong, does not entirely remove responsibility. *Qui s'excuse s'accuse.* To excuse implies something which needs excuse—something which is disapproved though it may not call for moral indignation or punishment.

V

I have now to discuss what so far I have taken for granted—the nature of moral responsibility and in particular its dependence on free will. I have already made the obvious point that so far as a man is in any way or degree free in willing, the volition must proceed from himself. It follows that to that extent also we may rightly attribute it to him and deal with him as its author, approving or disapproving of his behaviour. But though this first step cannot be left out, it carries us only a very little way. It does not touch

---

[3] The compulsion in resisting which he shows his freedom is, however, only a test; his act would have been equally free with no compulsion to be overcome, if he would have done the same act had there been compulsion.

any of the more difficult problems. It justifies approval or disapproval, but it gives no help in deciding how the disapproval should be felt or expressed. Our attitude towards the person whose behaviour we disapprove may be purely one of regret or pity, expressing itself in an endeavour to show him by reasoning and persuasion why his conduct is in our view wrong, so that he may be brought to realize its wrongness and feel towards it the same disapproval which we feel ourselves. On the other hand our attitude towards him and his conduct may be one of moral indignation, in some cases finding its appropriate expression in the infliction of some form of penalty. Both these contrasted ways of dealing with a wrongdoer are based on moral disapproval. Even when we only pity and are not angry we do so because we disapprove.

It is an important practical problem of Ethics to decide in principle when and how far each of these different ways of expressing disapproval is appropriate in preference to the other. I shall here confine the issue to moral as distinct from legal or quasi-legal responsibility, and consider primarily the responsibility of the individual for his own voluntary behaviour rather than the need for preserving social order by preventing or suppressing conduct inconsistent with it; the two questions are, however, not easily separable.

On what general principle are such problems to be decided? I do not find that I have any ready-made set of intuitions to guide me. I do not, for instance, find it intuitively evident that wrong-doing is somehow compensated by inflicting pain on the offender and calling it punishment. In itself this seems to me to be merely adding one evil to another. Considering punishment only in relation to the individual who is punished, it seems to me justifiable only to the extent to which it makes for his moral welfare; it is justifiable only so far as it is better for himself as a moral agent to be punished than not to be punished. On the same principle, the method of persuasion is to be preferred to that of punishment if and so far as it fulfils the same purpose.

Broadly speaking, and allowing for qualifications and exceptions, blame and punishment are properly, though not exclusively, applicable when the wrongdoer recognizes that he is doing wrong and so sins against his own conscience. The recognition that a certain course is wrong is not for him a sufficient motive for rejecting it. It is the purpose of blame and punishment to make good this deficiency. This it may do in two very different ways. One of them consists simply in introducing fear as a motive. The offender is to be deterred from similar behaviour in the future by fear of the disagreeable consequences attached to it, and others are to be similarly deterred by "making an example" of him. Legally this deterrent function of punishment, as a standing threat, is very important. But ethically it is obviously most unsatisfactory. It leaves the offender morally in as bad a state as before—perhaps even in a worse state. If he refrains from similar offences in the future, it is not from fear of doing wrong, but from fear of being found out. But there is another way in which punishment may work, if it is judiciously applied, which does satisfy ethical demands. It may bring home to the wrong-doer more fully and vividly the wrongness of his act, so that he may abstain from similar acts in the future not from fear of the penalty, or at any rate not merely from fear of it, but because he recognizes the act to be wrong. In order to work in this way the punishment must be such as to make the individual realize how his conduct is viewed by the community of which he is a member. It must bring home to him the moral resentment and indignation which his conduct arouses in others, or at any rate in some authority which he respects, so that he may come to judge and condemn himself as they judge and condemn him. Administered as if it were a dose of medicine it will fail. I am ready to admit that crime is a moral disease. But punishment, if it is to be the remedy for this disease, must be, and be recognized as, an expression of moral indignation.

From this account of the function of punishment it is easy to understand its relation to responsibility as dependent on freedom. So far as its aim is merely to deter, the only sense in which freedom is presupposed is that in which all volitions are free just because they are volitions. But so far as its aim is to bring about a change of heart, we must in punishing take into account degrees of free will, corresponding to degrees in which the passing volition expresses the general trend of the will in the self as a whole. It is possible that when the passing impulse or passion is over and the man comes to himself, he will fully and effectively repent his conduct, so that his own remorse is adequate punishment, and he will sin no more in this way under equal or even greater temptation. In such cases (provided always that we are considering only the individual offender himself and his moral welfare) blame and punishment coming from others is unjustified, because the purpose which alone justifies them is fulfilled without them. It is irrational to take measures to make the offender rue his act when he sufficiently rues it already. While this is an extreme case which probably does not often occur, there are many approximations to it in actual life. A man may be more or less predisposed to repent, so that the right degree of blame and punishment will make him do so fully and effectively. Ideal justice would demand that each case should be treated on its own merits. But while this might be possible if we had only to consider the offender and his moral welfare, in practice there are other considerations which have to be taken into account. For instance, it may be important for the preservation of social order that penal laws should in general be uniformly administered. But even this legal justice may leave some measure of discretion to the judge.

We have yet to consider the case of the man who does wrong meaning to do right and believing that he is doing right—the case in which what is willed is sometimes in technical language said to be objectively wrong but subjectively right. The question is whether a man who acts according to his conviction is blameworthy at all, and if so on what grounds and in what way. *Prima facie* it may seem that he cannot be blameworthy at all. His error being only an error of judgment, the only proper course, it will be said, is to try to set him right by persuasion, and also, if necessary, to take measures to prevent him from doing harm to others or to himself. But we ought not to be indignant with him, since such indignation cannot conduce to his moral wellbeing. It will only arouse his resentment.

This view takes for granted that no one can be justly blamed in any way or degree for intellectual error. But this assumption needs qualification. We must first take account of the way in which the erroneous belief arises. It may be due to want of care in the endeavour to find out what is true or right and to avoid bias and prejudice. So far as the error is due to such negligence the person who commits it is to be blamed for it, and sometimes very strongly blamed, in order to discourage such moral slackness in himself and in others. Secondly, we have to consider the way in which the belief once formed continues to be held. A man may cling to his own view with perverse obstinacy from other motives than love of truth. He may refuse to consider seriously the possibility that he may be wrong, and so make himself impervious to rational persuasion, and a fit object of moral resentment. All of us transgress more or less in this way. To take an instance of error which does not involve practical issues, the convinced earth-flattener may refuse to listen to the most careful and patient reasoning, or listen to it only in order to discover more or less ingenious devices for getting round it, his interest being not in finding out the truth but in avoiding the admission that he can be mistaken. He is then pig-headed or conceited or arrogant, and these are moral vices, not merely intellectual errors. As such they properly deserve punishment by neglect, ridicule or contempt. The method of persuasion being inapplicable, such means are all that are left for working against perverse obstinacy in those who are guilty of it, and for counteracting their influence on others.

Where the question is not merely theoretical, but concerns important practical issues, moral resentment is stronger, and may legitimately find expression in more drastic ways. What we call bigotry or fanaticism come under this head. The words themselves suggest condemnation and reproach. The bigot who cruelly persecutes those who disagree with him is not acquitted of blame merely because he is convinced that he is right. We are justified in feeling morally indignant with him and in expressing our indignation in all ways which will shake his unwarranted self-sufficiency and self-complacency. Even if we do him little or no positive good, it is better both for himself and for others to bring home to him the moral resentment aroused by his conduct than to leave him unchallenged and unopposed, as if he did not deserve blame at all.

Bigotry and fanaticism are extreme cases of a fault which in minor degrees is common to all of us. None of us consistently takes pains enough to determine what is right and what is wrong, and none of us keeps himself free as he should from bias and prejudice, so as to be entirely ready to listen to reasons which show him to be wrong. Though some measure of this fault is incident to human nature, it is blameworthy and we ought to do our best to correct it in ourselves and others. But we should all admit that the common failing ought not to be specially visited on any single individual by moral indignation and punishment, unless he shows it in a marked and obtrusive way. This follows from my view of the function of moral indignation and punishment as being to maintain and promote the moral welfare of the offender and others. It would do more harm than good to apply extreme measures in the attempt to correct a fault common to all human beings.

But what are we to say if the man in whom the desire to do right is so completely dominant that he takes all the care he can to distinguish what is right from what is wrong, and is ready to give adequate attention to reasons which may show that what he has taken to be right is not so? If in some particular he wills what is wrong, then we ought not to treat his volition as if it were right. To this extent we ought to disapprove. But moral resentment and punishment are entirely unjustified. The only proper course is to give him the enlightenment which he himself above all things desires. The will of such a person would be as free as that of any human being. For the self as a whole, being completely unified by the dominant desire to do right for its own sake, would have reached the highest level of moral unity, and it would be effectively brought to bear on practical issues involving the choice between right and wrong. As he is free, so he is responsible in a higher degree than he would be if he were liable to blame and punishment. It is just because he can be made the judge in his own case that he does not deserve or need to be compelled to account for his conduct to others. Where, on the contrary, blame and punishment are justly inflicted, the responsibility for his offence is partly taken over by those who blame and punish him.

Ethical Judgments and Avoidability *

C. L. STEVENSON

I

In a paper entitled "The Emotive Meaning of Ethical Terms" [1] I have pointed out that ethical statements are used to influence people, that they change or intensify people's attitudes, rather than describe what these attitudes already are. The influence is mediated not by some occult property which the ethical terms mean, but simply by their *emotive* meaning, which fits them for use in suggestion.

In the present paper we must put this analysis to an important test. We must see whether it permits us to make intelligible the relationship between ethical judgments and the "freedom" of the will.

Our question arises from such commonplace instances as the following: A. "You ought not to have done that." B. "But I simply couldn't help it!" It is clear that if A believes B, he will immediately withdraw his ethical judgment. No one judges a man for actions which he "couldn't help," or which, in other words, he was not "free" to alter. But why? What relation is there between "You ought not to have done it" and "I couldn't help it" which permits the one to be a generally accepted *reason* for rejecting the other? This is our central question. A great part of our attention, however, will be devoted to a preliminary question: What does "I couldn't help it" mean, when used to oppose ethical judgments?

II

Instead of the awkward expressions, "I couldn't help it," and "I was not free to do otherwise," it will be more convenient to use the expression, "My action was not avoidable." Our preliminary task, then, will be to define the word "avoidable."

Since the main difficulties about avoidability arise when we speak of actions which occurred in the past, we can simplify matters by defining the word for such contexts only. The definition is as follows:

"A's action was avoidable" means If *A had made a certain choice,*

---

* Reprinted by kind permission of the author and the editor from *Mind*, 47, 1938.
[1] *Mind*, vol. xlvi, no. 181, Jan. 1937 [pp. 415 ff. this volume].

which in fact he did not make, then his action would not have occurred.

We shall see that this definition is acceptable, at least in general outline. It is by no means surprising or novel. Hobbes [2] gave the same definition, and was partly anticipated by Aristotle.[3] But modern theorists, even though well acquainted with the definition, frequently reject it. It is thought to be relevant and important elsewhere, of course, but of no importance in making clear what sort of avoidability is presupposed by an ethical judgment. Since we shall accept a definition which is often deliberately rejected, we must carefully test it, for the ethical contexts here in question, to make sure that our departure from current trends of thought is not mistaken.

For example: An army officer has failed to win a battle. His commander tells him that he ought not to have failed. He replies that his failure was unavoidable. We must determine whether the circumstances under which the commander would accept this reply would be the same, regardless of whether he understood "avoidable" in a common-sense way, or in accordance with the definition.

Suppose that the officer had been confronted with overwhelming odds. The commander would then acknowledge, in common-sense fashion, that the officer's failure was not avoidable. Nor would it be, according to the definition. It is not true, as "avoidability" in the defined sense would require, that if the officer had chosen differently, the failure would have been prevented. It would have occurred no matter what the officer had chosen.

Suppose that the failure was due not to overwhelming odds, but only to the officer's leading his men into a needlessly exposed position. The commander would then say that the failure was avoidable. And so it would be, according to the definition. For if the officer had chosen differently— if he had chosen to keep his men in a less exposed position—the failure would have been prevented.

Suppose, as before, that the failure was due to the officer's leading his men to a needlessly exposed position. And suppose that the officer insisted, contrary to the commander's contention, that the failure was *not* avoidable, giving the following argument: "I acknowledge that if I had chosen to keep my men away from the exposed position, I should have prevented the failure. But I *couldn't choose* to do so. There were causes operating which made me choose just as I did. My choice, my actions, and the resulting failure were an inevitable outcome of natural law. Hence the failure was unavoidable." The commander would not listen for a moment, but would dismiss the argument as ridiculous. And so he would be entitled to do, if he used "avoidable" in the defined sense. An "avoidable" action, according to the definition, is one which would not have resulted *if* (contrary to fact) a different choice had been made. Now clearly, what would have resulted if

---

[2] *Leviathan*, pt. 2, ch. xxi. A more detailed discussion will be found in Hobbes' *The Questions Concerning Liberty, Necessity, and Chance.*

[3] *Nicomachean Ethics*, bk. 3, ch. i.

a man had chosen differently has nothing to do with whether or not his actual choice was determined. Similarly, the fact that rivers would have been lower if there had been less rain has nothing to do with whether or not the actual amount of rainfall was determined. According to the definition, then, arguments which seek to prove unavoidability by reference to determinism are to be dismissed as ridiculous, just as the commander would dismiss them.

In these three cases the proposed definition has proved consonant with common usage. There are other examples which will require us to revise the definition, but since these bring in nothing which will invalidate what is immediately to follow, they can be neglected until later on (section V).

A more important point now arises. The definition must do more than retain the customary denotation of "avoidable." It must also permit us to answer our central question. It must enable us to explain why avoidable acts alone are open to ethical judgment.

We shall soon see that the definition permits an extremely simple answer to this question. And yet this is generally denied. Theorists have repeatedly objected to the definition on the ground that it makes impossible any answer whatsoever. The objection has in part been anticipated by our army officer, in the last of the above cases; but in order to be safely rid of it, let us summarize it more fully:

"It is utterly beside the point," the objection proceeds, "to speculate about impossibilities. The proposed definition leads us to do this; but if avoidability is to be related to ethical judgments, it must deal only with the results of choices which were *possible*, granted the actual laws and causes that were operating. Suppose that a man's choice and his consequent actions were rigidly determined. He would then be a victim of circumstances, a victim of whatever hereditary and environmental factors produced the choice. It would be absurd to hold him responsible. It would be doubly absurd to 'prove' him responsible by pointing out that his action was 'avoidable' in the defined sense—by pointing out, in effect, that *if* his heredity and environment had yielded a different choice, his action would not have occurred. This conditional assertion, however true, leaves him no less a victim of circumstances in the *actual* case, hence not responsible, not open to judgment. The definition fails to make the relationship between avoidability and ethical judgments in any way intelligible. Indeed, no definition will succeed in this respect unless it refers to indeterminism; for only acts proceeding from choices which were not causally inevitable can sanely be considered open to judgment."

The last part of this objection is easily refuted. Reference to indeterminism, which the objection considers salutary, will throw no light on the difficulty. If a man's choice was not determined, it was theoretically unpredictable. The man himself could not have foreseen his choice, nor taken any steps to prevent it. It would not have sprung from his personality, but from nothing at all. He would still be a victim, not of natural forces, but of chance. What room is there here for an ethical judgment? [4]

The more destructive part of the objection is equally at fault. The contrary to fact conditions which occur in the definition of "avoidable" are by no means irrelevant. If they seem to be, it is because of the confusion which my preceding paper [5] sought to correct—a confusion about the meaning of ethical terms. The paradox which the objection attributes to the definition of "avoidable" is in fact due to a faulty analysis, tacitly presupposed, of the meaning of "right," "wrong," and "ought." If we dispel this confusion, the plausibility of the objection will vanish.

III

Let us recall, then, that ethical judgments have a quasi-imperative force, because of their emotive meaning. They influence people's attitudes, rather than describe what these attitudes already are.

Our chief purpose in influencing people's attitudes, obviously enough, is to lead them to *act* in a way which they otherwise would not. We tell a boy that he ought not to eat a green apple, in order to keep him from eating it. Our purpose is much the same when we make ethical judgments of something which has already been done. If the boy has eaten the green apple, we tell him that he ought not have done so. We are not, to be sure, trying to do anything about that particular action, which is past and gone. But we are trying to prevent similar actions in the future. The emotive meaning of "ought" greatly assists us. It enables us to build up in the boy an adverse attitude to his act, making him recall it, say, with an unpleasant feeling of guilt. The feeling becomes associated not with the past act alone, but with all others like it. It deters the boy from eating any more green apples. (We usually add to our ethical judgment the remark, "See that you don't do it again," and repeat our ethical judgment after the apple has made the boy ill, when his pain makes it easier to build up unpleasant associations with the action. These subsidiary devices, to say nothing of all forms of punishment, serve the same purpose as ethical judgments, although they operate in a different way.)

Other cases are only slightly more complicated. We often make ethical judgments of characters from a novel. By building up in the hearer, through ethical judgments, an adverse attitude to an imaginary character, we prevent the hearer from taking this character as a model for his own subsequent conduct.

When the purpose of modifying actions is not consciously present, it is latent. In other words, if a person is reminded that such a purpose will

---

[4] It is not necessary to develop this point, since it has been made time and again by others. For a particularly clear treatment, see C. D. Broad's booklet entitled *Determinism, Indeterminism, and Libertarianism* (Camb. Univ. Press, 1934).
[5] *Op. cit.*

not be served by the ethical judgment he is making, he will acknowledge that he is wasting his time in making it. (This is not true for certain senses of the ethical terms; but since these have no relation to avoidability, we need not consider them.)

It will be clear, then, that *ethical judgments look mainly to the future.* Even when they are made of past or imaginary acts, they still serve a dynamic purpose—that of discouraging (or encouraging) similar acts later on.

It is precisely here that ethical judgments become related to avoidability. Ethical judgments are used to modify actions of the kind judged. But the kind of action which can be modified in this way is limited. Judgments often induce men to give money to charity, but never make men add a cubit to their stature. If we tell a man that he ought to give to charity, our judgment may serve its purpose. If we tell him that he ought to add to his stature, our judgment will not serve its purpose. Since we are unwilling to talk aimlessly we confine our ethical judgments to actions of the first sort, to those which ethical judgments are likely to modify. But only avoidable acts, in the sense defined, are likely to be modified by ethical judgment. Hence only they are judged. Such, in brief, is the answer to our central question.

We must consider more carefully, however, why ethical judgments control avoidable acts alone. Let us return to the example about the army officer:

Suppose that the officer's failure was avoidable—that a different choice of his would have prevented it. From this it follows, granted uniformity of nature, that failure will in fact be prevented, in any future cases of the same sort, if the officer then makes the requisite choice. Of course no future cases will be of exactly the same sort as the past one, but some may be roughly so. It is *probable* that the officer will not fail if he is led to choose differently in these cases. The officer will be led to choose differently, quite possibly, by the quasi-imperative force of the commander's ethical judgment. A judgment of his past failure will make him ashamed of himself, and induce him to choose differently in any roughly similar case that may arise. In this way the ethical judgment will diminish the probability of future failures. To generalize: a judgment of an avoidable act is likely to control actions of the kind judged.

Suppose, however, that the failure was unavoidable. By steps of reasoning like those above, it follows that failure will probably occur, in future cases of roughly the same sort, even if the officer chooses differently. An ethical judgment will not serve, therefore, to prevent failures. It will exert its influence only through the mediating step of controlling the officer's choice, and this will not be enough. To generalize: a judgment of an unavoidable act will not control actions of the kind judged.

The relation between "You ought not to have done that" and "It was unavoidable" now looses its aura of mystery. The latter statement is recognized as a *reason* for giving up the former because it shows, if true, that the former will not serve its purpose. The relationship is not logical, but psychological. It is a psychological fact that people are unwilling to make purposeless ethical judgments.

The following analogy may be helpful: A says, "Please open the window." B replies, "I can't; it is built into the window frame." B's statement may properly be called a "reason" which is psychologically related to A's imperative. It leads A to withdraw the imperative as useless in serving any purpose. In a similar way the statement, "It was unavoidable," leads a person to stop making an ethical judgment.

These considerations introduce no unusual features into ethical methodology. In my previous paper we saw that empirically verifiable reasons, when used to support or oppose an ethical judgment, are always related to the judgment psychologically.[6] This is to be expected. A man uses an ethical judgment in order to exert an influence. He can be "refuted" only by being led to exert a different kind of influence, or else to exert no influence at all. Empirical reasons change his beliefs about the consequences or effectiveness of his influence, and in this manner *may* change the kind of influence which he afterwards exerts. Whether or not the reasons will effect this change depends upon the man's temperament. It so happens that men are temperamentally much alike in being unwilling to judge unavoidable actions. The close relationship between avoidability and ethical judgments depends upon this psychological fact.

The answer to our central question has now been given, at least in outline. Very little of it is new. The definition of "avoidable" is a familiar one, and even the explanation of how avoidability is related to ethical judgments is familiar, not in connection with the present problem, but in analogous cases presented by theories of punishment. Preventive and reformatory theories have long made clear that punishment of unavoidable acts serves no purpose. All that has been overlooked is that ethical judgments, being used dynamically, have also a preventive and reformatory function. Theorists have been blinded to this obvious fact by their neglect of emotive meanings.

IV

Let us now digress a little and decide whether ethics need concern itself about the indeterminism of the will.

---

[6] This generalization may at first seem too broad. If a man said "Go away and stay here," we should object to his imperative for a logical reason. May we not object to ethical judgments, then, for a logical reason? Yes, but our reason *would* be logical, not an *empirically verifiable* one logically related to the judgment. It would therefore constitute no exception to the generalization.

There are exceptions, but quite trivial ones. Should a man make some very curious ethical judgment, we might reply, "Come, you don't feel so yourself." According to my previous paper, this would be an empirical reason logically related to the judgment.

It is clear that ethical judgments do not presuppose indeterminism. They presuppose only avoidability, which depends solely upon the results of choice, not upon the absence of its causes.

It would seem, rather, that ethics presupposes determinism. Ethical judgments must control actions through the mediating step of controlling a man's choice. If the man's choice were not determined, it would not be controlled in this manner, or in any manner. Ethical judgments would be powerless to influence people's conduct. Isn't determinism necessary to provide ethical judgments with any function?

A moment's reflection will show that this is not strictly the case. We must presuppose at least a "partial" determinism, but need not necessarily presuppose a "complete" determinism. The meaning of these terms will be clear from the following example: The motion of the sun would be called "partially" determined if, from an exhaustive knowledge of laws and circumstances, we could predict that it would rise tomorrow at some time between five and six o'clock, say, but could not predict more specifically than this. It would be "completely" determined, if we could predict that it would rise, say, at exactly five-fifteen. Now ethics presupposes only the partial determination of a man's choice, for this still permits his choice to be influenced by an ethical judgment. Our judgment could not lead him to do exactly what we wanted, but it could lead him roughly in that direction.

Partial determinism is a trivial assumption, too obvious to deserve proof. The only point of dispute has been about whether choice is completely determined, or only partially so. Since either alternative is compatible with our explanation of how ethical judgments are related to avoidability, we may conclude that the dispute about determinism is irrelevant to ethics, so far as it deals with general presuppositions.

Why have so many theorists *thought* that ethics presupposed indeterminism? One reason, as has been intimated, is that they overlooked the quasi-imperative force of ethical judgments. They did not see that ethical judgments look to the future. Instead, then, of placing the connection between avoidability and ethical judgments in the future—instead of seeing that avoidable acts alone will subsequently be controlled by judgment—they looked to the past for a connection. Quite naturally, they could find an explanation only by making *choice* a mystery, as if it were somehow alterable even when it was irrevocably in the past. Some began to talk of indeterminism, and others, seeing that this really didn't help, became unintelligibly metaphysical.

Perhaps an equally important reason for the confusion lies in the emotional state of mind from which ethical judgments proceed. The purpose of modifying actions, which attends an ethical judgment, is usually latent. Our introspectable state of mind may at times be one of indignation, fear, or even blind hatred. These emotions often help us to attain our latent purpose by giving our ethical judgment a forceful spontaneity. If we pause to consider the causes of the act judged, our feelings become stultified.

Our ethical judgment becomes less convincing. What we are inclined to do, instead of finding causes, is to invent fictions, which strengthen our feelings by giving them semipoetic expression. We pretend that the action came, without more remote causal antecedents, from the man we are judging himself. He is "just naturally mean." His conduct has nothing to do with social pressure, or an unfortunate childhood. He dimly reminds us of the villain in an old-fashioned melodrama. Fictions of indeterminism, which give our feelings a more ready point of focus, are sometimes indispensable to the effectiveness of our ethical judgment. This may be an important source of error. How easy it would be to confuse these fictions, so prominent in consciousness, with the propositional meaning of the judgment. One might readily be tempted to say that the presupposition of indeterminism is found in the very "meaning" of ethical statements themselves. Perhaps theorists have been led in this way to give indeterminism an entirely unwarranted importance.

V

Several deliberate over-simplifications were made in sections II and III which must now be corrected.

The main simplification occurs in the definition of "avoidable." Let us see, by example, how the definition must be changed.

Suppose that our army officer would have prevented the failure only if he had given his men vigorous encouragement. He would not have had sufficient energy to encourage them unless he had had an extremely strong desire to do so. He would not, at the time, have had so strong a desire. Under these circumstances we should have to acknowledge, according to the definition, that the failure was "unavoidable." The officer would not have prevented it merely by *choosing* to encourage his men. He would have needed, as well, a strong desire to succeed in doing so, which he would not have had. A different choice alone would have been unavailing. And yet, although the failure was "unavoidable" according to our definition, it would not be called so by the commander, who would find no occasion for withholding ethical judgment.

In order to be more conventional the definition must be given as follows: "A's action was avoidable" has the same meaning as "If A had chosen a certain different alternative, and if he had had a sufficiently intense interest in bringing about what he chose, then his action would have been prevented." ("Interest" is here used, following Mr. R. B. Perry, to mean any kind of desire, aversion, etc.)

This new definition leaves the relationship between avoidability and ethical judgments essentially the same. In the above example the commander sees that failure may not occur in the future, other circumstances being roughly similar, if he can make the officer have a more vigorous desire to encourage his men. The commander's ethical judgment will serve to build up such a desire. It is likely to serve its purpose of preventing future failures.

We may now correct an unsound assumption made in section III. The main contention there, to repeat, was that avoidable acts alone are judged because they alone may be controlled by judgment. This required the assumption that ethical judgments control actions only through the mediating step of controlling a man's choice; for "avoidable" was then defined in terms of *choice* only. But at present "avoidable" is defined with reference to interests, as well as choice. Hence we may replace the unsound assumption by the correct one: Ethical judgments control actions not only by modifying a man's choice, but in a more general way by intensifying his interests.

The definition of "avoidable" is still too simple, however, as may be seen from the following example:

A man is progressively becoming addicted to opium. At first we say that his taking it is "avoidable," but as he grows more and more addicted to it, we say that it is "less and less avoidable," until at last we say that it is "unavoidable." Our definition fails to provide a meaning for "less avoidable." It fails further in requiring us to say that the man's taking opium never becomes "unavoidable"; for at any time it remains the case that if he chose to stop, and desired to with *enough* vigour, he would stop.

The definition is easily qualified: The stronger a man's interest must be, in order to prevent the action, the "less avoidable" his action becomes. When it must be extremely strong, the action ceases to be called "avoidable." These qualifications complicate our problem only very slightly. The less avoidable a man's action is, the more difficult it is for us to build up his interest in a way that would modify the action. Hence we parallel the decreasing avoidability by becoming increasingly more hesitant to make an ethical judgment. A low degree of avoidability becomes unavoidability when the intensity of the required interest becomes greater than any which our ethical judgment can build up. Judgment of avoidable acts still depends upon the probability of controlling the acts by judgment.

The example of the opium eater raises a further question: If his action was avoidable, just when must the choice and interest have had to occur, in order to have prevented it? Immediately before the action, or at *any previous* time? If we place no restriction on the time (and the definition does not) then his taking opium *was* avoidable even when he was in the last stages of the habit; for if he had chosen to stop taking it from the very beginning, even with a very slight interest in stopping, he would not have taken it thereafter.

The following qualification will suffice: When the conditions which existed at the time when the choice and interest would have prevented the action, and which were essential, no less than the choice and interest, in preventing the action, were of a sort that will not even roughly occur again, then the action is not called "avoidable." This obviously takes care of the above case. The opium eater will never again be at the beginning stages of his habit, if he is now in the last stages. The reasons for suspending judgment are equally obvious. If the beginning stages will not recur, and if they, no less than the effects of ethical judgment, will be essential to prevent his action, then his action cannot be controlled by ethical judgment.

We must next consider some more complicated cases. A man is sometimes excused from ethical judgment, though by no means always, because of his ignorance. If the failure of our army officer, for instance, would have been prevented by a certain choice, but if he had no reason to forsee that it would, even on the basis of excellent knowledge of the circumstances confronting him, his commander would probably make no adverse ethical judgment.

We need not trouble to decide whether this case requires us to revise the definition. It will be sufficient to see why the officer would not be judged. This is clear enough. A judgment would spur the officer on to make some change in his later procedure. The only significant change that he could make would be to acquire more knowledge thereafter. A judgment of the failure, then, would be tantamount, so far as its effective imperative force is concerned, to the judgment, "You ought not to have been so ignorant." By hypothesis, however, the officer had taken great care in acquiring knowledge. Perhaps a certain amount of ignorance was unavoidable (in the sense as above qualified). Perhaps it was avoidable only to a low degree. Perhaps it was "avoidable only at too great a cost." (In other words, if the officer had taken steps to acquire more knowledge, he would have had to neglect something else, and hence would have brought on even greater disaster.) For any of these reasons the commander might suspend judgment of the failure. Judgment would make no desired change.

We have been assuming throughout that ethical judgments have no other purpose than to control actions of the kind judged. It is important to note that there are many exceptions to this. For example: A, whose social position is rivalled by that of B, makes many adverse ethical judgments of B's actions whenever he is talking to B's friends. His purpose is not to control these actions, but rather to increase his own prestige by decreasing that of his rival. In general, an ethical judgment of a man's actions may be used to alter the man's social position. As in the preceding cases, however, such judgments usually serve no purpose when the actions judged are unavoidable. A will not induce B's friends to give B's social position to someone else unless someone else would have acted in a way more to their liking. If B's actions were unavoidable, this would *usually* not be the case.

Yet the matter is not always so simple. Suppose B has become so strongly addicted to alcohol that his taking it is now unavoidable. A might then judge B's conduct, and with effect, even though the conduct was unavoidable. The reason is clear. A's judgment will be tantamount, in its imperative force, to the combined judgment and reason, "We ought not to give B a preeminent social position, because he is a drunkard." In this form the judgment is of an avoidable act (our giving B a preeminent social position) and has the purpose of controlling actions of the kind judged. The later judgment is not strictly identical with the former; hence the former constitutes a genuine exception to our previous account. But the reader will doubtless see for himself how a perfectly accurate account would have to proceed.

A final remark is pertinent, to summarize and extend what has been in question throughout the paper. We have asked the question, "Why, as a matter of fact, are ethical judgments commonly limited to avoidable acts?" We have found that this is because ethical judgments of unavoidable acts would serve no purpose. Apart from definitions, our inquiry has been psychological. We have not asked the question, "*Ought* ethical judgments to be limited to avoidable acts?" This is an entirely different question. It is an ethical question, not a psychological question relevant to ethics.

In order to distinguish the latter question from the former, it may be well briefly to answer it. I answer, without hesitation, that ethical judgments *ought* to be so limited. It must be understood that this statement is essentially persuasive. I use it in order to influence people to disapprove of judging unavoidable acts. My purpose is to induce people to *continue* to judge avoidable acts alone, as they now usually do. In order to make my influence permanent, I shall have to support it by reasons. The main reason is this: judgments of unavoidable acts do not serve their purpose. It so happens, in this case, that the causal explanation of why people now do restrict their judgments to avoidable acts, and the reason why they ought to, coincide. Perhaps this reason will be insufficient to make permanent my influence. Perhaps the reader has very curious purposes, or approves of acting in a purposeless fashion. I should then have to point out other matters of fact, which might more successfully direct his approval in the way I wish. In the end I might have to resort to persuasive oratory. But I trust that in the present case this will not be necessary.

Free-Will and Psychoanalysis *

JOHN HOSPERS

O Thou, who didst with pitfall and with gin
Beset the Road I was to wander in,
   Thou wilt not with Predestined Evil round
Enmesh, and then impute my Fall to Sin!
   —Edward FitzGerald, *The Rubaiyat of Omar Khayyam.*

. . . IT IS EXTREMELY common for nonprofessional philosophers and
iconoclasts to deny that human freedom exists, but at the same time to have
no clear idea of what it is that they are denying to exist. The first thing
that needs to be said about the free-will issue is that any meaningful term
must have a meaningful opposite: if it is meaningful to assert that people
are not free, it must be equally meaningful to assert that people *are* free,
whether this latter assertion is in fact true or not. Whether it is true, of
course, will depend on the meaning that is given the weasel-word "free."
For example, if freedom is made dependent on indeterminism, it may well
be that human freedom is nonexistent. But there seem to be no good
grounds for asserting such a dependence,** especially since lack of causation is the furthest thing from people's minds when they call an act free.
Doubtless there are other senses that can be given to the word "free"—such
as "able to do anything we want to do"—in which no human beings are
free. But the first essential point about which the denier of freedom must
be clear is *what* it is that he is denying. If one knows what it is like for
people not to be free, one must know what it *would* be like for them to *be*
free.

Philosophers have advanced numerous senses of "free" in which countless acts performed by human beings can truly be called free acts. The most
common conception of a free act is that according to which an act is free if
and only if it is a *voluntary* act. But the word "voluntary" does not always
carry the same meaning. Sometimes to call an act voluntary means that we
can do the act *if* we choose to do it: in other words, that it is physically and

* Section 2 and part of Section 3 of the article "Meaning and Free-Will" in *Philosophy and Phenomenological Research*, Vol. X, 1950. Reprinted by kind permission
of the editor.
   ** [See this volume, the essays by Stout and Stevenson immediately preceding this
one.]

psychologically possible for us to do it, so that the occurrence of the act follows upon the decision to do it. (One's decision to raise his arm is in fact followed by the actual raising of his arm, unless he is a paralytic; one's decision to pluck the moon from the sky is not followed by the actual event.) Sometimes a voluntary act is conceived (as by Moore [1]) as an act which would not have occurred if, just beforehand, the agent had chosen not to perform it. But these senses are different from the sense in which a voluntary act is an act resulting from *deliberation*, or perhaps merely from *choice*. For example, there are many acts which we could have avoided, if we had chosen to do so, but which we nevertheless did not *choose* to perform, much less *deliberate* about them. The act of raising one's leg in the process of taking a step while out for a walk, is one which a person could have avoided by choosing to, but which, after one has learned to walk, takes place automatically or semi-automatically through habit, and thus is not the result of choice. (One may have chosen to take the walk, but not to take this or that step while walking.) Such acts are free in Moore's sense but are not free in the sense of being deliberate. Moreover, there are classes of acts of the same general character which are not even covered by Moore's sense: sudden outbursts of feeling, in some cases at least, could not have been avoided by an immediately preceeding volition, so that if these are to be included under the heading of voluntary acts, the proviso that the act could have been avoided by an immediately preceding volition must be amended to read "could have been avoided by a volition or series of volitions by the agent *at some time in the past*"—such as the adoption of a different set of habits in the agent's earlier and more formative years.

(Sometimes we call *persons*, rather than their acts, free. Stebbing, for example, declares that one should never call acts free, but only the doers of the acts.[2] But the two do not seem irreconcilable: can we not speak of a *person* as free *with respect to a certain act* (never just free in general) if that *act* is free—whatever we may then go on to mean by saying that an act is free? Any statement about a free act can then be translated into a statement about the doer of the act.)

Now, no matter in which of the above ways we may come to define "voluntary," there are still acts which are voluntary *but which we would be very unlikely to think of as free*. Thus, when a person submits to the command of an armed bandit, he may do so voluntarily in every one of the above senses: he may do so as a result of choice, even of deliberation, and he could have avoided doing it by willing not to—he could, instead, have refused and been shot. The man who reveals a state secret under torture does the same: he could have refused and endured more torture. Yet such acts, and persons in respect of such acts, are not generally called free. We say that they were performed *under compulsion*, and if an act is performed under compulsion we do not call it free. We say, "He wasn't free because

---

[1] *Ethics*, pp. 15–16 [p. 37 this volume].
[2] *Philosophy and the Physicists*, p. 212.

he was forced to do as he did," though of course his act was voluntary.

This much departure from the identification of free acts with voluntary acts almost everyone would admit. Sometimes, however, it would be added that this is all the departure that can be admitted. According to Schlick, for example,

> Freedom means the opposite of compulsion; a man is *free* if he does not act under *compulsion*, and he is compelled or unfree when he is hindered from without in the realization of his natural desires. Hence he is unfree when he is locked up, or chained, or when someone forces him at the point of a gun to do what otherwise he would not do. This is quite clear, and everyone will admit that the everyday or legal notion of the lack of freedom is thus correctly interpreted, and that a man will be considered quite free . . . if no such external compulsion is exerted upon him.[3]

Schlick adds that the entire vexed free-will controversy in philosophy is so much wasted ink and paper, because compulsion has been confused with causality and necessity with uniformity. If the question is asked whether every event is caused, the answer is doubtless yes; but if it is whether every event is compelled, the answer is clearly no. Free acts are uncompelled acts, not uncaused acts. Again, when it is said that some state of affairs (such as water flowing downhill) is necessary, if "necessary" means "compelled," the answer is no; if it means merely that it always happens that way, the answer is yes: universality of application is confused with compulsion. And this, according to Schlick, is the end of the matter.

Schlick's analysis is indeed clarifying and helpful to those who have fallen victim to the confusions he exposes—and this probably includes most persons in their philosophical growing-pains. But *is* this the end of the matter? Is it true that all acts, though caused, are free as long as they are not compelled in the sense which he specifies? May it not be that, while the identification of "free" with "uncompelled" is acceptable, the area of compelled acts is vastly greater than he or most other philosophers have ever suspected? (Moore is more cautious in this respect than Schlick; while for Moore an act is free if it is voluntary in the sense specified above, he thinks there may be another sense in which human beings, and human acts, are not free at all.[4]) We remember statements about human beings being pawns of their early environment, victims of conditions beyond their control, the result of causal influences stemming from their parents, and the like, and we ponder and ask, "Still, are we really free?" Is there not something in what generations of sages have said about man being fettered? Is there not perhaps something too facile, too sleight-of-hand, in Schlick's cutting of the Gordian knot? For example, when a metropolitan newspaper headlines an article with the words "Boy Killer is Doomed Long before He Is Born," [5] and then goes on to describe how a twelve-year-old boy has been sentenced to prison for the murder of a girl, and how his parental background includes

---

[3] *The Problems of Ethics*, Rynin translation, p. 150.
[4] *Ethics*, Chapter 6, pp. 217 ff.
[5] *New York Post*, Tuesday, May 18, 1948, p. 4.

records of drunkenness, divorce, social maladjustment, and paresis, are we still to say that his act, though voluntary and assuredly *not* done at the point of a gun, is free? The boy has early displayed a tendency toward sadistic activity to hide an underlying masochism and "prove that he's a man"; being coddled by his mother only worsens this tendency, until, spurned by a girl in his attempt on her, he kills her—not simply in a fit of anger, but calculatingly, deliberately. Is he free in respect of his criminal act, or for that matter in most of the acts of his life? Surely to ask this question is to answer it in the negative. Perhaps I have taken an extreme case; but it is only to show the superficiality of the Schlick analysis the more clearly. Though not everyone has criminotic tendencies, everyone has been moulded by influences which in large measure at least determine his present behavior; he is literally the product of these influences, stemming from periods prior to his "years of discretion," giving him a host of character traits that he cannot change now even if he would. So obviously does what a man is depend upon how a man comes to be, that it is small wonder that philosophers and sages have considered man far indeed from being the master of his fate. It is not as if man's will were standing high and serene above the flux of events that have moulded him; it is itself caught up in this flux, itself carried along on the current. An act is free when it is determined by the man's character, say moralists; but what if the most decisive aspects of his character were already irrevocably acquired before he could do anything to mold them? What if even the degree of will power available to him in shaping his habits and disciplining himself now to overcome the influence of his early environment is a factor over which he has no control? What are we to say of this kind of "freedom?" Is it not rather like the freedom of the machine to stamp labels on cans when it has been devised for just that purpose? Some machines can do so more efficiently than others, but only because they have been better constructed.

It is not my purpose here to establish this thesis in general, but only in one specific respect which has received comparatively little attention, namely, the field referred to by psychiatrists as that of unconscious motivation. In what follows I shall restrict my attention to it because it illustrates as clearly as anything the points I wish to make.

Let me try to summarize very briefly the psychoanalytic doctrine on this point.[6] The conscious life of the human being, including the conscious decisions and volitions, is merely a mouthpiece for the unconscious—not directly for the enactment of unconscious drives, but of the compromise

[6] I am aware that the theory presented below is not accepted by all practicing psychoanalysts. Many non-Freudians would disagree with the conclusions presented below. But I do not believe that this fact affects my argument, as long as the concept of unconscious motivation is accepted. I am aware, too, that much of the language employed in the following descriptions is animistic and metaphorical; but as long as I am presenting a view I would prefer to "go the whole hog" and present it in its most dramatic form. The theory can in any case be made clearest by the use of such language, just as atomic theory can often be made clearest to students with the use of models.

between unconscious drives and unconscious reproaches. There is a Big Three behind the scenes which the automaton called the conscious personality carries out: the id, an "eternal gimme," presents its wish and demands its immediate satisfaction; the super-ego says no to the wish immediately upon presentation, and the unconscious ego, the mediator between the two, tries to keep peace by means of compromise.[7]

To go into examples of the functioning of these three "bosses" would be endless; psychoanalytic case books supply hundreds of them. The important point for us to see in the present context is that *it is the unconscious that determines what the conscious impulse and the conscious action shall be.* Hamlet, for example, had a strong Oedipus wish, which was violently counteracted by super-ego reproaches; these early wishes were vividly revived in an unusual adult situation in which his uncle usurped the coveted position from Hamlet's father and won his mother besides. This situation evoked strong strictures on the part of Hamlet's super-ego, and it was this that was responsible for his notorious delay in killing his uncle. A dozen times Hamlet could have killed Claudius easily; but every time Hamlet "decided" not to: a free choice, moralists would say—but no, listen to the super-ego: "What you feel such hatred toward your uncle for, what you are plotting to kill him for, is precisely the crime which you yourself desire to commit: to kill your father and replace him in the affections of your mother. Your fate and your uncle's are bound up together." This paralyzes Hamlet into inaction. Consciously all he knows is that he is unable to act; this conscious inability he rationalizes, giving a different excuse each time.[8]

We have always been conscious of the fact that we are not masters of our fate in every respect—that there are many things which we cannot do, that nature is more powerful than we are, that we cannot disobey laws without danger of reprisals, etc. We have become "officially" conscious, too, though in our private lives we must long have been aware of it, that we are not free with respect to the emotions that we feel—whom we love or hate, what types we admire, and the like. More lately still we have been reminded that there are unconscious motivations for our basic attractions and repulsions, our compulsive actions or inabilities to act. But what is not welcome news is that our very acts of volition, and the entire train of deliberations leading up to them, are but façades for the expression of unconscious wishes, or rather, unconscious compromises and defenses.

A man is faced by a choice: shall he kill another person or not? Moralists would say, here is a free choice—the result of deliberation, an action consciously entered into. And yet, though the agent himself does not know it, and has no awareness of the forces that are at work within him, his choice is already determined for him: his conscious will is only an instrument, a

[7] This view is very clearly developed in Edmund Bergler, *Divorce Won't Help*, especially Chapter I.

[8] See *The Basic Writings of Sigmund Freud*, Modern Library Edition, p. 310. (In *The Interpretation of Dreams*.) Cf. also the essay by Ernest Jones, "A Psycho-analytical Study of Hamlet."

slave, in the hands of a deep unconscious motivation which determines his action. If he has a great deal of what the analyst calls "free-floating guilt," he will not; but if the guilt is such as to demand immediate absorption in the form of self-damaging behavior, this accumulated guilt will have to be discharged in some criminal action. The man himself does not know what the inner clockwork is; he is like the hands on the clock, thinking they move freely over the face of the clock.

A woman has married and divorced several husbands. Now she is faced with a choice for the next marriage: shall she marry Mr. A, or Mr. B, or nobody at all? She may take considerable time to "decide" this question, and her decision may appear as a final triumph of her free will. Let us assume that A is a normal, well-adjusted, kind, and generous man, while B is a leech, an impostor, one who will become entangled constantly in quarrels with her. If she belongs to a certain classifiable psychological type, she will inevitably choose B, and she will do so even if her previous husbands have resembled B, so that one would think that she "had learned from experience." Consciously, she will of course "give the matter due consideration," etc., etc. To the psychoanalyst all this is irrelevant chaff in the wind—only a camouflage for the inner workings about which she knows nothing consciously. If she is of a certain kind of masochistic strain, as exhibited in her previous set of symptoms, she *must* choose B: her super-ego, always out to maximize the torment in the situation, seeing what dazzling possibilities for self-damaging behavior are promised by the choice of B, compels her to make the choice she does, and even to conceal the real basis of the choice behind an elaborate facade of rationalizations.

A man is addicted to gambling. In the service of his addiction he loses all his money, spends what belongs to his wife, even sells his property and neglects his children. For a time perhaps he stops; then, inevitably, he takes it up again. The man does not know that he is a victim rather than an agent; or, if he sometimes senses that he is in the throes of something-he-knows-not-what, he will have no inkling of its character and will soon relapse into the illusion that he (his conscious self) is freely deciding the course of his own actions. What he does not know, of course, is that he is still taking out on his mother the original lesion to his infantile narcissism, getting back at her for her fancied refusal of his infantile wishes—and this by rejecting everything identified with her, namely education, discipline, logic, common sense, training. At the roulette wheel, almost alone among adult activities, chance—the opposite of all these things—rules supreme; and his addiction represents his continued and emphatic reiteration of his rejection of Mother and all she represents to his unconscious.

This pseudo-aggression of his is of course masochistic in its effects. In the long run he always loses; he can never quit while he is winning. And far from playing in order to win, rather one can say that his losing is a *sine qua non* of his psychic equilibrium (as it was for example with Dostoyevsky): guilt demands punishment, and in the ego's "deal" with the super-ego the super-ego has granted satisfaction of infantile wishes in return for the self-damaging conditions obtaining. Winning would upset the neurotic equilibrium.[9]

A man has wash-compulsion. He must be constantly washing his hands —he uses up perhaps 400 towels a day. Asked why he does this, he says, "I need to, my hands are dirty"; and if it is pointed out to him that they are not really dirty, he says "They feel dirty anyway, I feel better when I wash them." So once again he washes them. He "freely decides" every time; he feels that he must wash them, he deliberates for a moment perhaps, but always ends by washing them. What he does not see, of course, are the invisible wires inside him pulling him inevitably to do the thing he does: the infantile id-wish concerns preoccupation with dirt, the super-ego charges him with this, and the terrified ego must respond, "No, I don't like dirt, see how clean I like to be, look how I wash my hands!"

Let us see what further "free acts" the same patient engages in (this is an actual case history): he is taken to a concentration camp, and given the worst of treatment by the Nazi guards. In the camp he no longer chooses to be clean, does not even try to be—on the contrary, his choice is now to wallow in filth as much as he can. All he is aware of now is a disinclination to be clean, and every time he must choose he chooses not to be. Behind the scenes, however, another drama is being enacted: the super-ego, perceiving that enough torment is being administered from the outside, can afford to cease pressing its charges in this quarter—the outside world is doing the torturing now, so the super-ego is relieved of the responsibility. Thus the ego is relieved of the agony of constantly making terrified replies in the form of washing to prove that the super-ego is wrong. The defense no longer being needed, the person slides back into what is his natural predilection anyway, for filth. This becomes too much even for the Nazi guards: they take hold of him one day, saying "We'll teach you how to be clean!" drag him into the snow, and pour bucket after bucket of icy water over him until he freezes to death. Such is the end-result of an original id-wish, caught in the machinations of a destroying super-ego.

Let us take, finally, a less colorful, more everyday example. A student at a university, possessing wealth, charm, and all that is usually considered essential to popularity, begins to develop the following personality-pattern: although well taught in the graces of social conversation, he always makes a *faux pas* somewhere, and always in the worst possible situation; to his friends he makes cutting remarks which hurt deeply—and always apparently aimed in such a way as to hurt the most: a remark that would not hurt A but would hurt B he invariably makes to B rather than to A, and so on. None of this is conscious. Ordinarily he is considerate of people, but he

---

[9] See Edmund Bergler's article on the pathological gambler in *Diseases of the Nervous System* (1943). Also "Suppositions about the Mechanism of Criminosis," *Journal of Criminal Psychopathology* (1944) and "Clinical Contributions to the Psychogenesis of Alcohol Addiction," *Quarterly Journal of Studies on Alcohol*, 5: 434 (1944).

contrives always (unconsciously) to impose on just those friends who would resent it most, and at just the times when he should know that he should not impose: at 3 o'clock in the morning, without forewarning, he phones a friend in a near-by city demanding to stay at his apartment for the weekend; naturally the friend is offended, but the person himself is not aware that he has provoked the grievance ("common sense" suffers a temporary eclipse when the neurotic pattern sets in, and one's intelligence, far from being of help in such a situation, is used in the interest of the neurosis), and when the friend is cool to him the next time they meet, he wonders why and feels unjustly treated. Aggressive behavior on his part invites resentment and aggression in turn, but all that he consciously sees is others' behavior towards him—and he considers himself the innocent victim of an unjustified "persecution."

Each of these acts is, from the moralist's point of view, free: he chose to phone his friend at 3 a.m.; he chose to make the cutting remark that he did, etc. What he does not know is that an ineradicable masochistic pattern has set in. His unconscious is far more shrewd and clever than is his conscious intellect; it sees with uncanny accuracy just what kind of behavior will damage him most, and unerringly forces him into that behavior. Consciously, the student "doesn't know why he did it"—he gives different "reasons" at different times, but they are all, once again, rationalizations cloaking the unconscious mechanism which propels him willy-nilly into actions that his "common sense" eschews.

The more of this sort of thing one observes, the more he can see what the psychoanalyst means when he talks about *the illusion of freedom*. And the more of a psychiatrist one becomes, the more he is overcome with a sense of what an illusion this free-will can be. In some kinds of cases most of us can see it already: it takes no psychiatrist to look at the epileptic and sigh with sadness at the thought that soon this person before you will be as one possessed, not the same thoughtful intelligent person you knew. But people are not aware of this in other contexts, for example when they express surprise at how a person whom they have been so good to could treat them so badly. Let us suppose that you help a person financially or morally or in some other way, so that he is in your debt; suppose further that he is one of the many neurotics who unconsciously identify kindness with weakness and aggression with strength, then he will unconsciously take your kindness to him as weakness and use it as the occasion for enacting some aggression against you. He can't help it, he may regret it himself later; still, he will be driven to do it. If we gain a little knowledge of psychiatry, we can look at him with pity, that a person otherwise so worthy should be so unreliable—but we will exercise realism too, and be aware that there are some types of people that you cannot be good to in "free" acts of their conscious volition, they will use your own goodness against you.

Sometimes the persons themselves will become dimly aware that "something behind the scenes" is determining their behavior. The divorcee will sometimes view herself with detachment, as if she were some machine (and indeed the psychoanalyst does call her a "repeating-machine"): "I know I'm caught in a net, that I'll fall in love with this guy and marry him and the whole ridiculous merry-go-round will start all over again."

We talk about free will, and we say, for example, the person is free to do so-and-so if he can do so *if* he wants to—and we forget that his wanting to is itself caught up in the stream of determinism, that unconscious forces drive him into the wanting or not wanting to do the thing in question. The analogy of the puppet whose motions are manipulated from behind by invisible wires, or better still, by springs inside, is a telling one at almost every point.

And the glaring fact is that it all started so early, before we knew what was happening. The personality-structure is inelastic after the age of five, and comparatively so in most cases after the age of three. Whether one acquires a neurosis or not is determined by that age—and just as involuntarily as if it had been a curse of God. If, for example, a masochistic pattern was set up, under pressure of hyper-narcissism combined with real or fancied infantile deprivation, then the masochistic snowball was on its course downhill long before we or anybody else know what was happening, and long before anyone could do anything about it. To speak of human beings as "puppets" in such a context is no idle metaphor, but a stark rendering of a literal fact: only the psychiatrist knows what puppets people really are; and it is no wonder that the protestations of philosophers that "the act which is the result of a volition, a deliberation, a conscious decision, is free" leave these persons, to speak mildly, somewhat cold.

But, one may object, all the states thus far described have been abnormal, neurotic ones. The well-adjusted (normal) person at least is free.

Leaving aside the question of how clearly and on what grounds one can distinguish the neurotic from the normal, let me use an illustration of a proclivity that everyone would call normal, namely, the decision of a man to support his wife and possibly a family, and consider briefly its genesis, according to psychoanalytic accounts.[10]

Every baby comes into the world with a full-fledged case of megalomania—interested only in himself, acting as is believing that he is the center of the universe and that others are present only to fulfill his wishes, and furious when his own wants are not satisfied immediately no matter for what reason. Gratitude, even for all the time and worry and care expended on him by the mother, is an emotion entirely foreign to the infant, and as he grows older it is inculcated in him only with the greatest difficulty; his natural tendency is to assume that everything that happens to him is due to himself, except for denials and frustrations, which are due to the "cruel, denying" outer world, in particular the mother; and that he owes nothing to anyone, is dependent on no one. This omnipotence-complex, or illusion

[10] E.g., Edmund Bergler, *The Battle of the Conscience*, Chapter I.

of non-dependence, has been called the "autarchic fiction." Such a conception of the world is actually fostered in the child by the conduct of adults, who automatically attempt to fulfill the infant's every wish concerning nourishment, sleep, and attention. The child misconceives causality and sees in these wish-fulfillments not the results of maternal kindness and love, but simply the result of his own omnipotence.

This fiction of omnipotence is gradually destroyed by experience, and its destruction is probably the deepest disappointment of the early years of life. First of all, the infant discovers that he is the victim of organic urges and necessities: hunger, defecation, urination. More important, he discovers that the maternal breast, which he has not previously distinguished from his own body (he has not needed to, since it was available when he wanted it), is not a part of himself after all, but of another creature upon whom he is dependent. He is forced to recognize this, e.g., when he wants nourishment and it is at the moment not present; even a small delay is most damaging to the "autarchic fiction." Most painful of all is the experience of weaning, probably the greatest tragedy in every baby's life, when his dependence is most cruelly emphasized; it is a frustrating experience because what he wants is no longer there at all; and if he has been able to some extent to preserve the illusion of non-dependence heretofore, he is not able to do so now—it is plain that the source of his nourishment is not dependent on him, but he on it. The shattering of the autarchic fiction is a great disillusionment to every child, a tremendous blow to his ego which he will, in one way or another, spend the rest of his life trying to repair. How does he do this?

First of all, his reaction to frustration is anger and fury; and he responds by kicking, biting, etc., the only ways he knows. But he is motorically helpless, and these measures are ineffective, and only serve to emphasize his dependence the more. Moreover, against such responses of the child the parental reaction is one of prohibition, often involving deprivation of attention and affection. Generally the child soon learns that this form of rebellion is profitless, and brings him more harm than good. He wants to respond to frustration with violent aggression, and at the same time learns that he will be punished for such aggression, and that in any case the latter is ineffectual. What face-saving solution does he find? Since he must "face facts," since he must in any case "conform" if he is to have any peace at all, he tries to make it seem as if he himself is the source of the commands and prohibitions: the *external* prohibitive force is *internalized*—and here we have the origin of conscience. By making the prohibitive agency seem to come from within himself, the child can "save face"—as if saying, "The prohibition comes from within me, not from outside, so I'm not subservient to external rule, I'm only obeying rules I've set up myself," thus to some extent saving the autarchic fiction, and at the same time avoiding unpleasant consequences directed against himself by complying with parental commands.

Moreover, the boy [11] has unconsciously never forgiven the mother for his dependence on her in early life, for nourishment and all other things. It has upset his illusion of non-dependence. These feelings have been repressed and are not remembered; but they are acted out in later life in many ways —e.g., in the constant deprecation man has for woman's duties such as cooking and housework of all sorts ("All she does is stay home and get together a few meals, and she calls that work"), and especially in the man's identification with the mother in his sex experiences with women. By identifying with someone one cancels out in effect the person with whom he identifies—replacing that person, unconsciously denying his existence, and the man, identifying with his early mother, playing the active rôle in "giving" to his wife as his mother has "given" to him, is in effect the denial of his mother's existence, a fact which is narcissistically embarrassing to his ego because it is chiefly responsible for shattering his autarchic fiction. In supporting his wife, he can unconsciously deny that his mother gave to him, and that he was dependent on her giving. Why is it that the husband plays the provider, and wants his wife to be dependent on no one else, although twenty years before he was nothing but a parasitic baby? This is a face-saving device on his part: he can act out the reasoning "See, I'm not the parasitic baby, on the contrary I'm the provider, the giver." His playing the provider is a constant face-saving device, to deny his early dependence which is so embarrassing to his ego. It is no wonder that men generally dislike to be reminded of their babyhood, when they were dependent on woman.

Thus we have here a perfectly normal adult reaction which is unconsciously motivated. The man "chooses" to support a family—and his choice is as unconsciously motivated as anything could be. (I have described here only the "normal" state of affairs, uncomplicated by the well-nigh infinite number of variations that occur in actual practice.)

Now, what of the notion of responsibility? What happens to it on our analysis?

Let us begin with an example, not a fictitious one. A woman and her two-year-old baby are riding on a train to Montreal in mid-winter. The child is ill. The woman wants badly to get to her destination. She is, unknown to herself, the victim of a neurotic conflict whose nature is irrelevant here except for the fact that it forces her to behave aggressively toward the child, partly to spite her husband whom she despises and who loves the child, but chiefly to ward off super-ego charges of masochistic attachment. Consciously she loves the child, and when she says this she says it sincerely, but she must behave aggressively toward it nevertheless, just as many children love their mothers but are nasty to them most of the

[11] The girl's development after this point is somewhat different. Society demands more aggressiveness of the adult male, hence there are more super-ego strictures on tendencies toward passivity in the male; accordingly his defenses must be stronger.

time in neurotic pseudo-aggression. The child becomes more ill as the train approaches Montreal; the heating system of the train is not working, and the conductor pleads with the woman to get off the train at the next town and get the child to a hospital at once. The woman refuses. Soon after, the child's condition worsens, and the mother does all she can to keep it alive, without, however, leaving the train, for she declares that it is absolutely necessary that she reach her destination. But before she gets there the child is dead. After that, of course, the mother grieves, blames herself, weeps hysterically, and joins the church to gain surcease from the guilt that constantly overwhelms her when she thinks of how her aggressive behavior has killed her child.

Was she responsible for her deed? In ordinary life, after making a mistake, we say, "Chalk it up to experience." Here we should say, "Chalk it up to the neurosis." *She* could not help it if her neurosis forced her to act this way—she didn't even know what was going on behind the scenes, her conscious self merely acted out its assigned part. This is far more true than is generally realized: criminal actions in general are not actions for which their agents are responsible; the agents are passive, not active—they are victims of a neurotic conflict. Their very hyper-activity is unconsciously determined.

To say this is, of course, not to say that we should not punish criminals. Clearly, for our own protection, we must remove them from our midst so that they can no longer molest and endanger organized society. And, of course, if we use the word "responsible" in such a way that justly to hold someone responsible for a deed is by definition identical with being justified in punishing him, then we can and do hold people responsible. But this is like the sense of "free" in which free acts are voluntary ones. It does not go deep enough. In a deeper sense we cannot hold the person responsible: we can hold his neurosis responsible, but *he is not responsible for his neurosis*, particularly since the age at which its onset was inevitable was an age before he could even speak.

The neurosis is responsible—but isn't the neurosis a part of *him?* We have been speaking all the time as if the person and his unconscious were two separate beings; but isn't he one personality, including conscious and unconscious departments together?

I do not wish to deny this. But it hardly helps us here; for what people want when they talk about freedom, and what they hold to when they champion it, is the idea that the *conscious* will is the master of their destiny. "I am the master of my fate, I am the captain of my soul"—and they surely mean their conscious selves, the self that they can recognize and search and introspect. Between an unconscious that willy-nilly determines your actions, and an external force which pushes you, there is little if anything to choose. The unconscious is just *as if* it were an outside force; and indeed, psychiatrists will assert that the inner Hitler (your super-ego) can torment you far more than any external Hitler can. Thus the kind of freedom that people want, the only kind they will settle for, is precisely the kind that psychiatry says that they cannot have.

Heretofore it was pretty generally thought that, while we could not rightly blame a person for the color of his eyes or the morality of his parents, or even for what he did at the age of three, or to a large extent what impulses he had and whom he fell in love with, one *could* do so for other of his adult activities, particularly the acts he performed voluntarily and with premeditation. Later this attitude was shaken. Many voluntary acts came to be recognized, at least in some circles, as compelled by the unconscious. Some philosophers recognized this too—Ayer [12] talks about the kleptomaniac being unfree, and about a person being unfree when another person exerts a habitual ascendancy over his personality. But this is as far as he goes. The usual examples, such as the kleptomaniac and the schizophrenic, apparently satisfy most philosophers, and with these exceptions removed, the rest of mankind is permitted to wander in the vast and alluring fields of freedom and responsibility. So far, the inroads upon freedom left the vast majority of humanity untouched; they began to hit home when psychiatrists began to realize, though philosophers did not, that the domination of the conscious by the unconscious extended, not merely to a few exceptional individuals, but to all human beings, that the "big three behind the scenes" are not respecters of persons, and dominate us all, even including that *sanctum sanctorum* of freedom, our conscious will. To be sure, the domination by the unconscious in the case of "normal" individuals is somewhat more benevolent than the tyranny and despotism exercised in neurotic cases, and therefore the former have evoked less comment; but the principle remains in all cases the same: the unconscious is the master of every fate and the captain of every soul.

We speak of a machine turning out good products most of the time but every once in a while it turns out a "lemon." We do not, of course, hold the product responsible for this, but the machine, and via the machine, its maker. Is it silly to extend to inanimate objects the idea of responsibility? Of course. But is it any less so to employ the notion in speaking of human creatures? Are not the two kinds of cases analogous in countless important ways? Occasionally a child turns out badly too, even when his environment and training are the same as that of his brothers and sisters who turn out "all right." He is the "bad penny." His acts of rebellion against parental discipline in adult life (such as the case of the gambler, already cited) are traceable to early experiences of real or fancied denial of infantile wishes. Sometimes the denial has been real, though many denials are absolutely necessary if the child is to grow up to observe the common decencies of civilized life; sometimes, if the child has an unusual quantity of narcissism, every event that occurs is interpreted by him as a denial of his wishes, and

[12] A. J. Ayer, "Freedom and Necessity," *Polemic* (September–October 1946), pp. 40–43.

nothing a parent could do, even granting every humanly possible wish, would help. In any event, the later neurosis can be attributed to this. Can the person himself be held responsible? Hardly. If he engages in activities which are a menace to society, he must be put into prison, of course, but responsibility is another matter. The time when the events occurred which rendered his neurotic behavior inevitable was a time long before he was capable of thought and decision. As an adult, he is a victim of a world he never made—only this world is inside him.

What about the children who turn out "all right?" All we can say is that "it's just lucky for them" that what happened to their unfortunate brother didn't happen to them; *through no virtue of their own* they are not doomed to the life of unconscious guilt, expiation, conscious depression, terrified ego-gestures for the appeasement of a tyrannical super-ego, that he is. The machine turned them out with a minimum of damage. But if the brother cannot be blamed for his evils, neither can they be praised for their good; unless, of course, we should blame people for what is not their fault, and praise them for lucky accidents.

We all agree that machines turn out "lemons," we all agree that nature turns out misfits in the realm of biology—the blind, the crippled, the diseased; but we hesitate to include the realm of the personality, for here, it seems, is the last retreat of our dignity as human beings. Our ego can endure anything but this; this island at least must remain above the encroaching flood. But may not precisely the same analysis be made here also? Nature turns out psychological "lemons" too, in far greater quantities than any other kind; and indeed all of us are "lemons" in some respect or other, the difference being one of degree. Some of us are lucky enough not to have a gambling-neurosis or criminotic tendencies or masochistic mother-attachment or overdimensional repetition-compulsion to make our lives miserable, but most of our actions, those usually considered the most important, are unconsciously dominated just the same. And, if a neurosis may be likened to a curse of God, let those of us, the elect, who are enabled to enjoy a measure of life's happiness without the hell-fire of neurotic guilt, take this, not as our own achievement, but simply for what it is—a gift of God.

Let us, however, quit metaphysics and put the situation schematically in the form of a deductive argument.

1. An occurrence over which we had no control is something we cannot be held responsible for.

2. Events E, occurring during our babyhood, were events over which we had no control.

3. Therefore events E were events which we cannot be held responsible for.

4. But if there is something we cannot be held responsible for, neither can we be held responsible for something that inevitably results from it.

5. Events E have as inevitable consequence Neurosis N, which in turn has as inevitable consequence Behavior B.

6. Since N is the inevitable consequence of E and B is the inevitable consequence of N, B is the inevitable consequence of E.

7. Hence, not being responsible for E, we cannot be responsible for B.

In Samuel Butler's Utopian satire *Erewhon* there occurs the following passage, in which a judge is passing sentence on a prisoner:

> It is all very well for you to say that you came of unhealthy parents, and had a severe accident in your childhood which permanently undermined your constitution; excuses such as these are the ordinary refuge of the criminal; but they cannot for one moment be listened to by the ear of justice. I am not here to enter upon curious metaphysical questions as to the origin of this or that—questions to which there would be no end were their introduction once tolerated, and which would result in throwing the only guilt on the tissues of the primordial cell, or on the elementary gases. There is no question of how you came to be wicked, but only this—namely, are you wicked or not? This has been decided in the affirmative, neither can I hesitate for a single moment to say that it has been decided justly. You are a bad and dangerous person, and stand branded in the eyes of your fellow countrymen with one of the most heinous known offenses.[13]

As moralists read this passage, they may perhaps nod with approval. But the joke is on them. The sting comes when we realize what the crime is for which the prisoner is being sentenced: namely, consumption. The defendant is reminded that during the previous year he was sentenced for aggravated bronchitis, and is warned that he should profit from experience in the future. Butler is employing here his familiar method of presenting some human tendency (in this case, holding people responsible for what isn't their fault) to a ridiculous extreme and thereby reducing it to absurdity.

Assuming the main conclusions of this paper to be true, is there any room left for freedom?

This, of course, all depends on what we mean by "freedom." In the senses suggested at the beginning of this paper, there are countless free acts, and unfree ones as well. When "free" means "uncompelled," and only external compulsion is admitted, again there are countless free acts. But now we have extended the notion of compulsion to include determination by unconscious forces. With this sense in mind, our question is, "With the concept of compulsion thus extended, and in the light of present psychoanalytic knowledge, is there any freedom left in human behavior?"

If practicising psychoanalysts were asked this question, there is little doubt that their answer would be along the following lines: they would say that they were not accustomed to using the term "free" at all, but that if they had to suggest a criterion for distinguishing the free from the unfree, they would say that a person's freedom is present *in inverse propor-*

[13] Samuel Butler, *Erewhon* (Modern Library edition), p. 107.

tion to his neuroticism; in other words, the more his acts are determined by a *malevolent* unconscious, the less free he is. Thus they would speak of *degrees* of freedom. They would say that as a person is cured of his neurosis, he becomes more free—free to realize capabilities that were blocked by the neurotic affliction. The psychologically well-adjusted individual is in this sense comparatively the most free. Indeed, those who are cured of mental disorders are sometimes said to have *regained their freedom:* they are freed from the tyranny of a malevolent unconscious which formerly exerted as much of a domination over them as if they had been the abject slaves of a cruel dictator.

But suppose one says that a person is free only to the extent that his acts are *not unconsciously determined at all,* be they unconscious benevolent *or* malevolent? If this is the criterion, psychoanalysts would say, most human behavior cannot be called free at all: our impulses and volitions having to do with our basic attitudes toward life, whether we are optimists or pessimists, tough-minded or tender-minded, whether our tempers are quick or slow, whether we are "naturally self-seeking" or "naturally benevolent" (and *all the acts consequent upon these things*), what things annoy us, whether we take to blondes or brunettes, old or young, whether we become philosophers or artists or businessmen—all this has its basis in the unconscious. If people generally call most acts free, it is not because they believe that compelled acts should be called free, it is rather through not knowing how large a proportion of our acts actually are compelled. Only the comparatively "vanilla-flavored" aspects of our lives—such as our behavior toward people who don't really matter to us—are exempted from this rule.

These, I think, are the two principal criteria for distinguishing freedom from the lack of it which we might set up on the basis of psychoanalytic knowledge. Conceivably we might set up others. In every case, of course, it remains trivially true that "it all depends on how we choose to use the word." The facts are what they are, regardless of what words we choose for labeling them. But if we choose to label them in a way which is not in accord with what human beings, however vaguely, have long had in mind in applying these labels, as we would be doing if we labeled as "free" many acts which we know as much about as we now do through modern psychoanalytic methods, then we shall only be manipulating words to mislead our fellow creatures.

Moral Freedom in Recent Ethics*

H. D. LEWIS [1]

I

THE PROBLEM of moral freedom has not been conspicuous in recent ethics. This is surprising. For the ideas which present it in its most formidable shape, the ideas of ought, responsibility, and of ultimate praise or blame, have been given much prominence in recent ethical controversy.

There have, it is true, been some notable discussions of moral freedom. Among these are Volume 3 of the *Ethics* of Nicolai Hartmann, Professor Broad's inaugural lecture, *Determinism, Indeterminism, and Libertarianism*, the middle chapters of Professor C. A. Campbell's *Scepticism and Construction* and the same author's inaugural lecture, *In Defence of Free Will*. Some papers on the same topic, such as Professor A. K. Stout's *Free Will and Responsibility*,[2] and Mr. R. E. Hobart's *Free Will as Involving Determination*,[3] both incidentally putting the case for determinism, have appeared from time to time. But these are exceptions, and they seem right off the main lines of recent ethical controversy.

More truly indicative of the present position is the fact that the problem of freedom is barely mentioned in two of the most influential ethical books of recent years. Professor G. E. Moore's *Principia Ethica* [4] and Sir David Ross's *The Right and the Good*. The lack is not felt very sharply in the former case. For Moore is much more concerned with the idea of value than with that of rightness or obligation. In this work he takes it that right can be defined in terms of a relation to goodness,[5] and the values which seem to impress him most are those of aesthetic enjoyment and personal affection.[6] But *The Right and the Good*, stressing the uniqueness and

---

* Reprinted by kind permission of the author and the editors from the *Proceedings of the Aristotelian Society*, 47, 1947–48.

[1] This essay is also included in his book, *Morals and Revelation*, published by George Allen and Unwin, 1951.

[2] *Proceedings of the Aristotelian Society*, 37, 1937–38 [pp. 537 ff. this volume].

[3] *Mind*, 1934.

[4] The problem of freedom is touched upon in the course of discussing Kant's view of the "autonomy of the Practical Reason" on page 127 of *Principia Ethica*. It is not discussed at all in *The Right and the Good*.

[5] *Principia Ethica*, p. 18 [p. 78 this volume], cf. p. 147.

[6] op. cit. p. 18.

ultimacy of duty, seems to call especially for a discussion of freedom which is not forthcoming.

In his later book, *Ethics*, Moore gives the ideas of right and wrong a more independent status; in support of his view that the acts which *are* right are those which produce most good, although this is not what we *mean* by calling them right, Moore is also induced to insist that the judgments which we pass upon motives are a different sort from those in which actions are pronounced right or wrong,[7] and that moral praise or blame may turn upon the worth of the motive in a way that leaves the rightness of an action unaffected. But Moore does not draw a perfectly sharp distinction here. All that he maintains is that a man's praiseworthiness does not depend "*entirely* or *always* upon his motive,"[8] this being, furthermore, apparently due to the fact that moral praise and condemnation are regarded as utilitarian devices for ensuring right conduct.[9] In consequence, although the positions we have noted lead in the *Ethics* to a short chapter on freedom, it is not strange that the author is uncertain whether freedom of choice is required in ethics,[10] and believes in the main that, if it is, it must be compatible with "the principle that everything has a cause."[11] The ideas of responsibility and obligation do not stand out very distinctly as unique ethical conceptions. But the matter is far otherwise in the case of Ross. He is concerned especially with the ideas of rightness and obligation, and, setting himself to oppose any utilitarian account of either rightness or moral worth, he contends strongly for the ultimacy of both these ethical conceptions. We should therefore expect his arguments to take a very close account of the problem of freedom. But this is not in fact the case.

In his more recent volume, *The Foundations of Ethics*, Ross does indeed devote a chapter to this topic. But he turns to the task with obvious reluctance." No discussion of fundamental questions of ethics," he declares, "would be complete without some discussion of the problem of free will; and I must therefore say something about the subject, even if I do not feel that I have anything very new to contribute."[12] The problem, we are told, "has been once more brought to the front by the appearance among physi-

---

[7] *Ethics*, p. 184–185.

[8] *Ethics*, p. 189.

[9] Stressing the distinction between "what is right or wrong, on the one hand, and what is morally praiseworthy or blameworthy on the other," Moore declares: "What we should naturally say of a man whose action turns out badly owing to some unforeseen accident when he had every reason to expect that it would turn out well, is not that his action was right, but rather that he *is not to blame*. And it may be fully admitted that in such a case he really *ought* not to be blamed; *since blame cannot possibly serve any good purpose, and would be likely to do harm*" (*Ethics*, p. 193—last italics mine). Compare p. 189: we ought to blame a man less when there is "less need to deter him by blame." See also pp. 215 and 216.

[10] The uncertainty has since been removed. See G. E. Moore's "Reply to my Critics" in *The Philosophy of G. E. Moore*, p. 624.

[11] Moore's admission of perplexity as to the sense in which this is possible (*Ethics*, p. 221) is repeated in *The Philosophy of G. E. Moore*, p. 626.

[12] *Foundations of Ethics*, p. 208.

cists of the doctrine known as that of indeterminacy." [13] But surely the problem should have been brought to the front for Ross by the prominence to which he himself has helped to bring the idea of obligation in recent ethics. He finds it easy to show that the doctrine of indeterminacy in physics has little relevance to any ethical question. [14] The rest of the chapter is mainly concerned with the alleged "intuition of freedom" and does not bear very closely on strictly ethical matters. [15] The crucial question of freedom and *responsibility* is put off to a few pages at the end, [16] and they bring us to the confession:

"In remorse we are acutely aware that, whatever our outward circumstances may have been, we have ourselves been to blame for giving way to them where a person of better character would not have done so. I cannot pretend that this satisfies the whole of our natural thought about responsibility, but I think that in claiming more, in claiming that a moral agent can act independently of his character, we should be claiming a metaphysical impossibility.

"A philosophical genius may some day arise who will succeed in reconciling our natural thought about freedom and responsibility with acceptance of the law of causality; but I must admit that no existing discussion seems to be very successful in doing so." [17]

No passage could typify better the attitude usually adopted today towards the problem of freedom. This, it is thought, is the problem which offers least prospect of solution; it is here that we are most prone to "argue about it and about" to no purpose; the deadlock is complete. In the meantime there are other fields where our labours will not go unrewarded, there are problems which will repay discussion. Such are the problems of "the nature of goodness," of "rightness and obligation," of "the relation of the morality of actions to their rightness" or of "motive to intention," of "*prima facie* rightness to one's full obligation," the problem of "subjective" and "objective" duty, and of utilitarian versus intuitionist views of duty. These are problems which have been very keenly discussed of late, not only in such books as those I have instanced, but also in a spate of most acute papers in philosophical journals. In the meantime the problem of

---

[13] op. cit. p. 208.

[14] He also shows that it is fraught with much confusion.

[15] See below, section III.

[16] Even these are mainly concerned with a view that Ross rejects, namely, Mr. Wisdom's view that the idea of pre-existence affects the problem. [The reference is to John Wisdom's *Problems of Mind and Matter*, Cambridge University Press, chap. 8 —Ed.]

[17] *Foundations of Ethics*, p. 251. It is significant also that the volume closes with the following words: "It seems to me that something like half of our ordinary thinking on moral questions implies a belief in the indetermination of the will, and something like half a belief in its determination; and I have neither found elsewhere nor discovered by my own reflections any adequate solution of this difficulty. But the truth can never be inconsistent with itself, and we may hope that better thinking will in the long run remove this apparent contradiction, as sound thinking has already removed many others."

freedom is postponed or, at best, set aside for quite separate treatment, often very perfunctory. But this, I submit, and it is the main contention of this paper, is just what we cannot do. It would be foolish to complain that philosophers do not provide a solution of the problem of freedom; on the contrary one admires the frankness with which they confess themselves bewildered by it; if they see no way to mitigate our perplexity, then we must say: "It is unfortunate but there is no help for it." But what does seem equally plain is that if there is uncertainty as to what we should think about moral freedom, if we remain on the horns of the dilemma, then it is equally impossible to make progress with many other fundamental ethical problems. In particular, some view about freedom is presupposed in any attitude we adopt towards the question of obligation; if we suspend judgment in the one case we should do so in the other. The problem of freedom is not one we can isolate, it is essentially bound up with others; and this, I think, a prime source of confusion in recent ethics. For while there is little direct attack on the problem of freedom, the problem itself winds itself subtly in and out of arguments which take little clear cognisance of it. These prove on examination to be essentially attempts to fit the idea of moral choice into a view of conduct which, as I hope to show, does not admit of choice in the way required by a "categorical imperative." This will be evident if we now turn to a topic which has been much discussed in recent years.

II

This is the celebrated distinction between "the morality of the action and the rightness of the act." And the first point that I should like to make is that, in one sense or other, a distinction of this kind seems to me unavoidable. One crucial factor here is that of the fallibility of ethical judgments. It seems beyond all reasonable controversy that we may be mistaken as to what is our duty.[18] All cases of moral perplexity and all attempts to educate and enlighten our own consciences or those of other persons presuppose this. There is therefore clearly some sense in which it is possible for us to be fully conscientious, to be loyal to our duty and worthy of the highest praise, and at the same time to be acting in a way that is wrong. May we not also do what is "materially" right for "the wrong reason"? What is altogether involved in loyalty to duty is another matter; we need not decide that issue to see that moral worth must be divorced from doing what is right in some sense of those terms. This paradox, as Moore shows so well,[19] is not in the least vicious; and it is quite ineradicable.

But as we have also suggested, the present argument commits us to no special view of the criterion of moral worth. Does this depend on our

---

[18] There is, however, much reluctance to admit this without ambiguity. See my "Obedience to Conscience," *Mind*, July, 1945.

[19] *Ethics*, Chapter V.

motives or on some free and "unmotivated" willing? The issue remains open so far as the independence of moral worth on "material" or outward rightness is concerned. For what this mainly establishes is that moral ignorance is not a moral defect.

But there is a further argument that is used in support of the distinction between moral worth and rightness. And it is this that touches our present discussion closely. It is the argument that we cannot control our motives and that, therefore, we are only under an obligation to do a certain act, not to do it from a particular motive. Ross has much recourse to this argument, both in *The Right and the Good* [20] where the distinction we are considering now finds its most celebrated statement, and in *The Foundations of Ethics*.[21]

Before indicating what I think is the real implication of this argument I should like to turn first to the question whether it is true that we cannot control a motive.

It seems plain to me that Ross has the best of it here. Is it not quite certain, as he says, that we cannot feel sorrow at will or summon up a feeling of benevolence as required? We do feel sorrow or we don't, we feel amiably disposed or we do not; there is nothing to be done in the matter at the moment of acting. Our feelings and desires are what they are, that is all we can say. Admittedly a person may set himself in the way of having certain feelings in the future, although this, as we shall see, is not quite so straightforward a matter as it seems. But there is clearly some sense in which a feeling can be cultivated; the way I act now will affect my character and modify my motives in the future. But it seems plain to me that I cannot command a certain feeling immediately; much less am I able "at a moment's notice to make it effective in stimulating me to act." [22]

This matter has not, however, been so plain to others, and several writers have joined issue with Ross at this point. One of the best known of his opponents is H. W. B. Joseph in his *Some Problems in Ethics*, a book completed before the actual publication of *The Right and the Good*. The position which Joseph takes up is not easy to grasp. The substance of it, if I understand aright, is as follows. If I perform an act to which I am prompted by a motive such as "gratitude, affection, or benevolence" there is "a kind of goodness" [23] in the act which can also be regarded as the ground of its rightness. This is not the only way in which an act may be right. Usually the ground of rightness is productivity of good results.[24] But rightness may sometimes be due to motives in the way described. Certain acts ought to be done because of the motives from which, if done, they will be done. There is, moreover, one very special kind of motive always available here. It is "a sort of urgency" to act in a certain way arising from "the conscious-

[20] p. 5 [p. 166 this volume].
[21] pp. 45-46, cf. Chapter VI, especially p. 116.
[22] *The Right and the Good*, p. 5 [p. 166 this volume].
[23] *Some Problems in Ethics*, p. 47.
[24] op. cit. p. 28.

ness of a determinate obligation to do this in this situation." [25] This consciousness need not be very explicit, it may prompt a man to do something, "even without his saying to himself that he ought to do it," [26] and it must not be confused with "the consciousness of duty in general." [27] When therefore we review the possibilities before us in some situation, or seek to resolve some case of perplexity, we may find that a certain course should be followed because the special feeling of "urgency" to take it is being "preferred to or prevails over the contrary inclination." [28] Motive here makes the act right, but if we do that act because of the rightness which belongs to it in this way there will be moral worth as well as rightness in our action. "I shall have acted morally as well as rightly." [29] It seems therefore that I do control my motives to the extent of choosing to do (or not to do) the act which will have the right (or shall we say the right-making?) motive, and thus, in maintaining that we have duties to do certain acts from certain motives, we need not be deterred by the objection that "it is not in my power to feel a particular motive which I am not feeling, nor therefore to act from it." [30]

There is much here that calls for comment. [31] But what concerns us at the moment is the contention that, in choosing to do one act rather than another, the motive from which the act is done can be regarded as part of what I choose. If motive is given its usual meaning of some desire or feeling which moves us to act, the position is flatly contradictory. [32] It puts the cart before the horse in very shameless fashion. And this is indeed brought out by Joseph's own argument. For if I am to choose to do a certain act from a certain motive there must be some other motive which determines that choice; this, on Joseph's view, would be the "motive of duty." Now it is possible for an act to proceed from a combination of motives. But in that case we either think of one motive reinforcing another or of a number of desires pointing to the same conduct at the same time, any one of these being in itself stronger than any elements in my character which prompt me to a contrary action. We could then say that, if one of these desires were absent, the act would still be necessitated by one or more other desires

---

[25] op. cit. p. 50.
[26] op. cit. p. 50.
[27] op. cit. p. 50.
[28] op. cit. p. 51.
[29] op. cit. p. 48.
[30] op. cit. p. 46.
[31] For example, the question whether the "sort of urgency" envisaged by Joseph can mislead. If it cannot, and if it is bound up with the general sense of obligation, how can we ever be in moral perplexity—as we often are? Ross seems to me to put matters very conclusively when he observes, in his reply to Joseph, that the "urgency" he describes presupposes the belief that the act is right and cannot therefore be regarded as the ground of its rightness (*Foundations of Ethics*, p. 132).
[32] This was one of the main points stressed by Professor H. A. Prichard in his much-discussed article, "Does Moral Philosophy Rest on a Mistake"? *Mind*, 1912, p. 27. [Prichard's essay is reprinted on pp. 149 ff. of this volume, and the reference is to a passage on pp. 153–4.]

which point to it. But in that case the desires in question would need to be independent of one another. And this is just what Joseph's account does not provide. Neither, clearly, is he thinking of cases where devotion to duty is not effective without support from some other motive. The agent is presumed to have resolved to do his duty once its nature is plain to him. And so what we have, on Joseph's view, is a very curious double determination of the same act. For a person to be determined to do act "A" by the motive of duty, one has to presuppose his being already determined to do it by the motive of benevolence or "urgency." And this seems to me an altogether impossible position.

The downright inconsistency of Joseph's theory is somewhat obscured by a proneness of the author to speak of motive, on occasion (but on occasion only), not as a feeling or desire moving an agent to act in a certain way, but as a "feeling expressed" in action. So conceived, motive may well be the justification of right conduct. For a suitable expression of a feeling of affection, to take Joseph's instance,[33] may lead to a deepening of the feeling itself and enhance a close personal relationship in many ways. But here we are looking to the effects of actions. And the fact that an act may become a duty on account of its motive in the present unusual sense gives no justification for the very different view, but one which Joseph seems mainly anxious to hold, that it may be our duty to act from a certain motive in the normal meaning of the term. Against *this* view Ross's objection seems unanswerable. We cannot, in the moment of action, alter the balance of our feelings and desires.

The same point must be stressed in answer to a more recent critic of Ross, Mr. George Hughes. He takes up the subject in his paper on *Motive and Duty* [34] where he stresses especially the distinction between an impulsive or "involuntary act" and a willed or "fully deliberate act." In the latter case the self is aware of a number of desires or "potential motives" together, and "identifies itself with" one of them. The relation of act to motive is not therefore, in rational conduct, a simple example of efficient causation. It is not "diadic" but "triadic," for the self intervenes to "adopt" or "sanction" a motive and "give it its act." And if we leave out for the present, as I wish to do, the strictly libertarian view that there may be actions not determined by motives at all, the substance of Hughes's contention seems beyond dispute. It was a major contribution of the maligned idealists to the metaphysics of morals to show that the desires of a rational being oppose one another, not as isolated impulses with an independent force of their own, but as taken up into the unity of the self as a whole. But however important we regard this matter in itself, and however appropriate the terms "selection", "adoption", etc. may be in this context, the fact remains that I cannot, in any final sense, will my desires to be other than they are at a particular moment. They are as they are, and those which prevail, prevail.

[33] *Some Problems in Ethics*, p. 47.
[34] *Mind*, October, 1944, pp. 314–332.

When, therefore, I choose to do act "A" rather than act "B" to which I am also drawn, whatever else may be said of this choice, and we shall return to its difficulties shortly, it is plain that the motive which leads to the act has an ascendancy which I cannot alter at the moment of acting. It does not come immediately within the control of my will, however the self, *in other ways*, may be involved in its victory.

In addition to the general claim that the "adoption" of a desire by the self, in the process noted, provides the control required for responsibility, Mr. Hughes gives several examples of the way a suitable direction of attention may alter the balance of "potential motives." A dentist who has to perform a painful operation on a patient against whom he has a grudge may tell himself that it would be shameful to be moved to act by a desire to cause pain. He comes thus to act from the more worthy motive of doing what the case in hand requires, the amount of pain inflicted remaining the same. There seems thus to be a change in motive only. In other examples the agent is thought to evoke a new motive by suitable reflections. But there is nothing here which Ross would deny, for the examples afford nothing different from the cultivation of motives which he admits. That the cultivation may be almost instantaneous in some cases does not affect the main issue. What the dentist does is not directly to summon up a motive but to direct his thought in a way that brings about a rapid change of motive. And this is admitted by Hughes himself when he notes that, in this case, "two acts are involved," [35] the self-admonition of the dentist and the subsequent operation. The problem of evoking motives also draws attention from the main issue, for the question is not whether I can summon up a motive which I do not feel at all, but whether, with the aid of new motives or without them, I can alter the balance of my desires in the moment of action. The words "summon up" may be misleading here. But there can be no serious doubt about Ross's intention. The important point is that there is never a direct control of desire. We are thus more likely to find the weak point in Ross's defences if we concentrate on the relation between the predominant motive and the alleged choice of action.

And here the arguments of Hughes and Joseph and others who take a similar view, although not successful in their immediate aim of showing that the motives of actions can be controlled in a way which admits of there being duties to act from certain motives, have none the less an ominous bearing on Ross's position as a whole. The thought behind the positions we have noted is that motive and act stand in a peculiarly intimate relation. Joseph goes so far as to deny that they can be considered apart,[36] action being for him a "self-realising process." [37] This is, no doubt, an

---

[35] *Mind*, 1944, p. 320.

[36] "But no act exists except in the doing of it, and in the doing of it there is a motive; and you cannot separate the doing of it from the motive without substituting for action in the moral sense action in the physical, mere movements of bodies." *Some Problems in Ethics*, p. 38.

[37] op. cit. p. 55.

extreme view. And Ross has not found it difficult to meet the criticism as it stands. In his reply to Joseph he observes, first, that an act, considered in abstraction from the motive, is not a mere physical change: "Besides motive and a physical change there is a third thing—the setting oneself to bring about a change." [38] But this never happens, on Ross's view, except as we are moved by some motive: "all intentional acts are motived acts." [39] The real question is then whether we can "*consider* the act independently of the motive." [40] Ross maintains emphatically that we can, just as the shape of a body may be considered apart from its size, although the one would not exist without the other. And we have ourselves endorsed one important reason for adjudging rightness independently of motive. But it still seems true that the relation of a motive to an act is of such a peculiarly intimate kind that, if I could not have willed "at a moment's notice" to have another motive, *my act could not be other than it is either.* In so far as I cannot finally control the one I cannot control the other. Ross's argument thus proves too much—for his theory. For if he is to argue that "ought" has no application to motives because "we cannot desire a certain end at will" [41] it seems to follow also that ought has no application to conduct in any regard.

As an *argumentum ad hominem* the contentions of the writers we have noted have therefore considerable force. As Professor Field observes, also writing in criticism of Ross, "In any sense in which we can choose what action we shall do, we can choose what motive we shall act from." [42] In his reply, Ross contends that we choose to do an act "on the assumption" that the motive for doing it will be forthcoming when the time comes to do the act, as we may choose to walk down the High Street on the assumption that the High Street will still exist "when the time comes at which I mean to take the walk." [43] This argument I find very unconvincing. For how can we be thought to make a choice at all except in so far as, and at the time when, we are moved by the motive to do the act? Of course we do speak in a rough way of deciding to do something some time in advance of doing it. But this is a way of speaking which requires very careful analysis. As long as it is open to me not to do something, and it must be so on the present assumption until the motive is forthcoming, I cannot strictly be said to have chosen to do it. What does happen, however, is that I am so certain that I shall continue to desire to do something when the time comes that I take certain steps beforehand to facilitate the execution of it. I may also put the issue out of my mind on the assumption that it will be plain to me when the time comes. But to say more than this, to speak as if one could actually choose to perform a certain act beforehand on the assump-

[38] *Foundations of Ethics*, p. 128.
[39] op. cit. p. 127.
[40] op. cit. p. 127.
[41] *Foundations of Ethics*, p. 46.
[42] "Kant's First Moral Principle," *Mind*, 1932, p. 33.
[43] *Foundations of Ethics*, p. 138.

tion that the motive will be forthcoming, involves the same sort of distortion of the relation of act to motive as that which speaks of choosing to act from a certain motive. How can there be a choice except in so far as the motive moves us to make it?

Field's contention then stands. From it he draws the conclusion that we *can* act from one motive rather than another, and that therefore we may (and do) have a duty to do so. But it seems to me quite certain that Ross is right in holding that we cannot choose to act from a certain motive, and that, therefore, we must draw a very different conclusion from Field, and one that Ross himself is very far from drawing. It is that the idea of obligation cannot be fitted at any point into the normal view of conduct as the expression of motive and character. When, therefore, moral philosophers debate as to whether rightness qualifies "acts" or "actions from certain motives," they are bound to drive one another round in an endless circuit. Both sides to the controversy appeal to a postulate which has no bearing on conduct as conceived in terms of their problem. It would thus have been better *to ask at the start* in what way the idea of obligation presupposes freedom. A great deal of ingenious but misplaced argumentation might then have been avoided.

III

This is, indeed, evident without going outside the writings of Sir David Ross himself. For the difficulties which beset his side of the controversy we have just discussed seem to be emphasised by his own account of the alleged "intuition of freedom." The view which he presents as adequate both to a determinist view of conduct and to the sense of freedom which we have in the moment of action, is the common view of freedom as "self-determination." The distinction between mental and physical causation is stressed, and we are shown that "what choice depends upon, and reveals, is not the strength of isolated desires but the trend of the whole character, of the whole system of more or less permanent desires." [44] "It is the universe of my desires that determines my action, and not the strongest single desire." [45] This is of great importance for the understanding of desire and character. But if it also gives us the freedom that is most distinctive of human action we should expect this to be the freedom which makes us morally accountable. In that case the freedom required by responsibility, and presupposed in the maxim "I ought, therefore I can," concerns the inner determination of conduct in the way of motive and character, and not the more outward aspect of actions to which Ross restricts the ideas of "ought" and "rightness" when the problem of "I ought, therefore I can" becomes insistent.

This suggests a much closer relation between the idea of obligation

[44] *Foundations of Ethics*, p. 228.
[45] *Foundations of Ethics*, p. 229.

and the idea of moral worth than Ross is normally prepared to allow. Admittedly there must be *a* sense of obligation in which the discharge of it is independent of the worth of the will. For, as we have noted, it is possible to do what is "materially" wrong with the best intention. And in this sense also rightness presupposes freedom of a sort. For we never ask of any act whether it is right except on the assumption that it is an act which it is possible for us to do; no one asks "is it right to swim the Atlantic?" [46] But if the idea of obligation is to be retained in any ultimate sense, if there is to be a true "categorical imperative," it seems plain that there must also be a sense in which doing what is right is immediately tantamount to having moral value, there must be an internal loyalty to duty (or betrayal of it) on which the worth of the will directly depends. This is the common presumption of ordinary thought, and the conviction that ordinary thought is thoroughly justified here, has been the main cause of the dissatisfaction felt at Ross's divorce of obligation from moral goodness.

The point at which Ross asserts most emphatically that the conditions of moral worth are other than the conditions of doing one's duty—in any sense—is in regard to the much-discussed "infinite regress argument." [47] He holds that it is contradictory to say "You ought to act from the sense of duty" because this must mean "It is my duty to do act 'A' from the sense that it is my duty to do Act 'A.'" But as has been pointed out by Professor L. A. Reid [48] and Mr. George Hughes [49] there is no contradiction here except on the supposition that we are using the term duty in the same sense in both parts of the proposition. That the meaning of duty which will resolve the paradox is a duty to act from a certain motive—in Hughes's version to do the act which seems to the agent right (the subjectively right act) "from the belief (or sense) that it is objectively right" [50]—seems to me also much mistaken for the reasons adduced above. But it seems none the less plain that if we are to speak of duty at all there is a sense of doing one's duty, and that much the most important, which is distinct from any form of rightness described by Ross, including one sense of doing what seems to us right; and that is the doing of what is right *qua* right. And it is the freedom involved here, that is, in that resolution to do one's duty *as such* on which moral worth depends directly, that mainly matters in ethics. The problem of freedom thus arises directly from the fact that we are subject to moral praise or blame. It is a postulate of moral worth (if that carries with it genuine praise or blame) *in precisely the same way* as it is a postulate of duty, and it must, therefore, qualify conduct *directly in that aspect of it*

---

[46] Some critics of Ross have assumed that he regards rightness as standing in no relation whatsoever to the agent. I think it is for this reason that Mr. Falk, in his "Obligation and Rightness" in *Philosophy*, July, 1945, wonders whether "fittingness of acts to situations" is "the description of anything real at all," p. 146.

[47] *Foundations of Ethics*, p. 119. *The Right and the Good*, p. 5.

[48] *Creative Morality*, p. 46.

[49] *Mind*, 1944, p. 332.

[50] op. cit. p. 324.

in respect of which we hold ourselves open to blame. But, according to Ross, our "actions are morally good when and because they proceed from certain motives" [51] or as "manifestations of character"—"the larger and grander bearer of moral goodness." [52] It is character and desire, therefore, that should be free. By suggesting this and turning attention to the inner determination of the will, the view of freedom as self-determination affords a corrective to Ross's general account of obligation. But it also tosses us on to another horn of a dilemma. For Ross has also argued, quite convincingly as it seems to me, that we are not able to control our motives in the way required by moral obligation.

We are brought to a similar impasse when we consider two other main considerations adduced by Ross in his account of the intuition of freedom.

First he stresses the power that we have to "cause any one of two or more changes in the state of affairs." [53] This will sometimes be a "change in the condition of our own mind; but far more often a change of something in the physical world," such changes being "caused by first causing a change in the state of one's own body." [54] It seems beyond dispute that we have this power, whatever the final account to be given of the relation between mind and body. We find from experience that we are able to move about and to lift and carry various objects. Such powers are of course very limited, and illness or death may immediately deprive us of them. But life would not be possible at all, it would not be recognizable for the thing it is, if our actions never produced the effects we intended. So much is plain. It may also be allowed that the control of mind over body involves genuine activity as distinct from mere necessary connection, it is "immanent" and not "transeunt" causation. But does this explain the supposed intuition of freedom? If it does should we not conclude that the intuition is illusory in the extreme? For it gives us no sort of freedom which is distinctive of human action. It has no bearing on the inner springs of volition, and if it were the decisive factor in our assurance of freedom, then, incidentally, it would be hard to see what need there is to stress the unity of desire and character, etc., in connection with the problem. The freedom to "effect changes in the state of affairs" belongs in fact to irrational creatures as well as to human beings. But any freedom in which we are seriously interested when considering the nature of man must be freedom which characterises distinctively human activities. This is especially the case when we consider moral freedom. For the power to do what we purpose can have little significance here.[55] It seems quite an elementary principle in ethics that conduct is not to be appraised in terms of its actual conse-

[51] *Foundations of Ethics*, p. 290.
[52] op. cit. p. 293.
[53] op. cit. p. 231.
[54] op. cit. p. 231.
[55] But compare A. E. Taylor, *Elements of Metaphysics*, Bk. IV, ch. iv., and H. Gomperz, "Individual, Collective and Social Responsibility," *International Journal of Ethics*, Vol. XLIX, p. 329.

quences. This principle is, moreover, quite fundamental to Ross's account of moral goodness and rightness, and he himself insists that "the question whether the mind can control the body is irrelevant to the question of the freedom of the will. . . . Suppose that a man had, without knowing it, lost the power of speech. He could still set himself, or make the effort, to tell the truth, or alternatively set himself to tell a lie. . . . Morally, both the act and the decision to act are just the same as they would be if the control over the body still existed." [56] It seems, therefore, that the real issue is whether we are free in "setting ourselves" to do one thing or the other, but once the enquiry proceeds in this way to the more distinctive features of action which make it what it is for human beings, is it not also plain that we cannot omit the inner determination of choice in considering whether or not it is free?

Ross, finally, assures us that "possibility is always related to a judger, and that to say 'so and so may happen' is just to say 'I don't know that it won't.'" [57] Here again there would normally be little to dispute. For when we make judgments such as "It may rain tomorrow," we do not for a moment think that there is here an open possibility in *rerum natura*. What we mean is that the conditions, so far as we have been able to ascertain them, do not preclude rain. As a psychological, in distinction from the merely logical, condition of making such a judgment of possibility we must also be aware of conditions which make it likely that it will rain; the possibility must be a "real" one. But both these conditions are assured in the case of character and conduct without recourse to libertarian views. For even in anticipating immediate actions of our own there is always some possibility of error. "The situation is never *exactly* like any in which we have been in the past," [58] and hidden elements in our character may reveal themselves without warning. "Thus so long as *any* interval, however short, separates the present moment from that at which the act will be done, we do not now *know* what the relative strength of the different motives will be when the latter moment arrives; and therefore do not *know* what we shall do, though we may of course think it highly probable that we shall do a certain act rather than any other." [59]

About this there need be no argument. We may also allow that possibility in this sense is of much practical importance in certain regards. No one is likely to put out his best effort in some undertaking if he is either too confident or too despondent about the prospect of success. To quote Ross's analogy, "Of the candidates in an examination, those who are most likely to make the needed effort are neither those who feel sure that they will pass nor those who feel sure that they will fail, but those who know that they do not know whether they will pass or fail." [60] This has its

[56] *Foundations of Ethics*, p. 234.
[57] op. cit. p. 235.
[58] *Foundations of Ethics*, p. 236.
[59] op. cit. p. 236.

parallel in most spheres of interest. And the determinist can, with complete consistency, urge that possibility in the present sense is "just that which is needed to induce us to keep our moral armour in the best possible repair." [61]

But can this be the possibility that makes us responsible, is it in this way that we are to interpret the maxim "I ought therefore I can"? Surely not, for that is not a possibility which actions share with any and every event. It is a possibility required in a special manner by moral praise or blame, and are we to say that the *rationale* of praise or blame is mainly to be found in unavoidable limits of finite knowledge? Does responsibility rest on no foundation more secure than ignorance? It would be more dignified to repudiate our responsibility altogether than to cling to so unsubstantial a replica of it as that. Moreover, we hold ourselves accountable, if at all, quite as much for our actions in the past, where the outcome is no longer in doubt, as for those we have yet to perform and whose nature is uncertain. In other words, the freedom for which we have a serious concern, especially where ultimate ethical questions are at issue, must be a genuine attribute of conduct itself, not a relation to a judger.

So much so that it is extremely surprising to find so doughty and clear-sighted a champion of objectivist ethics as Sir David Ross so willing to capitulate to the relativist on what seems the most vital point of his theory as a whole.

Nor is he very happy about it himself. He adds: "But the phrase 'it is possible that I shall do what is right, and possible that I shall do what is wrong' does not do full justice to our actual thought when it takes its usual form 'I can do what is right,' though it expresses part of what that thought involves." [62] For a man is not the 'mere spectator of the play of forces' within him. "We say not merely 'I may do right, and I may do wrong,' but 'I *can* do right and I *can* do wrong.' What exactly does this mean?" [63]

It means, we are told, that "if a certain condition is added to conditions already present in me, I shall do so and so," [64] and the unfulfilled condition "consists of my wishing to do this." [65] " 'I can do this or that' means 'I shall do this if I want, and I shall do that if I want'—'want' being here a brachylogy for 'want predominantly.' " [66] But if this is to add anything at all to the view that we are free in so far as we can execute a purpose, a view we have already found to be quite unsatisfactory, it must somehow represent freedom as turning on the fact that conduct is an expression of want or desire. We are thus again driven back on the inner determination of conduct in the way of desires or motives. But we have also seen, as very apt pupils of Ross himself, that the process of being moved to act by a certain motive

[60] and [61] op. cit. p. 239.
[62] *Foundations of Ethics*, p. 239.
[63] op. cit. p. 240.
[64] [65] and [66] op. cit. p. 241.

is not free in the way required by the idea of 'ought' or 'duty.' So the dead-lock seems complete.

To examine other arguments by which it is attempted to reconcile freedom with determinism would take us farther afield than we can venture in this paper. It must suffice for the present to show how the critic of de-terminist views of moral responsibility finds support in recent arguments about obligation and rightness which take little account directly of the problem of freedom. But I should like to conclude with some comments on the position that faces us in ethics if the main contentions of this paper are sound.

IV

In the first place we seem to be committed to a much more serious and sympathetic consideration of the alternative presented by the libertarian than is usually accorded to it by philosophers. For it is very hard to rid ourselves of the conviction that there is ultimate moral responsibility. Much that is of supreme worth in the life of man, and especially in religion, seems to turn upon it. If thus there prove to be insuperable difficulties in the way of accommodating this conviction to any form of determinism, and on that score, I, for one, have little doubt, the indeterminist has a very strong *prima facie* case to be considered—a great deal stronger than would appear from the cursory treatment of the position in ethical writings.

To go exhaustively into this matter would however require consider-able space. The following comments must suffice for the present.

(a) A great many who call themselves indeterminists and libertarians, especially among the protagonists of Liberal Theology, turn out on exami-nation to be no more than qualified determinists. This seriously confuses the issue. If the libertarian is to be heard, let it be on the claim that there is an unambiguous "open possibility," and that some of our actions at least could have been other than they are although everything else in the universe was the same. Mere rebuttal of the cruder forms of determinism is quite another matter, and makes no substantial difference to the present issue.

(b) It seems to be inordinately easy to travesty the libertarian view. Some, for example, ascribe to the libertarian the belief in a mysterious 'once for all' choice, or a choice at birth. This is the view subjected to criticism by a recent contributor to *Mind*.[67] The libertarian, it is urged, proceeds in the following way. He insists that we cannot be considered responsible for a particular action because it is due to our character at the time, and this is, in part at least, the result of our own actions in the past. If, therefore, I am to be praised or blamed, it must be for the past conduct that made me the sort of person I am today. But what I did in the past was also the result of the sort of person I was then, and this I could not help, because it was, in turn, the result of past actions on my part

[67] P. Nowell Smith, *Mind*, January, 1948.

and that of others. And it is here, the writer concludes, "that the temptation to invoke a metaphysical *deus ex machina* becomes inviting. If we proceed on the assumption that, to be moral, an action must be uncaused, either we shall find a genuinely uncaused action at the beginning of the chain or we shall not. If we do not, then, according to the libertarian, there can be no moral praise and blame at all (and it was to account for these that Libertarianism was invented); and, if we do, then we must suppose that, while almost all our actions are caused, and therefore amoral, there was in the distant past some one action that was not caused and for which we can justly be praised or blamed. This bizarre theory has in fact been held; but the objections to it are clear. We praise and blame people for what they do now, not for what they might have done as babies, and any theory of moral responsibility must account for this." [68] But, we must reply, does any philosopher of repute today hold the preposterous theory discussed in this passage? It may be that the theory 'has in fact been held.' Support in some quarter or other can be found for the most fantastic views; and religious thinkers come perilously near the notion of a 'once for all choice' when they ascribe the wickedness of man to a 'fall' which is prior to his history on earth. But this is hardly a view to which the supporters of indeterminism would normally subscribe. What they hold is that there are *several* choices made from time to time in the course of our lives as mature human beings. And it is to this view, in the form in which it is held by philosophers whose work commands respect, that criticism should be directed, not to the caricature of it in the notion of an 'infantile choice.' The failure to appreciate this is all the more inexcusable because statements of the libertarian view are easily available in recent ethical books by philosophers of considerable standing such as E. F. Carritt and C. A. Campbell. There may not be many who agree with these thinkers. But if it is considered worth while at all to criticise the libertarian view, one should at least take the trouble to refer to the form in which it appears in the work of its most worthy exponents. This brings me to a point of much importance.

(c) On some counts, at least, such indeterminists as have ventured to take the field in recent years seem to have been very successful. They have answered some criticisms quite conclusively. Among these is the objection, usually considered the most formidable of all, that the libertarian view is incompatible with the observed continuity of conduct. It is taken to imply that "any action could come from any person at any time," that so far as his character is concerned a man can entirely "trammel up the consequences" of his action. And if it were the case that the libertarian did hold that belief, or if he were in consistency committed to it, his position would indeed be quite preposterous. All his conduct would belie his theory, for we can hardly act at all apart from the presumption that other persons and ourselves will behave in certain ascertainable ways in particular circumstances. We do rely on one another in practice, and a world in which we did not

[68] op. cit. p. 51.

do so would be a world of madmen. In so far, therefore, as it is assumed that the indeterminist repudiates all connection between conduct and a continuous character, it is most understandable that he should usually be dismissed with contempt. But he need not hold anything so foolish, and he rarely does so today. His position only requires that there should be genuine choice *within limits*, the limits prescribed by conscience and character. To the extent that moral convictions summon us to courses of action opposed to the predominant trend of our characters, the libertarian holds that there is a free choice before us. We may make an "effort of will" to defeat the weakness of our character as formed at a particular time; but not otherwise. It is not suggested that we can disregard both conviction and character. When therefore I rest assured that my friend X will not cheat at cards, this will be, on the libertarian view, because I know him well enough to be reasonably certain that such conduct will not be in accordance either with his nature or his principles. In *this* regard there will be no occasion for moral choice where he is concerned. In the same way we rule out preposterous actions by persons whose sanity we have no reason to doubt. This leaves ample room for moral choice, and however severe the other difficulties which confront the libertarian, he seems thus to have a perfectly adequate answer to those who accuse him of absurd violations of the obvious continuity of conduct. So complete and so final is the answer, and so well has it been stated by recent writers,[69] that it is indeed surprising we have not heard the last of the objection. In fact it is still very prominent in discussions of moral freedom.[70]

(d) But if we are to follow the libertarian here, a clear distinction will need to be drawn between the properly moral worth (or badness, as the case may be) of genuine acts of choice and good or bad qualities of character. A kindly disposition does not lose its importance by being no longer regarded as the subject of distinctively moral praise. It may in fact indirectly reflect moral worth, since we have a duty to cultivate a good character. But in itself it must be classed with non-moral values, and as such it will lose nothing of its lustre.

In consistency with this view the libertarian will also require to insist that moral worth must be appraised, not in terms of the end achieved in our actions or even of the content willed, but in terms of the effort required to obey our own consciences. For the end at which we aim, the content willed, can only reflect directly certain qualities of character. The aims of Gandhi were much nobler than those of most persons, but this was probably due in great measure to natural endowment and environment. His circumstances helped to make him the sort of person he was, he was naturally more tenacious of purpose than most men and more attracted to great ends. This may entitle us to say that he was a supremely virtuous or saintly person, but that will still have to be discounted by the libertarian in appraisement of

[69] e.g., by C. A. Campbell, *Scepticism and Construction*, Chapter V.
[70] cf. Ross's *Foundations of Ethics*, p. 230.

strictly moral worth. For the latter would only be exhibited on those occasions when Gandhi's natural strength of character proved insufficient to the demands made upon him by his ideals. No one can be certain what those occasions were. For however firm and heroic Gandhi's resolution may have been, no one could judge from anything in the overt nature of his conduct whether, in relation to his formed character as a whole at the time, he was not really acting in the line of least resistance. Only he himself, or God, could know that, although there is the presumption that no one is so richly endowed by nature as to rise to the heroic triumphs of a Gandhi without having at some stages to reinforce the natural bent of his character by free efforts of will. This latter need would arise more often perhaps in his case, not in the matter of sustained physical endurance, but on the occasions when he had to incur the obloquy and distrust of his own friends and followers by calling off campaigns which he himself had originally inspired (as happened especially when the non-violent campaign of 1922 seemed unlikely to take the course Gandhi himself expected). It is, among other reasons, because free efforts of will are presupposed in this way that 'saintliness' has its especial appropriateness in describing a nature such as that of Gandhi. But one has always to remember that, if we are to adhere consistently to the libertarian view, a high degree of moral worth may be attained by persons of more ordinary qualities of character for actions which would cost Gandhi nothing in the way of strictly moral effort and thus reflect no strictly *moral* credit upon him. This makes properly *moral* censure or approval very unreliable; we can presume a measure of moral evil in actions which seem contrary to what we have every reason to regard as the agent's own convictions, these being, however, by no means so easy to ascertain as is commonly supposed—how far was Hitler morally wicked and how far the victim of absurd delusions? The injunction to 'judge not' is thus reinforced by the libertarian view, although there is nothing in that view to preclude strong expression of disapproval of outward action as likely to lead to more enlightened views or better characters.

Understood as involving these consequences, there can be no denying that there is something of a paradoxical nature in the libertarian view of moral worth. It does not altogether accord with our ordinary judgments and reactions, but may not the answer here be that there is much confusion in these latter which a sound moral analysis may help to remove; ethical reflection has certainly helped us in other respects to adopt more enlightened attitudes. Again, it may be felt that the cultivation of moral qualities is precluded on the libertarian view, and that this contradicts what we normally think about moral education and training. But again it may be answered that such training is not precluded where qualities of character are concerned, and there is no reason to be negligent of these when their importance in their own way is appreciated. It is not for us to create opportunities of moral triumph for ourselves by weakening our characters any more than we should rejoice over pain and privation because they afford opportunities of acquiring merit in relieving them. There will in any case be plenty of temptations for creatures situated as we are without inducing them artificially, especially since the conquest of certain kinds of temptation exposes us to others—the temptations of St. Paul or Gandhi may not be those of ordinary men, but they may be acute nonetheless. In these ways then, and by stressing the difference between properly moral effort and mere physical or intellectual effort or the effort involved when one strain in our nature subdues another, careful analysis of the libertarian view may show that in the long run it conforms more closely than is commonly supposed by philosophers to what we normally feel impelled to believe about the moral life.

But while the course for the libertarian is clear in these respects, his success is not so easily assured in other ways. In particular an especially formidable objection presents itself in the question, 'Is there not a metaphysical requirement that everything should be determined in some way?' The libertarian will not, any more than other moral philosophers who know their business, wish to deny the normal continuity of events, including most human actions. He only makes an exception of acts of moral choice. If he went beyond this his position would soon become absurd. For action is only possible in a stable world. But do the exceptions the libertarian makes jeopardise his faith in the continuity of other actions and events? The position is sharpened if it is believed that, outside the sphere of free choice there is *necessary* determination. I should certainly hold that there is such necessitation. Nor is this a matter that could be established empirically. For no observations can be relevant to the determination of a question about the relation of events in general. Our principle has to be known *a priori*, and I feel confident that it is known in that way. But to claim to know *a priori* that there is causal determination, and also to limit its operation, is certainly a bold undertaking. I think it is an undertaking in which the libertarian need not despair of success, and that a highly valuable clue to the procedure he ought to adopt may be found in Nicolai Hartmann's conception of a 'plus of determination' striking into other modes of determination without altogether suspending them. But to consider these matters properly would require, not only a careful examination of Hartmann's view, but also study of further formidable metaphysical issues. That can hardly be attempted here. And we are in any case concerned now with the ethical rather than the more metaphysical aspects of the problem of freedom. Not that the two can be divorced in a final account. But I think that the most that our present purpose requires is that acknowledgment be made of the formidable difficulties which confront the libertarian at the metaphysical level. If he feels that he has not the resources to meet them, he must have no illusions as to what he must eventually forfeit.

This brings me to the point I wish most to stress in closing this paper.

If we find that we have to reject the libertarian view, then we must also be ready to sacrifice much that is usually considered important in ethics, including the common conception of guilt and responsibility. Drastic changes will be needed at several points in our ethical thought, and to some extent also in practice. These changes must be carried out boldly and thoroughly. Otherwise we shall only perpetuate the sort of confusion in which, as we have contended above, some of the best ethical thinking is entangled today. There is hardly a greater need in ethics at present than this of considering closely what has to be sacrificed if we surrender the notion of ultimate responsibility. And if the task is neglected by those who do not despair of applying meaningful ethical distinctions to conduct, they may find it undertaken for them more ruthlessly and carelessly by others. The way will be open for the positivist, the Freudian or the advocate of "evolutionary," "scientific," ethics. Their pruning will be far too severe. For if we surrender the values that turn on final responsibility, it does not follow that all will be lost. There will still be important distinctions of value. Nor will these be confined to knowledge and aesthetics, although the latter will henceforth be more typical of values in general. Character and conduct of a certain kind will still have the highest worth and call for cultivation through training and environment. Among the best qualities of character, moreover, will be the desire to do what is fitting to the situation as a whole. And, if we are mindful what we are about, we may call this, if we please, the "sense of duty." Its worth will not depend directly on sound judgment, much less on correct information. The question what sort of conduct is "materially" correct will be a further one. In these ways ethical theory will wear much the same appearance as it usually presents today in such writings as we have mentioned in this paper. It will require no sacrifice of any of the main contentions of *Principia Ethica*. But it will have no room for guilt and remorse or for merit and demerit in any distinctive and ultimate sense not resembling, for example, the pride or despair of the artist. It must not embarrass itself with a "categorical imperative" or any of its preconditions.

Such ethics will approximate closely to the ethical thinking of the Greeks. And the problem of freedom will present itself in the same way, in essentials, as it appears in their theories. It will have much to try the mettle of philosophers. But it will not be altogether bewildering. The main values will depend largely, as in Greek thought, on harmony and adjustment, great goodness will go with enlightenment, and the supreme evil will be "the lie in the soul" as affecting personal relationships as well as understanding of nature. This may lack much we have usually held to be yet more important. That it is an ignoble view no one conversant with Greek thought will suppose.

Neither, incidentally, will it be very hard to accommodate it to certain modes of Christian thought. In some ways it will greatly simplify the procedure of traditional theology. For a great deal of the ethical thinking of traditional theology seems to the present writer to be a Socratic ethic into which there have been infused ideas of guilt and blame incompatible with it.

"If a man could *see* evil as it is," says a prominent and very influential theologian of the present day, "he would not *really* be evil." [71] Unfortunately he proceeds, in the time-honoured way of theologians, to vilify man for his blindness (incurred through a "fall" in which each one is involved with the whole of his kind). This, as it stands, I submit, carries very little real conviction to anyone not committed to the perpetuation of a set of doctrines. But the general Christian view of man's blindness, and his salvation by "grace," present no special difficulty on a Socratic ethic from which we strictly exclude the notions of guilt and blame. On the contrary, they vastly deepen such an ethic. There is also much precedent for this course in traditional theology itself. For many theologians approximate it in the distinction between sin and guilt. This, again, will not do as it stands. For apart from the fact that "sin" is almost certain to convey the idea of guilt to the ordinary man, the latter notion is still accorded a place, and that within a system which does not allow of genuine freedom of choice, however prone theologians may be to persuade themselves that it does. Guilt, like the "categorical imperative," simply cannot be accommodated at all within a deterministic scheme.

To set these observations on religious thought in their proper context would however take us very far afield. The most that this paper attempts is a plea for the bolder consideration of the problem of freedom and obligation, together with more determination to follow the "wind of the argument" whithersoever it takes us. Sir David Ross expresses the hope "that a genius will some day arise who will succeed in reconciling our natural thought about freedom and responsibility with acceptance of the law of causation." But what if the task is plainly an impossible one? Would it not then be the wiser course to turn from it altogether, and set our house in order as best we can with what remains to us? That is considerable. But considerable also is the surrender to be made of ordinary ethical beliefs if we conclude that the law of causality holds universal sway.

[71] Emil Brunner, *Divine Imperative*, p. 75.

Guilt and Freedom *

꙳

H. D. LEWIS [1]

MORAL PHILOSOPHERS do not seem to have had a great deal to say about guilt, and it would be easy to compile an impressive list of ethical treatises in which the subject is not mentioned at all. In recent ethics especially it has suffered much neglect. In theology, on the other hand, the problem of guilt has always remained to the fore, and of late it has also elicited the very lively interest of the psychologist. It is the moralist who remains aloof.

This is as regrettable as it is strange. For however important the problem of guilt may be, in some of its bearings, for religious thought or psychology, it is first and foremost an ethical problem. And when the moralists are reluctant to tackle some ethical question, and are content to hand it over to other disciplines, such as theology or psychology, which have an interest in it, the properly ethical features of that question are apt to be either overlaid altogether by extraneous considerations or distorted into some quasi-ethical religious or psychological form. Of this the treatment of the problem of guilt is an excellent example.

We have thus to insist at the start that our problem is essentially an ethical one. It is also a problem of first importance.

This is so for several reasons. (1) Some of the most crucial issues in theological controversy have turned on the nature of guilt, and the course which the discussion of these matters has taken has been such as would have been substantially improved by bolder intrusion into the field of theology by moral philosophers—especially in recent times. (2) The rapid advance of psychology in our time, and in particular the fascinating, if also somewhat uncritical, theories of the psycho-analysts, have added much to the plausibility of the view that a fully satisfactory account of guilt can be given in purely psychological terms; this alone would justify a fresh investigation. (3) Questions of penal reform and other matters of even more urgent and far-reaching importance, such as the problem of war-guilt and the treatment of "guilty nations," set our problem among the more pressing practical issues of this age. There is hardly another field where the philoso-

* Reprinted with minor changes by kind permission of the author and the editors from the *Proceedings of the Aristotelian Society, Supplementary Volume* 21, 1947.
 [1] This essay is also included in his book *Morals and Revelation*, George Allen and Unwin, 1951.

pher, by close and impartial analysis can have a more immediate and beneficial influence on practice, nor any where the challenge to come out of
the ivory tower is plainer. (4) Some of the matters most keenly debated in
ethics today, and especially the question of rightness and moral worth on
which so much ingenuity has been expended, could have been viewed more
clearly from the start if the implications of guilt, as involved in the nature
of moral evil, had been more carefully and boldly considered in connection
with those matters. (This, although not taken up very fully in this paper—
I have discussed it elsewhere—will, I hope, be plainer in due course.)

We have thus a vast field of investigation before us, and it will only
be possible to touch very briefly on some of the matters mentioned above.
My aim will be to centre attention as far as possible on the strictly ethical
nature of the problem of guilt. The crucial question here is that of freedom.
In presenting it I beg your indulgence in traversing some rather familiar
ground for a little.

I

The problem of moral freedom was never an acute one for the Greeks.
This was because they thought of the moral life in terms of a goodness which
men are by nature disposed to pursue. Aristotle typified well the attitude
of his contemporaries when he made the conceptions which he had found
useful in his study of natural life also fundamental for ethics. There is a
growth which is natural to man, there is a certain capacity, to be thought
of not merely as a power but also as a tendency, which it is his function to
fulfil. The 'potential' stands in this relation to the 'actual,' that the un-
organised passions and impulses which constitute the raw material of goodness acquire a final form with an inevitability so inherent to the nature of
man that it is not fundamentally different from the inevitability by which
an acorn becomes an oak tree. Admittedly reason makes a difference, and
no one would confuse the naturalism of Aristotle with that of Hobbes
or Hume. Reason enters into the Supreme Good in the form of 'Contemplation' and the requirements of practical life are discerned by the exercise
of Practical Wisdom in a way that makes reason the master much more
than the 'slave of the passions.' Even so, the end that is proper to man remains one to which he is directed by his nature; and the problem of ethics
is, therefore, the problem what is the nature of man and in what environment can he become most truly himself, most truly what he really wants
to be.

This represents no substantial departure from the teaching of Plato.
For although Plato does not set out like Aristotle to define the Supreme
Good in terms of our own aspirations, but rather gives the Form of the
Good a completeness and reality of its own, he is, none the less, convinced
that man finds in the Form of the Good what is most akin to the distinctive
constituent of his own nature—his reason. And in virtue of this likeness the

'Good' has an irresistible attraction for anyone who properly understands its nature.

This approach to ethical problems was facilitated for the Greeks by the absence of a sharp distinction between moral and non-moral values, such as we are familiar with today. They were indeed brought easily to the idea of one Supreme Good to be exhibited in the whole of life, and the fundamental principles of their ethical theories did not, therefore, deviate markedly from the principles implied in the attainment of estimable qualities and accomplishments generally. Analogies with some art or craft have a significant recurrence in the most important contexts of Greek moral philosophy. The pursuit of moral worth thus presented itself to the Greeks with at least such inevitability as we find in the cultivation of some gift in whose exercise a man is bound to take the greatest delight.

An obvious reflection of this view is the Socratic maxim 'Virtue is Knowledge.' But Plato and Aristotle understood well that this maxim could not be accepted without qualification. It did not accord altogether with experience. For very often we seem, at any rate, to choose the worse course knowing the better. For this problem Plato found an answer, satisfactory to him, in the distinction between genuine knowledge and opinion. It is only when we rely on uncertain opinions, on ideas derived at second-hand or conventions on whose purpose we have not ourselves reflected, that our conduct may not be in line with our principles. When we really understand, when the nature of the good is properly the possession of our own minds, then we are certain to model our conduct upon it. This did not satisfy Aristotle. He pointed out [2] that many persons hold their fallible beliefs with the same firmness and assurance as others their certain knowledge. But his own treatment of the subject does not take us very far. He observed, quite rightly, that passion or fear may induce a momentary blindness and that, again, we often fail to perceive the application of some general principle to our own case. But this is not the whole of the matter—far from it. There remain the much more important cases where we seem deliberately and calmly to do what we know to be wrong. And the fact that Aristotle manages only to touch the fringes of the problem shows that he did not concern himself deeply with it, notwithstanding the downright admission in one context that we do sometimes choose the worse course knowing the better. It is moreover hard to see what alternative to the Platonic solution is possible on Aristotle's theory of goodness.

We can still admit that Aristotle's principles fully allowed him to supply a very necessary corrective to the superficial views of the Sophists and their assumption that goodness, as well as intellectual excellence, could be produced by teaching alone. He was quite entitled to stress the importance of discipline and training. For he was not bound to regard this training of the will as a factor altogether apart from the process of ethical enlightenment. The value of the training and its perpetuation in the right sort

[2] *Ethics*, Book VII, 1146b.

of habit could be thought to lie in the deepening of Practical Wisdom to which it led, and the consequent fuller devotion to the good. This in the main seems to be the view that Aristotle does hold. At any rate there is no certain indication of the contrary such as would show a real appreciation of the issues involved in the problem of deliberate wrong-doing.

But whether or not it be held that the typical Greek view of the nature of goodness allows of some deviation from a 'Socratic ethics,' there is certainly required by it the ascription of virtue and vice altogether to some combination of the factors of enlightenment, training, and environment. There is no room for genuine rebellion. On the contrary, as Professor A. E. Taylor reminds us, the principle "that goodness is in the soul what health and fitness are in the body" is really at the bottom of all Greek thinking on morality.[3]

It has to be stressed that, to the extent that the Greeks were compelled to take some account of deliberate wrong-doing, they were driven to do so by the fact that experience seems to present us with instances of it. Men did apparently choose the worse course, and however perplexing the fact might be, it had to be accommodated somehow in ethical theories. But the thought that a power of making the wrongful choice may itself be a condition of virtue does not seem to have occasioned serious misgiving. Deliberate wickedness presented itself mainly as a fact of experience, not *as an ethical postulate*. And this is a most significant way in which the problem of freedom had not for the Greeks the acuteness which it usually has for us.

There would still be *a* problem of freedom. On its more theoretical side this would be the problem of deciding how we must understand and describe men's independence of their environment in so far as they are also clearly determined by their environment or, as it used to be put, not unfairly as it seems to me, 'organic to their world.' Art supplies an obvious illustration. The poet is in one sense the creature of his age, of his immediate environment, and of traditions that reach into remotest ages of the past, but he is also supremely free. The influences that affect him are assimilated by his mind with a completeness that makes his creations distinctively his own. The more sensitive he is the more are factors of the world about him brought into rich combinations and transformed as they become parts of a unique individuality. But just what can we mean by individuality here, and what can we say in a final sense about the distinctness of persons at this level? These are important questions, and they have been very fruitfully discussed by philosophers, not least in fairly recent times. They have the greatest importance for speculative thought, and they enter deeply into religious questions.

On the practical side there are such problems as those of the statesman and the educator when they have to decide how far it is wise to interfere with the spontaneous development of mind and character if the finest qualities are to be elicited. How may instruction be effective without being

[3] *Aristotle*, p. 105.

mechanical or biased, how is society to give support to the arts and sciences without affecting the free play of the mind; in what measure should efficiency in matters of government be sacrificed when that seems necessary for the political education of a people; and again, a most acute problem at the moment, how far should we venture to influence one another in matters of religious belief? These are also questions of great moment, and here, as on the theoretical side, there is a great deal to be learnt from the Greeks.

For not only had the Greeks a distinctive feeling for the integration and harmony required for the development of persons in the present sense, and especially in those aspects of men's lives that are most easily assimilated to aesthetic pursuits, they also provided us with specific principles and conceptions of the greatest importance in this context. Plato's comparison of the education of the soul to the 'nurture' of a plant upon which we cannot impose a form of our own but which can be brought to its richest bloom by careful tending under suitable climatic conditions and in the right soil, the insistence upon the importance of general environment as well as direct instruction, and Aristotle's conception of 'the mean,' of a fittingness to one's own nature and one's circumstances discerned by the insight that comes with experience and devotion to the good, are obvious indications of ways in which our grasp of the problem of freedom in the sense in question at the moment, in all its aspects, is enhanced by the study of Greek thought. But here we have, none the less, not at all the problem of freedom that men have in mind when they speak of freedom as a postulate of ethics, however much the latter may be intertwined in practice with such problems as confront the parent or the statesman.

II

The problem of moral freedom in the proper sense is one that arises when the idea of duty, obligation, law, of a 'categorical imperative,' of guilt and remorse, of ultimate praise or blame, are made central to ethical thought. These are ideas we have derived mainly from Hebrew attitudes and habits of thought, deepened by Christian teaching, and preserved, with not unimportant distortions, in traditional theology. Their presupposition found classical expression in Kantian ethics and in the celebrated maxim, 'I ought, therefore I can.' It was unfortunate that certain beliefs about the life of man arrived at on independent epistemological and metaphysical grounds prejudiced the presentation of this principle, and its implications, by Kant himself. For he seems in some regards forced to the conclusion that only the good will is free, and even that its freedom consists in some timeless once for all act—whatever that may mean in relation to the conduct of men. This has helped to perpetuate those theological distortions of ethical principles at which I have hinted above. But Kant did distinguish between the 'holy will' and the 'good will' which, in spite of being 'objectively determined,' is 'not necessarily in unison with the law.' [4] And it seems plain to me that, in spite of the unfortunate bifurcation of our nature into the 'pure' and the 'empirical' selves, Kant's conception of moral obligation turned essentially on a genuine conflict between duty and interest. What he was struggling to fit into his system, not always, it must be admitted, with conspicuous success, was the conviction of the ordinary man that if there be such a thing as duty, if there is genuine moral responsibility, then it must be the case, not only that we are able to perform certain actions, but also, as Professor Broad has stressed,[5] that we *need not* perform them.

Philosophers have not found it easy to determine how precisely we must conceive the freedom of choice which duty thus seems to require, and how far we can be said to enjoy it. During the last century it was common to seek a solution of the problem by combining the Greek view with that of Kant, a most unnatural yoking of principles which the idealists endeavoured to force upon ethics in other ways also—with much ingenuity and persistence, and to the great confusion of moral philosophy. Man, it was urged, is free because he is 'self-determined,' his desires direct his conduct, not in isolation from one another, but as taken up into the unity of 'the self as a whole'; influences from outside himself affect him only as they are assimilated into his own nature; his own past, as well as the environment to which he is organic, determines him only as brought to life anew in the continual shaping of character, and a motive takes its final form in the very process of issuing in action. There is thus no mechanical determination in the flow of conduct in accordance with character, a matter but little appreciated in Associationist psychology such as that of Bain and Mill which Bradley trounces so severely in his *Ethical Studies* and his *Logic*. But when every allowance has been made for the sounder psychology of the idealist view of character, are we much nearer a solution of the properly ethical problem of freedom? What we are offered is only a superior way of being determined, it is in essentials the same sort of freedom as is exhibited in knowledge or in art; it presents itself with greater completeness in good conduct than in bad, as the terms 'self-mastery' and 'consistency' as applied in the praise of conduct suggest. But the freedom which obligation seems to require is not itself in any way a part of the goodness of the action as symmetry would be an element in the beauty of a picture. It is the freedom to choose to do the action or not to do it, and it is not a whit affected when we choose the bad.

There is thus no solution of the problem of *moral* freedom by noting that there is usually a perfectly innocent paradox of freedom and necessity in rational experience. Admittedly freedom and necessity do meet wherever there is thought. We see the truth by making it our own in active thought, but the more we do so the more we are bound to think in a certain way, to submit to the structure of truth itself. Our freedom is also conformity

[4] *Principles of the Metaphysic of Ethics*, ed. Abbott, p. 37.
[5] In his *Determinism, Indeterminism, and Libertarianism*.

to law. The artist is most creative when he sees that he *must* do just this and not that, when he is most held to his way; we love those to whom we are drawn, and give ourselves with most abandon when we are already in thrall; in religion there is also a 'service' which is 'perfect freedom,' a 'perfect law of freedom,' a 'law which is my delight.' But the necessity of duty is not of this order at all. It is not itself also freedom, but rather *presupposes* it, it is the 'must' of command, not of conformity, and it implies that we need not conform. It does not vary with attainment, as in art or knowledge. The wicked are fully as free as the good. Their freedom is in that regard absolute. It is a 'liberty of indifference,' a liberty, not to go one way, the ideal way, but several.

Viewed in this way, moral evil is unlike any other; it is not a functional disorder or disease, it is not like our shortcomings in art or knowledge, for it can be brought home to the individual as his own disobedience or rebellion; it is guilt, a wilful violation of law, and thus reprehensible as no other evil can be. Moral value in turn is obedience, and calls for a distinctive sort of praise. But our terms are apt to confuse us here, for our usage of 'merit' is very ambiguous. A man may acquire merit as an athlete, a poet, or a statesman. But guilt, mainly because of its more strictly forensic origin, represents more truly that peculiar quality of moral distinctions which sets them in sharp opposition to other values because of the special way they rest on the will of the individual—hence we speak more of the problem of guilt than of merit. The Greeks had little consciousness of guilt, at least so far as the teaching of their main philosophers goes—Greek drama has a somewhat different tale to tell. And so there was no sharp distinction for them between aesthetic and moral good. But if we are to draw that distinction, and think of moral wickedness as violation of a law or imperative, we must not content ourselves with the freedom which matters most on a Greek view of ethics. And although this appears so plain it is not idle to stress it at some length. For the view of freedom as self-determination is still the view normally accepted by ethical writers, not excepting those who give prominence to the idea of obligation. But what we must presuppose for the latter purpose—and the word 'presuppose' is important here—is a freedom to go one way or the other, a freedom of open choice.

III

But here we may encounter the objection that, in the light of a better understanding of the nature of guilt, it will be seen that the postulate of freedom is no longer required, or that at any rate it comes in such a modest shape as to relieve the philosopher of the perplexities which this postulate has usually caused him in the past. This is thought to be especially the case when regard is had to the advances of recent psychology. At this point it behoves us therefore to consider more precisely how guilt must be understood.

Now the idea of guilt is one we most commonly encounter in a legal context; and here a person is guilty if he has contravened the 'law of the land' and incurred a penalty. But legal guilt and ethical guilt are by no means the same. It is possible to have the one without the other, as in the case of a person who breaks the law on conscientious grounds. How then must we conceive of guilt in the ethical sense?

There seems to be this at least in common to legal and ethical guilt, that a person is guilty when, in some way or another, he has done what is wrong. But there are several senses of 'doing what is wrong' in ethics. Sir David Ross distinguishes three.[6] (a) My act may be wrong by being out of accord with the actual requirements of a situation, or (b) by being out of accord with the requirements of the situation as I understand them, or (c) by being contrary to what I myself take to be my duty. These distinctions are required because we may be mistaken both about the facts of a situation and in our evaluation of them. Do we become guilty, then, by doing what is wrong in any of these senses? Not, it seems plain, in senses (a) and (b). And the reason seems to be that failure in these respects reflects no discredit directly on the agent, and that seems also, therefore, to be involved in the idea of guilt. What, then, of (c)? Here Ross's position is peculiar. For one of his main reasons for regarding (c) as the most important meaning of a failure to discharge our duty (and that in which "obligation" may be substituted for duty) is that it is the one in which blame is incurred, and blame is incurred because we *can* "set ourselves" or intend to do what we think is right, whereas we cannot guarantee the result. But Ross does not think that rightness or wrongness in the present sense is a direct indication of our moral quality. He argues that we may do what we think is right merely to suit our convenience or from thoroughly unworthy motives, and that our conduct would, then, be morally indifferent or bad, as the case may be. When we do what we think is *wrong* there is *some* evidence of moral wickedness, but motive must here also be taken into account in a complete evaluation. But it seems to me certain that conduct does not deserve blame except in strict proportion to moral disvalue, and that no one is guilty in the ethical sense except as he is also morally bad. I conclude, therefore, that guilt is some betrayal of what I take to be my duty by which my conduct becomes directly morally evil and blameworthy.

The conditions of guilt are therefore precisely the same as the conditions of moral evil, but we must not allow the notion of guilt to drop out in considering the nature and conditions of moral evil, for we shall then be inclined to overlook the peculiarity of moral evil, as so many moral philosophers have done, and assimilate it to other forms of evil which do not presuppose a special kind of wrong-doing and do not expose us to blame.

But the reference to the blameworthy nature of guilty conduct raises

[6] *Foundations of Ethics*, Chapter VII. Ross speaks mainly of "right act" but what he says obviously holds *mutatis mutandis* of "wrong act."

at once the question whether an exhaustive account of it may not be given —as in the case of legal guilt—in terms of the attitudes we closely associate with it, namely blame, condemnation, remorse, and righteous indignation. Some would include also overt punishment, but this raises some further rather complicated questions, and I leave it aside for the moment. But whether we have punishment into the picture or not, we can hardly think of guilt without thinking at the same time of blame and condemnation. And many have, therefore, concluded that what is most distinctive of guilt can be defined in terms of these reactions.

If that were in fact possible our ethical problems would be very much simplified. For it would follow that these reactions could themselves be exhaustively described in psychological terms, and this, in its turn, would give us the main indication of the nature of guilt which would also need to be naturalistic; from this, as we shall see below, would result a fairly easy solution of the problem of freedom. But this is not what we normally think. We think normally and, I believe, rightly, that blame and condemnation do not define guilt, but rather presuppose it. They are attitudes and reactions appropriate to guilt, but guilt comes first. This means that the latter is an ultimate ethical conception not to be wholly described in psychological terms. Moral blame and condemnation therefore derive their significance from it, not it from them. They are attitudes which have a peculiar irreducible ethical appropriateness to guilt. And as such they do not open up a possibility of defining guilt; but they aid our reflection about it, in particular by throwing into relief the contrast between guilt and other kinds of shortcomings which do not call for blame. And this, as we have noted, has special importance for the understanding of moral evil.

A vigorous protest must next be entered against the procedure of several eminent moral philosophers who, without any wish to put ethical ideas into jeopardy, but rather the reverse, have seriously prejudiced their case by defining responsibility as liability to punishment, and guilt as the meriting of it. Bradley is a good example. The position is in some ways redeemed by the fact that punishment is not itself conceived wholly, or even mainly, in utilitarian terms. There is retributive punishment, the appropriateness of which is distinctively ethical. But the case for retention of guilt as a properly ethical notion is made to depend on what seems to me, to say the least, a highly doubtful conception, namely that of retributive justice. I believe that something like the theory of retributive punishment may well be true, as I hope to suggest later, but I am certainly far from convinced that any situation is directly improved by infliction of pain on a guilty agent. But this does not vitally affect the problem of moral evil and guilt itself. The question of punishment is a separate issue for any account of moral evil which is not utilitarian. For punishment would have no special appropriateness (allowing for the moment that it has) were it not for the prior irreducible nature of moral evil.

If we overlook this, as Bradley and those who follow his lead are much inclined to do, we may find that we have moved unwittingly near to the naturalistic position, and it is because they have travelled further in that direction than they realised, I believe, that the thinkers in question find it so easy, as a rule, to reconcile freedom with determinism. This is why I think it important to keep the problems of responsibility and guilt distinct from the problem of punishment, except, of course, to the extent that punishment is bound to have a very central place in any naturalistic theory of guilt.

IV

But the view that guilt may be fully described in psychological terms, and that the representation of it as wrongfulness of a distinctively ethical character is an illusion—in the sense, for example, in which Freud regards religion as an illusion—may take a somewhat different form in the attempt to account for guilt, not so much in terms of the attitudes and reactions of other persons to our conduct, but in terms of certain states and reactions of the guilty person himself. This view of guilt has been given much prominence in recent attempts to account for ethical ideas exhaustively in psychological terms, but I do not think it is hard to show that it is only superficially attractive.

The first matter that falls to be emphasised here is the stubbornness of the belief that guilt is real, and that it is not to be described exhaustively in terms either of punishment or of the reactions of the agent himself. Illusion there may be, but it certainly dies very hard. The voice of vulgar opinion, whose prestige is rightly very high in ethics, speaks here in no unmistakable terms. The ordinary person, by no means so elusive a creature as is sometimes thought, draws a very sharp distinction between his shortcomings in art, or in matters of the intellect or good taste, and wrongdoing; and if it be suggested that the judgment to be passed on the latter is illusory, or can be exhaustively described in terms of fear and punishment or similar matters, he will be much offended, taking it as an affront to his dignity as a moral being. He believes that some conduct has an attribute of guilt which implies that it is evil in a deep and peculiarly revolting way. The "guilty" are not merely a menace, they are evil; and the evil nature of their actions is not at all on the level of some functional disorder or disease. It is deep and ultimate.

A reflection of this may be found in the procedure of some philosophers who, not themselves unsympathetic to subjectivist theories of non-moral good, have also held very firmly that moral good and moral evil are *sui generis* and ultimate! This may not be an easy position to defend. But at any rate it bears witness to the deep-rooted nature of the conviction that guilt and moral evil are ultimate and irreducible.

But someone may object here that the report of common experience is that, on occasion, we *feel* guilty or have a *sense* of guilt; and that might be taken to suggest that guilt is some feeling of uneasiness or fear due to anticipation—not very explicit perhaps—of some kind of punishment. This is, however, to ascribe far too great a significance to an ambiguous phrase. The consciousness of guilt will normally arouse some distressing emotion, of which remorse is by far the most distinctive and the most appropriate. And for the rough designations with which we are normally content the mere emotion may well give the best indication of the experience as a whole. But clearly we could not have guilty feelings unless, in the first place, we thought that we *were* guilty. This does not, of course, prove that guilt cannot itself be described, in the final account, in terms of our own emotions. But it does mean that such psychological accounts of guilt must have room for the distinction between the feelings consequent on guilt and the state which occasions them. And the fact that this distinction has to be drawn robs the popular expression "feeling of guilt" of any immediate support it might give to the notion that guilt can be exhaustively described in terms of our emotions.

Furthermore, "feeling" is itself a term notorious for its ambiguous usage in common parlance. We say "I have a feeling that the weather will clear," "I feel I ought to visit so and so," when clearly we mean primarily "I think that," etc., however much the thought may be prompted by feelings or accompanied by them.

V

It is not, therefore, so simple a matter to dispose of the belief that guilt is "a terrible reality"—and a properly ethical one. But, it may be urged, it is just here that psychology, and especially recent psychology, comes to our aid. It can be shown that there are many hidden anxieties and fears whose subtle and elusive operations create the impression that there is some distinctive ethical guilt when in fact there is nothing that we cannot, on close analysis, reduce to some emotional reaction. On this basis some thinkers, and especially followers of Freud, have maintained that guilt is to be conceived, in the last resort, as "a need for punishment" induced in part by "conditioning" when certain acts have come to be associated with punishment and we feel a doom hanging over us if punishment is not forthcoming, relieved when it has been administered. A subtler feature of the same phenomenon is the introjection into our "super-ego" of the relief experienced by those who punish us for offending against them by doing them some harm. This happens mainly in early years, and especially in the relations of children to their parents. It becomes in due course one of the most influential factors in our lives, and affords the clue to many social and pathological problems which we might be inclined to oversimplify if we overlooked the fundamental character of the "need for punishment" and the complicated forms which it takes, for example in the inhibitions resulting from the Polycrates [7] complex, or in the operation of vicarious punishment in cases where we have projected our own guilt on to others.

Now it cannot be denied that recent psychology has taught us a great deal in these ways about ourselves. Not that we must straightway endorse its main conclusions, even when presented without any ethical implications. For there is much to invite serious criticism in both the procedures and the findings of psychology, especially of the psycho-analytic type. An exaggerated and somewhat distorted importance is ascribed, for example, to the vicissitudes of our lives in infancy as a clue to later and more mature states. No doubt the formative influences of early years need to be carefully studied, and they can throw very special light on our subsequent history. But we must not overlook the fact that there is development; and that mature experiences remain opaque to inspection on the basis of early factors alone. Admittedly, the more elusive elements in the constitution of adult life will often be found in the experiences we are apt to forget most completely, and it is tempting to the psychologist to seek explanation of what he fails to understand in adult experience in matters which are least accessible to our consciousness. But he does so at his peril, however remarkable some of the discoveries obtained in this way may be. For apart from the fact that conclusions about early years must be drawn with the greatest caution, there is a genuine reforming of the main traits in our nature in the continual flow of life from infancy to maturity. Even in cases of grave maladjustment or mental disorder, the main clue may be found in some event of adolescence or maturity that does not involve the days of our infancy in any special way. Nor is the preoccupation with abnormal psychology, so noticeable among the Freudians, a help to the achievement of a balanced understanding of mature states. In addition there is a proneness to force the evidence into preconceived patterns, as well as some foolishness in the practice of psycho-analysis, resulting sometimes in no inconsiderable harm. But when objections of this sort have been pressed to the uttermost limit, there remain some truly impressive achievements to be put to the credit side of empirical psychology today. We have been shown as never before how to look below the surface for a better understanding of ourselves, and the rudiments at least of a new technique are being evolved. And this leaves us with the question whether, cured of its more extravagant and fanciful tendencies, psycho-analysis can provide an explanation of guilt along the lines suggested. While we cavil at much in the present formulation of the explanation, can we accept it in principle?

If we can, then we must be very clear what we are about. For the upshot of our conclusion will be that moral distinctions, as we normally think of them, will have to be adjudged to be quite without substance, and banned for the mischievous confusions they engender. About this there should be no prevarication. There will be no room for ethics in that aspect

[7] cf. Flügel: *Man, Morals and Society*, p. 151.

of it which we ordinarily regard as having most depth and importance, namely the study of obligation and moral good and evil. We must turn from these matters with the firmness, if also with something of the gentle sadness, with which Plato abandoned the poets. Our fondness for a noble illusion must not dim our eyes to the course we must take, for the brightest illusions are often potent of the greatest harm. And here the psychologists themselves must stand most rebuked. For they have not always understood their own procedures, and have written as though they were treating of properly ethical problems when in fact they were seriously impugning the validity of ethical ideas. Professor Flügel is a good example. His usurpation of the place of the moralist, in his recent *Man, Morals, and Society*, wears a most innocent appearance. For he gives no clear indication of the ethically barren land to which he proposes to lead us. One might often gather that his purpose was to treat of psychological matters subsidiary to distinctively ethical principles, and such expressions as "wrongdoing," "moral factors," "budding moral sentiments," "moral and social influences," "moral development," "a very genuine moral conflict," to select a few examples at random, appear in a disconcertingly normal shape in a context where they have suffered complete transformation. We are also disarmingly told at the start that, as psychology "is a positive, not a normative discipline," the author has "no concern with values as such," [8] but this does not deter him from asserting later, in much completer consistency with his main theme, that "we must substitute a cognitive and psychological approach for an emotional and a moral one." [9] Of the easy assimilation of Scriptural sayings into a context most incompatible with their true purport Hobbes himself might well be proud. But the result of this is most seriously to darken counsel, and prejudice fair estimation of the author's claims. If, therefore, we find that the notion of guilt is reducible to psychological terms, there must be the fullest and most unambiguous repudiation of its claims to strictly ethical significance, and of all that is associated with it in ethics. To waver in that matter is fatal.

But are we reduced to such a pass? Is that involved in the concessions we have made to the psychologist? By no means. We may freely admit that there are such fears and desires as he describes, and that they take shape through the complicated processes which psycho-analysis reveals; formative influences may be deeply hidden from us in aspects of our personal history which we have mostly forgotten. But this is no bar to there being *in addition* guilt of a genuinely ethical kind incurred in certain ways. Most of what the psychologist avers may be allowed without touching the properly ethical question. And, indeed, the significance of much that we are told about the repression of guilt and its projection on to others, and similar processes, may be vastly deepened and extended if such operations are performed, not merely on desires and fears but, also, on a true consciousness

---

[8] op. cit. p. 11.
[9] op. cit. p. 255.

of guilt and its accompanying emotions. It must be a more serious matter, and presumably one where subtler and more determined resistance would be offered to therapeutic treatment, to suppress real guilt and drive remorse itself underground to erupt elsewhere, than to treat the pseudo-guilt of the psychologist in similar fashion. Furthermore, one wonders whether pseudo-guilt, with its roots in fear and retaliation, would have quite the tone that it has were it not for resemblance to genuine guilt. But without pressing this attack too deeply into the ranks of the analysts, and remaining mainly on the defensive, we may at least insist that there is nothing conclusive in their teaching about introjected emotions and subsequent projection, etc., as it bears on the problem of whether guilt, in the properly ethical sense, is real or illusory. This question could never be finally settled by recourse to the psychologist alone, for the essence of the claim to be determined is that there is something not to be directly encompassed by psychology. To leave the final decision here to the psychologist himself is to beg the question in completest fashion. Our doubts can only be finally resolved by reflection on what we do mean when we think of guilt. This reflection is conducted fairly only when the facts adduced by psycho-analysis are kept steadily before us. But, for my own part, I must admit that the presence of a plausible alternative account in psychological terms avails little to shake my conviction that guilt is a distinctively ethical mode of wrong-doing to which blame and remorse have an appropriateness of an irreducible ethical nature.

VI

But if we are to think of guilt in this fashion there must be no illusions about the conditions which render it possible. For, as we have stressed, no conduct is open to blame unless it is free, and it is a fair rejoinder to an accusation to declare that we "could not help" what we did. But what sort of freedom is this? It would be easy to reply if we could think of the moral law as in some way analogous to the "law of the land," and, therefore, as having its sanction in the fact that we may be proceeded against or punished in some way, or if blame could be wholly described in psychological or naturalistic terms. For the most we would need on that view would be the sort of avoidability which would give point to the reactions in question. Its nature has been very clearly presented by several writers, including Mr. Charles Stevenson in his recent *Language and Ethics*. As he notes, an action need only be avoidable, for the present purpose, in the sense that we could have acted differently had we wished. It is folly to be angry with a man for not giving us the moon, or to punish him. Our action could not mend the matter at all. But we may well be angry with someone who strikes us a blow, and take measures against him; for that may prevent a recurrence. It will also deter others by affecting their wishes.

But this position is not quite as straightforward as it seems, and there are some aspects of it which its advocates would do well to ponder more closely than they commonly do. In particular we need to distinguish two meanings of the notion of freedom to act differently had we wished. For this may mean either (a) freedom to intend something other than what we do intend, or (b) freedom to carry our intention into effect. For the purpose of (a) we must, of course, take 'intention' in the strict sense in which it is equivalent to actually 'setting ourselves' to achieve some end, and not merely the forming of designs which we may or may not implement—intending in the sense in which 'hell is paved with good intentions.' But, taking intention in the strict sense, we have to ask whether it is meaningful to speak of freedom to intend. And it seems to me that it is not meaningful for anyone to do so if he also believes, as most philosophers do, that our conduct is invariably determined by our desires and feelings (strictly, of course, by our character as a whole). For in that case we can point to nothing over and above the fact that there are intentions (prompted by desire, etc.) which could be described as freedom to intend. Nothing need be said beyond the fact that we do intend. If it be objected that we need to distinguish between actions such as those of the kleptomaniac or the lunatic and the deliberate misdeeds of the thief, then we must answer that the former do not act or intend in the strict sense at all. If the kleptomaniac or the pervert have some strain in their nature which just makes it impossible for them to behave rationally in certain regards (and I suspect that the excuse is to be invoked with justice in fewer cases than is popularly supposed today), then they are, to that extent, in precisely the same position as the madman or the child, and their behaviour is not action in the proper sense at all. If someone cavils at this, and prefers simply to speak of free as distinct from impulsive or non-voluntary action, then I have no serious quarrel with him. But what I do wish to insist upon is that, within action in the proper sense of the behaviour of rational beings, there is nothing which the determinist can describe as freedom to act or intend over and above the fact that we do intend certain things in particular states of mind, others in others. This does not directly invalidate the view of freedom we are now discussing. Intentions can be modified by punishment and rewards, and all that we need to do for the purpose of the present view, so far as intention is concerned, is to point this out. The question of a postulate of freedom just does not arise at this point for the determinist.

But it is otherwise when we turn to the 'freedom to do' in the sense of freedom to execute a purpose. And it is this freedom, it seems to me, which matters on the view that describes responsibility in terms of liability to punishment in the way indicated. It matters in two ways. Firstly, it might be held that certain intentions have such little likelihood of being fulfilled in practice that there would be little purpose in seeking to modify them. But it is not easy to provide examples of this, since the wicked intentions which we could wholly disregard would almost certainly be the behaviour of a madman and not of a sane human being. But the 'freedom to do' will have much importance in another way—an indirect way. It will be important as a clue to the outside observer as to what an agent really intends. It is plain that no one can intend to do what he considers impossible. And therefore, in respect to matters which there is a general presumption that they are not amenable to control by our will, the agent will at once be exonerated on the ground that he shares this general assumption. Let us suppose that a burglar breaks into a hotel and quickly overpowers and gags the night porter. If, then, the porter be reproached for not giving the alarm, he can obviously reply. 'But I could not.' We normally accept this, but if we had reason to believe (possibly by having some 'psychic' knowledge of what was actually passing in the man's mind) that the porter was not really convinced that he was effectively gagged, but was remaining inactive out of fear of further attacks upon himself, the fact that in actual fact he was effectively silenced would not affect such censure as we might pass on his conduct. For, still keeping to the present view of responsibility, the porter's reluctance to risk his safety in the common interest might be modified in the future by our disapproval, and others, similarly placed, might be induced to show a bolder front. As Hobbes, taking substantially the present view of punishment, observed, it is "not only the unjust facts, but the designs and intentions to do them (though by accident hindered), are Injustice; which consisteth in the pravity of the will, as well as in the irregularity of the act." [10] It is intentions, and not outward action, that we can modify directly by punishment; and, for this purpose, all that we *strictly* need is knowledge of the precise nature of the intention. The law does not always allow this. The penalty for murder is different, in this country, from the penalty for 'attempted murder.' But there are various matters which help to account for this. Legal enactments have not yet rid themselves wholly of elements that have survived from primitive times. The morality of strict retribution, an eye for an eye, a life for a life, persists in some ways in the social codes of enlightened peoples. And the legislator has to take some account of this. Punishment, in matters of such seriousness as murder, may also need to be administered in part as a relief to public emotions which might otherwise find more sinister and unruly expression. It might also be pointed out, in the case of murder, that there is an element of doubt as to whether the criminal intended to maim or to kill, and that in being given a lighter sentence when the victim has not actually died, the criminal may be getting the benefit of this doubt. There does not seem, however, to be a very good case for this, at any rate in the instances where the eventual fate of the criminal turns on the skill and effort of doctors in saving the life of the victim. To what extent considerations such as these make it reasonable to discriminate between intention and the actual commission of a crime need not be considered closely here. For it is plain that, apart from very exceptional cases, it is intention that matters for the legislator as for the moralist; for it is by punishing (or rewarding) intentions

[10] *Leviathan*, ch. 30.

that we can modify the conduct of our fellows in the future. If we knew the intentions directly we could disregard the effects, *but this rarely*, if ever, happens, and therefore we have in actual practice to take account of what people can, or can not, actually accomplish, as helping to determine what is the nature of their intentions.

But the fact that the postulate of freedom, as it arises on the present view of responsibility, is of this somewhat incidental nature, while it does not strictly overthrow the view that responsibility can be conceived in the way we are discussing now, shows how far removed it is from what we normally think. For there can be cases in which punishment would be quite appropriate in the absence of the freedom that matters on this view—the freedom to effect an intention. This would happen in cases where some evil intention had been frustrated by factors not anticipated by the agent—if, for example, his gun had misfired or he had been struck by paralysis. But we normally take the relation between the postulate of freedom and responsibility to be much more direct and invariable than that. And this brings me to the matter which needs most to be stressed in regard to the view that responsibility, in the properly moral sense, can be fully described in legal or quasi-legal terms as liability to be punished or rewarded, namely the extent to which it is a departure from what we normally feel bound to believe.

A recent contributor to *Mind*,[11] Mr. P. Nowell-Smith, puts the essence of the view we are now discussing very clearly. He writes: "If a man steals because he has decided to do so, we can prevent his doing so again by causing him to decide otherwise. If he expects to be punished, then in addition to the motive that tends to make him steal there will be a powerful motive tending to make him refrain. Now the fear of punishment has no such influence on the kleptomaniac; on the other hand, psycho-analysis, by removing the subconscious cause of his tendency to steal, may achieve the desired result. Nor is this merely an interesting but unimportant distinction between kleptomaniacs and thieves; it is the very basis for the distinction."[12] But can we accept this? Does it not overlook something quite fundamental? Do we not believe that, whether or not the theft is one where punishment is appropriate (whether as a deterrent or, if we accept the retributive view, for its own sake), the conduct of the thief acquires immediately an evil quality, not possible in the case of the kleptomaniac, in virtue of wilful violation of an obvious duty? Is not this the fundamental consideration where moral distinctions are concerned, and is not the denial of this a repudiation of all that we normally understand by moral good and evil, however the writer may conceive the ends in terms of which the suitability of modifying conduct by punishment and reward is determined? There are, moreover, cases in which punishment would be the best way of restraining children, lunatics, or animals. But clearly we do not consider

[11] January, 1948.
[12] op. cit. p. 60.

the latter to be responsible in the properly moral sense. But if we do not, and if we are to hold that there is more to the distinction between the thief and the kleptomaniac than Nowell-Smith suggests, then it is not so apparent that we have an easy solution of the problem of moral freedom in terms of the freedom to do something other than we do if we so desire.

VII

The course described, however, has attractions, not only for supporters of naturalistic ethics, but also for others who are much less entitled to pursue it. Sir David Ross, for example, is firmly opposed to any attempt to define ethical ideas wholly in terms of our own reactions or those of other people. And in conformity with this he admits that the 'freedom to do,' in the sense of a power to carry our purposes into effect, has little significance for ethical theory. For we blame those who have failed to carry out a wicked intention quite as much as those who succeed. Yet Ross seems to think that a freedom to intend to do something if that is what we most desire will suffice in ethics. But if we are right in our previous argument, it is very hard to give any meaning to this freedom to intend if, like Ross, we hold a determinist view of the way our intentions are formed.

Account has already been taken earlier of Ross's distinction between three senses of right and wrong action. He argues that obligation in the strict sense must refer to intention rather than outward performance, and so to rightness in the strictly subjective sense, because the most that we can really control is our own intention. We cannot guarantee the result. This is sound enough so far as it goes. But it is an odd view to adopt if we also believe that we are bound to intend in accordance with what we most desire at the time. Ross himself has insisted that we do not control our emotions and desires; we cannot 'summon up' motives at will, although we may cultivate them. But that makes it strange to argue that we control our intentions in any sense which would not also apply to the motives which are believed to determine them.

The main reason for Ross's failure to appreciate this is the divorce of moral worth, as he understands it, from any sense of doing one's duty, and the assumption that blame applies to the latter in a way which does not concern the former. But we have maintained that this is very mistaken. The wrongful action by which blame is incurred is also the guilty and morally evil action, and if Ross does not think that emotions and desires are free in the sense which entitles us to say that we have obligations in respect of them, he is also precluded from making moral worth turn, in any measure, upon these features of character, or upon character as a whole. But he is also debarred from ascribing it solely to intentions. For the most plausible view for anyone to hold, if he believes that intentions are invariably determined by character, is that account must be taken of motives as well as intentions in making distinctions of moral value. From this dilemma there seems no escape short of the bolder course of affirming that moral worth belongs to actions which are free in a way in which neither motives nor actions 'from' certain motives are free; in other words, we have to presuppose a power to act independently of our desires and character—a freedom of genuinely open choice. To relegate the problem of freedom to the sphere of a particular meaning of wrongful action, even a legitimate one, in which it does not indirectly affect moral worth, affords no alleviation of the difficulties of the determinist. It only confuses the issue.

This is in fact one of the main sources of confusion in recent ethics where philosophers have been seriously at cross-purposes with themselves, especially in the controversy about the distinction between "the right act and the morality of the agent," by making extensive appeals to the postulate of freedom without clear recognition of its meaning as a choice between genuinely open alternatives.

This I have discussed more fully in an earlier paper.[13] But there is one matter not mentioned there which I should like to note now. It seems plain that conscience is fallible, and that, therefore, we may do what is wrong with the highest intentions. We normally think that our moral worth does not suffer in such cases, and this is one of the main reasons for the distinction between the "right act" and the "morality of the agent." But it only holds if we think of the conditions of moral value as differing sharply from the conditions of some non-moral good like knowledge. Why, otherwise, should ignorance exonerate? But conduct which is the expression of motives and character has the same inevitability as appears in the course of our thought. And since this is the view of conduct usually adopted by those who have recently stressed the distinction between "the right act and the worth of the agent," their opponents, proceeding on the same assumption, seem on equally strong ground in urging that moral ignorance is itself a moral defect, or, more ambiguously, that "we do not believe that everyone ought always to do what seems to him probably best." [14] There seems to be as much to be said on both sides as long as we seek to retain the idea of obligation within a deterministic view.

But to reject determinism is not to imply that any action may be expected from any man at any time; such a position would be as absurd as any position can be. All that is required is that there should be some occasions on which the flow of our conduct in accordance with character is arrested by a contrary claim of duty. This, in turn, also presents many difficulties, of which the greatest, to my mind, is that of reconciling genuine freedom of choice with what we also feel bound to think about causality. But this raises metaphysical questions which cannot be brought within the scope of this paper. I will content myself with the insistence that we can only retain the ideas of obligation and guilt as properly ethical ideas, if we

13 "Moral Freedom in Recent Ethics" [pp. 576 ff. this volume].
14 John Laird, "On Doing One's Best," *Philosophy*, January, 1931.

can also believe in actions which could have been other than they were although everything else in the universe had remained the same. I content myself with this because there is another aspect of our problem to which I should like to turn before I close.

VIII

As we have seen, it is when we think of moral evil as guilty or blameworthy conduct that we have also to regard it as wilful violation of law, as disobedience, and, thus, as involving absolute freedom of choice. But, very strangely, it is the persons who seem most assured that guilt is real, and who would most stoutly resist the attempt to reduce it to psychological terms, or to dismiss it as an illusion or some matter calling for mere therapeutic treatment—it is these, religious thinkers mostly and concerning themselves much more than the moralist with the problem of guilt, who also, as a rule, seem most emphatic in repudiating freedom. Even when they pay lip-service to freedom of choice, they belie it in their deepest and most distinctive convictions. This I shall call "the paradox of guilt." It is very deep and persistent, and it presents itself in fiction and general literature as well as in religious thought and reports of religious experience. Where there is the greatest assurance of guilt, there also we often find least concern for the individual and his freedom, and a consciousness of being in the grip of destiny. And, rightly understood, I believe that this has the greatest significance.

Some matters preliminary to the main explanation of this paradox are these.

There is a tendency for religious thinking to be more conservative than any other part of our thought. This is so for several reasons. But the most important reason, perhaps, is the fact that early religious experience carries a certain superficial authenticity which is absent from more mature religious life. This is because man is closer to Nature and more at her mercy. His life is less protected, and the world about him has not been so subdued to his thought as in more enlightened ages. He wages a more constant battle with reality, and there is thus a greater sense of awe and mystery, of the pressure upon him of alien, unrelenting powers and of a world not made amenable to his own will. The problem of subsequent ages, and above all in religion, is to recover this sense of an alien reality, of what is not ourselves or dissolvable into the categories of our own thought, at the level of new attainments and the conquests of the mind, to bend back our powers into contact with things, and thus be more truly and deeply at one with reality than was possible in the cruder immediacy of primitive life. It is this that we seek in the present crisis of western society, but it is not easy of attainment. And the starker, if unedified, realism of remote times confers on their religious life in particular a genuineness which may be equally present in more sophisticated experiences, but is rarely so obvious. And, therefore, the religious ideas which have taken shape in earlier and darker periods of society are apt to carry with them afterwards a peculiar claim to be the most essential and authentic versions of religious truth. But primitive society pays little heed to the individual; it identifies him, in his moral activities, with his community, with his family or his tribe; and the inexorable rule of custom operates with little regard for such niceties as the distinction between the purposes and the effects of actions. Accidental wrong initiates as surely as the most open maliciousness the savage alternation of retribution and retaliation. It is thus not surprising that so much in our religious thought, hailing from this source and also made more inflexible by its origin, should lag behind more enlightened views about freedom and accountability.

In reinforcement of this, it is worthy of note here that the assertion of guilt incurred in other ways than by avoidable human action, is bolder in times of confusion, like the present, when there is a recrudescence of the primitive and pagan attitudes which lurk beneath the surface of our civilisation. This seems to point to a deep kinship, and not to a mere accident of the times, as might be well brought out from a close study of the course of religion in Europe of late.

But, further, there is a very important way in which it is natural for religion to fill us with a sense of unworthiness, to make us "as dust," "as nothing"; the fleeting and unsubstantial aspect of existence is contrasted with the permanent realities of religion. But this, as has often been remarked by writers on "the sublime" and "the holy," is not moral unworthiness, but, rather, a general sense of unworthiness induced by the confrontation of the individual with the absolute perfection which he senses in his religion. God is all, man is nothing, his "days are as grass, as a flower of the field so he withereth." But this general sense of the dependent and limited character of finite being, and sometimes of utter hollowness, is easily confused with a sense of moral unworthiness, especially in those undiscriminating formative periods in which the more permanent idiom of religious utterance is coined. Moreover, the sense of the distance of the finite creature from the absolute perfection of religion does sharpen a man's ethical consciousness also and make him more vividly aware of the evil nature of the sinful acts that he has performed. And this makes it easier for the feeling of nothingness with which we are overwhelmed in religion—but that is only one aspect of the matter—to present itself also as an all-pervasive consciousness of sin.

With the greater progress of religion other factors enter in. This in particular. As religion becomes more completely moralised, and takes its place as the main source of refinement in ethics, the individual often finds himself confronted with exacting ideals which he is not able to embody to the full in the circumstances of his time and his society. The visionary must carry his neighbour with him, and this means some lowering of standards, much as the socialist today has to belie his principles about the ownership of property until he can persuade his society to accept them as a rule of life for the community as a whole. Some compromise is unavoidable, and the structure of society itself, moreover, impedes moral effort in some ways—even if it helps it in others. Hence, to borrow the title of a notable book, we have "moral man and immoral society." But this adjustment to a more common denominator rests very uneasily on a sensitive conscience, and the more sensitive are also often the most prone to measure themselves, not by what is attainable in the special situation in which they are placed, but by the ideals which glow more brightly ahead, by "impossible ideals" and "patterns laid up in heaven." This also leads to a sense of sinfulness and guilt not resting on individual choice, a matter that is no less distressing to the individual because it has such little foundation. It is significant that the idea of a tainted and fallen nature became most distinctive of Christian thought when the church was passing through a similar crisis. The early disciples of Christ obeyed his revolutionary injunctions—much more revolutionary than we usually acknowledge—with a great deal of consistency. But by the third century the church, for good or ill (but more for ill, I think), had immersed itself more completely in the world, and had to regulate its life by a "relative" rather than an "absolute" law. It was then, in the teaching of St. Augustine and his successors, that the notion of a tainted nature, of unavoidable sin, and the hypostatising of the universal nature of man in the doctrines of the Fall and of universal guilt acquired their ascendancy in Christian theology. They have had most prominence subsequently in times of similar crises, in the nationalist upheavals of the 15th century and in great modern wars when Christian ideals are most obviously strained.

This is not without its sinister aspect. For the idea of unavoidable sin is easily exploited. It presents an attractive way of turning the edge of inconvenient standards. The ideals remain in our midst but go unregarded. And Christians have in fact often, singly or collectively, sometimes with more, sometimes with less, deliberation sheltered from the rigorous exactions of their Christian allegiance behind the doctrine of the radical corruption of man and the domination of his life by impersonal evil forces. Something of the glow of the ideals is retained, or, at the level (rare, I believe) of crude expediency, their prestige, without too inconvenient an exaction of obedience. Such accommodation accounts for more in the history and thought of Christianity than is commonly realised. Along with this there go a delight in denunciation, in exploitation, without great emotional and spiritual cost, of the dramatic possibilities of a tragic situation, and, by a subtle inversion of pride, in vilification of self. Of these there is much evidence at present. The result is twofold. On the one hand, we have an alienation of religion, and often of ethics, from the business of living, a serene irresponsibility; ideals become, not rules of practice, but standards by which we are judged and condemned, salvation in turn being mediated in the cosmic drama of religion independently of our will. On the other hand, we have a sullen despair and pessimism, an enervating sense of the futility of all human endeavour. Both attitudes are very marked today, and they call for the bold and sustained intervention of the moral philosopher. But I mention these matters here mainly because of the lease of life which is lent in these ways also to the paradox of guilt.

But we have yet to offer the main explanation of this paradox and the reason for its significance. This presents itself when we consider the function of morality in the economy of life as a whole. Mention has already been made of the need to discover reality anew, and at a new power. And it is here that morality serves us so well, for its discipline is unlike any other, not excluding that of suffering and pain. For, although reality impinges upon us in pain with a peculiar insistency, this is because in a measure it has become ourselves. It is subjectively mediated, as also in perception where the pressure of reality upon us is rudest. Even in art where reality is made anew, where it is most individualised and expressive, and when the day-to-day rigidity of things is broken, when they stir and become articulate, even there our minds are only turned outwards to reality, as plants to the light, because of its fascination. Art could do nothing with us if it had no appeal. Neither would there be forgetfulness of self in personal attachments were not our affections involved. But morality knows nothing of this, there is no subtle transformation here, no fusion of reality with self. Morality provides no lodgment for the real in our own affections. And this is why the sense of reality is sustained by the moral life, and kept from distortion. Duty does not beguile, it commands; it can have no lure. What is not self is starkly before us, insistent, not to be denied; we are left with it as in an utter void. If we prevail there is a tremendous sense of exultation, a heightening of all our powers; the sheer, rugged, external shape of reality recedes; it is serene again. If we fail there is a diminution of our powers, a desolation, a kind of doom or death which is the penalty of sin. From this we may escape in part by sharp awareness of guilt and confession, and by the thrusting of the evil nature of surrender to self deep into our consciousness in condemnation and remorse; [15] and by grace, even more, the inward flow of reality begins again. What we are told of this in religion is often repellent, because the idiom and structure of religious thought hardened so much at the time when it was still mingled with a barbaric ethic. But the alienation of self from reality in moral failure is often so overwhelming, and most of all for religious minds, that we come to regard that failure, not as the cause, but as the effect, of some general impotence, of a doom in which we are caught up, of evil forces warring in all our members. Hence it is that the deepest consciousness of moral evil, and the sharpest recognition of it as guilt, often carries with it the belief so contradictory of all morality, that our guilt is itself the working out of some radical weakness in our own nature.

---

[15] It is by confusion with this that the notion of retributive punishment acquires some plausibility.

This, and much else in the relations of morality and religion, and of both to all forms of experience, we shall understand much better when religious thought is able to mount to the level of our other attainments. We shall then have the clue to the crisis of which so much is heard today, but which is not quite so peculiar to our time as is thought.

H. D. Lewis on the Problem of Guilt[*]

G. A. PAUL

1.—*Is it specially difficult to give a naturalistic account of the meaning of "guilty"?*

Mr. Lewis thinks it is much more difficult than giving a naturalistic account of the meaning of "good." I am not convinced by the reasons he gives for this, and from his own definition of "guilty" we can see that it is not so. He says that when we say that a man is guilty we mean that he has done something morally *bad* for which it is morally *fitting* that he should be blamed and feel remorse. So it is only if we think it much more difficult with "bad" or "fitting" than with "good" that we shall think it much more difficult with "guilty" than with "good."

Whether it is possible at all to give a naturalistic account of the meaning of any of these terms at all—"good," "bad," "fitting," "guilty"—is a question we shall not discuss today, for we shall follow Mr. Lewis in wishing to avoid for the present "the general problem of naturalistic ethics."

2.—*Psychoanalysis: Does it aid the naturalist?*

After emphasising how stubborn is the ordinary man's belief that guilt cannot be fully described in psychological terms, Mr. Lewis says,[1] "It may be urged that it is just here that psychology, and especially *recent* psychology, comes to the aid" of the naturalist. Its aid consists in showing that "there are many hidden anxieties which *create the impression that there is some distinctive ethical guilt*, when *in fact there is nothing but some emotional reaction*. On this basis some thinkers, and especially followers of Freud, have maintained that guilt is to be conceived, in the last resort, as a 'need for punishment.' "

The aid is of two kinds:—

(1) A new naturalistic definition of "guilt," namely, need for punishment.

(2) A new explanation of how ordinary people come to believe that

* Reprinted by kind permission of the author and the editors from the symposium on "The Problem of Guilt," *Proceedings of the Aristotelian Society, Supplementary Volume* 21, 1947. The editors of the present volume wish to call attention to the fact that the essay to which Mr. Paul is replying has been printed above in a slightly revised form. However, by far the greater number of passages cited by Mr. Paul are to be found in the revised version.

[1] p. 181 [p. 607 this volume].

guilt is non-natural and distinctively ethical whereas in fact it is natural and psychological—"there are many hidden anxieties which create this impression."

I find it difficult to come to grips with Mr. Lewis here, for he does not support what he says from the writings of any Freudians. I hope that in time he will do so; for the present I shall content myself with a short discussion of what he says about (1), and with giving some documentary evidence that not all Freudians would claim to provide either (1) or (2).

2.1: *Does "guilt" mean need for punishment?*

2.11: "This question," says Mr. Lewis,[2] could never be finally settled by recourse to the psychologist alone, *for* the essence of the claim to be determined is that there is *something not to be directly encompassed by psychology.*" I agree, it cannot be settled by the psychologist, but not for the reason Mr. Lewis gives. He implies that guilt *is* directly encompassed by moral philosophy, and that therefore it is for the philosopher to settle the question. Similarly, I suppose, matter is directly encompassed by physics, and therefore it is for the physicist to settle the corresponding question about matter; and the self is directly encompassed by psychology, so it is for the psychologist to settle the corresponding question about the self. But we do not in fact believe this in the case of matter or of the self; and even if it were a question of deciding between two *naturalistic* definitions of "guilt," or even between two naturalistic definitions in *psychological* terms, we should still not think it a question for the psychologist to settle. Why not? We need only look at the form of the question, in Mr. Lewis's own words,[3] "what do *we* mean when *we* think of guilt?" It is not "what does *the psychologist* mean when *the psychologist* thinks of guilt?" Now it is not that about which the question is asked (the self, matter, guilt), but the kind of question asked about it that makes it one for the philosopher, namely, "What do we mean when we think of *x*?" It is philosophers who have put in the work on questions of this form.

So Mr. Lewis's point is:—Psychoanalysts have proposed a new naturalistic definition of "guilt." Do not be brow-beaten by their grand language and professional status. Judge their attempt by just the same criteria as you would any other definition.

2.12: When the new naturalistic definition, need for punishment, is judged in this way it is quickly seen to be in fact no help to the naturalist. The trouble is not that it is naturalistic but that it is not even a plausible attempt at a naturalistic definition, and it would surprise me to find a naturalist who, having tried his hand at defining "guilt," had not done better before ever the Freudian came to "help" him. Compare "needing punishment" with Mr. Lewis's definition,[4] "requiring blame and condemnation." The difference between "punishment" and "blame and condemna-

---

[2] p. 185 [p. 610 this volume].
[3] p. 185 [p. 610 this volume].
[4] p. 178 [compare p. 605 this volume].

tion" is comparatively unimportant here; the main point is to compare "needing" and "requiring." These two words are often used to mean the same, and in fact we would have understood Mr. Lewis very well if he had spoken of "requiring punishment" and "needing blame and condemnation." Mr. Lewis explains that "He *needs* punishment" means "Unpunished he *feels a doom* hanging over him, and *will experience relief only when* punishment has been administered," [5] and that "He *requires* punishment" means "Punishment would be *appropriate* to his conduct." [6] Probably "needing punishment" can pass for a definition of "guilty" only because "needing" [7] can be taken to stand not only for "*feeling* a doom, etc.," but for "being *appropriately* dealt with by." [8] But once it is decided that "needs" is to mean "*feels* a doom, etc.," the definition will not pass for a moment, for it is so obvious that often when we call a person guilty, so far from meaning this, we are well aware that the very last thing that will give him relief will be to be blamed, condemned, or punished; and what we are saying of him is, of course, as Mr. Lewis says, that *whether it will give him satisfaction or not* he *deserves* something of that kind.

2.2: *Do psychoanalysts in fact claim that "hidden anxieties create the [false] impression that there is some distinctive ethical guilt"?*

I cannot answer this question in general. All I do here, and it is very little, is to quote from Dr. Karin Stephen, [9] a Freudian analyst, showing that she at least does not make the claim, but does say something that might be mistaken for it, namely, that *in every psychogenic illness* hidden anxieties create the impression that the patient *has some guilt which in fact he does not have.*

She writes, "*Neurotic* guilt, a painful emotion which in some form is always present in psychogenic illness, thus results from the presence in the unconscious of repressed sexualised hostility. The neurotic behaves *as if* he had a bad conscience . . . Very often the patient is conscious of these feelings of guilt and worthlessness, and such feelings may weigh crushingly even on people *whose lives are apparently blameless or even estimable*" (p. 194). And "it does not even seem necessary that their temper should have *actually done serious damage:* it is enough that they intended to do it, and in their omnipotent fantasy they will seize upon outside events for which they were not really responsible and claim the guilt for these" (p. 196). "'I did injure and rob them, and I can never do enough to atone for it.' Miss M.'s belief that she *had actually killed her rival and hurt her mother* sprang, ultimately, from her strong wish that this should in fact be true. Throughout her childhood she was burdened by the need to atone for this guilty success. To recognise that *she was not to blame* meant giving up her secret triumph, and she was willing to do this" (p. 202).

[5] p. 181 [p. 607 this volume].
[6] p. 178 [p. 605 this volume].
[7] cf. the possible ambiguity of "*demands* recompense."
[8] "He needs a good talking to."
[9] *Psychoanalysis and Medicine: A Study of the Wish to Fall Ill* (Cambridge, 1933).

Dr. Stephen makes clear that her patient has not "actually done serious damage," has not "actually killed her rival," "is not to blame" for any such thing, is "not really responsible for" an outside event and so cannot rightly "claim the guilt for it." This way of speaking implies that Dr. Stephen is aware that a person may do serious damage, be to blame for it, recognise that she is to blame, and justifiably claim the guilt for it.

What Dr. Stephen does say here is that *in every case of psychogenic illness* there is something for which the sufferer wrongly claims the guilt. (I should not be surprised if she were prepared to suggest that *everyone* has something for which he *wrongly* claims the guilt.) Now this way of speaking suggests that of course there are also things for which people do *rightly* claim the guilt, that there are things for which people *really are to blame*.

Mr. Lewis says,[10] "It must be a more serious matter to suppress *real guilt* and drive remorse itself underground to erupt elsewhere, than to treat the *pseudo-guilt* of the psychologists in similar fashion." It will now be evident that what Dr. Stephen believes is suppressed is not indeed real guilt, but neither is it pseudo-guilt, it is neurotic guilt, a painful sense of guilt *unfitted* to the patient's real situation.

All this about guilt has been said without taking sides on the philosophical question whether guilt is a (i) non-natural and (ii) peculiarly ethical attribute. I believe that in the quotation above he wishes to say that it must be a more serious matter for a person who believes that guilt is non-natural and peculiarly ethical to suppress a feeling of guilt than for a person who believes that guilt is naturalistic and not peculiarly ethical. He has no evidence to give in favour of this, and equally I have none against it.

3.—*Religious Therapy and Psychoanalytic Therapy.*

At the beginning of the last section, on religion,[11] Mr. Lewis speaks of "the attempt to *dismiss* guilt as some matter calling for *mere therapeutic treatment*" as having been most stoutly resisted by religious thinkers. I think he means that the attempt has been made by Freudian psychotherapists.

Yet later in describing what some religious people do, he tells of a process hardly if at all distinguishable from therapeutic treatment: "From this desolation, a kind of doom or death which is the penalty of sin, *we may escape* in part by (1) sharp awareness of guilt and confession, and by (2) the thrusting of the evil nature of the surrender to self deep into our consciousness in condemnation and remorse; and by (3) grace, even more, the inward flow of reality begins again." [12] Of course there are mentioned here some features of the world not usually mentioned in an analysis, and it is meant that the person really has done the evil he claims to have

---

[10] p. 185 [p. 610 this volume].
[11] [p. 616 this volume.]
[12] [Cf. p. 619 this volume.]

done. Why will it not do to write, "Of this desolation *we may be cured* in part by sharp awareness, etc."? A neurotic but innocent patient goes to the analyst to escape his feeling of desolation; a normal but guilty man goes to the minister of religion to escape his feeling of desolation. In both cases the person consulted tries to enable the man to admit to himself what the situation really is, to see himself as he really has been. The analyst tries to get the innocent man to see that he has not done what troubles him and could hardly have avoided the wish to do it and that therefore he has no ground for his feeling of desolation and so in part to escape it. The minister of religion tries to get the guilty man to face the fact that he has deliberately done what troubles him, and that he has indeed good ground for his feeling of desolation, to regret it now and feel remorse for it, and so in part to escape his feeling of desolation.[13] Each is a treatment which may in part bring relief from suffering. To what differences between them does Mr. Lewis wish to point? What he mentions are (*a*) *awareness* of the guilt, (*b*) *confession* of the guilt, (*c*) *condemnation* of the guilt, and (*d*) *remorse* for the guilt. Each of these would, of course, be out of place with the neurotic patient since he is in fact mistaken in supposing himself guilty.

What this brings out is once more that what the psychoanalyst appears to be chiefly concerned with is unjustified feelings of guilt, and that no evidence has been given that when a person really is guilty the analyst tries to dismiss the guilt or regard remorse as out of place. But both the psychoanalyst and the minister of religion are concerned to bring relief.

4.—*Freewill: Mr. Lewis's argument:*

Mr. Lewis says [14] that "no conduct is open to blame unless it is free." As evidence he instances that "it is a fair rejoinder to an accusation to declare that we 'could not help' what we did," and that "blame seems out of place in art or knowledge just because there is not the requisite freedom." [15] His worry is that there may be no cases of the requisite freedom, and hence no cases of guilt, so that in blaming someone we would always be being unfair.

What freedom *is* requisite? Not just "freedom to carry out a purpose," [16] *once we have chosen to,* but "freedom *to choose.*" [17] (He speaks of this as "an *absolute* freedom of choice," [18] "an *open* choice," "a choice between *genuinely* open alternatives." [19])

What are we free to choose between? Not motives ("We cannot summon up motives at will" [20]). And if not motives, then not intentions ("It seems odd to suppose that our conduct is open to blame in regard to our

[13] Neither of these claims to be a description of all that happens. By no means.
[14] p. 186 [p. 610 this volume].
[15] p. 189 [pp. 602, 610 this volume].
[16] p. 186 [pp. 611 ff. this volume].
[17] p. 187 [pp. 611 ff. this volume].
[18] p. 187 [cf. pp. 614-5 this volume].
[19] p. 188 [cf. pp. 614-5 this volume].
[20] p. 187 [p. 614 this volume].

intentions, but not in the way our intentions are shaped by our motives." [21]

So what is required if we are ever to blame is "some conduct that is free in a way in which neither (*a*) motives nor (*b*) acts from certain motives are free," [22] "in other words a power *to act independently of our desires and characters*," "actions which could have been other than they were even although *everything else in the universe* had remained the same." [23] However, it is not that "*any* action may be expected from any man at any time," but that "there should be some occasions on which *the flow of our conduct in accordance with character* is *arrested by a contrary claim of duty*." [24]

There is not time to examine the steps of this argument, and all I intend to do is to say something short about (1) the conclusion and (2) the first steps.

4.1: *The conclusion:*

4.11: *The dilemma is worse than Mr. Lewis supposes:*

It is not merely that indeterminism (which would make it sometimes reasonable to blame people) is difficult to believe in,[25] but that indeterminism, just as much as determinism, seems to make it unreasonable ever to blame anyone. Mr. Duncan-Jones puts the point well in "Freedom: an Illustrative Puzzle" *Arist. Soc. Proc.* 1938–9, p. 108:—"If the particular decision that I make, within a certain range, is not determined, then my previous life might have had the precise character that it actually had and I might none the less have made a different decision: I am therefore not responsible for having made this precise decision. And so on. A fortiori, unrestricted indifference is inconsistent with responsibility.

"We therefore have a simple constructive dilemma. If determinism is true, people are not responsible, and if the liberty of indifference is true, people are not responsible; but either determinism or the liberty of indifference is true; therefore people are not responsible." *Cf.* Prof. Stebbing, *Philosophy and the Physicists*, ed. 1, p. 239:—"Suppose my acts of choice are spontaneous, uncaused, in no sense springing from what I am. How then can *I* be said to be responsible?" And *cf.* Prof. Broad, this volume p. 10:—"Just in so far as our volitions, etc., are undetermined they seem to fall under the heading of *mere accidental events that happen to us*, yet it is required that they should be expressions of our permanent inner nature."

4.12: *Mr. Lewis's final suggestion seems to be a case not of indeterminism but of determinism.*

It will have been noticed that Mr. Lewis suddenly scales down the requirement:—"All that is required is that there should be some occasions on which the flow of our conduct in accordance with character is arrested by a contrary claim of duty." [26] There is nothing here to suggest that

---

[21] p. 187 [cf. pp. 614–5 this volume].
[22] p. 187 [p. 615 this volume].
[23] p. 190 [pp. 615–6 this volume].
[24] p. 190 [p. 615 this volume].
[25] p. 190.
[26] p. 190 [p. 615 this volume].

even if the character and the claim of duty had remained the same the flow could have been other than arrested. It seems to be rather determinism than indeterminism: "the flow of x *in accordance with* y *is arrested by* z."

So far from helping to solve the difficulty, these points make it worse.

4.2: *The first step:*

Mr. Lewis rightly says, "It is a fair rejoinder to an *accusation* to declare that we *'could not help'* what we did." [27] But as people nearly always do in discussing freewill, he emphasises this side only, to the exclusion of the fact that it is further a fair rejoinder to such an *excuse* to claim that we "*could very well have helped*" what we did. We find cases in which a person could very well have helped it just as much as cases in which he could not help it. I wish to focus attention on these cases.

First I must instance cases of *being unable to help it:*—

(i) "We are not really to blame for our ignorance of psychical research. We cannot help it because we have not time to read so many articles."

(ii) "He could not help it. They forced it out of him. He was given the third degree."

(iii) "You can't blame him for saying anything that is in this so-called confession. They interrogated him ten hours a day for weeks on end. When that is done a man becomes different; he may even begin to believe some of the things they repeat to him."

(iv) "They secretly gave him some sort of drug, and he spoke and acted in a queer, dreamlike way. He was beyond helping what he said or did."

(v) "He just can't help taking things. The truth is he is a kleptomaniac. You know he has everything that money can buy, and he does not even want the things he takes. He gets completely miserable about the trouble it brings, and tries hard not to do it again, but it seems he just can't resist it. 'It just comes all over me,' he says."

Now follow cases of *being very well able to help it:*—

(i) "Couldn't help it? He could very well have helped it. He had received very good treatment at their hands and appeared perfectly normal in the witness box. He did not *have* to make that elaborate confession."

(ii) "He'll take anything he can lay his hands on, if he thinks he can get away with it. He has had every chance in life. He is just plain extravagant, a spendthrift."

(iii) A boy comes home late from a party. His mother blames him saying, "You knew perfectly well you had to come away at 10 o'clock and it's nearly 12." He replies, "I couldn't help it. They just kept on doing things and I didn't get a chance to come away." She says, "Didn't get a chance! There was nothing to prevent you from just getting up at 10 o'clock and excusing yourself." Boy: "Yes, but you know how difficult it is when they're wanting you to do things." Mother: "I know, you've just got to try." Boy: "But I did try, Mother, only I couldn't." Mother: "Well you've just got to try harder. It's no use telling me you couldn't help it. You could very well. You've just got to learn to come away from things." Boy: "But the flow of my actions in accordance with my character just didn't happen to be interrupted by a claim of duty."

These examples indicate some of the things we are trying to find out in trying to find out whether a person could have helped doing what he did, and hence in trying to find out whether he is to blame for doing it.

[27] p. 186 [p. 610 this volume].

"No conduct is open to blame unless it is free" and these indicate what we are in fact concerned with in trying to find out whether his conduct was free. There was no question that there are cases of *necessity*. Is there any question that there are cases of *freedom?*

Asked by a man whether the material world exists I hand him a stone. Does that resolve his doubt (and mine)? No, but it may help us to begin.

VIII

THE PROBLEM OF JUSTIFICATION

Prolegomena to a Theory of the Moral Criterion *

C. A. CAMPBELL

INTRODUCTION

Sɪɴᴄᴇ ʀᴇᴀᴅᴇʀꜱ of philosophical literature have become accustomed, by famous precedents, to the employment of the term "prolegomena" in a somewhat generous signification,[1] it may be as well to make it clear at the outset that the above title means no more than it says. I shall not stray beyond the limits of "mere" prolegomena. The positive theory of the moral criterion in whose ultimate interest, in a sense, the paper is written, will not appear.

That positive theory has, as a matter of fact, already appeared elsewhere, although somewhat sketchily, in a publication whose primary purport was metaphysical.[2] Among other defects in the form of the statement there given to it was, I think, a failure to prepare the way adequately by a systematic criticism of what may be called the "orthodox" way of conceiving the moral criterion. I am seeking to remedy that defect now. I shall try to show in this paper that the orthodox type of theory is in principle untenable. If the attempt succeeds, it will not, of course, establish the theory which I myself favour. The most that it can do will be to exhibit the need for something in the nature of a new constructive approach to this problem. But with such a result I should be well content. For, to speak plainly, I do not believe that ethical discussions of a fundamental kind can hope to make the slightest progress until the issues presented below have been squarely faced.

A few words will suffice to explain what I mean by the "orthodox" type of theory of the moral criterion. By "the moral criterion" I mean, of course, just what is ordinarily meant—the standard in terms of which the moral worth of conduct is to be estimated.

* Reprinted by kind permission of the author and the editors from the *Proceedings of the Aristotelian Society*, 37, 1936–7. The second half of this essay, reprinted in its entirety below, deals with the problem of free-will.

[1] Green's *Prolegomena to Ethics* is perhaps the most conspicuous example. The reader is tempted to ask "If this be mere 'prolegomena,' what is 'ethics'?"

[2] *Scepticism and Construction*, especially Ch. VII. Nothing said in the present paper, however, presupposes acquaintance with that work.

There is admittedly a large diversity in traditional accounts of the moral criterion. One school puts forward the greatest happiness of the greatest number, another the full development of human capabilities, another the attainment of certain (so-called) "intrinsic goods," another the observance of specific moral rules or laws—and so on. What concerns us here about these views, however, is not their differences, but a certain identity of conception which underlies the differences. All, or almost all, are agreed in holding that the moral standard is expressible in some definitive *content,* and that (speaking generally) conduct is to be judged morally good or morally bad according as it attains to or falls short of that *concrete* standard. This is what I mean by the "orthodox" type of theory—the type of theory which holds that the standard by which we should measure the moral worth of conduct is (whatever else it is) at least concrete, embodying a definitive content. To give it a label more indicative of its nature, we may call it alternatively the "concrete" type of theory.

Now it seems to me that there are at least two grounds, each adequate in itself, upon which *any* concrete theory of the moral criterion must be dismissed as invalid. In what follows I shall deal with each of these in turn as exhaustively as I can.

I

The first great difficulty which the "concrete" moralist has to face is as follows. It is very evident that, in whatever terms the concrete moralist chooses to define his standard, there will be many persons who do not, and even many persons who *cannot,* accept this standard as *their* standard. It is, let it be conceded, the latter class only which constitutes a problem. But it is a large class. Many circumstances—a particular cultural environment, a defective education, or perhaps sheer congenital stupidity—may prevent a man from being able to entertain as his moral standard, and thus as morally imperative upon him, the standard which the moral philosopher enunciates. Now, are we seriously going to maintain that such persons are morally good (and thus deserving of moral esteem) in so far as they attain to, and are morally bad (and thus deserving of moral blame) in so far as they fall short of, this standard which *they* do not and could not accept? If so, it would seem to follow that a man may deserve moral esteem for doing what he believes to be wrong, and moral blame for refraining from doing what he believes to be wrong. And this is an implication which might well give pause to even the most sophisticated moralist.

Let us, however, examine the situation more closely. For the issue is fundamental, and the concrete moralist will certainly not be satisfied with the simple statement of it given above.

We are all agreed, I presume, that an act proclaimed to be a duty by the standard of the philosophical moralist (it is, of course, a matter of indifference what moralist or what standard we take for the sake of example) might be sincerely denounced by a given individual (bred, perhaps, in a different ethical environment) as a gross violation of duty. It is obvious also that the act, believed to be morally wrong by the given individual, might be one towards which he is nevertheless strongly urged by his inclinations. It might, for instance, be the preservation of the life of a weakly infant. Now suppose that in such a case the man "yields to his inclinations" in "defiance of duty." What is our "concrete moralist" going to say to such an act? If he says that it is morally estimable, because it aims at an object approved by his concrete standard, *viz.*, the preservation of human life, he is assigning moral worth to an act which the agent performs "against his conscience." And so to judge is surely to play havoc with our moral consciousness. If, on the other hand, he declares the act to be morally blameworthy, on what grounds, we must ask, does he justify this judgement? Surely he is then playing havoc with his professed moral standard, which seems, *prima facie* at any rate, quite impotent to authorize an attitude of censure towards the act.

Has the concrete moralist any means of escape from this impasse? I do not believe that he has. But it is incumbent upon us to examine carefully any ways along which escape might conceivably be sought. As far as I can see there are four alternatives to be considered.

(1) Possibly he will take refuge in a distinction between judgement of the *man* and judgement of the *act*. The man, he may agree, must be judged bad, because acting against conscience. But the act, because directed to a right content, must be judged good. On the basis of this distinction, he may urge, justice can be done both to the procedure of the concrete moralist and to the objection that has been advanced above.

But despite the formidable authority which views of this kind can claim, it seems to me that they make no contribution whatever to the settlement of the problem which is engaging us. Our problem is that of the *moral* criterion. We are concerned with *moral* value. But an act, surely, has moral relevance only in so far as it is the expression of a *personal will*. Without doubt we can *consider* an act in abstraction from the will of the doer. But so considered, the act loses all moral status. When thus depersonalized it is no more liable to moral praise and blame than are sunshine and tempest. It is to *persons*, and persons alone, that all our moral judgements ultimately refer. An ethical theory which ignores this simple truth is an ethical theory which is beginning to lose sight of its own very *data*.

(2) The concrete moralist may object, again, that we have not adequately understood the nature of his standard. It is indeed "concrete," he may tell us, but it has *also* certain "formal" characteristics. These are meant to be taken for granted, as too obvious to require explicit statement. A will, to be a morally good will, must be directed to the right concrete content: but it must *also* be in accord with the agent's moral conscience. Moral value attaches to an act only if this formal condition as well as the material conditions are satisfied. The concrete moralist, accordingly, is not obliged to

acclaim as morally estimable an act such as the one that we have under review, in which a right content is willed against conscience.

When the criterion is so qualified the concrete moralist is certainly relieved from one grave embarrassment. But this is achieved only at the expense of plunging him into another no whit less serious. For the "formal" characteristics, which we are invited to "take for granted," fairly bristle with difficulties when we attempt to insert them within the framework of a "concrete" theory of the moral criterion.

The concrete moralist is now enabled to condemn the act (of preserving the weakly infant's life) in virtue of the "formal" aspect of his criterion. And in virtue of the "material" aspect of his criterion he—does what? The material aspect he can hardly treat as otiose. Presumably it must have *some* bearing upon the moral judgement he passes. The concrete moralist must say at least (one imagines) that this act is good *in so far as* the content willed is in accord with his (the moralist's) concrete standard. Thus he would not hesitate to say, I think, that this act is a *better* act than it would have been had the agent succumbed to an inclination which was *contrary* to the said standard. The act, then, may be said to be for the concrete moralist bad in one respect (its formal character), and good in another respect (its material character).

Now this may, at the first look, appear to be an innocent enough doctrine. There is certainly nothing reprehensible in the view that an act may have elements both of goodness and of badness constituent within it. But if we look a little closer, it becomes clear that the concrete moralist's position, as we have now to understand it, is in fact insupportable. For the two aspects which he includes within his moral criterion are left by him with absolutely no intelligible relationship between them: so that, when we attempt to pass judgement upon an act in terms of that criterion, we find that we are entirely without guidance as to the relative amounts of weight to be attached to each of the two aspects. Thus moral judgement in terms of this criterion has no real determining ground. If it becomes determinate, that determination will depend not upon any objective principle, but merely upon the judge's subjective preferences in regard to the "two aspects." We are left, indeed, with no moral criterion in the proper sense at all. What poses as a single criterion with two "aspects" turns out to be to all intents and purposes two independent criteria. And to have two independent criteria is not easily distinguishable from having no criterion at all.

To put the matter in a nutshell: if a moral criterion which has two aspects is to yield any *determinate* moral judgement at all, it is imperative that the value of the two aspects relatively to one another be clearly and closely defined. Thus if a given act (such as that which we have taken as our example) is bad in so far as it lacks the right formal character, and good in so far as it possesses the right concrete character, it should be clear that we have not got, even in principle, the means of deciding whether "on balance" the act is good or bad, much less of deciding *how* good or *how* bad it is, *until* we know (among other things) whether "content" or "conscientiousness" is the more important constituent of the criterion, and the degree of importance of each of these relatively to the other. But on these vital matters the concrete moralist leaves us absolutely without information.

(3) The concrete moralist may, once more, attempt to justify himself on the basis of a distinction between "subjective" and "objective" moral worth. We have accused him of being obliged to ascribe moral worth to certain acts done "against conscience." But, he may tell us, he does not ascribe to such acts moral worth *simpliciter*. Such acts, done against conscience but with a right content, are *objectively* good but *subjectively* bad: just as, if done in obedience to conscience but with a wrong content, they would be *subjectively* good but *objectively* bad. His "concrete" standard, he implies, is concerned with "objective" moral worth. But, recognizing as he does that "conscientiousness" has *some* moral value, and that it is an indefensible paradox to say that an act with a right content but done against conscience has *nothing* morally defective in it, he endeavours to meet the difficulty in a way satisfactory to all parties by granting that such an act, though "objectively" good, is "subjectively" bad.

This distinction between subjective and objective moral value is a prevalent device among moralists who have made the uncomfortable discovery that the straightforward application of their concrete standard yields certain results repugnant to the moral consciousness of mankind. But it is just another attempt to run with the hare and hunt with the hounds. Any plausibility which the device enjoys remains just so long as the precise meaning of the distinction posited is veiled in convenient obscurity. A brief inquiry into its possible meanings should suffice to show that this is the case.

What then, let us ask, can "subjective" as opposed to "objective" moral value mean?

It might possibly, I suppose, be taken to mean the moral value which attaches to the "subject," in virtue of the character of the personal will expressed in the act, contrasted with the moral value which belongs to the act simply in virtue of its "objective" content. But clearly this is just another form of the distinction between judging the "man" and judging the "act" which we have already dismissed as ethically irrelevant. Within the sphere of *moral* value no such distinction can exist, for the reason that it is to persons and persons alone that judgements of moral goodness and badness ultimately refer. What is here, in our present sense of the distinction, called "objective" moral value, attaching to the act considered in abstraction from the personal will expressed in it, is not any kind of moral value at all. The distinction, then, if we try to give this meaning to it, collapses utterly.

Let us try another meaning. "Subjective" moral value might be taken to mean a value which is not "grounded in the nature of things," as contrasted with "objective" moral value, which is so grounded. That is the meaning suggested by analogy with the use made of these terms in general axiological discussions, where "subjective" value normally means a value contingent upon personal desires, feelings, or likings, and without onto-logical foundation. But it seems perfectly clear that this meaning will not do at all in our present connection. I do not know, in the first place, what can be meant by a "moral" value—whether or not we qualify the expression by a disparaging adjective, such as "subjective" is here intended to be—which is contingent upon personal likings. But even if there were any such thing, nothing can be much more evident in the whole field of our value-judgements than that the moral value we attach to *conscientiousness* as such is *not* regarded as a value contingent upon anyone's personal likings. If "subjective" moral value is to mean this, then the distinction posited by the concrete moralist will not help him out of his difficulty in the smallest degree. For to dismiss the moral value of conscientiousness as "subjective," in *this* sense of the term, is not a bit more plausible than to deny its moral value altogether.

Is there any other meaning that might attach to the distinction between subjective and objective moral value? I know of none which could con-ceivably have a useful bearing upon our problem, and propose therefore to pass on to the consideration of a different line of defence.

(4) We come here upon what is, so far as I can see, the concrete moral-ist's last resource—his last possible device for countering our old difficulty that if we estimate the moral worth of actions by a concrete standard we shall be driven at times to judge some conscientious actions as morally bad and some actions done against conscience as morally good. But it is a re-source of which he will, I think, hesitate to avail himself. We have so far taken for granted the common implication of moral goodness with "praise-worthiness," and moral badness with "blameworthiness." The lines of criticism we have advanced have depended vitally upon the recognition of that implication's validity. But it is conceivable that the concrete moralist may attempt to short-circuit our criticisms and save his criterion by frankly repudiating this whole attitude of mind. He may tell us that the "moral standard" as he understands it is not intended to measure moral praise-worthiness or blameworthiness, and that all objections based on the as-sumption that it is are in consequence irrelevant. Moral goodness consists—to state his view succinctly and without refinements—in willing the right content, moral badness in willing the wrong content, and considerations of the act's possible praiseworthiness or blameworthiness have nothing what-ever to do with the matter. Thus the goodness of the will to preserve the weakly infant's life, in our example, is not in the least compromised by the fact that the agent acted against conscience. That may possibly be a ground of blameworthiness in the agent, but it has no bearing at all on the moral quality of the act.

Now, if the moralist is prepared to take this paradoxical line, and to adhere to it consistently—divorcing moral worth altogether from considerations of praise and blame—there is of course no question about the propriety of his adopting a "concrete" standard. But it *is* a paradox, and one that it would be particularly difficult to defend. It seems, indeed, to be one of that inexcusable kind which arises from using old words with new meanings. For better or for worse, the term "morality" has come to hold in our common speech a meaning which includes an intrinsic reference to the concepts it is here proposed to ignore. To speak of a "moral" goodness which has yet no claim upon our esteem, and a "moral" badness which is yet no just object of censure, would seem to the ordinary man to be an abuse of the convention of language. The ordinary man might admit, and no doubt should admit, the right of the philosopher to *refine upon* the meaning of words in common speech. But here we have, not a refinement, but a radical revision: not an incidental modification, but a fundamental transformation. And the ordinary man would be perfectly right, I think, in calling upon the philosopher to use some other and less misleading term for that which he chooses to miscall a "moral" standard.

It may well be the case, of course, that on the last analysis the concepts of moral praise and blame are meaningless, and "morality" as understood by the ordinary man a mere delusion. Such a view follows logically—despite occasional protestations to the contrary—upon any thoroughgoing Determinism. And if such a view should ever come to be generally accepted, one must concede that no valid objection could then be taken to the use of the term "morality" without implications of praise and blame: for no longer would that term be, by common tradition, preempted for use *with* these implications. It is hardly necessary to point out, however, that that hypothetical stage in the development of our ethical thinking has not been reached as yet. With a very few exceptions, those philosophers who have debated the problem of the moral standard have neither openly proclaimed nor tacitly implied repudiation of the notions of moral praise and blame. And this being the actual situation, the elementary duty of respecting the normal usage of words would seem to prohibit the philosopher from professing to deal with the "moral" standard while ignoring considerations of praise and blame.

It seems to me clear, then, that this last line of defence is quite ineffective, at least in the present context of ethical controversy. Our brief discussion of it, however, may have served a useful enough purpose by bringing into the open an assumption which underlies most of our criticism of the "concrete" moralists—the assumption that the latter, like ourselves, are concerned to find the proper standard for estimating moral goodness and badness in the accepted signification of these terms.

II

So much, then, for the *first* ground upon which, as it seems to me, all concrete theories of the moral standard must fail. I have stated the ground, and examined and rejected such possible lines of defence as it seemed worth while to consider. I pass now to the *second* ground, which is quite independent of the first.

The first ground, it will be remembered, rested upon the premise that, whatever be the concrete standard we select, there will always be some persons who just *cannot* entertain that standard as *their* moral standard. Our second ground does not require us to assume even so much as that. I am prepared to argue that, *even if all persons were to accept precisely the same concrete standard*, it must still be illegitimate to judge the moral worth of their conduct in terms of its approximation to that standard. It would be illegitimate, for the reason that this basis of judgement takes no account of certain factors of which any satisfactory moral judgement *must* take account, *viz.*, certain influences which have a facilitating or an obstructing effect upon the agent's achievement of his concrete standard but for which the *agent himself* cannot be held responsible.

That influences of the kind described exist is, I think, beyond all reasonable doubt. Indeed, it would be a good deal easier to make a case for the view that no *other* influences exist, than that *these* influences do *not* exist. For we are all agreed, I suppose, that how easy or how difficult an agent finds it in any given case to conform his will to his concrete standard is a matter which depends upon the relative strength of his relevant desires and aversions: and that desires and aversions are thus, so far, causal influences determining the act of will. And we are all likewise agreed, I suppose, that the relative strength of a man's desires and aversions is always in part at least dependent upon his inherited nature, and also upon manifold educational influences from external sources which we may epitomize in the phrase "environmental nurture." But the agent is not responsible either for his inherited nature or for his environmental nurture. It follows that if we insist upon appraising the moral worth of persons in terms of the approximation of their conduct to a given concrete standard—even if that standard be their *own* standard—we shall be passing judgement upon persons in respect of something for which they are at least in part not responsible. And since (by the very definition of responsibility) a man is properly subject to moral praise and blame only in respect of conduct for which he *is* responsible, it would seem that the impropriety of this manner of judging could hardly be more clear.

Let us, however, follow our previous practice and examine the possible lines of defence which the concrete moralist might take up against this criticism.

There is little doubt, I think, that the concrete moralist will deem the best defence to lie in attack. He will attack the view of responsibility that underlies our criticism. Our statement of the criticism implied the view that while conduct was (or might be) in part due to the agent himself, it was also due in part to "external" factors, and that moral responsibility could only with propriety be assigned to the agent in respect of the former part of conduct—since, clearly, a self cannot justly be praised or blamed save for that in his conduct which the *self* determines. This position may be challenged from more than one point of view.

(1) It may be argued that, even if we grant the reality of the distinction between that in a man's conduct which is due to his own individual initiative and that which is due to external factors, still it must be utterly impossible in practice to disentangle from the complicated web of human conduct how much is assignable to the one source and how much to the other. If we are determined to press this "puristic" notion of moral responsibility, it will be said, the logical result should be a suspension of moral judgement altogether.

We need spend very little time over this objection. Clearly, it points to a difficulty in the *practical application* of our criterion of moral responsibility, and does not have the faintest bearing upon the quite different question of whether that criterion is the *true* one. That the difficulty alleged in practical application does exist, no one would be foolish enough to deny—though it may be worth mentioning, in parenthesis, that the difficulty can be, and often is, exaggerated. But the only condition under which that difficulty could have the effect of casting doubt upon the validity of the criterion itself would be if there were some good reason for believing that the criterion of moral responsibility, and consequently of moral worth, *must* be one which human beings are in a position to apply accurately and adequately in practice. And no such reason appears to exist.

(2) An altogether more serious objection, which we shall have to consider at some length, is that our conception of moral responsibility is not merely inapplicable in practice, but is fallacious in principle, in that it rests upon an untenable view of the relation of the self to its heredity and its environment. That view assumes that the influence of heredity and environment upon conduct is an influence external to and independent of the self, whence it is inferred that the self is not responsible for whatever in its conduct is traceable to either of these sources. But such an assumption, it may be held, cannot be sustained.

Why not? On what grounds would the critic deny that the influence of congenital tendencies—for convenience we confine ourselves meanwhile to this factor—is rightly regarded as "external" to the self? There are, I think, a less and a more sophisticated line of argument open to him. Let us begin with the less sophisticated.

(*a*) He may say: How can it be possible to separate the self from something that is, after all, part of *its nature*? All the tendencies in a self, whether inherited or acquired, are constituents of the self, part of what the self *is*. A descriptive analysis of the nature of a particular self would have to include, indeed would be largely composed of, items of just this sort. It must be absurd, then, to try to treat such tendencies as something external to the self, and to try to regard conduct, in so far as it is determined by inherited tendencies, as being determined by something external to the self, and thus as not being that *self*-determined conduct for which, admittedly, the self is alone responsible.

This line of argument has a certain surface plausibility: but it will not bear close inspection. In a paper which sought to be constructive, it would be necessary to deal fully with the distinction between that in a self's "nature" for which the self is responsible and that in a self's "nature" for which it is not—a distinction which, for all its paradoxical verbal appearance, is one which is perfectly familiar to common sense and is constantly being applied in actual moral judgements. But at present it is sufficient for our purpose to say just this. Assuredly congenital tendencies are constituents in the self's "nature." But they are constituents that have a *causal history which long ante-dates the existence of the particular self*. Hence, in so far as an act is determined by them, the particular self can be regarded as only the *proximate* cause of the act. He is the "cause" only in the sense of being one link, or complex of links, in an indefinitely long and intricate chain of causes and effects. He, this particular finite self with an historical beginning in time, is not in respect of these determinants the *initiator* of the act. He is the kind of cause that is *also* an effect. And it is surely mere nonsense to suggest that this particular self is morally responsible for an act the causation of which must admittedly be referred to processes occurring long before this particular self in any sense "was."

(*b*) The more sophisticated line of argument would probably begin by acknowledging the justice of what we have urged above. Determination by the self's congenital tendencies is not, as such, determination by the self. If an act were referable for its determination solely to such factors, if it were, for example, purely "instinctive" action, it would be meaningless to hold the "self" responsible. No "self" has been engaged in the transaction. Presuming that the self were conscious of the act, it would be conscious of it merely as a process enacted *in* it, not as in any sense a process enacted *by* it. Such determination is, and is recognized by the self to be, merely "external" determination.

But, our critic would go on, all this is very little to the point. Both parties can agree that in acts of *this* sort the influence of congenital tendencies is external and the self is not responsible. But it is not acts of this sort—acts of the "instinctive" type—that constitute the *conduct* in which moral judgement is interested. It is *willed* acts in which moral judgement is, or is primarily, interested. And thus the real point at issue is whether congenital tendencies can exert an external influence upon acts of will.

Now on this point, it is argued, a negative answer follows from the very nature of "willing." It is of the very nature of willing to be a *self*-determining activity. The willed or motived act differs from the instinctive or merely impulsive act most fundamentally just in this, that the end willed must be conceived by the self as something which the *self* wants, i.e. (in the terminology common to this critic's psychology) as a good for the self, or a "personal good." There is no question, therefore, of the end in willing being externally imposed upon a passive self—whether by a congenital impulse or anything else. For there is no act of will unless the self consciously adopts the end as *its* end. It is thus that the agent is prepared to say, after a willed act, "It was *I* who acted, and *I* accept responsibility." In this sense, then, every willed act is "self-determined," and, because self-determined, is one for which the self cannot disclaim responsibility.

But surely there is no way of escape along this well-beaten track? What, after all, does the argument really prove? It proves that conduct, *qua* willed action, is always "self-determined" in the sense that the end aimed at must always be one which the self consciously adopts as its own good. This is true enough, so far as it goes. The present writer, at any rate, would not dispute it. But there are obviously important further questions which we are bound to ask concerning the determination of such acts: and on the answer to *these* questions, in the last resort, our problem really turns.

Thus we may reasonably ask *what it is* that determines a self to conceive one object rather than another as a "good" for it, and one object as a "greater good" for it than another object, and one object as the "greatest good" for it in a given situation. If we do ask this, the first answer will naturally be in terms of the self's desires and aversions. Indeed to desire an object, and to conceive an object as a good for the self, are, the critic would himself probably agree, just "two different modes of naming the same psychological fact"—if we may apply Mill's phrase in a new, and I think more valid, context. Which of several conceived goods in a given situation will be regarded by the self as the greatest good for it in that situation will depend, we may say, upon the relative strength of those of the self's desires and aversions which are relevant to the situation.

The answer so far, of course, amounts to very little. But it becomes more significant when we add the further and equally obvious point that a self's desires and aversions are themselves in part determined by the self's equipment of congenital tendencies. This, I presume, no one has ever been prepared to deny. And it allows us to say now that the congenital tendencies in a self are at least a factor in determining what in a given situation the self will conceive to be a good for the self—and, we must add, the degree of its goodness relative to other "personal" goods.

What follows? It follows that if all that is meant by the "self-determination" characteristic of all willing is that the end must be conceived as a good for the self, then this self-determination is not of a kind which necessarily carries with it the self's responsibility for the end willed. For the self, we have seen, is partly determined in its conception of what is a good for it, and of how good a good it is, by factors which are not within its control, *viz.*, its specific equipment of congenital tendencies.

Congenital tendencies do then exert a certain "external" influence upon the act of will—an influence for which the self cannot be held responsible. I have advanced a formal argument for this conclusion, but indeed it was perhaps hardly necessary. It might have been sufficient to point out by way of an illustration how intolerable is the position of the critic who would question it. I shall offer an illustration now, choosing one which will emphasize the importance for valid moral judgement of a right attitude to the issue before us.

We shall want to use in our illustration some conative tendency whose capacity to vary in power in the congenital equipment of different persons is beyond dispute. Perhaps it is the case that *all* such items in our congenital equipment are variable in this way. But, to be on the safe side, let us take one about which there can be no reasonable doubt. Nobody, so far as I know, questions that one person may be "by nature" more highly-*sexed* than another. As the sex urge is also one whose control is of high moral importance, it will be especially suitable to make our point in reference to the manifestations of this tendency.

Suppose, then, two persons A and B, of whom A is by nature "over-sexed," B by nature "under-sexed." Other things being equal, A will naturally have a stronger desire for sexual gratification than B will. When the urge is explicitly present in both, its object will be conceived by each as a "good" for the self; but by A as a *greater* "personal good" than by B. Will anyone deny this? Very well. A practical situation arises, common to A and B, in which sex-desire is stimulated, but its gratification is conceived by both agents to be contrary to what "duty" ordains. Will anyone deny that—other motive forces, of course, being presumed to be equal—it will be much harder for A than for B to will the end prescribed by duty? On the contrary, we all recognize that it will be much harder. And since the reason for the variation in difficulty goes back to the variation in force of the congenital sex-urge, here is as clear a case as one could wish of the influence exerted by congenital tendencies upon the agent's willing of his own concrete standard. In this particular instance, the congenital tendency in A is such as to be seriously obstructive to "successful" willing. And a valid judgement upon the moral worth of A's conduct *must*, I am insisting, make allowances for that obstruction—which A did not create—and accordingly *must not* judge the moral worth of A's conduct simply in terms of his success or failure in willing his concrete standard.

So far I have dealt with only one of the two factors external to the self which exercise a causal influence upon willing—"inherited nature." It would be mere wasted labour to lavish the same amount of detail upon the other factor—"environmental nurture." The same general principles apply. It cannot be denied that the individual self has no voice in determining in what environment, natural and social, he will be born and reared. It cannot be denied that the nature of these environmental conditions has an influence in determining a man's desires and aversions—what ends will seem good and bad to the agent, and how good and bad they will seem—and that it must in consequence have an influence in determining how easy or how difficult it will be for an agent to will his concrete moral standard. And if that is granted, it is all that our argument needs. (Our argument does not at all require us to deny, for example, that there are *also* factors determining our desires and aversions which *are* due to the individual self's initiative.)

It seems evident, then, that the critic's appeal to the "self-determination" involved in the act of will as such is powerless to disapprove the causal efficacy upon willing of the external factors we have been considering. I may remind the reader at this juncture of the conclusion I wish to draw. It is this, that if the moral worth of conduct is judged in terms of the conformity of the concrete content willed with even the agent's *own* standard, it is being judged in terms of something for which the agent himself is not more than partly responsible; since factors which are beyond his control exert a causal influence upon the content which he wills. A valid standard of moral judgement must be such that the agent is not judged in respect of anything for which he is not himself responsible. It must therefore be one which, unlike the "concrete" standard, allows us to discount the effect of these external factors—as in actual practice all serious moral judgement that we pass upon our fellows *does* try to discount it.

The assertion made in the last clause has been uttered before in the course of the paper, and I may be asked to provide some justification of it. I confess that its truth seems to me to be extremely clear. Admittedly our causal everyday "moral" judgements do not as a rule consider more, or much more, than the conformity of a man's willed content with a concrete standard. But it would be odd if they did—indeed impossible that they should. To make anything approaching accurate allowances for external factors presupposes a knowledge of individual personal circumstances which could only be gained, in most cases, by much time and labour. Obviously it would be ridiculous to expect such an inquisition to precede and inspire our everyday judgements. But I do invite the reader to give a plain answer to this plain question. Where—as must occasionally happen—he is seriously concerned to frame a deliberate judicial estimate of a man's moral worth (whether as exhibited in his character in general, or in respect of some particular act), does he not as a matter of course do his utmost to discover, and having discovered, to make allowances for, in his judgement, the influence exerted by heredity and environment? Does he not, in other words, tacitly recognize a real distinction between external and internal determinants within willed action itself, and endeavour to judge the man's moral worth solely on the basis of the internal determination involved?

But indeed the recognition of the inadequacy of our concrete standards, though not overt in our ordinary judgements, is never very far below the surface of our minds. Under suitable conditions it manifests its presence in even comparatively casual moral judgements. Often we hear of some person who has "gone to the bad" (as we say), and who, it is common knowledge, has been the victim of tainted parentage and vicious surroundings, and we say "Poor fellow! He didn't have a chance. He is more to be pitied than blamed." What do we mean when we speak thus? Clearly we mean this at least, that the person, in spite of the fact that he *did* formally *will* a series of "disgraceful" acts, was yet not the *author* of these acts in the sense required to establish his full moral responsibility.

I plead here only that we face squarely in our theoretical conception of moral responsibility, and consequently in our theoretical conception of the moral criterion, the implications of these allowances which every one of us does in practice introduce into his moral judgements.

Conclusion

This paper has, deliberately, set out to be no more than destructive. In concluding, however, I venture to suggest that the nature of the criticisms that have been urged does indicate the direction which any hopeful attempt at reconstruction must follow. I suggest that there are two questions of paramount importance with which any satisfactory ethics must endeavour to deal. (1) Is there any kind of activity, of moral significance, in the finite historical self for which that finite historical self can legitimately be regarded as *ultimately* responsible? If so, we shall find a basis for judgements of moral worth and the application of moral standards. If not, we should acknowledge in plain language that "morality" and "moral worth" are terms which can only be retained with a changed meaning—a meaning foreign to that of their normal usage. (2) Granting an affirmative answer to (1), what precisely is the relation of "concrete" standards, which clearly have *some* moral relevance, to the moral standard which emerges on the basis of the affirmative answer to (1)? But to these large questions, as I conceive them, not even a complete paper, much less the tail end of a paper, can be adequate to furnish a useful answer.

On the Idea of a Philosophy of Ethics[*]

On the Idea of a Philosophy of Ethics [*]

ᗯᐧᗯ

JAMES BALFOUR

IN THIS Appendix I propose to extend and apply the remarks on the Idea of a Philosophy in general contained in the first chapter of the Essay, to the Philosophy of Ethics in particular. But, in order to do so, it is necessary, in the first place, to correct an error which, in these days when Science and the Knowable are supposed to be co-extensive, is natural though not the less mischievous;—the error I mean by which Ethics is degraded to a mere section or department of Science. At first sight, and from some points of view, the opinion seems plausible enough. That mankind have passed through many ethical phases (for example) is a fact of history, and history belongs to science; that I hold certain moral laws to be binding is a fact of my mental being; and, like all other such facts, is dealt with by Psychology,—also a branch of science. Physiology, Ethnology, and other sciences all have something to say concerning the origin and development of moral ideas in the individual and in the race; it is not unnatural, therefore, that some men of science, impressed by these facts, have claimed, or seemed to claim, Ethics for their own.

To hold such a view would be a most unfortunate error; not to hold clearly and definitely its contrary may lead to much confusion; for though, as will appear, scientific laws form necessary steps in the deduction of subordinate ethical laws, and though the two provinces of knowledge cannot with advantage be separated in practice, still the truth remains that scientific judgments and ethical judgments deal with essentially different subject-matters.

Every scientific proposition asserts either the nature of the relation of space or time between phenomena which have existed, do exist, or will exist; or defines the relations of space or time which would exist if certain changes and simplifications were made in the phenomena (as in ideal geometry), or in the law governing the phenomena (as in ideal physics). Roughly speaking, it may be said to state facts or events, real or hypothetical.

An ethical proposition, on the other hand, though, like every other proposition, it states a relation, does not state a relation of space or time. 'I

* Reprinted by kind permission of the present Lord Balfour and the publishers from *A Defence of Philosophic Doubt*, Appendix. Hodder and Stoughton, 1912.

ought to speak the truth,' for instance, does not imply that I have spoken, do speak, or shall speak the truth; it asserts no bond of causation between subject and predicate, nor any co-existence nor any sequence. It does not announce an event; and if some people would say that it stated a fact, it is not certainly a fact either of the 'external' or of the 'internal' world.

One cause, perhaps, of the constant confusion between Ethics and Science is the tendency there appears to be to regard the psychology of the individual holding the moral law as the subject-matter of Ethics, rather than the moral law itself; to investigate the position which the belief in such a proposition as "I ought to speak the truth" holds in the history of the race and of the individual, its causes and its accompaniments, rather than its truth or its evidence; to substitute, in short, Psychology or Anthropology for Ethics. The danger of such confusion will partly be shown by the few remarks which, in order to carry out the train of thought begun in the first chapter, I have to make on the Idea of a Philosophy of Ethics: that is, on the "form which any satisfactory system of Ethics must assume, or be able to assume, whatever be its contents."

The obvious truth that all knowledge is either certain in itself, or is derived by legitimate methods from that which is so, has been already, perhaps, more than sufficiently insisted on; and this, which is true of knowledge in general, is of course also true of ethical knowledge in particular. A little consideration will enable us to go on, and state this further fact, which is peculiar to Ethics. "The general propositions which really lie at the root of any ethical system must themselves be ethical, and can never be either scientific or metaphysical." In other words, if a proposition announcing obligation require proof at all, one term of that proof must always be a proposition announcing obligation, which itself requires no proof. This truth must not be confounded with that which I have just dwelt upon, namely, that Science and Ethics have essentially different subject-matters. This might be so, and yet Ethics might be indebted for all its first principles to Science.

A concrete case will perhaps make clearer this axiom of ethical philosophy. A man (let us say) is not satisfied that he ought to speak the truth. He demands a reason, and is told that truth-telling conduces to the welfare of society. He accepts this ground, and apparently, therefore, rests his ethics on what is a purely scientific assertion. But this is not in reality the fact. There is a suppressed premiss required to justify his conclusion, which would run somewhat in this way, 'I ought to do that which conduces to the welfare of society.' And this proposition, of course, is ethical. This example is not merely an illustration, it is a typical case. There is no artifice by which an ethical statement can be evolved from a scientific or metaphysical proposition, or any combination of such; and whenever the reverse appears to be the fact, it will always be found that the assertion, which seems to be the basis of the ethical superstructure, is in reality merely the 'minor' of a syllogism, of which the major is the desired ethical principle.

If this principle be as true as it seems to me to be obvious, it at once alters our attitude towards a vast mass of controversy which has encumbered the progress of moral philosophy. So far as the proof of a basis of morals is concerned it makes irrelevant all discussion on the origin of moral ideas, or on the nature of moral sentiments; and it relegates to their proper sphere in Psychology or Anthropology all discussion on such subjects as association of ideas, inherited instincts, and evolution, in so far, at least, as these are supposed to refer to ultimate moral laws. For it is an obvious corollary from our principle, that the origin of an ultimate ethical belief never can supply a reason for believing it; since the origin of this belief, as of any other mental phenomenon, is a matter to be dealt with by Science; and my thesis is, that (negatively speaking) scientific truth alone cannot serve as a foundation for a moral system; or (to put it positively), if we have a moral system at all, there must be contained in it, explicitly or implicitly, at least one ethical proposition, of which no proof can be given or required.

In one sense, therefore, all Ethics is 'a priori.' It is not, and never can be, founded on experience. Whether we be Utilitarians, or Egoists, or Intuitionists, by whatever name we call ourselves, the rational basis of our system must be something other than an experience or a series of experiences; for such always belong to Science.

Limited indeed is the number of English Moralists who have invariably kept this in view. However foreign it may be to their various systems, an enquiry into origin or into the universality of moral ideas always appears to slip in—not in its proper place, as an interesting psychological adjunct, but —as having an important bearing on the authority of their particular principle. And the necessary result, of course, of these efforts to support ultimate principles, is, that they cease to be ultimate, and become not only subordinate, but subordinate to judgments which, if explicitly stated, would very likely appear far less obvious than they.

There is a whole school of Moralists, for example, who find or invent a special faculty, intellectual or sensitive, by which moral truth is arrived at; who would regard it as a serious blow to morality if the process by which ethical beliefs were produced was found to be common to many other regions of thought. Oddly enough, these are the very people whose systems are often called 'a priori.' Now if by this term be meant that the ordinary maxims of morality are (according to these systems) independent of experience, it is appropriate enough; but if it be meant that they are self-evident, it is a singular misnomer. For it is clear that on their systems rigidly interpreted those maxims derive their evidence, not from their own internal authority, but from the fact that they bear a certain special relation to our mental constitution; so that the ethical proposition which really lies at the root of their ethics is something of this sort:—'We ought to obey all laws the validity of which is recognised by a special innate faculty, whether called Conscience or otherwise.' Now, I do not deny that from a philosophical point of view such propositions as these are possible foundations of morals; but what I desire to point out is that such a phrase (to take a concrete case) as 'I ought to speak the truth because conscience commands it,' may have two widely different meanings, and may belong to two different systems of Ethics, not commonly distinguished. According to the first and most accurate meaning, 'I ought to speak the truth' is an inference, of which the major premiss must be, 'I ought to do what conscience commands,' and being an inference, cannot obviously be an a priori law. According to the second and inaccurate meaning, 'I ought to speak the truth' is in reality received on its own merits, and conscience is very unnecessarily brought in, either to add dignity to the law, or to account for its general acceptance among mankind, or for some other extra-ethical reason. The first of these views is open to no criticism from the point of view of ethical philosophy; so far as form is concerned it is unassailable. But I greatly suspect that most people who nominally found their morality on conscience really hold the second theory; and in that case, as I think, their statement is misleading, if not erroneous.

So far I have only given a negative description of the nature of an ethical proposition. I have said, indeed, that it announces obligation, but this statement is tautological; for if we knew in what obligation consisted there would be no difficulty in stating the meaning of ethical. Beyond this I have only said that an ethical judgment deals with an essentially different subject-matter from either Science or Metaphysics. Is it possible to say more than this? Is it possible to give any description of ethical propositions which shall add to our knowledge of their character? On general grounds it is plain that this can only be done, supposing that what are "commonly" called ethical propositions form part of a larger class of judgments which resemble them in being neither scientific nor metaphysical, but differ from them in some other respect. I myself hold this to be the case. I hold not only that the judgments commonly called ethical (but which, in spite of the clumsiness attendant on changing the meaning of a word in the middle of a discussion, I shall henceforward call "moral") have the two negative characteristics above mentioned in common with a larger class of judgments; but that the distinction between the two classes should be ignored by ethical philosophy, since it depends not on 'form' but on 'matter.' All judgments belonging to either of these classes I shall henceforth call ethical. Those commonly called ethical I shall describe as moral; the rest are either non-moral or immoral. Every possible judgment, then is either moral or non-moral or immoral. The terminology thus being defined, let me explain it, and at the same time my view of the subject.

If a man contemplates any action as one which he chooses to perform, he must do so either because he regards the action as one which he chooses for itself, or because he expects to obtain by it some object which he chooses for itself. And similarly, if he contemplates any object as one he chooses to obtain, he must do so either because he regards that object as chosen for itself, or because it may be a means to one that is. In other words, deliberate action is always directed mediately or immediately to something which is chosen for itself alone; which something may either be itself an action, or what I loosely term an object. Including both, then, under the term 'end,' I define an ethical proposition thus:—"An ethical proposition is one which prescribes an action with reference to an end." Nobody will deny that this definition is true of all moral propositions (most people, indeed, will think that it is too obvious to need stating); but they will probably say, and say truly, that it is also true of a great many propositions which are not usually called moral. Now my object is to show that the distinction between what are usually called moral propositions and that larger class which I have defined above, has no philosophic import, has nothing that is to do with the grounds of obligation. And for this purpose, let me analyse more carefully this larger class (which I call ethical) from a philosophic point of view, that is, with reference to the rational foundation and connection of its parts.

(1) Every proposition prescribing an action with reference to an end, belongs either explicitly or implicitly to a system of such propositions. (2) The fundamental proposition of every such system states an end, which the person who receives that system regards as final—as chosen for itself alone. (3) The subordinate propositions of that system are deduced from the fundamental proposition by means of scientific or theological minor premises. (4) When two such systems conflict, their rival claim can only be decided by a judgment or proposition not contained in either of them, which shall assert which of these respective fundamental 'ends' shall have precedence. (Ethics, then, rests on two sorts of judgments, neither of which can be deduced from the other, and of neither of which can any proof be given or required. The first sort declares an end to be final, the second declares which of two final ends is to be preferred, if they are incompatible. This second sort, of course, is not essential to an ethical system, but can only be required when an individual regards more than one end as final.) (5) No other sort of proposition can possibly lie at the root of an ethical system. (This is merely a restatement of the law dwelt on at the beginning of this discussion.)

Now in so far as this is a complete philosophical diagram of every ethical system, it must show the sort of authority on which every ethical proposition—every imperative—must rest. Yet since it is plain that this diagram takes no account of the differences there may be between moral and immoral ethical systems, how (it may be asked) can we account for the wide-spread delusion, that these differences affect the authority of the former? This question takes us far afield into the regions of Psychology and Anthropology, but the answer to it may perhaps be suggested as follows. The main reason for this error appears to be false analogy, unchecked by any clear apprehension of the nature of the rational or philosophical peculiarities of an ethical system. And in order to illustrate this, and at the same time to place the theory I am defending under as strong a light as possible, it may be as well to examine the exact bearing which "Universality" and the approval of "Conscience" (two of the chief characteristics of moral as opposed to non-moral or immoral systems) have on obligation.

My position, of course, is that they have no bearing—and in order to show this I offer the following analysis to the reader—taking Universality first. A law may be said to be Universal to in one of four senses. It may mean (first) that all intelligences regard themselves as bound by it. This meaning we need not further consider, not only because it is a scientific assertion, and therefore, as I have shown, incapable of becoming the foundation of an ethical system, but also because it is a scientific assertion now entirely discredited. It is quite out of fashion to maintain that Morality is the same in every race and every country, and therefore till, in the revolutions of thought, some one is found to re-assert this doctrine, we need not further discuss it.

The second possible meaning is, that by a universal moral law we mean one by which all intelligences "ought" to regard themselves as bound. This also we may dismiss because it amounts to saying that there is a moral law which obliges all intelligences to be bound by other moral laws. If it is, we are committed to an infinite series of moral laws, each commanding us to be bound by the preceding one. If it is not, then there can be a moral law which (in this sense) is not universal.

In the third place, by a universal moral law we may mean one which we think all men ought to obey. That we do think this of most moral laws, and that we do not think it of the other ethical laws, namely, the non-moral and the immoral ones, is tolerably certain. It remains to enquire whether the difference bears on obligation; and this enquiry, as it seems to me, may be settled by a very simple consideration. All intelligences means Me and all other intelligences. The first of these constituent parts would be bound by a law held by Me whether it were universal (in this sense) or not. The second would not be bound by a law held by Me whether it were universal in this sense or not. In other words, to be bound by a moral law (and this, by the way, brings out very clearly the difference between being ethically bound and legally bound) is exactly the same thing as to regard it as binding on you; it is not to regard it as binding on someone else; and it is not for someone else to regard it as binding on you; it has therefore, and it can have, no connection with Universality in this third sense.

It is, of course, open to anyone to assert that he recognises no imperative which is not universal (in this sense). This may very well be the fact, and I have no wish to deny it. What I deny is, that the connection between the two is other than empirical and accidental, or that it has any place in the philosophy of obligation.

The fourth and last meaning which I am able to attach to the word

Universal, when used of a law, is that it signifies that all people of 'well-constituted minds' do, as a matter of fact, regard themselves as bound by a law so qualified. Now, if 'well-constituted' is defined with reference to morality, and means 'holding the one true moral system,' a proposition that all true or right moral laws are universal, is frivolous and merely verbal. If it be defined with reference to something else—if it means for instance, sane, or well-educated, or Christian, or scientific, or anything non-moral, then the same arguments may be used to show that universality in this sense cannot be a ground of obligation, as I used when speaking of the first sense. For a proposition asserting that any considerable body of men, distinguished from the rest of mankind by some non-moral attribute, hold the same moral code, is very likely to be questionable, and being a scientific assertion, is quite certain to be irrelevant.

So much, then, for Universality. As regards Conscience, I have shown before, that to assume a special faculty which is to announce ultimate moral laws can add nothing to their validity, nor will it do so the more if we suppose its authority supported by such sanctions as remorse or self-approval. Conscience regarded in this way is not ethically to be distinguished from any external authority, as, for instance, the Deity, or the laws of the land. Now, it is plain that no external authority can give validity to ultimate moral laws, for the question immediately arises, why should we obey that authority? Only two reasons can be given. The first is, that it is "right in itself" to obey; the second is, that (through a proper use of sanctions) it will be for our happiness to obey. Now, the first of these is a moral law, which obviously does not derive its validity from the external authority, because the external authority is an authority only by means of it. And the same may be said of the second reason, substituting the words 'ethical but non-moral' for the word 'moral.' In neither case, then, is the external authority the ultimate ground of obligation.

The inevitable ambiguity which arises from the sudden extension of the meaning of the word 'ethical' to imperatives which are immoral or non-moral, makes it, perhaps, desirable that I should very concisely re-state, from another point of view, the main position I have been attempting to establish.

All imperatives, all propositions prescribing actions, have this in common:—That if they are to have any cogency, or are to be anything but empty sound, the actions they prescribe must be to the individual by whom they are regarded as binding, either mediately or immediately desirable. They must conduce, directly or indirectly, to something which he regards as of worth for itself alone. The number of things which are thus in themselves desirable or of worth to somebody or other is, of course, very great. Pleasure or happiness in the abstract, other people's pleasure or happiness, money (irrespective of its power of giving pleasure), power, the love of God, revenge, are some of the commonest of them, and every one of these is regarded by some person or other as an end to be attained for its own sake, and not as means to something else. Now, it is evident that to every one of the ultimate propositions prescribing these ends, and for which, as the ends are ends-in-themselves, no further reason can be given, there will belong a system of dependent propositions, the reasons for which are that the actions they prescribe conduce to the ultimate end or end-in-itself.

If, for instance, revenge against a particular individual is for me an end-in-itself, a proposition which prescribes shooting him from behind a hedge may be one of the subordinate or dependent propositions belonging to that particular system. But whereas the indefinite number of such systems is thus characterised by a common form, it is divided by ordinary usage into three classes, the moral, the non-moral, and the immoral, about the denotation of which there is a tolerable agreement. It would be universally admitted, for instance, that a system founded on the happiness of others was a moral system, while one founded on revenge was immoral; and, though there would be more dispute as to the members of the non-moral class, this is not a question on which I need detain the reader. The denotation then of these names being presumably fixed, what is the connotation? or to limit the enquiry, what is the connotation of a moral system? The apparent answers are as numerous as the number of schools of Moralists. But however numerous they may be, they can all be divided into two classes. The first class merely re-state the denotation;—in other words, announce the ultimate end-in-itself of the system, and so, properly speaking, give no answer at all. A Utilitarian, for instance, may simply assert that the greatest happiness of the greatest number is for him the ultimate end of action. If he stops there he evidently shows no philosophic reason for distinguishing the system he adopts from the countless others which exist, or have existed. If he attempts to give any further characteristic of his system, he then belongs to the second Class, who do indeed explain the connotation of the word 'moral' according to their usage of it, but whose explanations have, and can have, nothing to do with the grounds of action or the theory of obligation. The sanction of conscience, the emotion of approval, the expectation of reward, the feeling of good desert, glow of conscious merit—these are all most undoubtedly marks or characteristics of moral actions: how they came to be so, whether by education, association of ideas, innate tendency, or howsoever it has happened, matters nothing whatever, except to the psychologist; that they are so is certain, but the significance of the fact is habitually misunderstood. Are they simply the *causes* of good action? Then they have nothing to do with Ethics, which is concerned not with the causes but with the grounds or reasons for action, and would remain wholly unchanged if not a single man ever had done or could do right. Are they the *ends* of action? Is the fact that they are obtained by a certain course a valid reason for pursuing that course? In that case they stand to a person holding that opinion in precisely the same relation as money does to the miser, or revenge to the savage. They are the groundwork of an ethical system, and to state them is simply to denote what ethical system it is which is being alluded to. Are they finally, not ends of action, but merely marks by which certain actions may be known to belong to a particular system? In that case, and for that very reason, they can have nothing to do with the grounds or theory of obligation. Therefore, I am justified in asserting that though under the general name 'ethical' are included not only moral, but also non-moral and immoral systems, the distinctions regarded from the outside between these subdivisions are not essential, and have no philosophic import—which was the thing to be proved.

The second corollary concerns the functions of the Moral Philosopher. It is clear from what precedes, that it is *not* the business of the moral philosopher to account for the origin of moral ideas, or to analyse and explain that growth of sentiment which collects around the time-honoured maxims of current morality. These are topics which belong to Psychology. Neither is he expected to prove the propositions which lie at the root of any system of morals; for these are incapable of proof. Nor, for the same reason, can he justify the judgments which declare which of two final ends is to be preferred in case of conflict, or how much of one is to be preferred to how much of the others. Nor, in reality, has he any but a subordinate part to play in expounding or deducing the derivative rules of morality; and for this reason.

The deduction of any derivative rule is always necessarily in this form: 'the happiness of mankind ought to be promoted' (this, let us say, is the ultimate unprovable foundation of the system): 'monogamy promotes the happiness of mankind' (this is the scientific—in another system it might have been theological—minor premiss): 'therefore monogamy is a system which ought to be supported.' This is the required derivative rule. Now it should be clear that the only difficulty in deducing this conclusion from the first principle of the system lies in the difficulty of demonstrating the minor premiss; in other words, it lies in the difficulty of a certain sociological investigation, which the speculative moralist as such cannot be expected to undertake.

The important duties of the moralist, for he has important duties, arise from the confused state in which the greater part of mankind are with regard to their ethical first principles. The two questions each man has to ask himself are—What do I hold to be the ultimate ends of action? and —If there is more than one such end, how do I estimate them in case of conflict? These two questions, it will be observed, are questions of fact, not of law; and the duty of the moralist is to help his readers to discover the fact, not to force his own view down their throats by attempting a proof of that which is essentially, and by its very nature, incapable of proof. Above all, he must beware of substituting some rude simplification for (what may perhaps be) the complexity of nature, by deducing (as the Utilitarians do) all subordinate rules from one fundamental principle, when, it may be, this principle only approximately contains actual existing ethical facts.

Since these two questions can be answered, not by ratiocination, but only by simple inspection, the art of the moralist will consist in placing before the enquirer various problems in Ethics free from the misleading particulars which surround them in practice. In other words, his method will be casuistical, and not dogmatic.

It may perhaps seem strange that, after commenting at some length on the prevailing confusion between Ethics and Psychology, I should now have to announce that the business of the Ethical Philosopher (at least, so far as first principles are concerned) is as purely psychological as, according to the two preceding paragraphs, I make it out to be; and it may seem, therefore, as if the difference between my view and that of the Philosophers whom I have attempted to criticise is by no means essential or important. This however, is not the case. My complaint against these philosophers is that they appear to suppose that a psychological law can serve as a rational basis for an ethical system; so that their chief aim often seems to have been the establishment of their own particular views on the origin and nature of our moral sentiments. I, on the other hand, altogether deny the possibility of such a basis, and maintain that all that a moralist can do with regard to ethical first principles is, not to prove them or deduce them, but to render them explicit if they are implicit, clear if they are obscure. To do this effectually he must, of course, treat of ideas and notions, and his work will, therefore, in some sense be undoubtedly psychological. To make this statement complete, I should add, that (as appears by my next paragraph) there is no absurdity in supposing that a moralist may in the course of his speculations hit on some entirely new first principle which he has not held even obscurely before, but which commends itself to his mind as soon as it is presented to him.

The third corollary I draw is this—that there are only two senses in which we can rationally talk of a moral system being superior to the one we profess. According to the first sense, superior means superior in form, more nearly in accordance with the ideal of an ethical system just sketched out. According to the second sense, in which the superiority attaches to the matter of the system, it can only mean that the system is one of which we are ignorant, but which we should adopt if present to us. The superiority indicated is a hypothetical superiority.

Now it must be observed that the sense in which we speak of other hypothetical systems as being superior to our own, is by no means identical with that in which we speak of our own as being superior to that of other people. Looking back over history, we perceive a change and development of the moral ideas of the race in the direction of the systems which now prevail; and this change we rightly term an improvement. But, if, arguing from the past, we suppose that this improvement will continue through the indefinite future, we are misled by a false analogy. The change may very well continue, the improvement certainly will not. And the reason is clear. What we mean, or ought to mean, by an improvement in the past, is an approach to our own standard, and since any change at all corresponding in magnitude to this in the future must involve a departure from that standard, it must necessarily be a change for the worse.

In other words,—when we speak of another system as being superior (in matter) to our own, we speak of a possible system which we should accept if we knew it. When we speak of our own system being superior to that of some other person, we assert the superiority unconditionally, and quite irrespectively of the possible acceptance of it by that other person, supposing him to be acquainted with it. If then we believe that development will proceed in the future as it has done in the past, we must suppose that a time will come when the moral ideas of the world would be as much out of our reach, supposing them presented to us, as ours would be out of reach of primitive man. This is also true of scientific ideas: but there is this difference between them, that whereas the change in scientific ideas may be an improvement, that in moral ideas must be a degradation. The grounds of this distinction of course are obvious, *viz.*, that the standard of excellence in the case of scientific ideas is, or is supposed to be, conformity to an infinitely complex external world:—a conformity which may increase with every change in the ideas. The standard of excellence, on the other hand, in moral ideas must necessarily be conformity to our actual ideal, and this conformity must diminish with every change in the ideas.

The point would not perhaps have been worth dwelling on, if it was not that the discussion brings into strong relief the nature, so far as form is concerned, of the criterion of right, and also has some bearing on current theories of optimistic evolution, with which I confess it does not seem possible easily to reconcile it.

Ethics as Pure Postulate[*]

D. C. WILLIAMS

A MAN'S MORALS are his real rock-bottom axioms, and like the axioms which lie at the root of a purely logical system they are unarguable because they are at once apparently self-evident and apparently undemonstrable. On the other hand, axioms, we are told nowadays, are postulates, and postulates are not eternal truths but conventions whose choice is either entirely arbitrary or subservient to obscure and alogical conditions. It is no new suggestion, certainly, that logic and ethics are the same sort of thing. Let us examine here the more specific proposition that ethics must be completely a postulational system, perhaps the ultimate and quintessential postulational system, with the same peculiar rigor, coupled with the same peculiar arbitrariness, which one finds among the foundations of logic and mathematics. Even if this investigation discovers nothing new and startling about ethics, it is possible that it will throw light upon the problems of logic and of logical postulation.

In the first place, what more exactly is a postulational system? In the second place, what reasons can be advanced for supposing that ethics is a postulational system? And finally, what difference would result for ethics from the prevalence of this supposition?

It is widely assumed today that the materials, the processes, and the deliverances, of logic are not categorical but hypothetical, that is, they operate within a system of disembodied possibility. They develop infallibly the consequences of certain antecedents, but can never affirm these antecedents except in the attenuated sense in which the provisional acceptance of postulates and rules of procedure may be called affirmation. There are two principal metaphysical interpretations of this assumption: the theory of logical realism and the theory of instrumentalism. The theory of logical realism holds that logic, representing the system of all possible systems of possibilities, is a veridical description of a realm of eternal essences. Its hypothetical character reduces to the fact that the question which of these essences, and their relations, are embodied in existence, is more or less

* Reprinted with minor alterations by kind permission of the author and the editors from *The Philosophical Review*, 42, 1933. The reader's attention is called to the note added at the end of this paper in which Professor Williams states his present conception of these matters.

adventitious and irrational, and therefore extra-logical. To lay down a postulate is to choose one from among the infinite store of essences and pure propositions with a view to exploring its eternal connections. The theory of instrumentalism, on the other hand, holds that logic, being a human invention and a kind of fundamental grammar, is a compendious scheme of systematic behavior, composed of mainly linguistic conventions whose justification is their practical value in making more systematic and effective our transactions with each other and with the rest of the world. Its hypothetical character reduces to the fact that it is a system of *resolves* which we adopt tentatively into our behavior, and it is binding upon us in the strange and intimate way in which our own resolves are binding. All animal intelligence, or at least all which is accompanied by representative ideation, must be the resultant of two structural components—the pattern of the environment which the animal confronts, and the arbitrary pattern of the symbolic behavior with which he confronts it. The pattern with which he confronts it is logic, and within limits one pattern will do as well as another, provided he keeps it sufficiently flexible and consistent. To lay down a postulate is simply to decide upon a certain systematic course of behavior with respect to certain features of the world or with respect to certain other features of one's own behavior. Typically this behavior is verbal, and the resolve to adopt it is of the nature of a nominal definition. If we are to suppose that ethics is postulational, however, the verbal postulates of ordinary logic may be considered only special and subordinate cases of behavior-postulates in general, so that the universal authority is ethical.[1] We need not now choose definitely between these two theories of the nature of postulational truth.

One difference between the logical realist and the instrumentalist on the present issue might be that the former would regard ethics as a special case of logic while the latter would regard logic as a special case of ethics. The present analysis, however, must not be taken to expunge, even for the instrumentalist, a profound difference between what may be called 'intellectual' and 'ethical' postulates, in spite of the fact that it describes each of them as a practical resolve. This difference can be sufficiently described here as the fact that even a pure or ultimate intellectual postulate is contingent in a way in which a pure or ultimate ethical postulate is not. A typical intellectual postulate would be: "If I call them 'parallel lines,' I will call them 'incapable of intersection' "; and a typical ethical postulate would be: "I will express myself." [2] Either of these could be laid down subject to further conditions, and the first one, at least, ordinarily would be; but the initial disparity would remain, that the ethical principle, which declares

---

[1] This version of instrumentalism derives largely from a behavioristic understanding of C. I. Lewis's "heterodox theory of logistic," *Survey of Symbolic Logic*, 354 ff. See also his *Mind and the World Order*.

[2] These propositions are, of course, instrumentalese for "Parallel lines never meet" and "The good is self-expression."

for an unremittent and unconditional *end*, is 'categorical' to a degree to which the intellectual principle is not.

The principal reasons for supposing that ethics is in this sense postulational are so obvious and familiar that it would be hopelessly trite to attempt more than a swift catalogue of some of them.

It is notorious that few or none of those moral principles which have been, now and again, proclaimed in one society to be either innate and indispensable, or else guaranteed by the sublime authority of pure reason, have not been ignored or repudiated by other societies which are otherwise living under what look like highly developed moral systems of their own. The most striking phenomenon in the ethical field has been the inevitability and coerciveness of certain moral dicta in the view of some people and the absurdity and impotence of those same dicta in the view of others. The exponent of an ethical principle, finding it really impossible to discover for his fundamental doctrine any logical antecedents from which it can be inferred, must content himself with laboring the consequences which can be inferred from it, in the hope that these consequences will recommend themselves to the ethical bias of his listener. Otherwise the doctrine, supremely self-evident and imperative to its author, remains to everybody else inane and implausible, *possible* no doubt, but with a dead unattractiveness which is invincible. *De gustibus non est disputandum.* The iota of truth contained in this saw may be that the realm of values is characterized by encounters between ultimate sets of postulates, of resolves, or of will-attitudes.

In the second place, and in close psychological relation to the foregoing, is the familiar reflection that any analysis of an obligation or an imperative seems to leave out, or miss, the essence of the obligation or imperative, in a way more thorough than that in which the ordinary scientific analysis of an ordinary quality seems to leave out, or miss, the essence of the quality. The sanction, the real obligatoriness, of the obligation lies apparently in another dimension from any of its describable content. It is especially easy, for this reason, to suppose that goodness is an indefinable quality. It seems appropriate also to chastise as 'the naturalistic fallacy' the attempt to derive the Ought from the Is, for the Ought and the Is seem to be citizens of different realms of being. All this is to be expected on our supposition that the Ought is never contained in the object of a resolve but in the act of resolving. The whole difficulty is strikingly analogous to the notorious impossibility of expressing within a logistic system the *postulatedness* of the postulates, the adoptedness of the rules of procedure, the inferredness of the implications.[3]

In this connection the history of ethical theism bears interesting witness for us. Theists have generally supposed that God is not only the guardian, but actually the aboriginal legislator, of the good; yet the theistic

---

[3] Eaton's *General Logic* 37–46 and 388–389 comments on this situation. Its ethical analogue is suggested by W. M. Urban: "In the mere recognition of a good or value there is implied immediately the obligation to seek it." *Fundamentals of Ethics,* 241.

tendency has been increasingly, not to resort to God and his works to define the good, but to define God or judge his works by an independent and apparently autonomous criterion of the good. It is difficult to imagine that the ordinary believer could acknowledge the authority of a deity, no matter how overwhelming the latter's credentials might otherwise be, who did not conform to the more fundamental of the believer's antecedent ethical principles. The situation is of course ambiguous, and might be interpreted by the theory that right and wrong are metaphysically real and prior even to any divinity and his demands. Surely the more plausible opinion, however, in view of the patently local and relative character of these invincible rights and wrongs, is that they are insusceptible of being dictated to because they are the creatures of a person's ultimate postulates.

It is a grave question, indeed, whether the whole *reverend* character, the *holiness,* of Deity, in distinction from all irrelevant magnification of His power and glory, may not be such a function of postulation. It balks the ordinary conceptual apparatus to conceive a Being to whom worshipfulness should belong as an intrinsic predicate, as trinity, mercy, or omnipresence, for instance, can belong. Some such realization is being met today by the popular tendency to preserve to God an inherent holiness by interpreting the concept of God as a hypostatization of our own deepest and most vital interests and purposes.

It is, in the next place, one of the tragedies of ethical theory that there seems to be no conceivable *evidence* which would either verify or refute a doctrine of good and evil. Disputes about ethics hence seem to be purely verbal, that is, bottomless and quite unresolvable disputes about the meanings to be attached to familiar words. Both of these peculiarities are characteristic of nominal definitions and the postulational *a priori.* Nobody can well deny that whatever else the good is, it is that to which we are to subscribe ourselves. This means, in our scheme, that 'It is good that . . .' is a substitute locution for 'Be it resolved that . . .' The further, and still nominal, definition of 'the good,' therefore, amounts not merely to a decision with regard to an important point of linguistic usage, but literally to a resolution in behalf of a whole fundamental way of life, the *a priori* postulation of the ends of one's existence. Since the whole process of this ultimate postulation will be so primitive and unilluminated, it is natural that the postulator should get his postulates tangled with his empirical propositions and propose them for discussion as though they could be rationally interrogated.

I have suggested that the motives for the individualism, scepticism, and relativism, which are so ubiquitous in moral philosophy can be accounted for by our present opinion. It is not so obvious, but I think true, that our opinion accounts for and justifies the persuasiveness of such a naturalistic ethics as Perry's interest-theory. Perry declares consistently that it is sheer impulse or interest which confers goodness upon any mode of behavior, and so he avoids carefully the proposal to determine what mode of behavior is otherwise *worthy* of interest. Readers of his classical statements, however, will be sometimes disturbed by his apparent assumption that there is one mode of behavior intrinsically worthy of interest, namely the mode which is interested in the satisfaction of other interests, especially other people's interests. If my present proposal should carry the day, Perry would still be right in declaring that the good is what is postulated by a will-attitude, but he would be wrong in supposing that this fact is at all immediately determinative of what any of the postulates shall be. The postulate that other postulates and other people's postulates should be sacred is one which still requires a special act of postulation.

There are undoubtedly other lines of evidence than these which I have indicated. I do not pretend that any or all of them must be conclusive for anyone. I myself still incline to the opinion of Perry, at one extreme, and of T. H. Green, at the other, that Right and Wrong are more real than black and white, are metaphysically real, are the undergirders of the universe. Yet it becomes increasingly persuasive, as one contemplates the affair, that ethics possesses the same kind of self-evident certitude, and the same utter provinciality, as are possessed for instance by Euclidean geometry, and that it possesses them because it is a system of resolves rooted logically in certain fundamental resolves which are postulates, and which may be *pure* postulates in the sense that, although there may be *causes* of them, there literally is no *reason* for them. They are what happens, with the blank indemonstrability and the blank irrefutability of a natural event.

Indeed, it may seem to some that my preceding paragraphs elaborate on what is quite contemptibly obvious. I pass at once to the third of my subsidiary enterprises, to inquire what important consequences for ethics would flow from the doctrine thus laid down.

The most general and most striking consequence is that there can be no 'categorical imperative' in the traditional meaning of that phrase. Every imperative except the supreme postulate is hypothetical in that it is conditional upon the supreme postulate; and the supreme postulate, although categorical in the peculiar sense that it may be an unconditioned fiat, is still hypothetical in the two familiar senses that it is not only the conditional clause or hypothesis of a complex hypothetical proposition, but, no matter how unqualifiedly it is adopted by its uncritical author, it is only tentative from the point of view of the critical moralist. It is only one among countless possibilities, without benefit of metaphysical fact.

There are left two chief spheres of ethical inquiry. Ethics may take for granted any postulate, especially the current one, and develop the consequences of it. Some of these consequences could doubtless be deduced analytically from the postulate taken by itself. Philosophers who are obsessed with the notion that ethics ought to be demonstrated like mathematics would here find their opportunity, subject to the proviso that ethics, like mathematics, is helpless to demonstrate its postulates, which are its real principles and which are capable of infinite variety. Most of the consequences, and the more interesting ones, however, would be derived, not simply from the postulate, but complexly from the postulate taken in conjunction with probable propositions about matters of fact. Ethics would then consist in a methodical and reasonable exercise of the art of life, compounding the major and *a priori* premises which state the ends of action with the minor and *a posteriori* premises which state the means of action, in order to decide in typical instances upon the successful course of human behavior. It is widely considered that such a function is either below the ethicist's dignity, or above his ability. The theory is that everybody must decide such matters for himself and on the spur of the moment. I believe that this theory is false and that there is no reason why there should not be trained and technical moral consultants of a professional standing at least as high and useful as that of the trained and technical plumber.

The second vocation of the ethical philosopher, and I think the more appropriate one, would be, not to draw interminable consequences from the current ethical postulates, but to examine into the postulates; to seek out their possible variety; to inquire whether there may not be some conditions of ethical postulation, or even some principles for its criticism.

One way of devoting oneself to the study of ethical postulates would simply be to catalogue and systematize them. To this end, either one could work *a priori* and in the armchair, excogitating innumerable pure possibilities, or he could work after the fashion of the French sociological positivists, and draw up elaborate annotated lists of the varieties of ethical postulate which anthropologists have found in actual operation among the peoples of the earth.

The more interesting and ambitious way of studying ethical postulates, however, would be an inquiry into their conditions, their limitations, and the possibility of criticism of them and of choice among them.

Now, even without such criticism, it should be noted, the theory of the purely postulational character of ethics does not justify indiscriminate scepticism and relativism, as one might fear. The theory shows the theoretical possibility of abandoning any or all of the customary standards of morality, but it leaves possible, and encourages, a most stringent examination of the deductions drawn from the standards which are actually accepted or postulated. In point of fact, the real postulates of most of us are too deep down in us to be played with facilely. It is usually not quixotic to attempt to argue your neighbor into accepting your ethics, because, supposing a decent homogeneity of culture, your ethics is at bottom his ethics. You have the same postulates and principles, and one of you is merely blinded by a logical incompetence which the other may hope to overcome. The ordinary ethical relativist or sceptic is only a creature who is particularly blind and incompetent in this way, or is one whose agreement with the rest of the tribe subsists at a somewhat deeper level than is common.

The commonest mode by which both philosophers and laymen have actually chosen among consciously and scientifically formulated ethical postulates has therefore been a simple one. It has been merely to adopt from among them, consciously and verbally, those which are identical with the unconscious and unformulated code which is already operative in one's habitual behavior, that is, to "choose them under the guidance of conscience and common sense and the natural light of reason!" This is plainly a blank refusal to reconsider any of one's real ethical postulates, and is irrelevant to the deeper inquiry we are now proposing.

In contemporary logic the problems of postulational technique are turning out to be especially interesting and evasive. Our question is, what principles can ethics hope to discover for the postulational technique of moral practice?

Prima facie our hypothesis lays open several possibilities which we can take up one by one. It is possible, first, for example, that although ethical postulates cannot literally be proved or disproved by particular experience, they can be approved or disapproved pragmatically according to their ability to deal with particular experience. It is possible, second, that certain ethical postulates will be found to be, as a matter of fact, implicit and inevitable in the nature of living beings or of any being at all. It is possible, third, that a certain choice of ethical postulates will be dictated inexorably by ultimate logical principles. It is possible, fourth, that something intrinsic to the appetitive and demanding character of ethical postulation will furnish a principle by which the postulates must criticize themselves. But it is possible, fifth and finally, that ethical postulates are indeed pure postulates and can be brought under no compulsion and no canons of criticism at all.

Now, with regard to the first of these possibilities, there is a manner in which even an ultimate postulate can be submitted to the hurly-burly repudiation or vindication of workaday experience. A definition or a postulate cannot be literally contradicted by experience, but it can be kept helpless by experience—inert, empty, unworkable, a blunt and idle instrument. We might hope, at first sight, that by this crass pragmatic method the moralist could appraise his postulates. It requires only a moment, however, to discover the hiatus in this program, for all these pragmatic tests must rely finally and completely on a more primitive postulate, the postulate that only postulates which satisfy certain vital conditions are good postulates, and the question of the justification of the really ultimate ethical postulate remains open.

A much more general authority than particular pragmatic experience, which might serve as a limitation upon ethical postulation, is suggested by our possibility that the very nature of biological impulse, of life, or even of natural existence, involves a certain set of postulates. Things which must live and act in order to *be*, must surely postulate the worth or obligatoriness of living and acting if they are to continue to be. Living and being, in fact, are already a postulation to that effect. It may remain possible to abrogate

the postulate and to die, but it is certain that the world will never be popu-
lated by the recusants. A pure postulate, we said, has just the brute blank
force of that which happens, and it is therefore perhaps relevant for the
ethicist to inquire metaphysically what, in the nature of being, must happen.
No discovery of this sort can *ipso facto* lay a real obligation upon us, but it
can describe and predict the obligations we are born into.

The third possibility is that the principles of logic and the postulational technique of logic can provide a canon for ethical criticism. It is true
that all or virtually all of the maxims which have so far been discovered
for logical technique appear to be pragmatic, and so to depend, themselves,
upon moral or esthetic principles.[4] It may be that, in the nature of the case,
so far as logic is concerned, *anything* can be a postulate. But this is hardly
a closed issue, and it is possible that there are superordinate principles of
postulation which are applicable even in ethics.

The most obvious and the least pragmatic principle of postulational
technique is that postulates should not contradict one another. Unfortunately a little reflection suggests that inconsistency and its fruits can oppose
no veto to the postulates of persons who like that sort of thing—that is, to
persons who refrain from making the usual ethical postulate that contradiction is a demerit. On the other hand, deeper thought may establish that
there is a way in which the principle of non-contradiction cannot be gain-
said; that it is implicit in the very nature of postulation, since postulation
implies or means a *consistent* structure of thought or action. What is ostensibly the principle of non-contradiction comes rather late in some typical
schemes of logistic demonstration, and yet the principle is surely *used* from
the very beginning, and is indispensable to the very concept of system as
system.

We hear a great deal today of 'queer logics.' The question I am broach-
ing is: Are there not limitations on the queerness of logics? If there are,
logic sets itself absolute and untrespassable limits which are other than
ethical, and it is possible, although not certain, that these limits set boundaries also to ethical postulation. Ethical postulates would then be criticiz-
able at least by the principle of non-contradiction and perhaps by any
number of other principles, so that it is conceivable that only one postulate
or set of postulates can be devised to satisfy these principles; or even, if
one is pessimistic enough, that none can.

The discussion so far has avoided the question of the sanctions of
esthetics, which would afford perhaps a parallel problem to that of ethics.
At the present point, however, the suggestion must occur that the ultimate
logical conditions may be purely esthetic, and that the fundamental esthetic
sanctions, either directly or by way of logic, are legislative for ethics. The
standards of esthetics would then either be postulates, and all our questions
would arise with respect to *their* conditions or lack of conditions; or they

[4] See Eaton's *General Logic* 365–366 and 471–475.

would be categorical metaphysical propositions. The latter is an important likelihood, but it is contrary to the hypothesis we are examining, and so is not within the scope of our study.

There is, in the fourth place, one last procedure which I find difficult to define but which I think most likely to enable a profound and indefeasible *self*-criticism of ethical postulates. It is closely related to the logical and metaphysical reflections already outlined. It originates in the difference between an intellectual and an ethical postulate described above, from which it follows that whereas an intellectual postulate must be, so to say, indifferent to itself, indifferent to the scope of its consequences and to its fate among either essences or existences, an ethical postulate is not indifferent but is always and already not only a resolve but a resolve to demand, and intrinsically it demands fulfilment. A postulate-set which thwarts itself condemns itself. It can thwart itself empirically by embodying demands unlikely to be realized because they are out of accord with contemporary events. It can thwart itself metaphysically by embodying demands which run counter to the most pervasive and permanent characters of the universe. The first of these authorities, and even the second, may represent mere opportunism and the impossible assumption that whatever is is right. But there is a third which is more serious; for it would seem that an ethical postulate-set can thwart itself intrinsically, or *ethically*, or absolutely, by running counter to its own nature; by making incompatible demands, or demanding a slighter and poorer satisfaction than a postulate might. If this is so, a postulate-set ought to judge itself by the inexorable condition that a set should be rich in coherent consequences; not necessarily that it be merely opportune, immediately and practically successful, but that it *provide for* a maximum issue of success. The best postulate-set would be that set among all the numberless possibilities, which defined, and furnished the frame for, a maximum of fulfilment, which *postulated* the most; and it would be best in a sense in which, because of the very nature of postulation, all of its rival postulate-systems would have to concur. The suggestion is reminiscent of Leibniz's "best of all possible worlds," as that richest system of consequences which follows from the fewest and simplest antecedents, but it is a less arbitrary suggestion than his because of what is involved in the conative character of ethical postulates. At this point, perhaps, a postulational theory of right and wrong becomes indistinguishable from an objective or metaphysical theory of right and wrong.

There remains finally, however, the possibility that ethics is indeed based on *pure* postulates, that its last principles are creative and unquestionable fiats. Neither the ordinary maxims of unpractical logic, nor the great vicissitudes of world-climate, perhaps not even the inherent dialectic of their own appetite, can condition them more than provisionally, for an epoch or two.

We are going somewhere, and must choose where to go. We mean by 'the good' simply the way we choose to go. We mean by it no self-sufficient quality and no divine edict, and the only significant question is, Which way do we choose to go? It may be that at this blank last moment there is no room for the operation of anything but blind causes or blind caprice, so that the ethical philosopher can only watch the happening of these fiats, as the scientist watches the happening of eclipses or cyclones, and can chronicle and classify them with natural piety. On the other hand, it is conceivable that this moment provides for the exercise of some strange and unanalysable creativity, and that the ethical philosopher can claim for himself the duty of presiding at the choice which creates. Here, perhaps, is the ultimate office of the philosophical intelligence, not because there is a rigorous and subtle principle to be applied, but just because there is none. Here the final responsibility is accepted; here is the dreadful and desperate last freedom at the growing point of the universe.

I wrote this essay quite a while ago for a meeting of the Pacific Division of the American Philosophical Association, as just what it pretends to be: an experiment in ideas. I soon found intolerable its flavor of voluntarism and subjectivism, and the editors of the present volume have amiably allowed me this space to set some matters straight. There is, I now understand, no truth by postulate, resolution, or convention, either in logic or in ethics. Logic is a class of especially abstract analytic propositions each of which is 'true by definition,' not in the sense that we can change its truth value by changing our verbal habits (this is no more but no less the case with it than with a headline in today's newspaper), but in the sense that, because it is analytic and self-evident, a sharp intelligence can discern its truth by merely contemplating a single instance or, if you like, its mere 'meaning.' (I have meantime defended this view of logical truth in "The Nature and Variety of the *A Priori,*" *Analysis,* Vol. 5, 1938, pp. 85–94.) The first principle of ethics, on the other hand, is a material and synthetic proposition, or an alternation of rival hypotheses, about my own fundamental or final purpose, my root intention, preference, or commitment. The whole pursuit of ethics consists of using all available evidence, including the funded results of the sciences, in accordance with the principles of logic, first, to examine into this fundamental commitment (i.e., to find out 'what I really want'), and thereafter to deduce what acts in what circumstances are best conformable to it. (This diagnosis of ethics I sketched in a note, "The Meaning of 'Good,' " in *The Philosophical Review,* Vol. 46, 1937, pp. 416–26.) The supreme ethical premise *seems* a mere postulate or resolution, and thus something less than a statement of fact, and it *seems* to have an intrinsic moving appeal, and thus to be something more than a statement of fact, for the same reason for which certain conspicuous ethical schools today are persuaded that it is uniquely 'normative,' or that it denotes a unique non-natural quality, or that it is mere emotive sound and fury, designating nothing: namely, because it is about so intimate and ultimate a fact of my own conative life. A statement about a wheelbarrow is so remote and different from the wheelbarrow that nobody ever imputes the properties of the wheelbarrow to the statement— nobody supposes, for example, that the latter has legs or is merely transportative instead of descriptive. But my statement about my root commitment is so near the commitment, and has by association so many of the effects of the latter, that I easily confuse the two, and did, I fear, confuse them in the accompanying essay. The truth is then that such a statement is a flat description of a state of affairs, serenely true forever or false forever, like a statement about a planet or a peony. I may change, 'voluntarily' and perhaps 'arbitrarily,' any or all of my practical resolves, just as I may pick a peony or let it flourish, but what I say or believe about any of these processes is made true or false by the occurrence of the processes themselves and not by the saying or the believing nor by the will to say or believe. A verbal convention can no more 'postulate' a moral attitude than it can a planetary convulsion. One's own purposes, moreover, and particularly one's fundamental commitment, are not so amenable, neither so easily discovered nor so easily modified, as I perhaps once fancied. A complete psychology, indeed a whole metaphysics, would be requisite to tell me reliably what I really want, and the works of the greatest moralists, who have been also the greatest world-seers, are best understood as efforts to anticipate this prodigious result. The non-romantic reader of my essay may now proceed by ignoring my mistaken use of the language of fiat and conventionalism, and interpret everything following the fifth paragraph as a discussion of the propriety of regarding fundamental ethical premises, not as themselves resolves or postulates, but as propositions about ultimate resolves or commitments. Romantics and instrumentalists may still think that there was something in the original proposal.

DONALD C. WILLIAMS

Validation and Vindication
An Analysis of the Nature and the Limits
of Ethical Arguments *

ᴨᴨ⁀ᴨᴨ

HERBERT FEIGL

THE FOLLOWING schematic dialogue was constructed with the intention of illustrating some of the typical turns and twists which occur almost invariably when argument in moral issues is pursued through successive levels of critical reflection. A more systematic formulation of the philosophical conclusions that may be derived from a study of such justificatory arguments will be presented in the second part of this essay.

I. A DIALOGUE

A.: Under what conditions can war be morally justified?

B.: Under no conditions. I am a convinced pacifist and conscientious objector. There is no greater evil than war and deliberate killing.

A.: Would you rather be killed or enslaved than do any killing? Are there no circumstances, such as a need for self-defense that would justify killing?

B.: There are none.

A.: If you were saying that wanton killing and cruelty are to be condemned, I should heartily agree with you. But there are occasions in which killing is the only choice: a necessary evil, surely, but justifiable because it may be the lesser evil in the given circumstances.

The point of view of the radical pacifist is unreasonable. More lives might ultimately be saved, and greater happiness for a larger number of people might result if the innocent‘victims of aggression

---

* This essay is a revision of an earlier (hitherto unpublished and altogether different) version of my essay "De Principiis Non Disputandum . . . ?" included in *Philosophical Analysis*, edited by Max Black, Cornell University Press, Ithaca, N. Y., 1950. In "De Principiis. . . ." the problem of justification is discussed not only with reference to ethical principles but also in regard to the more fundamental principles of deduction, induction and the criterion of factual meaningfulness.—For an important analysis of closely related issues see also the essay by Wilfrid Sellars: "Language, Rules and Behavior," contained in the volume *John Dewey, Philosopher of Science and Freedom*, ed. S. Hook, The Dial Press, New York, 1950.

were to wage a victorious war upon the aggressor. This is essentially the same reasoning that I would apply to the situation in which, for example, a robber threatened my own life or that of a friend.

B.: I admit that all these are very unfortunate situations. My sincerest efforts would be devoted to prevent their very occurrence (by whatever suitable means: education, reform, arbitration, compromise, reconciliation, etc.). But once such a situation arises I still believe that one should not kill.

A.: How do you justify this position?

B.: How does one justify *any* moral judgment? Obviously by deriving it from the basic moral laws. Respect for the life, the rights, the happiness of others is surely such a basic norm, is it not?

A.: I shall be curious to find out how such basic moral laws are proved or established. But before we enter into this deep question, tell me how you defend such a rigid adherence to non-violence, even if you yourself may easily become the victim of aggression or war.

B.: I shall not invoke religious principles here. Perhaps I can convince you if I make you aware of the consequences of the pacifist attitude. Once practiced by many it would tend to spread by way of emulation and thus sooner or later eradicate the evil of killing altogether.

A.: This is an optimistic assertion concerning the probability of certain consequences. In any case it is a question of fact which is not easily decided. However, your disagreement with me seems to go beyond whatever we may think about the facts, namely the conditions and consequences of attitudes. True enough, in your last remark you have tried to establish a common basis of evaluation. You appealed to a humanitarian principle which I do share with you. Still, I think that to kill is morally better than to be enslaved. Since you disagree with me on this, it is obvious that we diverge in *some* of our basic norms. This divergence in attitude can apparently not be removed by considerations of fact.

B.: Are ethical principles then a matter of personal whim and caprice?

A.: I did not mean to imply this at all. As our own cases show, we tend to have very strong and serious convictions in these matters. Far from being chosen arbitrarily, our moral attitudes are a result of the culture and the subculture in which our personalities are formed.

B.: We are not necessarily conforming to the prevailing patterns. I for one, am certainly not. I arrived at my views by independent and serious reflection.

A.: I don't wish to dispute it. And yet your attitudes are a causal consequence of many factors: heredity, environment (physical, and especially social; the influence of parents, friends, teachers, attractive and abhorrent examples, crucial experiences, etc.) and, yes, your (more or less) intelligent reflection upon the facts as they impress *you-as-you-are*.

B.: If you are right, there are limits beyond which rational (i.e. logical and/or factual) argument cannot be extended. Intelligent reflection concerning means and ends, conditions and consequences operates within the frame of basic evaluations. Beyond those limits there could be only conversion by persuasion (rhetoric, propaganda, suggestion, promises, threats, re-education, psycho-therapy, etc.). There are also techniques of settlement of disagreements by way of compromise, segregation (separation, divorce) or higher synthesis. By "higher synthesis" I mean, for example, the abandonment or severe restriction of the sovereignty of individual nations and a transfer of all sentiments of loyalty to a world government. Only if none of these techniques succeeds, then indeed coercion by violence, alas, seems inevitable.— (Universal pacificism is the only solution! But that's not my point at the moment.)

A.: You have expressed my point of view very well. But you are obviously unwilling to agree to it.

B.: Indeed not. Everything in me cries out for a belief in objectively and universally valid standards of moral evaluation.

A.: You will not get very far if you assume some theological or metaphysical absolutes. Any reference to the revealed commands of a divine authority is futile. For you would have to tell how you can know those imperatives as divine; and even if you were to know them as such you would have to state a reason as to why anybody should obey them. The same criticisms apply to any alleged metaphysical insight into what man ought to be. And if you dismiss theological and metaphysical foundations for morality you will find it difficult to argue for standards that are independent of human needs and interests.

B.: It's precisely human needs and interests that provide a solid foundation for moral standards. In all cultures that we call 'civilized' there are essentially the same ideals of coöperation (as opposed to conflict), of helpfulness (as opposed to harmfulness), of love (as opposed to hatred), of justice (as opposed to inequity), and of perfection and growth (as opposed to stagnation and decay). Cultural relativity and the variability of human nature have been exaggerated. There is a significant core of essential features shared by all human beings. Human nature as it is constituted biologically and psychologically, and as it finds its existence in a context of interdependence with other human beings, could scarcely fail to develop just those ideals of morality. I admit that these ideals are only rarely fulfilled or even approximated in actual conduct. But they are *the* standards of ethical evaluation. It is with reference to this frame that we make our judgments of "good" and "bad," "right" and "wrong."

A.: Much as I share your ideals, I can't refrain from calling your attention to the fact that there are notable exceptions that restrict severely not only the universality of certain types of conduct (this is what you admitted), but also the universality of the very standards or ideals of morality. To many an ancient or oriental culture the idea of perfection or progress remained completely strange. The prevailing ideologies of capitalism and nationalism basically extol the ideals of competition over those of coöperation. Only superficially and often hypocritically do they pay lip service to humanitarian or Christian ideals. And the very principle of justice (in the sense of equal rights for all) has been flouted not only by tyrants, aristocrats and fascists but also by such eminent philosophers as Plato and Nietzsche. Our own divergence on the issue of radical pacificism is equally a case in point. There are countless further, possibly secondary and yet radical divergencies as regards attitudes toward civil liberties, sex and marriage, birth control, euthanasia, the rôle of religion (church and state), animals (vegetarianism, vivisection), etc., etc.

B.: Disregarding the secondary divergencies, I must say that the deviations from the more fundamental and true moral ideals are simply perversions and corruptions. Whoever denies the principles of justice and neighborliness is immoral. Kant was essentially right and convincingly logical in defining moral conduct by his categorical imperative. Only a principle that is binding for all and excludes any sort of arbitrary privilege and partiality can justifiably be called ethical. The ideals that I enumerated are the very essence of what is meant by "morality." To be moral consists precisely in placing oneself in the service of interests and ideals that transcend purely selfish purposes.

A.: This is what *you* mean by 'morality.' (And, of course, it is in keeping with traditional morality). But Nietzsche, for example, explicitly proposed a revolution in all traditional morality. Clearly, he considered his own value-system as the "true ethics." Are you not aware that you are begging the very question at issue? You speak of "true moral ideals"; you call certain views "immoral," "perverse," "corrupt"; you say that only certain types of principles can "justifiably be called ethical." You are using persuasive definitions [1] here. You call "moral" or "ethical" only such doctrines or principles as agree with your own convictions about what is *right*. The fascination with the *"logicality"* of Kant's categorical imperative may in part lie in its implicit appeal to some version of the principle of sufficient reason: If there is no reason to discriminate (as regards rights and obligations) between two persons then such discrimination is willful, arbitrary, un-

---

[1] This useful phrase was coined by C. L. Stevenson. In his book *Ethics and Language* (Yale University Press, 1944), p. 210 he explains it as follows:

"In any 'persuasive definition' the term defined is a familiar one, whose meaning is both descriptive and strongly emotive. The purport of the definition is to alter the descriptive meaning of the term, usually by giving it greater precision within the boundaries of its customary vagueness; but the definition does *not* make any substantial change in the term's emotive meaning. And the definition is used, consciously or unconsciously, in an effort to secure, by this interplay between emotive and descriptive meaning, a redirection of people's attitudes."

just. But far from involving strictly logical contradictions such "un-justifiable" discriminations would merely violate *one* (not as you would say "*the*") definition of justice. A reason for discrimination could always be found. That it may not be accepted as a "good," "relevant" or "sufficient" reason is but a consequence of the ethical principles or fundamental evaluations of some alternative system. Let me assure you again that I share your moral attitudes. But strongly as I feel about them, I see no need for, and no profit in defending them with bad logic. You cannot by some verbal magic establish justifica-tions for ideals which obviously are neither logically nor empirically unique. These ideals compete with genuine alternatives.

B.: I can't believe this. The ideals that I have listed are the ones that will benefit humanity in the long run. Not just a particular group, but all of mankind.

Moreover these ideals are comprised by the essence of *rationality*. Man, the rational animal, is by his very nature not only characterized by his capacity for adequate deductive and inductive thinking, but also by his sense of justice and his abhorrence of violence as a method for the settlement of disputes.

A.: You are still begging the question. Those who do not accept the principle of equality are not interested in *all* of mankind. Furthermore, your time-honored conception of human nature is clearly not an ac-count of actual fact, but of an ideal (by no means universally shared) which you utilize for a persuasive definition of MAN. You won't con-vince any serious opponents by mere *definitions*. But you might try to entice, persuade, educate or reform them in other ways. You may also hope that the increasing interdependence of all of mankind on this planet will eventually generate a fundamental uniformity in the principles of moral evaluation.

B.: You underestimate the rôle of experience in the settlement of moral conflicts and disputes. Those who have had an opportunity to experi-ence different ways of life soon learn to discriminate between the better and the worse. Experience in the context of needs and interests, of claims and counter-claims, of existing and emerging rights and ob-ligations in the social milieu soon enough mould the moral conscience of man. We do not live in a vacuum. The constant encouragements and discouragements of our actions and their underlying attitudes form the very atmosphere of the life in the family, the workshop, the market place, the tribunal, etc. Add to that the basic sympathy human beings feel for each other and you will have to admit that there is a large mass of empirical factors that operate in the direction of a common standard of social morality.

A.: If I may use a parallel drawn from the field of aesthetics, there are a great many people who prefer pulp-magazine stories to "good" litera-ture; or swing (jazz, jive or whatever is the fashion) to "great" music.

Similarly, there are plenty of people who have had an opportunity to experience both the ruthless and the kindly way of life and yet subscribe to the principles of the former. Kropotkin rightly, though somewhat sentimentally, pointed out that despite the cruel struggle for existence in the animal kingdom there is also a good deal of mutual help and self-sacrifice. If human sympathy were as fundamental as (he and) you claim it is, there could hardly be such views as those of Nietzsche, Hitler, and Mussolini on the "greatness" of war. Only by endorsing one norm against other possible alternatives can you avail yourself of the premises by which to validate the special moral precepts which are dear to your heart.

B.: You still have failed to give me a single good reason why I or you or anyone should adhere to even those moral principles which we happen to share. Your position is a skepticism that could easily lead to moral indifference and cynicism.

A.: And what sort of a reason do you expect me to give you? If I provided you with premises from which you could *deduce* our moral standards, you would ask me for a justification of those premises. And you surely don't want a reason in the sense of a motive. You are motivated already. You do not seriously entertain doubt as long as this motivation prevails. And nothing that I've said was intended to undermine it. The aim of my remarks was clarification; not education, fortification or edification. Too many philosophers have sold their birthright for a pot of message.

II. ANALYSIS AND CONCLUSIONS

The foregoing argument illustrates among other things the ever-present pitfalls of the *petitio principii* in the procedures of justification. If the radical pacifist is accused of an exaggerated value-fixation upon "reverence for life" he is free to retort that his opponent has a hypertrophied value fixation upon liberty or upon the survival of the greater number of persons. In order to condemn some value-fixations as inhumane, immoral or perverse, it is necessary to invoke some ideals or standards of humaneness, morality or normality. It is only with reference to such ideals or standards that we can justify the *approval* of thrift, honesty, friendship, the devotion to science or art, etc. and the *disapproval* of avarice, hypocrisy, belligerence, sexual aberrations, etc. From a purely factual psychological or socio-psychological point of view *all* value-fixations may be explained in terms of some causal-genetical principles, such as Wundt's "Heterogony of Purposes," Allport's "Functional Autonomy," or some other laws of motivation as formulated in psychoanalytic or behavioristic theories.

Let us suppose that socio-historical and anthropological research could show that there are basic invariant moral ideals embodied in otherwise diverse cultures. Even then it cannot be denied that the rank-order of the normative force of these ideals has varied with time, clime, and cultural conditions. Wise moral philosophers along with the great dramatists and novelists of the ages have always known that moral problems in their most poignant and irresoluble form consist in the conflict of good with good or right with right. The understandable hope for the demonstration of one unique set of standards in terms of which an objective and universally binding adjudication of all moral issues could be achieved, may well turn out to be chimerical. Only if certain basic—and to many people all-too-obvious—valuational premises are taken for granted, can we obtain the semblance of objective deducibility of more special moral rules. If, for example, we take for granted that the life of the species *homo sapiens* is to be preserved, that conflict and violence is to be minimized, then a great number of special precepts are derivable from these premises taken together with special facts and laws concerning human conditions and behavior. The truth implied in the critique of the "naturalistic fallacy" reduces to the truism that factual statements alone cannot possibly entail normative conclusions. Some normative premises are indispensable.

If rational argument, criticism or justification is to be distinguished from persuasion by means of the emotional and motivational expressions and appeals of language, what are the forms of such reasoning and what are its criteria of validity?

The classical doctrine of self-evidence as a criterion of validity or truth still exerts its powerful influence. Brentano, Husserl and the phenomenologists; G. E. Moore, C. D. Broad, W. D. Ross, A. C. Ewing and other recent English intuitionists have revitalized this ancient (and Cartesian) tradition. There is scarcely any space here even to remind the reader that this philosophical point of view is open to the most serious objections. Its relevance to the truth of the axioms of geometry have become suspect since the developments of the non-euclidean geometries and their application in modern physics and astronomy. More fundamentally, the recent developments in the philosophical foundations of logic and mathematics have shown that self-evidence is neither a necessary nor a sufficient condition for truth or validity. The better intentions of the intuitionists to the contrary notwithstanding, the doctrine of self-evidence is at fault precisely because it is psychologistic. The accent of self-evidence is a result of habituation. Basic principles or presuppositions which delimit a certain universe of discourse or specify a certain field of validating procedures acquire the appearance of absolute cogency and uniqueness, because they form the indispensable (and hence within this context unquestioned) *conditiones sine qua non* of the very enterprise which they make possible and for which they legislate. Finally, intuitive self-evidence cannot possibly be claimed to yield absolutely unique or indubitable knowledge. Notoriously and especially in regard to moral judgments (not to mention aesthetic evaluations) there is no unanimity on just *which* principles are self-evident. It requires some arrogance to claim one's own intuitions infallible, and the disagreeing intuitions of others as in need of revision (by "deeper reflection," "re-education," "enlightenment," etc.).

At this point one of the most crucial questions in all philosophy arises: Are the justifying principles of knowledge, i.e. the principles of deductive and inductive logic, as undemonstrable and as much lacking uniqueness as are the norms of moral judgments? If intuitive cogency is to be abandoned as a criterion of truth, are we not faced with an analogous plurality or relativity in regard to basic presuppositions in the field of cognition?

Only a few suggestions can here be made as regards these burdensome scruples.[2] Firstly, the validity of deductive or inductive inference is presupposed in ethical argument. But no distinctly ethical norms are required for the validation of knowledge-claims. Reasoning in matters of morality utilizes, as any reasoning must, principles of deductive inference when special cases are subsumed under general (in this case, moral) rules. And in any practical issue of moral choice, inductive inference is indispensable for the determination of the most likely consequences of actions. There is no question then, that in the context of validation, the principles of cognition are more fundamental than the norms of morality. In this sense we may safely claim the "primacy of *pure* reason." Secondly, despite the fashionable notions about "alternative logics" it can be shown that at least the rules of deductive inference possess a uniqueness which, even if not present in the same degree, is also characteristic of the rules of inductive inference.

In order to grasp this situation clearly, a fundamental distinction, often badly neglected or blurred beyond recognition, must now be drawn: When we speak of "justification" we may have reference to the legitimizing of a knowledge-claim; or else we may have in mind the justification of an action. The first case may be called "*justificatio cognitionis*" (validation) the second, "*justificatio actionis*" (vindication). The rules of deductive and inductive inference serve as the justifying principles in validation; purposes together with (inductively confirmed or at least confirmable) empirical knowledge concerning means-ends relations, or in the extreme, degenerate case with purely logical truths, serve as the basis of vindication (pragmatic justification). Only ends can justify means, even if in accordance with the well known slogan it will be admitted that a given end may not justify the utilization of every means for its attainment.

The word "reason" displays ambiguities similar to the word "justification." Besides naming a capacity of the human mind (part of which is the ability to state reasons) it is used in referring to causes and purposes, as well as to grounds of validation. Aristotle, Schopenhauer, and many thinkers between and after, have struggled to disentangle these and other meanings of "reason." Kant's distinction between the questions "*quid facti*" and "*quid juris*" has shed a flood of light on the basic issues of philosophy and has

---

[2] For a fuller discussion, cf. "De Principiis non disputandum . . . ?," See reference in footnote on p. 667.

since become indispensable for the analysis of the problems of epistemology and ethical theory.

The justifying principles (*justificantia*) for the establishment of knowledge-claims have been retraced to their ultimate foundations in the rules of inference and substitution in deductive logic. We cannot without vicious circularity disclose any more ultimate grounds of validation here. Similarly the rules of maximal probability in inductive inference form the ultimate validating basis of all empirical reasoning. Correspondingly the supreme norms of a given ethical system provide the ultimate ground for the validation of moral judgments. No matter how long or short the chain of validating inferences, the final court of appeal will consist in one or the other type of justifying principles. Rational argument presupposes reference to a set of such principles at least implicitly agreed upon. Disagreement with respect to basic principles can thus only be removed if the very frame of validation is changed.[3] This can occur either through the disclosure and explication of a hitherto unrecognized common set of standards, i.e. still more fundamental validating principles to which implicit appeal is made in argument, or it can be achieved through the pragmatic justification of the adoption of an alternative frame, or finally, through sheer persuasion by means of emotive appeals.

Validation terminates with the exhibition of the norms that govern the realm of argument concerned. If any further question can be raised at all, it must be the question concerning the pragmatic justification (vindication) of the (act of) adoption of the validating principles. But this is a question of an entirely different kind. The answers we can give to this sort of question are apt to appear trivial, but for the sake of philosophical clarification they are nevertheless indispensable and illuminating. If the logical reconstruction of justification is pursued as here suggested, then even an obvious, not to say utterly trivial, vindication will at least make fully clear which aims are attained by means of the adoption of some specified validating principles. Thus it is quite plain that the adoption of the rules of deductive inference is pragmatically justifiable in that only reasoning which accords with them can insure the transition from true propositions to other true propositions. No vicious circularity is involved here. We are not attempting the (impossible) validation of ultimate validating principles. We can afford, and could not possibly refrain from, using logic in a vindicating argument, precisely because we are here concerned with arguments about means-ends relations. There is a similar vindication, formulated by H. Reichenbach [4] for the adoption of the principle of in-

---

[3] For an extremely important and clarifying discussion of the distinction between questions within a presupposed frame and questions concerning the frame itself (in connection with closely related issues) cf. R. Carnap: "Empiricism, Semantics and Ontology," *Revue Internationale de Philosophie* 11, Jan. 1950.

[4] *Experience and Prediction*, University of Chicago Press, 1938; §§ 38, 39; also: "On the Justification of Induction," *Jl. of Phil.* 37, 1940, reprinted in Feigl and Sellars, *Readings in Philosophical Analysis*, Appleton-Century-Crofts, N. Y., 1949; and *The Theory of Probability*, University of California Press, 1949.

duction. The reasoning in both cases is purely deductive because of the extreme (degenerate) nature of the question at issue. In regard to induction the following holds: If there is an order of nature at all (and we don't know that there is and we don't know that there isn't—beyond the scope of actual observations) then the method of simplest generalization is the only method of which it can be demonstrated (deductively) that (1) it *can* (but of course need not) succeed in disclosing that order and (2) that it is self-corrective. This obvious, simple tautology provides a pragmatic justification of the adoption of the rule of induction for anyone who wishes to attain the two mentioned aims, namely to make true inductive inferences (e.g. predictions) and to be able to keep such inferences adaptable to the accumulating evidence.

It may be charged that our analysis is outrageously artificial; that we never have occasion to "choose" a basis of validation; that in real-life-situations we find validating and vindicating arguments so intimately fused, that their separation distorts severely the dialectics of both cognitive and valuative arguments. My reply is, firstly, that all logical analysis from Aristotle through Descartes down to our time necessarily consists of an artificial and schematic reconstruction [5] and its illuminating character depends precisely upon the disentanglement of factors or aspects which, though admittedly *fused* in ordinary argument are in danger of being *con*fused in philosophical reflection. Secondly, I would say that those who make the charge under discussion, characteristically resolve the problems of justification simply by a *fiat* of definition. Induction, for example, is said to need no justification because the rule of induction defines (at least in part) *what we mean* by "*justifiable inference.*" Similarly, as we have remarked already, such moral principles as those of justice or benevolence may be claimed to constitute (at least in part) *what we mean* by a "*(rational) morality.*" If this sort of analysis results in a clear explication of the legislative principles of a given domain of validation, I should gladly admit that it is a helpful step in the clarification of philosophical perplexities. But it should be equally clear that this procedure is apt to rest its case simply with a persuasive definition of certain key-terms such as "rational," "valid," "probable," "morally right," etc. Once aware of the persuasive character of these definitions one should wish, in all candor, to state why one finds them persuasive. And the answer to this question must clearly refer to one's interests, purposes or ideals. Thus, while vindication can never prove (validate) any principles of validation, it can clarify their role in the context of human thought and action.

The validating principles of deductive and inductive logic do not seem at all to have any plausible alternatives or competitors. This is so, very likely because in this age of science our conception of the criteria of valid and reliable knowledge have already been so sharply focussed and

---

[5] See my article "Logical Reconstruction, Realism and Pure Semiotic," *Philosophy of Science*, 17, 1950, pp. 186-195.

so severely purged of pre-scientific (non-scientific and unscientific) elements. The purposes of the cognitive enterprise are today so clearly delimited that its basic criteria (but of course not its special methods and techniques) have attained practically universal consent.

It is only too tempting to hope for a similarly universal code of morals. But in view not only of the stark realities of group and culture-centered ethical standards, but also because of the ever present quandaries regarding the priority between the several supreme standards ("prima facie obligation," i.e. the validating principles of moral judgments) within a given group or culture we can scarcely expect a universal unanimity of purposes which would vindicate a set of unique standards and a rigid order of priority among them for any and all questions of moral decision. At this point, I must concede, that the relativism implicit in the emotivist analyses (of Stevenson, for example) may prove insuperable. But beyond this important concession I would stress that the emotivist assimilation of moral issues to questions of personal taste and preference does not even begin to do justice to the nature of argument and justification in the moral realm of discourse. There is a great deal of validation in ethical arguments which is only too easily lost sight of, if attention is primarily fixed upon persuasion or vindication.

In analogy to the analysis of justification in the cognitive domain I suggest that moral judgments are to be reconstructed as knowledge-claims and as subject to validation (or invalidation) by virtue of their accordance (or non-accordance) with the supreme norms of a given ethical system. In order to carry out this reconstruction, judgments of right and wrong, and likewise statements of obligation and of rights, must be construed as empirical propositions. This is possible only after these typically normative terms (and other relatives and derivatives "good," "evil," "desirable," "condemnable," etc.) have been given a factual reference in addition to their positive or negative emotive appeals. This means that we make, in this context deliberately a legitimate device of what in other contexts must indeed be repudiated as the "naturalistic fallacy." [6] This amounts to construing moral norms in the logical form of general laws. But in contradistinction to the general laws of the empirical sciences the moral laws are not subject to confirmation or disconfirmation by empirical evidence—at least and certainly not in the same sense. Their logical character is rather that of basic definitions or conventions for the use of normative terms with reference to empirical aspects of conduct, intentions, attitudes, personality traits and social objectives. In regard to the factual content as well as in their critical function, normative moral terms are quite similar to such terms

[6] This fallacy was most infelicitously labeled by G. E. Moore. As I view the matter, Moore's criticism should have been directed against the confusion of motivative appeals with factual meaning; or more closely in keeping with Moore's intentions, against the confusion of the phenomenological "oughtness" (its relatives and opposites) with the empirical characteristics of conduct with which these intuitively given (and indeed phenomenologically unanalyzable) qualities of moral awareness are associated.

of medicine as "healthy," "diseased," "normal," "abnormal," "well-functioning," "mal-functioning," etc. Just as in questions regarding normality or abnormality in medicine we require a factual content (in addition to the emotive appeals) of these terms, in ethics. We need likewise factual reference in order to break through the circle of formal tautologies (such as "the good is that which it is right to accomplish") and to attach these formal-and-emotive terms to empirical aspects of the facts of individual and social life.

Only with a reconstruction of this sort can we escape the sterility of formalism in ethics. If we wish to know for example whether killing in self-defense is morally right, we cannot get an answer unless definite and empirically specified moral rules (including priority-rules as between standards) are provided as *justificantia cognitionis* of the *correctness* of the moral judgment at issue. Obviously the same considerations apply to questions of distributive and retributive justice, to the evaluation of the various virtues, of measures of social, legal, political reform, etc.

It is a simple consequence of the proposed analysis and reconstruction that it is futile to criticize one system of norms in terms of another which is logically incompatible with it. Validation of moral judgments always requires a set of given norms to which we must hold fast, at least temporarily, in order to examine the validity of more special moral judgements. As in the case of the justification of cognition, so here in the domain of ethics, the only further step concerns vindication. The purposes which may be adduced in vindicating arguments for a whole system of moral norms are embodied in the individual interests and social ideals which we have come to form in response to life experience. The principle of justice (the golden rule) or other implicit definitions of "right actions" may, for example, be vindicated by reference to the ideal of a peaceful, harmonious and coöperative society. Or the principle of benevolence may be vindicated by reference to the ideal of the greatest happiness of the greatest number. We see then that the perennial dispute between deontological and teleological theories in ethics may perhaps be settled by the recognition that the former are concerned with validation, the latter with vindication.

The present approach differs from both the intuitionistic and the emotivist point of view (and is in more than one way closer to the Kantian) in that the great variety of self-evident prima facie obligations countenanced by the intuitionists and the corresponding equally great variety of interest-fixations allowed for by the emotivists are supplanted by a relatively small number of basic norms and priority rules. Naturally, the task of demonstrating that this is an adequate and feasible reconstruction is enormous and has here been barely suggested. In contradistinction to the Kantian metaphysics of morals a plurality of alternative ethical systems is here envisaged as a matter of historical and contemporary fact. As long as there are changing and divergent terminal purposes and ideals there will be different systems of moral validation. The moral approval of a given ideal is of course trivially validated by the system which that ideal vindicates; and, contrariwise, trivially invalidated by an alternative incompatible system.—But enough has been said about the dangers of the petitio principii.

One final question: Does the pluralism and relativism implied in the preceding remarks rule out *objectivity* in ethics? As may be expected by now, the answer depends upon the precise meaning which one is going to connect with the term "objectivity."

The objectivity of the truths of arithmetic lies in their logical necessity. Anyone who understands the postulates and definitions of arithmetic and complies with the rules of deductive logic will concede the universal validity of arithmetical truth. The objectivity of propositions of factual knowledge means something different: the intersensual and intersubjective confirmation of knowledge-claims,—and everything that these phrases imply, especially the principles of confirmation. "Objectivity" in the moral domain may mean a variety of aspects: (1) The logical necessity inherent in validation. (2) The logical consistency of the norms of one system. (3) The factual objectivity of the characterization of the empirical features of attitudes, conduct, etc. which are the subject of moral appraisal. (4) The factual objectivity of statements regarding conditions-consequences and means-ends relations. (5) The factual objectivity of statements concerning human needs, interests and ideals as they arise in the social context. (6) The conformity of the norms with the basic bio-psycho-social nature of man, especially as regards the preservation of existence, the satisfaction of needs, and the facts of growth, development and evolution.[7] (7) The degree of universality with which certain moral norms are actually or potentially embodied in the conscience of man within given cultural groups or perhaps even in cultural groups of all times and climes. (8) The equality of all individual persons before the moral laws—as conceived in the universal applicability of these laws.

Crucial questions arise only in regard to the factual truth of the seventh point and the significance of the eighth. The actuality of universally common standards, as we have pointed out, is problematic. Only at the price of a precarious attenuation of meaning, if not of the risk of tautological vacuity, could one defend this claim. As to the potential convergence towards common standards we may allow for a cautious optimism. Finally, and perhaps most critically, there remains the question whether we shall mean by an "ethical norm" one which embodies a thorough-going impartiality. If so, then we have by definitional fiat implied the essence of the principle of justice the very conception of "moral law." But when we speak of the "ethics" of feudalism, or even of the "ethics" of Nazism, along with the "ethics" of christianity, or the "ethics" of democracy, we obviously utilize a different definition covering much more ground. Of course,

---

[7] This elementary but important point stressed in naturalistic ethics from Aristotle down to the philosophizing biologists of our time, is apt to be neglected by purely analytic philosophers.

we are free to declare that "fascist ethics" is a contradiction in terms; i.e. we may decide that a code of norms for the appraisal of conduct is to be called "ethics" only if it embodies at least the principles of benevolence and impartiality. But must we then not conclude that the word "ethics" itself is subject to persuasive definition?

Objectivity in Morals*

卅⌒卅

WILLIAM KNEALE

I

It is remarkable that we have to-day a number of philosophers who call themselves subjectivists in moral philosophy. For, although the name "subjectivist" is by no means new, philosophers have reserved it hitherto for their opponents, and usually for imaginary opponents at that. Perhaps the chief cause of the change which has taken place in recent years is the discovery of a distinction between descriptive and emotive meaning. In the past the only form of subjectivism considered by writers on moral philosophy was the suggestion that moral sentences such as "You ought to do that" were statements about the speaker's own attitude; and it was easy to refute this by pointing out that we discuss questions of morals in a way which would be unintelligent, and even unintelligible, if moral judgments were only reports of introspection. But those who now call themselves subjectivists maintain that the peculiarity of moral words is their expressive and evocative power. According to their analysis, a speaker who uses one of these words in an indicative sentence may be *stating* nothing at all, but is undoubtedly trying to *influence* others (and perhaps also himself) to adopt a certain attitude. This, they say, explains how there can be genuine disagreement about questions of morals and why discussion may produce results. If A tries to evoke one attitude in his hearers and B tries to evoke an incompatible attitude, their utterances are opposed, not indeed like contradictory statements, but rather like the efforts of men engaged in a tug-of-war. Language is not merely a vehicle for conveying information, but also an instrument for inducing approval or disapproval which will presently manifest itself in action; and if moral philosophy is to be distinguished from preaching, it must be the attempt to understand in detail how language serves this second purpose.

To some philosophers this recent development seems very dangerous. They think that no subjectivist can take moral distinctions seriously, and that if subjectivism spread beyond the study and the lecture room it would lead to moral anarchy and political tyranny. There are even some critics

* Reprinted by kind permission of the author and the editor from *Philosophy*, 25, 1950.

of subjectivism who profess to believe that it is the source of totalitarianism. This last charge seems to me absurdly unfair: Hegel's ugly child should not be laid on the doorsteps of other philosophers. Nor am I much impressed by fears about what might happen if the doctrine were widely accepted. No doubt some people who did not understand it properly would say, like Punch at the end of the puppet show, "The Devil is dead: we may all do as we like." But is the danger really any greater than that to be feared from general acceptance of the doctrine of self-realization or of St. Augustine's maxim *"Dilige Deum et fac quod vis"*? I do not see why anyone should cease to hate cruelty and to admire charity merely because he had read the writings of Mr. Russell or Mr. Stevenson. On the contrary, some tough-minded people who have hitherto felt rather embarrassed by references to morality may find that such reading liberates the preacher within them. Something of this sort happened last century to many who read Bentham's work, and the social results were in my opinion almost wholly good, although hedonistic utilitarianism is not a satisfactory theory of morals. There is at least this much truth in the emotive theory, namely, that the practical effect of the use of moral words depends largely on manner and tone of voice. If a philosopher says that "right" means *merely* so-and-so, his "merely" may have more effect than his definition. But if it seems to his hearers that, while abstaining from cant, he approves and disapproves heartily as they do themselves, they may swallow the most outrageous definitions of moral words and be none the worse for it, except intellectually.

I suggest then that we should not allow ourselves to be shocked by subjectivism, but examine it as dispassionately as we can. When I try to do this, I find myself more and more doubtful about the subjectivist's account of the way in which we use moral words, and I suspect my feeling is shared by a number of others who have made the same experiment. In this paper I wish to ask what sort of objectivity we should like to assert in our moral theory. Until this question can be answered, dispute on the main issue is useless, but the finding of an answer to this question may perhaps enable us to settle the main issue easily.

In order to avoid unnecessary complications I shall concentrate attention on words of the "ought," "right," "wrong" group, which are commonly thought to be moral in a special sense. It is true that moral philosophy is often supposed to include consideration of the nature of goodness and the making of a list of things which are good; but there is narrower usage according to which a moral question is properly one about conduct, e.g. a question of the form "What ought I to do in these circumstances?" When a man puts a question of this kind to a wise friend, he does not want a disquisition on the nature of virtue or the comparative worth of different motives. For it is to be presumed that he is already prepared to do what he ought to do, if only he can find out what that is. Nor will he be contented by remarks about the goodness of various possible states of affairs such as mutual affection between human beings. For, although considerations of this kind have some relevance, they do not by themselves provide an answer to his question. It is usually this narrower usage of the word "moral" we have in mind when we argue about objectivity in morals. We may even be prepared to agree that in some of its usages the word "good" can be explained satisfactorily in the way suggested by modern subjectivists. But the suggestion that sentences about obligation, rightness and wrongness have no objective reference sticks in our throats. I do not say yet that our reluctance to accept this suggestion is reasonable, but I report the facts as I find them, with the hope that I may presently be able to clarify them.

II

Those who try to defend objectivism in moral theory usually begin by pointing out that moral judgments about obligation, rightness, etc., look like assertions of fact. Here they are certainly right, for until recently no one tried to deny that these judgments are statements. But the important question is whether such judgments can be true or false in the ordinary sense; and on this we may perhaps argue as follows. When a man enjoys something such as a new kind of food, a book, a film, or a game, he may try to induce his friends to share his enjoyment; and if he says in this context that he has discovered something good, the word "good" may then be merely expressive and evocative. But no one can live for very long in a complex society without learning that it is impossible for him to make even his closest friends share all his tastes. And so are always prepared to break off a discussion about taste by saying "Let's agree to differ. You go your way and I'll go mine. It takes all sorts to make a world." Now if discussions about right and wrong were fundamentally of the same kind, it might be expected that we should sometimes break them off in the same way. But this never happens. So long as we regard an issue as one of morals, we cannot say "Let's agree to differ." And it is natural to suppose that we cannot do so because we are not concerned with taste only, but with truth.

If the subjectivist is careful in the defence of his position, he may admit that there is an important difference between discussion about moral questions and discussions about matters of taste, but reply that the argument I have set out above proves no more than a very firm resolve on the part of all men to *produce* unanimity of *attitude* on issues they call moral. He may even go farther and say that a question of morals is by definition one on which we are not prepared to compromise by admitting that we are made differently and cannot be brought into agreement. If this answer is correct, the assertion of objectivity in morals is only a muddled expression of the proselytizing zeal for which modern subjectivism makes full allowance. In order to complete his case the subjectivist would have to go on to explain why we tend to be tolerant of some differences of attitude but not of others, i.e. why we delimit the sphere of morals as we do. For al-

though the objects of which an individual expresses specifically moral approval or disapproval may be very varied, they are not usually a random
selection from the possible objects of interest. We know, for example,
that many people like listening to music and try to persuade their friends
to join them, but we should think it extremely odd if anyone declared
that listening to music was a duty and apparently held towards this activity
the same attitude as he held towards the care of his children. I shall not
attempt to decide here whether or not the subjectivist could offer a plausible solution of this difficulty, because it is more important for my present
purpose to return to the argument of the objectivists and consider what
they mean by talking about the truth of moral judgments.

The philosophers who have talked most in this strain are the intuitionists from Richard Price to Sir David Ross. They usually discuss judgments
of the rightness of acts, and they like to compare these with the apprehension of necessary truths in mathematics. Their reason for drawing such a
comparison is not hard to understand. Although we often make singular
judgments of rightness in the form "It would be right for you to do X
in these circumstances," we cannot treat these as assertions of mere matters
of fact. For we always maintain that it cannot be right to do X in given
circumstances unless it is also right to do X in any precisely similar set of
circumstances. That is to say, we do not think that the rightness of an
act is apprehended by an intuition analogous to sense-perception, as though
it were a quality belonging to a particular contingency. Admittedly some
philosophers have talked about moral sense, but on examination their theories always turn out to be doctrines of moral sentiment, i.e. versions of subjectivism. No one takes seriously the suggestion that we can discover the
rightness of an act as we discover the shrillness of a noise. If, then, we wish
to maintain that a singular judgment of rightness is capable of truth or falsity, we must suppose that the man who makes it first notices some non-
moral features of the situation and then recognizes that these entail the
rightness (or fittingness, as it is sometimes called) of some act which is
possible in that situation. According to this analysis, a singular judgment
of rightness is always the conclusion of a kind of syllogism, and may be
mistaken because of an error in either premise: purely moral knowledge
is always of universal propositions.

As presented in our day, this theory is opposed not only to subjectivism, but also to utilitarianism; but on the point which is of interest for my
present inquiry utilitarians do not differ from intuitionists. They too believe that moral judgments can be true or false, but they think that all the
universal moral propositions of the intuitionists which are really valid can
be brought under the single principle that it is always right to produce the
maximum good possible in the circumstances. Sometimes they suggest
that they have given a definition of rightness, but in this they are surely
mistaken. For if to say that an act is right means the same as to say that it
is productive of the maximum good, the utilitarian principle which is

supposed to introduce order and simplicity into moral theory reduces to the triviality that it is always productive of the maximum good to produce the maximum good. On the contrary, the status of our notion of rightness should be just as much a puzzle for the utilitarian as it is for the intuitionist, since both of them talk of it as though it were unanalysable.

Now many philosophers who are aware of this puzzle tell us that rightness is a non-natural quality, and that our notion of it is an innate idea or *a priori* concept. This assertion makes me very suspicious, but I do not propose to discuss it here, because I think it extremely unplausible to treat the notion of rightness as unanalysable. "Right," "wrong," "ought" and the other words of the same group are not peculiar to moral judgments, and it would be very strange indeed if their moral use were quite distinct from their use in other contexts such as the exposition of the law of the land. On the contrary, it seems obvious that the use of the words by moralists must be explained in the same way as their use by lawyers. Let us see where this suggestion leads us.

III

As used by lawyers and moralists the word "right" is equivalent to the phrase "in accordance with the law." Similarly "wrong" means the same as "not in accordance with the law," and "A ought to do X" means the same as "the law requires that A should do X." When the lawyer speaks in his professional capacity, the law to which he refers is the law of the land. When the moralist or the plain man of our day uses these words in a non-legal context, the law to which he refers is the moral law. We must consider presently why they should both use the same language, but it will be useful to notice first some consequences of this account of the way in which we use the so-called moral words.

"Obligatory," "non-obligatory," "right," and "wrong" can be arranged in a square of opposition, with "obligatory" and "wrong" as contraries and "right" and "non-obligatory" as sub-contraries. Since, however, any right action which was not non-obligatory would have to be obligatory and any non-obligatory action which was not right would have to be wrong, we can simplify the scheme and classify all actions under three headings, "obligatory," "indifferent" and "wrong," with "indifferent" as an abbreviation for "right but non-obligatory." These three headings correspond obviously to "necessary," "contingent" and "impossible" in the logic of modalities. Indeed, the modal words "must," "may" and "cannot" are often used in a moral sense. But whereas logicians talk a lot about contingent propositions, moral philosophers have very little to say about indifferent actions. It is true that intuitionists often refer to the right, but they seem to assume at times that it is identical with the obligatory, although the word "right" never has that sense in ordinary speech. This is curious and unfortunate. One might almost say that the older moral philoso-

phers had played into the hands of the subjectivists by concentrating attention on utterances which can with some plausibility be regarded as attempts
to evoke attitudes of approval or disapproval. For who would be inclined
to adopt an emotive theory of morals if he had started by considering such
moral utterances as "You may if you like, but you needn't"? I do not say
that it is impossible to extend the emotive theory to cover these cases; but
I think that any such extension makes the theory much less plausible. If
Mr. Stevenson's pattern of analysis is to be followed, the sentence I have just
quoted must mean something like "I shrug my shoulders at the thought of
your doing X. Do so likewise." This paraphrase is not at all emotive in
any ordinary sense, and in order to cope with it a subjectivist would have
to say that he understood "emotive" in a sense wide enough to cover "seda-
tive." It seems much simpler and more in accord with good usage to treat
moral utterances as we should treat corresponding statements by lawyers.

Now we all think that lawyers succeed in making statements by the
use of words like "ought" and "right." Let us suppose for example that
Mrs. A has let an unfurnished room in her house to Mr. B for occupation
by the latter as a living room. When Mr. B arrives he brings with him a
cat. This greatly distresses Mrs. A, because she has a pathological dislike
of cats, and she tells Mr. B that he must not keep the animal in her house.
Mr. B replies, correctly enough, that the cat is quiet, clean and well-
behaved, and he refuses to take it away. Mrs. A then goes to her solicitor for
advice. Now I do not profess to know the English law of tenancy, but I
think the solicitor might perhaps say something like this: "You *ought* to
leave the cat alone, so long as it does not enter your own living quarters,
and you *must* on no account put Mr. B's furniture in the street. But you
may give him three months' notice to quit. And if he doesn't remove himself and his cat at the end of that time, he will definitely be in the *wrong*."
When the solicitor uses the words "ought," "may" and "wrong," he is
talking about the way in which the law of England applies to the case, and
no one doubts that what he says is either true or false. As a good citizen,
he may perhaps use a tone of voice which is likely to work upon Mrs. A's
emotions and induce her to keep the peace; but that is not part of the service
for which he claims a fee. If he has the reputation of being a good solicitor,
that is because he is nearly always correct when he undertakes to say what
the law of England requires, allows or forbids in any particular case.

Similarly we all assume in our everyday life that moral advice may be
true or false. Let us suppose that Mrs. C has good reason for believing that
her lodger Mrs. D is unfaithful to Mr. D during the latter's absence as a
prisoner-of-war in a foreign country, and that she is so worried about the
matter that she goes to her clergyman to ask what she should do. She and
the clergyman are at one in disapproving of adultery, and she fully expects
him to begin his part of the conversation by shaking his head and saying
"Tut, tut." But that is not all she wants to hear from him. She can see that
there are various possible courses of action open to her (e.g. expostulating

with Mrs. D, writing to Mr. D, turning a blind eye), and she is quite ready
to believe that a person cleverer than herself might be able to think of other
alternatives. Furthermore, she is already so much worked up about the
affair that she is quite sincerely prepared to do what she ought to do,
however unpleasant that may be for herself, if only she can find out what
it is. This is where she expects help from the clergyman. If in these circumstances he says "You ought to do X," he purports to tell how the moral
law applies to the case. This is certainly what Mrs. C wants him to do. If
asked why she had consulted him, she would say that she thought he would
be able to answer her question correctly.

IV

There is a close analogy, then, between the ways in which the lawyer
and the moralist use such words as "right." This is not surprising, because
there was a time when men did not make any sharp distinction between the
moral law and the law of the land but spoke simply of the Law.

It is a comparatively new idea that there must be in each state some
authority, the sovereign, who makes laws from time to time for the subjects.
Even in modern England we retain the notion of a common law which was
not introduced by the act of any human legislator and has no known origin.
It is true that the judges are sometimes said to be legislators of the common
law because their judgments in particular cases are precedents binding on
their successors; but when they decide cases of a new kind the judges still
profess to be merely applying a pre-existing law. In the city states of classical antiquity and in the primitive societies which have been studied by
anthropologists during the past century there are many signs of similar
conceptions, and I have little doubt that if we could investigate the social
life of our remote ancestors we should find that this view of law was once
universal. For the notion of deliberate legislation seems to be a product of
the type of civilization which has flourished in the past five thousand years,
and we can scarcely suppose that men lived without any idea of law during
the five hundred thousand years before the time of Hammurabi. Very often
a traditional system of law is said to be of divine origin, but it is obvious that
we cannot treat all such stories as true, and we must therefore suppose that
some at least were invented after the event to explain why laws had been
accepted as binding.

Now an undifferentiated system of law may contain elements which
to our way of thinking are very different indeed. Thus injunctions against
killing fellow tribesmen are of a kind we should call moral, but caste rules
and rules requiring women to obey men look to us very like political pro-
visions for securing the advantage of one group at the expense of another,
and tabus about touching certain objects or uttering certain names appear
to us at the best like warning notices such as we put near high-tension wires.
It is a mistake, however, to suppose that the people who live under such a

system must be able to make these distinctions: even in our society there are people who cannot see any clear difference between a rule against lying and a rule against playing games on Sunday, and in some languages there exist no means for drawing such distinctions easily. How then did men come to make the distinctions which seem familiar to us? I have not the historical knowledge to answer this question properly, and I doubt whether it is possible to generalize safely about the cause of the transition in all the various societies where it has taken place. But I think that the change has usually had something to do with the recognition of the possibility of devising alternative sets of rules, and that this in turn has been suggested by the activities of kings as legislators. When after some period of disorder a new king establishes himself and proclaims rules, his action, though he wishes to be conservative, may lead men to think of the dependence of the law of the land on human will; and once they have reached that point, they have started on a path which leads to Rousseau and Bentham. For they may then conceive of a moral law distinct from the law of the land. The word "moral" suggested originally a connexion with *mores* or customs, and in some contexts, e.g. the descriptive work of anthropologists and sociologists, it is still applied to unwritten codes of almost any kind; but in the common usage of our day the moral law is supposed to be something more fundamental or natural than the law of the land, and this conception, expressed in various ways, has had great influence on human thought and practice during the past few thousand years. Long before the Stoics talked of the law of nature, Hammurabi asserted in the preamble to his laws for the land of Babylonia that the gods had delighted mankind by calling him, the renowned prince, the god-fearing Hammurabi, to establish justice in the earth, to destroy the base and the wicked, and to hold back the strong from oppressing the feeble.[1] For all its arrogance, this formula was an admission that his code could itself be judged by the standard of another law.

Although the notion of the moral law may have been evolved, as I believe, in contrast with the legislation of early sovereigns, it is not to be supposed that the moral law is always conceived as a set of general articles, each of them absolutely binding by itself. Sometimes, indeed, it is conceived in that way, particularly when it still has some connexion with religious belief; and one of the commonest sources of philosophical perplexity about morals is the discovery of apparent conflicts between duties, e.g. between the duty of telling the truth and the duty of helping a friend. But I do not think that this way of describing matters is essential to belief in a moral law. For men sometimes talk of that law as though it were a system of case law like the common law of England. According to a statement of Aristotle the Greeks often spoke of fairness or equity as something which could not be reduced to simple rules.[2] If this view is correct,

---

[1] Chilperic Edwards, *The World's Earliest Laws*, p. 13.
[2] *Nicomachean Ethics*, 1137 [b]13.

the ordinary moral rules about telling the truth, etc., are to be regarded as *rules of presumption*, i.e. rules which suffice to determine the issue if no countervailing considerations present themselves. Assuming, then, that we are entitled to use the word "law" in this connexion without committing ourselves to a set of quite independent moral rules, let us go on to consider in more detail how the moral law is contrasted with the law of the land.

V

In the first place the moral law is supposed to be stricter than the law of the land—at least in a well-ordered state. But this fact may sometimes be overlooked, because in every well-ordered state the law of the land contains many articles, e.g. the rule of the road, which are not ordinarily included in a formulation of the moral law. The correct account of the situation seems to be as follows. When we distinguish clearly between the moral law and the law of the land, we think of the latter as a system of rules to be enforced within the land by pains and penalties. We recognize, of course, that the restrictions imposed by the law of the land may sometimes be morally unjust, but when we believe that they are unjust, we believe that those in power ought to alter the law. This is as much as to say that nothing should be enforced as the law of the land which is not included within the moral law. If there is no moral obligation to observe traffic regulations which have been adopted by a certain process, then it is certainly wrong in the moral sense to enforce those regulations by pains and penalties, because to do so is an infringement of rightful liberty. But the fact that the traffic regulations are in a certain way arbitrary does not imply that there is no moral obligation to observe them. We have plenty of cases outside the sphere of state action where moral obligations have arisen from arbitrary conventions. Thus in England there is a moral obligation on any man wearing a hat to raise it when he meets an acquaintance, unless they have a mutual understanding to the contrary. Perhaps this has never been included before in a formulation of moral law, but that is only because such formulations usually deal with high generalities like respect for human personality. There are, of course, excellent reasons why some moral obligations should not be enforced by pains and penalties. If men were punished for not raising their hats, a large part of the good effect of hat-raising would be lost, and there would be an intolerable increase of police activity. But it is not always easy to draw the line, and there is plenty of room for intellectual disagreement about political questions between men of good will.

Secondly, the moral law is thought to differ from the law of the land in having no sanctions. Admittedly men have often believed in supernatural sanctions for the moral law, and it may be that in some stages of development they could not easily conceive a law distinct from the law of the land without thinking that it was enforced with pains and penalties by some divine sovereign. But in the later history of religions we find many state-

ments to the effect that the gods command what they do because it is
morally obligatory, and not *vice versa*. These show that the moral law is already conceived as something to which sanctions are not essential. Now
when this aspect of the moral law is clearly understood, there arises a new
interest in motives. This is natural enough. For if we institute sanctions
for a law, we arrange by our own act that fear of punishment (or hope of
reward) shall be a motive for men to observe the law; and we do this because we are determined that men shall observe the law for some reason or
other, no matter what. For the time being we are interested only in observance as such. But when we talk to men of a law without sanctions, we
assume that they may be moved to observe the law by motives which are
in some way intrinsically connected with the nature of the acts required by
the law, and we praise those qualities of character which dispose men on
the whole to observe the law spontaneously. Similarly we dispraise those
qualities which commonly dispose men to break the law; and in this connexion we may even dispraise qualities such as timidity and cupidity, which
sometimes dispose men to observe the law, but do so only within a system
of sanctions. This is not to say that the moral law enjoins or forbids motives
whereas the law of the land does not, but rather that the emergence of the
notion of moral law is very naturally accompanied by a new interest in
motives. There is neither coincidence nor confusion when we use the same
word "moral" in speaking of the moral law and of the moral character of
a man.

Thirdly, anyone who has attained a clear notion of the moral law thinks
of it as a system of orders which he himself concurs in giving. I say "anyone
who has attained a *clear* notion of the moral law," because various intermediate stages are possible. A man may begin by thinking of a law as imposed from without by a god for some reason about which it is useless to
inquire, but later come to say that the command of the god is intelligible
and even necessary. When he makes this transition, he asserts in effect that
the law has his consent, much as a subject in a dictatorship may express approval of some of the orders issued from above. If, however, a man regards
a command as something wholly alien, then it cannot be for him what we
call a moral law. This is not to say that he will not describe violation of
the law as sin or wrongdoing. For the use of such words is no proof that a
man has the characteristically moral attitude towards the violation. There
may still be lacking an element which the children in our own society acquire only after years spent under the control of adults, during which they
have heard such words quite often and perhaps also used them.

But the characteristics of the moral law which have been mentioned
so far are not enough to distinguish that law clearly from other systems of
orders. A man might utter a command of his own which was stricter than
anything in the law of the land but had no sanctions attached to it, and yet
not be thought by himself or others to be giving expression to the moral
law. He might say, for example, "Go to every concert of Bach's music

which occurs within five miles of your home." In order to complete our account of the moral law we must notice a fourth characteristic, more fundamental than all the others. The moral law is thought to be a set of commands which all reasonable men who possess the relevant information must concur in giving to themselves and their fellow men. If, as seems very unlikely, anyone expected all reasonable men to concur in a command to attend concerts of Bach's music, then he would regard that command as an article of the moral law. But this is not to say that it would in fact be an article of the moral law; for he might be mistaken in assuming that all reasonable men must concur in proclaiming it.

In the statement I have made above the word "reasonable" is all-important. We do not think that the accidental agreement of any number of men is sufficient to make what they will a moral law. We say rather that the moral law is what men promulgate in their capacity of reasonable beings; and part of what we mean by this is that the moral law is independent of the peculiar predilections which any man or group of men may have at any time. The law of the land may be, as Thrasymachus said, a set of orders designed by the sovereign to further his private interests, and the policy of a drug-addict may involve the deliberate sacrifice of all his long-term interests; but the moral law is supposed to be what a man would command if he were free from all the passions which lead to selfishness or imprudence. So far as relations between men are concerned, this is attested by many common usages such as the identification of moral justice with equity and its representation by a figure holding a pair of evenly balanced scales. It appears already in the charge of an Egyptian king to his vizier: "The abomination of the god is an exhibition of partiality. This is the instruction and thus shalt thou act: Thou shalt look upon him whom thou knowest like him whom thou knowest not, upon him who has access to thy person like him who is far from thy household." [3] When we treat imprudence as an offence against the moral law, we seem to assume that there can be something analogous to injustice in the effect of a man's present conduct on his own future life: the drunkard, we say, is his own worst enemy.

The close connexion of moral judgments with the notion of impartiality is illustrated in an interesting way by the conduct of civilized adults when they are angry. The adequate stimulus for anger is thwarting by another sentient being, as animals and young children show by their behaviour when they are prevented from getting what they want. But if a civilized adult exhibits naked anger when he cannot get what he wants, we look at him with surprise and begin to think that he is mentally diseased. For in our society the anger of adults is normally clothed as moral indignation, i.e. as a protest on behalf of an impersonal principle, and even those who profess to be so free from vulgar prejudice that they never make moral judgments discover a use for moral words when they are in a rage. The reason is obvious. A situation in which the desires of one human being clash

[3] Henri Frankfort and others, *Before Philosophy*, pp. 99–100.

with those of another is *par excellence* a situation calling for moral judgment. Our moral training has impressed this on us so firmly that anyone who
ignores it is thought mad; and so even anger which is in fact selfish mas-
querades as moral indignation. Perhaps Plato was deceived by this decent
pretence when he suggested that the spirited or self-assertive element is
specially fitted to play the part of policeman in the soul.

In order to explain the fourth and most important feature of the moral
law, many philosophers from Plato onwards have said that this law is given
by reason, which is each man's true self. Undoubtedly the legislator of the
moral law must be rational in the sense of being able to see connexions
and make generalizations; but it is not helpful to talk about reason as though
it were a little man inside all ordinary men; and it is a mistake to suppose,
as Kant did, that reason alone determines the content of the moral law. I
am not referring here to the old charge that Kant tried to deduce absolute
special rules from a purely formal principle; for it is possible that his critics
have misunderstood him on that point. My objection is rather that reason
is not a motive for anything, and so not a motive for the making of the
moral law. If we try to characterize the moral law by saying that it is the
will of a certain sort of lawgiver, we must be careful to describe the lawgiver in a way which makes his legislation intelligible. But the mere fact
of being rational would not explain why a man should issue orders of any
kind to his fellow men. In order to account for that we must suppose that
he has some interest, however impersonal, in what is about to take place
and wishes for one result rather than another. Perhaps those who talk of
practical reason suppose this to involve a desire for consistency. If so, they
are drawing attention to something which is indeed relevant to the formulation of the moral law. For we commonly say that an inequitable distribution of satisfactions is inconsistent. But equity may be achieved at various
levels of satisfaction. Having realized that it would be inconsistent to give
all men permission to use the road as they please, and inconsistent also, but
in a slightly different sense of that word, to give such permission to some
men but not to others, we might conceivably decide that no one should use
the road. If, instead of doing this, we introduce a rule for the division of
the road, we must surely be moved by a more complicated motive, namely,
by the desire to let men have what they want so far as that can be arranged
equitably.

Reasonableness, which makes men legislators of the moral law, is something more than rationality. For when in English we say that a man is
reasonable, we mean not only that he is capable of reasoning, but also that
he is *willing to consider reasons* for modifying his own preferences. If he
shows his reasonableness in relation to matters which will affect his own
future happiness, we call him prudent. But the more interesting case is that
in which a man's preferences are modified by consideration of the way
others will be affected. And here it seems to me we must introduce the
notion of sympathy to explain the possibility of any modification what-

ever. In the absence of sympathy no consideration of the interests of other men could amount to a reason for adopting a policy; and although men might still be prudent, there would be no reason why onlookers should approve their prudence. When we say that the moral law is the legislation of the reasonable man, we seem therefore to mean that it is, as Adam Smith suggested, a set of commands such as would be given by an impartial spectator who was endowed with sympathy and intelligence and possessed all relevant information.

The formula of Adam Smith is attractive because it does justice not only to the intentions of Rousseau and Kant, but also to those of the utilitarians, who were not such fools as their idealist critics would have us believe. And it has two other merits which are, I think, of great importance. In the first place, it provides a way of determining the content of the moral law. This is essential, because there would be no sense in talking as we do of what the moral law requires or permits or forbids, if our assertions could not be verified in any way. The analogy between the pronouncements of the moralist and those of the lawyer would break down, if it were not possible to distinguish between good and bad moralists in much the same way as we can distinguish between good and bad lawyers. Secondly, the theory explains how each man can come to regard himself as the giver of the moral law, with the legislator's own motive for observing it. For by an effort of the imagination anyone who is accounted a moral agent can put himself in the position of an impartially sympathetic spectator. This effort is made easier by the study of history and the hearing or reading of fiction; and that is one reason why story-telling in all forms is an extremely important part of education. It is a curious mark of Plato's blindness to the good things in his own society that he put forward in his *Republic* a plan for preventing men from exercising their imagination in a way which is essential for moral development.

VI

What bearing has all this on the question with which we started? We have discovered a sense in which it seems quite proper to talk of the truth or falsity of moral judgments, but we can scarcely expect the subjectivist to admit without more ado that our argument is fatal to his theory. He may allow the force of the analogy I have drawn between the clergyman's use of "ought" and the solicitor's, but go on to say: "Your analogy does not justify you in claiming that moral judgments are ever true in the ordinary sense. For the moral law is not objective, since it cannot be ascertained in a purely intellectual fashion, as the law of the land may be. When you say that it requires this or that, you are really acting then and there as a legislator of sorts, but expressing your legislation in a way designed to secure the concurrence of others." If I am right in thinking that the subjectivist will take this line, the question about objectivity in morals reduces to this: Is there any good sense in which we may properly speak of the moral law as objective?

Obviously the moral law cannot be objective in the same sense as a fact or law of natural science. That is to say, it cannot be independent of all minds. For the moral law is a system of orders, and it makes no sense to say that there might be orders although there were no minds. Kant was clearly right when he talked of imperatives in his account of morality, and it is very strange that some philosophers in our time have gone back to talking about facts of obligation which are not derivative from orders. I can only suppose that they are muddled about the possible meanings of "objective." In the context which concerns us the word must mean something like "impartial," "free from bias," "independent of personal taste," or, more explicitly, "common to all reasonable men." But with this use of the word we all surely wish to maintain that the moral law is objective. For it is just nonsense to speak of Jones's moral law and Smith's moral law, or of the British moral law and the Russian moral law, although there may, of course, be differences of opinion about the content of the moral law, just as there are differences of opinion about the foundations of mathematics or about Lord Keynes's theory of employment. The modern subjectivists are right in saying that we want others to agree with us in our moral judgments, but they fail to see that we expect agreement here as of right on the ground that these judgments are not merely expressions of our own preferences or those of our group, but applications of a law to which all men commit themselves when they claim to be reasonable.

In primitive societies, whether of savages or of schoolboys, the social pressure towards conformity with established standards of all kinds is strong and undiscriminating. And the result may be a quite remarkable degree of uniformity, even in what we should regard as minor matters of taste. If the archaeologists are to be believed, the style of pottery decoration has sometimes remained unaltered within a community for centuries. But during the historical period which has seen the emergence of the idea of an independent moral law there has been also a very notable growth in the spirit of tolerance. This is not to say that men do not now practise persuasion as much as they did, but rather that they realize better what they are about and are more ready to admit the possibility of failure in some connexions. In art criticism, for example, there are now few outside the Royal Academy who display the undifferentiated vehemence we may suppose to have been common among cave-men. Most of us recognize that some differences are inevitable among those who share a very complex culture, and in certain contexts we may even welcome variety of attitude. I have no taste for music, but I am glad that others find enjoyment in it. That is to say, I yield to their persuasion so far as to say that listening to music is good provided no one is made to listen against his will. Similarly, although I try to bring others to like philosophy, when I meet people who are very resistant I am satisfied if I can induce them to admit that my activity is respectable. So far as I know, the ancient Greeks were the first to adopt such a policy of tolerance with full consciousness of what they were about. It was just this tolerance that Plato condemned in his *Republic* as the peculiar vice of the democratic man. But Plato was a reactionary, as Professor Popper has argued in *The Open Society and Its Enemies*. Although he had learnt from Socrates the notion of a moral law without sanctions, he proposed in effect a return to primitive uniformity through deliberate indoctrination and secret police action. In this he was surely misguided. For the notion of a specifically moral law seems to be inseparably bound up with the policy of mutual tolerance.

According to Plato's argument in the *Republic*, democracy is worse than oligarchy and next to the bottom in the scale of constitutions because it does not provide for the permanent subordination of one element in the state to another according to plan and so prepares the way for tyranny, or subordination without plan. But this is a caricature of the way of life he professes to describe. If a man adopts the policy of allowing the greatest possible satisfaction of diverse interests, he is committed to regulating the distribution of satisfactions by some principle independent of all the competing interests, that is to say, by some conception of moral law: when we adopt toleration as a rule of life, we must be prepared to suppress the intolerant. And conversely, no one would talk of a moral law who had not conceived a society in which there was inevitable diversity of interests and therefore the possibility of conflicts calling for impartial arbitration. We may perhaps speak of an interest in the observance of the moral law. But this interest is of a higher order, in the logical sense, than all other interests, and a man's advocacy of it is not to be treated like a recommendation for a sauce or a sonata.

Although I am convinced by these considerations that it is proper to speak of the moral law as objective, I can understand that a subjectivist may still feel impatient and wish to reply somewhat as follows: "At the best all this is just a lay sermon in favour of a certain way of life. But, being a professional philosopher, you have tried to pass off your sermon as a philosophical analysis by the device which Mr. Stevenson calls persuasive definition. When such different persons as a Buddha and a Thug utter words like 'right,' all that is common in their usages is the emotive function, i.e. the expressing and evoking of approval. You want to take advantage of that for your preaching, but, instead of admitting openly what you are about, you say that a right act is by definition one in accordance with the will of an impartially sympathetic spectator. I might perhaps be prepared to agree with you in *attitude*, that is to say, I might be ready to join with you in urging men to approve only such actions as would be approved by an impartially sympathetic spectator; but I must insist that it is a mistake to suppose that in ordinary English the word 'right' has the descriptive meaning you suggest."

Such an objection is based on a misunderstanding. I have not tried to maintain that the word "right" always means "in accordance with the will of an impartially sympathetic spectator." On the contrary, I have said that it means "in accordance with the law" and that the nature of the law under reference must be judged from the context. I might have gone further and said that almost all the words we use in expressing moral judgments have non-moral usages (consider, for example, "good," " heroic," "noble," "gentle," "virtue," "vice" and "fault"); but I have deliberately tried to concentrate attention on those words which involve reference to a law, because these seem to be most important in a discussion of objectivity. Furthermore, I have suggested that the notion of a specifically moral law appeared comparatively late in the development of the human race. No doubt men who spoke of the law in earlier times often gave some moral flavour to their remarks, but the distinction which philosophers of our day are apt to take for granted seems to be the work of moralists and philosophers in historical times; it is not clear even yet to all ordinary men. If, then, we wish to explain the nature of the moral law, we must consider how the expression "moral law" and its connected phrases have been used by those responsible for the innovation. Although I have not tried to justify it by detailed consideration of the usage of Confucius, Buddha, Socrates and the rest, I think the formula I have suggested is at least a fair approximation to the definition we need. Anyone who wishes to criticize it should remember that it is *not* intended to cover all that anthropologists sometimes call morality when they are discussing the unwritten codes of primitive peoples, but only what men call morality in those cultures which distinguish moral law from mere tradition.

It is true, of course, that those who speak of the moral law often behave as though they were trying to induce their fellow men to adopt the point of view of an impartially sympathetic spectator. But this is natural enough according to my account of the situation. For anyone who has already adopted the point of view of an impartial spectator may be expected to wish that his fellow men all had a sufficient motive for observing the moral law he enunciates from that point of view. And the only motive which is sufficient in all circumstances to produce obedience to a law without sanctions is the motive of the legislator of the law. For if anyone asks "Why should I obey the moral law?", we cannot give him a general answer by reference to other motives. And if he does not already possess the motive I have just described as sufficient to produce obedience on all occasions, we cannot supply it by argument. Our only course therefore is to try to induce it in him by appropriate education of a non-argumentative kind. If presently we come to the conclusion that this can never be done, we say that he is morally insane. All this we may concede to the subjectivists. Perhaps we may even go farther and admit that the introduction of the notion of a moral law was itself only a means to the spreading of the attitude of impartial sympathy. For when men first talked of a law without sanctions, they were undoubtedly using the word "law" in a new and rather strange way. Their usage was justified by the possibility of separating out certain features of the old undifferentiated notion of law; but it could scarcely have occurred to anyone who had not started with the notion of a law enforced by sanctions; and its chief value in discourse is that it enables us to talk easily of acts whose performance we desire from a certain point of view, and so helps us to maintain ourselves and others in that point of view.

I hope these concessions will placate subjectivists. But I wish to say again in conclusion that they are not at all inconsistent with a claim of objectivity for the moral law. For it seems clear to me that the only sense in which I want to claim objectivity for the moral law is that which I have tried to indicate. And in this sense the moral law is objective by definition. If we overlook this, we miss what is distinctively moral in moral judgments.

SUGGESTED FURTHER READINGS

BOOKS

AYER, A. J., *Language, Truth, and Logic*, Oxford University Press, 1936; 2nd ed., London, Victor Gollancz, Ltd., 1946.

BERGLER, EDMUND, *The Battle of the Conscience*, Washington Institute of Medicine, 1948.

BOSANQUET, BERNARD, *Some Suggestions in Ethics*, London, The Macmillan Co., 1918.

BRADLEY, F. H., *Ethical Studies*, Oxford, The Clarendon Press, 2nd ed., 1927.

BRENTANO, F., *The Origin of the Knowledge of Right and Wrong*, Westminster, A. Constable & Co., Ltd., 1902.

BROAD, C. D., *Five Types of Ethical Theory*, New York, Harcourt, Brace & Co., Inc., 1930.

———, *Determinism, Indeterminism, and Libertarianism*, Cambridge Univ. Press, 1934.

CAMPBELL, C. A., *In Defense of Free-will*, Inaugural Lecture, delivered at the University of Glasgow.

———, *Scepticism and Construction*, New York, The Macmillan Co., 1931.

CARRITT, E. F., *The Theory of Morals*, New York, Oxford University Press, 1928.

———, *Morals and Politics*, New York, Oxford University Press, 1935.

———, *Ethical and Political Thinking*, Oxford, The Clarendon Press, 1947.

DE BURGH, W. G., *From Morality to Religion*, London, Macdonald & Evans, 1938.

———, *The Life of Reason*, London, Macdonald & Evans, 1949.

DEWEY, JOHN, *Human Nature and Conduct*, New York, Henry Holt & Co., 1922.

———, *The Quest for Certainty*, New York, Minton, Balch & Co., 1929.

———, *Experience and Nature*, New York, W. W. Norton Co., 1929.

———, *The Theory of Valuation*, International Encyclopedia of Unified Science, University of Chicago Press, 1939.

———, AND JAMES TUFTS, *Ethics*, rev. ed., New York, Henry Holt & Co., 1932.

EWING, A. C., *The Morality of Punishment*, London, Kegan, Paul, Trench, Trubner & Co., 1929.

———, *The Definition of Good*, New York, The Macmillan Co., 1947.

———, *The Individual, the State, and World Government*, New York, The Macmillan Co., 1947.

FIELD, G. C., *Moral Theory*, London, Methuen & Co., 1921.

———, *Studies in Philosophy*, Bristol, J. W. Arrowsmith, Ltd., 1935.

FREUD, SIGMUND, *Beyond the Pleasure Principle*, New York, Boni & Livewright, 1922.

GREEN, T. H., *Prolegomena to Ethics*, 1st ed., Oxford, The Clarendon Press, 1883; 3rd ed., 1890.

GROTE, J., *An Examination of the Utilitarian Philosophy*, Cambridge, Deighton, Bell & Co., 1870.

HALL, E. W., *The Analysis of Value*, London, Routledge and Kegan Paul, 1952.

HARTMANN, N., *Ethics*, 3 vols., New York, The Macmillan Co., 1932.

HUXLEY, T. H. AND JULIAN, *Touchstone for Ethics*, New York, Harper and Brothers, 1947.

JOSEPH, H. W. B., *Some Problems in Ethics*, Oxford, The Clarendon Press, 1931.

KÖHLER, W., *The Place of Value in a World of Fact*, New York, Liveright Publishing Corp., 1938.

LAIRD, JOHN, *A Study in Moral Theory*, London, G. Allen & Unwin, 1926.

——, *The Idea of Value*, Cambridge University Press, 1929.

——, *An Inquiry into Moral Notions*, London, G. Allen & Unwin, 1935.

LEWIS, C. I., *An Analysis of Knowledge and Valuation*, La Salle, Illinois, Open Court Publishing Co., 1946.

LEWIS, H. D., *Morals and Revelation*, London, G. Allen and Unwin, 1951.

MARTINEAU, JAMES, *Types of Ethical Theory*, Oxford, The Clarendon Press, 1885.

MOORE, G. E., *Principia Ethica*, Cambridge University Press, 1903.

——, *Ethics*, London, Oxford University Press, 1911.

——, *Philosophical Studies*, New York, Harcourt, Brace & Co., 1921.

——, *The Philosophy of G. E. Moore* (ed. Schilpp), Evanston, Northwestern University Press, 1942.

OGDEN, C. K., AND RICHARDS, I. A., *The Meaning of Meaning*, New York, Harcourt, Brace & Co., 1923.

OSBORNE, H., *Foundations of the Philosophy of Value*, Cambridge University Press, 1933.

PAP, ARTHUR, *Elements of Analytic Philosophy*, New York, The Macmillan Co., 1949.

PARKER, D. H., *Human Values*, New York, Harper and Brothers, 1931.

PATON, H. J., *The Categorical Imperative*, London, Hutchinson's University Library, 1948.

PERRY, R. B., *General Theory of Value*, Cambridge, Harvard University Press, 1926.

POPPER, K. R., *The Open Society and Its Enemies*, London, G. Routledge & Sons, Ltd., 1945.

PRALL, D. W., *A Study in the Theory of Value, University of California Publications in Philosophy*, Volume 3, 1921.

PRATT, J. B., *Reason in the Art of Living*, New York, The Macmillan Co., 1950.

PRICHARD, H. A., *Duty and Interest*, New York, Oxford University Press, 1928.

——, *Duty and Ignorance of Fact*, London, Proceedings of the British Academy, 18, 1932.

——, *Moral Obligation*, New York, Oxford University Press, 1950.

PRIOR, A. N., *Logic and the Basis of Ethics*, Oxford, The Clarendon Press, 1949.

RAPHAEL, D. D., *The Moral Sense*, London, Oxford University Press, 1947.

RASHDALL, H., *Is Conscience an Emotion?*, Boston, Houghton Mifflin Co., 1914.

——, *Theory of Good and Evil*, 2nd ed., Oxford, The Clarendon Press, 1928.

ROSS, SIR DAVID, *The Right and the Good*, Oxford, The Clarendon Press, 1930.

——, *Foundations of Ethics*, London, Oxford University Press, 1939.

RUSSELL, BERTRAND, *The Philosophy of Bertrand Russell* (ed. Schilpp), Evanston, Northwestern University Press, 1944.

SANTAYANA, GEORGE, *The Life of Reason: Reason in Morals*, New York, Charles Scribner's Sons, 1905.

——, *Winds of Doctrine*, London, J. M. Dent & Co., 1913.

SCHILPP, P. A. (ed.), *The Philosophy of G. E. Moore*, Evanston, Northwestern University Press, 1942.

——, *The Philosophy of Bertrand Russell*, Evanston, Northwestern University Press, 1944.

SCHLICK, MORITZ, *The Problems of Ethics*, New York, Prentice-Hall, Inc., 1938.

SHARP, F. C., *Ethics*, New York, Appleton-Century-Crofts, Inc., 1928.
SIDGWICK, HENRY, *The Methods of Ethics*, 6th ed., New York, The Macmillan Co., 1901.
STACE, W. T., *The Concept of Morals*, New York, The Macmillan Co., 1937.
STEVENSON, CHARLES L., *Ethics and Language*, New Haven, Yale University Press, 1943.
TOULMIN, S., *Reason in Ethics*, Cambridge University Press, 1950.
UNIVERSITY OF CALIFORNIA ASSOCIATES, *Knowledge and Society*, New York, Appleton-Century-Crofts, Inc., 1938.
WESTERMARCK, E., *Origin and Development of the Moral Ideas*, London, The Macmillan Co., 1906.
———, *Ethical Relativity*, New York, Harcourt, Brace & Co., 1932.
WISDOM, JOHN, *Problems of Mind and Matter* (Chapter 8), Cambridge University Press, 1934.

ARTICLES AND ESSAYS

The following abbreviations are used in this list:

Arist. Proc. for *Proceedings of the Aristotelian Society*
Arist. Suppl. for *Aristotelian Society, Supplementary Volume*
Ethics for *International Journal of Ethics*
Jl. of Phil. for *The Journal of Philosophy*
Phil. and Phen. Res. for *Philosophy and Phenomenological Research*
Phil. Rev. for *The Philosophical Review*
Phil. Stud. for *Philosophical Studies*

ABRAHAM, L., "The Logic of Ethical Intuitionism, *Ethics*, 44, 1933-4.
AIKEN, H. D., "Definitions of Value and the Moral Ideal," *Jl. of Phil.*, 42, 1945.
———, Review of Stevenson's *Ethics and Language*, *Jl. of Phil.*, 42, 1945.
———, "A Pluralistic Analysis of the Ethical 'Ought,'" *Jl. Phil.*, 58, 1951.
ALEXANDER, S., "Is the Distinction between 'Is' and 'Ought' Ultimate and Irreducible?", *Arist. Proc.*, Old Series, Vol. 2 No. 1, 1892.
———, "Morality as an Art," *Journal of Philosophical Studies*, 3, 1928.
AYER, A. J., "Freedom and Necessity," *Polemic*, 1, 1946.
———, "The Nature of Moral Judgements," *Horizon*, 1948.
BARNES, WINSTON H. F., "Intention, Motive, and Responsibility" (symposium). *Arist. Suppl.*, 19, 1945.
———, "Ethics without Propositions," *Arist. Proc.*, 48, 1948.
BEARDSLEY, E., "Imperative Sentences in Relation to Indicatives," *Phil. Rev.*, 53, 1944.
BERGMANN, G., "Logical Atomism, Elementarism and the Analysis of Value," *Phil. Stud.*, 2, 1951.
BLAKE, R. M., "The Ground of Obligation," *Ethics*, 38, 1927-8.
———, "Why Not Hedonism? a Protest," *Ethics*, 37, 1926-7.
BOHNERT, H. G., "The Semiotic Status of Commands," *Philosophy of Science*, 1946.
———, "Lewis' Attribution of Value to Objects," *Phil. Stud.*, 1, 1950.
BLACK, MAX, "Some Questions about Emotive Meaning," *Phil. Rev.*, 57, 1948.
BRANDT, R., "An Emotional Theory of the Judgment of Moral Worth," *Ethics*, 52, 1941-2.
BROAD, C. D., "Is 'Goodness' a Name of a Simple Non-natural Quality?" *Arist. Proc.*, 34, 1933-4.
———, "Conscience and Conscientious Action," *Philosphy*, 15, 1940.

BROAD, C. D., "Certain Features in Moore's Ethical Doctrines," Essay 1 in Schilpp (ed.), *The Philosophy of G. E. Moore*, 1942.

——, Review of Julian Huxley's *Evolutionary Ethics*, Mind, 53, 1944. (Also reprinted in Feigl and Sellars, *Readings in Philosophical Analysis*.)

——, "Some of the Main Problems of Ethics," *Philosophy*, 21, 1946. (Also reprinted in Feigl and Sellars, *Readings in Philosophical Analysis*.)

——, "Hägerström's Account of Sense of Duty and Certain Allied Experiences," *Philosophy*, 26, 1951.

——, Review of H. A. Prichard's *Moral Obligation*, Mind, 60, 1951.

BRAITHWAITE, R. B., "Belief and Action," *Arist. Suppl.*, 20, 1946.

——, "Verbal Ambiguity and Philosophical Analysis," *Arist. Proc.*, 28, 1927–1928.

BRODBECK, MAY, "Towards a Naturalistic 'Non-naturalistic' Ethic," *Phil. Stud.*, 2, 1951.

BUCHLER, JUSTUS, "Russell and the Principles of Ethics," Essay 16 in Schilpp (ed.), *The Philosophy of Bertrand Russell*, 1944.

CAMPBELL, C. A., "Reason and the Problem of Suffering," *Philosophy*, 10, 1935.

CARRITT, E. F., "Thinking Makes It So," *Arist. Proc.*, 30, 1929–30.

CLARKE, M. E., "A Phenomenological System of Ethics," *Philosophy*, 6, 1931.

CROSS, R. C., "The Emotive Theory of Ethics" (symposium), *Arist. Suppl.* 22, 1948.

DE BURGH, W. G., "Right and Good," *Philosophy*, 6, 1931.

DENNES, W. R., "Conflict," *Phil. Rev.*, 55, 1946.

DEWEY, JOHN, "The Logic of Judgments of Practice," *Jl. of Phil.*, 12, 1915.

——, "The Objects of Valuation," *Jl. of Phil.*, 15, 1918.

——, "Valuation and Experimental Knowledge," *Phil. Review*, 31, 1922.

——, "The Meaning of Value," *Jl. of Phil.*, 22, 1925.

——, "Valuation, Judgments, and Immediate Quality," *Jl. of Phil.*, 40, 1943.

——, "Further as to Valuation as Judgment," *Jl. of Phil.*, 40, 1943.

DUNCAN-JONES, A. E., "Notes for a Treatise on Ethics," *Arist. Proc.*, 44, 1943-4.

——, "Intention, Motive and Responsibility" (symposium), *Arist. Suppl.*, 19, 1945.

——, "Freedom: an Illustrative Puzzle," *Arist. Proc.*, 39, 1938-9.

——, "Ethical Words and Ethical Facts," *Mind*, 42, 1933.

——, Review of C. L. Stevenson, *Ethics and Language*, Mind, 54, 1945.

FALK, W. D., "Obligation and Rightness," *Philosophy*, 20, 1945.

——, "Intention, Motive, and Responsibility," (symposium) *Arist. Suppl.*, 19, 1945.

FEIGL, H., "De Principiis . . . ," Essay in Max Black, (ed.), *Philosophical Analysis*, Ithaca, Cornell University Press, 1950.

FRANKENA, W. K., "Obligation and Value in the Ethics of G. E. Moore," Essay 3 in Schilpp (ed.), *The Philosophy of G. E. Moore*, 1942.

——, "Ewing's Case against Naturalistic Theories of Value," *Phil. Rev.*, 57, 1948.

——, "Arguments for Non-naturalism about Intrinsic Value," *Phil. Stud.*, 1, 1950.

——, "Obligation and Ability," Essay in Max Black, (ed.), *Philosophical Analysis*, Ithaca, Cornell University Press, 1950.

FRANKS, O. S., "Choice," *Arist. Proc.*, 34, 1933-4.

FIELD, G. C., "Kant's First Moral Principle," *Mind*, 41, 1932.

——, "Is Moral Progress a Reality?" *Philosophy*, 6, 1931.

FINDLAY, J. N., "Morality by Convention," *Mind*, 53, 1944.

GARNETT, A. C., "Relativism and Absolutism in Ethics," *Ethics*, 54, 1943-4.

————, "Deontology and Self-Realization," *Ethics*, 51, 1940-1.

————, "Freedom and Responsibility in Moore's Ethics," Essay 6 in Schilpp (ed.), *The Philosophy of G. E. Moore*, 1942.

————, "Phenomenological Ethics and Self-Realization," *Ethics*, 53, 1943.

GINSBERG, M., "The Function of Reason in Morals," *Arist. Proc.*, 39, 1938-9.

GOMPERZ, H., "Some Simple Thoughts on Freedom and Responsibility," *Philosophy*, 12, 1937.

————, "Individual and Collective Responsibility," *Ethics*, 50, 1939-40.

————, "When Does the End Sanctify the Means?" *Ethics*, 54, 1943-4.

HALL, E. W., "A Categorical Analysis of Value," *Philosophy of Science*, 14, 1947.

————, "Stevenson on Disagreement in Attitude," *Ethics*, 58, 1947.

HAMPSHIRE, S., "Fallacies in Moral Philosophy," *Mind*, 58, 1949.

HARDY, W., "Ethical Naturalism," Henrietta Hertz Lecture, *British Academy Lectures*, 1945-6.

HARROD, R. F., "Utilitarianism Revised," *Mind*, 45, 1936.

HART, H. L. A., "The Ascription of Responsibility and Rights," *Arist. Proc.*, 49, 1948-9.

HARVEY, J. W., "The Problem of Guilt" (symposium), *Arist. Suppl.*, 21, 1947.

HAY, W. H., "Stevenson and Ethical Analysis," *Phil. Rev.*, 56, 1947.

HENLE, P., "Method in Ethics," *Ethics*, 54, 1943.

HOBART, R. E., "Free-will as Involving Determinism and Inconceivable without It," *Mind*, 43, 1934.

HOOK, SIDNEY, "A Critique of Ethical Realism," *Ethics*, 40, 1929-30.

HUGHES, G., "Motive and Duty," *Mind*, 53, 1944.

JACKSON, REGINALD, "Practical Reason," *Philosophy*, 17, 1942.

————, "Kant's Distinction between Categorical and Hypothetical Imperatives," *Arist. Proc.*, 43, 1942-3.

————, "Bishop Butler's Refutation of Psychological Hedonism," *Philosophy*, 20, 1945.

KAPLAN, A., "Are Ethical Judgments Assertions?" *Phil. Review*, 51, 1942.

KLEIN, MELANIE, "The Early Development of Conscience in the Child."

LAIRD, JOHN, "Rationalism in Ethics," *Journal of Philosophical Studies*, 4, 1929.

————, "On Doing One's Best," *Philosophy*, 6, 1931.

————, "Other People's Pleasure and One's Own," *Philosophy*, 16, 1941.

LAMONT, W. D., "Duty and Interest," *Philosophy*, 16, 17; 1941, 1942.

————, "Justice: Distributive and Collective," *Philosophy*, 16, 1941.

LEWIS, H. D., "Is There a Social Contract?" *Philosophy*, 15, 1940.

————, "Obedience to Conscience," *Mind*, 54, 1945.

————, "Does the Good Will Define Its Own Content?" *Ethics*, 58, 1947-8.

————, "Collective Responsibility," *Philosophy*, 23, 1948.

MABBOTT, J. D., "The Concept of Politics," *Philosophy*, 13, 1938.

————, "Is Anthropology Relevant to Ethics?" *Arist. Suppl.*, 20, 1946.

————, "True and False in Morals," *Arist. Proc.*, 49, 1948-9.

MACBETH, A., "Is Anthropology Relevant to Ethics?" (symposium), *Arist. Suppl.*, 20, 1946.

MACDONALD, MARGARET, "The Language of Political Theory," *Arist. Proc.*, 41, 1940-1.

————, "Natural Rights," *Arist. Proc.*, 47, 1946-7.

MACLAGEN, W. G., "Punishment and Retribution," *Philosophy*, 14, 1939.

McGILVARY, E. B., "Freedom and Necessity in Human Affairs," *Ethics*, 45, 1934-5.

MILLER, DICKINSON S., "Moral Truth," *Phil. Stud.*, 1, 1950.

MUIRHEAD, J. N., "Is the Distinction between 'Is' and 'Ought' Ultimate and Irreducible?" (symposium), *Arist. Proc.*, Old Series, Vol. 2, No. 1, 1892.

OSBORNE, H., "Definition of Value," *Philosophy*, 6, 1931.

PAP, A., "Determination and Moral Responsibility," *Jl. of Phil.*, 43, 1946.

——, "The Verifiability of Value Judgments," *Ethics*, 56, 1946.

PARKER, DEWITT H., "On Value," *Phil. Review*, 38, 1929.

——, "Value as Any Object of Any Interest," *Ethics*, 40, 1929–30.

——, "The Metaphysics of Value," *Ethics*, 44, 1933–4.

——, "Value and Existence," *Ethics*, 48, 1937–8.

——, "Reflections on the Recent Crisis in Theory of Value," *Ethics*, 58, 1947.

PATON, H. J., "The Alleged Independence of Goodness," Essay 4 in *The Philosophy of G. E. Moore*, 1942.

——, "Can Reason Be Practical?" Henrietta Hertz Lecture, *Proceedings of the British Academy*, 1945.

——, "The Emotive Theory of Ethics" (symposium), *Arist. Suppl.*, 22, 1948.

PERRY, C., "The Arbitrary as a Basis for Rational Morality," *Ethics*, 43, 1932–3.

PERRY, R. B., "Value as an Objective Predicate," *Jl. of Phil.*, 28, 1931.

——, "Value as Simply Value," *Jl. of Phil.*, 28, 1931.

——, "A Theory of Value Defended," *Jl. of Phil.*, 28, 1931.

——, "Real and Apparent Value," *Philosophy*, 7, 1932.

——, "Value and Its Moving Appeal," *Phil. Rev.*, 41, 1932.

POPKIN, R., "Ethical Naturalism and Hedonics," *Jl. Phil.*, 1951.

PRICHARD, H. A., "Duty and Ignorance of Fact," Henrietta Hertz Lecture, *Proceedings of the British Academy*, 18, 1932.

——, "The Meaning of 'Agathon' in Aristotle's Ethics," *Philosophy*, 10, 1935.

RAPHAEL, D. D., "Equality and Equity," *Philosophy*, 21, 1946.

RASHDALL, H., "Can There Be a Sum of Pleasures?" *Mind*, 8, 1899.

REID, J. R., "A Definition of Value," *Jl. of Phil.*, 23, 1931.

RICE, P. B., "Objectivity in Value Judgments," *Jl. of Phil.*, 40, 1943.

ROBINSON, R., "The Emotive Theory of Ethics," *Arist. Suppl.*, 22, 1948.

ROGERS, A. K., "Principles in Ethics," *Phil. Rev.*, 29, 30, 1920.

ROSS, W. D., "The Nature of Morally Good Action," *Arist. Proc.*, 29, 1928–9.

——, "The Ethics of Punishment," *Journal of Philosophical Studies*, 4, 1929.

RUSSELL, BERTRAND, "Good and Bad," *Polemic*, 1, 1946.

RUSSELL, L. J., "Ideals and Practice," *Philosophy*, 17, 1942.

——, "Is Anthropology Relevant to Ethics?" (symposium), *Arist. Suppl.*, 20, 1946.

RICHARDS, I. A., "Emotive Meaning Again," *Phil. Rev.*, 57, 1948.

SAVERY, W., "A Defense of Hedonism," *Ethics*, 45, 1934–5.

SELLARS, W. S., Review of Arthur Pap's *Elements of Analytic Philosophy*, *Phil. and Phen. Res.*, 17, 1950.

——, "Language, Rules, and Behavior," in Sidney Hook, (ed.), *John Dewey: Philosopher of Science and Freedom*, New York, Dial Press, 1950.

SHARP, F. C., "Voluntarism and Objectivity in Ethics," *Phil. Rev.*, 50, 1941.

SIDGWICK, HENRY, "Is the Distinction between 'Is' and 'Ought' Ultimate and Irreducible?" (symposium), *Arist. Proc.*, Old Series, Vol. 2 No. 1, 1892.

SPROTT, W. J. H., "Psychology and the Moral Problems of Our Time," *Philosophy*, 23, 1948.

STEVENSON, C. L., "Persuasive Definitions," *Mind*, 47, 1938.

——, "Moore's Arguments against Certain Forms of Ethical Naturalism," Essay 2 in Schilpp (ed.), *The Philosophy of G. E. Moore*, 1942.

——, "Meaning: Descriptive and Emotive," *Phil. Rev.*, 57, 1948.

STOCKS, J. L., "Will and Action in Ethics," *Philosophy*, 13, 1938.

——, "Moral Values," *Journal of Philosophical Studies*, 4, 1929.

STOUT, G. F., "Is the Distinction between 'Is' and 'Ought' Ultimate and Irreducible?" *Arist. Proc.*, Old Series, Vol. 2 No. 1, 1892.

STRAWSON, P. F., Review of Ewing, *The Definition of Good, Mind*, 58, 1949.
SWABEY, W. C., "Westermarckian Relativity," *Ethics*, 52, 1941–2.
———, "Non-normative Utilitarianism," *Jl. of Phil.*, 40, 1943.
TOULMIN, S., "Knowledge of Right and Wrong," *Arist. Proc.*, 51, 1950–51.
URBAN, W. M., "Value Propositions and Verifiability," *Jl. of Phil.*, 34, 1937.
URMSON, J. D., "Grading," *Mind*, 59, 1950.
WILLIAMS, D. C., "The Meaning of 'Good,'" *Phil. Rev.*, 46, 1937.